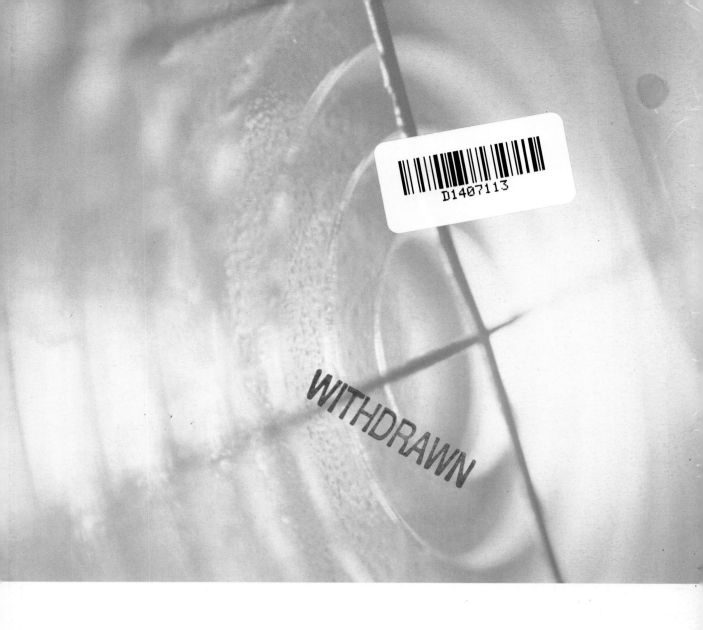

Quantitative Methods for Business and Management

second edition

Quantitative Methods for Business and Management

Second Edition

Frank Dewhurst

The **McGraw·Hill** Companies

London Boston Burr Ridge, IL Dubuque, IA Madison, WI New York San Francisco St. Louis
Bangkok Bogotá Caracas Kuala Lumpur Lisbon Madrid Mexico City Milan Montreal
New Delhi Santiago Seoul Singapore Sydney Taipei Toronto

Quantitative Methods for Business and Management, Second Edition
Frank Dewhurst
ISBN-13 978-0-07-710902-8
ISBN-10 0-07-7010902-3

 **Education**

Published by McGraw-Hill Education
Shoppenhangers Road
Maidenhead
Berkshire
SL6 2QL
Telephone: 44 (0) 1628 502 500
Fax: 44 (0) 1628 770 224
Website: www.mcgraw-hill.co.uk

British Library Cataloguing in Publication Data
A catalogue record for this book is available from the British Library

Library of Congress Cataloguing in Publication Data
The Library of Congress data for this book has been applied for from the
Library of Congress

Acquisitions Editor: Kirsty Reade
Head of Development: Caroline Prodger
Marketing Manager: Marca Wosoba

Text Design by Ken Vail Graphic Design, Cambridge UK
Cover design by Fielding Design
Typeset by MCS Publishing Services Ltd, Salisbury, Wiltshire
Printed and bound in Spain by Mateu Cromo

First edition published in 2002

ISBN-13 978-0-07-710-902-8
ISBN-10 0-07-7010902-3

Brief Table of Contents

Detailed Table of Contents

Preface

The intended audience

The primary target audience for this book is first year undergraduates on Business Studies and Management degree programmes. In particular, the book is intended for students who have little skill or confidence in statistics and mathematics. The material and treatment will also appeal to first year undergraduates on related undergraduate programmes (e.g. Economics, Accounting, Marketing, and joint degree programmes with these disciplines). Although the majority of the target audience will have GCSE or equivalent Mathematics, few will have taken Mathematics beyond GCSE and, two years on, will probably have forgotten the majority of the Mathematics and Statistics from their GCSE course.

The book may also appeal to similar non-degree study programmes, for example BTEC courses in business and finance and for professional bodies, such as the Chartered Institute of Cost and Management Accountants, the Chartered Institute of Public Finance and Accountancy, the Institute of Chartered Accountants, the Chartered Insurance Institute, the Institute of Financial Services and the British Institute of Management. Given the practical treatment of the material through spreadsheets and the use of mini-cases it may also be of use on MBA and taught MSc programmes, and for practising managers.

A justification for the book

Several trends in the tertiary education sector indicate that a text of the this nature is required. The last 10 years have seen an expansion of students entering further and higher education, particularly in vocationally based programmes, and this is set to increase as a result of UK government policy. Many new programmes are being – or are soon to be – launched, and the philosophy of lifelong learning will lead to a greater demand for basic self-learning materials in the tertiary sector, particularly using practical and example-based material. Higher education institutions are questioning the use of traditional teaching/lecturing methods and considering self-centred learning methods, particularly through the use of IT, because of competing demands for limited resources (e.g. research targets), and many of these institutions are expanding into the distance learning market, which will also require suitable self-centred learning material.

Given the increasing ownership of PCs by individuals and institutions, and the use of standard office software, there is a justification for using this software and the web as supplementary vehicles for delivery of learning material. Microsoft Office is the *de facto* standard, and Excel, in particular, is ideal for manipulating and displaying quantitative data. This book aims to provide students with the skill to use Excel as a spreadsheet tool, which is likely to be the prevalent software they will employ in the workplace.

Although there are numerous textbooks aimed at this market, few have the breadth of coverage required by the diverse range of courses, include a large number of worked examples and exercises, or take full advantage of the use of spreadsheets. No single book currently on the market offers all these features.

The pedagogical style

Mathematics is a language, and as with learning any language it is important to practise regularly, which is best achieved by undertaking exercises and trying to think and communicate as much as possible in the language.

Therefore, this book is thoroughly example-based. Mathematical concepts, notation and methods will only be introduced as and when necessary, and generalisations will be made from specific practical examples. This book avoids using formal mathematical derivations and proofs; instead empirical (i.e. example-based) justifications are given both to motivate the reader and to introduce the material. However, for the interested reader, some formal proofs and derivations can be found on the associated CD-ROM and web pages at: **www.mcgraw-hill.co.uk/ textbooks/dewhurst**

In addition to realistic and worked examples to present and illustrate the material in the main body of the text, there is a high proportion of exercises at the end of each section to reinforce the material. There are mini-cases to bring together and illustrate realistic applications in Business and Management.

Throughout the book the reader is guided by the author to any prerequisite material and to the relevant Excel workbooks by the use of icons placed in the left-hand margin. The notation and symbols used throughout this book are fully explained below.

In order to see how the material in the text has been presented for optimum clarity and accessibility, please take a look at the Guided tour on pp. xvi–xvii, which highlights the learning features in the text.

This book has been designed to meet most forms of learning and can be:
- Read from cover to cover to gain a comprehensive introduction to Quantitative Methods.
- Mapped onto typical courses by selecting relevant chapters or sections in each chapter. At the start of each section, the necessary prerequisite reading has been listed, and to cater for different course structures, topics are cross-referenced throughout.
- Used as a workbook to reinforce lecture courses, or used as a self-learning text.
- Used with or without the supporting Excel workbooks. As the book is aimed at a practical appreciation and application of Quantitative Methods the majority of illustrative worked examples and exercises are to be found on the CD-ROM and at the Online Learning Centre website. The reader can work through text, work through the worked illustrative examples and undertake the exercises while sat at their PC.
- Used as a reference and revision book. A comprehensive index at the end of the book enables the reader to use the book as a reference for their continued studies.

How to use this book

Unlike other courses where you will be expected to read several books, you will need only this book for an entire module or course unit. Because the chapters are as free standing as possible, your course tutor may recommend reading the book in a different sequence: for example you might be told to read Section 15.3 after reading Chapter 12.

This book is based on the idea of learning by doing. Every concept is illustrated by worked examples, which should be worked through either manually (i.e. with a pen and paper) or by using a spreadsheet or calculator. Do not be surprised if you do not understand something on first reading; few people do. Just go back and work through it again. The end-of-section exercises are to reinforce your understanding of the subject matter.

Although sections are as free standing as possible, some require a thorough understanding of previous sections. These prerequisites are listed at the start of each section. When you need to refer back to the prerequisite material, you will find an icon (000) in the left margin to indicate the page on which it is discussed.

Finally, do not worry if you find the notation daunting at first. Just regard it as just another language, for mathematics is simply the international language of numbers.

The structure of this book

This book is split into three parts. Each part opens with a brief description of its contents, and closes with a summary and some mini case studies, which demonstrate typical applications of what you have learned. Each chapter opens with a list of objectives and contents and ends with a review. The chapters are divided into sections: each starts with a list of prerequisites and ends with exercises.

Part A (The foundations of Quantitative Methods) considers basic mathematical concepts (i.e. numbers, arithmetic, measurement, notation, algebra) and introduces statistics (i.e. data collection and descriptive statistics). Despite encountering some of this material at school, you may have forgotten it, not fully understood it, or found it was not applied to business and management. Some of it will probably be new to you.

Part B (Models and analysis for business and management) covers the application of statistics, probability and mathematics to business and management, including finance, economics, production, operations, marketing, psychology, and other social sciences of management. Although some of the mathematics appears in A/S and A level Mathematics, and may or may not be new to you, many of the applications will be new.

Part C (Modelling and analysing decisions) extends the application of statistics and mathematics to problem solving for decision-makers, and will probably be new to you. This includes introductions to basic decision analysis, investment appraisal techniques, and operational research.

The conventions used in this book

In addition to the 000 icon, the icon indicates an Excel worksheet that contains a worked example or the inbuilt formulas in Excel, which can be found on the enclosed CD-ROM and online at **www.mcgraw-hill.co.uk/textbooks/dewhurst**. The first number in the icon refers to the workbook and the second to the relevant worksheet; in this case, the first worksheet in the workbook file **Chapter2.xls**.

Equations are numbered sequentially in each section in each chapter (e.g. (**3.2.10**) refers to the 10th equation in Section 2 of Chapter 3), and key formulas are highlighted in blue tint. Worked examples are also numbered sequentially (e.g. **Example 11.1.2** refers to the 2nd worked example in Section 1 of Chapter 11), and likewise for all tables and figures.

Student CD-ROM

The book is accompanied by a free student CD-ROM, which provides students with the examples from the text in the form of Excel spreadsheets, to enable them to gain a fuller understanding of how the software application is used for quantitative methods. To enable the use of Excel to be integrated with the text, spreadsheet icons in the left-hand margin of the book lead students towards the corresponding Excel spreadsheet on the CD-ROM. The CD-ROM also contains additional material including derivations and proofs of formulae, alternative tools and techniques of Quantitative Methods and solutions to exercises.

Online Learning Centre

The Online Learning Centre for the book has been developed to support lecturers who wish to use the text to teach, and students who wish to learn Quantitative Methods.

Materials for lecturers include PowerPoint slides and handouts for use in lecture presentations or seminars and full solutions to the problems in the book. A test bank containing 50 extra questions per chapter will also be available.

To help students practise the tools and techniques of Quantitative Methods, example data sets, sample exam questions and online self-assessment tests are available at the associated website: **www.mcgraw-hill.co.uk/textbooks/dewhurst**.

Acknowledgements

First and foremost, I would like to thank my wife (Diane) and children (Duncan and Jessica) for their infinite support and patience over the two years that it took to bring the first edition to fruition, and for their continued support in the production of this second edition.

Second, I would like to acknowledge colleagues both past and present who in some cases have unknowingly provided support. In particular, I would like to mention Stewart Gartside (retired), whose unlimited enthusiasm for and approach to the subject acted as a catalyst for the book, and Nathan Proudlove for the laborious task of proof-reading and for his useful comments.

I would also like to thank the editorial team of McGraw Hill for their patience.

Finally, I would like to thank my parents because ... if it wasn't for them I wouldn't have been here to do it!

Frank Dewhurst

Publisher's acknowledgements

The publishers would also like to thank the following reviewers for their help during the development of the book:

Adrian Boucher, University of Birmingham
David Coates, University of Loughborough
Neville Hunt, University of Coventry
Jill Johnes, University of Lancaster
Ulrike Inge Kussing, Stellenbosch University, South Africa
Tony Lewis, Oxford Brookes University
Michael List, Kingston University
Chris Shoostarian, University of Luton
Gary Simpson, Aston University
Stephanie Stray, University of Warwick
Niaz Wassan, University of Kent

CD contents

Examples Illustrative Excel examples used in the book (ChapterX.xls)

Solutions Solutions to end of section exercises
Solutions to mini-cases

Tables Binomial distribution (Binomial.xls)
Chi-squared distribution (Chi-square.xls)
Poisson distribution (Poisson.xls)
Normal distribution (Normal.xls)
Student's *t*-distribution (Students-t.xls)

Data sets Bank transactions
Cans of baked beans
Employees salaries and ages
Hospital Admissions
Sales for three department stores
Store transactions

Appendices
1.1	Introduction to Excel
2.1	Logarithms
2.2	Summation
3.1	Row Operations for solving systems of equations
3.2	Pivoting for solving systems of equations
3.3	Pivoting to find the inverse matrix
5.1	The group mode formula
5.2	Short-cut variance and standard deviation formula
5.3	Sample variance
6.1	Formula for Binomial probabilities
6.2	Formula for Poisson probabilities
8.1	Slope and intercept of regression line
9.1	The exponential function
10.1	Formula for roots of a quadratic
12.1	Continuous compounding formula
12.2	Compounding period and rate formulae
12.3	Sum of a geometric series
14.1	The Simplex method

OLC contents

In addition to the contents of the CD-ROM, additional material is available for lecturers and students including Powerpoint slides and sample examination questions. These can be found at:

www.mcgraw-hill.co.uk/textbooks/dewhurst

See Technology to enhance teaching and learning on page xviii for more details.

Guided Tour

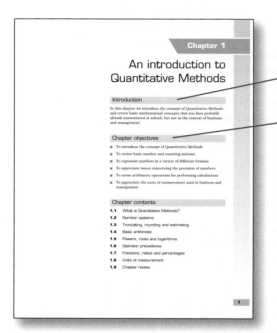

Chapter Introduction: Introduces the key topics to be covered in the chapter

Chapter objectives: Help students to understand the learning outcomes they should achieve by the end of the chapter.

Section Prerequisites: Each chapter is divided into modular sections. At the beginning of each section, a list of topics identifies what students should have mastered before beginning the new section

Examples: The text is full of examples that work through each new technique so students have a clear demonstration of each calculation to follow.

Margin References: These signposts lead students back to earlier pages to enable them to recap techniques and methods they have previously covered in the book.

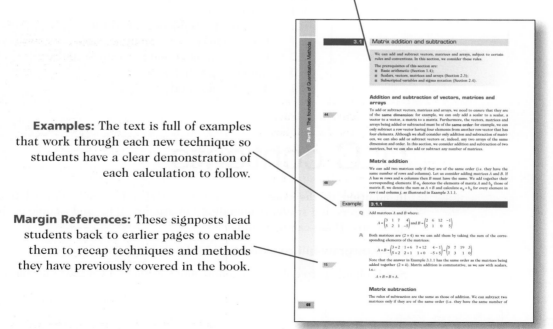

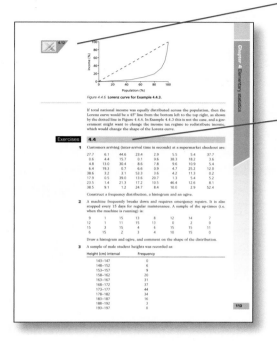

Excel Links: Margin icons also point students to the corresponding Excel example on the accompanying CD-ROM, integrating the use of spreadsheets throughout the text.

Exercises: End-of-section exercises encourage students to put their learning into practice. The exercises test their understanding and application of the quantitative techniques in the chapter.

Chapter Review: A summary section draws together the quantitative methods that students should have mastered at the end of the chapter.

Case Exercises: At the end of each part, case problems encourage students to apply the techniques from the text to a business situation, and to practise the use of quantitative techniques for decision-making.

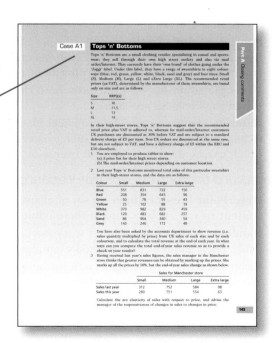

Technology to enhance learning and teaching

Visit www.mcgraw-hill.co.uk/textbooks/dewhurst today

Online Learning Centre (OLC)

After completing each chapter, log on to the supporting Online Learning Centre website. Take advantage of the study tools offered to reinforce the material you have read in the text, and to develop your skills in a fun and effective way.

Resources for students include:

- **Self-test questions** – each chapter has 12–15 multiple choice or true/false questions, for testing your progress quickly and easily.
- **Excel Spreadsheet** – Chapter by chapter Excel workbooks corresponding to the examples included in the book. Follow the Excel margin references in the textbook, and download the relevant file to see the example in Excel and read mini-tutorials on each technique.
- **Solutions to chapter exercises** – a set of solutions for the exercises in each chapter enables you to check you've solved each question correctly.
- **Additional exercises** – a set of 3–5 extra questions per chapter with answer guidelines for more problem-solving practice.
- **Appendices** – 18 self-contained sections offers some extra topics or formulae for those that wish to cover more advanced material, plus an introduction to Excel.
- **Mini-case solutions** – all the answers to the end of part mini-cases allow you to check that you've solved the business problem.
- **Datasets** – 6 new sets of data in Excel files, which include the type of data that you could be expected to handle in an organisation – such as store transactions, hospital admissions and salary information – which can be used as a basis for exercises.

Password-protected Lecturer resources include:

- **PowerPoint Presentations** – a set of chapter-by-chapter presentations which can be edited to tailor the content to suit each lecture in the module. Includes diagrams, graphs, key formulae and explanations.
- **Handouts** – chapter-by-chapter worksheets that can be provided to students to help their independent study. Each handout uses worked examples to illustrate each technique and calculation.
- **Exam questions** – a bank of extra test questions that lecturers can use for assignments, quick assessments or for exam purposes.
- **Access to all student resources for Blackboard, WebCT or other course management programme.** Ask your rep for more information.

Student CD-ROM

This book is also accompanied by a student CD allowing readers to use the Excel files as they progress through the book, and enabling them to check their progress with the exercise solutions provided.

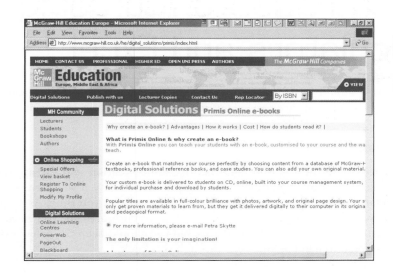

For lecturers:
Primis Content Centre

If you need to supplement your course with additional cases or content, create a personalised e-Book for your students. Visit

www.primiscontentcenter.com

or e-mail

primis_euro@mcgraw-hill.com

for more information.

Study Skills

We publish guides to help you study, research, pass exams and write essays, all the way through your university studies. Visit

www.openup.co.uk/ss/

to see the full selection and get £2 discount by entering promotional code **study** when buying online!

Computing Skills

If you'd like to brush up on your Computing skills, we have a range of titles covering MS Office applications such as Word, Excel, PowerPoint, Access and more.

Get a £2 discount off these titles by entering the promotional code **app** when ordering online at

www.mcgraw-hill.co.uk/app

An introduction to using calculators and Excel

Although you should be familiar with and happy to undertake manual calculations, most calculations are carried out using a calculator or a computer.

Calculators

All calculators perform addition, subtraction, multiplication and division and have a memory for storing numbers. You might already have a so-called 'scientific' calculator with many more functions designed to save you time. As all calculators have different functions or ways of implementing them, you need to become confident in using your calculator, and you should keep the calculator's reference manual to hand as you work through this book.

Computers

As a student you are likely to use a PC for day-to-day office tasks using 'office application' software. The standard is Microsoft Office, which comprises Word (a word processor), Excel (a spreadsheet), Access (a database) and PowerPoint (for presentations). You will probably have already encountered Microsoft Office at school or college, and in the first year of your studies you may be given basic training in using such software.

Most managers use spreadsheets for their day-to-day calculations. Although not originally designed for undertaking Quantitative Methods (they were originally designed for accounting purposes), they are widely used in this way on a day-to-day basis and often as a front-end to more specialised application packages.

Spreadsheets and Microsoft Excel

A spreadsheet consists of boxes called cells in which we type numbers, text or formulae. Cells can be formatted to be general (i.e. contain anything) or to contain specific types of number (e.g. currency, time) or just text.

The position of a cell is determined by its column reference letter (i.e. A, B, C, etc.) and row reference number (e.g. 1, 2, 3): so the top left cell is A1, and the cell below and to its immediate right is B2 (as shown in Figure i).

Spreadsheets not only enable us to undertake calculations but also have inbuilt functions similar to those on 'scientific' calculators. In this book we refer only to Excel, although other spreadsheets (e.g. Lotus and Quattro) have similar functions. If you have never used Excel, you should read the following two subsections 'Using Microsoft Excel' and 'Configuring button bars in Excel'.

Using Microsoft Excel

There are several ways of launching Excel:
- If there is an **Excel shortcut icon** on the desktop, double-click it.
- Use the **Start button** and select **Open Office Document** or **New Office Document** and double-click **Blank Workbook**.
- Use the **Start button** and select **Programs**, **Microsoft Office**, **Microsoft Excel**.
- Double-clicking on an existing Excel file will launch Excel and open the file.

Figure i shows a typical Excel screen, and the labels indicate the main features, many of which are used in all Windows-based applications.

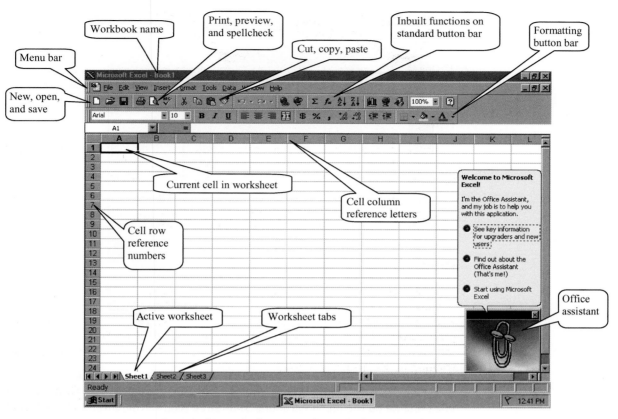

Figure i **The main features of an Excel workbook.**

Configuring button bars in Excel

If you cannot see the standard and/or the formatting bar under the menu bar, select **View** from the menu bar, then **Toolbars** and tick the Standard and Formatting pull-down menu items (as shown in Figure ii). The Standard and Formatting bars can be side by side or stacked by clicking and dragging the move pointer (i.e. ✛) and releasing the mouse button at the appropriate location.

Obtaining help in Excel

If you position the cursor on a button, it tells you what the button is for. You can obtain help by clicking on the Help button (i.e. 🔃), on **Help** and **Index** from the menu bar for specific help, or on the **Office Assistant**. To remove the Office Assistant, click on its close button (i.e. ✖). Help facilities can be activated while you are processing a workbook.

Opening, naming and saving Excel files

Before creating a spreadsheet, familiarise yourself with the screen and the pull-down menus and buttons. Many of the features and buttons operate as in Microsoft Word and other Windows-based applications. A new or existing file is called a **workbook** and consists of one or more **worksheets**; think of it as the pages (worksheets) of a book, marked up with rows and columns.

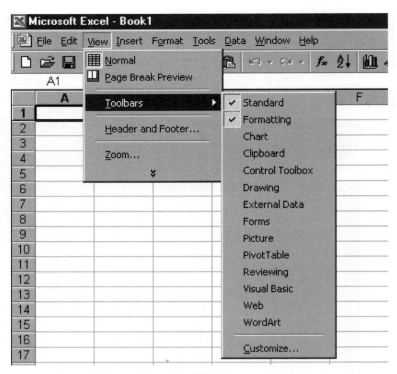

Figure ii **Configuring the Standard and Formatting button bars.**

Excel names all new files (workbooks) **Book1.xls** and shows **Book 1** above the menu bar. To change this to something more meaningful (e.g. MyAccounts.xls), click on **File** on the menu bar followed by **Save As...** Having given your workbook a new name, any subsequent work you do on it can be saved using the **save button** (i.e. 🖫).

Any previously saved workbook can be opened by double-clicking on it. If you are already running Excel, click on **File** on the menu bar, followed by **Open**; alternatively, click on the **Open** button (i.e. 🖿). To start a new workbook, simply click on the **New workbook** button (i.e. 🗋).

Renaming worksheets

Each worksheet is accessed by clicking on the tabs at the bottom of the screen labelled Sheet 1, Sheet 2, etc. and renamed by clicking on **Format**, **S̲heet** and **Rename** (as shown in Figure iii).

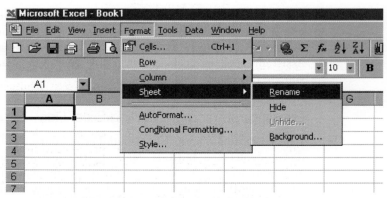

Figure iii **Renaming a worksheet.**

Entering numbers, text and formulae into a cell

To enter text, numbers or a formula into a cell, click on a cell and the cell reference appears in the Name box (Figure iv). As you type, the contents of the cell also appear in the formula bar (Figure iv). When you have finished, click on the **green tick** (i.e. ✔), press the **Enter key**, or click on a different cell. Clicking on the **red cross** (i.e. ✘) cancels what you typed, while clicking on the **equals symbol** (i.e. =), or keying the equals symbol before any text, allows you to enter a formula.

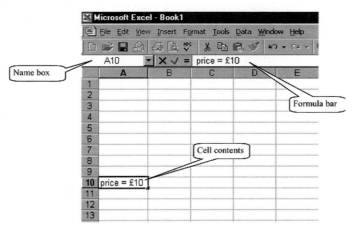

Figure iv **Typing in the contents of a cell.**

Editing and changing the contents of cells

To change the contents of a cell, point at it, press the **F2** key and change the contents as required. Click on the **green tick** (i.e. ✔) or press the **Enter key** to confirm.

The editing facilities in Excel are similar to those in other Windows-based applications. To edit (i.e. move, copy, delete) cell entries or change them in some way (e.g. underline, bold, change font or size), highlight the first cell by clicking on it and drag the mouse to highlight the block of cells you wish to edit. To change all cells, click **Edit** on the menu bar followed by **Select All**. To edit one or more columns (or rows), simply click on the column (or row) labels.

To change the appearance of highlighted cells, click on the relevant button (e.g. **B** for bold, *I* for italics, U̲ for underline, the font style and/or font size arrow buttons, i.e. Arial ▾ 10 ▾ etc.). To delete the contents of a highlighted cell, press the **Delete (Del)** key.

To left-, centre- or right-justify cell contents, highlight the appropriate cells and click on the relevant button (i.e. ≣ ≣ ≣). You can merge adjacent cells by clicking the **merge button** ⊞ . As in most Windows-based applications, there are several ways to edit:

(a) Click on **Edit** on the menu bar followed by **Cut** (to delete or move) or **Copy** (to copy), then move to a new cell and click on **Edit** and **Paste**.
(b) As in (a), except use the appropriate buttons (i.e. ✂ 🖹 📋).
(c) As in (a), except use the right mouse button to select **Cut**, **Copy** or **Paste**.
(d) To move contents from one cell to another, you can drag and drop. Highlight the cells to be moved, release the left mouse button, click the left mouse button on the edge of the highlighted range of cells, keep it depressed and

drag them to the new location. Once in position, release the left mouse button.

You can undo most changes using **Edit**, **Undo** or the **Undo button** (i.e. ↶ ▾).

Filling cells

From the menu bar, select **Edit** followed by **Fill** to fill a row (fill **Right**) or fill a column (fill **Down**) with the same number, text or formula. To fill a row or column with a series of numbers (e.g. dates), choose fill **Series...** (having first highlighted the range of cells you want to fill and either the cell to be copied or the one with the first number/date, etc. in the series).

Borders and colours

To draw boxes around cells, to highlight a single cell or range of cells, click the arrow next to the **Border** button (i.e. ▦ ▾), select the type of border and press the **Enter key**. You can give cells a background colour by using the **Fill color** button (i.e. 🎨 ▾).

Printing worksheets

Before printing a spreadsheet, click on **File** on the menu bar and then click on **Print Preview** or click the **Print Preview** button (i.e. 🔍), to ensure the spreadsheet displays what you want it to; otherwise, click the **Close** button in Print Preview and undertake the appropriate changes.

To print part of your spreadsheet, click on **File** on the menu bar, then **Page Setup...** and click on the **Sheet** tab at the top of this dialog box, revealing a new dialog box with a box titled **Print Area**. Having clicked in this box, either **drag the mouse over the cells** that you want to print (you might have to move the dialog box out of the way) or type in the cell references. Once again, click the **Print Preview** button to check that you have selected the appropriate area of the worksheet.

To print your worksheets, click on **File** on the menu bar followed by **Print...** to get the usual Windows dialogue box for selection of printer and pages to print, etc.

Closing and leaving Excel

To leave Excel, click on **File** on the menu bar followed by **Exit**, or click the **Close** button. If you have not already saved your file, you will be prompted to do so.

Inbuilt functions and tools

Many of Excel's useful features (e.g. formatting cells, using functions and formulae, drawing charts) are described in the spreadsheets on the enclosed CD-ROM and also online at **www.mcgraw-hill.co.uk/textbooks/dewhurst**

Data Analysis ToolPak and Solver Add-Ins

In addition to its standard set of inbuilt functions, Excel also has **Data Analysis** tools and a powerful tool called **Solver** (which may or may not have been installed on your version of Excel).

To check their installation, select **Tools** and see whether **Data Analysis...** and **Solver...** appear in the drop-down menu (Figure v). If they do, click on Data Analysis... and see whether a scrollable dialogue box appears. Do the same with Solver... and see whether the Solver parameter dialogue box appears.

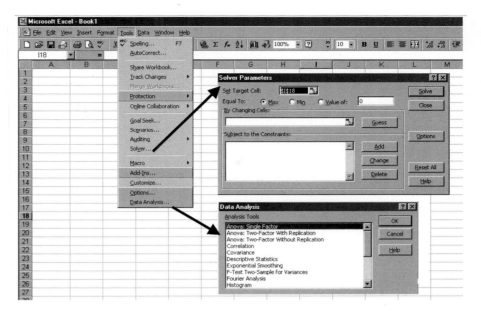

Figure v **Checking for the installation of the ToolPak and Solver.**

If they do not appear on the **Tools** drop-down menu, you will need to install them from the Excel installation disks. To do this, click on **Tools** and select **Add-Ins...** from the pull-down menu (Figure vi). Check **Analysis ToolPak**, **Analysis ToolPak-VBA** and scroll down the list to check **Solver** and then click **OK** and follow the instructions.

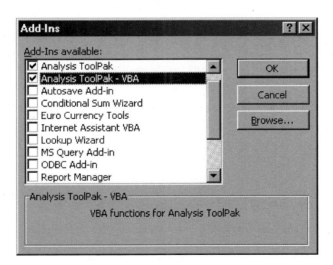

Figure vi **The Add-Ins dialogue box.**

A note on the use of spreadsheets on the enclosed CD-ROM

The spreadsheet files on the CD (e.g. Chapter 1.xls) cannot be changed or saved onto the CD.

If you want to change any of the spreadsheets on the CD, then save them to your hard disk together with any changes. You will always be able to obtain the original versions by going back to the CD.

The foundations of Quantitative Methods

The first part of this book covers the underlying mathematical and statistical notation and concepts used in Quantitative Methods. Most, but not all, of the material in this part of the book is covered at school, and is therefore revision. However, some of the material in this part will be new to most readers, even those who have taken mathematics beyond GCSE (UK) or the equivalent. Even though you may be familiar with some of the concepts, you might find that the notation, approach taken and certainly the applications to Business and Management will be new to you. Therefore you are strongly advised to read through the chapters appropriate to your studies and you might need to refer back to this part of the book when you progress to the later chapters. Most courses in Quantitative Methods will expect you to be familiar with the notation and concepts in the whole of Chapter 1, the first half of Chapter 2, Chapter 4 and Chapter 5. To reinforce your understanding of the notation and concepts, you should undertake the end of section exercises and attempt the mini-cases at the end of this part of the book.

Part contents

An introduction to Quantitative Methods

Introduction

In this chapter we introduce the concept of Quantitative Methods and review basic mathematical concepts that you have probably already encountered at school, but not in the context of business and management.

Chapter objectives

- To introduce the concept of Quantitative Methods
- To review basic number and counting systems
- To represent numbers in a variety of different formats
- To appreciate issues concerning the precision of numbers
- To revise arithmetic operations for performing calculations
- To appreciate the units of measurement used in business and management

Chapter contents

What is Quantitative Methods?

Quantitative Methods was first used by scientists as a catch-all phrase for ways of dealing with experimental observations. But what has this to do with business and management?

Although business and management are not pure sciences, many of their underlying disciplines involve scientific ideas. For example, accounting, economics and production and operations management are based on the pure science of mathematics, and marketing and human resource management are based in the behavioural sciences of psychology and sociology. All these disciplines make observations about their environment (e.g. the effects of advertising on markets) and describe and analyse them to provide information. The process of observing, describing, analysing and drawing conclusions forms the basis of scientific methodology. When we apply this process to management we call it Management Science. So, to understand Quantitative Methods, it is necessary to have some appreciation of scientific methodology.

Scientific methodology

When we undertake a study, we need to think about what it is for and how we are going to do it. First, we identify the scope, aims and objectives of the study (e.g. to test the effect of a new marketing strategy on end-of-year sales). We then collect relevant data (e.g. by surveying high-street shoppers). Having collected our data, we might just describe them or we might seek to analyse them scientifically, and this could involve building a model (a simplification or abstraction of reality). In physics or engineering we often encounter analogue models (e.g. a scaled-down version of a jet engine), while in business or management we often use iconic models (e.g. a flowchart) or a symbolic model (e.g. a system of mathematical equations).

Having built, tested and refined a model, we then experiment with it under different operating conditions. From an analysis of data and a model, we might then make inferences about reality (e.g. the cost-effectiveness of advertising on TV, in the national press, or both, over 1 year). We then draw conclusions and report (e.g. write a report and make recommendations to the marketing director). We might also become involved in implementation (e.g. mounting an advertising campaign on TV rather than in the national press). Figure 1.1.1 summarises this basic scientific methodology using an iconic model.

So what is Quantitative Methods?

Although most of us would use the basic scientific methodology in Figure 1.1.1, we might follow only the left-hand path (i.e. describe the data) by simply saying what was observed in a **qualitative** manner (e.g. by telling the marketing director that most people would buy the product if it was advertised on TV). Although providing some information, this is not very convincing. It would be better to ask how many items people would buy if the product was advertised on TV at a particular price. When we ask such questions, we are measuring quantities (i.e. number of items bought at a certain price) and are using **Quantitative Methods**. In this way, we can describe our observations in greater detail (e.g. 60% of UK households would buy the product if advertised on TV at £5) and follow the right-hand paths in Figure 1.1.1, culminating in more convincing arguments and greater support to managers. As Quantitative Methods employs statistical

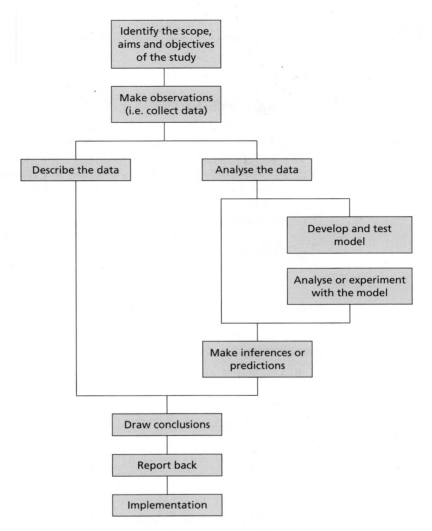

Figure 1.1.1 **An iconic model of a typical scientific methodology.**

and mathematical concepts, it is closely related to the topics of Business Statistics or Business Mathematics. When applied to modelling decision situations, we talk about Operational Research, Decision Analysis and Decision Science.

Help, I never understood maths at school

Although it may be some time since you did any mathematics, if you followed the logical approach described above you have jumped the first hurdle. Most of the mathematics and statistics in business and management are relatively simple and based on common sense. The mathematics you did at school was often abstract and not applied to business and management. **This book assumes you have forgotten any mathematics you came across at school**. The mathematics and statistics in this book are fully illustrated by worked examples, and also implemented on Excel spreadsheets as if by practising managers. If you have never used Excel, or if you need a refresher, you should read the Introduction to Excel for Quantitative Methods, which can be found on the CD and on the associated website **www.mcgraw-hill.co.uk/textbooks/dewhurst**. Formal mathematics is kept to a minimum, but some proofs and derivations of formulae can also be found on the associated website **www.mcgraw-hill.co.uk/textbooks/dewhurst**. The idea behind this book is **learning by doing**, and you are encouraged to work through the worked examples and exercises in the book and the spreadsheets on the CD.

Number systems

When we deal with quantities we are really dealing with numbers because we represent measurements of quantities using numbers. For example, the quantity of money borrowed by a company in 1 month might be £2,000 or the quantity of steel used by a car manufacturer per year might be 80,000 tonnes. Therefore we need to understand what we mean by numbers. This section reviews number systems encountered in business and management.

The prerequisites of this section are:
■ What is Quantitative Methods? (Section 1.1).

The decimal system

Most of us count in **denary** (i.e. the decimal counting system), which has ten distinct **digits**:

0, 1, 2, 3, 4, 5, 6, 7, 8, 9

In this system, all quantities are expressed by using these ten digits and other symbols. For example, the number 202 consists of the digits 2 and 0 arranged in a particular sequence, whereas the number 220 consists of the same digits arranged differently. Although the digits in both 202 and 220 are the same (i.e. 2 and 0) it is not only the digits themselves but also their position in the sequence that make up a particular number. To understand what a particular number means, we write it in **expanded notation**, as shown in Example 1.2.1.

Example | **1.2.1**

Q What does the decimal number 628 actually mean?

A The positions of the digits tell us that this number has:

six **hundreds**	i.e.	$6 \times 100 = 600$
two **tens**	i.e.	$2 \times 10 = 20$
and eight **units**	i.e.	$8 \times 1 = 8$

We see this more clearly in Table 1.2.1, in which the columns are written as multiples of 10.

Table 1.2.1 **Expanded number notation for hundreds, tens and units.**

Hundreds (100s)	Tens (10s)	Units (1s)
6	2	8

Condensed and expanded notation

The number **628** can be thought of as a **condensed form** of Table 1.2.1. For numbers having digits on either side of the hundreds and units columns, we usually insert special symbols. For example, the number 6280 is written as 6,280 where the **comma** indicates thousands or higher numbers. The **decimal point** in

0.628 indicates that the number is smaller than 1 (i.e. smaller than unity) and that we are dealing in tenths, hundredths, thousandths, etc.

If we insert a new column to the left of the 'hundreds' column in Table 1.2.1 it will contain 'thousands' (i.e. 1,000s) while columns to the right of the 'units' column will contain 'tenths' (i.e. 0.1ths, because $1/10 = 0.1$): see Table 1.2.2. If we move left in Table 1.2.2, the columns increase by factors of 10, while, if we move right, we divide by factors of 10.

Table 1.2.2 **General expanded notation.**

←	Thousands	Comma	Hundreds	Tens	Units	Decimal point	Tenths	→
Multiply previous column by 10	1,000s	,	100s	10s	1s	.	0.1s	Divide previous column by 10

When writing a number in expanded notation, each column must contain a digit so that the position of the comma and decimal point can be fixed. If a number does not have a digit in a particular column then we insert a 0 (i.e. zero). For example, 'eighteen thousand, one hundred and five pounds and six pence' in expanded notation is shown in Table 1.2.3, and therefore is written as **£18,105.06** in condensed notation.

Table 1.2.3 **Expanded notation for 18,105.06.**

Ten thousands (10,000s)	Thousands (1,000s)	,	Hundreds (100s)	Tens (10s)	Units (1s)	.	Tenths (0.1s)	Hundredths (0.01s)
1	8		1	0	5		0	6

By using ten digits, where each column in expanded notation represents a multiple or division of a factor of 10, then we say we are counting in **base ten** or **denary**.

Exponential notation

The column headings of Tables 1.2.1, 1.2.2 and 1.2.3 will need a lot of space to accommodate expanded notation: for example, in Table 1.2.4 the next left-hand column would be headed 'hundred thousands' (i.e. 100,000s) and the next right-hand column would be headed 'thousandths' (i.e. 0.001s). When using large or very small numbers, this form of notation becomes unwieldy and prone to mistakes by missing out zeros.

Remember that 100 is '10 times 10' (i.e. $10 \times 10 = 100$) and that the two zeros in 100 result from the two zeros in the multiplication 10×10. Instead of writing 100 as 10×10, we could say we are multiplying 10 twice and abbreviate this as 10^2, where the small superscript number 2 represents the number of multiples or the fact that 100 contains two zeros. Next, consider 1000, which is $10 \times 10 \times 10$; we could abbreviate this as 10^3 to denote three multiplications of 10 or the fact that 1,000 contains three zeros. So 10^1 must simply be 10 because it contains one zero. This is called **exponential notation**. The small (i.e. superscript) number representing multiplications of ten (i.e. the number of zeros) is called the **exponent**. Using exponential notation we can write the tens, hundreds, thousands, etc. columns of the expanded notation table as shown in Table 1.2.4.

Table 1.2.4 **Exponential notation for tens, hundreds and higher multiples of ten.**

Ten thousands (10,000s)	Thousands (1,000s)	,	Hundreds (100s)	Tens (10s)	Units (1s)	.	Tenths (0.1s)	Hundredths (0.01s)
10^4	10^3		10^2	10^1				

Exponential notation can be extended to deal with the units, tenths, hundredths, etc. columns. We define the units column as 10^0 because **unity** (i.e. 1 unit) contains no zeros. For tenths, hundredths, etc. (i.e. numbers to the right of the decimal point or below unity), we place a '−' symbol in front of the exponent. To be consistent with our notation, we should also place a '+' symbol in front of the exponent for numbers to the left of the decimal point (i.e. above unity). Table 1.2.5 shows this exponential form of notation for all the columns of Table 1.2.4.

Positive exponents to the left of the decimal point

Table 1.2.5 **Exponential notation for multiples of ten.**

Ten thousands (10,000s)	Thousands (1,000s)	,	Hundreds (100s)	Tens (10s)	Units (1s)	.	Tenths (0.1s)	Hundredths (0.01s)
10^{+4}	10^{+3}		10^{+2}	10^{+1}	10^0		10^{-1}	10^{-2}

Any number with an exponent of zero is unity (i.e. 1)

Negative exponents to the right of decimal point

An easy way to remember how exponential notation works is to think of numbers to the left of the decimal point as being multiples of 10 and of those to the right as being divisions by ten:

$$1\,0\,0\,0\,0\,0 = 10 \times 10 \times 10 \times 10 \times 10 = 10^{+5} \text{ i.e. five multiplications of ten}$$
$$1\,0\,0\,0\,0 = 10 \times 10 \times 10 \times 10 \qquad = 10^{+4} \text{ i.e. four multiplications of ten}$$
$$1\,0\,0\,0 = 10 \times 10 \times 10 \qquad = 10^{+3} \text{ i.e. three multiplications of ten}$$
$$1\,0\,0 = 10 \times 10 \qquad = 10^{+2} \text{ i.e. two multiplications of ten}$$
$$1\,0 = 10 \qquad = 10^{+1} \text{ i.e. ten itself}$$
$$1 = 1 \qquad = 10^0 \text{ i.e. unity}$$
$$0.1 = 1/10 \qquad = 10^{-1} \text{ i.e. one division by ten}$$
$$0.01 = 1/100 \qquad = 10^{-2} \text{ i.e. two divisions by ten}$$
$$0.001 = 1/1,000 \qquad = 10^{-3} \text{ i.e. three divisions by ten}$$
$$0.0001 = 1/10,000 \qquad = 10^{-4} \text{ i.e. four divisions by ten}$$
$$0.00001 = 1/100,000 \qquad = 10^{-5} \text{ i.e. five divisions by ten}$$

Usually, we do not write the '+' symbol for multiples, as this is considered the default, but we always prefix the exponent by '−' when we are dividing by tens.

Scientific notation

Some calculators and computers express numbers in a different form because the display or screen is unable to handle long sequences of digits. This is called

scientific notation and uses exponential notation to abbreviate the way in which numbers are displayed. Consider 180,000, which we can write as $18 \times 10{,}000$. Using exponential notation this can be written as 18×10^4. This is called the **scientific form** of the number. In general, scientific notation has a **mantissa** (e.g. 18), **base** (e.g. 10) and **exponent** (e.g. 4), i.e.

Mantissa $\times$ base^{exponent}	*(1.2.1)*

Usually, the mantissa has only one digit or no digits before the decimal point. For example, 180,000 can be written as $1.8 \times 100{,}000$, and in scientific form this would be 1.8×10^5, where 1.8 is the mantissa, 10 is the base and 5 is the exponent.

Most calculators and some computers abbreviate this notation further by not displaying the base number (e.g. 10) at all, whereas others replace it with a letter (often the letter E is used). Example 1.2.2 illustrates typical ways in which numbers are displayed in scientific notation.

Example | **1.2.2**

Q   Write the decimal numbers (a) 812,000,000 and (b) 0.000,000,008,12 using scientific notation.

A   (a)   If we write 812,000,000 as $8.12 \times 100{,}000{,}000$ and then as: 8.12×10^8
we might see this displayed as: 8.12E 8
or: 8.12E + 08
or: 8.12E 08
If we write 812,000,000 as $0.812 \times 1{,}000{,}000{,}000$ and then as: 0.812×10^9
we might see this displayed as: 0.812E 9
or: 0.812E + 09
or: 0.812E 09

   (b)   If we write 0.000,000,008,12 as $8.12/1{,}000{,}000{,}000$ and then as: 8.12×10^{-9}
we might see this displayed as: 8.12E − 9
or: 8.12 − 09
If we write 0.000,000,008,12 as $0.812/100{,}000{,}000$ and then as: 0.812×10^{-8}
we might see this displayed as: 0.812E − 8
or: 0.812 − 08

In a spreadsheet, it is possible to format one or a number of cells to display numbers in a variety of ways, including scientific notation.

Other number systems

It is claimed we count in base 10 (i.e. use the denary or decimal system) because we have 10 fingers or digits. However, there are many other number or counting systems: for example, both time and the degrees of a circle are measured using a base of 60 (i.e. minutes and seconds). Three other number bases or counting systems are extremely important as a result of using computers, and are worth mentioning briefly.

Binary

Our recent dependence on calculators and, more importantly, computers hardly needs comment. All calculators and computers are essentially made up of switches, which can be in one of two states, either ON or OFF. If we denote these two states by 0 and 1 (say 0 for ON and 1 for OFF) then we have a two-digit (i.e. **binary**) counting system. As with the denary system, we can consider binary expanded notation with columns containing exponents of 2, instead of 10, as illustrated in Table 1.2.6. Once again, we write unity (i.e. 1) as 2^0 and we have positive exponents for binary numbers to the left of unity and negative exponents for binary numbers to the right.

Table 1.2.6 **Exponential form of binary**

←	2^{+4}	2^{+3}	2^{+2}	2^{+1}	2^0	2^{-1}	2^{-2}	→
Multiply previous column by 2	$2 \times 2 \times 2 \times 2$	$2 \times 2 \times 2$	2×2	2	1	$\frac{1}{2}$	$\frac{1}{4}$	Divide previous column by 2
	16	8	4	2	1	0.5	0.25	

Example **1.2.3**

Q Write the binary number 10011 in expanded notation and calculate the decimal equivalent.

A First, we need to put the binary digits into the appropriate columns of Table 1.2.6, and then we can calculate the appropriate decimal equivalent of each column, as shown in Table 1.2.7:

Table 1.2.7 **Converting 10011 binary to decimal.**

Exponents	2^4	2^3	2^2	2^1	2^0	
Binary digits	1	0	0	1	1	
i.e.	1×2^4	0×2^3	0×2^2	1×2^1	1×2^0	Binary exponential notation
i.e.	1×16	0×8	0×4	1×2	1×1	Decimal digits
i.e.	16	0	0	2	1	Decimal values

We can now add up the decimals in each column to get the decimal equivalent of the binary number 10011 (i.e. $16 + 0 + 0 + 2 + 1 = 19$).

Octal and hexadecimal

Binary notation is extremely cumbersome because long sequences of digits are required for relatively small decimal numbers: for example, 694 in decimal notation is equivalent to 1010110110 in binary. Because of this, most computer switches are placed in banks of 8 or 16. Most computers use either the **octal** counting system (i.e. **base 8**) or the **hexadecimal** counting system (i.e. **base 16**). In the octal system, the eight digits 0, 1, 2, 3, 4, 5, 6 and 7 are used, while the hexadecimal system has sixteen digits: 0, 1, 2, 3, 4, 5, 6, 7, 8, 9, A, B, C, D, E and F.

Exercises **1.2**

1 Write the following numbers in exponential notation:
    (a) 10,000   (b) 10,000,000   (c) 0.01
    (d) 0.00001   (e) One tenth   (f) One thousandth.

2 Write the following numbers in scientific notation and identify the mantissa and exponents in each case:
    (a) 365,000,000   (b) 50 billion   (c) 0.05
    (d) 0.000052.

3 Write the following numbers in expanded notation:
(a) 3.1612×10^2 (b) 0.513×10^6 (c) $66.25E\,2$
(d) 98.45×10^{-2} (e) $594E-8$ (f) $18.95E-4$.

4 Calculate the following:
(a) 2^3 (b) 2^6 (c) 8^2
(d) 2^{-1} (e) 2^0 (f) 2^{-2}
(g) 16^2.

5 Represent the following in binary exponential notation:
(a) 16   (b) 64   (c) 4^3
(d) 8^4 (e) 16^2 (f) 0.125.

6 Convert the following binary numbers to decimal:
(a) 100   (b) 1001   (c) 10011
(d) 11001

| 1.3 | Truncating, rounding and estimating |

Many measurements in business and management are often approximate or taken to a limited degree of precision: for example, when working in UK currency (i.e. pounds sterling and pence) we usually only work to at most two decimal places. When we present our calculations, we might reduce the degree of precision to avoid the confusion of lots of digits: for example, in the end-of-year accounts the annual profits of a company might be presented to the nearest £ million. The number of digits in a number can be reduced in two ways: **rounding off** or **truncating**. In this section, we look at these processes and the issues surrounding their use.

The prerequisites of this section are:
- Number systems (Section 1.2).

Rounding

When we round numbers, the most extreme right-hand digits are dropped and the preceding digit is either left alone or increased: for example, the number 365.218 might be **rounded up** to 365.22 to give the nearest number with two **decimal places** (d.p.). This might be done if the quantity being measured is cash. However, if we want to round the number to the nearest **integer** (i.e. whole number) then we might **round down** to 365. This might be done when calculating the number of working days per year.

Problems occur when the digit to be rounded is 5 (e.g. in rounding 86.325 to two decimal places). Usually such half-way points are rounded up, so that 86.325 would be rounded up to 86.33.

Rounding does not apply solely to decimal places (e.g. a company's published accounts may present figures rounded to the nearest £1,000). When making calculations, we must always present the result with the same degree of precision as the original numbers. Errors that occur in rounding are called **rounding errors**. Example 1.3.1 illustrates how they occur.

| Example | 1.3.1 |

Q Calculate the result of (a) multiplying the number 0.666666 by itself and compare it with the result when (b) the number is rounded to three decimal places before the multiplication.

A (a) $0.666666 \times 0.666666 = 0.444443556$

However, the answer must have the same number of decimal places that we started with. The number 0.666666 has six decimal places and the answer should be rounded to 0.444444.

(b) Rounding 0.666666 to three decimal places gives 0.667 and $0.667 \times 0.667 = 0.444889$

The results of multiplication must have the same number of decimal places as the numbers being multiplied and rounding to three decimal places gives 0.445.

Note that if we round the answer in (a) to three decimal places we get 0.444. The difference between the answers in (a) and (b) (i.e. $0.445 - 0.444 = 0.001$) is called the rounding error.

Truncating

Truncating is simply chopping off unrequired digits. If we truncate 365.218 to five **significant figures** we get 365.21. Calculators and computers truncate numbers stored in memory (e.g. RAM), and therefore organisations that use such devices (e.g. banks) might use truncated figures. Errors can occur with truncating as they do when rounding. Example 1.3.2 illustrates how truncation errors occur.

Example	**1.3.2**

Q Calculate the result of adding the numbers 15.001 and 15.999, (a) before truncating and (b) after truncating to two significant figures.

A (a) $15.001 + 15.999 = 31$;

(b) truncating 15.001 gives 15 and truncating 15.999 gives 15 and $15 + 15 = 30$.

The difference (i.e. $31 - 30 = 1$) is the **truncation error**. Note that rounding to the nearest integer (i.e. 15 and 16) before adding gives the same as the untruncated answer (i.e. $15 + 16 = 31$).

There are inbuilt functions available in most spreadsheets for rounding, rounding up, rounding down and truncating.

Estimating

When undertaking calculations, we need to know whether the answer is 'in the right ball park'. Sometimes we might just want a ball-park figure. In such cases, we estimate the 'order of magnitude' by rounding to make the calculations easy and then add or subtract a small amount to take account of the rounding error, as illustrated in Example 1.3.3.

Example	**1.3.3**

Q Calculate the total annual wage paid to an employee earning £4.15 per hour for 40 hours per week.

A If we assume 52 working weeks per year then:

The total annual wage is $= 52 \times 40 \times 4.15$

$$= 8,632$$

To check our calculation or simply to have a ball-park figure, we might round the number of weeks to 50, leave the hours at 40 per week giving $50 \times 40 = 2,000$ (check by calculating $4 \times 5 = 20$ and multiplying by $10 \times 10 = 100$ giving 2,000) and then multiply by 4 to give 8,000. An alternative way would be to note that $4 \times 4 = 16$, multiplied by 10 gives 160 and multiplied by 50 gives 8,000.

A better estimate can be found by taking the remainders after rounding (i.e. 2 from 52 and 0.15 from 4.15) and multiplying them (i.e. $2 \times 0.15 = 0.3$). Because this should have been done when we multiplied 50×40 to get 2,000 then we multiply 2,000 by 0.3 giving a further 600 (i.e. $0.3 \times 2,000 = 600$). So a better estimate is $8,000 + 600 = 8,600$.

Exercises **1.3**

1 For each of the following numbers:
(a) 256.172   (b) 13.35972   (c) 3,014.9142

(i) round up to two decimal places;
(ii) round down to two decimal places;
(iii) round to two decimal places.

2 Repeat Question 1 above but round each number to the nearest integer.

3 Truncate the numbers given in Question 1:
(a) to five significant figures;
(a) to two significant figures.

4 Estimate the following and check the accuracy of your estimates on a calculator or spreadsheet:
(a) 102×36.5 (b) half of 40 times 3.50   (c) 3.142^3

5 The end-of-year accounts of a company include total costs of £15.659 million and total income (revenue) of £36,258,400. What are the end-of-year profits (i.e. total revenue − total costs) in millions rounded to two decimal places?

1.4 Basic arithmetic

Having discussed numbers, let us now consider how they are manipulated or used. The most common forms of number manipulation are the four basic arithmetic operations of:

- **addition**;
- **subtraction**;
- **multiplication**;
- **division**.

These are easily performed on all calculators and computers. There are commonly accepted conventions or laws governing these operations, which are inbuilt in all calculators and computers. In this section, we review these arithmetic operators and the rules and laws governing their use.

The prerequisites of this section are:
- Number systems (Section 1.2);
- Truncating, rounding and estimating (Section 1.3).

The sign of a number

The simplest operator is that of changing the sign of a number: for example, changing from $+8$ to -8. Most calculators have a single key to do this (labelled '±'). A related operator is the modulus operator, which removes or ignores the sign of a number to give its absolute value. The modulus operator is denoted by two vertical lines, one on each side of the number, for example $|-3| = 3$. Because these

13

Chapter 1 An introduction to Quantitative Methods

operators act on a single number they are known as **unary operators**. But what does the sign of a number indicate? The best way to think of this is along a scale:

Numbers below zero are negative	*Zero*	*Numbers above zero are positive*
$-5 \quad -4 \quad -3 \quad -2 \quad -1$	0	$+1 \quad +2 \quad +3 \quad +4 \quad +5$

Numbers below (to the left of) 0 are negative and numbers above (to the right of) 0 are positive. Positive numbers are considered the default and are not prefixed by the '+' sign. However, the '−' sign is always used for numbers below 0.

Most other operators work on pairs of numbers (i.e. **binary operators**): for example, addition, subtraction, multiplication and division. The symbols used for these operations are usually written as '+', '−', '×' and '÷' respectively, with the numbers being operated on appearing on either side of the symbol.

Addition and subtraction

The symbol '+' denotes addition of numbers: for example, we write $5 + 3$ to denote the addition of 3 to 5. When adding numbers together we are taking their **sum** and refer to the operation as **summation**.

The symbol '−' denotes subtraction of numbers: for example, we write $5 - 3$ when subtracting 3 from 5. When subtracting numbers we are taking their **difference**, and we refer to the operation as the **process of taking differences**. Addition (i.e. summation) and subtraction (i.e. difference) symbols are found on all computer keyboards. However, for multiplication and division of numbers, a variety of symbols are used.

Multiplication

The traditional symbol for multiplication is '×': for example, '5 multiplied by 3' is written as 5×3. Sometimes, the multiplication symbol is omitted or replaced by a full stop so that 5.3 is the same as 5×3 (**do not confuse this with the decimal point**). Computers, to avoid confusion with the letter 'x', use the asterisk (i.e. *). So we write $5 * 3$ instead of 5×3. Sometimes, we call the operation of multiplication the process of calculating the **product** of numbers. From now on, we shall use * to denote multiplication or the process of calculating the product of numbers.

Division

The traditional symbol for division is '÷': for example, '5 divided by 3' is written $5 \div 3$.

Note that division of 5 by 3 results in a **recurring** decimal (i.e. 1.66666 ...), written as **1.66˙** (the dot above the last digit indicates that the digit 6 continues indefinitely). We could also round it to seven decimal places to give: 1.6666667.

The division symbol is often replaced both in written form and on the computer. Sometimes, the number to be divided is underlined, with the divisor being placed directly below:

$\dfrac{5}{3}$ is the same as $5 \div 3$

Written like this and left unevaluated (i.e. not calculated as 1.667 to three decimal places), we call this a **fraction** or a **quotient**. A fraction is essentially the unevaluated division of two numbers. The top number is called the **numerator** and the bottom number is the **denominator**. All fractions take the form:

$$\frac{\text{Numerator}}{\text{Denominator}} \qquad\qquad (1.4.1)$$

As we saw in Section 1.2 the '/' (i.e. forward slash) is often used to denote division or fractions and is always used on computers. For example, **5/3** is the same as **5 ÷ 3**. From now on, we use '/' to denote division.

When the numerator is 1 (i.e. unity), we call the fraction a **reciprocal** or **inverse**: for example, 1/3 is the reciprocal or inverse of 3. Division can also be viewed as multiplication by the reciprocal of the denominator: for example, 5/3 can be written as:

$$5 * \frac{1}{3}$$

The commutative law

When we add or multiply numbers the order in which the numbers are written down does not matter: for example, $5 + 3$ is the same as $3 + 5$ (i.e. both calculations give 8) and $5 * 3$ is the same as $3 * 5$ (i.e. both give 15). This is the **commutative law**. Clearly, if the law applies to addition then it must also apply to multiplication because multiplication is just repeated addition.

However, subtraction and division are **not commutative**: for example, $5 - 3$ is 2 but $3 - 5$ is -2, and 5/3 is 1.667 (to three d.p.) but 3/5 is 0.6.

Comparison operators

Operators used for comparisons are also binary operators: for example, the **equality** operator (i.e. '=') is a binary operator because $10^2 = 100$ operates on 10^2 and 100, which are either side of the '='.

We often encounter other comparison operators in business and management. Sometimes we compare numbers on the basis of **less than** or **greater than**. The symbol '<' means 'less than' and '>' means 'greater than': for example, $3 < 5$ (i.e. 3 is less than 5) or $5 > 3$ (i.e. 5 is greater than 3). We use the same symbols on computers. Sometimes we compare numbers on the basis of **less than or equal to** or **greater than or equal to**. The symbol '≤' means 'less than or equal to' and '≥' means 'greater than or equal to'. To make these comparisons on a computer, we use two keys for each operator. For 'less than or equal to' we press the '<' followed by the '=' keys, and for 'greater than or equal to' we press the '>' followed by the '=' keys. Note that these two operators are **never** written down as '=<' or '=>'. These four comparison operators ('<', '>', '≤', '≥') are called **inequalities**, and we speak of **strict inequalities** when dealing with '<' (i.e. strictly less than) and '>' (i.e. strictly greater than).

The opposite of equal is **not equal** and is usually written as '≠'. On a computer we press the '<' followed by the '>' key. So 5 <> 3 means $5 \neq 3$ (i.e. 5 is not equal to 3).

Sometimes we want to say that two numbers are approximately the same and we use the symbol ≈ (approximately equal to), for example, $\frac{2}{3} \approx 0.67$.

Rules of arithmetic

Basic arithmetic operations apply to all numbers, but we have to be careful, particularly when dealing with negative numbers, fractions and decimals. There are some **basic rules** to remember:

Subtracting a negative number is the same as adding	*(1.4.2)*

For example, $5 - -10 = 5 + 10 = 15$

Multiplying or dividing a positive number by a negative number gives a negative number	*(1.4.3)*

For example, $2 * -5 = -10$ and $5/-10 = -0.5$

> Multiplying or dividing a negative number by a positive number gives a negative number
>
> (1.4.4)

For example, $-2 * 5 = -10$ and $-5/10 = -0.5$

> Multiplying or dividing a negative number by a negative number gives a positive number
>
> (1.4.5)

For example, $-2 * -5 = 10$ and $-5/-10 = 0.5$

Division by zero

When we divide by very small numbers we get very large numbers: for example, $1/0.00000000000000002 = 50,000,000,000,000$, which is extremely large. If we divide by extremely small numbers (i.e. almost zero) then the result will be larger still; in fact, we might say infinitely large. When we try to divide by zero we may consider the answer to be infinitely large and simply call it **infinity**. We use '∞' to denote infinity. If we try to divide by zero on a computer we get a message '**#DIV/O!**', which indicates that arithmetically we cannot have a sensible number.

Exercises 1.4

1 Calculate the following 'by hand' and check your results on a calculator or spreadsheet:

(a) $5 - 3$ (b) $5 - 13$ (c) $54 - 80$

(d) $54 - -8$ (e) $4 * -2$ (f) $-4 * -2$

(g) $8/-3$ (h) $-8/-3$ (i) $8 * 2 + 3$

(j) $8 * 2 + 8 * 3$ (k) $3 * 3 + 4 * 4$ (l) $7 * 7$

(m) $16/2 + 15/3$ (n) 16 plus 15 all divided by 5

(o) $3 * 16 + 2 * 15$ all divided by 6   (p) $1.5 * 1.5$.

2 Which of the following statements are true and which are false?

(a) $4 * 4 = 2 * 2 * 2 * 2 * 2 * 2$ (b) $4 * 18 > 7 * 10$

(c) $120/40 < 2 * 3$ (d) $4 * 3 + 4 * 2 = 20$

(e) My age $\leqslant$ the oldest person I know

(f) A quintet contains $>$ six musicians

(g) Two litres $\geqslant 1$ imperial gallon.

1.5 Powers, roots and logarithms

> There are several other binary operators, found on most calculators and computers used in business and management. In this section we look at them and how they are used.
>
> The prerequisites of this section are:
> - Number systems (Section 1.2);
> - Basic arithmetic (Section 1.4).

Exponents and powers

In Section 1.2 we came across exponents, and saw, for example, that 100 can be written as 10^2 because $100 = 10 * 10$. Exponential notation is essentially a shorthand form of notation for repeated multiplication, where the exponent represents the number of times that a number is multiplied by itself. We also call the exponent the **power** of a number: for example, for $2^3 = 2 * 2 * 2 = 8$, we say that 8 is 2 raised to the power (i.e. exponent) of 3. The number being raised to a power is called the **base** (e.g. for 2^3, 2 is the base and 3 is the power or exponent). When we enter such calculations on a computer and some calculators, we cannot use superscripts (i.e. small numbers typed above the base); instead we use the symbol '^'. For example, we enter $2 \wedge 3$ on a computer to write 2^3. This is a binary operator because it applies to two numbers: the base (e.g. 2) and the exponent (e.g. 3).

Positive powers and exponents

In Section 1.2 we came across positive powers and exponents. Some powers or exponents have specific names: for example, the power or exponent 2 is called the **square** of a number, and we say $5^2 = 5 * 5 = 25$ is five squared. Similarly, the power or exponent 3 is called the **cube** of a number, and we say $5^3 = 5 * 5 * 5 = 125$ is five cubed.

Example **1.5.1**

  1.5

Q Calculate: (a) 5 squared and (b) 2 raised to the power of 7.

A (a) $5^2 = 5 * 5 = 25$ (b) $2^7 = 2 * 2 * 2 * 2 * 2 * 2 * 2 = 128$.

Negative powers and exponents

In Section 1.2 we also came across negative exponents (repeatedly dividing by a number): for example, $10^{-1} = 1/10 = 0.1$ and $2^{-3} = 1/2^3 = 1/8 = 0.125$.

In Section 1.4 we saw that a fraction could be written as multiplication by a reciprocal: for example, the fraction **5/3** can also be written as:

$$5 * \frac{1}{3}$$

Using negative exponents, we write this as **5 * 3⁻¹**, i.e. $5 * 3^{-1}$.

Example **1.5.2**

1.5

Q Write down the fraction 5/9 using exponential notation.

A $5/9 = 5 * \dfrac{1}{9} = \dfrac{5}{3*3} = \dfrac{5}{3^2} = 5 * 3^{-2}$

Roots

The reverse operation of raising to a power is that of **rooting**: for example, the **square root** of 100 is 10 because $10^2 = 100$, and the **cube root** of 8 is 2 because $2^3 = 8$. We use '$\sqrt[2]{}$' to denote the square root of a number and '$\sqrt[3]{}$' for the cube root of a number. For example, we write $\sqrt[2]{100} = 10$ (because $10 * 10 = 100$) and $\sqrt[3]{8} = 2$ (because $2 * 2 * 2 = 8$). When we write the square root symbol, we often omit the exponent in front of it and write '$\sqrt{}$'. For example, we often write $\sqrt{100} = 10$ instead of $\sqrt[2]{100} = 10$. This square root symbol does not appear on some calculators, and never appears on computer keyboards. When using a computer, we type in a special abbreviation to calculate square roots (e.g. SQRT). Remember from Section 1.4 that two negative numbers multiplied together give a positive answer and that two positive numbers multiplied together give a positive answer. Therefore the square root of a number can be either positive or negative:

$\sqrt[2]{100} = +10$ or -10 because $+10 * +10 = 100$ and $-10 * -10 = 100$. Note that it is not possible to calculate the square root of a negative number (e.g. $\sqrt{-1}$), and we say that negative numbers have no **real roots** because there is no real number that we can multiply by itself to give a negative number.

When we calculate higher roots (e.g. cube roots) on a computer or calculator, we use a different approach.

Reciprocal powers and exponents

Exponential notation (Section 1.2) can be extended to denote roots by using reciprocal exponents. Raising a number to a reciprocal power denotes the root of that number. The following are equivalent statements:

$$\sqrt{9} = \sqrt[2]{9} = 9^{1/2} = 9^{0.5} = 3 \qquad \text{because } 3 * 3 = 9$$
$$\sqrt[3]{8} = 8^{1/3} = 8^{0.333333} = 2 \qquad \text{because } 2 * 2 * 2 = 2^3 = 8$$

To calculate the root of a number on a calculator or computer, we first write the number in exponential format with a reciprocal exponent.

Example **1.5.3**

Q Calculate: (a) the fourth root of 16 and (b) the square root of -4.

A (a) Using traditional arithmetical notation, we want to calculate $\sqrt[4]{16}$. However, we cannot enter this on a calculator or computer keyboard. We write the calculation in exponential notation and then do the calculation (i.e. $16^{1/4} = 16^{0.25} = 2$). We can check this is correct by calculating $2^4 = 2 * 2 * 2 * 2 = 16$.

(b) Using traditional arithmetical notation, we want to calculate $\sqrt[2]{-4} = \sqrt{-4}$. Using the $\sqrt{}$ or SQRT on a calculator or computer gives an error message, because we cannot calculate the square root of a negative number.

Rules of exponents

There are useful rules for dealing with numbers written in exponential form. These apply only to numbers that have the same base, but apply to all exponents (positive, negative, reciprocal, etc.).

The first rule applies to multiplying numbers in exponential form:

> When multiplying two numbers in exponential format, we add the exponents *(1.5.1)*

For example, we calculate $10^2 * 10^3$ by:

$$10^{2+3} = 10^5 = 100 * 1,000 = 100,000$$

The second rule applies to dividing numbers in exponential form:

> When dividing two numbers in exponential format, we subtract the exponents *(1.5.2)*

For example, we calculate $10^2/10^3$ by:

$$10^{2-3} = 10^{-1} = 100/1,000 = 0.1$$

The third rule applies to raising numbers in exponential form to a power:

> When raising two numbers in exponential format to a power, we multiply the exponents *(1.5.3)*

For example, $10^2 * 10^2 * 10^2$ is calculated by:

$$10^{3*2} = 10^6 = 100 * 100 * 100 = 1,000,000$$

Logarithms to base 10

We may wish to know what exponent of a base produces a particular number: for example, what is the exponent of 10 that gives 10,000? Hopefully, you can see that the answer is, of course, 4, because there are four zeros in 10,000 (i.e. $10 * 10 * 10 * 10$).

The arithmetical operation to find exponents of 10 is known as taking the **logarithm to base 10** and written **$\log_{10}$**. So we write $\log_{10}(10,000) = 4$, because 10,000 has four zeros. If we want the power of 10 that gives 10,000,000, then this is 7 and is written as: $\log_{10}(10,000,000) = 7$, because 10,000,000 has seven zeros. Similarly, $\log_{10}(10) = 1$, because 10 has only one zero.

Remember that any number with an exponent of zero is unity (i.e. 1), and so:

$$\log_{10}(1) = 0.$$

We looked earlier at negative powers. Recall that 0.01 is 1/100 and is written

$$\frac{1}{100} = \frac{1}{10^2} = 10^{-2}$$

So $\log_{10}(1/100)$ is -2 and, similarly, $\log_{10}(0.001) = -3$ and $\log_{10}(0.1) = -1$, etc.

Some logarithms to base 10 are shown in Table 1.5.1:

Table 1.5.1 **Some logarithms to base 10.**

$\log_{10}(1/1000)$ =	$\log_{10}(0.001)$ =	-3
$\log_{10}(1/100)$ =	$\log_{10}(0.01)$ =	-2
$\log_{10}(1/10)$ =	$\log_{10}(0.1)$ =	-1
	$\log_{10}(1)$ =	0
	$\log_{10}(10)$ =	1
	$\log_{10}(100)$ =	2
	$\log_{10}(1000)$ =	3

From Table 1.5.1 we can see that numbers between 1 and 10 have logarithms between 0 and 1 (e.g. $\log_{10}(5) = 0.69897$). It is possible to have fractional or decimal powers when dealing with roots. In general, to calculate the logarithm of a number, we use a calculator or a computer, which has more than one logarithm button or function.

Logarithms to other bases

In Section 1.2 we came across other number and counting systems, for example binary (i.e. base 2). We can also define logarithms to base 2, and these are written: **$\log_2$**. Typical values of $\log_2$ are shown in Table 1.5.2.

Table 1.5.2 **Some logarithms to base 2.**

$\log_2(1/8)$	$= \log_2(0.125)$	$= -3$	
$\log_2(1/4)$	$= \log_2(0.25)$	$= -2$	
$\log_2(1/2)$	$= \log_2(0.5)$	$= -1$	
	$\log_2(1)$	$= 0$	
	$\log_2(2)$	$= 1$	
	$\log_2(4)$	$= 2$	
	$\log_2(8)$	$= 3$	

The natural logarithmic base (Euler's constant)

The number 2.718 (to three decimal places) occurs in nature (e.g. in growth patterns of plants and animals); it is called the **natural** or **exponential constant**, and is denoted by 'e'. This number is considered further in Sections 6.4 and 9.4, but for now let us simply accept that it is used when calculating logarithms. It was first identified by a mathematician called Napier, who is credited with discovering logarithms. However, another mathematician, Euler, is believed responsible for accurately defining the number, and he gave it the first letter of his name. Logarithms to base e (i.e. 2.718 to three decimal places) are called **natural** or **Naperian logarithms** and are denoted by **log$_e$**.

Look at a calculator or the list of functions available on a spreadsheet, and you find two types of logarithm: there are logarithms to base 10 (i.e. log$_{10}$ or simply **log**) and logarithms to base e (i.e. log$_e$ or simply **ln**).

When using logarithms, we must use the correct base. However, we can convert logarithms from one base to another.

Rules of logarithms

Logarithms are related to exponents, and the rules for exponents (i.e. rules (1.5.1)–(1.5.3)) can be translated into equivalent rules for logarithms. These apply to any base (e.g. 10 or e = 2.718).

> The logarithm of the product of two numbers is the sum of the logarithms of each number *(1.5.4)*

For example, $\log(3 * 5) = \log(3) + \log(5)$

> The logarithm of a fraction is the difference between the logarithm of the numerator and the logarithm of the denominator *(1.5.5)*

For example, $\log(3/5) = \log(3) - \log(5)$

> The logarithm of the exponent of a number is the product of the exponent and logarithm *(1.5.6)*

For example, $\log(3^5) = 5 * \log(3)$

Table 1.5.3 shows typical squares, cubes, square roots, cube roots, logarithms to base 10 and logarithms to base e.

1.5

Table 1.5.3 **Some squares, cubes, roots and logarithms.**

Number	Square	Cube	Square root ($\sqrt{}$)	Cube root ($\sqrt[3]{}$)	$\log_{10}$	$\log_e$
−10	100	−1,000	No real root	−2.154	Undefined	Undefined
−5	25	−125	No real root	−1.710	Undefined	Undefined
−1	1	−1	No real root	−1.000	Undefined	Undefined
−0.5	0.25	−0.125	No real root	−0.794	Undefined	Undefined
0	0	0	0.000	0.000	Undefined	Undefined
0.25	0.125	0.015625	0.500	0.630	−0.602	−1.386
0.5	0.25	0.125	0.707	0.794	−0.301	−0.693
1	1	1	1.000	1.000	0.000	0.000
2	4	8	1.414	1.260	0.301	0.693
3	9	27	1.732	1.442	0.477	1.099
4	16	64	2.000	1.587	0.602	1.386
5	25	125	2.236	1.710	0.699	1.609
10	100	1,000	3.162	2.154	1.000	2.326
100	10,000	1,000,000	10.000	4.642	2.000	4.605

Exercises

1.5

1 Calculate the following:

(a) 8^0 (b) 10^{-2} (c) $4^{0.5}$

(d) 10^{-1} (e) $4^{-0.5}$ (f) $\sqrt{4}$

(g) $\dfrac{1}{\sqrt{4}}$ (h) Cube root of 8 (i) $\log(1)$

(j) $\log(10,000,000)$ (k) $\log(5)$.

2 Which of the following statements are true and which are false?

(a) $16^0 = 4^4$ (b) The cube root of 27 is 9

(c) $\log(100)$ is the power of 10 giving 100 (d) $16^{0.25} = 2$

(e) $1/9 = 3^{-2}$ (f) $1/2 = 8^{-3}$

(g) $2^{-1.5} =$ cube root of 4 (h) $\text{SQRT}(-4) = -2$

(i) $\log(-10) = -1$.

1.6

Operator precedence

When using arithmetic operations, we adhere to accepted conventions. These are programmed in all calculators and computers, and are called arithmetic **operator precedence**.

The prerequisites of this section are:
- Number systems (Section 1.2);
- Basic arithmetic (Section 1.4);
- Powers, roots and logarithms (Section 1.5).

Operator precedence

By default, multiplication has **precedence** over addition, as illustrated in Example 1.6.1.

Example 1.6.1

Q Evaluate $6 + 9 * 2$.

A The value of: $6 + 9 * 2$ is found by adding 6 to the product of 9 times 2, giving: $6 + 18 = 24$.

To perform addition before multiplication (i.e. change the order of precedence), we indicate that the order in which we undertake calculations is different from the accepted convention by using brackets (or parentheses), as shown in Example 1.6.2.

Example 1.6.2

Q Evaluate $(6 + 9) * 2$.

A The brackets tell us to calculate the sum of $6 + 9$ before we undertake the multiplication.

Therefore we write: $(6 + 9) * 2 = 15 * 2 = 30$.

All the arithmetic operations discussed in the previous sections can be placed into groups, each group of operators having precedence over the other group. These groupings are shown in Table 1.6.1.

Table 1.6.1 **Operator precedence groupings.**

Group	Operators
1	Brackets and unary sign change
2	Raising to the power or exponent and taking logarithms
3	Multiplication and division
4	Addition and subtraction
5	Comparison ($=, <, >, \leqslant$ and $\geqslant$)

All operators within each **group** have **equal precedence**, and **group 1 has the highest priority**. If we have a **sequence of arithmetic operations** to undertake then the operations are considered from the **left to the right**. The mnemonic **BOMDAS** helps us remember the first four main groups of operator precedence:

Table 1.6.2 **BOMDAS mnemonic.**

	Operators
B	Brackets and unary sign change
O	Raising to power or exponent and taking logarithms **O**f
MD	Multiplication and **D**ivision
AS	Addition and **S**ubtraction
	Comparison ($=, <, >, \leqslant$ and $\geqslant$)

Example 1.6.3 illustrates operator precedence.

1.6.3

Q Calculate the following:

(a) $25 - 6 * 2$ (b) $(25 - 6) * 2$ (c) $25 - 6^2$

(d) $(25 - 6)^2$ (e) $(8/3)^2$ (f) $8^2/3$

(g) $8^{2/3}$ (h) $8 \wedge 2/3$.

A (a) Reading from the left, we have subtraction and then multiplication. Multiplication is in group 3 and subtraction is in group 4, so we undertake multiplication first (i.e. $6 * 2 = 12$). Now, we have $25 - 12$, and doing the subtraction gives 13.

(b) The brackets change the order of precedence. Brackets are in group 1, so we undertake the arithmetic enclosed in the brackets first (i.e. $(25 - 6) = 19$). We then multiply by 2, giving $19 * 2 = 38$.

(c) Here, we have subtraction and then raising to a power. Raising to a power is in group 2 and subtraction is in group 4, and so we raise to the power first (i.e. $6^2 = 36$). Now, we have $25 - 36$, giving -11.

(e) The brackets change the order of precedence, and we undertake the arithmetic in the brackets first, i.e. $(25 - 6) = 19$. We then raise this to the power, giving $19^2 = 19 * 19 = 361$.

(e) The brackets have priority, and we calculate $8/3 = 2.667$ (to three decimal places) first. We then raise to the power, giving $2.667 * 2.667 = 7.113$ (to three decimal places).

(f) Raising to a power is in group 2 and division is in group 3, so we calculate 8^2 first, giving $8 * 8 = 64$. We then undertake the division, giving $64/3 = 21.333$ (to three decimal places).

(g) Note that the fraction $2/3$ is a power (i.e. a superscript) to the number 8. Strictly speaking, this should be written in brackets, and the entire calculation written as $8^{(2/3)}$. Calculating the fraction first gives 0.667 (to three decimal places); we then raise to the power (i.e. $8^{0.667} = 4$).

(h) Recall from Section 1.5 that '$\wedge$' is used on computers for powers or exponents. So this is the same as (f). If we calculate $8^{(2/3)}$ on a computer, we must include the brackets and write this as '$8 \wedge (2/3)$'.

1.6

1 Calculate the following:

(a) $3 * 5 - 150/10$ (b) $256 - 2 * 3 \wedge 2$ (c) $256 - (2 * 3) \wedge 2$

(d) $(25/5 + 15/3)^2$ (e) $(25/5)^2 + (15/3)^2$ (f) $\log(5/2)$

(g) $(-5) \wedge 3$.

2 Which of the following are true and which are false?

(a) $18 * 2 - 9 * 3 = 9 * (2 * 2 - 1 * 3)$

(b) $4 \wedge 2 - 3 \wedge 2 = (4 - 3) \wedge 2$

(c) $8/3 - 4/3 = (8 - 4)/3$

(d) $3 \wedge 4 = (3 \wedge 2) * (3 \wedge 2)$

(e) $10/3 - 5/6 = (10 * 6 - 5 * 3)/(3/6)$

(f) $10/3 - 5/6 = 1/3 * (10 - 5/2)$

(g) $\log(5)/\log(2) = \log(5/2)$

(h) $-(-2) \wedge 3 = -8$.

3 A storeroom is 3.5 m high, 15 m wide and 50 m long. It is used for storage of A4, standard-quality copy paper, which arrives on pallets 3 m^2 and 3 m high, each containing 25,000 reams. The pallets are stacked vertically. How many full pallets and how many million reams can be stored?

| 1.7 | Fractions, ratios and percentages |

In Section 1.4 we came across fractions and defined them as the unevaluated division of two numbers (i.e. we did not undertake the calculation). In this section, we consider different types of fraction (e.g. percentages), related concepts (e.g. ratios), how we calculate them, and how they are used in business and management.

The prerequisites of this section are:
- Number systems (Section 1.2);
- Basic arithmetic (Section 1.4);
- Operator precedence (Section 1.6).

Fractions

In Section 1.4 we defined a fraction to be the unevaluated division of two numbers:

$$\text{Fraction} = \frac{\text{Numerator}}{\text{Denominator}}$$

If the fraction yields a number less than 1 (unity), then we talk of **proper fractions** (e.g. $2/4 = 0.5$), whereas **improper fractions** have values greater than 1 (e.g. $4/2 = 2$). In either case, we represent them in several ways: for example, 6/9 can be simplified to 2/3, because both the numerator and the denominator can be divided by 3. In its original form, 6/9 is called a **vulgar fraction**, whereas in its latter form (i.e. 2/3) we say that it has been **simplified**.

Ratios

A ratio is a different way of expressing a fraction. A fraction is the ratio of a numerator to a denominator. We represent the ratio in the simplest possible arithmetic terms by looking for the lowest whole numbers for the numerator and denominator of the equivalent fraction. We write a ratio in the form:

| Ratio = Numerator : Denominator | (1.7.1) |

The relationship between fractions and ratios is illustrated in Example 1.7.1.

| Example | 1.7.1 |

Q Represent the number 0.5 as a ratio.

A The decimal 0.5 is the fraction 0.5/1. However, the numerator (i.e. 0.5) is not an integer (i.e. whole number). To make the numerator a whole number, we multiply by 2; the denominator must be multiplied by the same amount, so that 0.5 is written as $\frac{1}{2}$. As this is the simplest fractional representation of 0.5, we also say this is the ratio of 1 to 2, written $1 : 2$.

Percentages

The ratio of one number to another is not altered if both numbers (i.e. numerator and denominator) are multiplied by a common factor. If we express the fraction so that the denominator is always 100, then we talk of a **percentage**. We use the '%' to denote percentages. So a percentage is a fraction with a denominator of 100:

$$\text{Percentage (\%)} = \frac{\text{Numerator}}{100} \qquad (1.7.2)$$

Example

1.7.2

Q Represent $\frac{1}{4}$ as a percentage.

A To make the denominator of this fraction 100, we multiply by 25 (i.e. $4 * 25 = 100$).

Multiplying the numerator by 25 gives 25. So 25/100 is the same as the simple fraction $\frac{1}{4}$, and we say that this is 25%.

Using percentages

Percentages are used to find parts or fractions of quantities. To find a percentage of a quantity, we multiply by the percentage and divide by 100, as shown in Example 1.7.3.

Example

1.7.3

Q What is 12% of £80?

A As 12% is 12 hundredths, then we want 12 hundredths of £80:

$$80 * \frac{12}{100} = \frac{960}{100} = £9.60.$$

To find percentages of quantities, we divide by 100 at some stage of the calculation: so, in effect, we move the decimal point two places to the left. In Example 2.6.3, we could have obtained the result by calculating:

$$£80 * 0.12 = £9.60$$

This is because 12/100 = 0.12 is obtained by moving the decimal point from 12.0 to 0.12.

Applications of percentages

In business and management, percentages are widely used. Sales managers and personnel staff use percentages, as do accountants and economists. A percentage added to the quantity is called a **mark-up** and if subtracted is called a **mark-down**.

Mark-ups

When dealing with fees and commissions on sales or interest on savings and loans, a mark-up is added to the original quantity. Another mark-up is the inclusion of duty or taxes: for example, VAT (**value added tax**) is a mark-up for certain items. In the UK, many items are taxed at $17\frac{1}{2}$% VAT, and the original price of an item is marked up by $17\frac{1}{2}$% to make it inclusive of VAT. Examples 1.7.4 and 1.7.5 illustrate the concept of a mark-up.

1.7.4

Q A bank gives 4% interest at the end of each year on any sum left in a deposit account for a whole year. If Mr Smith opens such a deposit account with £20,000, what is the balance in the account at the end of one year?

A The interest at the end of the year is found by calculating 4% of £20,000:

$$\text{Interest gained} = 20{,}000 * \frac{4}{100} = \frac{80{,}000}{100} = £800$$

So, at the end of the year, Mr Smith's account will hold the original deposit (i.e. £20,000) and the interest gained (i.e. £800):

End-of-year balance = £20,000 + £800 = £20,800

With bank accounts the original deposit is called the **principal**, and the percentage mark-up is called the **interest rate**. These concepts are considered further in Section 12.1.

Common factors

The amount in Mr Smith's account (see Example 1.7.4) can be calculated another way. Because multiplying any number by 1 (unity) has no effect, we could write the initial deposit of £20,000 as: $20{,}000 * 1$

The interest gained was found by calculating: $20{,}000 * \dfrac{4}{100}$

Adding the initial deposit and interest gained gives:

$$\text{End-of-year balance} = 20{,}000 * 1 + 20{,}000 * \frac{4}{100} = 20{,}000 + 800 = 20{,}800$$

Note that 20,000 is a **common factor** to both multiples (i.e. 1 and 4/100) on the left-hand side (**LHS**) of the calculation. If we take the common factor of 20,000 outside a bracket we can write:

$$\begin{aligned}
\text{End-of-year balance} &= 20{,}000 * (1 + 4/100) \\
&= 20{,}000 * (1 + 0.04) \\
&= 20{,}000 * (1.04) \\
&= 20{,}000(1.04) \\
&= £20{,}800
\end{aligned}$$

> We usually omit the multiplication symbol when we use brackets.

1.7.5

Q What is the retail price of a computer system quoted as £2,500 excluding VAT?

A VAT of $17\frac{1}{2}$% is added to the quoted price to obtain the retail price:

Retail price = Original price + Tax to be added

$$= 2{,}500 + 2{,}500 * \frac{17.5}{100} = 2{,}500 + 437.5 = 2{,}937.5$$

Using common factors, we can write this as:

$$= 2{,}500 * 1 + 2{,}500 * \frac{17.5}{100} = 2{,}500 + 437.5 = 2{,}937.5$$

Taking the common factor of 2,500 outside a bracket, we write this as:

$$\begin{aligned}\text{Retail price} &= 2{,}500 * (1 + 17.5/100)\\ &= 2{,}500 * (1 + 0.175)\\ &= 2{,}500(1.175)\\ &= \pounds 2{,}937.50.\end{aligned}$$

So, when calculating mark-ups we take the percentage mark-up, divide it by 100, then add it to 1 (unity) before multiplying the original amount.

Marking down

Marking down works in the opposite way to marking up, and is used to calculate discounts (see Example 1.7.6).

Example **1.7.6**

Q The normal retail price of a product sold in a shop is £5, but will be reduced by 10% for a 'cash' purchase. What price does the consumer pay for cash?

A The price for cash is calculated by:

$$\text{Cash price paid} = \text{Original price} - \text{Discount given}$$

$$\text{Cash price paid} = 5.00 - 5.00 * \frac{10}{100} = 5.00 - 0.50 = \pounds 4.50$$

Using common factors, we can write:

$$\text{Cash price paid} = 5.00 * 1 - 5.00 * \frac{10}{100}$$

Taking the common factor of £5 outside a bracket, we write:

$$\begin{aligned}\text{Cash price paid} &= 5.00 * (1 - 10/100)\\ &= 5.00 * (1 - 0.1)\\ &= 5.00 * 0.9\\ &= \pounds 4.50.\end{aligned}$$

Another mark-down is the deduction of taxes (e.g. income or profit tax), for conversion of gross into net amounts: for example, a gross income of £20,000 becomes £14,000 net after income tax of 30% is deducted. Reducing balance depreciation is another mark-down: for example, a machine valued this year at £10,000 has an accounting book value of £9,800 next year after depreciation of 2% per annum. The concept of depreciation is considered in Section 12.3.

Elasticity

Another application of fractions and percentages in economics is the concept of elasticity. Price elasticity of demand is a measure of the sensitivity or responsiveness of demand to changes in price. It is often simply defined to be:

$$\text{Elasticity} = \frac{\text{percentage change in quantity demanded}}{\text{percentage change in price}} \qquad (1.7.3)$$

The basic concept of elasticity is illustrated in Example 1.7.7.

Example   **1.7.7**

Q   Over one year the price of a product increased from £10 to £12, and, as a result, annual sales of this product fell from 1,000 to 800 units. How is demand affected by price?

A   The change in price is $12 - 10 = 2$ and the percentage change in price is $2/10 = 20\%$. The change in demand is $800 - 1,000 = -200$ and the percentage change in demand is $-200/1,000 = -20\%$. The minus sign indicates a fall in demand for the increase in price. (There are other ways of calculating the % change: see Section 10.3.) Applying equation (1.7.3), we calculate the elasticity of demand as $-20/20 = -1$. The negative number indicates that demand falls as prices increase, and the size of the number indicates the degree of sensitivity. In this case, a one-unit increase in price reduces demand by one unit. Economists would say this product exhibits **unit elasticity** around these prices.

Exercises   **1.7**

1   Represent the following fractions as ratios and percentages:
(a) 1/10   (b) 1/2   (c) 3/15
(d) 40/8   (e) −10/15   (f) 0.2/10.

2   Represent the following percentages as simplified fractions and as decimals:
(a) 15%   (b) 17.5%   (c) 0.5%
(d) $33\frac{1}{3}\%$ (e) $4\frac{1}{4}\%$ (f) −0.8%.

3   Calculate the following:
(a) 10% of £45,000.
(b) The price of an item priced at £15 ex VAT.
(c) The percentage increase in price from 10p to 12p.
(d) The interest gained at the end of a year on a deposit account, containing £5,000 at the start of the year, if the interest rate on deposits is 6% p.a.
(e) The book value of a machine worth £150,000 after 1 year's depreciation at 2% p.a.
(f) The percentage decrease in people in employment if employment fell from 1.5 million to 1.2 million.
(g) A 12% increase in growth from a capital base of £200,000.

4   At the start of the millennium, £1,000 was placed in a bank deposit account. Calculate the total amount in the account at the end of each of the subsequent 10 years, if interest of 5% p.a. is added at the end of each year and no money is withdrawn.

1.8   ## Units of measurement

In the previous sections, numbers and arithmetic were considered with no reference to the units of measurement being used. When measuring quantities, the numbers represent only size or magnitude, and do not refer to what is actually being measured.

The prerequisites of this section are:
- What is Quantitative Methods? (Section 1.1);
- Number systems (Section 1.2);
- Basic arithmetic (Section 1.4);
- Factors, ratios and percentages (Section 1.7).

Units of measurement

The units of measurement for money, are, of course, the appropriate units of currency (e.g. pounds sterling (£) or US dollars ($)). When dealing with other quantities (e.g. manufacturing output) other units are used, such as units of weight, length, area, volume or time.

When applying arithmetic to numbers resulting from measuring quantities, ensure that the units are the same: for example, pounds sterling cannot be added to US dollars to give a total amount of money in pounds sterling. US dollars should, of course, be converted to pounds at the current exchange rate to yield a meaningful result for the total amount of money in pounds sterling. Spreadsheets have inbuilt facilities for converting Fahrenheit to Centigrade, miles to kilometres, etc., and exchange rates can be found on the Internet, in most newspapers and at banks.

We often use abbreviations for very large and small quantities: for example, when dealing with £1,000s we shorten this to £1k (for one 'kilo' pounds sterling). Table 1.8.1 lists other abbreviations that we use in quantitative methods.

Table 1.8.1 **Measurement unit abbreviations.**

Prefix	Multiplier		Abbreviation
tera	$1E + 12 =$	1,000,000,000,000	T
giga	$1E + 09 =$	1,000,000,000	G
mega	$1E + 06 =$	1,000,000	M
kilo	$1E + 03 =$	1,000	k
hecto	$1E + 02 =$	100	h
deka	$1E + 01 =$	10	e
deci	$1E - 01 =$	0.1	d
centi	$1E - 02 =$	0.01	c
milli	$1E - 03 =$	0.003	m
micro	$1E - 06 =$	0.000006	u
nano	$1E - 09 =$	0.000000001	n
pico	$1E - 12 =$	0.000000000001	p

Even when using the same units of measurement it is sensible to express them to the same base before applying any arithmetic, so as to avoid errors, as shown in Example 1.8.1.

Example 1.8.1

Q The contents of two containers weigh 18 kg and 500 g, respectively. What is the total weight?

A Use either kilograms or grams before applying arithmetic. We express the total weight as either:

18 kg + 0.5 kg = 18.5 kg or 18,000 g + 500 g = 18,500 g.

When applying arithmetic, such as multiplication or division, the results often yield different units of measurement, as shown in Example 1.8.2.

Example **1.8.2**

Q An operative receives £1,000 for 40 hours' work. What is the hourly rate of pay?

A The hourly rate of pay is calculated by division as:

$$\frac{1,000}{40} = 25$$

Since earnings are in £s and time in hours, then the units of measurement of rate of pay are:

$$\frac{\text{£s}}{\text{Hours}} \text{ i.e. £s per hour}$$

The rate of pay is 25 pounds (sterling) per hour.

Exercises **1.8**

1 Convert the following:
  (a) 15 lb to kilograms   (b) 10 gallons to litres
  (c) 1 kg to lb   (d) 2 miles to kilometres
  (e) 5 litres to pints   (f) 50 degrees Fahrenheit to Celsius.

2 (a) If the nominal annual rate of interest charged on loans is 24% p.a., what is the nominal monthly rate of interest?
  (b) If the rate of growth of an economy is stated as 25% p.a., what is the equivalent nominal daily growth rate?

3 In the UK, the speed of a car is stated in miles per hour (mph). If a car is accelerating, what units of measurement are used to indicate the rate of acceleration?

4 In the UK, the fuel consumption of a particular car is stated as 40 mpg on an urban cycle. What is the equivalent for this car in France, where fuel consumption is stated as litres per kilometre?

5 Why is computer memory (RAM) stated as: 16 MB, 32 MB, 64 MB, 128 MB, etc.? A PC has 512 MB RAM and a 160 GB disk. How many bytes of memory does it have? What is the capacity of the disk in KB and in bytes using scientific notation?

6 A delivery vehicle has a fuel-tank capacity of 200 litres, and average fuel consumption is 18 mpg. How many miles does the vehicle travel on a full tank? If the vehicle makes 20 return journeys between its depot and customers, who are all within a 150 mile radius of the depot, what is the maximum number of refuels required? If the cost of fuel is 90p per litre, what is the total fuel cost for making the 20 deliveries?

1.9 # Chapter review

In this chapter we reviewed the basic concepts of counting, number systems and arithmetic and considered several typical applications in business and management. Many basic errors of judgement in business and management happen because these basic concepts are not fully understood or are applied incorrectly.

Chapter 2

From numbers to symbols

Introduction

This chapter begins with a review of the basic concepts of mathematical notation and then introduces the concept of algorithms. Methods for solving equations are reviewed, and an extended form of algebraic notation is introduced. The concepts of algebra, vectors, matrices, arrays and sets and their applications in business and management are also introduced.

Chapter objectives

- To review mathematical notation
- To review the concept of algebra
- To introduce the concept of an algorithm
- To review methods for solving equations
- To solve simultaneous equations
- To review the concepts of scalars, vectors, matrices and arrays
- To introduce subscripted and sigma notation
- To represent sets
- To undertake operations on sets
- To use Venn diagrams
- To recognise factorials, permutations and combinations
- To recognise binomial coefficients

Chapter contents

Algorithms, variables and algebra

In life, and certainly in business and management, we undertake calculations. In Chapter 1, we came across the meaning of numbers and their arithmetic. This arithmetic is often performed over and over again on different numbers (e.g. in calculating mark-ups/mark-downs of prices). Often, the rules and procedures in performing calculations remain the same, and it is only the raw numbers or data that change. In this section, we consider how to write down the ways we undertake calculations so we can communicate these procedures to other people and apply them to any numbers.

The prerequisites of this section are:
■ Basic arithmetic (Section 1.4);
■ Powers, roots and logarithms (Section 1.5);
■ Operator precedence (Section 1.6);
■ Fractions, ratios and percentages (Section 1.7).

Algorithms

Repetitive tasks have been reduced by the advent of computers, which apply a step-by-step approach, using a set of instructions, to undertake calculations. A set of instructions for undertaking calculations is called an **algorithm**. Not only do we write algorithms to instruct a computer to undertake calculations, we also use them to generalise calculations, and to communicate our calculations to other people. Example 2.1.1 illustrates a simple algorithm.

Example | **2.1.1**

Q You are too busy and so want a friend to calculate the end-of-year balance for an account in which you deposited £10, 1 year ago. The account pays interest of 8% at the end of each year.

A In Section 1.7 we calculated the balance in such a deposit account, and so you could give your friend a set of instructions, similar to the following:

1 Identify the amount deposited (in this case £10);
2 Calculate the interest on the deposit (in this case at 8% per year);
3 Add the interest to the original amount to calculate the end-of-year balance;
4 Write down the answer.

More specifically, you could write the instructions as:

1	Identify the amount deposited	i.e. 10	(in £s)
2	Calculate the interest	i.e. $10 * \dfrac{8}{100} = 0.8$	(in £s)
3	Add the interest to the original amount	i.e. $10 + 0.8 = 10.8$	(in £s)
4	Write down the answer.	i.e. 10.80	(in £s)

This set of instructions could easily be generalised for any amount deposited for one year, by providing boxes for the appropriate parts of the calculation. We could have a box labelled d for the amount deposited, a box labelled i for the interest gained and a box labelled b for the end-of-year balance. Instead of performing operations (calculations) on specific numbers, we could apply them to the boxes. The complete set of generalised instructions is called an **algorithm**. The algorithm for Example 2.1.1 is shown below as Algorithm A1.

Algorithm A1

Step	Instruction	Box	Operation	Value
1	Identify the amount deposited	d	Let $d =$	10
2	Calculate the interest	i	$i = d * 8/100 =$	0.8
3	Calculate the balance	b	$b = d + i =$	$10 + 0.8$
4	Write down the answer		Answer $b =$	10.8

Algorithms coded to run (or be executed) on a computer are called computer programs. A spreadsheet is a generic program that uses labelled boxes for undertaking repetitive calculations. In a spreadsheet, the labelled boxes take the form of cells and are labelled according to the rows and columns in which they appear.

Variables

In Algorithm A1, the boxes labelled d, i and b are called **variables**, because they do not represent a particular number (i.e. their contents can vary). We use variables in mathematics because we often want to perform the same set of calculations on different numbers: for example, we could use Algorithm A1 for calculating balances from making different deposits (e.g. £50, £100 and £1,200).

We use lower-case letters for variable names or labels (e.g. $x, y, z, a, b, c, t, v, u$). As these variables are essentially just boxes, which contain numbers, so arithmetic operations (Chapter 1) apply equally well to variables. When we use variables, rather than specific numbers, we are using **algebra**.

In spreadsheets (e.g. Excel), we put numbers (and also symbols and instructions) into cells, and these cells can be thought of as variables because they can contain any number (symbol or instruction).

Algebra

Using algebra, the statement:

Take any two numbers and add them together (i.e. find their sum)

might be written:

$$x + y \qquad\qquad (2.1.1)$$

where x and y are two variables for the two numbers being added together (i.e. summed). Statements in this symbolic form '$x + y$' are called **algebraic expressions**. We can store the result in another variable, say z, and write:

$$z = x + y \qquad\qquad (2.1.2)$$

An algebraic expression containing variables and the 'equals' symbol, for example (2.1.2), is called an **equation**.

When we write algebraic expressions, we omit the 'multiplication' symbol and the 'raise to the power' symbol: for example, $x * y$ is simply written as xy and $x \char`^ y$ as $x^y$. However, when using algebraic expressions on a computer, we always include the 'multiplication' and 'raise to the power' symbols (i.e. $*$ and $\char`^$). Algebraic expressions can include all the other arithmetic operations from Sections 1.4 and 1.5, as illustrated by Example 2.1.2.

Example **2.1.2**

Q If the manufacturing cost of a product is £20 per unit and the weekly amount (i.e. the budget) available for production is £5,000, represent the production possibilities as an algebraic expression for any production quantity.

A If we let x denote the general weekly production quantity for this product, then the cost of producing x units is found by multiplying the number of units produced (i.e. x) by the unit cost of £20:

$$\text{Cost of production} = 20x \qquad (2.1.3)$$

If all the budget can be spent, then we can equate the cost of production to the weekly budget:

$$20x = 5{,}000 \qquad (2.1.4)$$

If, on the other hand, we prefer not to spend all the budget, we could instead write:

$$20x \leqslant 5{,}000 \qquad (2.1.5)$$

This latter algebraic expression (2.1.5) is called an **inequality**, rather than an equation.

The number multiplying x in expressions (2.1.4) and (2.1.5) is called a **coefficient**, and in this specific case we say it is the **coefficient of x**.

Solving and simplifying algebraic problems

With equalities and sometimes inequalities, we need to determine values for the variables that make the algebraic statement true, and we talk about **solving equations** or **simplifying expressions**: for example, equation (2.1.4) has a unique solution, as illustrated in Example 2.1.3.

Example **2.1.3**

Q Find the maximum production quantity that can be afforded this week for the budget given in Example 2.1.2.

A We want to solve equation (2.1.4) to find a value for x. We can simply divide both sides of equation (2.1.4) by the coefficient of x:

$$\frac{20x}{20} = \frac{5{,}000}{20}$$

This clearly gives:

$$x = 250$$

We have solved equation (2.1.4) and found that the maximum production quantity of the product, if all this week's budget is spent, is 250. We could similarly solve or simplify inequality (2.1.5):

$$x \leqslant 250$$

This tells us that the weekly production quantity cannot exceed 250 units.

We often rearrange algebraic expressions (as in Example 2.1.3) to find their solution. Some basic guidelines for solving or simplifying algebraic expressions are:

1   Try to get all the variables on the left-hand side (LHS) and a single number on the right-hand side (RHS).
2   Avoid having variables as denominators (i.e. below a division line) by multiplying both sides by the variable or powers of the variable.
3   Can we multiply or divide both sides of an equation by a number, variable or bracket to simplify the expression?
4   Can we take common factors outside brackets to simplify the expression?
5   Try multiplying out brackets to simplify the expression.
6   Remember, whatever you do to one side of an expression you must do to the other.
7   Having solved an equation, substitute your answer back in the original expression to check that you have done it correctly.

The use of these basic guidelines is illustrated in Example 2.1.4.

Example 2.1.4

Q   Find a value for x that satisfies the following algebraic expressions:

(a) $x + 2 = \dfrac{9}{(x + 1)} + 1$

(b) $4(x - 1) - (x - 1)^2 = 5 - x$

(c) $x^2 + 4x - 5 = (x + 1)(x - 1)$.

A   (a) First, we label the equation so that we can refer to it:

$$x + 2 = \frac{9}{(x + 1)} + 1 \qquad (2.1.6)$$

Next, let us attempt to put all the variables on the LHS and all the numbers on the RHS. We start by subtracting 1 from both sides of equation (2.1.6):

$$x + 1 = \frac{9}{(x + 1)} \qquad (2.1.7)$$

Now multiply both sides of equation (2.17) by $(x + 1)$ to give:

$$(x + 1)(x + 1) = 9 \qquad (2.1.8)$$

i.e. $(x + 1)^2 = 9$

We now square-root both sides of equation (2.1.8), remembering from Section 1.5 that a square root can be either positive or negative, to get:

$$(x + 1) = \pm 3 \qquad (2.1.9)$$

We no longer need the bracket, and subtracting 1 from both sides of equation (2.1.9) gives:

$$x = 2 \text{ or } x = -4$$

Let us check the original expression (2.1.6) to see if we have the correct answers. When $x = 2$, the LHS of equation (2.1.6) gives $2 + 2 = 4$ and the RHS gives $9/(2 + 1) + 1 = 4$. When $x = -4$, the LHS of equation (2.1.6) gives $-4 + 2 = -2$ and the RHS gives $9/(-4 + 1) + 1 = -2$.

17

(b) First, we label the equation so that we can refer to it:

$$4(x - 1) - (x - 1)^2 = 5 - x \qquad (2.1.10)$$

This time we have a common factor $(x - 1)$ on the LHS of equation (2.1.10), and we can take this common factor outside a bracket:

$$(x - 1)(4 - (x - 1)) = 5 - x \qquad (2.1.11)$$

The bracket $(4 - (x - 1))$ can be simplified to $(4 - x + 1) = (5 - x)$, remembering from Section 1.4 that subtracting a negative number is the same as adding. We now have:

$$(x - 1)(5 - x) = 5 - x \qquad (2.1.12)$$

We now have a common factor of $(5 - x)$ on both sides of equation (2.1.12). We need to be careful, because if $x = 5$, then both sides of equation (2.1.12) are zero, and therefore one possible solution is $x = 5$.

However, if $x \neq 5$ then we can divide both sides of equation (2.1.12) by $(x - 5)$ to get:

$$(x - 1) = 1 \qquad (2.1.13)$$

We no longer need the bracket, and equation (2.1.13) is satisfied by $x = 2$.

Therefore we have two solutions: $x = 5$ and $x = 2$.

Let us check the original expression (2.1.10) to see whether we have the correct answers. When $x = 5$, the LHS of equation (2.1.10) is zero and the RHS is also zero. When $x = 2$, the LHS of equation (2.1.10) is 3 and the RHS is also 3.

(c) Again we label the equation so that we can refer to it:

$$x^2 + 4x - 5 = (x + 1)(x - 1) \qquad (2.1.14)$$

In this case, there is no obvious common factor on either side of equation (2.1.14), and we multiply out the brackets on the RHS of the equation. When we multiply out brackets, we must multiply all the contents of both brackets:

$$(x + 1)(x - 1) = x * x + 1 * x - 1 * x - 1 * 1 = x^2 - 1$$

We can now replace $(x + 1)(x - 1)$ by $x^2 - 1$ in equation (2.1.14), giving:

$$x^2 + 4x - 5 = x^2 - 1 \qquad (2.1.15)$$

We can now subtract x^2 from both sides of equation (2.1.15) to get:

$$4x - 5 = -1 \qquad (2.1.16)$$

Adding -5 to both sides of equation (2.1.16) gives:

$$4x = -1 + 5 = 4 \qquad (2.1.17)$$

Dividing both sides of equation (2.1.17) by 4 gives the solution:

$$x = 1$$

Again, let us check the original expression (2.1.14) to see whether we have the correct answer. When $x = 1$ the LHS of equation (2.1.10) is zero and the RHS is also zero.

Exercises 2.1

1 (a) A firm advertises computers at £800 plus VAT. What is the price that you actually pay? (Note: the standard VAT rate is 17.5%.)

(b) Write down an algebraic expression for the total price including VAT of any good that is sold for £x excluding VAT.

2 If $x = 2$ and $y = 7$, calculate the following:

(a) $5(x + y)$　　　　　　(b) $5x^2 - y$　　　　　　(c) y^x

(d) x^y　　　　　　　　(e) $(x - y)(x + y)$　　　　(f) $x^2 - y^2$.

3 Algebraically rearrange the following expressions to express y in terms of x:

(a) $y + 5 = x - 10$　　(b) $x = (y - 2)/3$　　　(c) $x = y^3$

(d) $(x - 2)(y - 4) = 10$.

4 Simplify the following expressions by taking out lowest common denominators and using brackets:

(a) $2x - 6$　　　　　　(b) $4(x + 2) + (x + 2)^2$　　(c) $P(1 + i) + P(1 + i)i$.

5 Solve the equations:

(a) $3x = 9$　　　　　　(b) $(x - 4)^2 = 4(5 - 2x)$　　(c) $(x - 1)(x + 2) = 0$.

2.2 Simultaneous and systems of equations

In Section 2.1 we considered how equations arise and how to solve them by finding values for their variables. Sometimes, we have two or more equations to solve at the same time, in which case we talk of **simultaneous** and more generally **systems** of equations. In this section, we consider how simultaneous and systems of equations arise and how they can be solved.

The prerequisites of this section are:
- Algorithms, variables and algebra (Section 2.1).

Simultaneous equations

When two equations have to be solved, we have **simultaneous equations**, and any solutions must satisfy both equations at the same time. Example 2.2.1 illustrates how simultaneous equations can arise.

Example 2.2.1

Q A firm manufactures two products, widgets and wodgets. Both products require capital (money) to pay for the materials and labour (hours) in the production process. A single widget requires £5 of capital and 3 hours of labour, whereas a single wodget requires £2 of capital and 4 hours of labour. If only £60 of capital and 50 hours of labour are available today, how many units of each product can be produced to fully utilise the available resources (i.e. capital and labour)?

A First, we label the quantities of widgets and wodgets that the firm might produce. We shall let x be the number of widgets and y the number of wodgets that might be produced today. The cost of producing x widgets is £$5x$, the cost of producing y wodgets is £$2y$, and the total budget available is £60. So we can write an equation for the budget (capital) as:

$$5x + 2y = 60 \text{ (capital)} \tag{2.2.1}$$

Similarly, the labour required to produce x widgets is $3x$ hours whereas that to produce y wodgets is $4y$ hours, but only 50 hours are available. So we can write an equation for labour as:

$3x + 4y = 50$ (labour). *(2.2.2)*

Solving simultaneous equations

To solve simultaneous equations, we want to find values of the variables that satisfy both equations: for example, in Example 2.2.1 we want to find values of x and y that satisfy equations (2.2.1) and (2.2.2) at the same time (i.e. simultaneously).

We could use trial and error by guessing a value for x and calculating a value for y: for example, if we try $x = 1$ in equation (2.2.1), we get $5 + 2y = 60$, which gives $y = 55/2 = 27.5$, and if we try $x = 1$ in equation (2.2.2), we get $3 + 4y = 50$, which gives $y = 46/4 = 11.5$. Clearly, y cannot be both 27.5 and 11.5 at the same time. We could keep making further guesses until we eventually find a solution. However, this trial-and-error approach may take quite some time. A better approach is to solve these simultaneous equations.

One method of solving simultaneous equations is to eliminate one of the variables by subtracting multiples of the equations. There are various ways of doing this, but a foolproof way of solving simultaneous equations (which can be extended to solve any number of equations) is shown in Algorithm A2.

Algorithm A2

Operation	Instruction
1	Write down and label the equations (1) and (2), respectively, with the first variable labelled x and the second variable labelled y.
2	Divide equation (1) by the coefficient of x in equation (1) and call this equation (3).
3	Multiply equation (3) by the coefficient of x in equation (2) and call this equation (4).
4	Subtract equation (4) from equation (2) and call this equation (5).
5	Divide equation (5) by the coefficient of y in equation (5) and call this equation (6). This gives the value for y.
6	Multiply equation (6) by the coefficient of y in equation (3) and call this equation (7).
7	Subtract equation (7) from equation (3) and call this equation (8). This gives the value for x.

Example **2.2.2**

Q Use Algorithm A2 to solve the simultaneous equations in Example 2.2.1 (to find the production quantities of widgets and wodgets).

A

Operation	Instruction	Result	
1	Write down and label the equations	$5x + 2y = 60$	Equation (1)
		$3x + 4y = 50$	Equation (2)
2	Divide equation (1) by 5	$x + 0.4y = 12$	Equation (3)
3	Multiply equation (3) by 3	$3x + 1.2y = 36$	Equation (4)
4	Subtract equation (4) from equation (2)	$0 + 2.8y = 14$	Equation (5)
5	Divide equation (5) by 2.8	$y = 5$	Equation (6)
6	Multiply equation (6) by 0.4	$0.4y = 2$	Equation (7)
7	Subtract equation (7) from equation (3)	$x = 10$	Equation (8)

So the firm can produce up to 10 widgets and 5 wodgets today, given the available capital and labour.

An improved algorithm

We can improve our basic algorithm for solving simultaneous equations (i.e. Algorithm A2) by making a few observations. The first operation is nothing more than setting up (i.e. labelling) the equations in an appropriate way to apply the algorithm, and we do this once at the beginning. Notice how similar operations 5, 6 and 7 are to operations 2, 3 and 4. In fact, the instructions are the same, and it is only the equation references that are different (operations 5, 6 and 7 are a repetition of operations 2, 3 and 4, but operating on different equations). In our new and improved algorithm (Algorithm A3) below we shall call the setting up (i.e. labelling) of the equations Step 0, and then we shall have three other steps (Steps 1, 2 and 3), which we shall undertake twice (the first time we undertake them will be equivalent to operations 2, 3 and 4 and the second time will be equivalent to operations 5, 6 and 7 in Algorithm A2). When we repeat steps in an algorithm we say that we are performing an **iteration**, and such algorithms are said to be **iterative**. In Algorithm A3 we shall perform two iterations on Steps 1, 2 and 3.

Algorithm A3

Stage	Steps	Instructions and comments
Initialise	0	Initialise the procedure by writing down and labelling the equations (1) and (2), and labelling the variables x and y.
Iteration 1	1	Divide equation (1) by the coefficient of x in equation (1), and call this equation (3).
	2	Multiply equation (3) by the coefficient of x in equation (2), and call this equation (4).
	3	Subtract equation (4) from equation (2), and call this equation (5).
Iteration 2	1	Divide equation (5) by the coefficient of y in equation (5), and call this equation (6).
	2	Multiply equation (6) by the coefficient of y in equation (3), and call this equation (7).
	3	Subtract equation (7) from equation (3), and call this equation (8).

Applying Algorithm A3 to Example 2.2.1 gives:

Stage	Steps	Results	Action
Initialise	0	$5x + 2y = 60$	Equation (1)
		$3x + 4y = 50$	Equation (2)
Iteration 1	1	$x + 0.4y = 12$	Equation (3) = Equation (1)/5
	2	$3x + 1.2y = 36$	Equation (4) = 3 * Equation (3)
	3	$0 + 2.8y = 14$	Equation (5) = Equation (2) − Equation (4)
Iteration 2	1	$y = 5$	Equation (6) = Equation (5)/2.8
	2	$0.4y = 2$	Equation (7) = 0.4 * Equation (6)
	3	$x = 10$	Equation (8) = Equation (3) − Equation (7)

In Examples 2.2.1 and 2.2.2 we had two equations with two unknown variables (i.e. x and y) and found a unique solution to the problem. Some simultaneous equations do not have a solution, whereas others might have many. Examples 2.2.3 and 2.2.4 illustrate cases where we cannot find a unique solution.

Example 2.2.3

Q Solve the simultaneous equations:

$$5x + 2y = 60 \tag{2.2.3}$$
$$10x + 4y = 50 \tag{2.2.4}$$

A Look at the LHS of equation (2.2.4): we see that it is a multiple of (in this case, double) the LHS of equation (2.2.3), and so we are looking for values of both x and y that satisfy, simultaneously, $5x + 2y = 60$ and $5x + 2y = 25$. Clearly, this is not possible. So these simultaneous equations do not have a solution.

Example 2.2.4

Q Solve the simultaneous equations:

$$5x + 2y = 60 \tag{2.2.5}$$
$$15x + 6y = 180 \tag{2.2.6}$$

A In this case, equation (2.2.6) is a multiple of (i.e. three times) equation (2.2.5). So we simply have one equation (i.e. $5x + 2y = 60$), and there is an infinite number of possible solutions. To find any one of these solutions, we choose a value for x (e.g. $x = 2$), and then calculate the value for y (e.g. $y = 25$).

Solving systems of equations

Sometimes, we have more than two equations and/or more than two unknowns to solve. We can generalise from the simultaneous equations in Examples 2.2.1, 2.2.3 and 2.2.4.

If the number of equations and the number of variables are the same (say n), then, unless one equation is a multiple of another, we can usually find a solution to the system of equations, and we can extend our algorithms to do so. For example, for a system with three equations in three unknowns (i.e. $n = 3$), we shall have to perform three iterations comprising five steps after initialisation (Step 0).

2.2

If we have more equations than unknowns, we may not have a solution to the system of equations. When we have more unknowns than equations, usually there is at least one solution, but our methods (e.g. Algorithm A3) do not apply and we have to resort to trial and error.

In Section 3.5 we look for another method for solving systems of equations employing matrices, and other methods can be found on the CD and on the associated website **www.mcgraw-hill.co.uk/textbooks/dewhurst**.

Exercises 2.2

1 An inkjet printer uses two types of cartridge, black and colour, costing £15 and £20 each, respectively. If a budget of £100 is available for cartridges, represent the purchase decision algebraically. How many different solutions are there to spending the budget, and what are these solutions? Which solution would you choose and why?

2 If the price of product A is 50% more than product B, represent the relationship between the price of A and B as an algebraic expression. If a consumer, purchasing one unit of each product, spends £100, what are the prices of the two products?

3 If the GDP (gross domestic product) of Scotland is double that of Northern Ireland, a quarter that of England, but four times that of Wales, what are the GDPs of each if the UK GDP is £11.5 billion?

4 Solve the following systems of equations:
(a) $y = 1$
$x + 5y = 8$

(b) $2x + y = 6$
$x + y = 4$

(c) $2x + 4y + 4z = 22$
$x + 3y + z = 10$
$4x + y + 2z = 12$

(d) $a + 2b + c = 8$
$a + b = 3$
$a + c = 5.$

5 Write a simple algorithm to calculate the selling price of an item that has a normal retail price of £R pounds, but is marked down by D% when sold for cash. Implement this algorithm for items having normal retail prices of £50, £120 and £250, with a mark-down of 15% for cash.

6 **This question can only be undertaken on a spreadsheet**.
A useful feature in computing is the IF statement, which changes things depending on whether a statement is true or false: for example, in Excel if we type **=IF(A1 > 20, 50, 55)** in cell B1, then cell B1 will contain 50 if the contents of cell A1 exceed 20, otherwise it will contain 55. We can use such statements for calculating the price of an item that is marked down when certain quantities are purchased: this is called **quantity discounts at price breaks**. Use conditional statements to devise an algorithm for calculating the cost of purchasing items that normally retail at £100, having the following quantity discounts:

Price-break quantity	Discount
1–9	0%
10–99	10%
100 or more	15%

2.3 Scalars, vectors, matrices and arrays

So far, we have considered quantities on a single scale of measurement: for example, we have measured the price of an item in £s, the length of an object in metres, its weight in grams or kilograms, etc. In this section, we represent quantities using several scales of measurement.

The prerequisites of this section are:
■ Basic arithmetic (Section 1.4).

Scalars

When we have single scales of measurement (e.g. the retail price of a single item in £s) we use **scalars**. A **scalar quantity** represents only the magnitude or size of a particular item on a **single scale of measurement**.

Vectors

In some cases, we have **two scales of measurement**: for example, in specifying the location of a customer on a map we might use the distance from the office (in miles) and the direction (in compass points). Another example are the sales figures (in £s) for different periods of time (days, months, quarters or years). When we have two scales of measurement we use **vectors**, which appear as several numbers presented in a row or a column. These numbers are called the **elements** of the vector and are scalar quantities. We surround the elements of a vector by brackets or parentheses and denote the entire vector by a bold lower-case letter. Example 2.3.1 illustrates how vectors arise and the notation we use.

Example **2.3.1**

Q The profits of the clothing department of a high-street store in Manchester, at the end of each quarter, are as shown in Table 2.3.1.

Table 2.3.1 **Quarterly sales for the clothing department of a Manchester store last year in £s.**

Quarter 1	Quarter 2	Quarter 3	Quarter 4
900	1,000	1,200	800

Represent these data in the form of a vector.

A Each quarter's profits are scalar quantities (measured in £s), but we have a second scale of measurement – time (i.e. quarters of a year). We represent these data as a vector. There are two forms of vector: a **column vector** and a **row vector**. Let us denote our vector by **s** to represent 'sales':

$$\mathbf{s} = \begin{pmatrix} 900 \\ 1,000 \\ 1,200 \\ 800 \end{pmatrix} \text{ or } \mathbf{s} = \begin{bmatrix} 900 \\ 1,000 \\ 1,200 \\ 800 \end{bmatrix} \text{ for column vectors}$$

$$\mathbf{s} = (900 \ 1,000 \ 1,200 \ 800) \text{ or } \mathbf{s} = [900 \ 1,000 \ 1,200 \ 800] \text{ for row vectors}$$

Sometimes, we separate the elements of a row vector by commas to avoid confusion, for example:

$$\mathbf{s} = (900, 1000, 1{,}200, 800).$$

Matrices

There are situations where three scales of measurements are used, requiring both rows and columns. A **matrix** is a collection of numbers appearing in rows and columns, which result from taking measurements along three measurement scales. We use a form of notation similar to vector notation. Its constituent numbers are called the **elements** of the matrix, and, as with vectors, they are scalar quantities. We surround them by brackets or parentheses, and denote the entire matrix by an upper-case letter. Example 2.3.2 illustrates how matrices arise and the notation we use.

Example

2.3.2

Q The retail store considered in Example 2.3.1 has three departments, and their quarterly sales figures for last year are shown in Table 2.3.2.

Table 2.3.2 **Quarterly sales for each department of a Manchester store last year in £s.**

Department	Quarter			
	1	2	3	4
Clothing	900	1,000	1,200	800
Hardware	1,100	1,400	900	700
Food	8,000	8,000	9,000	12,000

Represent these data in the form of a matrix.

A In this case, one scale of measurement is sales volume in £s, the second is time in quarters of a year, and the third is the specific department of the retail store. Essentially, we take the numbers from Table 2.3.2 and surround them by brackets or parentheses to form a matrix. If we use S to denote the sales matrix then:

$$S = \begin{pmatrix} 900 & 1{,}000 & 1{,}200 & 800 \\ 1{,}100 & 1{,}400 & 900 & 700 \\ 8{,}000 & 8{,}000 & 9{,}000 & 12{,}000 \end{pmatrix} \quad \text{or}$$

$$S = \begin{bmatrix} 900 & 1{,}000 & 1{,}200 & 800 \\ 1{,}100 & 1{,}400 & 900 & 700 \\ 8{,}000 & 8{,}000 & 9{,}000 & 12{,}000 \end{bmatrix}$$

The matrix in Example 2.3.2 has three rows and four columns, and we say it is of 'size (or order) of 3 by 4' or simply a (3×4) matrix. Note that a **spreadsheet** is essentially a matrix.

Arrays

The sales figures in Example 2.3.2 could have been represented by three separate row vectors (i.e. one for each department) or four separate column vectors (i.e. one for each quarter). So we can view matrices as an extension of vectors, and a vector can be viewed as a matrix having a single row or column. Similarly, a vector can be viewed as an extension of scalar notation because a scalar has only one row and column.

It is, of course, possible to have four or even more measurement scales, and then we talk of **arrays**. An array is a collection of numbers that result from taking measurements along several scales of measurement. Once again, its constituent numbers are called **elements** and, as with vectors and matrices, they are scalar quantities. Matrices, vectors and scalars are special cases of arrays. Example 2.3.3 illustrates how arrays arise and the notation we use.

Example 2.3.3

Q The company that owns the retail store in Example 2.3.2 has another two such stores in Birmingham and London. The entire set of quarterly sales figures for the three departments of all stores is shown below. Represent these data as an array:

$$\begin{pmatrix} 600 & 1,200 & 1,200 & 1,000 \\ 1,000 & 1,400 & 800 & 800 \\ 7,000 & 6,500 & 11,000 & 12,000 \end{pmatrix} \text{London}$$

$$\begin{pmatrix} 700 & 1,100 & 1,100 & 900 \\ 1,100 & 1,400 & 900 & 700 \\ 7,000 & 6,000 & 12,000 & 11,000 \end{pmatrix} \text{Birmingham}$$

$$\begin{pmatrix} 900 & 1,000 & 1,200 & 800 \\ 1,100 & 1,400 & 900 & 700 \\ 8,000 & 8,000 & 9,000 & 12,000 \end{pmatrix} \text{Manchester}$$

A We could represent these data with an array having: (a) three rows (one for each department); (b) four columns (one for each quarter); and (c) three matrices (one for each location). This is a $(3 \times 4 \times 3)$ (i.e. a '3 by 4 by 3' array). Such an array could be stored as a **workbook**, with each matrix on a different sheet.

Array dimension

To measure how large an array is, in terms of the amount of numbers that it contains, a vector needs a single number to say how many numbers are in the row or column; a matrix needs two numbers, one for the number of rows and the other for the number of columns; and the array in Example 2.3.3 needs three numbers – one for rows, one for columns and another for the number of matrices. This is called the **dimension** of the array. So a vector is 1-dimensional, a matrix is 2-dimensional, and the array in Example 2.3.3 is 3-dimensional. Note that, using this definition, a scalar logically has no dimension. In general, we can have arrays of any number of dimensions. Although it is not possible to visualise more than 2-dimensional arrays, higher-order dimensional arrays do exist.

Exercises 2.3

1 How many scales of measurement have each of the following?
(a) a scalar   (b) a vector   (c) a matrix   (d) a 5-dimensional array

2 Desktop PCs Ltd have three assembly plants, located in the UK, Germany and Australia. Each plant manufactures a range of PCs for different markets (HomeCD, HomeDVD, Gamer, Office Workstation, Graphics Workstation, Network Server, Mailserver and Internet Server). The weekly sales of each model by each plant are to be collected for future analysis. What type and size of array would you use?

3 How many elements are in:
(a) a (4×52) matrix   (b) a $(3 \times 4 \times 5 \times 1 \times 2)$ array
(c) the array in Question 2

4 Write down an appropriate array for the cost of purchasing up to a quantity of 20 of an item that normally retails at £100 and is subject to the following quantity discounts (recall Question 6 of Exercises 2.2):

Price break quantity	1–4	5–9	10–14	15 or more
Discount	5%	10%	15%	20%

5 A game of 'toss' is being played by Anne and Brian. On Anne's turn, she tosses a coin and Brian has to guess whether it shows heads or tails. If the coin shows a head and Brian guesses correctly, Anne pays Brian £3; if the coin shows a tail and Brian guesses correctly, Anne pays Brian £2; but if Brian guesses incorrectly, he pays Anne £5. Such games are called **two-person zero-sum games**, and the winnings for any game can be written as elements of a matrix called the **pay-off matrix**. Write down the pay-off matrix for Anne for the different outcomes (i.e. heads or tails).

6 Recall from Sections 1.7 and 2.1 that if you leave £1 in a deposit account providing an annual rate of growth of 10%, then after one year you will have £1 plus 10p interest, giving a total of £1.10. If you leave this to grow for a further year, you will have £1.10 plus 11p interest, giving £1.21 after 2 years. Create a matrix to show the future values after 1, 2, 3, ..., 10 years of £1 deposited at 1%, 2%, ..., 20% interest.

7 A supermarket sells three different brands of tea: Tips, Leaf and Blend. The next time a customer who usually buys Tips visits the supermarket s/he has a 50% chance of buying Tips again, 30% of buying Leaf but only 20% of buying Blend. However, a customer who usually buys Leaf has a 60% chance of buying Leaf again, 10% of buying Tips and 30% of buying Blend. A customer who usually buys Blend has a 30% chance of buying it again, a similar chance of buying Leaf and 40% of buying Tips. This is called a **chance transition matrix**. Write down the chance transition matrix for a customer on their next visit to the supermarket.

8 The study of the flow of money between industries and sectors in an economy is called **input–output analysis**. A small economy has three basic sectors: Manufacturing, Services and Energy, each producing outputs sold to each other and the consumer. On average, 1 unit of output from Manufacturing requires inputs of 0.3 units from the Energy sector, 0.2 from the Services sector and 0.1 of its own output as inputs. To produce 1 unit of energy, 0.2 are required from Manufacturing, 0.1 from Services and 0.1 from itself. The Services sector uses no Manufacturing inputs, 0.1 from Energy and 0.2 from its own sector. Write down a matrix (i.e. the **matrix of technical coefficients**), whose rows are inputs and whose columns are outputs for each sector.

2.4 Subscripted variables and sigma notation

In Section 2.1 we used variables to represent any number along a single scale of measurement (i.e. scalar), and in Section 2.3 we encountered several scales of measurement (i.e. vectors, matrices and arrays). The elements (i.e. contents) of these vectors, matrices and arrays are scalar quantities, and, as we saw in Section 2.1, are usually labelled by lower-case letters. However, when vectors, matrices and arrays have many elements, we quickly run out of lower-case letters and it is useful to label these elements to identify which row and/or column they appear in. Furthermore the usual alphabetic labelling of columns in spreadsheets becomes very cumbersome. We overcome these problems by using **subscripted variables**. In this section we look at variables with a single subscript, then variables with two subscripts, and finally generalise to any number of subscripts.

The prerequisites of this section are:

■ Scalars, vectors, matrices and arrays (Section 2.3).

Single subscripted variables and vector notation

To illustrate why and how we use single subscripts, we return to Example 2.3.1, in which we labelled the column vector of quarterly sales figures for a Manchester store with the bold lower-case letter **s**:

$$\mathbf{s} = \begin{pmatrix} 900 \\ 1{,}000 \\ 1{,}200 \\ 800 \end{pmatrix}$$

We label each element of this vector according to its position (in this case row) with a subscript number:

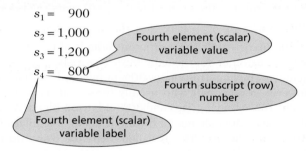

$s_1 = 900$
$s_2 = 1{,}000$
$s_3 = 1{,}200$
$s_4 = 800$

Fourth element (scalar) variable value

Fourth subscript (row) number

Fourth element (scalar) variable label

In general, we might label the elements of any vector, say **x**, as:

$$x_1, x_2, x_3, \dots, x_n,$$

where n denotes the number of elements in the vector (in Example 2.3.1 $n = 4$). Subscripts themselves can be variables, and we often use the variable i as a subscript for rows and j as a subscript for columns.

For a column vector, we might refer to the ith row:

$$\mathbf{x} = \begin{Bmatrix} x_1 \\ x_2 \\ x_3 \\ \vdots \\ x_i \\ \vdots \\ x_n \end{Bmatrix}$$

For a row vector, we might refer to the jth column:

$$\mathbf{x} = (x_1, x_2, x_3, \dots x_j, \dots, x_n)$$

We shall come across this form of subscripted notation in later chapters when we deal with statistics and modelling, particularly when the number of variables being used exceeds the number of letters in the alphabet.

42

Sigma notation

There is an abbreviated form of notation for summing the contents of subscripted variables. For example, suppose we wish to find the total annual sales for the data given in Example 2.3.1. Using subscripted variable notation, rather than the actual data, we calculate:

$$s_1 + s_2 + s_3 + s_4$$

Suppose we wish to add or sum together any number of subscripted variables:

$$\text{Sum} = x_1 + x_2 + x_3 + \cdots + x_n$$

Writing down this type of sum is very cumbersome, and so an abbreviated form of notation has been developed, using the Greek upper-case letter Σ (sigma) to denote summation:

$$\sum_{i=1}^{n} x_i = x_1 + x_2 + x_3 + \cdots + x_n \tag{2.4.1}$$

This means add or sum together all the contents of the subscripted variables x_i whose subscripts start with $i = 1$ and end with $i = n$.

Example | **2.4.1**

Q Write down an expression for the total sales of Example 2.3.1 using sigma notation.

A If we denote the vector of sales by **s** and the elements by s_1, s_2, s_3 and s_4, then we can write their sum (i.e. total) as:

$$s_1 + s_2 + s_3 + s_4$$

Using sigma notation, we write this as: $\displaystyle\sum_{i=1}^{4} s_i$

Calculating, we get: $\displaystyle\sum_{i=1}^{4} s_i = 900 + 1,000 + 1,200 + 800 = 3,900$

We often calculate the total of a set of numbers, so most calculators and spreadsheets have inbuilt functions for calculating such summations.

General subscripted notation

We can extend subscripted notation to refer to the elements of a matrix. For any matrix X, say, we label the elements with two subscripts, one for rows and the other for columns (i.e. x_{ij}). In general, we have n columns and m rows:

$$\left\{ \begin{array}{ccccccc}
x_{11} & x_{12} & \cdots & x_{1j} & \cdots & x_{1n-1} & x_{1n} \\
x_{21} & x_{22} & \cdots & x_{2j} & \cdots & x_{2n-1} & x_{2n} \\
\vdots & \vdots & \vdots & \vdots & \vdots & \vdots & \vdots \\
x_{i1} & x_{i2} & \cdots & x_{ij} & \cdots & x_{in-1} & x_{in} \\
\vdots & \vdots & \vdots & \vdots & \vdots & \vdots & \vdots \\
x_{m-11} & x_{m-12} & \cdots & x_{m-1j} & \cdots & x_{m-1n-1} & x_{m-1n} \\
x_{m1} & x_{m2} & \cdots & x_{mj} & \cdots & x_{mn-1} & x_{mn}
\end{array} \right\}$$

Therefore in general we have $(m \times n)$ (i.e. 'm by n' matrices).

To find the sum of the elements of a matrix we use abbreviated sigma notation to sum along both the rows and the columns, so using two summations (one for i

and another for j):

$$\sum_{i=1}^{m}\sum_{j=1}^{n} x_{ij} = \quad x_{11} + x_{12} + x_{13} + \cdots + x_{1n}$$

$$+ x_{21} + x_{22} + x_{23} + \cdots + x_{2n}$$

$$\cdots\cdots\cdots\cdots\cdots\cdots\cdots\cdots$$

$$\cdots\cdots\cdots\cdots\cdots\cdots\cdots\cdots$$

$$+ x_{m1} + x_{m2} + x_{m3} + \cdots + x_{mn} \qquad (2.4.2)$$

This means add or sum together all the contents of the subscripted variables x_{ij}. We begin by setting $i = 1$ and sum the variables for $j = 1$ to $j = n$, then we set $i = 2$ and add the sum of the variables for $j = 1$ to $j = n$. This process is continued until we set $i = m$ and finally add the sum of the variables for $j = 1$ to $j = n$.

Example 2.4.2

Q Write down the total sales for Example 2.3.2 using sigma notation.

A The sales matrix in Example 2.3.2 is:

$$S = \begin{pmatrix} 900 & 1{,}000 & 1{,}200 & 800 \\ 1{,}100 & 1{,}400 & 900 & 700 \\ 8{,}000 & 8{,}000 & 9{,}000 & 12{,}000 \end{pmatrix}$$

Using double subscripted notation, the element in the first row and column is referenced or labelled by $s_{11} = 900$, and the element in the bottom right-hand corner is labelled by $s_{34} = 12{,}000$.

The total sales are:

$$\text{Sum} = \quad s_{11} + s_{12} + s_{13} + s_{14}$$

$$+ s_{21} + s_{22} + s_{23} + s_{24}$$

$$+ s_{31} + s_{32} + s_{33} + s_{34}$$

$$= \sum_{i=1}^{3}\sum_{j=1}^{4} s_{ij}$$

Calculating, we get:

$$\sum_{i=1}^{3}\sum_{j=1}^{4} s_{ij} = \quad 900 + 1{,}000 + 1{,}200 + 800$$

$$+ 1{,}100 + 1{,}400 + 900 + 700$$

$$+ 8{,}000 + 8{,}000 + 9{,}000 + 12{,}000$$

$$= 5{,}100$$

The same form of notation is also used for arrays of any number of dimensions: for example, x_{ijk} refers to the element in the ith row, jth column and kth matrix of the 3-dimensional array X.

Exercises 2.4

1 Use subscripted notation to write down the elements of:
(a) a row vector **v** having five columns;
(b) a (3×4) matrix M;
(c) a $(2 \times 1 \times 3)$ array S.

2 For the row vector $\mathbf{v} = (5, 10, -2, 4, 18, 25, -5, 15, 7, 3, 0, 8)$ write down symbolically and calculate:

(a) the sum of all the elements;

(b) the sum of the first five elements;

(c) the sum of the last five elements;

(d) $v_1 + v_2 + v_3 + v_4 + v_5 - v_7 - v_8 - v_9 - v_{10}$.

3 For the matrix:

$$T = \begin{pmatrix} 1 & 7 & 4 & 15 \\ 12 & 3 & 16 & 7 \\ 2 & 8 & 10 & 4 \\ 6 & 5 & 11 & 13 \\ 14 & 0 & 17 & 9 \end{pmatrix}$$

write down an expression for and calculate the sum of:

(a) each column   (b) each row   (c) all elements.

4 For the sales data in Example 2.3.3, calculate:

(a) the total sales for each quarter for each city store;

(b) the total annual sales for each department for each city store;

(c) the total sales for each quarter for all stores;

(d) the total annual sales for each department for all stores.

2.5

Set notation, set properties and Venn diagrams

Scalars, vectors, matrices and arrays are ways of representing quantities that come from taking measurements. A more general concept, used to represent a collection of objects as a whole, is that of **sets**. The notation for sets is similar to that of matrices and arrays. As with matrices, we use upper-case letters for sets and lower-case letters for their contents (i.e. elements or members).

The prerequisites of this section are:
- Number systems (Section 1.2);
- Basic arithmetic (Section 1.4);
- Algorithms, variables and algebra (Section 2.1);
- Scalars, vectors, matrices and arrays (Section 2.3);
- Subscripted variables and sigma notation (Section 2.4).

Set notation

The contents of a set are enclosed in braces (i.e. {}). Two ways of writing down a set of objects are: **roster notation** and **set-builder notation**. Roster notation lists the elements (i.e. contents) of a set; set-builder notation defines the contents of a set by stating where the elements come from. With roster notation, the order in which we write the elements does not matter, but we do not repeat elements. Example 2.5.1 shows these forms of set notation.

Example | **2.5.1**

Q In Section 1.2, when counting in denary, we used ten digits. Represent them using roster and set-builder notation.

A If we let D denote the set of denary digits then, using roster notation, we write them as:

$$D = \{0, 1, 2, 3, 4, 5, 6, 7, 8, 9\}$$

Note that we can also write this as $D = \{0, 2, 4, 6, 8, 1, 3, 5, 7, 9\}$, but not as $D = \{0, 1, 3, 5, 7, 0, 9, 2, 4, 6, 8\}$ because we do not repeat elements.

Alternatively, we could say 'D is the set of all x such that x is a denary digit'. Using set-builder notation, we write this as:

$$D = \{x: x \text{ is a denary digit}\}$$

Special sets and notation

There are some special sets that we find useful, such as the **empty** or **null set** (i.e. the set that has no elements), denoted by $\emptyset$. Another is the **universal set**, the set of all elements under consideration, denoted by U. We use the symbol '$\in$' to denote membership of a set: so, for example, we write $2 \in D$ because 2 is a member of the set of denary digits D.

Venn diagrams

We represent sets pictorially by **Venn diagrams**. The universal set U is represented by a large rectangle and other sets by circles, as shown in Example 2.5.2.

Example	2.5.2

Q Let U be the universal set of all students who purchase this book in a particular year and P the set of people who read this chapter by the end of that year. Use a Venn diagram to represent these sets.

A

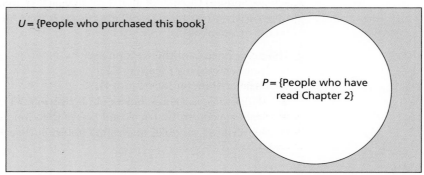

U = {People who purchased this book}

P = {People who have read Chapter 2}

Figure 2.5.1 **A simple Venn diagram.**

Set operations

There are certain operations that we can perform on sets, some of which are analogous to the arithmetic operations on scalars that we encountered in Section 1.4, whereas others are unique to sets.

Equality of sets

Two sets, say A and B, are equal if and only if they contain the same elements, and we write $A = B$, but if they are not equal, we write $A \neq B$, as with scalars.

Subsets

If sets are not equal then one set may contain, among other objects, all the elements of another set. If A and B are two sets, then we say that A is a **subset** of B (i.e. A is contained in B) if and only if every element of A is also an element of B, and we write $A \subseteq B$. Using set-builder notation, we say that A is a subset of B (i.e. $A \subseteq B$) if and only if whenever x is in set A (i.e. $x \in A$) then x is in set B (i.e. $x \in B$) for all objects x. Note that this definition **allows for subsets being equal**. Therefore, if $A \subseteq B$ and $B \subseteq A$, then we must have $A = B$. If there are no elements in set A that are also elements in set B, then A is not a subset of B, and we write $A \nsubseteq B$. If, in Example 2.5.2, everyone purchasing this book this year had also read this chapter by the end of the year then $P \subseteq U$.

Proper subsets

When subsets cannot be equal then we define the notion of a **proper** subset. Set A is a proper subset of B if and only if every element in A is also in B, but there is at least one element in set B that is not in set A: we write this as $A \subset B$. If A is not a proper subset of B, we write $A \not\subset B$. For example, the set of binary digits $B = \{0, 1\}$ is a proper subset of the set of denary digits $D = \{0, 1, 2, 3, 4, 5, 6, 7, 8, 9\}$, and so $B \subset D$.

Union of sets

To combine the elements of two or more sets, we use the operation of **union**. The union of A with B (or $A \cup B$) is the set of those elements that are either in set A or in set B and in both A and B. We write this as:

$$A \cup B = \{x : x \in A \text{ or } x \in B\} \qquad (2.5.1)$$

In English there are two meanings of the word 'or': the inclusive meaning, which is 'either' or 'both', and the exclusive meaning, which does not include 'both'. In mathematics, we only use the inclusive meaning. To remember the symbol, think of '$\cup$' for **u**nion. The union of two sets is shown by the shaded area in the Venn diagram in Figure 2.5.2.

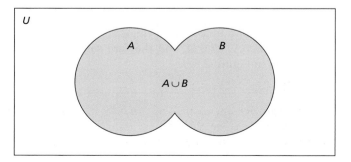

Figure 2.5.2 **The union of two sets.**

2.5.3

Q What is the union of the two sets A and B if $A = \{x: x$ is an odd denary digit$\}$ and $B = \{x: x$ is an even denary digit$\}$?

A In this case, we have: $A \cup B = \{x: x$ is a denary digit$\} = \{0, 1, 2, 3, 4, 5, 6, 7, 8, 9\}$ because the set of odd and even denary digits is the set of all denary digits.

Intersection of sets

To identify elements that are **only in both sets**, we use the operation of **intersection**. The intersection of A with B is the set consisting of those elements that are in both A and B. We write this as:

$$A \cap B = \{x: x \in A \text{ and } x \in B\} \tag{2.5.2}$$

The intersection of any two sets identifies their common elements, as shown by the shaded area of the Venn diagram in Figure 2.5.3.

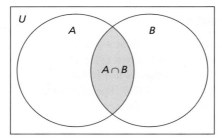

Figure 2.5.3 **The intersection of two sets.**

To remember the symbol, think $\cap$ for i**n**tersection.

2.5.4

Q What is the intersection of the two sets A and B if $A = \{1, 2, 3, 5, 6, 7\}$ and $B = \{0, 2, 4, 6, 8\}$?

A In this case, we have:

$$A \cap B = \{2, 6\}$$

because the only elements that appear in both sets are 2 and 6.

Disjoint sets

If two sets have no common elements, their intersection results in the empty or null set, i.e. $A \cap B = \emptyset$, and they are said to be **disjoint**, as shown in the Venn diagram in Figure 2.5.4.

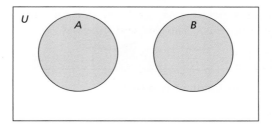

Figure 2.5.4 **Two disjoint sets.**

Example 2.5.5

Q How would you describe the intersection of the sets $A = \{x: x$ is an even denary digit$\}$ and $B = \{x: x$ is an odd denary digit$\}$?

A We see there are no common elements to both sets, and so the intersection is the empty set:

$$A \cap B = \varnothing$$

Therefore the sets are disjoint.

Complement of a set

The set of elements that are in the universal set U but not in a specific set, say A, are called the **complement** of set A, which is denoted by $\overline{A}$; the line above the label or name of the set is called an 'overbar'[1]:

$$\overline{A} = \{x: x \text{ is not in } A\} = \{x: x \notin A\} \qquad (2.5.3)$$

The shaded area in the Venn diagram in Figure 2.5.5 illustrates the complement of a set A.

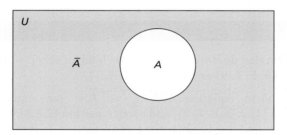

Figure 2.5.5 **The complement of a set.**

Example 2.5.6

Q If $U = \{0, 1, 2, 3, 4, 5, 6, 7, 8, 9\}$ and $A = \{1, 3, 5, 7, 9\}$, what is the complement of set A?

A In this case:

$$\overline{A} = \{0, 2, 4, 6, 8\}$$

because the elements 0, 2, 4, 6 and 8 appear in the universal set, but do not appear in set A.

de Morgan's properties

de Morgan's properties (or laws) relate to the union and intersection of complements of sets. They are written as:

$$\overline{A \cup B} = \overline{A} \cap \overline{B} \qquad (2.5.4)$$

---

[1] We use the **overbar** to represent several operations in mathematics; see Chapter 5 for an instance of another use.

that is, the intersection of the complements of two sets is the same as the complement of their union; and:

$$\overline{A \cap B} = \overline{A} \cup \overline{B} \qquad (2.5.5)$$

that is, the union of the complements of two sets is the same as the complement of their intersection.

de Morgan's properties are illustrated in Figure 2.5.6, where the shaded area represents $\overline{A \cup B} = \overline{A} \cap \overline{B}$.

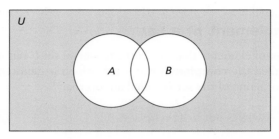

Figure 2.5.6 **de Morgan's properties.**

Example **2.5.7**

Q Confirm that de Morgan's properties hold for sets $U = \{0, 1, 2, 3, 4, 5, 6, 7, 8, 9\}$, $A = \{1, 3, 5, 7, 9\}$ and $B = \{1, 2, 3, 5, 7\}$.

A To confirm equation (2.5.4), we first use equation (2.5.1) to identify $A \cup B = \{1, 2, 3, 5, 7, 9\}$, and using equation (2.5.3) we get $\overline{A \cup B} = \{0, 4, 6, 8\}$. Next, we find $\overline{A} = \{0, 2, 4, 6, 8\}$ and $\overline{B} = \{0, 4, 6, 8, 9\}$ by using equation (2.5.3), and using equation (2.5.2) gives $\overline{A} \cap \overline{B} = \{0, 4, 6, 8\}$.

To confirm equation (2.5.5), we first use equation (2.5.2) to identify $A \cap B = \{1, 3, 5, 7\}$, and using equation (2.5.3) we get $\overline{A \cap B} = \{0, 2, 4, 6, 8, 9\}$. Next, we find $\overline{A} = \{0, 2, 4, 6, 8\}$ and $\overline{B} = \{0, 4, 6, 8\}$ by using equation (2.5.3), and using equation (2.5.1) gives $\overline{A} \cup \overline{B} = \{0, 2, 4, 6, 8\}$.

Counting elements in sets

In some cases, a set may have an unlimited number of elements (e.g. the set of grains of sand on a beach), and we say the set is **infinite**. When we can count the number of elements in a set, we say the set is **finite**. An example of a finite set is the empty or null set, which contains no elements. The set of binary digits is a finite set because it contains two elements, as is the set of denary digits, which contains ten elements. We use $n(A)$ to denote the number of elements in a set: for example, if $A = \{x: x$ is a denary digit$\}$ then $n(A) = 10$. Making use of unions and intersections, there is an obvious relationship between the number of elements in two intersecting sets:

$$n(A \cup B) = n(A) + n(B) - n(A \cap B) \qquad (2.5.6)$$

The use of equation (2.5.6), and how we count the number of elements in sets, are illustrated in Example 2.5.8.

Example | 2.5.8

Q A supermarket surveyed some of its customers and found that 25 bought strawberries and 15 bought cream. Only 10 bought both strawberries and cream. How many customers were surveyed?

A Let us define two sets:

A = {Customers buying strawberries}

B = {Customers buying cream}

We know that $n(A) = 25$ and $n(B) = 15$, and as the set of customers buying both is given by $A \cap B$, we also know that $n(A \cap B) = 10$. We can see this from the Venn diagram in Figure 2.5.7.

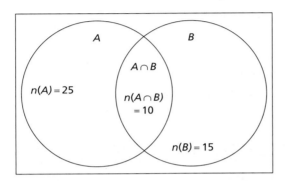

Figure 2.5.7 **Customers buying strawberries and cream.**

We can see the total number of customers surveyed from Figure 2.5.7. We know 25 bought strawberries and 15 cream, and so 40 bought strawberries or cream or both. Since 10 bought both, we use equation (2.5.6) to give $40 - 10 = 30$. So 30 customers were surveyed.

Exercises | 2.5

1 A company employs three sales representatives: Smith, Jones and Bloggs, each based at their homes, and each responsible for the customers in a 50-mile radius from their home. The customers within each sales representative's area are:

Sales representative	Customers within 50 mile radius
Smith	$A, B, F, G, J, K, O, P, T, W, X$
Jones	$C, D, E, F, H, I, J, L, P, U, Z$
Bloggs	$B, G, J, L, M, N, Q, R, S, V, Y$

(a) How many and which customers are visited by Smith or Jones?
(b) How many customers do both Smith and Jones have, and who are they?
(c) How many and which customers are visited only by Jones?
(d) How many and which customers are visited by Bloggs but not by Jones?
(e) How many and which customers are visited by neither Smith nor Jones?
(f) What is the set {Customers of Smith} ∪ {Customers of Jones}?
(g) What is the set {Customers of Bloggs} ∪ {Customers of Jones}?
(h) What is the set {Customers of Smith} ∩ {Customers of Jones}?
(i) What is the set {Customers of Smith} ∩ {Customers of Jones} ∪ {Customers of Bloggs}?
(j) How would you write 'the set of customers of Bloggs who are not customers of either Smith or Jones' in set notation, and which customers constitute this set?

2 Three newspapers A, B and C are published in a certain city. It has been estimated from a survey of the adult population in the city that:

20%	Read paper A
16%	Read paper B
14%	Read paper C
8%	Read both papers A and B
5%	Read both papers A and C
4%	Read both papers B and C
2%	Read all three papers

What percentage of adults read at least one of the newspapers?

Counting, factorials, permutations and combinations

In Section 2.5 we counted the number of elements in sets. We now introduce the general principle of counting (the multiplication principle) and consider some extensions of it, including factorials, permutations and combinations.

The prerequisites of this section are:
- Subscripted variables and sigma notation (Section 2.4);
- Set notation, set properties and Venn diagrams (Section 2.5).

Tree diagrams

We can count the number of ways that a set of tasks can be done by using **tree diagrams**, as illustrated by Example 2.6.1.

Example 2.6.1

Q In an office, there are 3 managers and 5 secretaries. The managers pass on to any of the secretaries their reports for word-processing, copying, etc. How many different ways might a management report be produced?

A Let us denote the three managers by M1, M2 and M3 and the five secretaries by S1, S2, S3, S4 and S5. All the possible ways that a report can be produced are shown by the tree diagram in Figure 2.6.1, from which we see there are $3 * 5 = 15$ possible ways of producing a report.

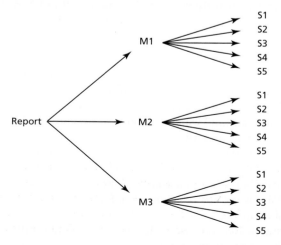

Figure 2.6.1 **A tree diagram for Example 2.6.1.**

The multiplication principle

In general we might have m tasks, each of which can be done in a different number of ways, which we denote with subscripted variables:

The first task can be undertaken in n_1 different ways

The second task can be undertaken in n_2 different ways

$\vdots$

etc.

$\vdots$

The last (i.e. mth) task can be undertaken in n_m different ways.

In Example 2.6.1, we had $m = 2$, $n_1 = 3$ and $n_2 = 5$, and from Figure 2.6.1 the total number of possibilities was found by $3 * 5 = 15$ (i.e. $n_1 * n_2$). In general, for m tasks, the total number of possibilities is:

$$n_1 * n_2 * n_3 * \cdots * n_m \qquad (2.6.1)$$

In Section 2.4 we used sigma notation for the summation of subscripted variables. There is a similar shorthand notation for the **product of subscripted variables**, for which we use the Greek upper-case letter Π (i.e. pi), and write (2.6.1) as:

$$\prod_{i=1}^{m} n_i = n_1 * n_2 * n_3 * \cdots * n_m \qquad (2.6.2)$$

In Example 2.6.1, we have:

$$\prod_{i=1}^{2} n_i = 3 * 5 = 15$$

Most spreadsheets have an inbuilt function for calculating the product of a set of numbers.

Factorials

In some cases, we need to determine the product of:

$1 * 2 * 3 * 4 * 5 * \cdots * n$ for any integer $n > 0$

This particular quantity is called the **factorial of n**, or more commonly **n factorial**, and is denoted $n!$:

$$n! = n * (n - 1) * (n - 2) * \cdots * 4 * 3 * 2 * 1 \qquad (2.6.3)$$

Note that we define $0!$ (zero factorial) to be 1 (i.e. $0! = 1$). Some factorials are:

$0! = 1$

$1! = 1$

$2! = 2 * 1 = 2$

$3! = 3 * 2 * 1 = 6$

$4! = 4 * 3 * 2 * 1 = 24$

etc.

Notice how, as n gets larger, $n!$ becomes even larger very quickly (e.g. $10! = 3,628,800$). Note also that if we multiply $n!$ by the next highest integer (i.e. $(n + 1)$) we get $n!(n + 1) = (n + 1)!$ The reason for this is that $n! = 1 * 2 * 3 * \cdots * n$ and $(n + 1)! = 1 * 2 * 3 * \cdots * n * (n + 1)$. Example 2.6.2 illustrates how factorials arise. Most spreadsheets and calculators have an inbuilt function for calculating factorials.

Example 2.6.2

Q How many different ways can a sales representative visit 4 customers in 1 day?

A First, consider the number of ways that the sales representative can visit 1 customer, say Mr *A* (there is only one, of course).

Next, consider two customers, Mr *A* and Mrs *B*. The sales representative might visit Mr *A* before Mrs *B*, or the other way round. So there are $2 * 1 = 2 = 2!$ possibilities.

Now consider three customers, Mr *A*, Mrs *B* and Ms *C*. If we **enumerate** (i.e. list) all the possibilities we get *ABC*, *BAC*, *CAB*, *ACB*, *BCA* or *CBA*, and so there are now $3 * 2 * 1 = 6 = 3!$ possibilities.

For four customers, there are $4! = 4 * 3 * 2 * 1 = 24$ possibilities (i.e. apply equation (2.6.3)). If you are not convinced, here is a list of all the possibilities for four customers:

ABCD or *ACBD* or *ADBC* or *ABDC* or *ACDB* or *ADCB*

BACD or *BCAD* or *BDAC* or *BADC* or *BCDA* or *BDCA*

CABD or *CBAD* or *CDAB* or *CADB* or *CBDA* or *CDBA*

DABC or *DBAC* or *DCAB* or *DACB* or *DBCA* or *DCBA*

Permutations

A **permutation** is an ordered arrangement of distinct objects. Example 2.6.3 illustrates how permutations arise.

Example 2.6.3

Q Suppose the sales representative in Example 2.6.2 has 5 customers to visit, Mr *A*, Mrs *B*, Ms *C*, Mr *D* and Ms *E*, and on any particular day he must visit 3 of them. How many ways can the visits be arranged?

A There are 5 possibilities (i.e. *A*, *B*, *C*, *D* or *E*) for the first customer.

In selecting the second customer, there are only 4 possibilities, because the representative will not visit the same customer twice on the same day.

In selecting the third customer, there are only 3 possibilities, because the representative has already visited 2 of the 5 customers.

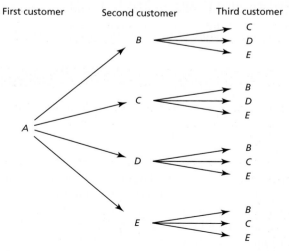

Figure 2.6.2 **A permutation for Example 2.6.3.**

The possibilities of starting with a visit to customer A are shown in Figure 2.6.2. There are, of course, similar possibilities for the representative starting with B, C, D and E.

In Figure 2.6.2, we see that there are $4 * 3 = 12$ possibilities of starting visits with customer A. However, the sales representative could start with any of the 5 customers (i.e. A, B, C, D or E), so there are $5 * 4 * 3 = 60$ possibilities in all.

The permutation notation and formula

In general we denote r permutations from n objects, ^nP_r. In Example 2.6.3, we have $^nP_r = 5 * 4 * 3 = 60$, where $n = 5$ and $r = 3$. In general, we define a permutation as:

$$^nP_r = n * (n - 1) * (n - 2) * \cdots * r \tag{2.6.4}$$

However, there is an easier way of writing this. From equation (2.6.3), we know that:

$$n! = n * (n - 1) * (n - 2) * \cdots * 3 * 2 * 1 \tag{2.6.5}$$

Applying equation (2.6.5) to $(n - r)!$ gives:

$$(n - r)! = (n - r) * (n - r - 1) * (n - r - 2) * \cdots * 3 * 2 * 1 \tag{2.6.6}$$

If we divide (2.6.5) by (2.6.6) we get:

$$\frac{n * (n - 1) * (n - 2) * (n - 3) * \cdots 3 * 2 * 1}{(n - r) * (n - r - 1) * (n - r - 2) * \cdots * 3 * 2 * 1} = n * (n - 1) * (n - 2) * \cdots * r$$

Therefore we can write equation (2.6.4) as:

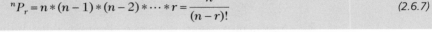

$$^nP_r = n * (n - 1) * (n - 2) * \cdots * r = \frac{n}{(n - r)!} \tag{2.6.7}$$

2.6

Most spreadsheets and calculators have inbuilt functions for calculating permutations.

Combinations

With permutations, we distinguish between the order in which objects are presented. In Example 2.6.2, the selection ABC was different from ACB, BAC, BCA, CAB and CBA. In some situations, the order is not important and we just wish to count the number of unordered possibilities; we call this a **combination**. Example 2.6.4 illustrates how combinations arise and how we count them.

Example | **2.6.4**

Q Suppose the sales representative in Example 2.6.3 is not concerned about how the visits are arranged. How many ways can 3 customers be selected from 5 on each day?

A As we do not distinguish between ABC, BAC and CAB, etc., we have only 10 possibilities:

(a) ABC (b) ABD (c) ABE
(d) ACD (e) ACE (f) ADE
(g) BCD (h) BCE (i) BDE
(j) CDE.

The combination notation and formula

We use a notation similar to that for permutations, and denote the general combination of r objects out of n objects by ^nC_r. To derive a formula for counting combinations, recall from dealing with factorials that r objects can be listed in $r!$ different ways. The number of permutations of r objects out of n objects must therefore be $r!$ times the number of ways that r objects can be combined from n objects (i.e. $r! * {}^nC_r = {}^nP_r$) and so we can write:

$$^nC_r = \frac{^nP_r}{r!} \qquad\qquad (2.6.8)$$

Using equation (2.6.7), we can also write:

$$^nC_r = \frac{^nP_r}{r!} = \frac{n!}{r!(n-r)!} \qquad\qquad (2.6.9)$$

 2.6

Many spreadsheets and calculators have inbuilt functions to help us calculate combinations.

Exercises 2.6

1 In Catlogshop retail outlets, customers pick and pay for items at an EPOS (electronic point of sale).[2] Once the order has been processed, the customer goes to a collection point to wait for the items. Between purchase and collection, the item is picked from the warehouse by a 'picking' operative, and carried to the collection point by a 'warehouse' operative, who places it on a shelf in the collection area; then the 'counter' staff pass it on to the customer. On one particular day, there are 2 picking operatives, 2 warehouse operatives and 3 counter staff. How many ways are there of satisfying a customer order?

2 A sales representative visits 6 clients in 1 day. If the clients can be visited in any order, how many ways are there to do this?

3 A production process consists of 10 machines M1, M2, ..., M10. A product must be processed on each machine, but only once. How many routes might it take?

4 In Gotham City Council, all committees must have a quorum of 5, of which 3 must be elected councillors. How many ways are there to do this if there are only 12 elected councillors?

5 A medical secretary has to type up 20 case notes and reckons that only 5 can be done each day. How many ways of typing reports are there today, tomorrow and each subsequent day?

2.7 Pascal's triangle and binomial coefficients

In Section 2.6 we counted the number of ways r objects can be chosen from a set of n objects. If order was unimportant then this was called a combination, denoted by ^nC_r. One method of displaying these combinations is **Pascal's triangle**. These combinations (i.e. the numbers in Pascal's triangle) also occur when we multiply out algebraic expressions of the form $(x + a)^n$, and they are then known as binomial coefficients. This section looks at Pascal's triangle and why and how binomial coefficients arise.

---

[2] System used by retail outlets to record information electronically.

The prerequisites of this section are:

■ Algorithms, variables and algebra (Section 2.1);
■ Subscripted variables and sigma notation (Section 2.4);
■ Counting, factorials, permutations and combinations (Section 2.6).

Pascal's triangle

The entries in Pascal's triangle are calculated by putting unity (i.e. 1) down the two diagonal sides, and then creating each new row in turn, by adding together an adjacent pair of numbers from the previous row, as shown by the arrows in the rows labelled $n = 1$, $n = 2$ and $n = 3$ in Figure 2.7.1. The required combination is read from the triangle by looking at the **entry on row n** and up the **diagonal labelled r**.

In Example 2.6.4, the combination for selecting $r = 3$ out of $n = 5$ is $^5C_3 = 10$, shown boxed in the Pascal triangle in Figure 2.7.1.

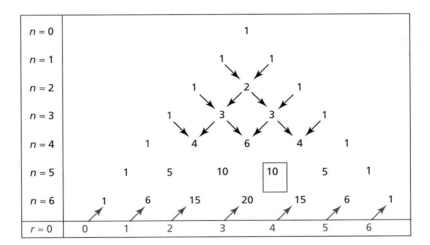

Figure 2.7.1 **Part of Pascal's triangle.**

Binomial coefficients

The values in Pascal's triangle or from the combinations formula (i.e. ^nC_r) in equation (2.5.9) are known as **binomial coefficients**, and are used in the **binomial theorem**. This is used when we want to **expand** (i.e. multiply out) algebraic expressions containing brackets with exponents: for example, to expand $(x + 1)^2$. We can simply multiply out the brackets, as illustrated in Example 2.7.1. However, when we have large exponents, this can be extremely time consuming.

| Example | 2.7.1 |

Q   Expand the expressions (a) $(x + 1)^2$ and (b) $(x + 1)^3$.

A   Multiplying out the brackets we get:

(a) $(x + 1) * (x + 1) = x^2 + x + x + 1 = x^2 + 2x + 1$ (2.7.1)

(b) $(x + 1) * (x + 1)(x + 1) = (x^2 + 2x + 1) * (x + 1)$

$$= x^3 + 2x^2 + x + x^2 + 2x + 1$$

$$= x^3 + 3x^2 + 3x + 1.$$ (2.7.2)

59

The binomial theorem

The coefficients in equations (2.7.1) and (2.7.2) can be read from a row of Pascal's triangle in Figure 2.7.1. Those in equation (2.7.1) appear in row $n = 2$ and those in equation (2.7.2) appear in row $n = 3$. In general, the coefficients appear in that row of Pascal's triangle determined by the power in the algebraic expression.

In general, to expand expressions of the form $(x + y)^n$, then we use the binomial theorem:

$$(x+y)^n = {}^nC_0 x^n + {}^nC_1 x^{n-1}y^1 + {}^nC_2 x^{n-2}y^2 + {}^nC_3 x^{n-1}y^3 + \cdots + {}^nC_{n-1}x^1 y^{n-1} + {}^nC_n y^n$$

$$(2.7.3)$$

Example 2.7.2

Q Expand expression $(x + 1)^4$, using the binomial theorem.

A From Pascal's triangle, or using equation (2.6.9), the coefficients are:

   1, 4, 6, 4, 1

and using equation (2.7.3) the expanded expression is:

   $x^4 + 4x^3 + 6x^2 + 4x + 1.$

Binomial identities

Binomial coefficients have some useful properties for use in counting sets:

$${}^nC_r = {}^nC_{n-r} \qquad (2.7.4)$$

$${}^nC_r = {}^{n-1}C_r + {}^{n-1}C_{r-1} \qquad (2.7.5)$$

$$\sum_{r=0}^{n} {}^nC_r = 2^n \qquad (2.7.6)$$

These properties are illustrated in Examples 2.7.3, 2.7.4 and 2.7.5.

Example 2.7.3

Q How many ways are there of choosing any 3 out of 5 customers?

A We already know that we can simply calculate: ${}^5C_3 = 10$

Alternatively, we could count the number of ways that 2 customers are not selected from 5 (i.e. ${}^5C_{5-2}$), given by equation (2.7.4).

Example 2.7.4

Q If in Example 2.7.3 the customers are labelled A, B, C, D and E, how many visits do not include A?

A We know from Example 2.7.3 that ${}^5C_3 = 10$ and the visits to customer A will be ${}^4C_2 = 6$, so the visits that do not include customer A are $10 - 6 = 4$. This is found from equation (2.7.5): ${}^{n-1}C_r = {}^nC_r - {}^{n-1}C_{r-1}$.

Example | **2.7.5**

Q How many subsets are there in a set containing 6 elements?

A We can simply add the numbers in row 6 of Pascal's triangle in Figure 2.7.1, giving 64, or alternatively use equation (2.7.6), which gives $2^6 = 64$.

Exercises | **2.7**

1 Expand the following expressions:
(a) $(x + 1)^5$ (b) $(x + 2)^4$ (c) $(x + y)^3$

2 What is the coefficient of x^4 in the expansion of $(2x + 1)^6$?

3 In how many ways can a committee of 8 men and 5 women be formed if there are 10 men and 11 women eligible to sit on the committee?

4 A street contains 16 houses on the west side and 10 on the east side. A pollster has to visit 4 houses on the west and 3 on the east. How many ways can the pollster meet the target?

5 How many subsets are in sets containing:
(a) 5 elements? (b) 10 elements?

6 If a set contains 5 elements, how many subsets contain:
(a) an even number of elements?
(b) an odd number of elements?

2.8 | ## Chapter review

In this chapter we used the language of mathematics to generalise calculations from numbers (arithmetic) to variables (algebra), and we encountered instructions in the form of algorithms to undertake repeated calculations on variables. We extended algebra to deal with several scales of measurement by using vectors, matrices and arrays, and in Section 2.4 we generalised even further by using subscripted notation and sigma notation. We can extend the concept of algebra to deal with vectors, matrices and arrays, and this is considered in the next chapter.

Sometimes, we want to identify and count things – for example to identify and count the number of customers that a sales representative can visit in one day, to plan an itinerary – and to do so we use the concept of sets. We also use sets to design algorithms and calculate probabilities (Chapter 6). Other applications of sets and counting also appear in later chapters. The branch of mathematics that deals with sets is called **combinatorial mathematics** or **combinatorics**.

Although some of the notation and formulae may, at first, appear daunting, they are necessary when undertaking calculations manually. However, when calculators or computers are used, the notation is unnecessary because many spreadsheets and calculators have inbuilt functions for calculating factorials, permutations and combinations.

Let us briefly reflect on the process of generalisation we have followed. We began with scalars and generalised to arrays of any dimension and then to sets. We shall come across this process of generalisation time and time again; it is one of the most powerful features in the language of mathematics. Furthermore, though we may not be able to visualise a particular mathematical concept (e.g. a 4-dimensional array), mathematics can not only handle such abstract concepts, it can also provide useful tools or mechanisms for representing real phenomena that we encounter in business and management.

Chapter 3

Matrix algebra

Introduction

In Section 2.1 we extended our use of arithmetic from numbers to variables, by means of algebra. In Section 2.3 we encountered vectors, matrices and arrays, when we have several scales of measurement. In this chapter we extend our use of arithmetic and algebra to deal with vectors and matrices.

We can apply the concepts of addition and subtraction to matrices, and we can redefine the operation of multiplication, but there is no direct analogy with scalar division. Instead, we define an operation called inversion. Because matrices are different from scalars, it is also possible to define other operations on matrices that cannot be applied to scalars: for example, it is possible to transpose a matrix. There are also some special matrices, which are useful.

Matrices are widely used, especially in Economics and particularly for representing systems of equations such as those encountered in Section 2.2.

Chapter objectives

- To add and subtract vectors and matrices
- To multiply vectors and matrices
- To find the determinant and inverse of a matrix
- To transpose vectors and matrices
- To recognise and use identity, null and unit vectors and matrices
- To use matrix methods for solving systems of equations

Chapter contents

Matrix addition and subtraction

We can add and subtract vectors, matrices and arrays, subject to certain rules and conventions. In this section, we consider these rules.

The prerequisites of this section are:
- Basic arithmetic (Section 1.4);
- Scalars, vectors, matrices and arrays (Section 2.3);
- Subscripted variables and sigma notation (Section 2.4).

Addition and subtraction of vectors, matrices and arrays

To add or subtract vectors, matrices and arrays, we need to ensure that they are of the **same dimension**: for example, we can only add a scalar to a scalar, a vector to a vector, a matrix to a matrix. Furthermore, the vectors, matrices and arrays being added or subtracted must be of the **same order**: for example, we can only subtract a row vector having four elements from another row vector that has four elements. Although we shall consider only addition and subtraction of matrices, we can also add or subtract vectors or, indeed, any two arrays of the same dimension and order. In this section, we consider addition and subtraction of two matrices, but we can also add or subtract any number of matrices.

Matrix addition

We can add two matrices only if they are of the same order (i.e. they have the same number of rows and columns). Let us consider adding matrices A and B. If A has m rows and n columns then B must have the same. We add together their corresponding elements. If a_{ij} denotes the elements of matrix A and b_{ij} those of matrix B, we denote the sum as $A + B$ and calculate $a_{ij} + b_{ij}$ for every element in row i and column j, as illustrated in Example 3.1.1.

Example | **3.1.1**

Q Add matrices A and B where:

$$A = \begin{pmatrix} 3 & 1 & 7 & 4 \\ 5 & 2 & 1 & -5 \end{pmatrix} \text{ and } B = \begin{pmatrix} 2 & 6 & 12 & -1 \\ 2 & 1 & 0 & 5 \end{pmatrix}$$

A Both matrices are (2×4) so we can add them by taking the sum of the corresponding elements of the matrices:

$$A + B = \begin{pmatrix} 3+2 & 1+6 & 7+12 & 4-1 \\ 5+2 & 2+1 & 1+0 & -5+5 \end{pmatrix} = \begin{pmatrix} 5 & 7 & 19 & 3 \\ 7 & 3 & 1 & 0 \end{pmatrix}$$

Note that the answer in Example 3.1.1 has the same order as the matrices being added together (2×4). Matrix addition is commutative, as we saw with scalars, i.e.:

$$A + B = B + A.$$

Matrix subtraction

The rules of subtraction are the same as those of addition. We can subtract two matrices only if they are of the same order (i.e. they have the same number of rows and columns). We subtract their corresponding elements. If a_{ij} denotes the elements of matrix A and b_{ij} those of matrix B, we denote the subtraction as $A - B$ and calculate $a_{ij} - b_{ij}$ for every element in row i and column j, as illustrated in Example 3.1.2. As with matrix addition, the resulting matrix has the same order as the matrices being subtracted.

Matrix subtraction is not commutative, as we saw with scalars, i.e.:

$$A - B \neq B - A$$

Example 3.1.2

Q Subtract B from A, and A from B where:

$$A = \begin{pmatrix} 3 & 1 & 7 & 4 \\ 5 & 2 & 1 & -5 \end{pmatrix} \text{ and } B = \begin{pmatrix} 2 & 6 & 12 & -1 \\ 2 & 1 & 0 & 5 \end{pmatrix}$$

A Both matrices are (2×4) so we can subtract them:

$$A - B = \begin{pmatrix} 3-2 & 1-6 & 7-12 & 4+1 \\ 5-2 & 2-1 & 1-0 & -5-5 \end{pmatrix} = \begin{pmatrix} 1 & -5 & -5 & 5 \\ 3 & 1 & 1 & -10 \end{pmatrix}$$

$$B - A = \begin{pmatrix} 2-3 & 6-1 & 12-7 & -1-4 \\ 2-5 & 1-2 & 0-1 & 5+5 \end{pmatrix} = \begin{pmatrix} -1 & 5 & 5 & -5 \\ -3 & -1 & -1 & 10 \end{pmatrix}$$

Matrix addition and subtraction are performed very easily on a spreadsheet.

 3.1

Exercises 3.1

1 For the matrices:

$$X = \begin{pmatrix} 10 & 7 \\ 1 & 2 \\ 4 & 3 \end{pmatrix}, \quad Y = \begin{pmatrix} 2 & 5 \\ 9 & 3 \\ 1 & 6 \end{pmatrix} \text{ and } Z = \begin{pmatrix} 3 & 12 \\ 8 & 7 \\ 5 & 2 \end{pmatrix}$$

calculate the following:
(a) $X + Y$ (b) $X - Y$ (c) $Y + X$
(d) $Y - X$ (e) $X + Y + Z$ (f) $X + Y - Z$
(g) $X - Y + Z$ (h) $X - (Y + Z)$.

2 For matrices and vectors:

$$A = \begin{pmatrix} 1 & 7 & 3 \\ 1 & 6 & 2 \\ 4 & 3 & 8 \end{pmatrix}, \quad I = \begin{pmatrix} 1 & 0 & 0 \\ 0 & 1 & 0 \\ 0 & 0 & 1 \end{pmatrix}, \quad U = \begin{pmatrix} 1 & 1 \\ 1 & 1 \\ 1 & 1 \end{pmatrix}, \quad X = \begin{pmatrix} 2 & 5 & 3 \\ 1 & 3 & 8 \end{pmatrix}$$

$$\mathbf{p} = (1 \ 2 \ 3), \quad \mathbf{q} = (4 \ 1 \ 9), \quad \mathbf{s} = (7 \ 0 \ 1 \ 5 \ 9)$$

Are the following calculations possible, and if not explain why. Otherwise, calculate the answer:
(a) $A + A$ (b) $A + I$ (c) $U + X$
(d) $U + I$ (e) $X + \mathbf{p}$ (f) $\mathbf{p} + \mathbf{q}$
(g) $\mathbf{p} + \mathbf{s}$ (h) $\mathbf{q} - \mathbf{p}$ (i) $\mathbf{p} - \mathbf{q}$
(j) $\mathbf{p} + \mathbf{q} - \mathbf{s}$.

Matrix multiplication

Unlike addition and subtraction, we cannot simply extend scalar multiplication to matrices; instead, we redefine the operation of multiplication for vectors and matrices. In this section, we consider the rules for multiplying vectors, matrices and arrays.

The prerequisites of this section are:
- Basic arithmetic (Section 1.4);
- Scalars, vectors, matrices and arrays (Section 2.3);
- Subscripted variables and sigma notation (Section 2.4);
- Matrix addition and subtraction (Section 3.1).

Matrix multiplication

Matrix multiplication is more involved than matrix addition and subtraction, and requires different conditions to be satisfied. We can multiply a vector, matrix or indeed any array by a scalar; we can multiply a matrix by a vector; and we can multiply a matrix by a matrix. However, we need to be very careful when multiplying vectors and matrices, and we must check that the operation is possible.

Multiplying vectors, matrices and arrays by a scalar

When multiplying a vector, matrix or any array by a scalar, we multiply all the elements of the matrix by the scalar. We write the scalar in front of the vector or matrix: for example, if x is a scalar and A is a matrix, we simply write xA and calculate $x * a_{ij}$ for every element in matrix A, as illustrated in Example 3.2.1.

Example | **3.2.1**

Q For the scalar $s = 5$, the vector $\mathbf{v} = (2 \quad 1 \quad -2)$ and the matrix $W = \begin{pmatrix} 1 & 2 & 1 \\ 3 & 4 & 2 \\ 2 & 0 & 5 \end{pmatrix}$, calculate:
(a) $s\mathbf{v}$ (b) sW.

A (a) $s\mathbf{v} = 5 * (2 \quad 1 \quad -2) = (5*2 \quad 5*1 \quad 5*-2) = (10 \quad 5 \quad -10)$

(b) $sW = 5 * \begin{pmatrix} 1 & 2 & 1 \\ 3 & 4 & 2 \\ 2 & 0 & 5 \end{pmatrix} = \begin{pmatrix} 5*1 & 5*2 & 5*1 \\ 5*3 & 5*4 & 5*2 \\ 5*2 & 5*0 & 5*5 \end{pmatrix} = \begin{pmatrix} 5 & 10 & 5 \\ 15 & 20 & 20 \\ 10 & 0 & 25 \end{pmatrix}$

Multiplying vectors and matrices

When we multiply vectors and matrices together, we redefine multiplication. Furthermore, vector and matrix multiplication is not commutative (i.e. for any two matrices A and B, $AB \neq BA$). So we distinguish between **pre-multiplication** and **post-multiplication**. Matrix B is pre-multiplied by matrix A when we calculate AB, whereas matrix B is post-multiplied by A when we calculate BA. The process of vector or matrix multiplication is difficult to write down in words, but it is quite easy to understand. We begin by considering the multiplication of two vectors, as shown in Example 3.2.2, and then generalise to the process of multiplying matrices.

Example 3.2.2

Q Pre-multiply the vector $\mathbf{w} = \begin{pmatrix} 1 \\ 6 \\ 2 \end{pmatrix}$ by the vector $\mathbf{v} = (5 \quad 4 \quad -3)$.

A We want to calculate:

$$\mathbf{vw} = (5 \quad 4 \quad -3) * \begin{pmatrix} 1 \\ 6 \\ 2 \end{pmatrix}$$

To obtain the answer we add together (i.e. sum) the products of the corresponding elements in each vector. That is, we multiply the first element of each vector (i.e. find the product of the first element of each vector), and then add this to the product of the second element of each vector, and then add this to the product of the third element of each vector:

$$\mathbf{vw} = (5 \quad 4 \quad -3) * \begin{pmatrix} 1 \\ 6 \\ 2 \end{pmatrix} = 5 * 1 + 4 * 6 - 3 * 2 = 5 + 24 - 6 = 23$$

Multiplying a vector by a matrix

If we look carefully at how we calculated the product of the two vectors in Example 3.2.2 we can see the rules for multiplying two vectors together. First, we observe that we can only undertake this operation if the number of rows in the second vector (e.g. $\mathbf{w}$) is the same as the number of columns in the first vector (e.g. $\mathbf{v}$). In Example 3.2.2 vector $\mathbf{w}$ has 3 rows and vector $\mathbf{v}$ has 3 columns. Second, we can also observe that this process has resulted in a single number (i.e. a scalar).

Let us now consider pre-multiplying a matrix by a vector. If we follow the same process then the number of rows in our matrix will have to be the same as the number of columns in the vector, otherwise we cannot perform the operation. Example 3.2.3 illustrates the process.

Example 3.2.3

Q Pre-multiply the matrix $W = \begin{pmatrix} 1 & 9 \\ 6 & 7 \\ 2 & 8 \end{pmatrix}$ by the vector $\mathbf{v} = (5 \quad 4 \quad -3)$.

A We want to calculate:

$$\mathbf{v}W = (5 \quad 4 \quad -3) * \begin{pmatrix} 1 & 9 \\ 6 & 7 \\ 2 & 8 \end{pmatrix}$$

To apply the process we used in Example 3.2.2, we think of matrix W as being made up of two column vectors:

$$\begin{pmatrix} 1 \\ 6 \\ 2 \end{pmatrix} \quad \text{and} \quad \begin{pmatrix} 9 \\ 7 \\ 8 \end{pmatrix}$$

We end up with two scalars. The first from calculating:

$$(5 \quad 4 \quad -3) * \begin{pmatrix} 1 \\ 6 \\ 2 \end{pmatrix} = 5*1 + 4*6 - 3*2 = 23$$

and the other from calculating:

$$(5 \quad 4 \quad -3) * \begin{pmatrix} 9 \\ 7 \\ 8 \end{pmatrix} = 5*9 + 4*7 - 3*8 = 49$$

That is:

$$\mathbf{v}W = (5 \quad 4 \quad -3) * \begin{pmatrix} 9 \\ 7 \\ 8 \end{pmatrix} = (5*1 + 4*6 - 3*2 \quad 5*9 + 4*7 - 3*8)$$

$$= (5 + 24 - 6 \quad 45 + 28 - 24)$$

$$= (23 \quad 49).$$

Multiplying a matrix by a matrix

If we look carefully at our calculation in Example 3.2.3, we see that this process resulted in a vector with two columns. It had two columns because matrix W has two columns.

Let us now consider multiplying two matrices together. If we follow the same process again then the number of rows in one matrix will have to be the same as the number of columns in the other matrix, otherwise we cannot perform the operation. Example 3.2.4 illustrates the process of pre-multiplying a matrix by another matrix.

Example | **3.2.4**

Q Pre-multiply the matrix $W = \begin{pmatrix} 1 & 9 \\ 6 & 7 \\ 2 & 8 \end{pmatrix}$ by the matrix $V = \begin{pmatrix} 5 & 4 & -3 \\ 1 & 2 & 7 \end{pmatrix}$

A We want to calculate:

$$VW = \begin{pmatrix} 5 & 4 & -3 \\ 1 & 2 & 7 \end{pmatrix} * \begin{pmatrix} 1 & 9 \\ 6 & 7 \\ 2 & 8 \end{pmatrix}$$

To apply the process we used in Example 3.2.3, we need to think of matrix V as consisting of two row vectors:

$$(5 \quad 4 \quad -3) \text{ and } (1 \quad 2 \quad 7)$$

each of which multiplies W, which can be thought of as consisting of two column vectors:

$$\begin{pmatrix} 1 \\ 6 \\ 2 \end{pmatrix} \text{ and } \begin{pmatrix} 9 \\ 7 \\ 8 \end{pmatrix}$$

Let us apply this process to each of these vectors. This time, we end up with four scalars:

$$(5 \quad 4 \quad -3) * \begin{pmatrix} 1 \\ 6 \\ 2 \end{pmatrix} = 23 \quad \text{and} \quad (5 \quad 4 \quad -3) * \begin{pmatrix} 9 \\ 7 \\ 8 \end{pmatrix} = 49$$

$$(1 \quad 2 \quad 7) * \begin{pmatrix} 1 \\ 6 \\ 2 \end{pmatrix} = 27 \quad \text{and} \quad (1 \quad 2 \quad 7) * \begin{pmatrix} 9 \\ 7 \\ 8 \end{pmatrix} = 79$$

This is:

$$VM = \begin{pmatrix} 5 & 4 & -3 \\ 1 & 2 & 7 \end{pmatrix} \begin{pmatrix} 1 & 9 \\ 6 & 7 \\ 2 & 8 \end{pmatrix} = \begin{pmatrix} 5*1+4*6-3*2 & 5*9+4*7-3*8 \\ 1*1+2*6+7*2 & 1*9+2*7+7*8 \end{pmatrix}$$

$$= \begin{pmatrix} 5+24-6 & 45+28-24 \\ 1+12+14 & 9+14+56 \end{pmatrix}$$

$$= \begin{pmatrix} 23 & 49 \\ 27 & 79 \end{pmatrix}$$

General matrix multiplication

If we now look carefully at Example 3.2.4, we can see the general rules for multiplying matrices. If we want the product AB of two matrices and matrix A is of order $(n \times m)$ then matrix B must have m rows but it can have any number of columns, say o. The resulting matrix will then be of order $(n \times o)$, (i.e. it will have n rows and o columns). The ith row and jth column of the resulting matrix will have elements calculated from:

$$a_{i1} * b_{1j} + a_{i2} * b_{2j} + a_{i3} * b_{3j} + \cdots + a_{im} * b_{mj} \qquad (3.2.1)$$

Using subscripted notation, we write this as:

$$\sum_{k=1}^{m} a_{ik} b_{kj} \qquad (3.2.2)$$

 3.2

Some spreadsheets have an inbuilt function for multiplying matrices.

Raising matrices to a power

As with scalars, we can raise a matrix to a power. Because raising to a power is just repeated multiplication, then it also applies to matrices. Recall that matrix multiplication of two matrices A and B is possible only if B has the same number of rows as the number of columns of A. So, to multiply a matrix by itself, it is possible only if it has the same number of rows as columns (i.e. a **square matrix**). Example 3.2.5 illustrates how square matrices can be raised to a power.

Example   3.2.5

Q For the matrix $C = \begin{pmatrix} 2 & 3 \\ 5 & 1 \end{pmatrix}$ find (a) C^2 and (b) C^3

A (a) $C^2 = \begin{pmatrix} 2 & 3 \\ 5 & 1 \end{pmatrix}\begin{pmatrix} 2 & 3 \\ 5 & 1 \end{pmatrix} = \begin{pmatrix} 2*2+3*5 & 2*3+3*1 \\ 5*2+1*5 & 5*3+1*1 \end{pmatrix} = \begin{pmatrix} 19 & 9 \\ 15 & 16 \end{pmatrix}$

(b) $C^3 = \begin{pmatrix} 2 & 3 \\ 5 & 1 \end{pmatrix}\begin{pmatrix} 2 & 3 \\ 5 & 1 \end{pmatrix}\begin{pmatrix} 2 & 3 \\ 5 & 1 \end{pmatrix} = \begin{pmatrix} 19 & 9 \\ 15 & 16 \end{pmatrix}\begin{pmatrix} 2 & 3 \\ 5 & 1 \end{pmatrix}$

$= \begin{pmatrix} 19*2+9*5 & 19*3+9*1 \\ 15*2+16*5 & 15*3+16*1 \end{pmatrix}$

$= \begin{pmatrix} 83 & 66 \\ 110 & 61 \end{pmatrix}$

Exercises   3.2

1 For $A = \begin{pmatrix} 3 & 2 \\ 4 & 1 \\ 5 & 2 \end{pmatrix}$ and $B = \begin{pmatrix} 1 & 2 & 4 \\ 3 & 1 & 9 \end{pmatrix}$, calculate the following or state why the operation is not valid:

(a) $A + B$ (b) AB (c) BA (d) A^2.

2 For $P = \begin{pmatrix} 1 & 2 \\ 3 & 5 \end{pmatrix}$ and $Q = \begin{pmatrix} -5 & 2 \\ 3 & -2 \end{pmatrix}$, calculate:

(a) PQ (b) QP (c) P^2 (d) Q^3.

3 The percentage chances of customers switching between three different brands of tea are:

	Tips	Leaf	Blend
Tips	50	30	20
Leaf	10	60	30
Blend	40	30	30

(a) Write these chances in matrix form with decimal elements.

(b) A survey in a supermarket revealed that the numbers of customers who bought Tips, Leaf and Blend last week were 300, 150 and 200, respectively. You can calculate the number of customers expected to buy each brand this week by simply post-multiplying the matrix in part (a) by a row vector of last week's purchases. Calculate the expected sales of the three brands of tea this week. Calculate the expected sales of the three brands of tea next week.

(c) How might you write down the calculations undertaken in (b) using matrix algebra?

4 The proportions of inputs and outputs between three sectors of an economy are shown below:

INPUTS	OUTPUTS		
	Manufacturing	Services	Energy
Manufacturing	0.1	0.0	0.2
Services	0.2	0.2	0.1
Energy	0.3	0.1	0.1

(a) Write these in the form of a matrix.
(b) If the annual output levels of the three sectors are £300m, £500m and £200m, respectively, what are the levels of Manufacturing, Services and Energy available to household consumers? *Hint*: The answer must be the annual output from each sector less the inputs used by each of the three sectors.
(c) Represent the calculations undertaken in (b) using matrix algebra.

3.3 Special matrices

There are a number of special matrices that have useful properties.

The prerequisites of this section are:
- Matrix addition and subtraction (Section 3.1);
- Matrix multiplication (Section 3.2).

Null vectors, matrices and arrays

Null vectors, matrices and arrays have all their elements **zero**: for example,

$$\begin{pmatrix} 0 & 0 & 0 \\ 0 & 0 & 0 \\ 0 & 0 & 0 \end{pmatrix} \text{ is a } (3 \times 3) \text{ null matrix and } \begin{pmatrix} 0 \\ 0 \\ 0 \\ 0 \end{pmatrix} \text{ is a null column vector.}$$

Null vectors and matrices have the same effect as 0 in scalar arithmetic: that is, addition or subtraction of the null vector or matrix makes no difference, whereas multiplication by a null vector or matrix results in a zero vector or matrix. Example 3.3.1 illustrates the effect of multiplying a matrix by a null vector and null matrix. Note that null vectors, matrices and arrays can be of any order (i.e. they can have any number of elements).

Example 3.3.1

Q Pre-multiply the matrix $\begin{pmatrix} 2 & 3 & 0 \\ 5 & 1 & 4 \end{pmatrix}$ by the appropriate (a) null vector and (b) null matrix.

A (a) $(0 \quad 0)\begin{pmatrix} 2 & 3 & 0 \\ 5 & 1 & 4 \end{pmatrix} = (0*2+0*5 \quad 0*3+0*1 \quad 0*0+0*4) = (0 \quad 0 \quad 0)$

(b) $\begin{pmatrix} 0 & 0 \\ 0 & 0 \end{pmatrix}\begin{pmatrix} 2 & 3 & 0 \\ 5 & 1 & 4 \end{pmatrix} = \begin{pmatrix} 0*2+0*5 & 0*3+0*1 & 0*0+0*4 \\ 0*2+0*5 & 0*3+0*1 & 0*0+0*4 \end{pmatrix} = \begin{pmatrix} 0 & 0 & 0 \\ 0 & 0 & 0 \end{pmatrix}$

Unit vectors, matrices and arrays

The **unit** vector or matrix has all its elements equal to unity (i.e. 1): for example,

$$\begin{pmatrix} 1 & 1 & 1 \\ 1 & 1 & 1 \\ 1 & 1 & 1 \end{pmatrix} \text{ is a } (3 \times 3) \text{ unit matrix and } \begin{pmatrix} 1 \\ 1 \\ 1 \\ 1 \end{pmatrix} \text{ is a unit column vector.}$$

As with null vectors, matrices and arrays, unit vectors, matrices and arrays can be of any order (i.e. they can have any number of elements). If a matrix is multiplied by a unit vector or a unit matrix then the elements in each column of the matrix are summed, as illustrated in Example 3.3.2.

Example 3.3.2

Q Pre-multiply the matrix $\begin{pmatrix} 2 & 3 & 0 \\ 5 & 1 & 4 \end{pmatrix}$ by the appropriate (a) unit vector and (b) unit matrix.

A (a) $(1 \quad 1) \begin{pmatrix} 2 & 3 & 0 \\ 5 & 1 & 4 \end{pmatrix} = (1*2+1*5 \quad 1*3+1*1 \quad 1*0+1*4)$

$= (7 \quad 4 \quad 4)$

(b) $\begin{pmatrix} 1 & 1 \\ 1 & 1 \end{pmatrix}\begin{pmatrix} 2 & 3 & 0 \\ 5 & 1 & 4 \end{pmatrix} = \begin{pmatrix} 1*2+1*5 & 1*3+1*1 & 1*0+1*4 \\ 1*2+1*5 & 1*3+1*1 & 1*0+1*4 \end{pmatrix}\begin{pmatrix} 7 & 4 & 4 \\ 7 & 4 & 4 \end{pmatrix}$

The identity matrix

The **identity matrix** is a **square matrix** with the same property as 1 (unity) in scalar arithmetic. The identity matrix has 1's down its leading diagonal and 0's elsewhere, is denoted by I, and can be of any order (i.e. it can have any number of rows or columns). Therefore the (3×3) identity matrix is:

$$I = \begin{pmatrix} 1 & 0 & 0 \\ 0 & 1 & 0 \\ 0 & 0 & 1 \end{pmatrix}$$

As with the unit scalar (i.e. 1), if we pre-multiply a matrix, say A, by the appropriate identity matrix the result is the same as the original matrix:

$$IA = A \tag{3.3.1}$$

Note that if A is a square matrix, then we can also write:

$$AI = A \tag{3.3.2}$$

The effects of multiplication by the identity matrix are shown in Example 3.3.3.

3.3

Example 3.3.3

Q Pre-multiply and post-multiply the matrices (a) $\begin{pmatrix} 2 & 3 \\ 5 & 1 \end{pmatrix}$ and (b) $\begin{pmatrix} 2 & 3 & 0 \\ 5 & 1 & 4 \end{pmatrix}$ by the appropriate identity matrix.

A (a) $\begin{pmatrix} 1 & 0 \\ 0 & 1 \end{pmatrix}\begin{pmatrix} 2 & 3 \\ 5 & 1 \end{pmatrix} = \begin{pmatrix} 1*2+0*5 & 1*3+0*1 \\ 0*2+1*5 & 0*3+1*1 \end{pmatrix} = \begin{pmatrix} 2 & 3 \\ 5 & 1 \end{pmatrix}$

$\begin{pmatrix} 2 & 3 \\ 5 & 1 \end{pmatrix}\begin{pmatrix} 1 & 0 \\ 0 & 1 \end{pmatrix} = \begin{pmatrix} 2*1+3*0 & 2*0+3*1 \\ 0*2+1*5 & 5*0+1*1 \end{pmatrix} = \begin{pmatrix} 2 & 3 \\ 5 & 1 \end{pmatrix}$

(b) $\begin{pmatrix} 1 & 0 \\ 0 & 1 \end{pmatrix}\begin{pmatrix} 2 & 3 & 0 \\ 5 & 1 & 4 \end{pmatrix} = \begin{pmatrix} 1*2+0*5 & 1*3+0*1 & 1*0+0*4 \\ 0*2+1*5 & 0*3+1*1 & 0*0+1*4 \end{pmatrix}$

$= \begin{pmatrix} 2 & 3 & 0 \\ 5 & 1 & 4 \end{pmatrix}$

$\begin{pmatrix} 2 & 3 & 0 \\ 5 & 1 & 4 \end{pmatrix}\begin{pmatrix} 1 & 0 \\ 0 & 1 \end{pmatrix}$ is not possible.

3.3

1 For $A = \begin{pmatrix} 3 & 2 \\ 4 & 1 \\ 5 & 2 \end{pmatrix}$ and $B = \begin{pmatrix} 1 & 2 & 4 \\ 3 & 1 & 9 \end{pmatrix}$, calculate the following or state why the operation is not valid:

(a) IA (b) BI (c) I^2 (d) I^3

2 For $P = \begin{pmatrix} 1 & 2 \\ 3 & 5 \end{pmatrix}$, $Q = \begin{pmatrix} -5 & 2 \\ 3 & -1 \end{pmatrix}$, $\mathbf{u} = (1 \quad 1)$ and $U = \begin{pmatrix} 1 & 1 \\ 1 & 1 \end{pmatrix}$, calculate:

(a) $\mathbf{u}P$ (b) $\mathbf{u}Q$ (c) U^2 (d) U^3
(e) PU (f) UP (g) QU (h) $\mathbf{u}U$

3.4 Special matrix operations

There are some special operations that apply only to vectors, matrices and arrays. In this section we look at the transposition, determinant and inversion operations.

The prerequisites of this section are:
- Matrix multiplication (Section 3.2);
- Special matrices (Section 3.3).

The transpose matrix

Transposition is not possible with scalars, and applies only to vectors, matrices and arrays. The **transpose of a matrix** is simply the 'turning around' of a matrix, so that the rows become columns and vice versa. For a matrix, say A, the transpose is denoted by:

A^T *(3.4.1)*

The transpose is illustrated in Example 3.4.1. Some spreadsheets have an inbuilt function for transposing a matrix.

3.4

Example | 3.4.1

Q Find the transpose of the matrix:

$$D = \begin{pmatrix} 3 & 2 \\ 6 & 4 \\ 5 & 7 \\ 1 & 9 \end{pmatrix}$$

A The transpose is simply:

$$D^{\mathrm{T}} = \begin{pmatrix} 3 & 6 & 5 & 1 \\ 2 & 4 & 7 & 9 \end{pmatrix}$$

Note that if we transpose D^{T}, then we return to the original matrix D.

The inverse matrix

In Section 1.5 we viewed division of scalars as multiplication by a reciprocal (i.e. a number raised to the power −1). So, for any scalar, say x, we have:

$$x * \frac{1}{x} = xx^{-1} = 1 \quad \text{(i.e. unity)}$$

We use a similar notation in matrices, by denoting A^{-1} to be the **inverse** of matrix A. Because we are raising a matrix to a power, we can only find the inverse of a **square** matrix; however, **not all square matrices have an inverse**. If a square matrix has an inverse, then any square matrix (e.g. A) multiplied by its inverse (i.e. A^{-1}) results in the identity matrix (i.e. I).

$$AA^{-1} = I \text{ or } A^{-1}A = I \tag{3.4.2}$$

Example | 3.4.2

Q Show that $A^{-1} = \begin{pmatrix} -0.0770 & 0.2310 \\ 0.3846 & -0.1500 \end{pmatrix}$ is the inverse of the matrix $A = \begin{pmatrix} 2 & 3 \\ 5 & 1 \end{pmatrix}$.

A We can use equation (3.4.2) to check that one matrix is the inverse of another, by multiplying the two matrices together:

$$A^{-1}A = \begin{pmatrix} -0.0770 & 0.2310 \\ 0.3846 & -0.1500 \end{pmatrix} * \begin{pmatrix} 2 & 3 \\ 5 & 1 \end{pmatrix}$$

$$= \begin{pmatrix} -0.0770 * 2 + 0.2310 * 5 & -0.0770 * 3 + 0.2310 * 1 \\ 0.3846 * 2 + -0.150 * 5 & 0.3846 * 3 + -0.1500 * 1 \end{pmatrix}$$

$$= \begin{pmatrix} 1 & 0 \\ 0 & 1 \end{pmatrix}$$

or, alternatively:

$$A^{-1}A = \begin{pmatrix} 2 & 3 \\ 5 & 1 \end{pmatrix} * \begin{pmatrix} -0.0770 & 0.2310 \\ 0.3846 & -0.1500 \end{pmatrix}$$

$$= \begin{pmatrix} 2 * -0.0770 + 3 * 0.3846 & 2 * 0.2310 + 3 * -0.1500 \\ 5 * -0.0770 + 1 * 0.3846 & 5 * 0.2310 + 1 * -0.1500 \end{pmatrix}$$

$$= \begin{pmatrix} 1 & 0 \\ 0 & 1 \end{pmatrix}$$

The determinant of a matrix

Not all square matrices have an inverse – for example, when one row of a matrix is a multiple of another row of the same matrix. To check whether a square matrix does have an inverse we can calculate its **determinant**. If the **determinant of a square matrix is zero** then one row of a matrix is a multiple of another and consequently it does **not** have an inverse. It is easy to calculate the determinant of a (2×2) matrix, and this is illustrated in Example 3.4.3.

The determinant of a (2×2) matrix

The determinant of a (2×2) matrix, say $A = \begin{pmatrix} a_{11} & a_{12} \\ a_{21} & a_{22} \end{pmatrix}$, is denoted by $|A|$, and found by calculating

$$|A| = a_{11} * a_{22} - a_{12} * a_{21} \tag{3.4.3}$$

Example **3.4.3**

Q Calculate the determinant of matrix $A = \begin{pmatrix} 5 & 2 \\ 3 & 4 \end{pmatrix}$, and comment on whether A has an inverse.

A Using equation (3.4.3) gives:

$$|A| = 5 * 4 - 2 * 3 = 20 - 6 = 14$$

Because this determinant is **not** zero, the matrix $A = \begin{pmatrix} 5 & 2 \\ 3 & 4 \end{pmatrix}$ has an inverse.

Co-factors

If we want to calculate the determinant of larger matrices then we need to introduce the concept of **co-factors**. A co-factor is the determinant of part of a matrix (i.e. a sub-matrix) obtained by removing a row and column and prefixed by a '+' or '−' sign. Because co-factors are obtained from matrices, we denote them by upper-case letters and use subscripts to denote the row and column that were deleted to form them. The sign of the co-factor alternates according to the sign of the adjacent element, starting with '+' in the top left-hand corner. In general for the matrix:

$$A = \begin{pmatrix} a_{11} & a_{12} & a_{13} & \cdots & a_{1n} \\ a_{21} & a_{22} & a_{23} & \cdots & a_{2n} \\ \vdots & \vdots & \vdots & \vdots\vdots\vdots & \vdots \\ a_{n1} & a_{n2} & a_{n3} & \cdots & a_{nn} \end{pmatrix}$$ there are $n * n = n^2$ possible co-factors.

The first co-factor is obtained from deleting row 1 and column 1 from the original matrix A, to give:

$$A_{11} = + \begin{vmatrix} a_{22} & a_{23} & \cdots & a_{2n} \\ \vdots & \vdots & \vdots\vdots\vdots & \vdots \\ a_{n2} & a_{n3} & \cdots & a_{nn} \end{vmatrix}$$

A second co-factor is obtained from deleting row 1 and column 2 from the original matrix A, to give:

$$A_{12} = - \begin{vmatrix} a_{21} & a_{23} & \cdots & a_{2n} \\ \vdots & \vdots & \vdots\vdots\vdots & \vdots \\ a_{n1} & a_{n3} & \cdots & a_{nn} \end{vmatrix}$$

Another co-factor is obtained from deleting row 2 and column 1 from the original matrix A, to give:

$$A_{21} = - \begin{vmatrix} a_{12} & a_{13} & \cdots & a_{1n} \\ \vdots & \vdots & \vdots\vdots\vdots & \vdots \\ a_{n2} & a_{n3} & \cdots & a_{nn} \end{vmatrix}$$

and so on until all n^2 co-factors have been written down.

Example 3.4.4

Q Write down all the co-factors of matrix $W = \begin{pmatrix} 1 & 2 & 1 \\ 3 & 4 & 2 \\ 2 & 0 & 5 \end{pmatrix}$

A Matrix W is a (3×3) matrix and therefore will have $3 * 3 = 9$ co-factors, which are:

$$W_{11} = + \begin{vmatrix} 4 & 2 \\ 0 & 5 \end{vmatrix} = 20, \quad W_{12} = - \begin{vmatrix} 3 & 2 \\ 2 & 5 \end{vmatrix} = -11, \quad W_{13} = + \begin{vmatrix} 3 & 4 \\ 2 & 0 \end{vmatrix} = -8$$

$$W_{21} = - \begin{vmatrix} 2 & 1 \\ 0 & 5 \end{vmatrix} = -10, \quad W_{22} = + \begin{vmatrix} 1 & 1 \\ 2 & 5 \end{vmatrix} = 3, \quad W_{23} = - \begin{vmatrix} 1 & 2 \\ 2 & 0 \end{vmatrix} = 4$$

$$W_{31} = + \begin{vmatrix} 2 & 1 \\ 4 & 2 \end{vmatrix} = 0, \quad W_{32} = - \begin{vmatrix} 1 & 1 \\ 3 & 2 \end{vmatrix} = 1, \quad W_{33} = + \begin{vmatrix} 1 & 2 \\ 3 & 4 \end{vmatrix} = -2.$$

Notice the alternating sign of the co-factors in example 3.4.4.

The general determinant of a matrix

The determinant of any matrix is found by taking the first row co-factors (i.e. A_{11}, A_{12}, A_{13} etc.) and the first row elements (i.e. a_{11}, a_{12}, a_{13}, etc.), and calculating:

$$|A| = a_{11} * |A_{11}| - a_{12} * |A_{12}| + a_{13} * |A_{13}| - \ldots \text{ etc} = \sum_{j=1}^{n} a_{1j} * |A_{1j}| \qquad (3.4.4)$$

We alternately add and subtract because of the sign of the co-factors, as illustrated in Example 3.4.5.

Example 3.4.5

Q Calculate the determinant of matrix $W = \begin{pmatrix} 1 & 2 & 1 \\ 3 & 4 & 2 \\ 2 & 0 & 5 \end{pmatrix}$.

A The first row co-factors are given in Example 3.4.4, and using equation (3.4.4) gives:

$$|W| = 1 * \begin{vmatrix} 4 & 2 \\ 0 & 5 \end{vmatrix} - 2 * \begin{vmatrix} 3 & 2 \\ 2 & 5 \end{vmatrix} + 1 * \begin{vmatrix} 3 & 4 \\ 2 & 0 \end{vmatrix}$$

We can use equation (3.4.3) to calculate the co-factors:

$$|W| = 1*(4*5 - 0*2) - 2*(3*5 - 2*2) + 1*(3*0 - 2*4) = -10.$$

If we have large matrices it is extremely time consuming to calculate the determinant in this way, because we need to calculate all the appropriate co-factors until we reach the (2 × 2) matrices so that we can apply equation (3.4.3). Some spreadsheets have an inbuilt function for calculating the determinant of a matrix.

3.5

Finding the inverse matrix using co-factors

It is possible to calculate the inverse of a matrix using determinants and co-factors. In this method we need to calculate all the co-factors of a matrix and divide them by the determinant of the original matrix. These form the elements of a new matrix, which we transpose to obtain the inverse matrix. The inverse of the general (3 × 3) matrix:

$$A = \begin{pmatrix} a_{11} & a_{12} & a_{13} \\ a_{21} & a_{22} & a_{23} \\ a_{31} & a_{32} & a_{33} \end{pmatrix}$$

is given by:

$$A^{-1} = \frac{1}{|A|} \begin{pmatrix} A_{11} & A_{12} & A_{21} \\ A_{21} & A_{22} & A_{23} \\ A_{31} & A_{32} & A_{33} \end{pmatrix}^{\mathrm{T}}$$

and remember that the signs of co-factors alternate according to:

$$\begin{pmatrix} + & - & + \\ - & + & - \\ + & - & + \end{pmatrix}$$

Example   **3.4.6**

Q   Find the inverse of matrix $W = \begin{pmatrix} 1 & 2 & 1 \\ 3 & 4 & 2 \\ 2 & 0 & 5 \end{pmatrix}$ using co-factors and determinants.

A   From Example 3.4.4, we have the co-factors:

$$W_{11} = 20 \qquad W_{12} = -11, \qquad W_{13} = -8$$
$$W_{21} = -10, \qquad W_{22} = 3, \qquad W_{23} = 4$$
$$W_{31} = 0, \qquad W_{32} = 1, \qquad W_{33} = -2$$

From Example 3.4.5, we know that $|A| = -10$. Therefore the inverse matrix is:

$$A = -\frac{1}{10} \begin{pmatrix} 20 & -11 & -8 \\ -10 & 3 & 4 \\ 0 & 1 & -2 \end{pmatrix}^{\mathrm{T}}$$

$$= \begin{pmatrix} -2 & 1 & 0 \\ 1.1 & -0.3 & -0.1 \\ -0.8 & -0.4 & 0.2 \end{pmatrix}.$$

The inverse of a (2 × 2) matrix

The method of co-factors simplifies when we have a (2 × 2) matrix. In such cases the co-factors are found simply by swapping the two diagonal elements and changing the signs of the others.

So the inverse of the general (2 × 2) matrix $A = \begin{pmatrix} a_{11} & a_{12} \\ a_{21} & a_{22} \end{pmatrix}$ is given by:

$$A^{-1} = \frac{1}{|A|} \begin{pmatrix} a_{22} & -a_{12} \\ -a_{21} & a_{11} \end{pmatrix}$$

Using equation (3.4.3) we can write the inverse for any (2 × 2) matrix as:

$$A^{-1} = \frac{1}{(a_{11} * a_{22} - a_{12} * a_{22})} \begin{pmatrix} a_{22} & -a_{12} \\ -a_{21} & a_{11} \end{pmatrix} \qquad (3.4.5)$$

Example 3.4.7

Q Find the inverse of the matrix $A = \begin{pmatrix} 5 & 2 \\ 3 & 4 \end{pmatrix}$.

A Using equation (3.4.5) gives: $A^{-1} = \frac{1}{(5*4 - 2*3)} \begin{pmatrix} 4 & -2 \\ -3 & 5 \end{pmatrix} = \frac{1}{14} \begin{pmatrix} 4 & -2 \\ -3 & 5 \end{pmatrix}$

Clearly, the method of co-factors will be very time consuming for large matrices. Other methods for calculating the inverse matrix can be found on the CD, and on the associated website **www.mcgraw-hill.co.uk/textbooks/dewhurst**. Some spreadsheets have an inbuilt function for calculating the inverse.

3.6

Exercises 3.4

1 For $A = \begin{pmatrix} 3 & 2 \\ 4 & 1 \\ 5 & 2 \end{pmatrix}$ and $B = \begin{pmatrix} 1 & 2 & 4 \\ 3 & 1 & 9 \end{pmatrix}$, calculate the following:

(a) A^{T} (b) B^{T} (c) $A - B^{\mathrm{T}}$

2 Calculate the determinant of the matrix $P = \begin{pmatrix} 1 & 2 \\ 3 & 5 \end{pmatrix}$ to find out whether it has an inverse and if so find the inverse.

Check that your inverse matrix is correct.

3 For the matrix in question 2 calculate the following:

(a) $P^{\mathrm{T}}P^{-1}$ (b) $(P^{-1})^{\mathrm{T}}P$

4 Calculate the determinant of matrix A.

$$A = \begin{pmatrix} 1 & 0 & 0 \\ 3 & 1 & 5 \\ -2 & 0 & 1 \end{pmatrix}$$

3.5 Using matrices to solve systems of equations

One useful application of matrices is to solve systems of equations.

The prerequisites of this section are:
- Simultaneous and systems of equations (Section 2.2);
- Matrix multiplication (Section 3.2);
- Special matrix operations (Section 3.4).

The matrix form of a system of equations

Any system of equations can be represented by matrices and vectors, as illustrated by Example 3.5.1.

Example **3.5.1**

Q In Example 2.2.2, we solved the equations:

$$5x + 2y = 60$$
$$3x + 4y = 50$$

Represent this system of equations in matrix form and check your answer.

A We represent the simultaneous equations as the product of a matrix of coefficients of variables post-multiplied by a vector of variables (unknowns) equal to a vector of right-hand sides of the equations:

$$\begin{pmatrix} 5 & 2 \\ 3 & 4 \end{pmatrix} \begin{pmatrix} \mathbf{x} \\ \mathbf{y} \end{pmatrix} = \begin{pmatrix} 60 \\ 50 \end{pmatrix}$$

Matrix of coefficients Vector of unknowns Vector of right-hand sides

We can check this is the matrix representation by applying matrix multiplication to get back to the original system of equations:

$$\begin{pmatrix} 5 & 2 \\ 3 & 4 \end{pmatrix} \begin{pmatrix} x \\ y \end{pmatrix} = \begin{pmatrix} 5*x + 2*y \\ 3*x + 4*y \end{pmatrix} = \begin{pmatrix} 60 \\ 50 \end{pmatrix}$$

The general matrix form

Let A be the matrix of coefficients, $\mathbf{x}$ the vector of unknowns and $\mathbf{b}$ the vector of right-hand sides. We then write these simultaneous equations in matrix form:

$$A\mathbf{x} = \mathbf{b} \tag{3.5.1}$$

In Example 3.5.1, we had:

$$A = \begin{pmatrix} 5 & 2 \\ 3 & 4 \end{pmatrix}, \quad \mathbf{x} = \begin{pmatrix} x \\ y \end{pmatrix} \text{ and } \mathbf{b} = \begin{pmatrix} 60 \\ 50 \end{pmatrix}$$

In general, we might have a system of n equations in n unknowns, i.e.:

$$
\begin{array}{ccccccccc}
a_{11}x_1 & + & a_{12}x_2 & + & a_{13}x_3 & + & \cdots & + & a_{1n}x_n & = & b_1 \\
a_{21}x_1 & + & a_{22}x_2 & + & a_{23}x_3 & + & \cdots & + & a_{2n}x_n & = & b_2 \\
a_{31}x_1 & + & a_{32}x_2 & + & a_{33}x_3 & + & \cdots & + & a_{3n}x_n & = & b_3 \\
\vdots & & \vdots & & \vdots & & \vdots & & \vdots & & \vdots \\
a_{n1}x_1 & + & a_{n2}x_2 & + & a_{n3}x_3 & + & \cdots & + & a_{nn}x_n & = & b_n
\end{array}
$$

So we can represent any system of n equations with n unknowns in matrix form, using equation (3.5.1):

$$
\begin{pmatrix}
a_{11} & a_{12} & a_{13} & \cdots & a_{1n} \\
a_{21} & a_{22} & a_{22} & \cdots & a_{1n} \\
a_{31} & a_{32} & a_{32} & \cdots & a_{3n} \\
\vdots & \vdots & \vdots & \vdots & \vdots \\
a_{n1} & a_{n2} & a_{n3} & \cdots & a_{nn}
\end{pmatrix}
\begin{pmatrix}
x_1 \\ x_2 \\ x_3 \\ \vdots \\ x_n
\end{pmatrix}
=
\begin{pmatrix}
b_1 \\ b_2 \\ b_3 \\ \vdots \\ b_n
\end{pmatrix}
$$

We solve such systems of equations in matrix form by modifying the methods encountered in Section 2.2.

Using the inverse matrix to solve systems of equations

If the matrix of coefficients in equation (3.5.1) has an inverse (i.e. its determinant is non-zero), then we can use it to find the solution to the system of equations.

If we multiply equation (3.5.1) by the inverse of the coefficient matrix (if it exists), we get:

$$A^{-1}A\mathbf{x} = A^{-1}\mathbf{b} \tag{3.5.2}$$

Using equation (3.4.2) (i.e. $A^{-1}A = I$) we can write equation (3.5.2) as

$$I\mathbf{x} = A^{-1}\mathbf{b} \tag{3.5.3}$$

We also know, from equation (3.3.1) of Section 3.3, that multiplication by the identity matrix has no effect (i.e. it is like multiplying a scalar by unity), so we can write equation (3.5.3) as:

$$\mathbf{x} = A^{-1}\mathbf{b} \tag{3.5.4}$$

Equation (3.5.4) tells us that if we pre-multiply the vector of right-hand sides by the inverse of the coefficient matrix of a system of equations, we can find the solution to the system of equations in the form of a vector. This is illustrated in Example 3.5.2.

Example 3.5.2

Q Show that $A^{-1} = \begin{pmatrix} 0.285714 & -0.142860 \\ -0.214286 & 0.357143 \end{pmatrix}$ is the inverse of $A = \begin{pmatrix} 5 & 2 \\ 3 & 4 \end{pmatrix}$, and use the inverse matrix to solve the simultaneous equations in Example 3.5.1.

A First, check that A^{-1} is the inverse of A by using equation (3.4.2):

$$\begin{pmatrix} 0.285714 & -0.142860 \\ -0.214286 & 0.357143 \end{pmatrix}\begin{pmatrix} 5 & 2 \\ 3 & 4 \end{pmatrix}$$

$$= \begin{pmatrix} 0.285714*5 - 0.142860*3 & 0.285714*2 - 0.142860*4 \\ -0.214286*5 + 0.357143*3 & 0.214286*2 + 0.357143*4 \end{pmatrix}$$

$$= \begin{pmatrix} 1 & 0 \\ 0 & 1 \end{pmatrix}$$

Because A^{-1} is the inverse of A, we can use equation (3.5.6) to solve the system of equations:

$$\begin{pmatrix} 0.285714 & -0.142860 \\ -0.214286 & 0.357143 \end{pmatrix}\begin{pmatrix} 60 \\ 50 \end{pmatrix} = \begin{pmatrix} 10 \\ 5 \end{pmatrix}.$$

Several alternative matrix methods have been devised for solving systems of equations and some of these can be found on the associated CD and website **www.mcgraw-hill.co.uk/textbooks/dewhurst**.

Exercises 3.5

1 Solve the simultaneous equations:

$$4x + 3y = 11$$
$$2x + y = 5$$

2 Rearrange the equations and solve them:

$$q = 23p - 860$$
$$q = -11p + 1{,}010$$

3 Confirm that matrix B is the inverse of matrix A:

$$A = \begin{pmatrix} 1 & 0 & 0 \\ 3 & 1 & 5 \\ -2 & 0 & 1 \end{pmatrix} \text{ and } B = \begin{pmatrix} 1 & 0 & 0 \\ -13 & 1 & -5 \\ 2 & 0 & 1 \end{pmatrix}$$

and solve the system of equations:

$$x = 5$$
$$3x + y + 5z = 30$$
$$-2x + 2z = -5.$$

4 Find the determinant and inverse of the matrix $\begin{pmatrix} 1 & 1 & 2 \\ 2 & 1 & 0 \\ 1 & 2 & 2 \end{pmatrix}$ and use the inverse to solve the equations:

(a) $x + y + 2z = 1$ (b) $x + y + 2z = 2$
    $2x + y = 2$ $2x + y = 5$
    $x + 2y + 2z = 3$ $x + 2y + 2z = 4$

5 Find the equilibrium prices p_1, p_2 and p_3 of the three interdependent products, which satisfy the equations:

$$2p_1 + 4p_2 + p_3 = 77$$
$$4p_1 + 3p_2 + 7p_3 = 114$$
$$2p_1 + p_2 + 3p_3 = 48.$$

6 Three products X, Y and Z are to be processed through a production system comprising three machines. The unit processing times (hours) of each product on each of the machines and the total production time available on each machine are given below. How many items of X, Y and Z can be produced?

Unit production time (hours) for:

	X	Y	Z	Total available time (hours)
Machine 1	1	2	3	15
Machine 2	1	3	3	15
Machine 3	3	3	1	20

3.6 Chapter review

In this chapter we extended arithmetic operations and algebra to vectors, matrices and arrays. We encountered some special operations that apply only to matrices for example, the determinant and the inverse. We used the inverse matrix, when it existed, to solve systems of equations. We often encounter systems of equations in matrix form, particularly in Economics, Operational Research and Decision Analysis, and we look at some such applications in Part C. There are several alternative matrix methods available for finding the inverse of a matrix and for solving systems of equations, such as Gauss–Jordan pivoting, and some of these methods can be found on the CD and on the website **www.mcgraw-hill.co.uk/textbooks/dewhurst**.

Elementary statistics

Introduction

In the previous chapters we saw the need for information to assist and support managers in their decision-making. Information is not just data. Data consist of numbers or other attributes of a situation that when analysed become useful information. In this chapter we review the basic concepts of statistics, and in particular methods of data collection and presentation.

Chapter objectives

- To introduce statistical concepts
- To introduce methods of data collection
- To introduce methods of presenting data

Chapter contents

The meaning and nature of statistics

There are two basic meanings of the word **statistics** in everyday use. The most common meaning, which we write in lower case (i.e. 'statistics'), relates to a particular set of data, usually prefixed by a specific source (e.g. UK Government transport statistics). In its singular form, 'statistic' usually refers to a characteristic of a set of data or a sample (e.g. the average age of employees in the UK). If we start the word with a capital letter (i.e. 'Statistics') then we mean an applied branch of mathematics, covering the study of methods of data collection, data presentation and analysis. In this section, we review the branch of mathematics known as Statistics, and in particular the concept of a Statistical study. We also briefly consider the underlying issues of data collection, covered in greater detail in the remainder of this chapter.

The prerequisites of this section are:
- An introduction to Quantitative Methods (Chapter 1);
- Algorithms, variables and algebra (Section 2.1).

Descriptive statistics

For a Statistical study we use the standard scientific methodology described in Chapter 1. However, in this and the next chapter we are concerned only with a subset of the methodology (i.e. collecting, describing, summarising and presenting data), called **Descriptive Statistics**. This involves:
- planning and designing the study;
- collecting data;
- describing and presenting data;
- summarising data.

In this chapter we look at the first three issues, and in Chapter 5 we consider how we summarise data.

The full scientific methodology in Chapter 1 also involves the analysis of data, and this aspect of Statistics is often called **Inferential** or **Inductive Statistics**. There are many ways to analyse data, depending on our purpose (i.e. the type of information we want), and some of these are considered in Part B.

Planning and designing a statistical study

Before collecting any data, we need to **plan and design** the collection of data very **carefully**, and need to consider:
- the **scope** (i.e. breadth) and the **purpose** of the study (e.g. should we consider the sales at all stores or a single store to measure typical sales?);
- the **resources** (e.g. what time, money and staff are available for collecting data?);
- what **type of data** is required (e.g. are figures required to the nearest penny or do we want to know preferences for a particular range of products?);
- how **accurate** do we want to be? (we might trade measurement accuracy against the cost of collecting the data);
- what **data sources** are available? (e.g. do we need to collect the data or have the data already been collected for another purpose?);
- how **reliable** are the data sources (e.g. are the people being interviewed honest?);

- if we need to collect data, what **method** or measuring instruments should we use (e.g. surveys), and how should we use them (e.g. interviews or questionnaires?);
- how can we **validate** the data-collection exercise (e.g. undertake a pilot survey)?

Types of data

Before we collect data, we need to understand what data are. As we saw in Chapter 1, they fall into two broad categories:

- **quantitative** data result from counting or measuring, are represented by numbers, and are sometimes called numerical data (e.g. the number of people in a bus queue or the salaries of employees);
- **qualitative** data may or may not contain numbers (e.g. the job titles of employees or the type of car owned by an individual).

There is another form of data that falls between these two. For example, the positions of contestants at the end of a race are numbered (i.e. 1st, 2nd, 3rd, etc.), but we cannot say the contestant in second place was twice as slow as the winner. To distinguish between these different types of data, we use the categories: **nominal**, **ordinal** and **cardinal**. Further categories can also be defined (e.g. **discrete** and **continuous**). All these categories are described below.

Nominal data

Nominal (also called **categorical**) data are qualitative and consist of names or responses that may be labelled with letters or numbers. We cannot rank nominal data (i.e. say one thing is always better or bigger than another) or make statements about their differences (i.e. how much one thing is bigger than another). This is the weakest form of measurement. Here are examples of nominal data measuring instruments:

Q1   Have you a valid driving licence? (Yes or No)   [   ]

Q2   Tick which political party you voted for at the last election:

Labour   [   ]

Conservative   [   ]

Lib-Dem   [   ]

Nationalist   [   ]

Independent   [   ]

Other   [   ] (please specify)

Q3   Tick which type of mortgage you have:

Repayment   [   ]

Endowment   [   ]

Interest only   [   ]

Pension   [   ]

Q4   Circle your preferred takeaway meal:

Chinese   Curry   Pizza   Fish and chips

Ordinal data

Ordinal data are sometimes said to be qualitative, but may be considered quantitative, and consist of responses that may be labelled with letters or numbers, enabling us to rank things in order. We still cannot make statements about their differences (i.e. how much one thing is bigger than another). Ordinal data are a stronger form of measurement than nominal data. For example:

Q1 What was your grade in the Quantitative Methods exam?
(A, B, C, D, E or F) ☐

Q2 How satisfied are you with your new computer? (circle your response below)

Very satisfied   Fairly satisfied   Neutral

Fairly unsatisfied   Very unsatisfied

Q3 Put these takeaway meals in order of preference (1 as most preferred and 4 as least preferred):

Chinese ☐   Curry ☐   Fish and chips ☐   Pizza ☐

Quantitative data

Quantitative data are the strongest form of measurement and result from counting a number of objects or responses (e.g. the number of faulty items produced) or from physically measuring something (e.g. time). Quantitative data are often called **cardinal** or **numerical data**. We can rank numbers and make statements about their differences (i.e. by how much one thing is bigger than another).

Discrete data

Discrete data usually result from counting or measuring to a specific degree of precision (e.g. two decimal places), but can result from labelling observations (e.g. types of takeaway meal). Here are some examples:

- the number of cans of baked beans sold in the UK last year;
- the price of a can of beans in a supermarket today;
- the age of a person in years;
- the sizes of clothes (e.g. small, medium, large, extra large).

Continuous data

Continuous data result only from measuring (length, weight, etc.). They can be measured and recorded to any degree of precision, unlike discrete data. Most continuous data are measured on a **ratio scale** (i.e. there is a true zero point on the scale of measurement, e.g. length, weight, time). However, it is possible to measure on an **interval scale** where there is no fixed zero point: for example, calendar time (Roman, Gregorian, Hebrew, etc.). Note that, although Fahrenheit and Celsius have fixed zero points, they are not absolute (e.g. 20 °F is not twice 10 °F), but if we measure in degrees Kelvin we are using a ratio scale in which 'absolute zero' is −273 °C.

Sometimes, for convenience, we represent measurements in a discrete manner when we could measure on a continuous scale (e.g. weights of loose vegetables are continuous but they may be measured to the nearest gram). When the units of measurement are small, the distinction between discrete and continuous disappears.

Range of values and variables

The data collected may well cover all the possible values (e.g. students might get any one of the possible grades A, B, C, D, E or F in an exam). However, sometimes our observations may not cover all theoretical possibilities (e.g. although you may have money in your bank account, other people may not, and you might incorrectly conclude that a bank account can only be greater or equal to zero; it can also be negative, i.e. in the red).

In Chapter 2, when we measured or counted something we stored the results in variables. Such variables can therefore be qualitative, quantitative, nominal, ordinal, cardinal, discrete, continuous, etc.

We indicate the possible (i.e. theoretical) **range of values** that a variable can take inside square brackets. For discrete variables, we could simply list all possibilities, but, in other cases, we just show the upper and lower values of the range (Figure 4.1.1). Recall from Section 1.4 that we say very large numbers are infinite and we denote them by ∞. Continuous variables often have a full range of values (i.e. $[-\infty, +\infty]$).

Variable	Possible range of values
Colours of the rainbow	[Red, orange, yellow, green, blue, indgo, violet]
Day in a month	[1, 31]
Car mileage	[0, +∞]
Bank balance	[−∞, +∞]

Figure 4.1.1 **Ranges of some typical variables.**

Sometimes, set notation (Section 2.5) is used to indicate the range of values.

Describing and presenting data

With **small amounts of data**, we can present all the data in a table or in pictures (e.g. charts, graphs, pictograms). In Section 4.3 we look at ways of presenting and describing small amounts of data. However, sometimes there is too much data and we need to **reduce** them to present it graphically. Data reduction can be done while collecting 'raw' data (e.g. annual salaries in intervals of £500 rather than individual salaries), or it can be done later. In such cases, we talk of **grouped** data as opposed to **ungrouped** data. Methods of data reduction (i.e. grouping data) and presenting grouped data are considered in Section 4.4.

Exercises **4.1**

You need variables for recording the following data:
(a) the height of a person
(b) the gender of a person
(c) the distance travelled by a sales representative
(d) the available disk capacity on a PC
(e) the lifetime of an electrical component
(f) the price of a can of beans in a supermarket
(g) the country of registration of an oil tanker
(h) the number of children in a household
(i) the annual sales of a particular product
(j) the position of a company in the FTSE
(k) the temperature of a freezer in degrees Celsius

1 Classify each variable according to whether it is qualitative or quantitative.

2 Identify the possible range of values for each variable.

3 Identify the type of data in each case.

4 Classify each variable according to whether it is continuous or discrete.

5 Which discrete variables might be considered continuous and why?

6 Which continuous variables might be considered discrete and why?

Sampling and data collection

Rarely do we need to collect all possible data relevant to a study (i.e. the **population**). If the entire population is small, the results are important and the costs can be justified, then data may be collected from the entire population. Although a **census** is supposed to collect data about the entire population of a country, some people will be missed because of errors, and others will intentionally avoid the census. Censuses are rarely undertaken, because of limited time and resources, so we usually take a representative **sample** from a population. In this section, we consider some different types of sample and methods of collecting them.

The prerequisites of this section are:
- Number systems (Section 1.2);
- Truncating, rounding and estimating (Section 1.3);
- Fractions, ratios and percentages (Section 1.7);
- Algorithms, variables and algebra (Section 2.1);
- The meaning and nature of statistics (Section 4.1).

Sampling from a population

When collecting sample data, we must identify the population from which our samples are to be drawn (e.g. if we wanted student opinions about their finances, should we include full-time, part-time and day-release students?). If we do not identify the appropriate population for our samples, then any conclusions we draw about the population will be meaningless. When an appropriate population can be identified (e.g. all full-time undergraduate students in the UK this year), we then need to obtain a list of it. Such lists (e.g. electoral register, special agencies, telephone directories, maps) are called **sample frames**. If the sample frame is inadequate because some items are missing or have been ignored, then the samples might not be representative of the population and are said to be **biased**.

We denote the **population size** by N and label every item in the sample frame from 1 to N. We denote the **sample size** by n and select the 1st, 2nd, 3rd, etc. until we have sampled the nth item. Clearly, $n < N$, otherwise we would be taking a census.

Having identified the sample frame, we might find that the data have already been collected. Many government departments and agencies collect data (e.g. census, retail prices, unemployment figures), as do many industries and trade associations (e.g. house prices, consumer preferences). These are known as **secondary data**. Secondary data should be carefully scrutinised because they may contain transcription (e.g. typing) errors and may have been collected for a different purpose. When we collect our own data these are called **primary data**. Primary data may be collected **internally** within an organisation (e.g. from company accounts) or **externally** (e.g. a survey of customers). We must avoid bias by identifying possible survey errors and dealing with them accordingly (this is addressed at the end of this section).

Types of sampling

There are two basic kinds of sample:

- **Non-random** (or non-probabilistic) **samples** are chosen on the basis of convenience or cost. There are many types (e.g. judgemental, quota and systematic), and these are described below. Despite convenience and cost, they are subject to bias and lack of accuracy, and so any generalisations (i.e. inferences) we make from them are doubtful.
- **Random** (or probabilistic) **samples** are chosen on the basis of known chances or probabilities of events occurring. The concept of probability is discussed in Chapter 6. There are several types of random sample (e.g. simple with or without replacement, stratified, and cluster) and these are described and illustrated below.

Judgemental (non-random) sampling

In many situations, only a **judgemental** sample is available. In these cases, the opinions of experts in a particular field are elicited and used to provide information. Such judgemental sampling is used by governments or in legal situations where there is no other way of obtaining data.

Quota (non-random) sampling

In **quota** sampling, we structure the sample so that it has the same characteristics as the population, to avoid taking large samples. It is broken down into subsamples to reflect subsets of the sample frame or population, as illustrated in Example 4.2.1.

Example | **4.2.1**

Q A market research bureau is conducting a high-street survey of shopping habits of 1,000 adults in a town. The electoral register contains 45% males, 20% of whom are aged 18–25. How many males should be interviewed, and how many aged 18–25? How should the survey be conducted? Will this be a representative survey?

A The sample frame consists of the entire voting population of the town. Any sample of 1,000 people should contain 450 (i.e. $0.45 * 1,000$) males, and of these 90 (i.e. $0.2 * 450$) should be aged 18–25. Each interviewer should be given a quota, and one might be given the quota for males aged 18–25. Once this interviewer has reached the quota, no more 18–25-year-old males should be interviewed. This may not be a representative sample of the population or even of that subset of the population, because the 90 selected males aged 18–25 may all just have walked out of college.

Systematic (pseudo-random) sampling

In a **systematic** sample, the population is divided by the desired sample size into k groups:

$$k = \frac{N}{n}$$

where k is rounded to the nearest integer (i.e. whole number). We randomly select (see below) the first item or person from the first group of k items and then select every kth item or person from the sample frame.

4.2.2

Q A quality-control department requires a daily sample of 30 items from 600 finished items per day on a production line. Suggest a systematic sampling procedure and discuss whether it is appropriate.

A The sample frame consists of the daily output of 600 items. In this case, there are $k = 600/30 = 20$ groups. We randomly select a number between 1 and 20 (say 12) and sample item number 12, then sample item number 32 (i.e. $12 + 20$), then sample item number 52 (i.e. $12 + 2 * 20$), and so on.

Although this appears to be random sampling, it is in fact pseudo-random sampling because some items are not available for selection from the sample frame (e.g. items 10, 20, 30, etc. are not sampled). Any unknown patterns in the data could introduce bias (e.g. a fault in the production process might affect only odd-numbered items).

Simple random sampling

In a **simple random sample**, any person or item has the same chance of being selected. We could generate a series of random digits (e.g. 5, 20, 38, 1, 9) and select the 5th, 20th, 38th, 1st and 9th person or item. Simply picking a person or item 'at random' is not random, as we all have preferences (even for numbers). In the long run, a true random sample yields a representative sample, and simple random samples must be fairly large to avoid bias. Sets of random numbers are available in most statistical textbooks, but it is easy to generate random numbers or random integers in a spreadsheet or by using a calculator.

Sampling with and without replacement

When sampling **with replacement**, once an item is selected, it is returned to the sample frame and has the same chance (i.e. $1/N$) of being selected again. When we sample **without replacement**, then any sampled item is not returned to the sample frame, and the chances of being selected from the sample frame increase from $1/N$ on the first draw to $1/(N-1)$ on the second, etc. until we reach the nth item, which has a chance of $1/(N-n)$.

Stratified (random) sampling

This is a combination of quota sampling and random sampling, and is illustrated in Example 4.2.3. As with quota sampling, the N items in the population are subdivided into subpopulations called strata, according to common characteristics. Simple random samples are taken from each of the strata, and then combined to give the total sample.

4.2.3

Q A company has 400 employees and wants to survey 25 employees about car parking. Previous surveys elicited a response rate of 60%, and personnel records show that of all employees 30% are office, 50% are skilled and 20% are unskilled workers. How should a stratified sample be selected?

A The sample frame comprises the 400 employees. First, divide the sample frame into three subpopulations: 120 (i.e. 0.3 * 400) office workers, 200 (i.e. 0.5 * 400) skilled workers and 80 (i.e. 0.2 * 400) unskilled workers. Number each of the 120 office workers 1–120, each of the skilled workers 1–200 and each of the unskilled workers 1–80.

As 25 personnel are to be surveyed and a 60% response rate is expected, then: $0.6x = 25$ and so

$x = 25/0.6 = 41.67 = 42$ employees should be surveyed:

13 (i.e. $0.3 * 42 = 12.6$, rounded to 1 d.p.) should be office workers

21 (i.e. $0.5 * 42 = 21$) should be skilled workers

8 (i.e. $0.2 * 42 = 8.4$ rounded to 1 d.p.) should be unskilled workers

We then randomly sample without replacement as follows:

13 from the office workers numbered 1 to 120

21 from the skilled workers numbered 1 to 200

8 from the unskilled workers numbered 1 to 80.

Cluster (random) sampling

In a **cluster** sample we have several clusters, each representative of the entire population. Clusters can occur naturally (e.g. electoral districts, counties, regions, cities, towns, streets or even families). A random sample of clusters is then taken, and all items in each selected cluster are then studied. Cluster sampling is extremely cost-effective, particularly if the population is spread over a large geographical area. However, cluster sampling requires large sample sizes to obtain results of accuracy similar to that of simple random sampling or stratified sampling. There is a variation of cluster sampling known as **multi-stage** sampling, in which we select items from the clusters by random sampling, as illustrated in Example 4.2.4.

Example | **4.2.4**

Q A financial institution is surveying pension schemes in the PVCu industry. The PVCu industry consists of 1,600 companies spread throughout the UK. The financial institution wants to select 200 employees from a total population of 80,000. How could the cluster samples be selected?

A We base the clusters on the companies (numbered from 1 to 1,600) as they are likely to be representative of the population, although some companies may differ.

If, initially, we assume that each company contains $80,000/1,600 = 50$ employees and, since the desired sample size is 200, this suggests selecting only four companies. However, four companies from 1,600 is unlikely to be representative, and we would have to sample every single employee in each company. Furthermore, each company may not have 50 employees. If instead we assume a 50% response rate from each company then we would need to select 8 companies (clusters). We then use random numbers to select 8 clusters from 1,600 and this completes the first stage. Having selected 8 clusters, each employee is then assigned a number from 1 to 50 and, using random numbers, we select 25 employees from each company. This completes the second stage and achieves the sample size of 200 employees. These employees are then identified from personnel records and

Chapter 4 Elementary statistics

93

interviewed. If we expect a lower response rate from each company then we can recalculate the number of clusters and the sample accordingly.

Methods of collecting data

There are a variety of primary methods for collecting data, including:

- observation;
- experiments or tests;
- surveys.

Each of these methods is now described.

Observation

With inanimate objects (e.g. products or machines), animals or data files the only means of collecting data is by observation (e.g. counting, timing or monitoring). Even with people, there are situations where observation is the most reliable approach. Indeed, studies show that people frequently exaggerate or try to please when questioned (e.g. people claim to wear seat belts but observation suggests otherwise). When observing people, ethical issues arise. However, gaining consent from someone prior to observation can result in different behaviour.

Longitudinal studies make observations over long periods of time, usually many years. They are very expensive and generally used for sociological (e.g. social trends), health (e.g. effects of immunisation programmes) and physical surveys (e.g. structural changes to buildings).

Experiments or tests

As with observation, we refer to the animals or people in the experiment as **subjects**. When testing, say, the effectiveness of a new product or drug, we need to be aware of issues of experimental design (e.g. selecting the hypothesis to be tested and the test group). Such issues are considered in Chapter 6.

Surveys

Surveys question respondents about their beliefs, attitudes, preferences, etc. by **interviews** and **questionnaires**.

Interviews can be personal (i.e. face to face) or via telephone or the Internet. They are the most reliable means of obtaining accurate information, they have a high response rate (typically 80%), and the interviewer can explain what is required. However, interviewers need training to obtain reliable responses without introducing bias (e.g. helping the respondent to answer, or influencing the respondent by comments, facial expression or intonation). Personal interviewing is extremely expensive owing to interviewer time, travelling, subsistence and training. Telephone and Internet interviews are cheaper, and respondents can be selected at random by telephone number or through cookies. However, bias is present because not all the population is contacted (some may not have a phone, they may be ex-directory, or they may not have Internet access).

Questionnaires can be posted, presented personally, collected or sent via e-mail. The advantages are that large samples can be taken cheaply. However, the response rate is low (typically 20%). To increase response rate, rewards (e.g. prizes, gifts) or personal contact (e.g. follow-up calls) may be used, but may introduce bias. Questionnaires are prone to bias because of poorly worded questions, and because certain members of society (e.g. retired people, house-parents, people unhappy about a service or product) are the most likely to reply.

Nevertheless, questionnaires are the most frequently used means of collecting data (see the discussion of **measurement errors** below about their design).

Panel surveys monitor changes over time and are used in marketing research, politics and quality management. A panel is selected and asked a series of questions on different occasions. Examples are focus groups, consensus building, brainstorming and Delphi. They tend to be expensive, they rely on small samples, and changes in the make-up of the panel can result in bias.

Survey errors

Surveys are subject to error. Reduction of such errors is costly, leading to a trade-off between error reduction and cost. There are four types of survey error:

- **Coverage error** – inadequate sample frame (e.g. out-of-date telephone directory); respondents may be excluded from the survey.
- **Non-response error** – not everyone responds, and an unrepresentative sample brings bias (e.g. upper and lower socio-economic classes often fail to respond; people may be ill, on holiday, moved job or house, be out of the country, not at home, etc.). Non-responses should be followed up (e.g. further visit, telephone call, letter, e-mail).
- **Sampling error** – cost and chance dictate who is or which items are included in the sample. Therefore we make statements about the margin of (sampling) error (e.g. the poll is within ±2 percentage points of the actual votes).
- **Measurement error** – results from poorly designed surveys or questionnaires (e.g. badly worded questions) or from incorrectly calibrated instruments. These must be calibrated before, during and after use. Surveys and questionnaires should be well designed and validated by a pilot study (i.e. small-scale trial to identify any problems) before being applied.

Guidelines for surveys and questionnaires

The following guidelines, although by no means exhaustive, should be considered when undertaking surveys and questionnaires:

- **A questionnaire should ask related questions in a logical sequence** (if questions are presented at random, respondents lose interest).
- **Keep questions brief, simple and unambiguous** (if respondents do not understand a question, they give convenient rather than true answers).
- **Avoid hypothetical and conditional questions** (such as 'if you won the lottery would you first pay off your mortgage, buy a new car or have the holiday of a lifetime?'). The respondent may not have thought about it.
- **Avoid leading questions** (such as 'do you agree that broadsheet newspapers report news more accurately than tabloids?'). Respondents may try to conform rather than give their honest opinion.
- **Avoid vague questions** (such as 'do you usually drink more wine or beer?'). Respondents may drink neither. Does the 'more' refer to glasses, alcoholic content, frequency, etc?.
- **Ask positive questions and avoid apologies** (such as 'I hope you don't mind me asking but do you usually buy a daily paper?' Instead you could simply ask 'Did you buy a daily paper today?').

Exercises   **4.2**

1   You have been asked to consider how house prices have changed throughout the country. The government publishes average house prices for different categories of house in different regions at the end of each year. What type of data would you use, and how might you select an appropriate sample?

2 Undertake a 'quota sample' about student attitudes to the entertainment facilities provided by the student union. 80% are undergraduates and 60% are male. You expect to survey 10% of the student population, about 10,000 per year. Determine the sizes of the quotas and discuss how you might test the sample.

3 As chief auditor, you need to estimate the average size of orders received over the last financial year. You have a list of all 8,500 orders received this year. How might you obtain a representative sample?

4 For (i) the income of teachers, (ii) the effectiveness of a new stop-smoking campaign, (iii) the effectiveness of a new drug for lowering cholesterol levels:
(a) suggest appropriate types of data to collect
(b) identify a suitable sampling frame
(c) suggest how you might select a suitable sample
(d) suggest appropriate survey methods

5 You undertake a study into the likely sales of a new computer game. What types of data might you collect, and how might you classify the data? How might you identify a suitable sample frame and select a suitable sample? What type of survey might you conduct to collect the data?

6 You survey 150 students about library use, book borrowing and purchasing in your university. In the university, 60% of all students are male, 75% are undergraduates, 40% are in technology departments, 25% in pure science departments and the remainder in arts/social sciences departments. Of all students, 30% live within $\frac{1}{2}$ mile of the campus, 25% live between $\frac{1}{2}$ and 1 mile and the rest live over a mile away. How would you conduct a quota sample survey?

4.3 Presenting and describing small datasets

A dataset can be presented as words and numbers, but often we use a **table** or **pictures**. Sometimes we use both, because we usually draw a picture from a table. In this section, we use tables and pictures to describe small datasets. We consider large datasets in Section 4.4.

The prerequisites of this section are:
- Number systems (Section 1.2);
- Basic arithmetic (Section 1.4);
- Fractions, ratios and percentages (Section 1.7);
- Scalars, vectors, matrices and arrays (Section 2.3);
- The meaning and nature of statistics (Section 4.1);
- Sampling and data collection (Section 4.2).

Tables

A table is an array containing text and/or numbers. We encountered tables in Chapters 1 and 2, particularly in Section 2.3, where we considered vectors, matrices and arrays. Certain conventions and guidelines should be followed when constructing a table. Some guidelines are:
- Always give the table a title.
- If the table is one of several tables or diagrams in a report, essay, book, etc. clearly number the table for cross-referencing.
- Use borders, underlining, shading, etc. to structure the table and make it easy to read.
- Lay out the table neatly, with columns and rows in line.
- Clearly distinguish between the title, row and column headings and the main body of data.

42

- When presenting numbers, always right-justify or use the same format for all numbers in a row or column to make comparisons easy.
- If necessary, use footnotes to explain abbreviations and conventions used.
- If appropriate, state the source from which the data was drawn.

Table 4.3.1 illustrates these conventions and guidelines.

Table 4.3.1 **A comparison of shopping costs.**

Table reference in this document

Column titles

Table title

Product	How shopping costs compare		
	UK	France	Germany
Sirloin steak (per 500g)	4.80	5.03	5.03
Chicken breast (per kg)	6.99	5.00	6.10
Heineken cans (4 × 440 ml)	3.38	1.84	1.09
Coca-Cola (litre)	1.18	0.81	0.91
Mars bars 5 pack (5 × 65 g)	1.09	1.24	0.91
Colgate Total (100 ml)	1.79	1.45	1.22
Gillette Blue 2 (fixed blade) 10 pack	2.67	2.25	2.90
Häagen-Dazs ice-cream (500 ml)	3.69	2.04	2.44
Olive oil (per 500g)	1.85	1.77	1.37
Instant coffee granules (100g)	1.28	1.42	2.59
Kellogg's Cornflakes (750g)	1.38	2.20	1.40
Tuna (185 g)	0.47	0.36	0.45
Tropicana orange juice (1 litre)	1.99	1.32	1.22
Total basket	**£32.56**	**£26.73**	**£27.63**

Main body of data

Row title

Notes

Source: Sunday Times 8 October 2000

Notes: UK prices based on Tesco (where identical items not available the nearest equivalent was chosen).

All currencies converted to £ sterling on day of survey.

4.2

A spreadsheet is essentially an array or table consisting of cells in rows and columns, and is ideal for constructing tables, which can easily be inserted into word-processed documents. Most word-processors also have a facility for drawing tables.

Pictures

Despite being widely used for presenting data, tables do not always show underlying trends or enable comparisons. One way of presenting data pictorially is to use **charts**. There are five basic types of chart (**scattergrams**, **graphs**, **pie charts**, **bar charts** and **pictograms**), and each has variants or subtypes. As with tables, there are basic conventions and guidelines for drawing them:

- First, put the data into a table.
- Always give the chart a title.
- If the chart is one of several in a report, essay, book, etc., clearly number the chart for cross-referencing.
- Draw the chart neatly with a ruler on graph paper or use the chart-drawing facilities of a spreadsheet.
- Use borders, underlining, shading, etc. to make it easy to read.
- Where a chart has a horizontal and/or vertical axis, each should have a title, showing the units of measurement, and be clearly labelled with text or numbers. If an ordinal or cardinal scale is used, scales with equal intervals should be used. Think of an ordinal or cardinal axis scale as a ruler. The range of the scale should cover the dataset, often starting at zero, and should end just above the highest value. The interval should be chosen to make the chart easy to read, but not too large to confuse the reader.

- If more than one dataset is shown on a chart, each should be given a legend drawn using different symbols or colours.
- When presenting numbers, always right-justify or use the same format for all numbers.
- If necessary, use footnotes to explain abbreviations and conventions used.
- If appropriate, state the source from which the data was drawn.

Scattergrams

A **scattergram** (**XY scatter**, scatter diagram or plot) indicates trends in data (often over time) using a set of **rectangular** (sometimes called **Cartesian**) coordinates. Once axes are drawn and titles written, data are represented by marks (often crosses) at appropriate coordinates. Example 4.3.1 illustrates how to draw a typical scattergram from a table. Most spreadsheets have a facility for drawing scattergrams.

Example **4.3.1**

Q Pairs of sandals, sold in a retail store, were recorded at different prices as shown in Table 4.3.2. Draw a scattergram with sales on the vertical axis and price on the horizontal axis to show how sales vary with price.

Table 4.3.2 **Monthly sales of sandals.**

Month	Price	Sales
1	16	280
2	18	300
3	20	300
4	25	195
5	28	155
6	30	150
7	28	160
8	24	250
9	24	245
10	22	280
11	25	200
12	25	210

A Table 4.3.2 shows prices in the range [16, 30] and sales [150, 300]. Let us use £5 intervals for prices and intervals of 50 units for sales, and set the horizontal (price) axis range to [0, 50] and the vertical (sales) axis range to [0, 500]. We then draw the axes, label the chart and axes, and place marks at the coordinates given by price, and sales, i.e. (16, 280); (18, 300); (20, 300); etc. as shown in Figure 4.3.1.

Figure 4.3.1 indicates a pattern between sales and price. Sales increased as the unit price increased from £15 to £20; for prices beyond £20 per unit sales declined, and they then levelled off as unit price reached £30. The highest level of sales is at a unit price just below £20. This is of use to the sales manager when setting future prices for this sandal. We discuss this form of graphical analysis in greater detail in Part B.

Figure 4.3.1 shows all the data in the centre of the diagram. By using a smaller range for each axis and changing the interval, we see the relationship between sales and price in more detail. The scattergram in Figure 4.3.2 uses the same dataset, but its horizontal range is [15, 35] with £1 intervals and its vertical range is [100, 400] with an interval size of 50 units.

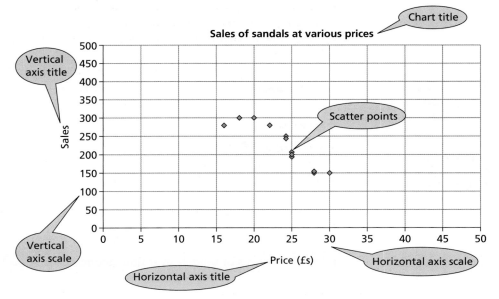

Figure 4.3.1 **Scattergram of sales of sandals at various prices.**

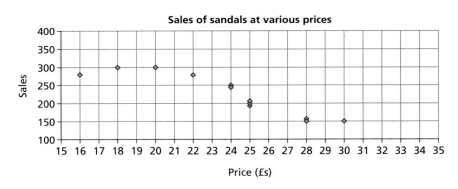

Figure 4.3.2 **A revised scattergram of sales at various prices.**

Graphs

A **graph** (or line graph) is similar to a scattergram except that we join up the points plotted from the table. Example 4.3.2 shows a typical graph. Most spreadsheets have a facility for drawing graphs.

Example | **4.3.2**

Q Draw graphs of (a) price over time, (b) sales over time, and (c) sales against price, for the data given in Table 4.3.2 in Example 4.3.1.

A Ensure that each axis represents only one scale of measurement. In this example, we have three scales of measurement (sales in units, price in £s and time in months). To keep the graphs as simple as possible with one horizontal and one vertical axis, we can draw three separate graphs: one showing sales over time, another price over time and a third showing sales against price. These are shown in Figures 4.3.3, 4.3.4 and 4.3.5, respectively.

(a) For the price over time graph, we take the (month, price) data pairs, i.e. (1, 16), (2, 18), (3, 20), etc., and plot their points as for a scattergram, but this time we join up the points as shown in Figure 4.3.3.

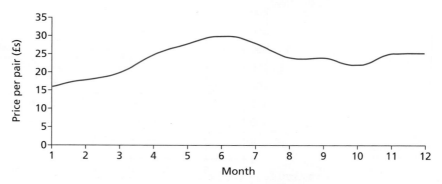

Figure 4.3.3 **Prices of sandals over time (months).**

Figure 4.3.3 shows that the highest unit price was in month 6 and the lowest in month 1, indicating that the sales manager set the highest price in early summer and then began to experiment in subsequent months.

(b) For the sales over time graph, we take the (month, sales) data pairs, i.e. (1, 280), (2, 300), (3, 300), etc., and plot and join up the points as shown in Figure 4.3.4.

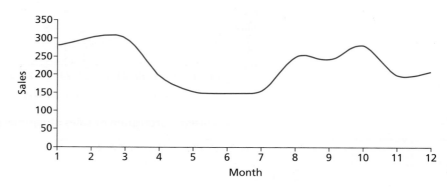

Figure 4.3.4 **Sales of sandals each month.**

Figure 4.3.4 shows the drop in sales in months 5–7, when we might have expected otherwise. This may be attributed to the increase in price (or perhaps a bad summer?).

(c) To see whether there is any relationship between sales and price, we might draw a curved line through the scatter points of Figure 4.3.1, as shown in Figure 4.3.5.

Figure 4.3.5 shows what might be happening in between the data points we plotted in Figures 4.3.1 and 4.3.2. If this curved line is representative, it suggests that highest sales occur at a unit price of £19. We discuss this use of scattergrams in more detail in Part B.

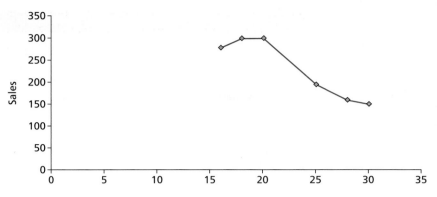

Figure 4.3.5 **Sales at different prices.**

Graphs can also be drawn with two vertical axes to help identify patterns and relationships. However, such graphs can be misleading if not drawn and annotated well, and can be very confusing. Figure 4.3.6 shows both price and sales over time (note the different vertical scales for sales and time and the legend to identify the two variables). Such graphs are not recommended but frequently appear in newspapers and magazines.

Figure 4.3.6 **Price and sales over time.**

Analysis of these graphs and the mathematical equations that 'model' this behaviour are considered in Part B.

Pie charts

Scattergrams and graphs are useful for showing the relationship between variables, but other pictures are more useful for showing how a set of data is classified. **Pie charts** are useful for showing how small sets of data are divided into categories. Generally, pie charts are useful only when there is only a small number of categories (at most 8). It is difficult to compare pie charts, so only single pie charts should be used to show how a single set of data is classified into categories.

A pie chart is essentially a circle divided into portions (i.e. the slices of a pie), where each portion represents a category or subdivision of the data. To draw a pie chart, first represent each category or subdivision as a percentage of the total. A circle contains 360°, and 1% contains $360/100 = 3.6°$. So we represent the angle of each portion of the circle (i.e. each slice of the pie) by multiplying its percentage by 3.6° (see example 4.3.3). Most spreadsheets have a facility for drawing pie charts.

4.3.3

Q The end-of-year sales (in £s) for three departments of a retail store are given in Table 4.3.3. Use pie charts to show how sales are divided between the departments.

Table 4.3.3 **Sales by department.**

Department	Sales
Clothing	25,000
Hardware	9,000
Food	37,000

A First, calculate the total sales from all three departments, then the percentage sales for each department and the angle of each slice of the pie by multiplying each percentage by 3.6 (Table 4.3.4).

Table 4.3.4 **Percentage sales and angles for data in Table 4.3.3.**

Department	Sales	% sales	Angle
Clothing	25,000	25,000/71,000 = 35%	35 ∗ 3.6 = 126°
Hardware	9,000	9,000/71,000 = 13%	13 ∗ 3.6 = 47°
Food	37,000	37,000/71,000 = 52%	52 ∗ 3.6 = 187°
Total =	71,000	100%	360°

We can draw different styles of pie chart (Figures 4.3.7 and 4.3.8).

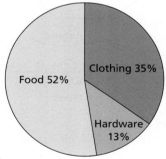

Figure 4.3.7 **A basic pie chart for the data in Example 4.3.3.**

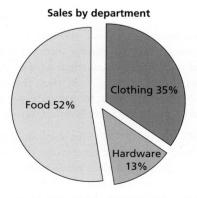

Figure 4.3.8 **An exploded pie chart for the data in Example 4.3.3.**

Bar charts

Like pie charts, **bar charts** are used to show categories within datasets. Categories are represented by bars on a set of horizontal and vertical axes, similar to those of a graph. Unlike pie charts, we can compare categories within different datasets by using multiple and stacked bar charts. When drawing bar charts start each scale at zero. Example 4.3.4 shows the use of bar charts. Most spreadsheets have a facility for drawing bar charts.

Example

4.3.4

Q Table 4.3.5 shows the quarterly sales data for three departments of a retail store last year.

Table 4.3.5 **Sales figures for each department of a retail store last year in £s.**

| Department | Quarter | | | |
	1	2	3	4
Clothing	900	1,000	1,200	800
Hardware	1,100	1,400	900	700
Food	8,000	8,000	9,000	12,000

Draw bar charts to compare (a) the sales of each department in each quarter and (b) the quarterly and annual sales of each department.

A (a) We could use a multiple bar chart with sales along the vertical and quarters along the horizontal having three bars (one for each department) (Figure 4.3.9).

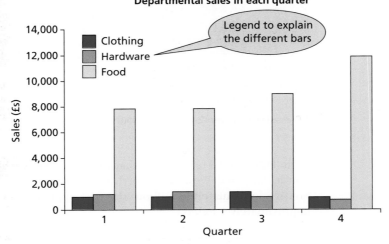

Figure 4.3.9 **A multiple bar chart for the sales data in Example 4.3.4.**

(b) Alternatively we could place departments along the horizontal axis and sales along the vertical axis, and draw a stacked bar chart to show quarterly and total sales for each department (Figure 4.3.10).

4.6

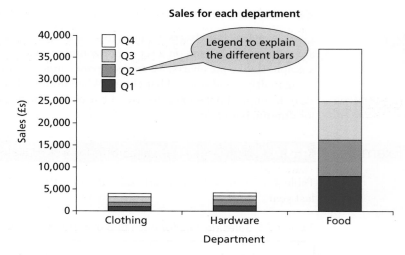

Figure 4.3.10 **A stacked bar chart for the sales data in Example 4.3.4.**

Pictograms

Pictograms are similar to bar charts, but the bars are replaced by pictures. They are very eye-catching, and are used in newspapers, magazines and for adverts. However, they are not very accurate, can give only a general impression, and are not recommended. They should never be used to represent small quantities or fractions, and badly drawn or thought-out pictograms can be very misleading. Figures 4.3.11 and 4.3.12 illustrate some pictograms.

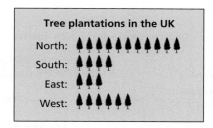

Figure 4.3.11 **Millions of hectares under trees in each region of the UK.**
(*Source*: **UK Forestry Commission 2000**)

From Figure 4.3.11, it is clear that the North had a higher area of trees than the South, East and West. The North had approximately 11 million hectares, the South approximately 4 million, the East approximately 3 million and the West approximately 6 million.

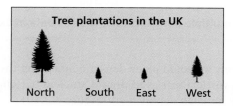

Figure 4.3.12 **Millions of hectares under trees in each region of the UK.**
(*Source*: **UK Forestry Commission 2000**)

Figure 4.3.12 tries to convey the same information as Figure 4.3.11. Both figures show the North had the highest area under trees and the West the second highest. However, in Figure 4.3.12, it is not obvious that the North had almost twice as much as the West, which had twice that of the East.

Exercises 4.3

1 The numbers of male and female students choosing the module 'Statistics for Managers' on a degree programme in Business Administration over the last 5 years are:

	Year				
	1	2	3	4	5
Male	32	35	30	32	34
Female	12	12	11	14	13

(a) What chart would you use to present the ratio of male to female students?
(b) What chart would you use to show how the ratio of male to female students has changed over the 5 years?
(c) How might you present the numbers of male and female students along with the total module size each year?

2 A poll of a sample of eligible voters gave the following results:

Political party	No. of votes
New Labour	258
Conservative	204
Liberal Democrat	42
Other	36
Undecided	60

Construct a suitable chart to compare the results.

3 The monthly sales volume of two products over the last year are:

Month	Product #1	Product #2
January	196	150
February	198	160
March	199	176
April	199	181
May	200	192
June	200	200
July	200	201
August	201	202
September	201	213
October	201	224
November	202	240
December	203	261

Construct a suitable chart to compare the monthly sales of the two products over time.

4 Quarterly sales (millions of units) in each of 3 years are:

	Quarter			
Year	1	2	3	4
1	38.2	39.0	38.8	44.6
2	43.4	43.8	46.0	52.0
3	52.2	53.8	56.4	60.6

Construct a chart to compare quarterly and total sales in each year.

Presenting and describing large datasets

In Section 4.3 we considered ways of presenting and describing small datasets using tables and charts. Sometimes, there may be too many data to tabulate in a meaningful way, and we would be unable to see any general patterns, trends, relationships, etc. To simplify the data, we use **data reduction** to obtain **grouped data**. In some cases, we may prefer to collect data in a reduced form rather than applying data reduction after data have been collected. Having collected the raw data and applied data reduction or collected the data in a reduced form, we can then tabulate and present them pictorially.

The prerequisites of this section are:
- Truncating, rounding and estimating (Section 1.3);
- Basic arithmetic (Section 1.4);
- Fractions, ratios and percentages (Section 1.7);
- The meaning and nature of statistics (Section 4.1);
- Sampling and data collection (Section 4.2);
- Presenting and describing small datasets (Section 4.3).

Data reduction

To reduce a large dataset, we identify **classes** in which we subdivide or **group** the data. We want sufficient classes to identify any patterns in the data. We would probably never want fewer than four classes, because any patterns would be lost, and never more than the number of items of data, because there would be only one data item in each class. Typically the number of classes is less than 20% of the number of data items. A basic guide would be to choose eight to ten classes and, if that is later found to be insufficient, repeat the data reduction process with a larger number of classes. To choose the classes, we consider the smallest and largest items of data and define a **class interval** or range (consisting of **class limits**) with **class boundaries** that distinguish which class each item of data falls into. The width of class intervals is related to the number of classes, and we can use Sturges's rule to get an approximate guide to the width of the class intervals and consequently the number of classes, i.e.

$$\text{Class interval width} \approx \frac{(\text{Largest data item} - \text{smallest data item})}{\log_2(\text{Number of data items})} \qquad (4.4.1)$$

It must be clear which class each item of data belongs to, and a good general rule is to choose class boundaries so they are one degree of precision higher than the data. For example, if data are collected to 2 d.p., we define the class boundaries to 3 d.p.

Example	**4.4.1**

Q The number of cans of baked beans sold each day in a London store have been recorded through their EPOS (Electronic Point of Sales) system over the last 2 months, and are shown in Table 4.4.1. Although there are only 60 items of data, it is not obvious whether there are any patterns, nor how the data can be tabulated to draw some form of chart. Apply data reduction to this set of data.

Table 4.4.1 **Daily sales of baked beans in a London store.**

142	108	42	108	180	102	52	106	102	88
136	100	50	94	164	130	44	88	168	105
160	156	84	90	152	114	80	82	98	121
116	132	74	60	138	150	56	58	60	126
124	152	76	62	112	156	90	64	163	47
96	164	82	60	120	183	88	64	181	65

A We have 60 items of integer data (i.e. whole numbers) and so we define the class boundaries to 1 d.p. The smallest item of data is 42 and the largest is 183. Therefore we can restrict our classes to have a lower class limit of 40 for the first class and an upper class limit of 199 for the last class. Applying Sturges's rule (equation 4.4.1) we get:

$$\text{Class interval width} \approx \frac{(183 - 42)}{\log_2(60)} \approx \frac{141}{6} = 23.5$$

Therefore we shall use a class interval width of 20, and we have 8 classes with the class boundaries shown in Table 4.4.2 because:

$$\text{Number of classes} \approx \frac{(199 - 40)}{20} = \frac{159}{20} \approx 8$$

Table 4.4.2 **Classes for Example 4.4.1.**

Class	Class interval	Lower boundary	Upper boundary
1	40–59	39.5	59.5
2	60–79	59.5	79.5
3	80–99	79.5	99.5
4	100–119	99.5	119.5
5	120–139	119.5	139.5
6	140–159	139.5	159.5
7	160–179	159.5	179.5
8	180–199	179.5	199.5

Tallies

Having chosen the classes, class ranges, limits and their boundaries, we produce a **tally** by counting (in groups of five) the number of items of data that fall into each class, as shown in Table 4.4.3:

Table 4.4.3 **Tally for Example 4.4.1.**

Class	Class interval	Lower boundary	Upper boundary	Tally
1	40–59	39.5	59.5	⌗ //
2	60–79	59.5	79.5	⌗ ////
3	80–99	79.5	99.5	⌗ ⌗ //
4	100–119	99.5	119.5	⌗ ⌗
5	120–139	119.5	139.5	⌗ ///
6	140–159	139.5	159.5	⌗ /
7	160–179	159.5	179.5	⌗
8	180–199	179.5	199.5	///

Frequency tables

From a tally, we count the number of items of data in each class and call this the **class frequency**. We then tabulate the reduced data into a **frequency distribution**, as shown in Table 4.4.4:

 4.7

Table 4.4.4 **Frequency distribution for Example 4.4.1.**

Class	Class interval	Frequency
1	40–59	7
2	60–79	9
3	80–99	12
4	100–119	10
5	120–139	8
6	140–159	6
7	160–179	5
8	180–199	3

> Check that the total frequency equals the number of items of data

Cumulative frequency

Sometimes, we want to calculate cumulative frequency (i.e. a running total of the sum of the frequencies). For Example 4.4.1, a cumulative frequency distribution is shown in Table 4.4.5:

4.7

Table 4.4.5 **Cumulative frequency distribution for Example 4.4.1.**

Class	Class interval	Frequency	Cumulative frequency
1	40–59	7	7 = 7
2	60–79	9	7 + 9 = 16
3	80–99	12	16 + 12 = 28
4	100–119	10	28 + 10 = 38
5	120–139	8	38 + 8 = 46
6	140–159	6	46 + 6 = 52
7	160–179	5	52 + 5 = 57
8	180–199	3	57 + 3 = 60

> We do not usually show the calculations in the table

Percentage cumulative frequency

We can also represent frequencies and cumulative frequencies as percentages. The % frequency and % cumulative frequency distributions for Example 4.4.1 are shown in Table 4.4.6:

Table 4.4.6 **% frequency and % cumulative frequency distributions for Example 4.4.1.**

Class	Class interval		% Frequency	% Cumulative frequency
1	40–59	7/60 = 0.1167	11.67	11.67
2	60–79	9/60 = 0.1500	15.00	26.67
3	80–99	12/60 = 0.2000	20.00	46.67
4	100–119	10/60 = 0.1667	16.67	63.33
5	120–139	8/60 = 0.1333	13.33	76.67
6	140–159	6/60 = 0.1000	10.00	86.67
7	160–179	5/60 = 0.0833	8.33	95.00
8	180–199	3/60 = 0.0500	5.00	100.00

> We do not usually show the calculations in the table

Histograms

We pictorially represent a frequency distribution or a percentage frequency distribution by a **histogram** (similar to a bar chart). However, we are now dealing with continuous data (i.e. the horizontal axis is measured on a continuous scale), so we do not put spaces between the bars. Strictly speaking, the bars of the histogram should be drawn at class boundaries. However, because class boundaries often have too many digits for the horizontal axis, we write down class limits or some other key values. Furthermore, we might not have equal class intervals, so the width of the bars may differ. In a histogram, it is the **area** rather than just the height of the bars that is used to represent the data. So the overall shape is determined by how the classes are defined. Figure 4.4.1 shows a histogram drawn from the data in Table 4.4.4. We can use the chart-drawing facilities of a spreadsheet to draw histograms.

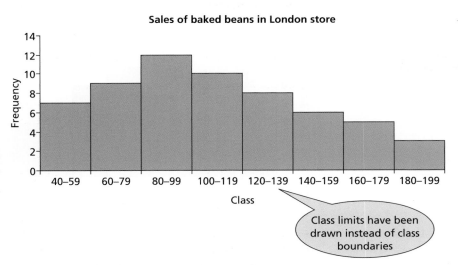

> Class limits have been drawn instead of class boundaries

Figure 4.4.1 **Histogram for Example 4.4.1.**

With unequal class intervals, we must ensure the histogram accurately represents the data. If, for example, one interval width is twice that of another, the height of the bar of the double interval should be halved to maintain the same area. Another problem occurs with open-ended classes, which may be 'less than' or 'greater than'. With open-ended classes, we must decide on class limits before we draw the histogram, and this will affect its shape (see Example 4.4.2).

Example 4.4.2

Q The numbers of cans of baked beans sold each day at a Birmingham store have been recorded as shown in Table 4.4.7. Present the data in the form of a histogram. How many days had sales in excess of 160 cans?

Table 4.4.7 **Sales of baked beans at a Birmingham store.**

Class	Class interval	Frequency
1	0–39	8
2	40–59	7
3	60–79	9
4	80–99	12
5	100–119	10
6	120–139	8
7	140–159	6
8	160–199	6
9	200 or more	10

A From Table 4.4.7 we see that most classes have an interval width of 20, but classes 1 and 8 have a width of 40 and class 9 is open ended. When drawing the bars for classes 1 and 8, we halve the height because their interval widths are double that of classes 2 to 7. To draw class 9, we decide on an upper class limit. As some classes have an interval width of 20 and others one of 40, we make the interval width for class 9 at least 40. To show how the choice of class limits affects the histogram, we consider two cases for class 9: the first has an upper class limit of 239 and the second, one of 299, resulting in the histograms in Figures 4.4.2 and 4.4.3, respectively.

4.9

Figure 4.4.2 **Histogram for Example 4.4.2.**

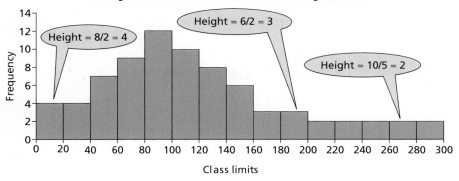

Figure 4.4.3 **Alternative histogram for Example 4.4.2.**

We can see how the choice of upper class limit for the open-ended class has affected the right-hand **tails** of these two histograms, but the information we can glean remains unchanged (e.g. the number of days that sales exceeded 160 cans was 6 + 10 = 16 out of 76).

Ogives

An **ogive** is a graph of cumulative or % cumulative frequency and shows the 'less than' or 'more than' distribution of a set of grouped data. The 'less than' % ogive for the data in Example 4.4.1 is shown in Figure 4.4.4.

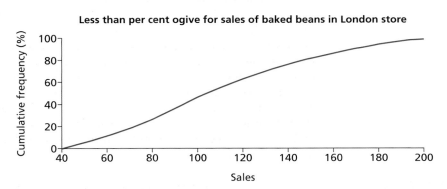

Figure 4.4.4 **Ogive for Example 4.4.1.**

From Figure 4.4.4 we see that for approximately 27% of days the London store sold fewer than 80 cans of baked beans.

Frequency polygons

A **frequency polygon** is a graphical representation of a frequency or % frequency distribution and is constructed from a histogram by plotting lines through the midpoint of the top of each bar in the histogram. To complete the graph, an 'imaginary' class having zero frequency is added at each end. Because they are derived from histograms, they are subject to the same problems encountered with unequal and open-ended classes. A frequency polygon for Example 4.4.1 is superimposed on the histogram in Figure 4.4.5. Note that we do not usually show the histogram on a frequency polygon. By making class intervals very small, the frequency polygon becomes a smooth continuous curve. In Part B, we encounter such graphs and use them to provide further information about a dataset.

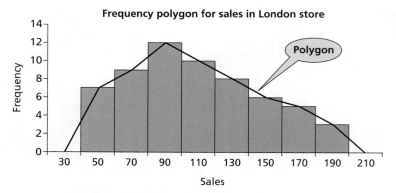

Figure 4.4.5 **Frequency polygon for Example 4.4.1.**

Lorenz curves

A **Lorenz curve** is a type of ogive in which both the horizontal and vertical axes represent cumulative percentages. They are used in economics to show the distribution of wealth or income for a population (see Example 4.4.3).

Example | **4.4.3**

Q Table 4.4.8 shows the percentage of the total national income earned by the UK population last year (i.e. 45% of earned only 5% of the total national earned income while 20% of the population earned 7% of the total national income). Construct a Lorenz curve to show the distribution of income across the population.

Table 4.4.8 **Incomes and population last year.**

% of population	% of total income
45	5
20	7
15	8
10	15
5	17
3	23
2	25

A To draw a Lorenz curve, create a table of cumulative % for both population and income (see Table 4.4.9) and then draw the ogive (see Figure 4.4.6).

Table 4.4.9 **Cumulative percentages for Example 4.4.3.**

% of population	% of total income	Cumulative % of population	Cumulative % of total income
		0	0
45	5	45	5
20	7	65	12
15	8	80	20
10	15	90	35
5	17	95	52
3	23	98	75
2	25	100	100

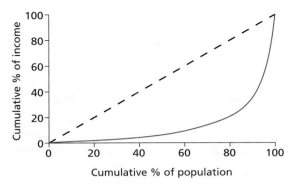

Figure 4.4.6 **Lorenz curve for Example 4.4.3.**

If total national income was equally distributed across the population, then the Lorenz curve would be a 45° line from the bottom left to the top right, as shown by the dotted line in Figure 4.4.6. In Example 4.4.3 this is not the case, and a government might want to change the income tax regime to redistribute income, which would change the shape of the Lorenz curve.

Exercises 4.4

1 Customers arriving (inter-arrival time in seconds) at a supermarket checkout are:

27.7	6.1	44.6	23.4	2.9	5.5	5.4	37.7
0.6	4.4	15.7	0.1	9.6	38.3	18.2	3.6
4.8	13.0	30.4	8.6	7.8	9.6	10.9	5.4
6.4	19.3	0.7	6.6	0.9	4.7	25.2	12.0
38.6	3.2	3.1	53.3	3.6	4.2	11.3	0.2
17.9	0.5	39.0	13.6	20.7	1.3	5.4	5.2
23.5	1.4	21.3	17.2	10.5	46.4	12.6	8.1
38.5	9.1	1.2	24.7	8.4	10.0	2.9	52.4

Construct a frequency distribution, a histogram and an ogive.

2 A machine frequently breaks down and requires emergency repairs. It is also stopped every 15 days for regular maintenance. A sample of the up-times (i.e. when the machine is running) is:

9	1	15	13	8	12	14	7
12	1	11	15	13	0	2	0
15	3	15	4	6	15	15	11
6	15	2	3	4	10	15	0

Draw a histogram and ogive, and comment on the shape of the distribution.

3 A sample of male student heights was recorded as:

Height (cm) interval	Frequency
143–147	0
148–152	6
153–157	9
158–162	20
163–167	31
168–172	37
173–177	44
178–182	34
183–187	16
188–192	3
193–197	0

(a) Construct a histogram, frequency polygon and 'greater than' ogive.

(b) What proportion of students are over 1.8 m tall?

4.5 | **Chapter review**

In this chapter we have encountered the meaning of the word 'statistics', and have seen how this word is used in different contexts. We have also considered what is meant by 'data' and the different types of data that are of interest to managers and decision-makers. Different sampling methods for collecting data were described and illustrated, and guidelines were given for undertaking surveys by which we collect data. We also encountered how data can be presented and described through the use of tables, charts and words to provide information for managers and decision-makers. We saw how in some cases, when we had large samples, it was useful to reduce the data before presenting and describing what had been observed. In the next chapter we consider methods of summarising sets of data to provide quantitative measures to describe our observations.

Chapter 5

Summary statistics

Introduction

In the previous chapter we considered methods of collecting data and how we could present and describe our observations through tables, charts and words. However, the use of tables, charts or words can often be too cumbersome when all that is required is some very simple measure to describe the data. Therefore we often wish to **summarise** data in some way, for example to find the average waiting time at a bus stop. We begin this chapter by considering such summary measures, which we call **measures of location**. Sometimes, a single measure cannot usefully describe a set of data. For example, the average wait at a bus stop might be 5 minutes but some people might have arrived at the bus stop just as a bus came whereas others might have waited an hour. Therefore we might also need to consider **measures of variation** for our data. Sometimes we want to make **comparisons** between different sets of data, particularly over time. Often it is not feasible to use tables or pictures as too many would be required. Instead, we use **index numbers** or **indices** to summarise the differences between sets of data. For example, the Retail Price Index (RPI) shows how the price of a basket of consumer goods differs from year to year. We look at these relative methods of describing data at the end of this chapter.

Chapter objectives

■ To introduce measures of location

■ To introduce measures of variation

■ To introduce index numbers

Chapter contents

Measures of location

This section considers how we can summarise a dataset by a single measure to represent a typical or average value of the dataset. Such measures are called measures of location. They can be calculated by using simple arithmetic from a table of data, by applying a formula, or by using inbuilt functions on calculators or spreadsheets. All these methods are considered in this section.

The prerequisites of this section are:
- An introduction to Quantitative Methods (Chapter 1);
- From numbers to symbols (Chapter 2);
- Elementary statistics (Chapter 4).

Measures of central location

Statements such as 'the average income' or 'the average age' are commonplace, but what is the 'average'? The statement 'The average annual income of employees is £100,000' might refer to a particular sector of the economy or to company directors, and so may not be 'typical' of all employees. The statement 'On average, UK households have two computers' is misleading, as many have only one (or none) and others four or five. The statement 'On average, the most preferred takeaway is curry' will have been derived from a qualitative survey and probably refers to the most popular takeaway meal. When dealing with a list of items (e.g. the 100 companies having the largest share value), we might think the typical or average is in the middle of the list once the items have been listed in order. All these are called **measures of central location** because they represent the centre of a dataset by a single quantity. Each measure is calculated in a different way, and one measure may be more appropriate than another depending upon the circumstances. The most common measures of central location used in Business and Management are:

- the **arithmetic mean** (or simply the **mean**), which is what we usually think of as the 'average';
- the **median**, which is the value in the middle once the data have been put in order;
- the **mode**, which is the most frequently occurring value in a dataset.

The arithmetic mean

The arithmetic mean (commonly called the **mean** or **average**) is calculated by taking the sum (i.e. total) of all observations and dividing it by the number of observations. We distinguish between the mean of a sample and the mean of a population because we sometimes use the mean of a sample to estimate the mean of the population from which the sample was taken.

Let us denote our observed values from sampling by $x_1, x_2, x_3, ..., x_n$, where n is the number of observations (or variables). Then we define the **mean of a sample**, $\bar{x}$, by:

$$\text{Mean of a sample, } \bar{x} = \frac{\sum_{i=1}^{n} x_i}{n}$$

(5.1.1)

For a population of N observations, we denote the **mean of a population** by μ:

$$\text{Mean of a population,} \quad \mu = \frac{\sum_{i=1}^{N} x_i}{N} \tag{5.1.2}$$

Most spreadsheets have inbuilt functions for calculating the arithmetic mean.

Example | **5.1.1**

Q What is the mean age of 20 employees whose ages are:

| 25 | 42 | 18 | 55 | 46 | 37 | 28 | 31 | 34 | 61 |
| 55 | 41 | 47 | 18 | 40 | 34 | 55 | 34 | 59 | 21 |

A We have $n = 20$ observations, and simply sum the ages and divide by $n = 20$. Using equation (5.1.1), we can label our variables as shown in Table 5.1.1.

5.1

Table 5.1.1 **The sum of employee ages.**

Employee	Variable label	Age
1	x_1	25
2	x_2	42
3	x_3	18
4	x_4	55
5	x_5	46
6	x_6	37
7	x_7	28
8	x_8	31
9	x_9	34
10	x_{10}	61
11	x_{11}	55
12	x_{12}	41
13	x_{13}	47
14	x_{14}	18
15	x_{15}	40
16	x_{16}	34
17	x_{17}	55
18	x_{18}	34
19	x_{19}	59
20	x_{20}	21
Sum =	$\sum_{i=1}^{20} x_i =$	781

Applying equation (5.1.1) we have:

$$\bar{x} = \frac{\sum_{i=1}^{20} x_i}{20} = \frac{x_1 + x_2 + x_3 + \ldots + x_{20}}{20}$$

$$= \frac{25 + 42 + 18 + 55 + \ldots 34 + 59 + 21}{20}$$

$$= \frac{781}{20} = 39.05 \text{ years.}$$

The median

The **median** is simply the number in the middle once the data have been put in order. An odd number of observations has a unique middle observation, which is the $(n + 1)/2$th item in an ordered list. For example, if we have five observations (i.e. $n = 5$), the middle number is the 3rd item because $(5 + 1)/2 = 6/2 = 3$. An even number has two central observations (i.e. items $n/2$ and $n/2 + 1$), and the median is estimated by taking their mean. For example, if we have six observations, we take the mean of the 3rd and 4th items. Most spreadsheets have inbuilt functions for calculating the median.

Example 5.1.2

Q   What is the median age of the 20 employees in Example 5.1.1?

A   First, we rank the data in order (Table 5.1.2).

Table 5.1.2 **The ages of the employees in Example 5.1.1 in rank order.**

Item	1	2	3	4	5	6	7	8	9	10	11	12	13	14	15	16	17	18	19	20
Age	18	18	21	25	28	31	34	34	34	37	40	41	42	46	47	55	55	55	59	61

Here, $n = 20$ and $(n + 1)/2 = (20 + 1)/2 = 10.5$, so we take the mean of the 10th and 11th items in the ranked list. These are 37 and 40 with mean $(37 + 40)/2 = 38.5$, and so the median = 38.5.

The mode

The **mode**, or modal value, is the most frequent observation. Datasets can have more than one modal value, and we then say that the dataset is multi-modal. Most spreadsheets have inbuilt functions for calculating the mode.

Example 5.1.3

Q   What is the modal age of the 20 employees in Example 5.1.1?

A   The most frequent ages are 34 and 55 (i.e. three aged 34 and three aged 55). So the dataset is **bimodal** with modes of 34 and 55.

Measures of central location for grouped data

If we have grouped data (i.e. classes and frequencies; see Section 4.4) and do not have raw data available, then we cannot accurately calculate the arithmetic mean, median or mode. We can only estimate them. We do this by calculating the **'group' arithmetic mean**, **'group' median** or **'group' mode**, or we might simply identify the **median class** or **modal class**.

The group arithmetic mean

The **group mean** is estimated by modifying equation (5.1.1) to take into account classes and their frequencies. With 'grouped' data, we assume 'typical' values for each class by taking the midpoint, as we did when drawing the frequency polygon, and call this x_i. If we denote the frequencies of each class by f_i and the number of classes by c, then calculate the group mean:

$$\text{Group mean}, \bar{x} = \frac{\sum_{i=1}^{c} (x_i * f_i)}{n} \qquad (5.1.3)$$

The total number of observations is found by summing all the frequencies (i.e. $n = \sum\limits_{i=1}^{c} f_i$) and so we can write equation (5.1.3) as:

$$\text{Group mean, } \bar{x} = \frac{\sum\limits_{i=1}^{c}(x_i * f_i)}{\sum\limits_{i=1}^{c} f_i} \qquad (5.1.4)$$

Example

5.1.4

Q Calculate the group mean of the data in Example 4.4.2.

A To draw the histogram in Example 4.4.2, we made assumptions about the last class boundary because the last class was open ended. One assumption was to make the last class interval 200–299, and we do the same here to estimate the group mean. First, we calculate the mid-points of each class, and then we tabulate the class mid-points, the frequencies and their products, as shown in Table 5.1.3.

Table 5.1.3 **Calculations for the group mean of Example 5.1.4.**

Class	Class range	Class median (x_1)	Frequency(f_i)	$x_i * f_i$
1	0–39	19.5	8	156.0
2	40–59	49.5	7	346.5
3	60–79	69.5	9	625.5
4	80–99	89.5	12	1,074.0
5	100–119	109.5	10	1,095.0
6	120–139	129.5	8	1,036.0
7	140–159	149.5	6	897.0
8	160–199	169.5	6	1,077.0
9	200–299	249.5	10	2,495.0
			$n = \sum\limits_{i=1}^{c} f_i = 76$	$\sum\limits_{i=1}^{c} x_i f_i = 8,802$

Using equation (5.1.4) the group mean is

$$\bar{x} = \frac{8,802}{76} = 115.8$$

The group median

The **median class** is the class containing the middle item of data. When we have grouped data, we have a large and usually an even number of items in a sample. When a sample has an even number of observations then the median is the $(n + 1)/2$th item in an ordered list. Therefore the median class is the class that would contain the $(n + 1)/2$th item.

There is a formula to estimate the median for grouped data, but it is not easy to remember. If we call the lower boundary of the median class L_m, the width of the median class interval W_m, the median class frequency f_m, and the cumulative frequency up to and including the median class CF_m, then the grouped median can be calculated by:

$$\text{Group median} = L_m + \frac{W_m}{f_m} * \left[\frac{(n + 1)}{2} + f_m - CF_m \right] \qquad (5.1.5)$$

Example **5.1.5**

Q Find the median class and calculate the group median for th[...] in Example 4.4.2.

A There are $n = 76$ observations, and the median is the $(76 + 1)/2 = 38.5$th item of data. To find the median class, we construct a cumulative frequency table (Table 5.1.4).

Table 5.1.4 **Cumulative frequencies for Example 4.4.2.**

Class	Class interval	Frequency	Cumulative frequency
1	0–39	8	8
2	40–59	7	15
3	60–79	9	24
4	80–99	12	36
5	100–119	10	46
6	120–139	8	54
7	140–159	6	60
8	160–199	6	66
9	200 or more	10	76

The cumulative frequency column shows that the 38.5th item is in class 5, and so we say the median is in the class interval 100–119: so this is the median class.

To find the group median, we note that the median is $38.5 - 36 = 2.5$ observations out of 10 in the 5th class. We can estimate it as being at the class boundary (i.e. 99.5) plus 2.5 tenths of the width of the 5th class (i.e. 20):

$$\text{Group median} = 99.5 + \frac{2.5}{10} * 20 = 104.5$$

This is precisely the same that we obtain if we use equation (5.1.5), i.e.

$$\text{Group median} = 99.5 + \frac{20}{10} * (38.5 + 10 - 46) = 99.5 + \frac{20}{10} * 2.5 = 104.5.$$

5.2

The group mode

The modal class is the class with the largest frequency. As with the group median, we estimate the **group mode** by first identifying the modal class. We then estimate where the mode would appear by drawing two crossing lines between the class boundaries on a histogram (Figure 5.1.1).

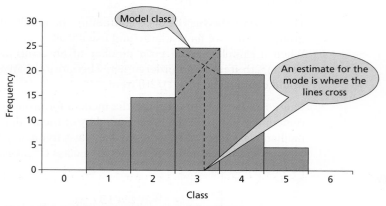

Figure 5.1.1 **Estimating the group mode.**

Rather than estimating the mode from the histogram, we can instead use a formula but, as with the group median, the formula is not easy to remember.

$$\text{Group mode} = L + \frac{W*(f-f_b)}{(f-f_b)+(f-f_a)} \qquad (5.1.6)$$

where W is the interval width of the modal class
   L is the lower class boundary of the modal class
   f is the frequency of the modal class
   f_a is the frequency of the class above the modal class
   f_b is the frequency of the class below the modal class

The derivation of this formula can be found on the CD, and on the associated website **www.mcgraw-hill.co.uk/textbooks/dewhurst**.

Example 5.1.6

Q Find the modal class and calculate the group mode for the data in Example 4.4.2.

A Table 5.1.5 shows that the highest frequency, 12, occurs in the fourth class (i.e. class interval 80–99), so this is the modal class.

Table 5.1.5 **Frequency distribution for Example 4.4.2.**

Class	Class interval	Frequency
1	0–39	8
2	40–59	7
3	60–79	9
4	80–99	12
5	100–119	10
6	120–139	8
7	140–159	6
8	160–199	6
9	200 or more	10

Graphically, we estimate the mode to be approximately 93 (Figure 5.1.2).

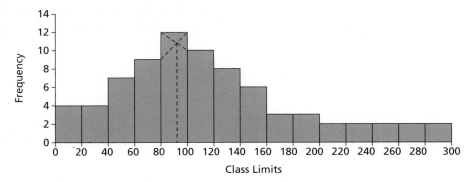

Histogram of sales of baked beans in Birmingham

Figure 5.1.2 **Histogram for Example 4.4.2.**

5.2

Using equation (5.1.6), we have: $W = 20, f = 12, f_a = 10$ and $f_b = 9$ giving:

$$\text{Group mode} = 79.5 + \frac{20*(12-9)}{(12-9)+(12-10)} = 91.5.$$

Which measure of central location?

Although there are no hard-and-fast rules about which measure of central location to use, each has different advantages and disadvantages and is used in different circumstances (e.g. for different types of data). The arithmetic mean (i.e. average) is the most widely used because it is easily calculated and can be used to develop theoretical concepts and models such as those considered in Part B, though, strictly speaking, it should be used only for cardinal data. However, the mean is greatly affected by extremely large or small values that may not be 'typical'. For example, most flight times between London and New York are similar, but one particular flight may have been delayed for hours, and if we included it in a calculation of average flight times, 'typical' flight times would be exaggerated. One way of dealing with such **outliers** is to give them less influence by taking a **weighted mean** (see below).

The median is less affected by extreme values and is therefore a more robust measure of 'typical' when a set of data contains extreme values, but it is not easily calculated and cannot be used to develop theoretical concepts and models.

The mode is unaffected by extreme values, but is more problematic than the median. When data are multi-modal, there is no single measure of central location and the mode can vary dramatically from one sample to another, particularly when dealing with small samples. As with the median, it cannot be used to develop theoretical concepts and models and so is used only for basic descriptive purposes.

The relationships between the mean, median and mode for different histograms are shown in Figures 5.1.3–5.1.5.

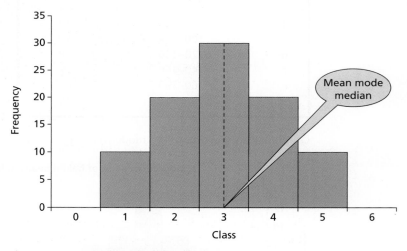

Figure 5.1.3 **A symmetrical distribution.**

Figure 5.1.3 shows a **symmetrical distribution**, i.e. the left-hand side **tail** is a mirror image of the right-hand side **tail** about the mean, median and mode, which are equal.

In Figure 5.1.4 the histogram is not symmetrical (i.e. it is **asymmetrical**) and is said to be **positively skewed** or skewed to the right (i.e. the mean is to the right of the median and the mode).

In Figure 5.1.5 the histogram is also asymmetrical and is said to be **negatively skewed** or skewed to the left (i.e. the mean is to the left of the median and the mode).

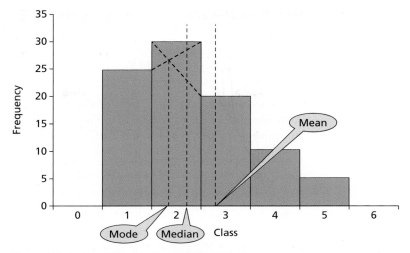

Figure 5.1.4 **A positively skewed distribution.**

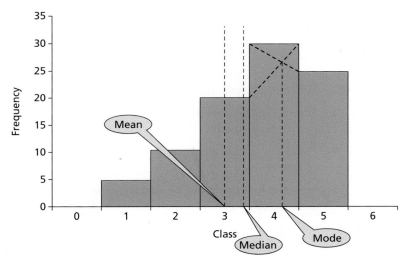

Figure 5.1.5 **A negatively skewed distribution.**

The weighted mean

The **weighted mean** is similar to the arithmetic mean, but more importance or emphasis (weight) is placed on some observations than on others. However, there is a problem in selecting the appropriate weights (i.e. the amount of influence) to place on each item of data.

We denote the weights by w_i so that each observation could be given its own unique weight. Equation 5.1.1 can be modified to include these weights:

$$\text{Weighted mean, } \bar{x}_w = \frac{\sum_{i=1}^{n} w_i x_i}{\sum_{i=1}^{n} w_i} \qquad (5.1.7)$$

Equation (5.1.7) is in effect the formula for the group mean in which the frequencies are the weights. In Example 5.1.7 we calculate the weighted mean with known weights.

Example 5.1.7

Q A particular CD can be bought from only one of two stores, HBP and Virgo. Last week, HBP sold 150 at £10 and Virgo sold 100 at £12. What was the average price paid for this CD last week?

A We cannot simply take the mean of the two prices (i.e. £11), because more people bought the CD from HBP than Virgo. We should take a weighted mean and apply equation (5.1.7), where $n = 2$, $x_1 = 10$, $x_2 = 12$ with weights $w_1 = 150$ and $w_2 = 100$:

$$\bar{x}_w = \frac{w_1 x_1 + w_2 x_2}{w_1 + w_2} = \frac{150*10 + 100*12}{150 + 100} = \frac{2{,}700}{250} = 10.80$$

So the average price paid for the CD last week was £10.80.

Exercises 5.1

1 Calculate the mean, median and mode of 4, 2, 7, 4, 5, 3, 5, 4, 3, 4.

2 The monthly sales (£s) achieved by ten sales representatives are:

| 13,548 | 16,894 | 20,768 | 17,650 | 45,421 |
| 31,258 | 15,497 | 15,657 | 35,638 | 27,145 |

Calculate the mean, median and mode and discuss the most appropriate measure of central location for a company report.

3 20 items have a mean value of £30 and 25 a mean value of £80. What is the mean value of them all?

4 Find the mean, mode and median of the datasets in questions 1, 2 and 3 of Exercises 4.4.

5 For the histogram below, calculate the mean, mode and median. What do these values tell you about the shape of the distribution?

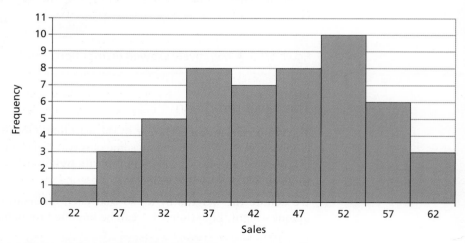

Figure 5.1.6 **Histogram of sales.**

6 Six breakfast-cereal boxes from a production process weigh:

> 405.4, 403.0, 405.6, 406.7, 402.9, 404.3

A second sample, taken later, found boxes weighing:

> 402.0, 408.6, 401.7, 406.7, 405.0, 403.5

Using measures of location, discuss how similar or different these samples are.

5.2 Measures of non-central location

> We may want to consider other locations in a set of data, such as how many employees earn the top 25% of all salaries or how many students are in the bottom 10% of all marks on an exam. Quarters of sets are called **quartiles**, and hundredths (i.e. percentages) are called **percentiles**.

Quartiles

Quartiles are widely used as measures of non-central location. Recall that the median is a value that divides an ordered dataset into two halves. Quartiles divide an ordered dataset into quarters. To calculate them, we first rank the data in order, as we did for the median. The first quartile has 25% of the data below it and 75% above it. The second quartile is the median (i.e. 50% below and 50% above). The third quartile has 75% below it and 25% above it. The fourth quartile is the largest observation (i.e. all the data are below it).

We defined the median to be located at the $(n + 1)/2$th position in a ranked or ordered list of n observations, and we now define quartiles in a similar way.

The **first quartile** is located at the $(n + 1)/4$th position in an ordered list. As with the group median, either we can calculate the first quartile class or we can use a formula to calculate a value for the group first quartile. We modify Equation (5.1.5) to calculate the value of the first quartile:

$$\text{1st quartile value} = L_{Q1} + \frac{W_{Q1}}{f_{Q1}} * \left[\frac{(n + 1)}{4} + f_{Q1} - CF_{Q1} \right] \qquad (5.2.1)$$

where L_{Q2} is the lower boundary of the class containing the 1st quartile
W_{Q1} is the width of the class containing the 1st quartile
f_{Q1} is the frequency of the class containing the 1st quartile
CF_{Q1} is the cumulative frequency up to and including the 1st quartile class

The **second quartile** is located at the $2 * (n + 1)/4$th $= (n + 1)/2$th position in an ordered list (i.e. the median). As the second quartile is the median then we can simply replace the subscript m by Q2 in equation (5.1.5), i.e.

$$\text{2nd quartile value} = L_{Q2} + \frac{W_{Q2}}{f_{Q2}} * \left[\frac{2 * (n + 1)}{4} + f_{Q2} - CF_{Q2} \right] \qquad (5.2.2)$$

where L_{Q2} is the lower boundary of the class containing the 2nd quartile (i.e. median)

W_{Q2} is the width of the class containing the 2nd quartile (i.e. median)

f_{Q2} is the frequency of the class containing the 2nd quartile (i.e. median)

CF_{Q2} is the cumulative frequency up to and including the 2nd quartile class

The **third quartile** is located at the $3 * (n + 1)/4$th position in an ordered list. Again, we can modify equation (5.1.5) to calculate it:

$$\text{3rd quartile value} = L_{Q3} + \frac{W_{Q3}}{f_{Q3}} * \left[\frac{3 * (n + 1)}{4} + f_{Q3} - CF_{Q3} \right] \qquad (5.2.3)$$

where L_{Q3} is the lower boundary of the class containing the 3rd quartile

W_{Q3} is the width of the class containing the 3rd quartile

f_{Q3} is the frequency of the class containing the 3rd quartile

CF_{Q3} is the cumulative frequency up to and including the 3rd quartile class

Quartiles for ungrouped data and grouped data are illustrated in Examples 5.2.1 and 5.2.2, respectively.

Example 5.2.1

Q Find the 1st, 2nd and 3rd quartiles of the data in Example 5.1.1.

A We first put the data in increasing order, as shown in Table 5.2.1.

Table 5.2.1 **The ranked data for Example 5.1.1.**

Item	1	2	3	4	5	6	7	8	9	10	11	12	13	14	15	16	17	18	19	20
Age	18	18	21	25	28	31	34	34	34	37	40	41	42	46	47	55	55	55	59	61

The 1st quartile is located at position $(20 + 1)/4 = 21/4 = 5.25$, and we could approximate the median by taking the 5th observation (i.e. 28). To be more precise, we could consider a value between the 5th and 6th observations, but 75% nearer to the 5th than the 6th observation. To calculate this, we can take a weighted mean of the 5th and 6th observations having 75% of 28 (the 5th observation) and 25% of 31 (the 6th observation), i.e. $0.75 * 28 + 0.25 * 31 = 28.75$.

The 2nd quartile (i.e. the median) is located at position $2(20 + 1)/4 = 10.5$. So we want the weighted mean of the 10th and 11th observations having 50% of each, i.e. $0.5 * 37 + 0.5 * 40 = 38.5$.

5.4

The 3rd quartile is located at position $3 * (20 + 1)/4 = 15.75$. So we want the weighted mean of the 15th and 16th observations having 25% of the 15th item and 75% of the 16th item, i.e. $0.25 * 47 + 0.75 * 55 = 53$.

Example 5.2.2

Q Find the 1st quartile for the data in Example 4.4.2.

A We tabulate the frequencies and cumulative frequencies (just as we did for the group median) as shown in Table 5.2.2.

Table 5.2.2 **Cumulative frequencies for Example 4.4.2.**

Class	Class interval	Frequency	Cumulative frequency
1	0–39	8	8
2	40–59	7	15
3	60–79	9	24
4	80–99	12	36
5	100–119	10	46
6	120–139	8	54
7	140–159	6	60
8	160–199	6	66
9	200 or more	10	76

We have $n = 76$ and $(n + 1)/4 = 19.25$, so class 3 contains the 1st quartile. Now apply equation (5.2.1) with $L_{Q1} = 59.5$, $W_{Q1} = 20$, $f_{Q1} = 9$ and $CF_{Q1} = 24$ to get:

$$\text{1st quartile value} = 59.5 + \frac{20}{9} * [19.25 + 9 - 24] = 68.94.$$

Percentiles

Percentiles are similar to quartiles, but we divide the ordered set of data into 100ths or percentages. The Pth percentile is the value with $P\%$ of the data below it and $(100 - P)\%$ above it. When $P = 25$ (i.e. the 25th percentile), it is the 1st quartile. The Pth percentile is located at the $P(n + 1)/100$th position in an ordered list of n observations, and we can modify equations (5.2.1) to (5.2.3) to obtain the formula:

$$P\text{th percentile value} = L_P + \frac{W_P}{f_P} * \left[\frac{P * (n + 1)}{100} + f_P - CF_P \right] \qquad (5.2.4)$$

where L_P is the lower boundary of the class containing the Pth percentile
W_P is the width of the class containing the Pth percentile
f_P is the frequency of the class containing the Pth percentile
CF_P is the cumulative frequency up to and including the Pth percentile

Example 5.2.3

Q Find the 40th percentile for the data in Example 4.4.2.

A We tabulate the frequencies and cumulative frequencies as we did for the group median and quartiles, as shown in Table 5.2.3.

Table 5.2.3 **Cumulative frequencies for Example 4.4.2.**

Class	Class interval	Frequency	Cumulative frequency
1	0–39	8	8
2	40–59	7	15
3	60–79	9	24
4	80–99	12	36
5	100–119	10	46
6	120–139	8	54
7	140–159	6	60
8	160–199	6	66
9	200 or more	10	76

We have $n = 76$ and $40 * (n + 1)/100 = 30.8$, so class 4 contains the 40th percentile (i.e. 40% of the data). Now apply equation (5.2.4) with $L_{40} = 79.5$, $W_{40} = 20, f_{40} = 12$ and $CF_{40} = 36$ to get:

$$\text{40th percentile value} = 79.5 + \frac{20}{12} * [30.8 + 12 - 36] = 90.83.$$

5.4

Exercises   **5.2**

1   Calculate the 1st and 3rd quartiles and 25th percentile of 4, 2, 7, 4, 5, 3, 5, 4, 3, 4.

2   Find 1st and 2nd quartiles of the datasets in questions 1, 2 and 3 of Exercises 4.4.

3   The waiting times in minutes at an ATM are:
4.21, 5.55, 3.02, 5.13, 4.77, 2.34, 3.54, 3.20,
4.50, 6.10, 0.38, 5.12, 6.46, 6.19, 3.79.
Calculate the mean, median, first and third quartiles, and comment on these measures of location

4   Waiting times at another ATM are:
9.66, 5.90, 8.02, 5.79, 8.73, 3.82, 8.01, 8.35,
10.59, 6.68, 5.64, 4.08, 6.17, 9.91, 5.47
Calculate the mean, median, first and third quartiles, and comment on these measures of location
Is it appropriate to make comparisons with the ATM in question 3?

5   The salaries of a sample of employees were recorded as:

Salary range (£s)	Frequency
5,000–7,999	1
8,000–10,999	5
11,000–13,999	7
14,000–16,999	13
17,000–19,999	45
20,000–22,999	128
23,000–25,999	134
26,000–28,999	97
29,000–31,999	75
32,000–34,999	91
35,000–44,999	56
45,000–54,999	32
55,000–64,999	3
65,000–74,999	6
75,000–99,999	1
100,000–124,999	0
125,000–199,999	1

Calculate the mean, median, mode, first quartile, third quartile and the 10th, 20th and 30th percentiles and comment on their usefulness.

5.3 Measures of variation

The previous section described datasets using a single measure of location. Such measures of location give no indication of how the data are 'spread'. For example, two samples of screws might both have a mean length of 2 cm, but the screws in the first sample might have lengths within ±1 mm whereas those in the second sample might be within ±5 mm. When comparing samples, it is important to know how the data are spread around the mean. In this section, we consider the most popular measures of 'spread' or **variation** and calculate them in a variety of ways. We can calculate measures of variation from a table of data, by applying a formula, or by using inbuilt functions on calculators or spreadsheets.

The prerequisites of this section are:

■ From numbers to symbols (Chapter 2);
■ Elementary statistics (Chapter 4);
■ Measures of location (Section 5.1).

Measures of variation

The histograms in Figures 5.3.1 and 5.3.2 have the same mean but come from different sets of data. The first has a smallest class limit of 5 and a largest class limit of 50, whereas the second has a smallest class limit of 10 and a largest class limit of 40. If the mean of these two datasets were presented without any further information (e.g. the histogram) then we might assume that the samples were very similar, when clearly they are not. Rather than referring back to the original data or some qualitative representation of it (e.g. a histogram), we use quantitative measures of 'spread' called **measures of variation**.

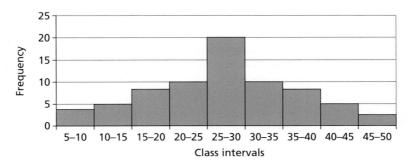

Figure 5.3.1 **Histogram with class limits from 5 to 50.**

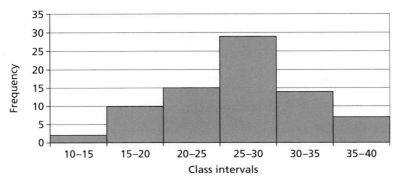

Figure 5.3.2 **Histogram with class limits from 10 to 40.**

Range

The simplest measure of variation is the **range**, the difference between the largest and smallest items in a dataset. Let us call the largest data item x_{max} and the smallest x_{min}, and define the range, which we often denote by R:

$$R = x_{max} - x_{min} \qquad (5.3.1)$$

The range of data in Figure 5.3.1 is $50 - 5 = 45$ and in Figure 5.3.2 is $40 - 10 = 30$. Most data are not at the extremes of the distribution, so the range is a poor indicator of 'spread'.

Interquartile range

The interquartile range overcomes some of the deficiencies of the range by looking at the difference between the 3rd and 1st quartiles. It is useful because it is less influenced by extreme values and it limits the range to the middle 50% of the values:

$$\text{Interquartile range} = Q_3 - Q_1 \qquad (5.3.2)$$

Box and whisker plots

A box and whisker plot is a visual representation of the median, interquartile range and range. Box and whisker plots are one example of Tukey's exploratory data analysis (EDA) tools. Example 5.3.1 illustrates a box and whisker plot.

Example | **5.3.1**

Q Construct box and whisker plots for the data:

18, 27, 34, 52, 54, 59, 61, 68, 78, 82, 85, 87, 91, 93, 100

A To draw a box and whisker plot we find the minimum and maximum of the data, calculate the median, 1st quartile and 3rd quartiles, and then represent them on a horizontal scale, i.e.

Minimum = 18

Maximum = 100

Median = 68

1st quartile = 52

3rd quartile = 87

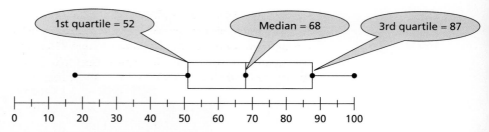

Figure 5.3.3 **Box and whisker plot.**

Deviations from the mean

The range and interquartile range, although indicating overall variation in a dataset, do not indicate its spread around the centre (i.e. mean, mode or median), and box and whisker plots give only a visual representation of the spread. The mean is the most commonly used measure of central location, but it can be atypical (see the histograms in Figures 5.3.1 and 5.3.2). So we need to measure the 'spread' of data around the mean to indicate how typical the mean is.

To do this, we could calculate the difference between each item of data and the mean (i.e. $\bar{x} - x_i$), i.e. the deviations from the mean, resulting in as many numbers as items of data! We could summarise these deviations by taking their mean:

$$\text{Mean of deviations} = \frac{\sum_{i=1}^{n}(\bar{x} - x_i)}{n} \qquad (5.3.3)$$

However, the mean of deviations from the mean is 0 because some numbers are above the mean and others below it (Example 5.3.2).

Example 5.3.2

Q Calculate both the mean and mean of deviations of 4, 7, 6, 2, 8, 3.

A The calculations are shown in Table 5.3.1.

Table 5.3.1 **Deviation from the mean.**

i	x_i	$\bar{x} - x_i$
1	4	$5 - 4 = 1$
2	7	$5 - 7 = -2$
3	6	$5 - 6 = -1$
4	2	$5 - 2 = 3$
5	8	$5 - 8 = -3$
6	3	$5 - 3 = 2$
Total (Σ) =	30	0
Mean =	$30/6 = 5$	$0/6 = 0$

The positive deviations, resulting from data items less than the mean, are cancelled out by the negative deviations, which come from data items greater than the mean.

We can overcome the problem of the mean of deviations being zero in two ways. First, we could simply ignore the sign of the deviations (by taking their absolute value) or, second, we could square the deviations (because the square of a negative number is positive). These two measures of variation are called the **Mean Absolute Deviation (MAD)** and **variance**, respectively.

Mean Absolute Deviation (MAD)

From Section 1.4 we denote the absolute difference between two numbers by placing them between two vertical lines (i.e. $|3 - 8| = 5$). We can modify equation (5.3.3) to calculate MAD for a sample:

$$\text{Mean Absolute Deviation of a sample} = \frac{\sum_{i=1}^{n} |\bar{x} - x_i|}{n} \qquad (5.3.4)$$

To calculate MAD for a population, we divide by the population size and sum over all the population (i.e. N), and use the population mean (i.e. μ) in equation (5.3.4):

$$\text{Mean Absolute Deviation of a population} = \frac{\sum_{i=1}^{N} |\mu - x_i|}{N} \qquad (5.3.5)$$

With grouped data, we modify the formula as we did when calculating the group mean of c classes with midpoints x_i and frequencies f_i. Modifying equation (5.3.4) for grouped data gives:

$$\text{Group Mean Absolute Deviation} = \frac{\sum_{i=1}^{c} f_i |\bar{x} - x_i|}{\sum_{i=1}^{c} f_i} \qquad (5.3.6)$$

Example | **5.3.3**

Q Calculate the group MAD for the data in Example 4.4.2.

A As we saw in Section 4.4, such calculations are best performed in a table (Table 5.3.2).

Table 5.3.2 **Calculations for MAD for Example 4.4.2.**

Class range							
				Median Frequency			
Class	From	To	x_i	f_i	$x_i * f_i$	$|\bar{x} - x_i|$	$f_i * |\bar{x} - x_i|$
1	0	39	19.5	8	156.0	96.32	770.53
2	40	59	49.5	7	346.5	66.32	464.21
3	60	79	69.5	9	625.5	46.32	416.84
4	80	99	89.5	12	1,074.0	26.32	315.76
5	100	119	109.5	10	1,095.0	6.32	63.19
6	120	139	129.5	8	1,036.0	13.68	109.47
7	140	159	149.5	6	897.0	33.68	202.11
8	160	199	179.5	6	1,077.0	63.68	382.11
9	200	299	249.5	10	2,495.0	133.68	1,336.84
		(Sums Σ) =		76	8,802.0		4,061.05

Group mean = 8,802/76 = 115.82

Group MAD = 4,061.05/76 = 53.43.

Variance

MAD cannot easily be used to develop statistical theory for making inferences about the population, such as those in Part B, and such problems are overcome by using **variance**. Instead of ignoring the sign of the deviations, as in equations (5.3.4) to (5.3.6), we square the deviations, resulting in three formulae:

$$\text{Variance of a sample } s^2 = \frac{\sum_{i=1}^{n}(\overline{x}-x_i)^2}{n} \qquad (5.3.7)$$

$$\text{Variance of a population } \sigma^2 = \frac{\sum_{i=1}^{N}(\mu-x_i)^2}{N} \qquad (5.3.8)$$

$$\text{Group variance } = \frac{\sum_{i=1}^{c}f_i(\overline{x}-x_i)^2}{\sum_{i=1}^{c}f_i} \qquad (5.3.9)$$

Standard deviation

By squaring deviations from the mean to calculate variance, we not only remove the negative sign but also change the magnitude of the numbers. We can square-root the variance to compensate, and we call this the **standard deviation**. Square-rooting equations (5.3.7)–(5.3.9) gives:

$$\text{Standard deviation of a sample } s = \sqrt{\frac{\sum_{i=1}^{n}(\overline{x}-x_i)^2}{n}} \qquad (5.3.10)$$

$$\text{Standard deviation of a population } \sigma = \sqrt{\frac{\sum_{i=1}^{N}(\mu-x_i)^2}{N}} \qquad (5.3.11)$$

$$\text{Group standard deviation } = \sqrt{\frac{\sum_{i=1}^{c}f_i(\overline{x}-x_i)^2}{\sum_{i=1}^{c}f_i}} \qquad (5.3.12)$$

We can algebraically rearrange equations (5.3.10)–(5.3.12) to provide so-called 'short-cut' formulae, which avoid calculating the mean (see **www.mcgraw-hill.co.uk/textbooks/dewhurst**).

Sample variance and sample standard deviation

To find the MAD, variance or standard deviation of a population or sample for descriptive purposes, we use equations (5.3.4)–(5.3.12). However, if we want to make **inferences about a population** from a sample (say, to estimate the population standard derivation of a population from the standard deviation of a sample), we use **sample variance** and **sample standard deviation** and modify equations (5.3.7) and (5.3.10) to have a denominator of **(n – 1) instead of n**. Do not confuse these with the variance (or standard deviations) *of* a sample. Sample variance and sample standard deviation are the best estimates of the variance and standard deviation of a population *from* a sample. When sample size (n) becomes very large, ($n-1$) becomes indistinguishable from n and so the distinction becomes irrelevant. (See **www.mcgrawhill.co.uk/textbooks/dewhurst** for an explanation of why we divide by ($n-1$) for sample variance and sample standard deviation.) We denote sample standard deviation by **stdev** and sample variance by **var**.

The modified formulae for **sample variance** and **sample standard deviation** are:

$$\text{Sample variance (var)} = \frac{\sum_{i=1}^{n}(\bar{x} - x_i)^2}{(n-1)} \tag{5.3.13}$$

$$\text{Group sample variance} = \frac{\sum_{i=1}^{c}f_i(\bar{x} - x_i)^2}{\left(\sum_{i=1}^{c}f_i\right) - 1} \tag{5.3.14}$$

$$\text{Sample standard deviation (stdev)} = \sqrt{\frac{\sum_{i=1}^{n}(\bar{x} - x_i)^2}{(n-1)}} \tag{5.3.15}$$

$$\text{Group sample standard deviation} = \sqrt{\frac{\sum_{i=1}^{c}f_i(\bar{x} - x_i)^2}{\left(\sum_{i=1}^{c}f_i\right) - 1}} \tag{5.3.16}$$

 5.6

Most spreadsheets have inbuilt functions for the variance of a population using equation (5.3.8), the standard deviation of a population using equation (5.3.11), the sample variance using equation (5.3.13) and the sample standard deviation using equation (5.2.15) (see Example 5.3.4).

Example 5.3.4

Q Find the variance and standard deviation for the data in Example 4.4.2.

A We use equations (5.3.9) and (5.3.12). If we want to make inferences about a population (e.g. the sales of baked beans in many stores or over longer periods of time), we calculate the sample variance and standard deviation using equations (5.3.14) and (5.3.16). These calculations are shown in Table 5.3.3.

5.6

Table 5.3.3 **Group variance and standard deviation.**

Class	Class range From	To	Median x_i	Frequency f_i	$x_i * f_i$	$(\bar{x} - x_i)^2$	$f_i * (\bar{x} - x_i)^2$
1	0	39	19.5	8	156.0	9,276.73	74,213.85
2	40	59	49.5	7	346.5	4,397.78	30,784.49
3	60	79	69.5	9	625.5	2,145.15	19,306.37
4	80	99	89.5	12	1,074.0	692.52	8,310.25
5	100	119	109.5	10	1,095.0	39.89	398.89
6	120	139	129.5	8	1,036.0	187.26	1,498.06
7	140	159	149.5	6	897.0	1,134.63	6,807.76
8	160	199	179.5	6	1,077.0	4,055.68	24,334.07
9	200	299	249.5	10	2,495.0	1,7871.50	178,714.68
			Sums (Σ) =	76	8,802.0		344,368.42

Group mean = 8,802/76 = 115.82

Group variance = 344,368.42/76 = 4,531.16

Group standard deviation = $\sqrt{4,531.16}$ = 67.31

Group sample variance = 344,368.42/75 = 4,591.58

Group sample standard deviation = $\sqrt{4,591.58}$ = 67.76

Coefficient of variation

The standard deviation of a set of measurements is sometimes used as an indicator of accuracy. If we repeatedly measure a quantity (e.g. the weight of a can of baked beans), we do not always expect the same results, and the amount of variation indicates the degree of accuracy in our measurements. The mean is often used as an indicator of 'typical', and standard deviation as an indicator of variation. The use of variation for measurement accuracy makes sense only if the typical size of the quantity is already known (e.g. a 454 g can of baked beans). If we have two samples, one with mean $\bar{x} = 3$ and standard deviation $s = 5$ and another with $\bar{x} = 150$ and $s = 1$, a standard deviation of $s = 5$ around a mean of $\bar{x} = 3$ suggests a great deal of variability, but $s = 1$ around a mean of $\bar{x} = 150$ suggests little variability.

To make comparisons of measurement accuracy, we need to express the magnitude of the variation relative to the size of the quantity being measured and we use a measure of relative variation, such as the **coefficient of variation (cv)** in which the standard deviation is scaled (i.e. divided) by the mean and represented as a percentage:

$$\text{Coefficient of variation (cv)} = \frac{\text{Standard deviation} \times 100}{\text{Mean}} \qquad (5.3.17)$$

Example

5.3.5

Q Over the last 6 months, the average price of Internet-based shares was £5.80 with a standard deviation of £1.50; Manufacturing share prices were £3.50 on average with a standard deviation of £0.80. Which shares had the highest relative variability?

A   Use equation (5.3.17) to see the relative variation in share prices:

For Internet shares $cv = 1.50/5.80 = 0.258621 = 25.86\%$

For Manufacturing shares $cv = 0.80/3.50 = 0.228571 = 22.86\%$

Internet shares have a higher relative variability, and we might infer that they represent a more risky investment.

Coefficient of quartile deviation

An alternative but less common measure of relative variation is the **coefficient of quartile variation**, defined as the interquartile range divided by the sum of the 1st and 3rd quartiles:

$$\text{Coefficient of quartile variation (cqv)} = \frac{Q_3 - Q_1}{Q_3 + Q_1} \qquad (5.3.18)$$

Exercises   **5.3**

1   Calculate the range, interquartile range, MAD, variance and standard deviation for questions 1, 2, 4 and 5 of Exercises 5.1.

2   Compare the variation in the two samples given in question 3 of Exercises 4.3.

3   The salaries of a sample of employees were recorded as:

Salary range (£s)	Frequency
5,000–7,999	1
8,000–10,999	5
11,000–13,999	7
14,000–16,999	13
17,000–19,999	45
20,000–22,999	128
23,000–25,999	134
26,000–28,999	97
29,000–31,999	75
32,000–34,999	91
35,000–44,999	56
45,000–54,999	32
55,000–64,999	3
65,000–74,999	6
75,000–99,999	1
100,000–124,999	0
125,000–199,999	1

Calculate the interquartile range and coefficient of quartile variation, and comment on their usefulness.

4   Reconsider your answer to question 7 of Exercises 5.1 by calculating appropriate measures of variation.

5.4 Index numbers

Index numbers show how data change over time relative to a fixed point (the base period). They are used to compare 'baskets' of goods over time. The RPI (Retail Price Index) shows how prices of consumer goods change over time, and the FTSE and Dow Jones indices show how share prices change. In this section, we consider how such indices are calculated and used.

The prerequisites of this section are:
- An introduction to Quantitative Methods (Chapter 1);
- From numbers to symbols (Chapter 2);
- The meaning and nature of statistics (Section 4.1);
- Sampling and data collection (Section 4.2);
- Measures of location (Section 5.1).

Index numbers

To calculate index numbers, we use subscripted variables with subscripts that refer to points in time. If p denotes the price of a product, we might label the prices at different points in time (periods):

p_1 the price in year 1
p_2 the price in year 2
p_3 the price in year 3
p_n the price in year n

To see how prices p_1, p_2, p_3, etc. have changed relative to a particular year (the **base period**), we denote the base period by p_0 and calculate indices as a percentage of it. Equation (5.4.1) calculates a simple price index in year n relative to the base year, and is illustrated by Example 5.4.1.

$$\text{Simple price index (in year } n) = \frac{p_n}{p_0} * 100 \qquad (5.4.1)$$

Example 5.4.1

Q Over the last three years, the share prices of a company have been £3.80, £3.90 and £3.75. Construct an index to show how share prices have changed.

A First, decide on a base year. Let us make it the first year, and apply equation (5.4.1) as shown in Table 5.4.1.

Table 5.4.1 **A simple price index.**

Year	Share price (£)	Ratio to base	Index
1	3.80	3.80/3.80 = 1.0000	1 * 100 = 100.00
2	3.90	3.90/3.80 = 1.0263	1.0263 * 100 = 102.63
3	3.75	3.75/3.80 = 0.9868	0.9868 * 100 = 98.68

Table 5.4.1 shows that in the second year the share price had risen by 2.63% (i.e. 102.63 – 100 = 2.63) relative to the base (year 1), whereas in the third year the share price was down by 1.32% (i.e. 98.68 – 100 = –1.32).

Weighted price indices

The simple price index, given by equation (5.4.1) and illustrated in Example 5.4.1, can compare only single items (e.g. the share price of one company). To compare a 'basket' of goods (as does the RPI), we could construct a price index by taking the average (e.g. mean) price of all the items in each year and extend equation (5.4.1) to calculate the ratio of one year's average prices to the average prices in a base year. However, some items in the 'basket' may be more important than others. Basic food items (e.g. bread, milk) are considered more important than non-essential items (e.g. biscuits, wine). We therefore use weighted indices by taking a weighted mean. If our 'basket' has m items each labelled by i, their weights by w_i and their prices in period n by p_{in}, then we can define the weighted price index:

$$\text{Weighted price index} = \frac{\sum_{i=1}^{m} w_i \left(\frac{p_{in}}{p_{i0}}\right)}{\sum_{i=1}^{m} w_i} \qquad (5.4.2)$$

The Retail Price Index

 5.7

The RPI is a base weighted price index used by the UK government to show how household expenditure changes over time with reference to a base year. Government agencies use it to identify inflation for calculating state pensions, etc. Table 5.4.2 shows an example RPI and Example 5.4.2 its use.

Table 5.4.2 **Part of an RPI.**

Item i	Weight w_i	Base year price (p_{i0})	This year's price (p_{in})	Ratio of p_{in} to p_{io}	Weighted price index
Food	158	35	36	36/35 = 1.03	158 * 1.03 = 162.5
Motoring	131	40	42	42/40 = 1.05	131 * 1.05 = 137.6
Housing	185	20	19	19/20 = 0.95	185 * 0.95 = 175.8
Clothing	77	34	36	36/34 = 1.06	77 * 1.06 = 81.5
Entertainment	21	10	12	12/10 = 1.20	21 * 1.20 = 25.2
Total $\Sigma w_i =$	572				$\Sigma w_i (p_{in}/p_{i0})$ = **582.54**

The RPI for this current year = 100 * 582.54/572 = 101.80, which shows that the RPI has increased by 1.8%.

Example	5.4.2

Q In the base year, average earnings were £20,000 and are currently £20,800. How has the purchasing power of wages changed?

A To answer this, use the RPI in Table 5.4.2. This year's wages are £20,800 and, taking the RPI into account, are equivalent to £20,800/1.018 = 20,432.22.

So wages have increased in 'real' terms by:

$$(20,432.22 - 20,000)/20,000 = 100\% * 432.22/20,000$$
$$= 2.16\%$$

Laspeyre's indices

Simple weighted indices consider changes in only one variable (e.g. price). Consumer expenditure may change not only because of price but also because of buying habits (e.g. quantities purchased). With two variables (e.g. price and quantity), we can use Laspeyre's base weighted index to compare changes in price (p) or quantity (q). These two indices are given by equations (5.4.3) and (5.4.4), and are illustrated in Example 5.4.3.

$$\text{Laspeyre's price index} = \frac{\sum_{i=1}^{m} q_{i0} p_{in}}{\sum_{i=1}^{m} q_{i0} p_{i0}} \qquad (5.4.3)$$

$$\text{Laspeyre's quantity index} = \frac{\sum_{i=1}^{m} q_{in} p_{i0}}{\sum_{i=1}^{m} q_{i0} p_{i0}} \qquad (5.4.4)$$

Example **5.4.3**

Q Table 5.4.3 shows the quantities purchased for three consumer goods over the last 4 years and Table 5.4.4 the prices paid for them. Calculate a Laspeyre's quantity and price index for each year, and discuss how consumer habits and prices have changed since Year 1.

Table 5.4.3 **Quantities purchased for goods A, B and C over 4 years.**

	Year 1	Year 2	Year 3	Year 4
A	700	650	750	600
B	250	250	200	150
C	800	1,200	14,000	1,600

Table 5.4.4 **Prices paid for goods A, B and C over 4 years.**

	Year 1	Year 2	Year 3	Year 4
A	54	54	56	62
B	114	116	120	124
C	182	190	202	222

A Laspeyre's quantity index (i.e. equation (5.4.4)) is best calculated in a table (Table 5.4.5) in which we hold the base period (Year 1) prices constant.

Table 5.4.5 shows an increase in sales of 33.08% between the first and second year.

Laspeyre's price index (i.e. equation (5.4.3)) is similarly best calculated in a table (Table 5.4.6), but now we hold the base period (Year 1) quantities constant.

5.8

Table 5.4.5 **Laspeyre's quantity index for Example 5.4.3.**

$q_n p_0 =$	Year 1	Year 2	Year 3	Year 4
A	700 * 54 = 37,800	650 * 54 = 35,100	50 * 54 = 40,500	600 * 54 = 32,400
B	250 * 114 = 28,500	250 * 114 = 28,500	200 * 144 = 22,800	150 * 144 = 17,100
C	800 * 182 = 145,600	1,200 * 182 = 218,400	14,000 * 182 = 2,548,000	1,600 * 182 = 291,200
$\Sigma\, q_n p_0$	211,900	282,000	2,611,300	340,700
$\Sigma\, q_0 p_0$	211,900	211,900	211,900	211,900
$\dfrac{\Sigma\, q_n p_0}{\Sigma\, q_0 p_0} =$	$\dfrac{211,900}{211,900}$	$\dfrac{282,000}{211,900}$	$\dfrac{2,611,300}{211,900}$	$\dfrac{340,700}{211,900}$
Laspeyre's quantity = index	100	133.08	1,232.33	160.78

Table 5.4.6 **Laspeyre's price index for Example 5.4.3.**

$q_n p_0 =$	Year 1	Year 2	Year 3	Year 4
A	700 * 54 = 37,800	700 * 54 = 37,800	700 * 56 = 39,200	700 * 62 = 43,400
B	250 * 114 = 28,500	250 * 116 = 29,000	250 * 120 = 30,000	250 * 124 = 31,000
C	800 * 182 = 145,600	800 * 190 = 152,000	800 * 202 = 161,000	800 * 222 = 177,600
$\Sigma\, q_0 p_n$	211,900	218,800	230,800	252,000
$\Sigma\, q_0 p_0$	211,900	211,900	211,900	211,900
$\dfrac{\Sigma\, q_0 p_n}{\Sigma\, q_0 p_0} =$	$\dfrac{211,900}{211,900}$	$\dfrac{218,800}{211,900}$	$\dfrac{230,800}{211,900}$	$\dfrac{252,000}{211,900}$
Laspeyre's price = index	100	103.26	108.92	118.92

5.8

Table 5.4.6 shows an increase in price of 18.92% between the first and the fourth years.

The Paasche indices

Over time Laspeyre's indices can get very high (e.g. because of continually increasing prices). One way of overcoming this problem is to change the base period (e.g. every 10 years). Another is to make comparisons with the present (i.e. current) time and use the current period as weights rather than the base period. We can compare two variables (e.g. price and quantity) over time using Paasche's current weighted index. These two indices are given by equations (5.4.5) and (5.4.6) and illustrated in Example 5.4.4. Paasche indices do not give a direct comparison of changes over time, and require more data to update than do Laspeyre's indices.

$$\text{Paasche price index} = \frac{\displaystyle\sum_{i=1}^{m} q_{in} p_{in}}{\displaystyle\sum_{i=1}^{m} q_{in} p_{i0}} \qquad (5.4.5)$$

$$\text{Paasche quantity index} = \frac{\displaystyle\sum_{i=1}^{m} q_{in} p_{in}}{\displaystyle\sum_{i=1}^{m} q_{i0} p_{in}} \qquad (5.4.6)$$

Example 5.4.4

Q Calculate Paasche indices for the data in Tables 5.4.3 and 5.4.4 for each year, and compare past and current prices, with Year 1 as the base year.

A Again, to find the Paasche quantity index (i.e. equation (5.4.6)) it is best to set the calculations out in a table. First, multiply the quantities by their corresponding prices to find $q_n p_n$ and take their sums. Then hold the base period quantities (Year $n = 1$) constant, multiply them by the prices to find $q_0 p_n$ and take their sums. Finally, divide the first sum by the second sum.

Table 5.4.7 **The Paasche quantity index for Example 5.4.4.**

$q_n p_n =$	Year 1	Year 2	Year 3	Year 4
A	700 * 54 = 37,800	650 * 54 = 35,100	750 * 56 = 42,000	600 * 62 = 37,200
B	250 * 114 = 28,500	250 * 116 = 29,000	200 * 120 = 24,000	150 * 124 = 18,600
C	800 * 182 = 145,600	1,200 * 192 = 228,000	14,000 * 202 = 2,828,000	1,600 * 222 = 355,200
$\Sigma q_n p_n$	211,900	292,100	2,894,000	411,000

$q_0 p_n =$	Year 1	Year 2	Year 3	Year 4
A	700 * 54 = 37,800	700 * 54 = 37,800	700 * 56 = 39,200	700 * 62 = 43,400
B	250 * 114 = 28,500	250 * 116 = 29,000	250 * 120 = 30,000	250 * 124 = 31,000
C	800 * 182 = 145,600	800 * 190 = 152,000	800 * 202 = 161,600	800 * 222 = 177,600
$\Sigma q_0 p_n$	211,900	218,800	230,800	252,000
$\dfrac{\Sigma q_n p_n}{\Sigma q_0 p_n} =$	$\dfrac{211,900}{211,900}$	$\dfrac{292,100}{218,800}$	$\dfrac{2,894,000}{230,800}$	$\dfrac{411,000}{252,900}$
Paasche quantity = index	100	133.50	1,253.90	163.10

Table 5.4.7 shows an increase in sales of 33.50% in the second year.

To calculate the Paasche price indices using equation (5.4.5), we again multiply the quantities by their corresponding prices to find $q_n p_n$ and take their sums. Then we hold the base period prices (Year $n = 1$) constant, multiply them by the prices to find $q_n p_0$, and take their sums. Finally we divide the first sum by the second sum, as in Table 5.4.8.

Table 5.4.8 **The Paasche price index for Example 5.4.4.**

$q_n p_n =$	Year 1	Year 2	Year 3	Year 4
A	700 * 54 = 37,800	650 * 54 = 35,100	750 * 56 = 42,000	600 * 62 = 37,200
B	250 * 114 = 28,500	250 * 116 = 29,000	200 * 120 = 24,000	150 * 124 = 18,600
C	800 * 182 = 145,600	1,200 * 190 = 228,000	14,000 * 202 = 2,828,000	1,600 * 222 = 355,200
$\Sigma q_n p_n$	211,900	292,100	2,894,000	411,000

$q_n p_0 =$	Year 1	Year 2	Year 3	Year 4
A	700 * 54 = 37,800	650 * 54 = 35,100	750 * 54 = 40,500	600 * 54 = 32,400
B	250 * 114 = 28,500	250 * 114 = 28,500	200 * 114 = 22,800	150 * 114 = 17,100
C	800 * 182 = 145,600	1,200 * 182 = 218,400	14,000 * 182 = 2,548,000	1,600 * 182 = 291,200
$\Sigma q_n p_0$	211,900	282,000	2,611,300	340,700
$\dfrac{\Sigma q_n p_n}{\Sigma q_n p_0} =$	$\dfrac{211,900}{211,900}$	$\dfrac{292,100}{282,000}$	$\dfrac{2,894,000}{2,611,300}$	$\dfrac{411,000}{340,700}$
Paasche price = index	100	103.58	110.83	120.63

Table 5.4.8 shows that there was an increase in price of 20.63% between the first and fourth years.

Generally, a Laspeyre index overestimates whereas a Paasche index underestimates the relative changes.

Exercises | **5.4**

1 Construct a simple quantity index, using period 1 as the base, for:

Period	Quantity
1	70
2	84
3	109
4	132
5	151

2 The consumer price index in the USA over a 5-year period is:

Year	CPI
1	100.5
2	113.5
3	125.1
4	132.6
5	136.6

Average monthly earnings for senior managers over the same period are:

Year	Earnings ($)
1	4,116
2	4,416
3	4,800
4	5,124
5	5,316

Calculate the 'real' earnings of senior managers in each year.

3 Sales of mini, small and medium family cars over a 3-year period and their prices are:

Sales (million units)	Year			
	1	2	3	4
Mini family	13.4	12.2	15.0	16.8
Small family	4.2	4.0	4.6	5.2
Medium family	8.0	8.6	8.6	9.0

Prices (£1,000s)	Year			
	1	2	3	4
Mini family	6.0	7.3	8.0	7.5
Small family	8.5	8.7	10.9	12.9
Medium family	9.3	12.7	12.5	11.9

(a) Calculate (i) a base weighted price index and (ii) a base weighted quantity index with year 1 as the base.

(b) Calculate (iii) a current period weighted price index and (iv) a current period weighted quantity index with year 3 as the base.

4   The Retail Price Index over the last 5 years was:

Year	RPI
1	100.0
2	113.5
3	125.1
4	132.6
5	136.6

The average weekly take-home pay of manual workers in each of these years was:

Year	Earnings
1	342.99
2	367.78
3	399.26
4	426.45
5	442.97

How has the purchasing power of manual workers changed over the last 5 years?

5.5   Chapter review

This chapter considered some typical quantitative ways of describing sets of data by using summary measures of location and variation to provide information for managers and decision-makers. If we want to use samples to make predictions about the population from which the samples were drawn, then we use sample statistics (e.g. sample mean and sample variance). This moves us into the realm of 'Inferential Statistics'. In Part B of this book we look at how we can use such samples and sample statistics to make inferences and provide further information for managers.

Closing comments

We have now completed the first part of this book and laid the foundations for the next two parts (i.e. B and C). There are three mini-case studies at the end of this part of the book, which reinforce the basic concepts learned in this part in a business and management context. Although these mini-case studies can be undertaken manually or by using a calculator, they would in practice be undertaken using a spreadsheet, and you are encouraged to do so. These mini-cases are based on the chapters of this part as shown below.

Case	Required reading
Case A1: Tops 'n' Bottoms	Chapters 1 and 4
Case A2: CompRus Ltd	Chapters 2 and 3
Case A3: Joowel's Store	Chapters 4 and 5

Case A1 — Tops 'n' Bottoms

Tops 'n' Bottoms are a small clothing retailer specialising in casual and sports-wear; they sell through their own high street outlets and also via mail order/Internet. They currently have their 'own brand' of clothes going under the 'Joggi' label. Under this label, they have a range of sweatshirts in eight colour-ways (blue, red, green, yellow, white, black, sand and grey) and four sizes: Small (S), Medium (M), Large (L) and eXtra Large (XL). The recommended retail prices (ex-VAT), determined by the manufacturer of these sweatshirts, are based only on size and are as follows:

Size	RRP(£s)
S	10
M	11.5
L	13
XL	14

In their high-street stores, Tops 'n' Bottoms suggest that the recommended retail price plus VAT is adhered to, whereas for mail-order/Internet customers UK purchases are discounted at 30% before VAT and are subject to a standard delivery charge of £5 per item. Non-UK orders are discounted at the same rate, but are not subject to VAT, and have a delivery charge of £5 within the EEC and £10 elsewhere.

1 You are employed to produce tables to show:
  (a) A price list for their high street stores.
  (b) The mail-order/Internet prices depending on customer location.

2 Last year Tops 'n' Bottoms monitored total sales of this particular sweatshirt in their high-street stores, and the data are as follows:

Colour	Small	Medium	Large	Extra large
Blue	551	831	732	150
Red	208	354	643	96
Green	50	78	55	43
Yellow	25	102	88	19
White	370	982	829	459
Black	120	483	682	257
Sand	86	904	340	54
Grey	143	246	172	48

You have also been asked by the accounts department to show revenue (i.e. sales quantity multiplied by price) from UK sales of each size and by each colourway, and to calculate the total revenue at the end of each year. In what ways can you compute the total end-of-year sales revenue so as to provide a check on your results?

3 Having received last year's sales figures, the sales manager in the Manchester store thinks that greater revenues can be obtained by marking up the prices. She marks up all the prices by 10%, but the end-of-year sales change as shown below.

	Sales for Manchester store			
	Small	Medium	Large	Extra large
Sales last year	312	752	584	98
Sales this year	280	751	554	63

Calculate the arc elasticity of sales with respect to price, and advise the manager of the responsiveness of changes in sales to changes in price.

Case A2 | CompRus Ltd

CompRus Ltd assemble and sell computers and develop, install and sell software to industrial clients. CompRus are organised into five departments, which are their major cost centres:

> Accounting
> Personnel
> Sales
> H/w production
> S/w production

1. The Accounting department are due to undertake an internal audit of each department but only have two qualified auditors. Assuming that the auditors will be split between the departments, how many ways are there of allocating the auditors to the departments?

2. The times for auditing each department have been estimated as follows:

Department	Time (weeks)
Accounting	3
Personnel	2
Sales	5
H/w production	3
S/w production	2

What is the quickest time by which the entire audit of all departments can be achieved, and how should the two auditors be allocated to the departments?

3. One outcome from the audit was the monthly costs of each department. These have been classified as direct costs (e.g. salaries and materials) and indirect costs (e.g. charges for the services received from the other departments), and were found to be:

Department	Direct costs	Indirect costs (%)		
		Accounting	Personnel	Sales
Accounting	600	25	15	15
Personnel	1,100	35	20	25
Sales	600	10	10	35
Hardware production	2,100	15	25	15
Software production	1,500	15	30	10

Formulate and solve the equations for calculating the total monthly operating costs of the Accounting, Personnel and Sales departments. Hence find the total monthly operating costs of the hardware and software production departments.

Case A3 | Joowel's Store

Joowel's Store Ltd are a high-street store selling a variety of accessories (e.g. rings, bags). As part of your studies you have been asked by Mrs Joowel, the store manager/owner, to provide information on the sales lines to help her make decisions on ordering, stocks and pricing. Mrs Joowel suggests that you survey the till roll for a typical Saturday, which has a record of sales by item value (£s) as follows:

5.25	69.99	11.99	13.88
9.98	21.25	29.97	7.75
21.50	9.97	34.95	13.89
74.96	4.65	34.98	49.99
23.85	4.50	7.19	14.99
11.97	9.97	7.44	61.98
5.99	19.97	12.49	4.35
1.23	68.99	12.95	8.12
0.97	4.35	7.49	8.90
5.69	0.49	13.39	41.69
10.48	11.99	35.95	4.44
22.95	24.99	4.44	9.85
1.29	6.50	8.99	18.63
1.69	11.99	16.30	67.29
2.19	24.99	64.88	6.99
2.77	3.99	3.97	3.57

Provide Mrs Joowel with appropriate information from this set of data.

Models and analysis for business and management

We have seen in Part A how quantities are measured, and how we can observe, collect and represent data in Business and Management. Once we have collected a set of data pertinent to a particular issue, we may be able to see a pattern, which can then be used to provide further information for managers to help them manage more effectively. We live in an uncertain world, so we try to make sense of the world by developing models based on the real world, on past experiences, and on what we believe has happened or might happen in the future.

Sometimes we can construct models from sample data that we encountered in Chapter 4, and from these we can make inferences about the population from which the sample was drawn. For example, we can estimate the average weekly national sales of a product from samples taken from a number of stores. We might be able to see a cause-and-effect relationship between two or more observed variables – a pattern over time – and be able to model and analyse this relationship to support planning decisions.

This part of this book considers how we can use the basic concepts that we encountered in Part A to model and analyse observations to provide further information for managers to help them manage more effectively.

To reinforce your understanding of the notation and concepts, you should undertake the end-of-section exercises and attempt the mini-cases at the end of this part of the book.

Part contents

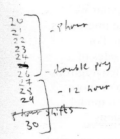

20
21
22   } – 8 hour
23
24
25   — double pay
26
27
28   } – 12 hour
29
30   } shifts

Chapter 6

Probability and statistical models

Introduction

In Chapters 4 and 5 we considered how data can be collected, presented and summarised. But how can we use these data to provide information? To make decisions, we need to identify the **outcomes** of **actions** and the **chances** of their happening. Any action has at least two outcomes (e.g. someone entering a store may or may not make a purchase, or a machine may or may not break down). Chances are usually expressed as percentages (e.g. a 30% chance of a breakdown today), but when they are represented in decimal form (e.g. 0.3) we talk about **probability**.

Chapter objectives

■ To introduce the concept of probability

■ To appreciate ways in which probability can be measured

■ To use established methods for calculating probability

Chapter contents

6.1 An introduction to probability

Probability was devised by mathematicians studying games of chance, but can provide information for managers about the likelihood of something happening or courses of action where there are risks and uncertainties.

The prerequisites of this section are:
■ Basic arithmetic (Section 1.4);
■ Fractions, ratios and percentages (Section 1.7);
■ Algorithms, variables and algebra (Section 2.1);
■ Subscripted variables and sigma notation (Section 2.4);
■ Set notation, set properties and Venn diagrams (Section 2.5);
■ Presenting and describing large datasets (Section 4.4).

The sample space and events

When we investigate what might happen, all outcomes must be identified. The set of all outcomes is called the **sample space**, which in some studies is finite whereas in others it is infinite. An **event** consists of one or more outcomes in a sample space, and it **occurs** when one of the outcomes of the sample space happens.

Example 6.1.1

Q A book company has an agreement with its customers to deliver the correct book within two working days of placing the order. Identify the possible outcomes, the sample space and the good and poor service events.

A Figure 6.1.1 illustrates the outcomes and the sample space. The good service event is shown lightly shaded, and the poor service event is darker.

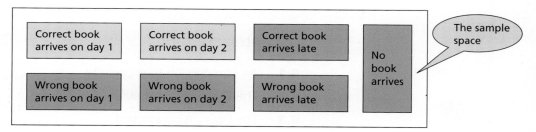

Figure 6.1.1 **Service-level outcomes for Example 6.1.1.**

Set notation for events

Instead of using a diagram for outcomes, sample space and events, we can use set notation (Example 6.1.2).

50

Example 6.1.2

Q Use set notation to represent the outcomes, sample space and events in Example 6.1.1.

A Let us denote the outcomes as follows:

  O_1 (correct book arrives on day 1)

  O_2 (correct book arrives on day 2)

  O_3 (correct book arrives late)

  O_4 (wrong book arrives on day 1)

  O_5 (wrong book arrives on day 2)

  O_6 (wrong book arrives late)

  O_7 (no book arrives)

and denote the sample space by S. As the sample space is finite, we can use Roster notation:

  $$S = \{O_1, O_2, O_3, O_4, O_5, O_6, O_7\}$$

The outcomes are the elements of the sample space, and here the sample space is the universal set. Let the good service event be $E = \{O_1, O_2\}$ and the poor service event be its complement $\{O_3, O_4, O_5, O_6, O_7\}$ (Figure 6.1.2):

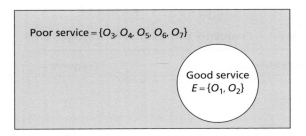

Poor service = $\{O_3, O_4, O_5, O_6, O_7\}$

Good service
$E = \{O_1, O_2\}$

Figure 6.1.2 **Good and poor service outcomes.**

Measuring probability

There are two interpretations of probability: **objective** and **subjective**.

In the **objective** interpretation we calculate probability from large samples, random trials or reasoned arguments. If we use reasoned arguments and what we already know how to estimate the chance of an event occurring, this is called 'a priori' probability. For example, with a 'fair' coin, we can reasonably expect the chances of getting a head or a tail are the same (i.e. a 50% chance), so we say that the 'a priori' probability of getting a head is 0.5. If we use a survey to estimate the chance of an event occurring, this is called the **empirical** probability. For example, if out of 5,000 customers only 2,000 made a purchase last week (i.e. 40%), the empirical probability of a customer making a purchase last week was 0.4. Objective probabilities are based on the relative frequency of an event occurring.

In the **subjective** interpretation we rely on personal opinion to estimate the chance of an event occurring. These estimates differ from person to person. For example, the owner of a new business might think the probability of making a profit in the first year of trading is 0.3, whereas his bank manager might think it is only 0.05. To elicit subjective probabilities, we can use **direct questioning** (e.g. by asking a sales representative 'What is the probability of making 100 sales this year?') or **indirect methods** (e.g. by asking 'Would you bet £100, £200 or £300 on making 100 sales this year?'). If the response was £200 we could infer that the probability is 200/600 = 0.333 (to 3 d.p.).

Probability as relative frequency

In Section 4.4, we represented data by a frequency distribution (i.e. table of observed events and their frequencies), which can be used to calculate **relative frequency** (i.e. the observed frequency of the event divided by the total frequency of all the events). This gives us only an estimate of probability because we usually only collect a sample (Example 6.1.3).

Probability notation

If we let P denote probability and E an event, then we denote the probability of E occurring by:

$$P(E) = \text{the probability that event } E \text{ occurs} \qquad (6.1.1)$$

Example | 6.1.3

Q The frequency distribution for a store's monthly sales of freezers over 5 years is shown in Table 6.1.1. Find the empirical probability of each event and the probability of selling three freezers each month.

Table 6.1.1 **Frequency distribution for Example 6.1.3.**

Monthly sales	Frequency
0	7
1	9
2	12
3	10
4	8
5	6
6	5
7	3
8 or more	0

A Define events as the number of freezers sold each month, and calculate the proportion of times we have observed each event (i.e. the relative frequency) (Table 6.1.2).

Table 6.1.2 **Probabilities of monthly sales for Example 6.1.3.**

Event	Frequency	Relative frequency	Probability
0	7	7/60 = 0.11667	0.11667
1	9	9/60 = 0.15000	0.15000
2	12	12/60 = 0.20000	0.20000
3	10	10/60 = 0.16667	0.16667
4	8	8/60 = 0.13333	0.13333
5	6	6/60 = 0.10000	0.10000
6	5	5/60 = 0.08333	0.08333
7	3	3/60 = 0.05000	0.05000
Total =	60	60/60	1

So the probability of selling three freezers each month, calculated from the relative frequency, is 0.16667.

Long-run relative frequency

Strictly speaking, we should define probability as relative frequency over a long period of time. In Example 6.1.3, we could improve our estimates by taking more samples over more years.

The properties of probability

We can identify the properties of probability by considering Table 6.1.2 and the definition of probability:

- the probability of any event occurring is a number between 0 and 1;
- if an event has a probability of 0, it will never occur;
- if an event has a probability of 1, it is certain to occur;
- the sum or total of the probabilities of all outcomes occurring is 1.

Types of event

Some events cannot occur if another has occurred. If you toss a coin and it comes down heads, it cannot show a tail at the same time. We call this a **mutually exclusive** event. Other events may be **non-mutually exclusive**. The selection of an ace or a heart from a pack of cards is not mutually exclusive. Although there is only one ace of hearts, there are 4 aces and 13 hearts.

Some events occur independently of others. The probability of winning on the National Lottery is not affected by the probability of it raining on the day the lottery is drawn. We call these **independent events**. However, some events are affected by or are conditional on other events. The probability of winning on the lottery is affected by the probability of buying a lottery ticket. We call these **dependent events**, and they have **conditional probabilities**.

How we calculate the probabilities depends on whether the events are mutually exclusive, independent or dependent.

Independent events

Independent events have no relationship between their probabilities. The probability of any two independent events occurring at the same time is smaller than the probability of each event occurring alone. The chances of winning both the lottery and the pools at the same time are less than the chances of winning either the lottery or the pools.

Relative frequency measures probability by counting the number of times an event occurs. The number of times two events can occur is the product of the number of times each event occurs. For any two independent events, say E_1 and E_2, we have:

$$P(E_1 \text{ and } E_2) = P(E_1) * P(E_2) \tag{6.1.2}$$

If the probability of winning any prize on the lottery is 0.002 and any win on the pools is 0.03, the probability of winning both at the same time is $0.002 * 0.03 = 0.0006$.

We can make similar statements about any number n of independent events E_1, E_2, E_3, ..., E_n:

$$P(E_1 \text{ and } E_2 \text{ and } \cdots E_n) = P(E_1) * P(E_2) * \cdots * P(E_n) \tag{6.1.3}$$

For example, the probability of winning four competitions is the product of the probability of a win in each.

Mutually exclusive events

When two events are mutually exclusive, the probability of one **or** the other occurring is higher than the probability of either occurring. We can show this using Venn diagrams for events E_1 and E_2 (Figure 6.1.3).

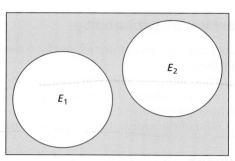

Figure 6.1.3 **Two mutually exclusive events.**

To find the probability of either event E_1 or event E_2 occurring, we consider the probabilities of outcomes in both sets (i.e. the probability of their union):

$$P(E_1 \text{ or } E_2) = P(E_1 \cup E_2) \tag{6.1.4}$$

We can use equation (2.5.6) to count the probability of both sets:

$$P(E_1 \text{ or } E_2) = P(E_1 \cup E_2) = P(E_1) + P(E_2) - P(E_1 \cap E_2) \tag{6.1.5}$$

Both events are mutually exclusive (i.e. disjoint because they do not intersect), so we know that $P(E_1 \cap E_2) = \varnothing$ (i.e. the empty set) and equation (6.1.4) gives:

$$P(E_1 \text{ or } E_2) = P(E_1) + P(E_2) \tag{6.1.6}$$

As the probability of getting a head when tossing a coin is 0.5 and that of getting a tail is also 0.5, the probability of getting either is $0.5 + 0.5 = 1$.

We can make similar statements about any number n of independent events E_1, $E_2, E_3, ..., E_n$:

$$P(E_1 \text{ or } E_2 \text{ or } E_3 \text{ or } \cdots E_n) = P(E_1) + P(E_2) + P(E_3) + \cdots + P(E_n) \tag{6.1.7}$$

When throwing dice, the probability of getting a 1 or 2 is $\dfrac{1}{6} + \dfrac{1}{6} = \dfrac{2}{6} = \dfrac{1}{3} = 0.333$ (to 3 d.p.).

Non-mutually exclusive independent events

Some events might not be mutually exclusive. Either event E_1 **or** event E_2 might occur **or both** might occur. Be careful not to double-count, because the probability of E_1 occurring includes the probability of both E_1 and E_2 occurring; likewise for E_2. The Venn diagram (Figure 6.1.4) shows two non-mutually exclusive events.

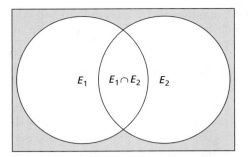

Figure 6.1.4 **Two non-mutually exclusive events.**

We count the probability of both events using equation (6.1.5):

$$P(E_1 \text{ or } E_2) = P(E_1 \cup E_2) = P(E_1) + P(E_2) - P(E_1 \cap E_2) \qquad (6.1.5)$$

From Figure 6.1.5 we see that $P(E_1 \cap E_2)$ is not empty, and we have:

$$P(E_1 \cap E_2) = P(E_1 \text{ and } E_2) \qquad (6.1.8)$$

Using equation (6.1.2), we write equation (6.1.8) as:

$$P(E_1 \cap E_2) = P(E_1 \text{ and } E_2) = P(E_1) * P(E_2) \qquad (6.1.9)$$

Substituting equation (6.1.9) into equation (6.1.5) gives:

$$P(E_1 \text{ or } E_2) = P(E_1) + P(E_2) - P(E_1) * P(E_2) \qquad (6.1.10)$$

The probability of picking a heart or an ace from a pack of cards is:

$$P(\text{heart or ace}) = P(\text{heart}) + P(\text{ace}) - P(\text{heart}) * P(\text{ace})$$

$$= \frac{13}{52} + \frac{4}{52} - \frac{13}{52} * \frac{4}{52} = 0.3077$$

Conditional probabilities

For any two events, we define the conditional probabilities:

$$P(E_1 | E_2) = \text{probability of event } E_1 \text{ occurring given that event } E_2 \\ \text{has occurred} \qquad (6.1.11)$$

$$P(E_1 | \overline{E_2}) = \text{probability of event } E_1 \text{ occurring given that event } E_2 \\ \text{has not occurred} \qquad (6.1.12)$$

Dependent events

Two events are said to be dependent if the occurrence or non-occurrence of one event changes the probability of occurrence of another event:

$$P(E_1) \neq P(E_1 | E_2) \neq P(E_1 | \overline{E_2}) \qquad (6.1.13)$$

$$P(E_2) \neq P(E_2 | E_1) \neq P(E_2 | \overline{E_1}) \qquad (6.1.14)$$

We can extend equation (6.1.2) to apply to two dependent events, which have conditional probabilities, by replacing one of the independent probabilities by the appropriate dependent probability:

$$P(E_1 \text{ and } E_2) = P(E_1) * P(E_2 | E_1) \qquad (6.1.15)$$

Equation (6.1.15) says that the probability of both dependent events occurring is the probability of one event occurring multiplied by the conditional probability of the other event occurring. If the probability that a person enters a shop is 0.4 and that a person in the shop makes a purchase is 0.3, the probability of the same person making a purchase in the shop is $0.4 * 0.3 = 0.12$.

Bayes' theorem

It does not matter how we label events. We could have written equation (6.1.15) as:

$$P(E_2 \text{ and } E_1) = P(E_2) * P(E_1 | E_2) \qquad (6.1.16)$$

As $P(E_1 \text{ and } E_2) = P(E_2 \text{ and } E_1)$ mean the same thing, the right-hand sides of equations (6.1.15) and (6.1.16) are equal:

$$P(E_1) * P(E_2 | E_1) = P(E_2) * P(E_1 | E_2) \qquad (6.1.17)$$

If we divide both sides of equation (6.1.17) by $P(E_2)$ we get:

$$P(E_1 | E_2) = \frac{P(E_1) * P(E_2 | E_1)}{P(E_2)} \qquad (6.1.18)$$

Equation (6.1.18) is known as **Bayes' theorem** and is used to calculate unknown conditional probabilities from known conditional probabilities.

Example 6.1.4

Q Two machines R1 and R2 insert and solder components on circuit boards. Machine R1 handles 35% of the components and has a 20% failure rate, while machine R2 handles 65% of the components with a 10% failure rate. If both machines fail, no circuit board is produced. What is the probability that a circuit board is faulty, and what is the probability that machine R1 caused a faulty circuit board?

A Let E_1 be the event that machine R1 inserted and soldered a component, E_2 the same event for machine R2, and E_3 the event that the circuit board is faulty. We know the probabilities:

$$P(E_1) = 0.35$$

$$P(E_2) = 0.65$$

$$P(E_3 | E_1) = 0.2$$

$$P(E_3 | E_2) = 0.1$$

To find the probability that a circuit board is faulty, we calculate the probability of machine R1 failing and a faulty board being produced using equation (6.1.15):

$$P(E_1 \text{ and } E_3) = P(E_1) * P(E_3 | E_1) = 0.35 * 0.2 = 0.07 \qquad (6.1.19)$$

The probability of machine R2 failing and a faulty board being produced using equation (6.1.15) is:

$$P(E_2 \text{ and } E_3) = P(E_2) * P(E_3 | E_2) = 0.65 * 0.1 = 0.065 \qquad (6.1.20)$$

As these are mutually exclusive events, we calculate the probability of a faulty board using equation (6.1.6):

$$P(E_3) = 0.07 + 0.065 = 0.135 \qquad (6.1.21)$$

Therefore the probability of a circuit board being faulty is 0.135.

The probability that a faulty circuit board was caused by machine R1 is $P(E_1 | E_3)$ and can be found by applying Bayes' theorem using equation (6.1.18):

$$P(E_1 | E_3) = \frac{0.35 * 0.2}{0.135} = 0.519 \qquad (6.1.22)$$

Probability distributions

In Section 4.4 we used a histogram to represent a frequency distribution. If we place probability, instead of relative frequency, on the vertical axis, we construct a **probability distribution**. Figure 6.1.5 shows a probability distribution for the relative frequencies calculated in Example 6.1.3.

As probability distributions are similar to the histograms in Section 4.4, we describe them in the same way. The probability distribution in Figure 6.1.5 is skewed to the right. Besides being able to qualitatively describe the shape of probability distributions, we can calculate their mean, variance and standard deviation as we did in Sections 5.1 and 5.3.

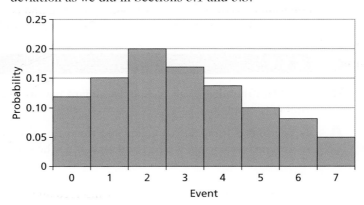

Figure 6.1.5 **A probability distribution for Example 6.1.3.**

The mean, variance and standard deviation of a distribution

In Section 5.1 we calculated the group mean (equation 5.1.4) by summing the mid-point of each class multiplied by its frequency and then divided by the total frequency. We apply the same approach to calculate the mean of a probability distribution. Instead of the mid-point of a class we have an event E, instead of frequency we have probability $P(E)$, and we sum over all the events (n):

$$\text{Mean of a probability distribution} = \frac{\sum_{E=1}^{n} E * P(E)}{\sum_{E=1}^{n} P(E)} \qquad (6.1.23)$$

As the total probability is 1 (i.e. $\sum_{E=1}^{n} P(E) = 1$), equation (6.1.23) becomes:

$$\text{Mean of a probability distribution} = \sum_{E=1}^{n} E * P(E) \qquad (6.1.24)$$

133

In Section 5.3 we calculated group variance (equation 5.3.9), and again we replace the mid-point of each class by E and the frequency by corresponding probability $P(E)$ to calculate the variance of a probability distribution:

$$\text{Variance of a probability distribution} = \frac{\sum_{E=1}^{n} P(E) * (\text{mean} - E)^2}{\sum_{E=1}^{n} P(E)} \qquad (6.1.25)$$

Again, as total probability is 1 (i.e. $\sum_{E=1}^{n} P(E) = 1$), equation (6.1.25) becomes:

$$\text{Variance of a probability distribution} = \sum_{E=1}^{n} P(E) * (\text{mean} - E)^2 \qquad (6.1.26)$$

133

In Section 5.3 we saw that standard deviation is simply the square root of the variance:

$$\text{Standard deviation of a probability distribution} = \sqrt{\sum_{E=1}^{n} P(E) * (\text{mean} - E)^2}$$

$$(6.1.27)$$

Example 6.1.5

Q Calculate the mean, variance and standard deviation of the probability distribution of Example 6.1.3.

 6.2

A In Sections 5.1 and 5.3 we calculated the mean, variance and standard deviation of grouped data using a table, and we can do the same here (Table 6.1.3):

Table 6.1.3 **Calculations for mean and variance for Example 6.1.3.**

E	Frequency	$P(E)$	$E * P(E)$	$(\text{Mean} - E)^2$	$P(E) * (\text{Mean} - E)^2$
0	7	7/60 = 0.1167	0 * 0.1167 = 0.0000	8.6044	1.0039
1	9	9/60 = 0.1500	1 * 0.1500 = 0.1500	3.7378	0.5607
2	12	12/60 = 0.2000	2 * 0.2000 = 0.4000	0.8711	0.1742
3	10	10/60 = 0.1667	3 * 0.1667 = 0.5000	0.0044	0.0007
4	8	8/60 = 0.1333	4 * 0.1333 = 0.5333	1.1378	0.1517
5	6	6/60 = 0.1000	5 * 0.1000 = 0.5000	4.2711	0.4271
6	5	5/60 = 0.0833	6 * 0.0833 = 0.5000	9.4044	0.7837
7	3	3/60 = 0.0500	7 * 0.0500 = 0.3500	16.538	0.8269
Total =	60	60/60 = 1	2.9333		3.9289

Applying equations (6.124), (6.126) and (6.127) gives:

Mean of probability distribution = 2.9333

Variance of probability distribution = 3.9289

Standard deviation of probability distribution = $\sqrt{3.9289}$ = 1.9821.

Discrete and continuous probability distributions

As with quantitative data (Section 4.1), we can classify events in two categories – discrete (e.g. the number of cans sold) and continuous (e.g. the time between customers entering a store). In Example 6.1.3 we had discrete data and obtained a **discrete probability distribution**, which consisted of rectangles. For continuous data (e.g. fuel consumption, time, distance) we construct **continuous probability distributions**, which have smooth curves (Figure 6.1.6).

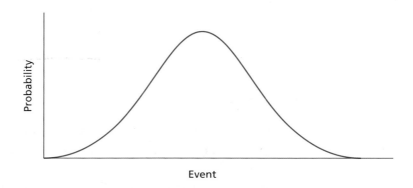

Figure 6.1.6 **A continuous probability distribution.**

Random variables

In Section 4.1 we considered nominal data (e.g. types of take-away meal), ordinal data (e.g. positions of companies in the FTSE), and cardinal data (e.g. the number of employees in a company). Events can be classified in the same way. We label events numerically even though they may not be quantitative (i.e. cardinal). In Section 2.1 we used variables to generalise from specific numbers, and we use **random variables** to generalise from specific random event numbers.

We use an upper-case X to denote a random variable and a lower-case x to denote a specific value. We write the probability of X being a particular number (i.e. x) as $P(X = x)$. We write the probability of X being greater than a specific number as $P(X > x)$, and we write the probability of X being between two particular numbers, say x_1 and x_2, as $P(x_1 < X < x_2)$: see Example 6.1.6.

Example	6.1.6

Q Use the probability distribution in Example 6.1.3 to calculate (a) $P(X = 1)$, (b) $P(X > 2)$ and (c) $P(2 < X < 5)$ and interpret their meanings.

A (a) From Table 6.1.2, we see that $P(X = 1) = 0.15$ (the probability of selling one freezer each month).

(b) To calculate $P(X > 2)$, we consider the probabilities of selling 3, 4, 5, 6 and 7 freezers each month. As these are mutually exclusive events, from equation (6.1.7) we have:

$$P(X > 2) = P(X = 3) + P(X = 4) + P(X = 5) + P(X = 6) + P(X = 7)$$
$$= 0.16667 + 0.13333 + 0.1 + 0.08333 + 0.05$$
$$= 0.53333$$

(the probability of selling more than two freezers per month).

(c) To calculate $P(2 < X < 5)$, we again use equation (6.1.7):

$$P(2 < X < 5) = P(X = 3) + P(X = 4)$$
$$= 0.16667 + 0.13333$$
$$= 0.3$$

(the probability of selling more than two but fewer than five freezers each month).

Mean, variance and standard deviation of discrete random variables

We calculate the mean, variance and standard deviation of random variables using equations (6.1.24), (6.1.26) and (6.1.27) respectively, and write these as:

$$\text{Mean of a random variable} = (\mu) = \sum_{x=1}^{n} x * P(X = x) \qquad (6.1.28)$$

$$\text{Variance of a random variable} = (\sigma^2) = \sum_{x=1}^{n} P(X = x) * (\mu - x)^2 \qquad (6.1.29)$$

$$\text{Standard deviation of a random variable} = (\sigma) = \sqrt{\sum_{x=1}^{n} P(E) * (\mu - E)^2} \qquad (6.1.30)$$

The area under a probability distribution

As the sum of probabilities is 1, the area under a probability distribution also is 1. Another way to find the probability of X being greater than a particular value (i.e. $P(X > x)$) is to consider the area under the right-hand tail of a probability distribution (Figure 6.1.7). To find the probability of X being less than or equal to a particular value (i.e. $P(X \leqslant x)$), we consider the area under the left-hand tail of a probability distribution, calculated by $1 - P(X > x)$. In Example 6.1.6(b), $P(X > 2) = 0.53333$, so $P(X \leqslant 2) = 1 - 0.53333 = 0.46667$ (Figure 6.1.7).

Cumulative probability distributions

In Section 4.4 we considered charts of cumulative frequency (i.e. ogives). To construct cumulative probability distributions, we similarly calculate a table of cumulative relative frequency and draw a chart (Table 6.1.4 and Figure 6.1.8). Cumulative probability distributions show the probabilities of X being less than or equal to a particular value (i.e. $P(X \leqslant x)$).

We can also use cumulative probability distributions to calculate probabilities (Example 6.1.7).

111

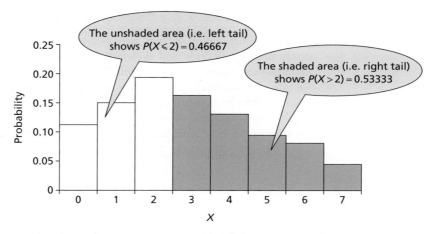

Figure 6.1.7 **The area under a probability distribution for Example 6.1.3.**

Table 6.1.4 **Cumulative probabilities for Example 6.1.3.**

Event	Probability	Cumulative probability
0	0.11667	0.11667
1	0.15000	0.26667
2	0.20000	0.46667
3	0.16667	0.63334
4	0.13333	0.76667
5	0.10000	0.86667
6	0.08333	0.95000
7	0.05000	1.00000

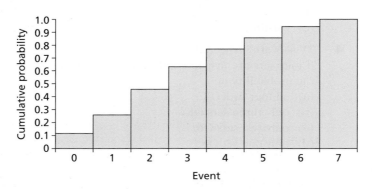

Figure 6.1.8 **A cumulative probability distribution for Example 6.1.3.**

Example 6.1.7

Q Use the cumulative probabilities in Table 6.1.3 to calculate the probabilities required in Example 6.1.6:

A (a) $P(X = 1) = P(X \leqslant 1) - P(X \leqslant 0) = 0.26667 - 0.11667 = 0.15$

(b) For $P(X > 2) = 1 - P(X \leqslant) = 1 - 0.46667 = 0.53333$

(c) For $P(2 < X < 5) = P(X \leqslant 4) - P(X \leqslant 2) = 0.766667 - 0.46667 = 0.3$.

Theoretical probability distributions

Over the years, many surveys have been undertaken, their empirical frequency distributions tabulated and their histograms and probability distributions drawn and analysed. Some empirical probability distributions have similar patterns, and we talk of **theoretical probability distributions**. They were originally studied to calculate the probabilities of winning and losing in games of chance (e.g. tossing coins, throwing dice, playing cards). They can also be used to estimate the probabilities of events occurring in business and management.

To obtain probabilities from theoretical probability distributions, we use:
- formulae;
- an inbuilt function of a spreadsheet or calculator;
- ready-made tables from these formulae (see the tables and Further Reading at the end of this book).

We consider all three in the remaining sections of this chapter.

Exercises 6.1

1 Cleanbryte manufacture washing powders and liquids for washing machines and want to introduce a new product:
(a) Define the study and identify the relevant sample space.
(b) How would you measure the probability that the new product achieves 10% of the market?

2 Comment on the sample space for each of the following studies:
(a) the annual amount of oil-seed rape grown in Europe;
(b) the percentage by which the stock market can change;
(c) the number of years before retirement of the employees of a company.

3 Define the following events:
(a) having a surplus or deficit on the UK balance of trade;
(b) being a doctor and being ill;
(c) earning a large salary and paying a high rate of tax.

4 TV sets are inspected as they leave the production line and labelled 'OK' or 'fail'. If four sets are inspected, describe the sample space, identify the outcomes and the probability of:
(a) all four sets OK;
(b) only three sets OK;
(c) only two sets OK;
(d) only one set OK;
(e) all sets fail the inspection.

5 Mr Smith has applied for a job at Balance & Sons Ltd, who typically interview 98% of candidates and headhunt the other 2%. They appoint only 4% of candidates and typically interview only 1% of those who are rejected. What is the probability that Mr Smith will be appointed?

6 For Questions 1 and 3 of Exercises 4.4 and Question 5 of Exercises 5.1, construct empirical probability distributions and calculate their mean, variance and standard deviation.

7 Construct an empirical probability distribution for the salaries of employees in Question 3 of Exercises 5.3 and use it to estimate the probabilities of:
(a) an employee earning a salary in the range £14,000 to £16,999;
(b) an employee earning less than £20,000;
(c) an employee earning £35,000 or more;
(d) an employee earning between £20,000 and £35,000.

Show the areas under the probability distribution corresponding to each event.

8 Construct a cumulative empirical probability distribution for the salaries of employees in Question 3 of Exercises 5.3 and use this to estimate the probabilities of events (a) to (d) in Question 7 above.

6.2 The Binomial distribution

Some sample spaces have only two mutually exclusive outcomes, for instance tossing a 'fair' coin. We refer to these outcomes as **success** (e.g. a head) or **failure** (e.g. a tail). We encounter such outcomes in situations such as these:

- inspecting products for quality, where each faulty item is considered a success and each acceptable item a failure;
- meeting deadlines and service-level agreements where success is achieved if they are met;
- forecasting sales to customers entering a store, where success occurs if they make a purchase.

We call these situations a **trial**, and we can count the number of successes in a number of trials. The probabilities of 1, 2, 3, etc. successes occurring in a number of trials (e.g. 3 heads in 5 tosses of a coin) are found from the **Binomial distribution**.

The prerequisites of this section are:

- Presenting and describing large datasets (Section 4.4);
- Measures of location (Section 5.1);
- Measures of variation (Section 5.3);
- An introduction to probability (Section 6.1).

The probabilities of outcomes

We use the Binomial distribution in 'either/or' situations that have a fixed number of trials and for which the probability of success is known and constant. We know all probabilities sum to 1 so if we denote the probability of success by $P(s)$, the probability of failure by $P(f)$ then $P(s) + P(f) = 1$. If we know $P(s)$ we can calculate $P(f)$, because $P(f) = 1 - P(s)$, and so we only need to consider $P(s)$ and, instead of writing $P(s)$ we simply write P (Example 6.2.1).

Example 6.2.1

Q An Internet company has recorded 200,000 'hits' to its website, of which 40,000 resulted in an on-line purchase. What is the probability of a 'hit' leading to a sale?

A Either a hit leads to a sale (success) or it doesn't (failure). We can calculate the probability of success from relative frequency:

$$P = \frac{40,000}{200,000} = 0.2$$

In this case, the probability of a failure (i.e. no sale) is $1 - 0.2 = 0.8$.

The Binomial distribution

We denote the number of trials by n. The shape of the Binomial distribution varies with P and n. For small values of P, the distribution is skewed to the right.

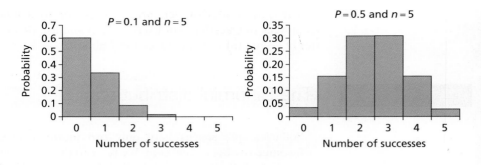

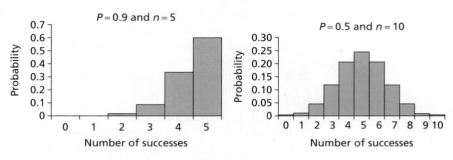

Figure 6.2.1 **Some Binomial distributions.**

Calculating Binomial probabilities

Let x denote the number of successes, and then the number of failures in n trials will be $(n - x)$. The probability of s successes in n trials can be calculated using equation (6.2.1). We define X as the number of successes x:

$$P(X = x) = P(x \text{ successes in } n \text{ trials}) = {}^nC_x * P^x * (1 - P)^{(n-x)} \qquad (6.2.1)$$

where ${}^nC_x = \dfrac{n!}{x! * (n - x)!}$ is the formula given in Section 2.6 for calculating the number of combinations of x out of n items.

If we put the combinations formula into equation (6.2.1), we have:

$$P(X = x) = P(x \text{ successes in } n \text{ trials}) = \frac{n! * P^x * (1 - P)^{(n-x)}}{n! * (n - x)!} \qquad (6.2.2)$$

The derivation of equations (6.2.1) and (6.2.2) can be found on the CD, and on the associated website **www.mcgraw-hill.co.uk/textbooks/dewhurst**.

Equations (6.2.1) and (6.2.2) are not easy to remember or use, and so tables of Binomial probabilities have been created. A typical table can be found at the end of this book and on the spreadsheet Binomial.xls on the enclosed CD. Most spreadsheets and some calculators have inbuilt functions for calculating equation (6.2.2).

Example 6.2.2

Q If the Internet company in Example 6.2.1 has 5 hits per day, calculate to 4 d.p. the probabilities of making: (a) no sales, (b) 1 sale, (c) 2 sales, (d) 3 sales, (e) 4 sales, and (f) 5 sales on any given day, and draw the probability distribution.

A We use the Binomial distribution to calculate these probabilities ($n = 5$) with a probability of success of

$$P = 0.2.$$

To apply equation (6.2.1), you need to remember that any number to power zero is 1 (Section 1.5), and that $0! = 1$ (Section 2.6):

(a) $P(X = 0) = \dfrac{5! * 0.2^0 * (1 - 0.2)^{(5-0)}}{0! * (5 - 0)!} = \dfrac{5 * 4 * 3 * 2 * 1 * 1 * 0.8^5}{1 * (5 * 4 * 3 * 2 * 1)} = 0.3277$

To use Binomial tables, look across row $n = 5$, $x = 0$ until you reach column $P = 0.2$, which shows $P(X = 0) = 0.3277$. Alternatively, use the inbuilt function available on a spreadsheet.

(b) $P(X = 1) = \dfrac{5! * 0.2^1 * (1 - 0.2)^{(5-1)}}{1! * (5 - 1)!} = \dfrac{5 * 4 * 3 * 2 * 1 * 0.2 * 0.8^4}{1 * (4 * 3 * 2 * 1)} = 0.4096$

Using Binomial tables look across row $n = 5$, $x = 1$ of the table until you reach $P = 0.2$, which shows $P(X = 1) = 0.4096$. Alternatively, use the inbuilt function available on a spreadsheet.

We obtain the remaining probabilities in a similar way, giving:

(c) $P(X = 2) = 0.2048$ (d) $P(X = 3) = 0.0512$
(e) $P(X = 4) = 0.0064$ (f) $P(X = 5) = 0.0003$

These probabilities are shown in Figure 6.2.2.

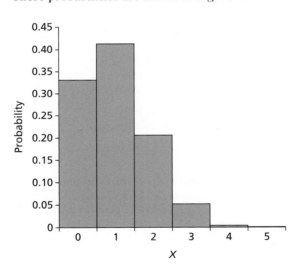

Figure 6.2.2 **The Binomial distribution for Example 6.2.2.**

Calculating probabilities of several events occurring

Sometimes, we want to find the probabilities of several events occurring. In Section 6.1 we did so by finding the appropriate area under the probability distribution (i.e. $P(X > x)$). In the Binomial distribution, outcomes and events are mutually exclusive, and so we can use equation (6.1.6) to sum the relevant individual probabilities (see Example 6.2.3).

Example   **6.2.3**

Q Using the data in Example 6.2.2, calculate the probabilities of: (a) making 2 or fewer sales per day; (b) making more than 2 sales per day; (c) making fewer than

2 sales per day; (d) making 2 or more sales per day; (e) making between 1 and 3 sales per day.

A As we know the probabilities from Example 6.2.2 we can apply equation (6.1.6) to sum the relevant probabilities:

(a) $P(2 \text{ or fewer sales per day}) = P(X \leqslant 2)$
$$= P(X = 0) + P(X = 1) + P(X = 2)$$
$$= 0.3277 + 0.4096 + 0.2048$$
$$= 0.9421$$

$P(X \leqslant 2) = 0.9421$ is the unshaded area in Figure 6.2.3.

(b) $P(\text{more than 2 sales per day}) = P(X > 2)$
$$= P(X = 3) + P(X = 4) + P(X = 5)$$
$$= 0.0512 + 0.0064 + 0.0003$$
$$= 0.0579$$

$P(X > 2) = 0.0579$ is the shaded area in Figure 6.2.3. We could have calculated $P(X > 2)$ from (a), because the sum of all probabilities (i.e. the total area under a probability distribution) is 1:

$$P(X > 2) = 1 - P(X \leqslant 2) = 1 - 0.9421 = 0.0579$$

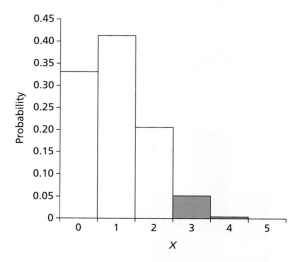

Figure 6.2.3 **$P(X \leqslant 2)$ and $P(X > 2)$ for Example 6.2.3.**

(c) $P(\text{fewer than 2 sales per day}) = P(X < 2)$
$$= P(X = 0) + P(X = 1)$$
$$= 0.3277 + 0.4096$$
$$= 0.7373$$

$P(X < 2) = 0.7373$ is the unshaded area in Figure 6.2.4.

(d) $P(2 \text{ or more sales per day}) = P(X \geqslant 2)$
$$= P(X = 2) + P(X = 3) + P(X = 4) + P(X = 5)$$
$$= 0.2048 + 0.0512 + 0.0064 + 0.0003$$
$$= 0.2627$$

$P(X \geqslant 2) = 0.2627$ is the shaded area in Figure 6.2.4. Again, we could have calculated $P(X \geqslant 2)$ from (c), because the sum of all probabilities is 1:

$$P(X \geqslant 2) = 1 - P(X < 2) = 1 - 0.7373 = 0.2627$$

(e) To calculate the probability of making between 1 and 3 sales per day we need to be careful. If we include 1 and 3 sales, we calculate $P(1 \leqslant X \leqslant 3)$ and:

$$P(1 \leqslant X \leqslant 3) = P(X = 1) + P(X = 2) + P(X = 3)$$
$$= 0.4096 + 0.2048 + 0.0512 = 0.6656$$

$P(1 \leqslant X \leqslant 3)$ is shaded in Figure 6.2.5.

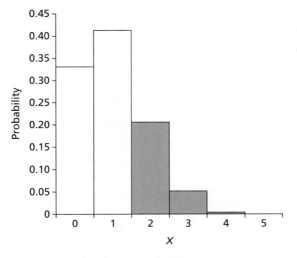

Figure 6.2.4 **$P(X < 2)$ and $P(X \geqslant 2)$ for Example 6.2.3.**

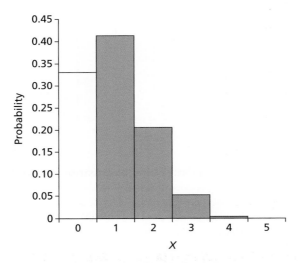

Figure 6.2.5 **$P(1 \leqslant X \leqslant 3)$ for Example 6.2.3.**

If we exclude 1 and 3 sales, we calculate $P(1 < X < 3)$ and $P(1 < X < 3) = P(X = 2) = 0.2048$.

Cumulative Binomial probabilities

In Section 6.1, we calculated cumulative probabilities and we can calculate cumulative Binomial probabilities, see Example 6.2.4.

Example 6.2.4

Q Calculate a table of cumulative probabilities and draw a cumulative probability distribution for the daily sales in Example 6.2.2. Use these cumulative probabilities to find the probabilities of: (a) making 2 or fewer sales per day; (b) making more than 2 sales per day; (c) making fewer than 2 sales per day; (d) making 2 or more sales per day; (e) making between 1 and 3 sales per day; (f) making exactly 2 sales per day.

A As we saw in Example 6.2.2, we can use equation (6.16) to sum Binomial probabilities (because the events are mutually exclusive). Table 6.2.1 shows the cumulative probabilities for Example 6.2.4, and Figure 6.2.6 shows the corresponding cumulative probability distribution.

Table 6.2.1 **Probabilities and cumulative probabilities for Example 6.2.4.**

x	Probability	Cumulative probability
0	0.3277	0.3277
1	0.4096	0.7373
2	0.2048	0.9421
3	0.0512	0.9933
4	0.0064	0.9997
5	0.0003	1.0000

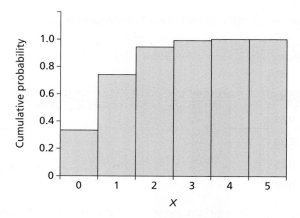

Figure 6.2.6 **The cumulative Binomial distribution for Example 6.2.4.**

(a) P(2 or fewer sales per day) = $P(X \leqslant 2)$ = 0.9421 from Table 6.2.1
(b) P(more than 2 sales per day) = $1 - P(X \leqslant 2) = 1 - 0.9421 = 0.0579$
(c) P(fewer than 2 sales per day) = $P(X \leqslant 1)$ = 0.7373 from Table 6.2.1
(d) P(2 or more sales per day) = $1 - P(X \leqslant 1) = 1 - 0.7373 = 0.2627$
(e) As we saw in Example 7.2.3, we need to be careful, and again we have two possibilities:

$$P(1 \leqslant X \leqslant 3) = P(X \leqslant 3) - P(X \leqslant 0) = 0.9933 - 0.3277 = 0.6656$$
$$\text{or } P(1 < X < 3) = P(X \leqslant 2) - P(X \leqslant 1) = 0.9241 - 0.7373 = 0.2048$$

(f) P(exactly 2 sales per day) = $P(1 < X < 3)$ as above.

Calculating probabilities from cumulative tables

In Examples 6.2.3 and 6.2.4 it was easy to calculate the probabilities because there were only five events. When we have many probabilities to calculate, we use ready-made formulae and cumulative tables (such a table can be found at the end of this book and on the spreadsheet Binomial.xls on the enclosed CD), or we can use the inbuilt function of a spreadsheet, see Example 6.2.6.

Example **6.2.6**

Q Following an advertising campaign, the Internet company in Example 6.2.1 now has 10 hits per day. What is the probability of making more than 7 sales per day?

A We know that $P(X > 7) = 1 - P(X \leqslant 7)$. From Binomial tables or using a spreadsheet with $x = 7$, $P = 0.2$ and $n = 10$, we find $P(X \leqslant 7) = 0.9999$. So $P(X > 7) = 1 - 0.9999 = 0.0001$ is the probability of making more than 7 sales per day.

The mean, variance and standard deviation of the Binomial distribution

We can calculate the mean, variance and standard deviation of the Binomial distribution using equations (6.1.28)–(6.1.30) (see Example 6.2.7). There are also specific formulae (see equations (6.2.3)–(6.2.5)) for the mean, variance and standard deviation of the Binomial distribution. The derivation of these can be found on the CD, and on the associated website **www.mcgraw-hill.co.uk/textbooks/dewhurst**.

Mean $(\mu) = n * P$	(6.2.3)

Variance $(\sigma^2) = n * P * (1 - P)$	(6.2.4)

Standard deviation $(\sigma) = \sqrt{n * P * (1 - P)}$	(6.2.5)

Example **6.2.7**

Q Calculate the mean and standard deviation of daily sales for the data in Example 6.2.2.

A To use equations (6.1.28)–(6.1.30), we lay the calculations out as a table (Table 6.2.2).

Table 6.2.2 **Calculations for mean and variance for Example 6.2.2.**

x	$P(X = x)$	$x * P(X = x)$	$P(X = x) * (\mu - x)^2$
0	0.3277	0.0000	0.3277
1	0.4096	0.4096	0.0000
2	0.2048	0.4096	0.2048
3	0.0512	0.1536	0.2048
4	0.0064	0.0256	0.0576
5	0.0003	0.0015	0.0048
Sum =		1	0.8

Using equations (6.1.28)–(6.1.30):

  Mean daily sales = 1

  Variance of daily sales = 0.8

  Standard deviation of daily sales = $\sqrt{0.8} = 0.894$

Alternatively, use equations (6.2.3)–(6.2.5):

  Mean daily sales = $5 * 0.2 = 1$

  Variance of daily sales = $5 * 0.2 * (1 - 0.2) = 0.8$

  Standard deviation of daily sales = $\sqrt{0.8} = 0.894$.

Using the Binomial distribution as a model

In Example 6.2.1 we empirically estimated the probability of success, and in Example 6.2.2 we used the Binomial distribution to calculate probabilities. We assumed that the Binomial distribution was a suitable model for the probability distribution of sales in the Internet company. We might want to see if this assumption holds. In Sections 5.1 and 5.3 we calculated the mean and variance (or standard deviation) of a sample, and we have equations (6.2.3)–(6.2.5) for the mean, variance and standard deviation of the Binomial distribution. By equating the mean of our sample to that of the Binomial distribution, we can calculate P for a particular number of trials. By comparing the standard deviation of the sample with that of the particular Binomial distribution, we can see whether the Binomial distribution can be used as a model of our sample. We could also calculate the Binomial probabilities of the model and compare them with the relative frequencies of the sample, as shown in Example 6.2.8.

| Example | **6.2.8** |

Q Use the Binomial distribution to model the monthly sales of freezers in Example 6.1.3.

A In Example 6.1.5 we calculated the mean of the distribution of monthly sales of freezers as 2.9333 for a sample size $n = 60$. So we want a Binomial distribution with a mean of 2.9333. Equation (6.2.3) gives:

$$\text{Mean} = n * P = 2.9333$$

The sample size $n = 60$ suggests $P = 2.9333/60 = 0.0489$.

Using Binomial tables, a spreadsheet, or equation (6.2.2), we calculate Binomial probabilities for each event for $P = 0.0489$ (Table 6.2.3).

Table 6.2.3 shows, for some events, that Binomial probabilities are different from empirical probabilities (e.g. the first event), whereas for others they are very similar (e.g. the second event) (see Figure 6.2.7).

Table 6.2.3 **Empirical and Binomial probabilities for Example 6.1.3.**

6.6

Event	Empirical probabilities	Binomial probabilities
0	0.1167	0.0494
1	0.1500	0.1523
2	0.2000	0.2311
3	0.1667	0.2297
4	0.1333	0.1683
5	0.1000	0.0969
6	0.0833	0.0457
7	0.0500	0.0181

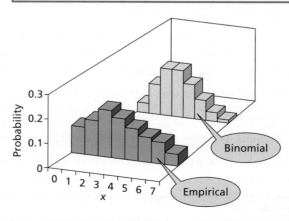

Figure 6.2.7 **Empirical and Binomial distributions for Example 6.1.3.**

We can quantify how closely the Binomial distribution matches the empirical distribution by comparing the variances of the two distributions and by considering the differences between the empirical and the Binomial probabilities (see Section 7.3).

Large numbers of trials and small probabilities

The main problem with using the Binomial distribution is that calculations become cumbersome when n becomes very large and P (success probability) is very small (Example 6.2.9). In such cases, we use other theoretical distributions.

Example 6.2.9

Q BRC, a roadside recovery service, guarantee to be at a breakdown within 2 hours, otherwise they refund £10. They have 2 million customers in any year and have been later than 2 hours only four times each year. What is the probability that BRC will spend their budget of £100 for refunds?

A We calculate the probability of a late recovery as relative frequency to be:

$$P = \frac{4}{2,000,000} = 0.000002$$

The budget is £100, and as each late recovery costs £10, the budget will cover only 10 late recoveries. To find the probability of experiencing 10 or more late recoveries out of 2 million, we calculate $P(X \geqslant 10)$ when $n = 2,000,000$. Such large values for n and small values for P do not appear in Binomial tables, and so we could use equation (6.2.2) to calculate $P(X = 0)$, $P(X = 1)$, $P(X = 2)$, etc. so that we could then calculate $P(X \geqslant 10) = 1 - P(X \leqslant 9)$. This calculation would have to be performed on a scientific calculator or a computer, and we might as well use the inbuilt function of a spreadsheet, which gives $P(X \geqslant 10) = 0.0081$.

 6.7

Exercises 6.2

1 A postal service finds that 5% of deliveries are late. An item later than 2 weeks is considered lost. Use the Binomial distribution to find the probability of an item being 1, 2, etc. days late. Construct a probability and cumulative probability distribution to calculate the probability of:
(a) an item being 3 days late
(b) an item being no more than 3 days late
(c) an item being more than 3 days late
(d) an item being 1 week late or more.

2 A product has a 10% chance of being defective. Use the Binomial distribution to find how many are defective from a sample of 20. What is the probability of finding 2 defective, and what is the mean number of defective products?

3 Twenty multiple-choice questions have 4 responses. A student who knows nothing about the topic selects random responses, while a knowledgeable student identifies the correct answer. Set the pass mark so that fewer than 1% of the former succeed. If students answer only half the questions correctly, how many will pass the test?

4 A rep. has a 50% chance of making a sale, gets a basic salary if 50% successful (i.e. makes one sale for every two customers), gets a bonus if 75% successful, and is sacked if less than 15% successful. Use the Binomial distribution to calculate the probability of:
(a) obtaining a bonus   (b) being sacked   (c) not being sacked.

5 A bus company has a fleet of 10-wheeled buses. Last week 50 buses were randomly sampled for tyre checks, and the numbers of illegal tyres on each bus were:

Number of failed tyres per bus	Frequency
0	22
1	16
2	5
3	4
4	3
5 or more	0

Construct an empirical probability distribution and find a suitable Binomial distribution to calculate the probability of:
(a) a bus having 2 failed tyres
(b) a bus having fewer than 2 failed tyres
(c) a bus having 3 or more failed tyres.

6.3 The Poisson distribution

The **Poisson distribution** occurs in business situations in which there are a few successes against a continuous background of failures or vice versa (i.e. few events in an interval), and has outcomes and single independent events that are mutually exclusive. Because of this, the probability of success P is very small in relation to the number of trials n, so we consider only the probability of successes. The following are examples of Poisson processes:
■ the number of industrial accidents per year;
■ the number of customers arriving at a checkout per minute;
■ the number of defects in a reel of cable;
■ the number of typographical errors in a book;
■ the number of broken threads in a roll of cloth;
■ the number of holes in a pipeline;
■ the number of damaged cans in a canning factory.

The prerequisites of this section are:
■ Powers, roots and logarithms (Section 1.5);
■ An introduction to probability (Section 6.1);
■ The Binomial distribution (Section 6.2).

Calculating Poisson probabilities

As with the Binomial distribution, we can use a formula to calculate the probability of x successes:

$$P(x \text{ success}) = \frac{e^{-\lambda} * \lambda^x}{x!} \qquad (6.3.1)$$

where e = the exponential constant (e = 2.718 to 3 d.p.)
λ = the mean number of successes
x = number of successes
$x!$ = factorial x

The derivation of this equation can be found on the CD and on the associated website **www.mcgraw-hill.co.uk/textbooks/dewhurst**.

As with Binomial probabilities, we use a formula (equation (6.3.1)), a table of Poisson probabilities (a typical table appears at the end of this book and in the file Poisson.xls on the accompanying CD), or an inbuilt spreadsheet function.

6.8

Equation (6.3.1) shows that the shape of the Poisson distribution is determined by a single parameter λ. When λ is small the distribution is skewed to the right, but as λ increases the distribution becomes more symmetrical (Figure 6.3.1).

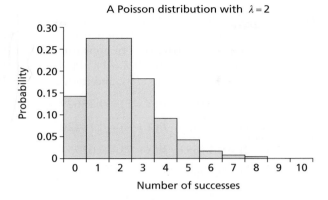

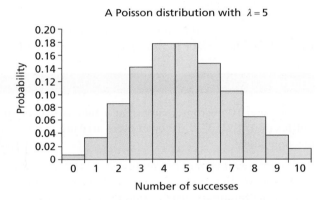

Figure 6.3.1 **Some typical Poisson distributions.**

The mean, variance and standard deviation

As in Section 6.2, we can calculate the mean, variance and standard deviation of the Poisson distribution using equations (6.1.29)–(6.1.30). However, there are also specific formulae. The mean and the variance of the Poisson distribution are calculated by equations (6.3.2) and (6.3.3); the standard deviation is the square root of the mean (equation 6.3.4):

$$\text{Mean } (\mu) = \lambda = n * P \tag{6.3.2}$$

$$\text{Variance } (\sigma^2) = \lambda = n * P \tag{6.3.3}$$

$$\text{Standard deviation } (\sigma) = \sqrt{n * P} = \sqrt{\lambda} \tag{6.3.4}$$

Applications of the Poisson distribution

The Poisson distribution is closely related to the Binomial distribution (Section 6.2), and can be used to approximate the Binomial distribution when $n > 20$ and when the mean is less than 5 (i.e. $n * P < 5$) (Example 6.3.1). Many business situations can be modelled by a Poisson process (Example 6.3.2).

Example 6.3.1

Q Use the Poisson distribution to calculate the probability that BRC (Example 6.2.9) will spend their refund budget of £100.

A First, we need to check that the conditions are satisfied. We have $n = 2,000,000$, and this is clearly larger than 20 whereas the mean $(\mu) = 4$ is less than 5. So we can use the Poisson distribution to approximate the Binomial distribution. We need to calculate $P(X = 0)$, $P(X = 1)$, $P(X = 2)$, ..., $P(X = 9)$ using equation (6.3.1), sum them to find $P(X < 9)$, and then calculate $P(X \geq 10) = 1 - P(X < 9)$:

$$P(X = 0) = 0.01832 \quad P(X = 5) = 0.15629$$

$$P(X = 1) = 0.07326 \quad P(X = 6) = 0.10420$$

$$P(X = 2) = 0.14653 \quad P(X = 7) = 0.05954$$

$$P(X = 3) = 0.19537 \quad P(X = 8) = 0.02977$$

$$P(X = 4) = 0.19537 \quad P(X = 9) = 0.01323$$

Summing gives $P(X \leq 9) = 0.99187$, so $P(X \geq 10) = 1 - P(X \leq 9) = 0.00813$. Alternatively, we could simply use the inbuilt function of a spreadsheet. This is the same as the answer in Example 6.2.9 if we round to 4 d.p.

Example 6.3.2

Q On average, 10 customers arrive at a takeaway every hour. What are the probabilities of 0, 1, 2, 3, ..., 10 customers arriving in any hour and no more than 5 in any one hour?

A Use the Poisson formula (equation 6.3.1), Poisson tables, or a spreadsheet with $\lambda = 10$ to calculate $P(X = 0)$, $P(X = 1)$, $P(X = 2)$, etc. (Table 6.3.1). Figure 6.3.2 shows the probability distribution for these events.

As with the Binomial distribution, we use equation (6.1.6) to sum probabilities because the outcomes and events are mutually exclusive. So the probability that no more than 5 customers arrive in any one hour is:

$$P(X \leq 5) = P(X = 0) + P(X = 1) + P(X = 2) + P(X = 3) + P(X = 4) + P(X = 5)$$
$$= 0.0000 + 0.0005 + 0.0023 + 0.0076 + 0.0189$$
$$= 0.0671.$$

Table 6.3.1 **Poisson probabilities for Example 6.3.2.**

x	Probability
0	0.0000
1	0.0005
2	0.0023
3	0.0076
4	0.0189
5	0.0378
6	0.0631
7	0.0901
8	0.1126
9	0.1251
10	0.1251

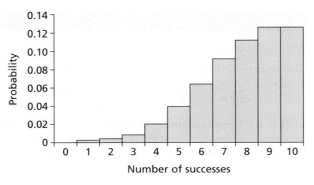

Figure 6.3.2 **Poisson probabilities for Example 6.3.2.**

Cumulative Poisson probabilities

6.8

Because n is very large, the sample space can contain an infinite number of events. To calculate probability $P(X \leqslant x)$ for any value (i.e. x), or the area under any part of the Poisson distribution, we could have an infinite number of additions to perform. As for the Binomial distribution, there are ready-made tables of cumulative probabilities (see the end of this book and the file Poisson.xls on the CD). Spreadsheets and some calculators have inbuilt functions for calculating cumulative Poisson probabilities. Example 6.3.3 illustrates how to use cumulative Poisson probabilities.

Example   **6.3.3**

Q   For the data in Example 6.3.2, find the probability (per hour) of: (a) 10 or fewer customers arriving; (b) more than 10 customers; (c) fewer than 10 customers; (d) 10 or more customers; (e) between 10 and 20 customers; (f) exactly 10 customers.

A   (a) $P(X \leqslant 10) = 0.5831$ from cumulative tables, spreadsheets or summing the probabilities in Table 6.3.1.

(b) $P(X > 10) = 1 - P(X \leqslant 10) = 1 - 0.5831 = 0.4149$.

(c) $P(X < 10) = P(X \leqslant 9) = 0.4579$ from cumulative tables, spreadsheets or summing the first 10 probabilities in Table 6.3.1.

(d) $P(X \geqslant 10) = 1 - 0.4579 = 0.5421$.

(e)   We consider two cases, depending upon how we interpret the word 'between':

$$P(10 \leqslant X \leqslant 20) = P(X \leqslant 20) - P(X \leqslant 9)$$

From cumulative tables or spreadsheets, we find $P(X \leqslant 20) = 0.9984$:

$$P(X \leqslant 20) - P(X \leqslant 9) = 0.9984 - 0.4579 = 0.5405$$

6.8

Or:

$$P(10 < X < 20) = P(X \leqslant 19) - P(X \leqslant 10)$$

From cumulative tables or spreadsheets, we find $P(X \leqslant 19) = 0.9965$:

$$P(X \leqslant 19) - P(X \leqslant 10) = 0.9965 - 0.5831 = 0.4134.$$

(f) $P(X = 10) = P(X \leqslant 10) - P(X \leqslant 9) = 0.5830 - 0.4579 = 0.1251$.

Using a Poisson distribution as a model

In Section 6.2 we used the Binomial distribution to model an empirical distribution. We can use the Poisson distribution in the same way and equate the mean of our empirical distribution to that of the Poisson distribution (Example 6.3.4).

Example 6.3.4

Q Use the Poisson distribution to model the data in Example 6.1.3.

A The mean of the empirical distribution of monthly sales of freezers is 2.933 (Example 6.1.5). Using this as the mean of a Poisson distribution, we can calculate Poisson probabilities (Table 6.3.2).

Table 6.3.2 **Empirical and Poisson probabilities for Example 6.3.4.**

Event	Empirical probabilities	Poisson probabilities
0	0.1167	0.0532
1	0.1500	0.1561
2	0.2000	0.2290
3	0.1667	0.2239
4	0.1333	0.1642
5	0.1000	0.0963
6	0.0833	0.0471
7	0.0500	0.0197

As we saw in Example 6.2.8, we can compare these distributions qualitatively (Figure 6.3.3).

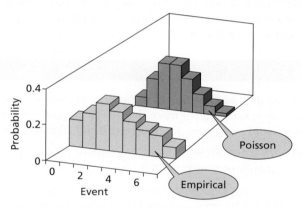

Figure 6.3.3 **Empirical and Poisson distribution for Example 6.3.3.**

If we compare Tables 6.2.3 and 6.3.2, we see that the probabilities in Table 6.3.2 are nearer to the empirical probabilities than those of Table 6.2.3. So the Poisson distribution is a better model of the empirical distribution than the Binomial distribution. We quantify such statements in Section 7.3.

Exercises 6.3

1 Rework Questions 1 and 2 of Exercises 6.2 using the Poisson distribution.

2 Model the breakdown distribution below as a Poisson process and compare the model with the empirical distribution.

No. of breakdowns	Frequency
0	100
1	70
2	45
3	20
4	10
5	5
6 or more	0

3 A furniture manufacturer buys screws in batches of 10,000, 1% of which are faulty. A delivery of screws is rejected if 7 or more faulty screws are found in a sample of 300. Use the Poisson distribution to calculate the probabilities of finding 0, 1, 2, 3, 4, 5, 6 and 7 faulty screws in a sample of 300. How many deliveries of such screws are considered unacceptable?

4 Patients arrive at an A&E department on average every 5 minutes. Use the Poisson distribution to calculate the probabilities of 0, 1, ..., 24 arriving per hour. What is the probability that no patients arrive and that more than 12 arrive per hour?

5 Rework Question 5 of Exercises 6.2 using a Poisson model.

6.4 | The Exponential distribution

In Section 6.3 we used the Poisson distribution to calculate the probability of $X = 0, 1, 2, ...$ events occurring over a specific period. The Poisson distribution is a discrete distribution because the events (e.g. customers arriving per hour) are whole numbers and therefore discrete quantities.

Instead of considering the number of customers arriving per hour, we could consider the time between arrivals. Theoretically, this can be between 0 (i.e. two customers arrive at the same time) and ∞. As time is a continuous variable in the range $[0, \infty]$, we have a continuous distribution. A frequency distribution for the times between arrivals in Example 6.3.2 is called an **Exponential distribution**, and is encountered in Operations Research when studying queues or reliability of systems (e.g. the time between break-downs).

The prerequisites of this section are:
- Powers, roots and logarithms (Section 1.5);
- An introduction to probability (Section 6.1);
- The Binomial distribution (Section 6.2);
- The Poisson distribution (Section 6.3).

Exponential and other continuous probability distributions

In continuous distributions, such as the Exponential distribution, the random variable X can be any value (unlike the Binomial and the Poisson distributions), so there are an infinite number of possible values of X. Therefore, the probability that the random variable X equals a specific value is zero (i.e. $P(X = x) = 0$, think about it!). So we view probability as the area under the distribution, and use cumulative probability tables. However, such tables could contain an infinite number of probabilities and are rarely found. As $P(X = x) = 0$, we consider only probabilities of the form $P(X < x)$, which for the Exponential function is given by:

$$P(X < x) = 1 - e^{-\lambda x} \qquad (6.4.1)$$

where x = the value of the continuous random variable for which we want to calculate probability;

e = the exponential constant ($e = 2.718$ to 3 d.p.);

λ = determines the shape of the exponential distribution (Figure 6.4.1).

As the total area under a probability distribution is 1, $P(X > x) = 1 - P(X < x)$, and so from equation (6.4.1) we have:

$$P(X > x) = e^{-\lambda x} \qquad (6.4.2)$$

Figure 6.4.1 shows two Exponential distributions and areas under the distribution. Spreadsheets and calculators have inbuilt functions for calculating equation (6.4.1).

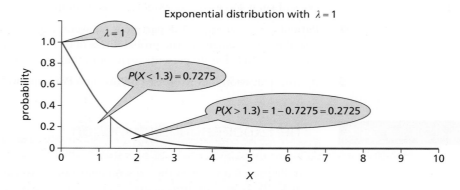

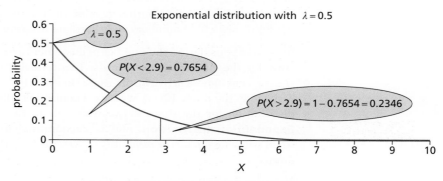

Figure 6.4.1 **Some Exponential distributions.**

The mean and standard deviation of the Exponential distribution

The Exponential distribution is inversely related to the Poisson distribution, so it is easy to find the mean and standard deviation. With the Poisson distribution, with a mean number of 10 customers arriving per hour, the mean interval must be 1/10 of an hour (i.e. every 6 minutes). So for the cumulative Poisson distribution given by equation (6.3.1) with a mean of λ, the corresponding Exponential distribution has a mean of $\mu = 1/\lambda$, and this is also the standard deviation, as shown by equations (6.4.3) and (6.4.4) (see Examples 6.4.1 and 6.4.2).

$$\text{Mean } (\mu) = \frac{1}{\lambda} \tag{6.4.3}$$

$$\text{Standard deviation } (\sigma) = \frac{1}{\lambda} \tag{6.4.4}$$

Example 6.4.1

Q For the data in Example 6.3.2, calculate the probability of inter-arrival times of: (a) less than 30 minutes; (b) more than 12 minutes; (c) between 12 and 30 minutes.

A As 10 customers arrived on average each hour, the mean of the Exponential distribution is $\mu = 1/10 = 0.1$ hours.

(a) An inter-arrival time of 30 minutes is 0.5 hours, and using equation (6.4.1):

$$P(X < 0.5) = 1 - e^{-0.1*0.5} = 1 - e^{-0.05} = 0.0488$$

(b) An inter-arrival time of 12 minutes is 0.02 hours, and using equation (6.4.2):

$$P(X > 0.2) = 1 - e^{-0.1*0.2} = 1 - e^{-0.02} = 0.020$$

(c) An inter-arrival time of between 12 and 30 minutes is:

$$P(0.2 < X < 0.5) = 0.0488 - 0.020 = 0.0288$$

Example **6.4.2**

Q In a continuous stream of products, the interval between defective products is recorded. On average, there is 1 in every 200. What is the probability that, a defective product having been found, the next 200 products are non-defective?

A The mean defective rate is $1/200 = 0.005$. To find the probability, we use equation (6.4.1):

$$P(X < 200) = 1 - e^{-0.005*200} = 1 - e^{-1} = 0.6321.$$

Exercises **6.4**

1 Calculate the mean inter-arrival time between patients arriving at the A&E department in Question 4 of Exercises 6.3. What is the probability that a patient arrives:
  (a) less than 30 seconds after the previous one?
  (b) more than 1 minute after the previous one?

2 The number of calls made to a call centre between 10 and 11 a.m. are:

No. of calls	Frequency
0	1
1	8
2	19
3	23
4	17
5	15
6	8
7	3
8	3
9	2
10	1

  (a) Calculate an empirical probability distribution.
  (b) Use the Poisson distribution to calculate the probabilities, and comment on its use as a model of the empirical distribution.
  (c) Calculate the probabilities that the time between calls is: (i) less than 1 minute; (ii) less than 2 minutes; (iii) greater than 2 minutes; (iv) between 1 and 2 minutes.

Many natural phenomena (e.g. the heights and weights of people, harvests, temperature and rainfall) and many business phenomena have a similar distribution, the **Normal distribution**. It is so called because it is what we 'normally' see in our daily lives. It is also called the **Gaussian distribution** after Gauss, who first described it.

The prerequisites of this section are:
- An introduction to probability (Section 6.1);
- The Binomial distribution (Section 6.2);
- The Poisson distribution (Section 6.3);
- The Exponential distribution (Section 6.4).

Calculating Normal probabilities

The Normal distribution is bell-shaped and symmetrical about its centre (the mean). The mean (μ) and standard deviation (σ) affect the shape of its distribution.

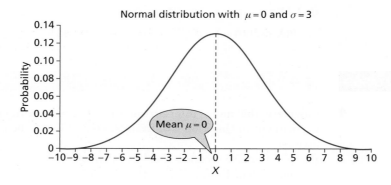

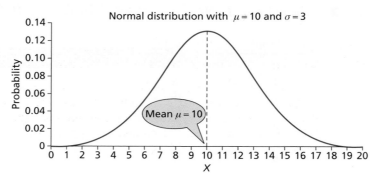

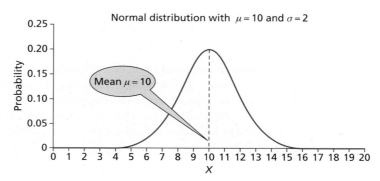

Figure 6.5.1 **Some Normal distributions.**

The mean positions the graph of the distribution along the horizontal axis, and the standard deviation stretches the graph away from the mean (Figure 6.5.1).

As with the Exponential distribution, there is an infinite number of Normal distributions (every pair of values for μ and σ yield a different distribution and graph), but all retain the characteristic bell shape around μ, and as the Normal distribution is continuous, $P(X = x) = 0$, we calculate only $P(X < x)$. Unlike the Exponential distribution, the formula for calculating the area under the Normal distribution is complex, and so we use tables, spreadsheets or calculators.

The Standard Normal distribution

Unlike the Exponential distribution, we can identify a **Standard Normal distribution** to which all Normal distributions are related. This has a mean $\mu = 0$ and a standard deviation $\sigma = 1$. All Normal distributions can be generated from this Standard Normal distribution through z, which relates the mean and standard deviation of any Normal distribution to the Standard Normal distribution by equation (6.5.1):

$$z = \frac{x - \mu}{\sigma} \tag{6.5.1}$$

The process of calculating z from x using equation (6.5.1) is called **standardisation**, and z is the **Standard Normal variable**. Spreadsheets and calculators have inbuilt functions for calculating equation (6.5.1).

Standard Normal tables

To find the areas under the Standard Normal distribution for $P(X < x)$, we use the Cumulative Standardised Normal distribution tables (see the end of this book and the file Normal.xls on the enclosed CD). However, other tables are available (see the note on the use of Standard Normal tables at the end of this section).

The use of the Standard Normal distribution to model sample data is illustrated in Examples 6.5.1–6.5.3.

Example 6.5.1

Q The weights of 2,500 cans of baked beans were measured to the nearest gram, and all were between 400 g and 500 g. The sample has a mean of 450 and a standard deviation of 18.38, and the distribution of weights is shown in Figure 6.5.2. What proportion of cans weigh under 430 g (i.e. what is the probability of a can weighing less than 430 g)?

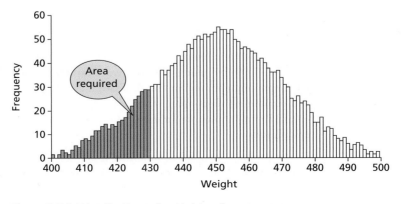

Figure 6.5.2 **Distribution of weights of cans.**

A   Once again, we look at the area under the left-hand tail of the distribution for weights below 430 g (i.e. $P(X < 430)$, shaded in Figure 6.5.2).

The histogram in Figure 6.5.2 looks similar to the Normal distribution, and so we use the Normal distribution as a model to calculate the probability of under-weight cans. But how do we find the appropriate parameters μ and σ for the model? By comparing our empirical distribution with the Standard Normal distribution, we see we can use equation (6.5.1) to find the appropriate values of the z variable. Figure 6.5.3 shows the empirical distribution and, superimposed, the Standard Normal distribution and the area under the curve we want to determine.

The Standard Normal distribution has a mean of zero that coincides with the empirical distribution mean of 450. We need to know what value of z lies underneath 430. Figure 6.5.3 shows this is near $z = -1$ (i.e. just below -1 standard deviations on the Standard Normal distribution). As we know the standard deviation of the empirical distribution is 18.38, we use equation (6.5.1) to calculate the corresponding standard deviation of the Standard Normal variable z:

$$z = \frac{430 - 450}{18.38} = \frac{-20}{18.38} = -1.09 \tag{6.5.2}$$

This is negative (i.e. $z < 0$) because 430 is less than 450 (the mean) and confirms we are looking at the left-hand tail in Figure 6.5.3.

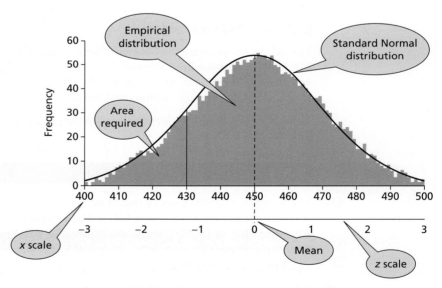

Figure 6.5.3 **The empirical and the Standard Normal distributions.**

We now find the area under the left-hand tail of the Standard Normal distribution for $z < -1.09$ by using cumulative Standard Normal distribution tables. By looking along the row for the first two digits (e.g. -1.0) and down the column for the remaining digits (e.g. 0.09), we find the area is $P(z < -1.09) = P(X < 430) = 0.1379$ (as shown in Table 6.5.1). Alternatively, we can use a spreadsheet or calculator.

So the probability of a can weighing less than 430 g is 0.1379 (i.e. 13.79% of cans weigh under 430 g) as shown in Figure 6.5.4.

Table 6.5.1 **Part of the cumulative Standard Normal distribution table.**

z	0.00	0.01	0.02	0.03	0.04	0.05	0.06	0.07	0.08	0.09
−1.7	0.0446	0.0436	0.0427	0.0418	0.0409	0.0401	0.0392	0.0384	0.0375	0.0367
−1.6	0.0548	0.0537	0.0526	0.0516	0.0505	0.0495	0.0485	0.0475	0.0465	0.0455
−1.5	0.0668	0.0655	0.0643	0.0630	0.0618	0.0606	0.0594	0.0582	0.0571	0.0559
−1.4	0.0808	0.0793	0.0778	0.0764	0.0749	0.0735	0.0721	0.0708	0.0694	0.0681
−1.3	0.0968	0.0951	0.0934	0.0918	0.0901	0.0885	0.0869	0.0853	0.0838	0.0823
−1.2	0.1151	0.1131	0.1112	0.1093	0.1075	0.1056	0.1038	0.1020	0.1003	0.0985
−1.1	0.1357	0.1335	0.1314	0.1292	0.1271	0.1251	0.1230	0.1210	0.1190	0.1170
−1.0	0.1587	0.1562	0.1539	0.1515	0.1492	0.1469	0.1446	0.1423	0.1401	0.1379
−0.9	0.1841	0.1814	0.1788	0.1762	0.1736	0.1711	0.1685	0.1660	0.1635	0.1611
−0.8	0.2119	0.2090	0.2061	0.2033	0.2005	0.1977	0.1949	0.1922	0.1894	0.1867
−0.7	0.2420	0.2389	0.2358	0.2327	0.2296	0.2266	0.2236	0.2206	0.2177	0.2148
−0.6	0.2743	0.2709	0.2676	0.2643	0.2611	0.2578	0.2546	0.2514	0.2483	0.2451
−0.5	0.3085	0.3050	0.3015	0.2981	0.2946	0.2912	0.2877	0.2843	0.2810	0.2776

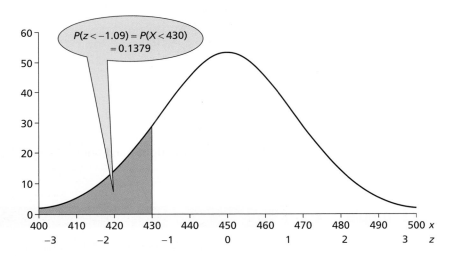

Figure 6.5.4 **Area under the left-hand tail.**

Example | **6.5.2**

Q What is the probability that a can in Example 6.5.1 weighs more than 480 g?

A Use equation (6.5.1) to calculate the corresponding standard deviation of the Standard Normal variable:

$$z = \frac{480 - 450}{18.38} = \frac{30}{18.38} = 1.63 \tag{6.5.3}$$

This time equation (6.5.3) is positive (i.e. $z > 0$) because 480 is greater than 450 (the mean) and confirms we are looking at the right-hand tail. Using cumulative Standard Normal tables, spreadsheets or calculator, we find:

$$P(X < 480) = P(z < 1.63) = 0.9484$$

However, we require $P(X > 480) = P(z > 1.63)$. As the area under the entire distribution is 1, we calculate:

$$P(X > 480) = P(z > 1.63)$$
$$= 1 - P(X < 480)$$
$$= 1 - P(z < 1.63)$$
$$= 1 - 0.9484$$
$$= 0.0516$$

So the probability of a can exceeding 480 g is 0.0516 (i.e. 5.16% of cans weigh over 480 g) as shown in Figure 6.5.5.

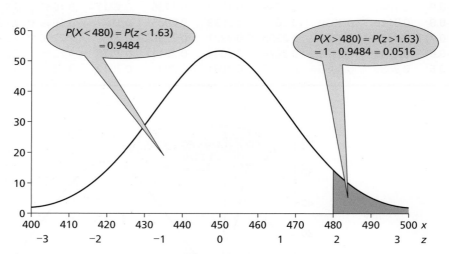

Figure 6.5.5 **Area under the right-hand tail of the distribution.**

| Example | **6.5.3** |

Q What proportions of cans in Example 6.5.1 weigh between 430 g and 480 g?

A We need to find the area shown in Figure 6.5.6. We know the two appropriate z values (i.e. $z = -1.09$ for $x = 430$ and $z = 1.63$ for $x = 480$) and the corresponding cumulative areas under the Standard Normal distribution (0.1379 and 0.9484, respectively). We subtract them to find the area between them (i.e. 0.9484 – 0.1379 = 0.8105) (Figure 6.5.6).

So $P(430 < x < 480) = P(-1.09 < z < 1.63) = 0.8105$ is the probability that cans weigh between 430 g and 480 g (i.e. 80.05% of cans weigh between 430 g and 480 g).

A note on the use of Standard Normal tables

(This can be skipped if you use only cumulative Standard Normal tables.)

As the Normal distribution is symmetrical about the mean, the area under the distribution each side of the mean is the same (i.e. 0.5). Because of this, some Standard Normal tables give the area under only one side of the distribution (see the file Normal.xls on the CD for such a table). Let us use such a Standard Normal table to rework Example 6.5.3.

To find the area between $z = -1.09$ and the mean ($z = 0$), we find the area corresponding to $P(z < -1.09)$ by looking up the table value for 1.09 (i.e. 0.1379) and

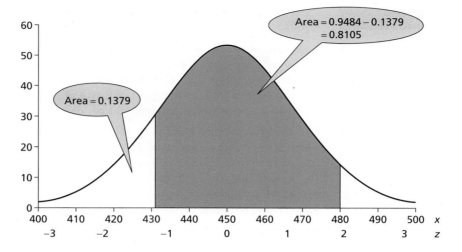

Figure 6.5.6 **Area between two values.**

subtract it from 0.5 (i.e. $0.5 - 0.1379 = 0.3621$), as shown on the left-hand side in Figure 6.5.7. To find the area between the mean ($z = 0$) and $z = 1.63$, we find the area corresponding to $P(z > 1.63)$ by looking up the table value for 1.63 (i.e. 0.0516) and subtract it from 0.5 (i.e. $0.5 - 0.0516 = 0.4484$), as shown on the right-hand side in Figure 6.5.7. The total area required is:

$$P(430 < x < 480) = 0.3621 + 0.4484 = 0.8105$$

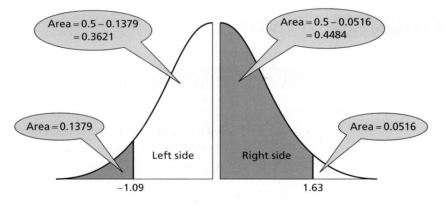

Figure 6.5.7 **Using one-tail Standard Normal tables.**

Approximating Binomial probabilities using the Normal distribution

In Section 6.3 we noted that the Poisson distribution cannot be used to model the Binomial distribution when n is large and $n * p > 5$. Figure 6.2.1 showed typical Binomial distributions, especially one when $p = 0.5$ and $n = 10$, which, although being discrete, has the characteristic bell shape of the Normal distribution.

In Example 6.3.1 we approximated Binomial probabilities by Poisson probabilities. However, we can also use the Normal distribution to model the Poisson distribution (when the mean number of successes is large), and this is why Binomial and Poisson tables do not cover a wide range of values.

6.5

1   A supermarket sells 500 loaves of bread with a standard deviation of 50 loaves. Assuming sales follow a Normal distribution, calculate the probabilities of:
  (a) sales being less than 450 on any day
  (b) the supermarket running out of loaves, if it starts a day with 600 loaves
  (c) sales being between 450 and 600 per day

2   Use the Normal distribution to calculate for the employees in Question 3 of Exercises 5.3 the probabilities of:
  (a) earning between £14,000 and £16,999
  (b) earning less than £20,000
  (c) earning £35,000 or more
  (d) earning between £20,000 and £35,000

Show the areas under the Normal distribution for each event and compare your answers with those for the empirical distribution in Question 7 of Exercises 6.1.

3   A particular web page takes 7 seconds to download on a 1 Mb broadband connection with a standard deviation of 2 seconds. Calculate the probabilities that the web page download times are:
  (a) less than 9 seconds
  (b) longer than 9 seconds
  (c) under 7 seconds or over 9 seconds
  (d) between 5 and 9 seconds
  (e) under 3.5 seconds

How much time will elapse before 10% of these web pages download?

Between what times will 95% of these web pages download?

6.6   ## Chapter review

In this chapter we considered the concept of probability, calculated the probability of an event occurring, and considered its underlying theory. In many situations we obtain empirical probabilities from sampling (e.g. quality inspections) and use empirical distributions to estimate the probability of an event occurring. We also encountered theoretical probability distributions and obtained probabilities from tables, spreadsheets and formulae.

We can use theoretical probability distributions to model the real world, and we do so by identifying the necessary parameters from a sample. We can also use one theoretical probability distribution to approximate the probabilities of another.

In the next chapter we test whether our models are representative of our samples, and we also see how probabilities can provide information to support managers in their decision-making.

Chapter 7

An introduction to inferential statistics

Introduction

In Chapter 5 we considered sampling (i.e. collecting data representative of a population), and we used tables, charts and summary statistics (i.e. descriptive statistics) to describe samples.

In Chapter 6 we considered probability and probability distributions, and obtained probabilities from empirical distributions of samples. We also considered using theoretical probability distributions to model empirical distributions.

The real purpose of sampling is to make predictions or inferences about the population from which the sample was taken. In this chapter we introduce inferential statistics.

Chapter objectives

- To appreciate the role of samples in making inferences about populations

- To estimate the population mean from samples, and calculate confidence intervals

- To appreciate the use of parametric methods to test hypotheses

- To recognise the role of non-parametric methods in testing hypotheses

Chapter contents

Estimating and confidence intervals

Statistical inference is concerned with making inferences from one or more samples about the population from which they were taken. One approach is to estimate the characteristics or parameters of a population from the characteristics or parameters of the sample(s). The simplest parameter to estimate is the population mean. We use such estimates for predicting and forecasting, and for monitoring and controlling processes (e.g. production processes), see Part C.

The prerequisites of this section are:
- Sampling and data collection (Section 4.2);
- Presenting and describing large datasets (Section 4.4);
- Measures of location (Section 5.1);
- Measures of variation (Section 5.3);
- The Normal distribution (Section 6.5).

Estimating the population mean

In Section 5.1 we denoted the mean of a random sample by $\bar{x}$ and the population mean by μ. We cannot simply estimate μ by $\bar{x}$ because two random samples from a population might have different means (Example 7.1.1).

Example 7.1.1

Q   Calculate the means of the two random samples in Table 7.1.1, which were randomly selected from the weights of 5,000 cans of baked beans.

Table 7.1.1 **Two samples of the weights (grams) of 25 cans.**

Sample 1	Sample 2
442	459
457	451
445	451
452	446
442	442
449	447
442	458
443	443
441	455
440	441
443	440
449	460
458	448
451	456
454	459
455	460
440	457
452	446
440	448
440	458
457	456
445	451
446	450
455	448
457	459

A Using equation (5.1.1), we calculate the mean of each random sample:

$$\bar{x}_1 = 447.8 \text{ and } \bar{x}_2 = 451.56.\text{grams}$$

The sampling distribution of sample means

The two means in Example 7.1.1 are sufficiently different to show that one random sample cannot be relied on to estimate the population mean accurately. The issue becomes more apparent if we take many random samples, calculate their means, and construct a **sampling distribution** to estimate the population mean (Example 7.1.2).

Example **7.1.2**

Q Table 7.1.2 shows the means of 50 random samples of the weights of 25 cans from the same population as the two random samples in Example 7.1.1. Investigate how the means of the 50 random samples differ by constructing a sampling distribution.

Table 7.1.2 **The mean weights (grams) of 50 samples of baked bean cans.**

Sample	Mean	Sample	Mean	Sample	Mean	Sample	Mean	Sample	Mean
1	447.80	11	451.36	21	450.32	31	448.72	41	450.44
2	451.56	12	450.08	22	450.36	32	450.88	42	450.44
3	450.12	13	451.64	23	452.04	33	448.80	43	449.12
4	448.68	14	447.60	24	449.20	34	447.56	44	451.12
5	450.56	15	449.12	25	448.80	35	449.64	45	450.92
6	449.20	16	450.96	26	447.92	36	448.56	46	450.64
7	451.76	17	448.20	27	450.36	37	449.12	47	450.20
8	449.64	18	450.16	28	452.40	38	451.64	48	450.32
9	450.24	19	447.48	29	449.36	39	450.12	49	451.52
10	451.40	20	451.12	30	449.28	40	449.16	50	450.88

A Using the approach in Section 4.4, we construct a frequency distribution of the sample means (Table 7.1.3).

Table 7.1.3 **Frequency distribution of means.**

Class	Frequency
447.00–447.99	5
448.00–448.99	6
449.00–449.99	11
450.00–450.99	17
451.00–451.99	9
452.00–452.99	2

Figure 7.1.1 shows a histogram drawn from Table 7.1.3.

Table 7.1.3 and Figure 7.1.1 show that the sample means vary from 447 to 452, with the most frequent in the range 450.00–450.99, which suggests that the mean of the sampling distribution of means is about 450.

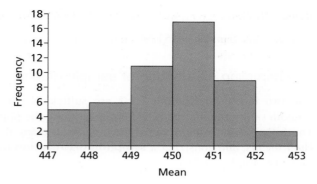

Figure 7.1.1 **A sampling distribution of means for Example 7.1.2.**

The sampling distribution of means for large numbers of samples

The histogram of the sampling distribution of means (Figure 7.1.1) is bell-shaped and looks similar to the Normal distribution (Section 6.5). With more than 30 random samples, we find the sampling distribution of means is Normally distributed, even though the population may not have any recognisable distribution, as shown by Figure 7.1.2.

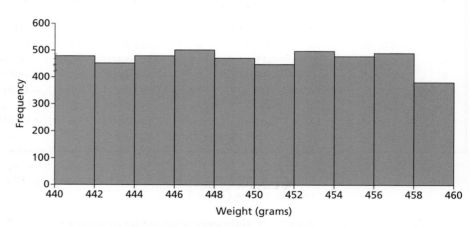

Figure 7.1.2 **Distribution of the weights (grams) of 5,000 cans of baked beans.**

The mean of the sampling distribution of means

Figure 7.1.1 shows how the means of samples can differ. However, by taking many random samples and the mean of the sampling distribution of the means (which we denote $\mu_{\bar{x}}$), we get a good approximation to the population mean (μ). We would expect $\mu_{\bar{x}} = \mu$ because many random samples will include more of the population (Example 7.1.3).

Example

7.1.3

Q Calculate $\mu_{\bar{x}}$ for the data in Table 7.1.2 and compare it with the population mean $\mu = 450.02$.

A Mean of sample means $\mu_{\bar{x}} = 449.97$

We can see that $\mu_{\bar{x}}$ is almost the same as μ (the mean of the population).

The standard deviation of the sampling distribution of the means

Although we expect that $\mu_{\bar{x}} = \mu$, we would not expect the standard deviation of the sampling distribution of the means $\sigma_{\bar{x}}$ to be similar to the standard deviation of the population (σ) because there is relatively little variation in the sample means. Although $\sigma_{\bar{x}} \neq \sigma$, there is a relationship between them:

$$\sigma_{\bar{x}} = \frac{\sigma}{\sqrt{n}} \qquad (7.1.1)$$

where n is the size of the random samples taken from the population (see Example 7.1.4).

Example

7.1.4

7.3

Q Calculate $\sigma_{\bar{x}}$ from Table 7.1.2 and compare it with the population standard deviation $\sigma = 6.04$.

A Using equation (5.3.15), $\sigma_{\bar{x}} = 1.27$. The standard deviations are very different, and σ is almost five times that of $\sigma_{\bar{x}}$ for a sample size $n = 25$, as indicated by equation (7.1.1).

The Central Limit Theorem

Before we return to estimating μ from $\mu_{\bar{x}}$, let us summarise our observations:

- In Example 7.1.2 the sampling distribution of 50 sample means is almost Normally distributed even though the population is not. Generally, the sampling distribution of the means is Normally distributed if the population is also Normally distributed, or at least 30 sampling units are used to construct it, or if the samples are almost as large as the population.
- In Example 7.1.3 the mean of the 50 sample means is almost equal to the mean of the population ($\mu_{\bar{x}} = \mu$).
- In Example 7.1.4 the standard deviation of the population, σ, is approximately five times that of the standard deviation of the sampling distribution of means $\sigma_{\bar{x}}$, and in general $\sigma_{\bar{x}} = \sigma/\sqrt{n}$. Sometimes $\sigma_{\bar{x}}$ is called the **standard error of the mean**.

Taken together these three statements are known as the **Central Limit Theorem**, and are illustrated in Figure 7.1.3 on page 194.

Modelling the sampling distribution of the means by the Normal distribution

In Section 6.5 we standardised any Normally distributed random variable X with mean μ and standard deviation σ to the Standard Normal distributed variable z using equation (6.5.1):

$$z = \frac{X - \mu}{\sigma} \qquad (6.5.1)$$

The Central Limit Theorem allows us to model the sampling distribution of the means using the Normal distribution, and so we can use equation (6.5.1) to standardise the sampling distribution of the means:

$$z_{\bar{x}} = \frac{\bar{x} - \mu_{\bar{x}}}{\sigma_{\bar{x}}} \qquad (7.1.2)$$

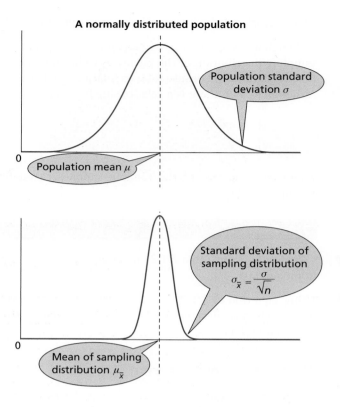

Figure 7.1.3 **The population and sampling distribution of the means.**

and because $\mu_{\bar{x}} = \mu$ and $\sigma_{\bar{x}} = \sigma/\sqrt{n}$, we can rewrite equation (7.1.2):

$$z_{\bar{x}} = \frac{\bar{x} - \mu}{\sigma/\sqrt{n}} \qquad (7.1.3)$$

Confidence intervals

So far, we can only estimate the population mean μ if we take large numbers of random samples. So, rather than looking for a single estimate for μ, we could estimate the interval in which it lies by using the Central Limit Theorem.

In Section 6.5 we looked up the value of $z_{\bar{x}}$ to find the area under the Standard Normal distribution from tables, or by using spreadsheets or calculators: for example, the probability that $z_{\bar{x}}$ lies between −1.96 and +1.96 (i.e. $P(-1.96 < z_{\bar{x}} < 1.96) = 0.95$) is shown in Figure 7.1.4.

To find $z_{\bar{x}}$ corresponding to an area under the standard Normal distribution, we use the tables in Section 6.5 but in the opposite way. To calculate the area shaded in Figure 7.1.4, we find the area under the two tails, $1 - 0.95 = 0.05$, but, because the Normal distribution is symmetrical, only half this (i.e. $0.05/2 = 0.025$) will appear under each tail. Looking up 0.025 in the Cumulative Standard Normal tables, we find $z_{\bar{x}}$ by looking left along the appropriate row (i.e. −1.9) and up the appropriate column (i.e. 0.06), giving $z_{\bar{x}} = -1.96$ (Table 7.1.4).

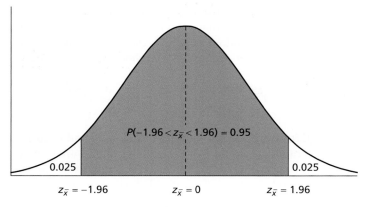

$$P(-1.96 < z_{\bar{x}} < 1.96) = 0.95$$

0.025   0.025

$z_{\bar{x}} = -1.96$ $z_{\bar{x}} = 0$ $z_{\bar{x}} = 1.96$

Figure 7.1.4 **The probability that $z_{\bar{x}}$ lies in the interval −1.96 to 1.96.**

Table 7.1.4 **Part of the Cumulative Standard normal table showing the value of z for 0.025.**

z	0.00	0.01	0.02	0.03	0.04	0.05	0.06	0.07
−4.0	0.0000	0.0000	0.0000	0.0000	0.0000	0.0000	0.0000	0.0000
−3.9	0.0000	0.0000	0.0000	0.0000	0.0000	0.0000	0.0000	0.0000
−3.8	0.0001	0.0001	0.0001	0.0001	0.0001	0.0001	0.0001	0.0001
−3.7	0.0001	0.0001	0.0001	0.0001	0.0001	0.0001	0.0001	0.0001
−3.6	0.0002	0.0002	0.0001	0.0001	0.0001	0.0001	0.0001	0.0001
−3.5	0.0002	0.0002	0.0002	0.0002	0.0002	0.0002	0.0002	0.0002
−3.4	0.0003	0.0003	0.0003	0.0003	0.0003	0.0003	0.0003	0.0003
−3.3	0.0005	0.0005	0.0005	0.0004	0.0004	0.0004	0.0004	0.0004
−3.2	0.0007	0.0007	0.0006	0.0006	0.0006	0.0006	0.0006	0.0005
−3.1	0.0010	0.0009	0.0009	0.0009	0.0008	0.0008	0.0008	0.0008
−3.0	0.0013	0.0013	0.0013	0.0012	0.0012	0.0011	0.0011	0.0011
−2.9	0.0019	0.0018	0.0018	0.0017	0.0016	0.0016	0.0015	0.0015
−2.8	0.0026	0.0025	0.0024	0.0023	0.0023	0.0022	0.0021	0.0021
−2.7	0.0035	0.0034	0.0033	0.0032	0.0031	0.0030	0.0029	0.0028
−2.6	0.0047	0.0045	0.0044	0.0043	0.0041	0.0040	0.0039	0.0038
−2.5	0.0062	0.0060	0.0057	0.0055	0.0054	0.0052	0.0052	0.0051
−2.4	0.0082	0.0080	0.0078	0.0075	0.0073	0.0071	0.0069	0.0068
−2.3	0.0107	0.0104	0.0102	0.0099	0.0096	0.0094	0.0091	0.0089
−2.2	0.0139	0.0136	0.0132	0.0129	0.0125	0.0122	0.0119	0.0116
−2.1	0.0179	0.0174	0.0170	0.0166	0.0162	0.0158	0.0154	0.0150
−2.0	0.0228	0.0222	0.0217	0.0212	0.0207	0.0202	0.0197	0.0192
−1.9	0.0287	0.0281	0.0274	0.0268	0.0262	0.0256	0.0250	0.0244
−1.8	0.0359	0.0351	0.0344	0.0336	0.0329	0.0322	0.0314	0.0307

So the probability that $z_{\bar{x}}$ lies between −1.96 and +1.96 is 0.95, and using equation (7.1.3):

$$P\left(-1.96 < \frac{\bar{x} - \mu}{\sigma/\sqrt{n}} < 1.96\right) = 0.95 \qquad (7.1.4)$$

i.e. $$P\left(-1.96 * \frac{\sigma}{\sqrt{n}} < \bar{x} - \mu < 1.96 * \frac{\sigma}{\sqrt{n}}\right) = 0.95 \qquad (7.1.5)$$

i.e. $$P\left(\bar{x} - 1.96 * \frac{\sigma}{\sqrt{n}} < \mu < \bar{x} + 1.96 * \frac{\sigma}{\sqrt{n}}\right) = 0.95 \qquad (7.1.6)$$

Equation (7.1.6) is a 95% **confidence interval** for the population mean μ and allows us to estimate the interval in which μ lies for a particular value of z, the mean of a random sample $\bar{x}$, the standard deviation of the population σ, and the sample size n. We are 95% confident that μ lies between the **confidence limits**:

$$\bar{x} - 1.96 * \frac{\sigma}{\sqrt{n}} \quad \text{and} \quad \bar{x} + 1.96 * \frac{\sigma}{\sqrt{n}} \tag{7.1.7}$$

But we still do not know the value of σ, and need some way of estimating it from a random sample. When random samples are large (i.e. $n \geqslant 30$), we would expect (because of greater population coverage) the standard deviation of a sample to be a good estimate of σ, provided we use equation (5.3.15) or the group standard deviation equation (5.3.16) (see Example 7.1.5):

$$s = \sqrt{\frac{\sum_{i=1}^{n}(\bar{x}-x)^2}{(n-1)}} \quad \text{or} \quad s = \sqrt{\frac{\sum_{i=1}^{c}f_i(\bar{x}-x)^2}{\left(\sum_{i=1}^{c}f_i\right)-1}} \tag{7.1.8}$$

Example | **7.1.5**

Q Calculate the standard deviations for the two random samples and the standard deviation of the combined samples in Table 7.1.1. Compare these with the population standard deviation of $\sigma = 6.04$.

A The standard deviations of the samples are 6.47 and 6.48, and the standard deviation of the combined sample is 6.68. These are higher than the population standard deviation.

Calculating confidence intervals for the population mean

By replacing σ by s in equation (7.1.6) and considering any value of z from the Standard Normal distribution, we get the general confidence limits for μ:

$$\bar{x} - z * \frac{s}{\sqrt{n}} \text{ and } x + z * \frac{s}{\sqrt{n}} \tag{7.1.9}$$

So a general confidence interval for μ is:

$$\bar{x} - z * \frac{s}{\sqrt{n}} < \mu < \bar{x} + z * \frac{s}{\sqrt{n}} \tag{7.1.10}$$

Example 7.1.6 uses equations (7.1.9) and (7.1.10) to calculate confidence intervals for μ. Spreadsheets and some calculators have an inbuilt function for this calculation.

Example | **7.1.6**

Q Use both samples in Table 7.1.1 to calculate (a) 95%, (b) 90% and (c) 99% confidence intervals for the mean weight of cans.

A We have a sample of size $n = 50$ (i.e. $n > 30$), with mean $\bar{x} = 449.68$ and standard deviation of $s = 6.68$.

(a) For a 95% confidence interval, we calculate confidence limits using equation (7.1.9). Figure 7.13 shows that an area of 0.95 under the Cumulative

Standard Normal distribution corresponds to $z = 1.96$. So the confidence limits are:

$$449.68 - 1.96 * \frac{6.68}{\sqrt{50}} = 447.83$$

and $\quad 449.68 - 1.96 * \frac{6.68}{\sqrt{50}} = 451.53$

So, using equation (7.1.10), a 95% confidence interval is $447.83 < \mu < 451.53$.

(b) For a 90% confidence interval, we use Cumulative Standard Normal tables to look up the value for z corresponding to the area $(1 - 0.9)/2 = 0.1/2 = 0.05$ shown under each tail in Figure 7.1.5. We find that 0.05 lies between $z = -1.64$ and $z = -1.65$, and so we can estimate $z = -1.645$.

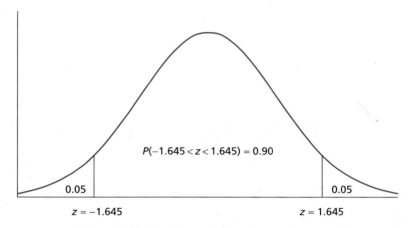

$P(-1.645 < z < 1.645) = 0.90$

0.05   0.05

$z = -1.645$ $z = 1.645$

Figure 7.1.5 **The probability that _z_ lies in the interval −1.645 to 1.645.**

Applying equation (7.1.9), the confidence limits are:

$$447.68 - 1.645 * \frac{6.68}{\sqrt{50}} = 448.13$$

and $\quad 447.68 - 1.645 * \frac{6.68}{\sqrt{50}} = 451.53$

So, using equation (7.1.10), a 90% confidence interval for μ is $448.13 < \mu < 451.23$.

(c) For a 99% confidence interval, we look up the value for z in the Cumulative Standard Normal tables corresponding to the area $(1 - 0.99)/2 = 0.01/2 = 0.005$, giving $z = -2.575$. Equations (7.1.9) and (7.1.10) give a 99% confidence interval for μ as $447.25 < \mu < 452.11$. Note that the intervals get wider as the level of confidence goes up.

One-tailed confidence intervals for the population mean

So far, we have considered **two-tailed confidence intervals**. Sometimes we want to consider the area under only one tail of the distribution (**one-tailed confidence intervals**). For example, we might want to be 95% confident that our cans weigh above 450 g to comply with trading standards regulations. Figure 7.1.6 shows the areas of interest for both 95% confidence intervals.

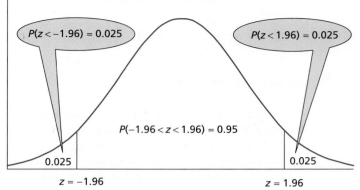

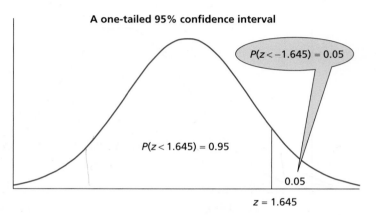

Figure 7.1.6 **Comparing one- and two-tailed 95% confidence intervals.**

Example | 7.1.7

Q Use the random samples in Example 7.1.1 to calculate the can weights for which we are: (a) 95% confident that the population mean μ is below; (b) 95% confident that μ is above; (c) 99% confident that μ is below; (d) 99% confident that μ is above.

A From Example 7.1.6 we know $n = 50$, $\bar{x} = 449.68$ and $s = 6.68$.

(a) From Figure 7.1.6 we know that $z = 1.645$, and so we are 95% confident that μ is less than $449.68 + 1.645 * \dfrac{6.68}{\sqrt{50}} = 451.23$.

(b) From Figure 7.1.6 we know that $z = -1.645$, and so we are 95% confident that μ is more than $449.68 - 1.645 * \dfrac{6.68}{\sqrt{50}} = 448.13$.

(c) To be 99% confident, we use Cumulative Standard Normal tables to find the z value for 0.01 ($z = 2.327$), and so μ is less than $449.68 + 2.327 * \dfrac{6.68}{\sqrt{50}} = 451.88$.

(d) To be 99% confident, we use Cumulative Standard Normal tables to find the z value for 0.01 ($z = -2.327$) and so μ is more than $449.68 - 2.327 * \dfrac{6.68}{\sqrt{50}} = 447.48$.

Confidence intervals for small samples (the t-distribution)

So far, we have used the Central Limit Theorem to calculate confidence intervals for the population mean, but it applies only when the population is Normally distributed or the sample size is large (i.e. $n \geqslant 30$). When the population is Normally distributed but the sample size is small ($n < 30$) we can use the **Student's t-distribution** to calculate confidence intervals. This distribution looks similar to the Normal distribution (see Figure 7.1.7), but its shape depends on a parameter called the **degrees of freedom**.

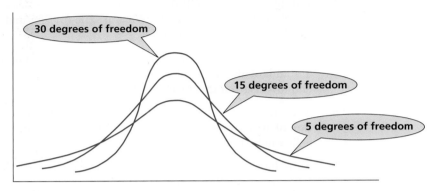

Figure 7.1.7 **Student's t-distribution for 5, 15 and 30 degrees of freedom.**

The degree of freedom is found by subtracting one from the sample size (i.e. $n - 1$). We use Student's t-distribution in the same way that we use the Normal distribution, but look up a value for t instead of z in equation (7.1.10) (see equation (7.1.11) and Example 7.1.8):

$$\bar{x} - t * \frac{s}{\sqrt{n}} < \mu < \bar{x} + t * \frac{s}{\sqrt{n}} \qquad (7.1.11)$$

Student's t-distribution tables can be presented in different ways. A typical table for two-tailed confidence intervals is given at the end of this book and on the spreadsheet t-Table.xls on the enclosed CD. In these tables, the rows relate to the degrees of freedom and the columns relate to the level of confidence. To look up a t value, we look along the row and down the column. Spreadsheets have inbuilt functions for calculating values for the Student's t-distribution and confidence intervals.

7.5

Example | **7.1.8**

Q A random sample of the heights of 10 undergraduate students has a mean of $\bar{x} = 1.82$ m with a standard deviation of $s = 20$ cm. Calculate a 95% confidence interval for the population mean.

A The height of adults is thought to be Normally distributed, and we shall use the t-distribution because the sample size is small (i.e. $n = 10 < 30$). For $n = 10$ we look along row $10 - 1 = 9$ degrees of freedom and down the 95% column, giving the t value of 2.2622. Applying equation (7.1.11) working in metres (20 cm = 0.2 m) gives the confidence interval:

$$1.81 - 2.2622 \frac{0.2}{\sqrt{10}} < \mu < 1.82 + 2.2622 \frac{0.2}{\sqrt{10}}$$

So we are 95% confident that the population mean (i.e. height of undergraduate students) lies in the interval $1.67 < \mu < 1.96$ m.

Estimating other parameters of a population

We can use the same concepts to estimate other characteristics of a population from a sample, such as the **proportion** of times that employees work overtime. These issues are beyond the scope of this book, and further details can be found in the Further reading at the end of this book.

Exercises | **7.1**

1 A random sample of 100 electrical leads have a mean length of 1 metre with a standard deviation of 1.2 cm. What are the (a) 95% and (b) 99% confidence intervals for the true mean length?

2 The average completion time of a task given to 60 employees is 6.4 minutes with a standard deviation of 30 seconds. What is the 95% confidence interval for employees given this task?

3 A hotline receives 60 calls of mean duration 4.5 minutes with a standard deviation of 30 seconds. What time durations can the hotline be 95% confident that all calls will be below?

4 A random sample of 10 invoices had a value of £60 with a standard deviation of £8. What is the 95% confidence interval for such invoices?

7.2 | ## An introduction to hypothesis testing

The previous section considered how we use statistical inference to estimate population parameters from a random sample, such as confidence intervals for the population mean from the mean of a sample. In this section we extend these ideas using hypothesis testing.

The prerequisites of this section are:
- Sampling and data collection (Section 4.2);
- Presenting and describing large datasets (Section 4.4);
- Measures of location (Section 5.1);
- Measures of variation (Section 5.3);
- The Normal distribution (Section 6.5).
- Estimating and confidence intervals (Section 7.1).

Hypothesis testing

When we have preconceived ideas about a population (e.g. that average life expectancy has increased over the last decade or average disposable income has decreased over the last 5 years), they are called **hypotheses**. We can **test hypotheses** by taking random samples to see whether there is evidence to support them. We never say we accept a hypothesis; instead, we say that it cannot be rejected. The hypothesis we set out to test is called the **Null Hypothesis**, which we denote by H_0. If it is rejected, we cannot reject an alternative to it, which we call H_1.

H_0 must be a simple and clear statement, whereas the alternative H_1 can be more vague, suggesting that some statement other than H_0 is true. A procedure for hypothesis testing is:
- accurately define a precise statement of the Null Hypothesis (H_0);
- take a random sample from the population;
- test to see whether the sample supports the Null Hypothesis (H_0);
- if the sample suggests that H_0 is improbable, then reject it but do not reject the alternative (H_1).

Example 7.2.1 illustrates a simple hypothesis test and the notation we use.

Example	**7.2.1**

Q Construct a Null Hypothesis that the mean weight of a can of baked beans is 450 g. What is the alternative hypothesis? How can we test H_0 using both samples in Table 7.1.1?

A H_0 is that $\mu = 450$ g and H_1 is that $\mu \neq 450$ g:

$$H_0: \mu = 450 \text{ g}$$

$$H_1: \mu \neq 450 \text{ g}$$

Applying equation (6.5.1), we calculate the mean of the combined random sample $\bar{x} = 449.68$ and test whether it is significantly different from $\mu = 450$ g, to decide whether to reject H_0.

Levels of significance

In Example 7.2.1 we considered whether there was a significant difference between the sample mean $\bar{x}$ and the population mean μ. As the sampling distribution of means is Normally distributed with a mean $\mu_{\bar{x}} = \mu$ (Section 7.1), we can instead consider any significant difference between $\bar{x}$ and $\mu_{\bar{x}}$ to see whether the difference between them can be explained by the variability we would expect to find in $\mu_{\bar{x}}$. As we can standardise any Normal distribution (Section 6.5) using equation (7.1.3), we only need to consider the appropriate Standard Normal distribution.

As standard deviation can be used to measure variability in a Normal distribution, it can also measure significance. So we could state how many standard deviations on either side of the mean we will accept before we reject our Null Hypothesis (using similar concepts to those in Section 7.1, when drawing control charts). Rather than stating significance in this way, we usually state it in percentage terms and identify the corresponding **acceptance and rejection regions** on the Normal distribution, which are similar to the confidence intervals that we met in Section 7.1.

We usually take 5% levels of significance, and occasionally we take 1% or 0.1% levels of significance. For example, a two-tailed 5% level of significance is equivalent to $z = \pm 1.96$ from Cumulative Standard Normal tables. So we do not reject the Null Hypothesis if the sample mean is within 1.96 standard deviations of μ, but we do if it is outside this range (Figure 7.2.1).

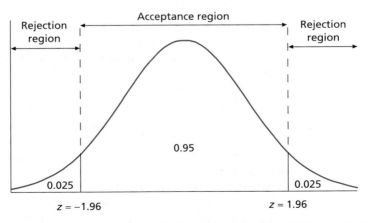

Figure 7.2.1 **Acceptance and rejection regions for 5% level of significance.**

Figure 7.2.1 shows that we can rearrange equation (7.1.10) to define a general acceptance region:

$$\mu - z * \frac{s}{\sqrt{n}} < \bar{x} < \mu + z * \frac{s}{\sqrt{n}} \qquad (7.2.1)$$

and by rearranging equation (7.2.1), we can define a general rejection region:

$$\mu - z * \frac{s}{\sqrt{n}} > \bar{x} > \mu + z * \frac{s}{\sqrt{n}} \qquad (7.2.2)$$

By comparing Figure 7.1.4 and Figure 7.2.1, we see the simple relationship between the level of confidence and the level of significance:

$$\text{Level of confidence} = 100\% - \text{level of significance} \qquad (7.2.3)$$

So a two-tailed 95% level of confidence is equivalent to a two-tailed 5% level of significance.

Example 7.2.2

Q Test the hypothesis in Example 7.2.1 at the (a) 5% and (b) 1% levels of significance.

A From Example 7.1.1 we have a sample size of $n = 50$. With a mean of $\bar{x} = 449.68$ and applying equation (5.3.15), we have a standard deviation of $s = 6.68$.

(a) Using equation (7.2.2), for a 5% level of significance the acceptance region is:

$$450 - 1.96 * \frac{6.68}{\sqrt{50}} < \bar{x} < 450 + 1.96 * \frac{6.68}{\sqrt{50}}$$

i.e. $448.15 < \bar{x} < 451.85$
As the sample mean $\bar{x} = 449.68$ is within this region, we do not reject the Null Hypothesis at the 5% level of significance, and there is insufficient evidence that $\mu \neq 450$.

(b) Using equation (7.2.2) for a 1% level of significance, the acceptance region is:

$$450 - 2.58 * \frac{6.68}{\sqrt{50}} < \bar{x} < 450 + 2.58 * \frac{6.68}{\sqrt{50}}$$

i.e. $447.56 < \bar{x} < 452.44$
As the sample mean $\bar{x} = 449.68$ is also within this region, we again do not reject the Null Hypothesis at the 1% level of significance.

Errors in hypothesis testing

No matter how large the sample, it always contains some uncertainty. In Example 7.2.2 we did not reject the Null Hypothesis (H_0) at the 5% level of significance, but we might have made the wrong decision. On the other hand, if we had rejected the Null Hypothesis but we should not have done so, then we would again have made the wrong decision.

So when we use a sample to test H_0 we can never be certain of the result, and might incorrectly reject H_0 or the alternative H_1. These two ways of making the wrong decision are called **Type I** and **Type II errors** (Figure 7.2.2).

134

		The null hypothesis (H_0) is:	
		True	False
The decision is:	Do not reject (H_0) (i.e. reject H_1)	Correct decision	Type II error
	Reject H_0 (i.e. do not reject H_1)	Type I error	Correct decision

Figure 7.2.2 **Type I and Type II errors.**

Type I or Type II errors depend on how the Null Hypothesis is formulated. To ensure that the probabilities of Type I and Type II errors are close to zero, we need to take large samples. With limited sample sizes, we have to compromise between these two types of error. We can calculate the probabilities of occurrence for each of the outcomes in Figure 7.2.2 (i.e. correct decision, Type I error or Type II error). The level of significance is the probability of committing a Type I error (e.g. at the 5% level there is a 5% chance of rejecting a true Null Hypothesis). The probability of a Type II error cannot be calculated this way and is beyond the scope of this book (see Further reading at the end of this book).

One-tailed hypothesis tests

So far we have considered only a Null Hypothesis in which we test whether a parameter is equal to a particular value. Sometimes we want to test whether a parameter is greater or less than a particular value, in which case we use one-tailed hypothesis tests. These are often to measure consumer or producer risk (e.g. if a can of baked beans is labelled 450 g, a consumer will complain about the weight only if it weighs less). So consumer associations set the Null Hypothesis at $H_0: \mu \geqslant 450$ g and the alternative at $H_1: \mu < 450$ g. One-tailed hypothesis tests are related to the one-tailed confidence intervals we met in Section 7.1 (see Figure 7.2.3 and Example 7.2.3).

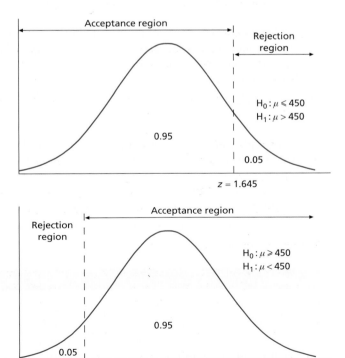

Figure 7.2.3 **One-tailed hypothesis tests for 5% level of significance.**

Example 7.2.3

Q A sample of 50 cans of baked beans have a mean weight of $\bar{x} = 447.54$ and a standard deviation of $s = 5.44$. Test a hypothesis for consumer risk at the 5% level of significance.

A The hypothesis test is one tailed with H_0: $\mu = 450$ g and H_1: $\mu < 450$ g. Applying equation (7.2.1) at the 5% level of significance with $z = 1.645$:

$$450 - 1.645 * \frac{5.44}{\sqrt{50}} < \bar{x}$$

i.e. $448.74 < \bar{x}$

The Null Hypothesis is rejected as the sample mean $\bar{x} = 447.54$ is outside the acceptance range.

Testing for the difference in two means

Sometimes we have two populations and want to know whether their means are the same (e.g. whether two machines have the same operating costs, or whether sales have increased after a marketing campaign). To do this we take a random sample from each population and test a hypothesis concerning the equality of the means of the two populations. We use subscripted notation to distinguish between each population mean, each sample mean, each sample size, and each sample standard deviation:

	Population 1	Population 2
Sample size	n_1	n_2
Sample standard deviation	s_1	s_2
Sample mean	$\bar{x}_1$	$\bar{x}_2$
Population mean	μ_1	μ_2

For large sample sizes the sampling distribution of the difference in means (i.e. $\bar{x}_1 - \bar{x}_2$) has a Normal distribution with a mean of zero, because our hypothesis is that $\bar{x}_1 = \bar{x}_2$ with standard deviation:

$$\sigma_{\bar{x}_1 - \bar{x}_2} = \sqrt{\frac{s_1^2}{n_1} + \frac{s_2^2}{n_2}} \qquad (7.2.4)$$

We can simply replace $s/\sqrt{n}$ in equations (7.2.1) and (7.2.2) by equation (7.2.4) and calculate the acceptance and rejection regions for the hypothesis test:

H_0: $\mu_1 = \mu_2$

H_1: $\mu_1 \neq \mu_2$

7.6

Spreadsheets have inbuilt functions for testing the difference between two sample means.

Example 7.2.4

Q The mean retail price of a game console in 30 stores in the UK is £180 with standard deviation of £14, whereas 40 stores in Spain had a mean price of £170 with a standard deviation of £10. Does the evidence from these surveys support the view that retail prices of the game console are the same in both countries?

A Applying equation (7.2.4) gives:

$$\sigma_{\bar{x}_1-\bar{x}_2} = \sqrt{\frac{s_1^2}{n_1} + \frac{s_2^2}{n_2}} = \sqrt{\frac{14^2}{30} + \frac{10^2}{40}} = 3.01$$

Applying a two-tailed hypothesis test at a 5% level of significance, we use equation (7.2.1) with $z = 1.96$, $\mu = 0$ and $\sigma_{\bar{x}_1-\bar{x}_2} = 3.01$:

$$0 - 1.96 * 3.01 < \bar{x}_1 - \bar{x}_2 < 0 + 1.96 * 3.01$$

i.e. $$-5.9 < \bar{x}_1 - \bar{x}_2 < 5.9$$

We have $\bar{x}_1 - \bar{x}_2 = £180 - £170 = £10$, which falls outside the acceptance region, and so we reject the hypothesis that the mean retail prices of the game console are the same in both countries.

Hypothesis testing using small samples

So far we have considered hypothesis testing only when we know a population is Normally distributed or when we have large samples. In Section 7.1 we used the Student's t-distribution to calculate confidence intervals for small samples. We can also apply the Student's t-distribution to testing hypotheses when we have small sample sizes by simply replacing the z value by the appropriate t value in equations (7.2.1) and (7.2.2). When you look up t values, remember that the level of significance is 100% less the level of confidence (e.g. a 95% level of confidence is equivalent to a 5% level of significance), that these tables apply only to two-tailed tests and that you will need to select the appropriate degrees of freedom.

Testing other hypotheses

Besides testing hypotheses about means, we can also devise hypothesis tests for other parameters (e.g. proportions and standard deviations), but these are beyond the scope of this book. Spreadsheets have inbuilt functions for such tests.

Exercises   **7.2**

1 The average salary of a firm's employees is thought to be £30,000. A random sample of 100 employees has a mean salary of £28,500 with a standard deviation of £7,600. Test the hypothesis at a level of significance of (a) 5% and (b) 1%.

2 Call-centre operators are told to spend no longer than 10 minutes on each call. A random sample of 40 operators found a mean call duration of 11.05 minutes with a standard deviation of 3 minutes. Test the hypothesis at the 1% level of significance.

3 The weight of a packet of biscuits is stated as 500 g. A sample of 200 such packets has a mean weight of 501 g with a standard deviation of 2.5 g. Test an appropriate hypothesis at the 5% level of significance.

4 An airline advertises 5 hour flights from Glasgow to Cairo. A sample of 30 such flights has a mean time of 5 hours 10 minutes with a standard deviation of 20 minutes. Test the hypothesis at the 5% level of significance using both Normal and Student t tables.

5 A firm has two plants (A and B). The trade union is concerned that different rates of pay apply at the two plants. Test an appropriate hypothesis at the 5% level of significance for these values:

Plant	Sample size	Mean rate of pay	Standard deviation
A	45	£25	£4.50
B	35	£23	£4.00

Non-parametric tests

In this chapter we have considered confidence intervals and testing hypotheses for a specific parameter of a population (e.g. the mean) when we have large samples or have assumed that the population was normally distributed. We call these **parametric tests**. Sometimes we want to test hypotheses for nominal data (e.g. job titles, types of vehicle) or ordinal data (e.g. position in the FTSE) when there is no appropriate parameter or when we do not know whether the population is Normally distributed. We call these **non-parametric tests** and introduce a new theoretical probability distribution to model our sampling distributions.

The prerequisites of this section are:
- Sampling and data collection (Section 4.2);
- Presenting and describing large datasets (Section 4.4);
- Measures of location (Section 5.1);
- Measures of variation (Section 5.3);
- Probability and statistical models (Chapter 6);
- Estimating and confidence intervals (Section 7.1);
- An introduction to hypothesis testing (Section 7.2).

The Chi-squared distribution

The **Chi-squared distribution** which is closely related to the Normal distribution, is often used for making comparisons, particularly between the contents of tables. It is derived from summing several independent squared Normal distributions, and is also found when dealing with variance, because variance also comes from considering squared differences.

Like Student's t-distribution (Section 7.2), the shape of the Chi-squared distribution is determined by the degrees of freedom (see Figure 7.3.1), and tables of frequently used Chi-squared probabilities are available. Note the similarity to the Normal distribution as the degrees of freedom increase.

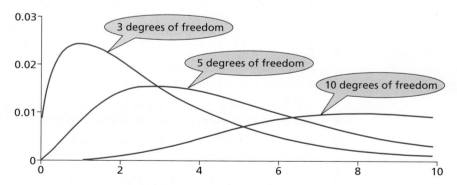

Figure 7.3.1 **Chi-squared distributions.**

The Chi-squared hypothesis test

The Chi-squared (χ^2) hypothesis test follows the approach used in Section 7.2, with some minor differences. First, we compare observed and expected frequencies in a frequency distribution over a number of classes. We denote observed frequencies by OF_1, OF_2, OF_3, ..., OF_n and expected frequencies by EF_1, EF_2, EF_3, ..., EF_n. By summing the squared differences between observed and expected frequencies and dividing by the expected frequencies, we calculate a χ^2 value as shown by equation (7.3.1) and Table 7.3.1.

Table 7.3.1 **Calculating the value of χ^2.**

Class number	Observed frequency	Expected frequency	$\dfrac{(OF_i - EF_i)^2}{EF_i}$
1	OF_1	EF_1	$\dfrac{(OF_1 - EF_1)^2}{EF_1}$
2	OF_2	EF_2	$\dfrac{(OF_2 - EF_2)^2}{EF_2}$
3	OF_3	EF_3	$\dfrac{(OF_3 - EF_3)^2}{EF_3}$
n	OF_n	EF_n	$\dfrac{(OF_n - EF_n)^2}{EF_n}$
			$\chi^2 = \displaystyle\sum_{i=1}^{n} \dfrac{(OF_i - EF_i)^2}{EF_i}$

$$\chi^2 = \sum_{i=1}^{n} \frac{(OF_i - EF_i)^2}{EF_i} \qquad (7.3.1)$$

Second, the χ^2 distribution requires that expected class frequencies are at least five (i.e. $EF_i \geqslant 5$), and so we might have to combine classes. Third, the Null Hypothesis is that there is no difference between the observed and expected frequencies (i.e. $\chi^2 = 0$). Instead of testing for an acceptance region, we test whether χ^2 is above or below a critical valve. If χ^2 is less than the critical value, we do not reject the Null Hypothesis, whereas if χ^2 is greater, we reject the Null Hypothesis. Finally, the degrees of freedom are calculated by equation (7.3.2):

$$\text{Degrees of freedom} = \text{number of classes} - 1 \qquad (7.3.2)$$

Note also that, if we estimate parameters in our calculations for Table 7.3.1 (e.g. the calculation of probabilities), we need to subtract the number of estimated parameters from equation (7.3.2).

We can now use χ^2 tables (see the end of the book or the file Chisquare.xls on the CD), or a calculator or spreadsheet, to test our hypotheses (Examples 7.3.1 and 7.3.2).

7.8

Example   **7.3.1**

Q A 5-year total of fatal industrial accidents is shown in Table 7.3.2. Are health and safety regulations being consistently adhered to at the 5% level of significance?

Table 7.3.2 **Annual industrial fatalities.**

Year	1	2	3	4	5
No of fatalities	310	350	290	420	380

A If they are, we should expect the same number of industrial fatalities each year (our Null Hypothesis H_0). The alternative hypothesis H_1 is that we do not find the same number. Over 5 years, the average number of fatalities is $\dfrac{310 + 350 + 290 + 420 + 380}{5} = 350$. We create a table to calculate χ^2 as shown in Table 7.3.3.

7.8

Table 7.3.3 **Calculating the value of χ^2.**

Year	Observed frequency	Expected frequency	$\dfrac{(OF_i - EF_i)^2}{EF_i}$
1	$OF_1 = 310$	$EF_1 = 350$	$(310 - 350)^2/350 = 4.57$
2	$OF_2 = 350$	$EF_2 = 350$	$(350 - 350)^2/350 = 0.00$
3	$OF_3 = 290$	$EF_3 = 350$	$(290 - 350)^2/350 = 10.29$
4	$OF_4 = 420$	$EF_4 = 350$	$(420 - 350)^2/350 = 14.00$
5	$OF_5 = 380$	$EF_5 = 350$	$(380 - 350)^2/350 = 2.57$

$$\chi^2 = \sum_{i=1}^{n} \frac{(OF_i - EF_i)}{EF_i} = 31.43$$

Table 7.3.3 has five classes, and we have estimated the expected frequency from the mean of the observation (i.e. we have estimated one parameter). So, from equation (7.3.2), we have $5 - 1 - 1 = 3$ degrees of freedom and at the 5% level of significance we find a critical value for χ^2 of 7.8147. Our calculated value is much higher than the critical value and so we reject the Null Hypothesis, suggesting that health and safety regulations are not being adhered to.

Example 7.3.2

Q At the 5% level of significance, is the Binomial distribution a good model of the empirical frequency distribution for monthly sales of freezers in Example 6.2.8?

A First, we calculate the expected frequencies from the Binomial distribution by multiplying the Binomial probabilities in Example 6.2.8 by the number of sales ($n = 60$) (Table 7.3.4). Note that these have been rounded to ease the calculations.

Table 7.3.4 **Frequency and probability distributions for Example 6.2.8.**

Monthly sales	Frequency	Empirical probabilities	Binomial probabilities	Expected frequencies
0	7	$7/60 = 0.12$	0.05	$60 * 0.05 = 2.97$
1	9	$9/60 = 0.15$	0.15	$60 * 0.15 = 9.15$
2	12	$12/60 = 0.20$	0.23	$60 * 0.23 = 13.87$
3	10	$10/60 = 0.17$	0.23	$60 * 0.23 = 13.78$
4	8	$8/60 = 0.13$	0.17	$60 * 0.17 = 10.10$
5	6	$6/60 = 0.10$	0.10	$60 * 0.10 = 5.81$
6	5	$5/60 = 0.08$	0.05	$60 * 0.05 = 2.74$
7	3	$3/60 = 0.05$	0.02	$60 * 0.02 = 1.09$
Total =	60	1	1	60

As some expected frequencies are less than 5, we combine the first two and last three classes to create a table to calculate χ^2 (Table 7.3.5).

Table 7.3.5 **Calculating the value of Chi-squared for Example 7.3.2.**

Monthly sales	Class number	Observed frequency	Expected frequency	$\dfrac{(OF_i - EF_i)^2}{EF_i}$
0 and 1	1	$OF_1 = 16$	$EF_1 = 12.12$	1.24
2	2	$OF_2 = 9$	$EF_2 = 13.87$	0.25
3	3	$OF_3 = 12$	$EF_3 = 13.78$	1.04
4	4	$OF_4 = 10$	$EF_4 = 10.10$	0.44
5, 6 and 7	5	$OF_5 = 14$	$EF_5 = 9.64$	1.97

$$\chi^2 = 4.95$$

To calculate the expected frequencies, we estimated one parameter (i.e. the probability of success) from the Binomial distribution and have $5 - 1 - 1 = 3$ degrees of freedom. From the χ^2 table at the 5% level of significance with 3 degrees of freedom, we find a χ^2 of 7.8147. Our calculated value is less than the critical value, so we cannot reject the Null Hypothesis. We conclude that the Binomial distribution is a good model for the empirical sales distribution.

Hypothesis tests of association

The χ^2 hypothesis test is also used for testing whether there is a relationship between the responses to two or more questions in a questionnaire. The responses are entered into a **contingency table** with r rows and k columns. Expected frequencies are calculated from relative frequencies and the degrees of freedom from equation (7.3.3) (see Example 7.3.3):

$$\text{Degrees of freedom for an } (r \times k) \text{ contingency table} = (r - 1) * (k - 1) \quad (7.3.3)$$

Example | **7.3.3**

Q A questionnaire found the responses shown in Table 7.3.6 about the health of 400 managers. Is there any relationship between the level of manager and the Body Mass Index (BMI)?

Table 7.3.6 **Body Mass Index.**

		Below	Average	Above
		Body Mass Index		
Level of manager	Junior	77	13	8
	Middle	145	58	27
	Senior	21	32	19

A The Null Hypothesis is that there is no difference in BMI between different levels of management. Table 7.3.6 is a (3×3) contingency table (i.e. $r = 3$ and $k = 3$). To calculate the expected frequencies, we first calculate the row and column totals, as shown in Table 7.3.7.

Table 7.3.7 **Row and column totals for Table 7.3.6.**

		Below	Average	Above	Column total
		Body Mass Index			
Level of manager	Junior	77	13	8	98
	Middle	145	58	27	230
	Senior	21	32	19	72
	Row total	243	103	54	400

Next, using the ideas from Section 6.1 we can calculate the expected frequency for each level of manager and BMI, as shown in Table 7.3.8.

Table 7.3.8 **Expected frequencies for Table 7.3.6.**

| | Expected Body Mass Index | | | |
	Below	Average	Above	Column total
Junior	$\dfrac{98*243}{400} = 59.54$	$\dfrac{98*103}{400} = 25.24$	$\dfrac{98*54}{400} = 13.23$	98
Middle	$\dfrac{230*243}{400} = 139.73$	$\dfrac{230*103}{400} = 59.23$	$\dfrac{230*54}{400} = 31.05$	230
Senior	$\dfrac{72*243}{400} = 43.74$	$\dfrac{72*103}{400} = 18.54$	$\dfrac{72*54}{400} = 9.72$	72
Row total	243	103	54	400

We can now calculate χ^2 as shown in Table 7.3.9.

Table 7.3.9 **Calculating χ^2 for Example 7.3.3.**

Class number	Observed frequency	Expected frequency	$\dfrac{(OF_i - EF_i)^2}{EF_i}$
1	77	59.54	5.1235
2	13	25.24	5.9320
3	8	13.23	2.0675
4	145	139.73	0.1991
5	58	59.23	0.0253
6	27	31.05	0.5283
7	21	43.74	11.8223
8	32	18.54	9.7719
9	19	9.72	8.8599
			Total = 44.3299

As Table 7.3.6 is a (3×3) contingency table, we use equation (7.3.3) to get $(3 - 1) * (3 - 1) = 4$ degrees of freedom. At the 5% level of significance the χ^2 critical value is 9.488. As our value exceeds this, we reject the Null Hypothesis and say there is a relationship between managerial level and BMI.

7.9

Exercises 7.3

1. Test the hypothesis that the Binomial distribution is a good model for the empirical distribution of failed bus tyres in Question 5 of Exercises 6.2.

2. Test the hypothesis that the distribution of machine breakdowns in Question 2 of Exercises 6.3 can be modelled by the Poisson distribution.

3. Test the hypothesis that the Poisson distribution is a good model for the empirical distribution of failed bus tyres in Question 5 of Exercises 6.2. Is the Binomial or the Poisson distribution the best model?

4. Test the hypothesis that the call frequency in Question 2 of Exercises 6.4 follows a Poisson process.

5. The table below shows responses from interviews of managers about career progression and their character. Test an appropriate hypothesis at the 5% level of significance.

Character	Rate of career progression			
	Slow	Average	Fast	Very fast
Aggressive	48	51	43	35
Moderate	22	42	59	57
Passive	15	22	33	13

7.4   Chapter review

In this chapter we considered inferential statistics (i.e. estimating, confidence intervals and hypothesis testing). To test hypotheses we need to specify a level of significance, and so these tests are also called **tests of significance**. In Sections 7.1 and 7.2 we considered only estimating and hypothesis testing for the population mean, but there are many other parameters we could estimate or test. In Section 7.3 we extended hypothesis testing to non-parametric tests, which test association and relationships. We consider the concepts of relationships in Chapters 8 and 9.

Here we have covered only the basic concepts of inferential statistics, and further details can be found in the further readings at the end of this book.

We have seen how some of the tools of inferential statistics are available as inbuilt functions in calculators and spreadsheets. However, these are often limited in scope, so we may have to use dedicated statistical packages (e.g. SPSS or Minitab) instead. Spreadsheets and statistical packages (e.g. SPSS and Minitab) also use the concept of p-values for hypothesis testing. A p-value is the smallest observed level of significance at which the Null Hypothesis can be rejected for a given set of data. Unless we are considering tests requiring the Normal distribution then it is difficult to calculate the p-value. A discussion of p-values is beyond the scope of this introductory book, and the interested reader is directed to the further readings at the end of the book.

Chapter 8

Modelling relationships

Introduction

In Chapter 4 we saw how datasets could be summarised and presented using tables and charts. In Chapter 6 we recognised underlying patterns in a dataset by looking at frequency distributions and histograms, and found that many histograms exhibit patterns that can be modelled by theoretical probability distributions to provide useful information to support managers in decision-making. In this chapter we extend this modelling process to other forms of chart (i.e. scattergrams and graphs).

Chapter objectives

- An appreciation of mathematical modelling of relationships between variables
- To recognise the role of dependent and independent variables in functions and equations
- To identify the equation, slope and intercept of a linear function
- To appreciate the methods available for finding appropriate linear models
- To appreciate how and where linear models can be used in business and management

Chapter contents

8.1 Relationships, functions and equations

96

In Section 4.3 we presented data relating to two variables using scatter-grams and found that, by drawing a line through the points on a scatter-gram, we could identify a pattern in the data. In this section we look at this concept in greater detail.

The prerequisites of this section are:
- Algorithms, variables and algebra (Section 2.1);
- Presenting and describing small datasets (Section 4.3).

When we see a pattern in a set of data, for example on a scattergram, we say the two variables in the scattergram are **related**. If the pattern suggests a relationship in which one variable depends on another, we identify an **independent variable** and a **dependent variable**. For example, the weekly sales volume of a particular product might depend upon its retail price. When we draw scatter-grams of related variables, we put the **independent variable** on the **horizontal axis** and the **dependent variable** on the **vertical axis** (see Example 8.1.1).

Example 8.1.1

Q Over 6 months a store has recorded the unit price at the start of the month and the sales volume at the end of the month, as shown in Table 8.1.1. Draw a scatter-gram and identify the relationship between sales volume and unit price charged.

Table 8.1.1 **Retail sales over a 6-month period for Example 8.1.1.**

Month	1	2	3	4	5	6
Unit price (£)	14	18	20	30	26	22
Sales volume	920	840	800	600	680	760

A The store can change (i.e. vary) the unit price, but the quantity sold will probably depend on the unit price. So unit price is the independent variable (because the store can choose the price independently) and sales volume is the dependent variable (because it depends on the unit price charged). So the scattergram has unit price p on the horizontal axis and sales volume s on the vertical axis (Figure 8.1.1).

Figure 8.1.1 **A scattergram of sales against unit price for Example 8.1.1.**

Figure 8.1.1 shows the relationship between sales and unit price and as expected, higher prices result in lower sales. This observed relationship can be used to provide further information. For example, the pattern in Figure 8.1.1 suggests that the store should expect sales of about 600 if the unit price was set at £28. We analyse such patterns in datasets in Chapter 10.

Functions and relationships

Using scattergrams to identify relationships is tedious, even when they are drawn on a spreadsheet, and the accuracy of any analysis will depend on the scale to which the scattergram is drawn. A better approach is to use an explicit means of representing the underlying relationship between variables using the concept of **functions**.

In Example 8.1.1, mathematically we could say that sales depend on or are a **function** of the unit price, and we might write:

Sales are a function of unit price

We abbreviate 'a function of' by $f()$ and put the independent variable p between the brackets:

$$s = f(p) \tag{8.1.1}$$

We label the **dependent variable y** (the vertical axis is usually called the **y-axis**) and the **independent variable x** (the horizontal axis is usually called the **x-axis**), and in general we write:

$$y = f(x) \tag{8.1.2}$$

We say that '**y is a function of x**' or '**y is related to x**' or '**y in terms of x**'.

To find an equation for the underlying pattern in the data, we assume the pattern will apply between and beyond the observed data (i.e. the scattergram points) (we consider the extent to which we can go beyond the data points in Section 8.4). Also, we need to be more precise about the underlying relationship. In Example 8.1.1, we can draw a straight line through our scatter points (Figure 8.1.2).

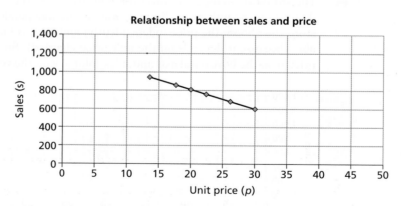

Figure 8.1.2 **Scattergram for Example 8.1.1 showing a line passing through all points.**

Figure 8.1.2 is now essentially a graph, because we have joined all the data and intermediate points by a solid line. A graph is a pictorial representation of a function, and can help us to decide whether a particular mathematical function is a suitable representation (i.e. model) of an underlying relationship. In the next section we consider the simplest mathematical function, the linear function.

Exercises **8.1**

1 A survey finds that sales of a product priced at £10 resulted in 900 units per week being sold. When priced at £20, only 800 units per week were sold, and at £30, only 700 units per week were sold. Represent these data on a scattergram.

2 The output and costs of operating a machine over the last 5 years are:

Year	1	2	3	4	5
Output (1,000s units)	40	54	48	62	60
Operating costs (£1,000s)	720	930	840	1,100	1,020

Using a scattergram, estimate the costs of producing 50,000 units per year. What are the unit operating costs of this machine?

3 The costs of operating a machine at different points in time are:

Age (years)	1	2	3	4	5
Operating costs	175	250	325	400	475

(a) Plot a scattergram of operating costs against age.
(b) Estimate the operating costs of a 10-year-old machine from the scattergram.
(c) Draw a line through all the points on the scattergram and estimate the operating costs of a brand new machine.
(d) Estimate the operating costs at 6-monthly intervals.

4 The prices and mileages of 1-year-old vans in the local newspaper are:

Mileage (1,000s)	Price (£1,000s)
1.6	23.6
12.4	19.8
14.7	20.5
24.2	17.7
22.6	18.1
37.2	16.1
32.8	14.8
9.2	18.9
6.5	21.4
0.2	24.5

Draw a scattergram and comment on the relationship between price and mileage.

5 A survey of patients visiting a local hospital results in the following data:

Age range	0–5	5–11	11–18	18–50	50–65	65+
Average no. of visits per year	25	12	5	2	10	45

Draw a scattergram of the average number of visits against median age and comment on the relationship.

8.2 Linear functions

In Section 8.1 we saw how we could represent the relationship between two variables. The simplest relationship that we might see on a graph is a straight line (i.e. a linear relationship).

The prerequisites of this section are:
- Algorithms, variables and algebra (Section 2.1);
- Simultaneous and systems of equations (Section 2.2);
- Presenting and describing small datasets (Section 4.3);
- Relationships, functions and equations (Section 8.1).

The linear function

Linear functions relate the dependent and independent variable by the equation:

Dependent variable = Slope of line * Independent variable + Constant   *(8.2.1)*

In general, we label the dependent variable y, the independent variable x, the slope of the line a and the constant b, giving:

$$y = ax + b \qquad (8.2.2)$$

Sometimes, the slope of a linear function is denoted by m and the constant by c, so you may come across equation (8.2.2) written as:

$$y = mx + c \qquad (8.2.3)$$

Figures 8.2.1 and 8.2.2 show typical graphs of linear functions. The graph of a linear function is called a **straight-line graph**.

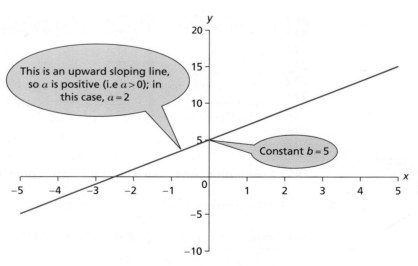

This is an upward sloping line, so a is positive (i.e $a > 0$); in this case, $a = 2$

Constant $b = 5$

Figure 8.2.1 **A graph of the linear function $y = 2x + 5$.**

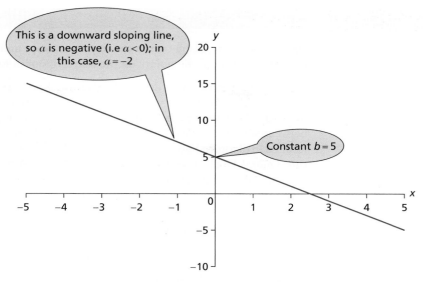

Figure 8.2.2 **A graph of the linear function** $y = -2x + 5$.

Figure 8.2.1 shows the graph is upward sloping when a is **positive** (i.e. $a > 0$), whereas in Figure 8.2.2 a is **negative** (i.e. $a < 0$) and the graph is downward sloping. The size of a determines the steepness of the slope. The constant b is where the line intercepts the *y*-axis: it is called the **y-axis intercept**, or just the **intercept** of the line.

Finding the equation of a line

From Figures 8.2.1 and 8.2.2 and equation (8.2.2) we see that, if we know the slope and intercept of a linear function, we have gained sufficient information to write down the equation of the function (Example 8.2.1).

Example	8.2.1

Q A machine manufactures plastic pipes for gas, water, etc. Before it produces any pipe, it is loaded with plastic granules and coloured dye, the cost of which is £5,000 irrespective of the amount of pipe to be produced. Costs for the electricity consumption of the machine are £10 per metre. What is the total cost function for manufacturing any quantity of this pipe?

A Whatever the quantity produced, there is a fixed set-up cost of £5,000, as well as the unit cost of £10 per metre. If we let x be the quantity of pipe in metres, then the variable cost is £10x. So total cost is fixed cost plus variable cost:

$$\text{Total cost} = 10x + 5{,}000 \qquad (8.2.4)$$

Equation (8.2.4) is a linear function with a slope of +10 (i.e. $a = 10$) and intercept of 5,000 (i.e. $b = 5{,}000$).

Finding the equation of a line from a graph

In Example 8.2.1 we could write the appropriate linear equation without doing any algebra because we knew the slope and intercept. If we have an accurate graph, we can find the slope and intercept and therefore write the linear equation (Example 8.2.2).

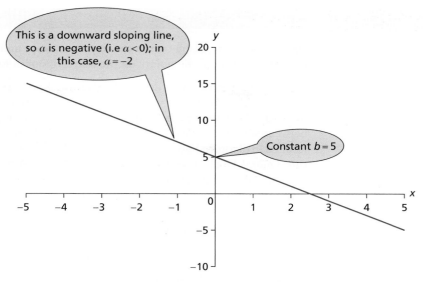

8.2.2

Q Draw an accurate graph to find the slope, intercept and hence the equation of the line drawn through the points on the scattergram in Example 8.1.1.

A Figure 8.2.3 shows a line drawn through the scatterpoints of Example 8.1.1. By extending the line to the vertical axis (shown dotted), we see it has an intercept of $b = 1,200$. We find the slope of the line by taking the difference in height between any two points on the line graph and dividing by the corresponding difference in distance between them. Let us label price p and sales s, rather than use the general labels x and y. So when $p = 20$, $s = 800$ and when $p = 30$, $s = 600$. Dividing the difference in height of the line graph (i.e. $800 - 600 = 200$) by the difference in its length (i.e. $20 - 30 = -10$), we find a slope of $a = 200/-10 = -20$, as shown by the triangle in Figure 8.2.3.

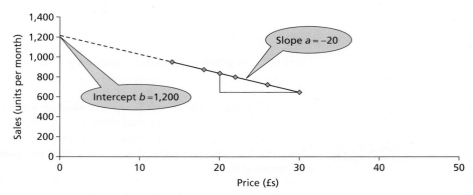

Figure 8.2.3 **The slope and intercept of a line joining the points.**

Using equation (8.2.2), we get the linear equation:

$$s = -20p + 1200 \tag{8.2.5}$$

Finding the equation of a line from the data

In Example 8.2.2 we were able to determine the slope and intercept because we had drawn an accurate graph. However, we can calculate the slope and intercept of a line without drawing a graph by using equation (8.2.2): see Example 8.2.3.

8.2.3

Q Use equation (8.2.2) to find the equation of the line that passes though all the scatterpoints in Example 8.1.1.

A The general linear equation, with p for price and s for sales, is:

$$s = ap + b \tag{8.2.6}$$

We want the line to pass through all the datapoints in Table 8.1.1:

Price (p)	Sales (s)
14	920
18	840
20	800
30	600
26	680
22	760

Putting each datapoint into equation (8.2.6) gives a **system of equations**:

$$920 = a * 14 + b \qquad \text{i.e.} \qquad 14a + b = 920$$
$$840 = a * 18 + b \qquad \text{i.e.} \qquad 18a + b = 840$$
$$800 = a * 20 + b \qquad \text{i.e.} \qquad 20a + b = 800$$
$$600 = a * 30 + b \qquad \text{i.e.} \qquad 30a + b = 600$$
$$680 = a * 26 + b \qquad \text{i.e.} \qquad 26a + b = 680$$
$$760 = a * 22 + b \qquad \text{i.e.} \qquad 22a + b = 760$$

In Section 2.2 we calculated the coefficients of a system of equations, in this case a (the slope) and b (the intercept), by solving the equations. However, to draw a line we need only two points on a graph. So we can select any pair of equations from the above list and solve them using any of the methods we encountered in Sections 2.2 or 3.5. For example, take the first two equations:

$$14a + b = 920 \tag{8.2.7}$$
$$18a + b = 840 \tag{8.2.8}$$

First, subtract equation (8.2.7) from equation (8.2.8) to give $4a = -80$, and so the slope of the line is $a = -80/4 = -20$. Next, multiply equation (8.2.7) by 18/14 and subtract equation (8.2.8) to give $b = 1,200$.

Exercises 8.2

1 Identify the slope and intercept of the following linear functions:
(a) $y = 5x - 10$ (b) $C = 500 + 10q$ (c) $D = 500 - 12p$

2 An enterprising student buys cans of cool soft drinks at 50p each and a coolbox for £15, and then sells the drinks to sunbathers. Write down a linear total cost function for his enterprise.

3 Plastic tube is extruded from three different machines according to tube length. Unit production costs for all three machines are 20p per centimetre, but set-up costs vary according to which machine is used:

Tube length (metres)	Set-up costs (£)
Less than 5	200
5 to 10	500
Greater than 10	800

Write down a cost function for producing tubes of length x metres.

4 At a unit price of £25 weekly demand for a product is 300 units, and at £40 it is 150 units. Find a linear relationship between weekly demand and unit price, and predict demand at £30. Rearrange the equation to find an expression for unit price in terms of quantity demanded. Identify the independent and dependent variables.

5 A firm will produce 290 items per week if it can sell them at a unit price of £50, and will increase production to 750 items per week if it can sell them at £70. Find a linear function for production quantity in terms of price (i.e. the supply function). However, market research indicates that only 240 items will be bought when the unit price is £70 and 460 items when the price is £50. Assuming that demand is linearly related to price, find a demand function for the product. Use these equations to find the equilibrium price (i.e. the unit price that satisfies both supplier and consumer).

6 A food contains colouring and thickener, costing £50 and £10 per kilo respectively. A production budget of £1,000 per day is allocated to the two ingredients. Write an equation for the production possibilities if the budget is to be fully spent. As the thickener is cheaper than the colouring, the production manager wishes to write the production possibilities as a function to determine quantities of colouring in terms of thickener. Find this function, and identify the slope and intercept of the line.

8.3 Least-squares linear regression

In the previous section we found the equation of a line passing through a set of data points by identifying the slope and intercept of the line drawn through the points on a scattergram. Sometimes the scattergram is such that we cannot draw a straight line through all data points, so we find a line that is as close as possible to the data points, called the **best-fit** line. The process of finding an equation to represent the best-fit pattern in a dataset is called **regression**. In this section we consider how we can find the best-fit line.

The prerequisites of this section are:
- Algorithms, variables and algebra (Section 2.1);
- Subscripted variables and sigma notation (Section 2.4);
- Presenting and describing small datasets (Section 4.3);
- Measures of variation (Section 5.3);
- Relationships, functions and equations (Section 8.1);
- Linear functions (Section 8.2).

A best-fit line

In Section 8.2 we considered examples in which it was possible to draw a line through all the relevant data, but sometimes we can only approximate a relationship between two variables by a linear function. To do this, we find the equation of the line that is as close as possible to the scatterpoints (Example 8.3.1).

Example 8.3.1

Q A company has recorded the output and costs of a production process, as shown in Table 8.3.1. What is the cost function of this process at any level of output, and what are the fixed and unit process costs?

Table 8.3.1 **Manufacturing costs and output over 5 years.**

Year	Output	Costs
1	50	2,500
2	95	1,800
3	200	5,500
4	120	2,800
5	150	4,500

A Figure 8.3.1 shows that the scatterpoints do not all fall on a straight line, which could be due to several factors. First, the data may not be accurate, because all costs have been rounded to the nearest £10. Second, the process may not be operating efficiently, and process costs may not be measured on the same basis.

Third, a linear function may be an inappropriate model for the total cost function. Finally, there may be other factors that contribute to cost. Although we may be unable to get more accurate data, we can question the use of a linear model (we consider alternative functions in Chapter 9). However, to identify the underlying relationship between total costs and output, we shall assume they have a linear relationship.

The best-fit line lies somewhere between all the data points (i.e. some will be above the line and others below). We could draw the line where we think it should be and read off the slope and intercept (Figure 8.3.1).

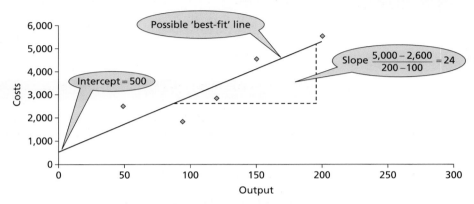

Figure 8.3.1 **A possible best-fit line for Example 8.3.1.**

Reading from the graph and denoting total cost by TC and output by x, we can estimate the total cost function as:

$$TC = 24x + 500 \tag{8.3.1}$$

From Equation (8.3.1) we estimate the fixed costs to be £500 and unit process costs to be £24.

Quantifying the best-fit line

The accuracy of the best-fit line depends on how good our scattergram is. Another approach would be to guess the slope and intercept of the best-fit line, and draw a graph of the line on the scattergram to see how close it is. We could apply trial and error until the line is as close as possible to all the points. However, this is a judgemental approach, and depends on how we measure 'close'.

To quantify the fit of the line to the scatterpoints we can use the measures Mean Absolute Error (MAE) and Mean Square Error (MSE), which are related to two measures of variation (i.e. MAD and variance) that we encountered in Section 5.3. Both can be used to measure the mean vertical differences between the scatterpoints and the equivalent points on the best-fit line. MAE considers the absolute difference, whereas MSE squares the differences.

MAE and MSE

We can extend the measures of variation we encountered in Section 5.3 by choosing an appropriate linear equation and calculating the y values on the line for the observed x values. To distinguish between the values given by the linear equation and the observed values, we denote the observed values by y and those of the linear equation with slope a and intercept b by y':

$$y' = ax + b \tag{8.3.2}$$

Using MAD (equation (5.3.4)), we define MAE:

$$MAE = \frac{\sum_{i=1}^{n} |y_i - y_i'|}{n} \qquad (8.3.3)$$

Using variance (equation (5.3.7)), we define MSE:

$$MSE = \frac{\sum_{i=1}^{n} (y_i - y_i')^2}{n} \qquad (8.3.4)$$

Both measures are illustrated in Example 8.3.2.

Example 8.3.2

Q Calculate the MAE and MSE for the best-fit line in Example 8.3.1, and show that MAD and MSE can be reduced by choosing other slopes and intercepts for the line.

A In Section 5.3 we noted that MAD and variance are easily calculated using a table (Table 8.3.2). However, we do not know whether this is the best-fit line, so we can try to find another line with a smaller MAE or MSE. In fact, the line $y = 25x + 500$ has an MAE = 555, and the line $y = 24x + 480$ has a lower MSE.

 8.3

Table 8.3.2 **The calculation of MAE and MSE for Example 8.3.1.**

Data point i	Observed values x_i	Observed values y_i	Line values $y_i' = 24x_i + 500$	Difference $(y_i - y_i')$	Absolute difference $|y_i - y_i'|$	Squared difference $(y_i - y_i')^2$
1	50	2,500	1,700	800	800	640,000
2	95	1,800	2,780	−980	980	960,400
3	200	5,500	5,300	200	200	40,000
4	120	2,800	3,380	−580	580	336,400
5	150	4,500	4,100	400	400	160,000
				Sum (Σ) =	2,960	2,136,800
					MAE = 592	MSE = 427,360

To find the smallest MAE or MSE is a tedious process and depends on how good our guesses are for the slope and intercept. A better approach would be to derive a formula for them; although this cannot be achieved using absolute differences, it can if we use MSE.

Least-squares linear regression

We can derive a formula for the slope a and the intercept b of the linear function that minimises MSE. This approach is called least-squares regression:

$$Slope = a = \frac{n \sum_{i=1}^{n} x_i y_i - \sum_{i=1}^{n} x_i \sum_{i=1}^{n} y_i}{n \sum_{i=1}^{n} x_i^2 - \left(\sum_{i=1}^{n} x_i\right)^2} \qquad (8.3.5)$$

$$\text{Intercept} = b = \frac{\sum\limits_{i=1}^{n} y_i}{n} - \frac{a \sum\limits_{i=1}^{n} x_i}{n} \qquad (8.3.6)$$

The derivations of these formulae can be found on the CD and on the associated website **www.mcgraw-hill.co.uk/textbooks/dewhurst**, and are illustrated in Example 8.3.3. Some calculators and spreadsheets have inbuilt functions to calculate the slope and intercept of the least-squares regression line.

8.4

Example 8.3.3

Q Use equations (8.3.5) and (8.3.6) to find the slope and intercept of the least-squares regression line for the data given in Table 8.3.1.

A We can perform the calculations in a table, as shown by Table 8.3.3:

Table 8.3.3 **Calculations for the least-squares regression line for Example 8.3.3.**

i	x_i	y_i	x_i^2	$x_i y_i$
1	50	2,500	2,500	125,000
2	95	1,800	9,025	171,000
3	200	5,500	40,000	1,100,000
4	120	2,800	14,400	336,000
5	150	4,500	22,500	675,000
Sums (Σ) =	615	17,100	88,425	2,407,000

8.4

Entering the 'sums' from Table 8.3.3 into equations (8.3.5) and (8.3.6) gives:

$$\text{Slope} = a = \frac{5 * 2{,}407{,}000 - 615 * 17{,}100}{5 * 88{,}425 - 615 * 615} = 23.764$$

$$\text{Intercept} = b = \frac{17{,}100}{5} - 23.764 * \frac{615}{5} = 497.066$$

Therefore the least-squares regression line is:

$$y' = 23.764x + 497.066 \qquad (8.3.7)$$

Exercises 8.3

1 The number of customers in 10 different areas and corresponding monthly sales of a product are:

Sales area	1	2	3	4	5	6	7	8	9	10
No. of customers	48	32	40	34	30	50	26	50	22	43
Sales volume	312	164	280	196	200	288	146	361	149	252

Plot a scattergram of sales volume against number of customers and find the equation of the best-fit line. Use your linear model to predict sales volume for areas having (a) 10 and (b) 60 customers.

2 Over the last 10 years, a bank's counter cash transactions per year (CCTs) have declined owing to increasing use of cash dispensers, credit cards, etc. in this way:

Year	1	2	3	4	5	6	7	8	9	10
CCT (million)	25	18	11	12	14	11	10	9	11	9

Use least-squares linear regression to model CCT over time.

3 Demand for tyres in each quarter over 4 years is as follows:

Year	Quarter 1	2	3	4
1995	672	636	680	704
1996	744	700	756	784
1997	828	800	840	880
1998	936	860	944	972

Draw a scattergram with quarters 1 to 16 on the horizontal axis and demand on the vertical axis and find the best-fit trend line. By joining the points within, but not between, each year can you identify a quarterly sales pattern? Such data are called 'time series' and are considered in more detail in Chapter 11.

8.4 Appropriateness and correlation

In this chapter we have considered simple linear regression and have found the regression equation (in linear regression the equation is, of course, a line) by finding the slope and intercept of the line that passes as close as possible to all the scatterpoints. Although we can quantify how close our linear equation is by measuring the distance of the scatterpoints from the best-fit line (i.e. MAE and MSE), these measures do not tell us how 'good' our linear function is as a model of the underlying pattern in the data. Furthermore, a linear equation may not fully explain the underlying relationship, and we might limit its use in some way or even use a different function. Sometimes there are several alternatives we could use as a model. In this section we measure the appropriateness of a function as a model of the relationship between variables in a dataset, and look at how we might set limits on its use. In the next chapter we consider other mathematical functions we can use when the linear function is inappropriate.

The prerequisites of this section are:
- Subscripted variables and sigma notation (Section 2.4);
- Presenting and describing small datasets (Section 4.3);
- Relationships, functions and equations (Section 8.1);
- Linear functions (Section 8.2).
- Least-squares linear regression (Section 8.3).

How good is the model?

The choice of equation to use as a model needs careful thought. It may be that a linear function is not always the most appropriate. The MAE and MSE tell us on average how close our chosen equation is to the scatterpoints, and are useful in comparing different models for a dataset, but they do not tell us how 'good' our chosen function is as a model of the underlying pattern in the data. However, we can use the **coefficient of determination** and the related concept of the **correlation coefficient**.

The coefficient of determination

This compares the sum of the squared differences between the height of the regression line (y') and their mean with the MSE. It is denoted by R^2:

$$R^2 = \frac{\left(n\sum_{i=1}^{n}x_iy_i - \sum_{i=1}^{n}x_i\sum_{i=1}^{n}y_i\right)^2}{\left[n\sum_{i=1}^{n}x_i^2 - \left(\sum_{i=1}^{n}x_i\right)^2\right]\left[n\sum_{i=1}^{n}y_i^2 - \left(\sum_{i=1}^{n}y_i\right)^2\right]}$$

(8.4.1)

The derivation of this formula can be found on the CD and on the associated website **www.mcgraw-hill.co.uk/textbooks/dewhurst**.

Although equation (8.4.1) seems complicated, it is similar to equation (8.3.5), except that we need to calculate the square of the y's and square the numerator. As with equation (8.3.5), we can use a table but add an extra column to it (Example 8.4.1). R^2 has values between 0 and 1, with zero representing no linear relationship between the variables and 1 representing a perfect linear relationship.

The correlation coefficient

The **correlation coefficient** (or **sample correlation**) is the square root of the coefficient of determination, and is calculated from equation (8.4.1):

$$r = \frac{\left(n\sum_{i=1}^{n}x_iy_i - \sum_{i=1}^{n}x_i\sum_{i=1}^{n}y_i\right)}{\sqrt{\left[n\sum_{i=1}^{n}x_i^2 - \left(\sum_{i=1}^{n}x_i\right)^2\right]\left[n\sum_{i=1}^{n}y_i^2 - \left(\sum_{i=1}^{n}y_i\right)^2\right]}}$$

(8.4.2)

The correlation coefficient takes values between −1 and +1. Values near +1 suggest a good positive correlation (i.e. y increases when x increases) and values near −1 a good negative correlation (i.e. y decreases when x increases). Some calculators and spreadsheets have inbuilt functions to calculate the coefficient of determination and the correlation coefficient.

8.5

Example **8.4.1**

Q Calculate the coefficient of determination and correlation coefficient for the data in Table 8.3.1.

A By extending Table 8.3.3, we obtain Table 8.4.1.

Table 8.4.1 **Calculations for the coefficient of determination for Example 8.4.1.**

i	x_i	y_i	x_i^2	x_iy_i	y_i^2
1	50	2,500	2,500	125,000	6,250,000
2	95	1,800	9,025	171,000	3,240,000
3	200	5,500	40,000	1,100,000	30,250,000
4	120	2,800	14,400	336,000	7,840,000
5	150	4,500	22,500	675,000	20,250,000
Sums (Σ) =	615	17,100	88,425	2,407,000	67,830,000

$$R^2 = \frac{(5*2,407,000 - 615*17,100)^2}{(5*88,425 - 615*615)*(5*67,830,000 - 17,100*17,100)}$$

$$= 0.772$$

So 77.2% of the squared deviations from the mean are accounted for by the least-squares regression line. As this is a high percentage, we say that our linear equation is a reasonably good model of the relationship between costs and output for the data in Table 8.3.1. Applying equation (8.4.2) gives $r = \sqrt{0.772} = 0.879$. As this is close to +1, it suggests that the model is a good representation of the relationship between costs and output, and that costs increase as output increases.

Appropriateness

Before we start any form of modelling, we first need to decide on the most appropriate model for our purposes, and then use techniques such as least-squares regression to find the appropriate equation. Although there are many alternative functions to consider as models, we might use a linear function to model any underlying trend. But we need to be aware of the limitations of the equations as models of the relationships between variables. We can restrict the **range of applicability** or the relevant **domain of a function** to suit our purposes (Example 8.4.2).

Example	**8.4.2**

Q Consider the linear equation $s = -20p + 1,200$ (equation (8.2.5)) and suggest a valid domain for its use as a model of sales in terms of price for the data given in Table 8.1.1.

A Let us extend equation (8.2.5) well beyond the dataset given by Table 8.1.1. First, consider what the model predicts for a price of zero (i.e. the retailer gives the product away). Putting $p = 0$ into equation (8.2.3) gives:

$$s = -20*0 + 1,200 = 1,200$$

When things are free, people tend to accept them. So, if the retailer has 20,000 potential customers per month then sales (actually, giveaways) would probably be 20,000 and not 1,200. Indeed, as the unit price approaches zero, most customers would buy it, and therefore we would not expect the linear model to predict sales at such low prices.

Next, consider the other extreme, when the price is very high. The linear model predicts that at £60 no one will buy it, as shown by extending the line in Figure 8.2.3 until it crosses the horizontal axis or, better still, by substituting $s = 0$ in equation (8.2.3):

$$0 = -20p + 1,200$$

i.e. $20p = 1,200$

i.e. $p = \dfrac{1,200}{20} = 60$

Again, this does not seem appropriate; there is always someone who will buy the product at any price (indeed, when a product becomes extremely expensive, it can become a status symbol). Note that for prices above £60 the model predicts negative sales, and this too does not seem reasonable.

To overcome this problem we could restrict the linear model to prices around the dataset: for example, in Example 8.1.1 we might use it for the price range between £5 and £55. We can make this explicit in our model by using inequalities:

$$s = -20p + 1,200 \text{ for } 5 < p < 55 \qquad (8.4.4)$$

In general, we refer to this price range as the 'range of applicability' or the relevant 'domain of the function'.

A second approach would be to use an entirely different function as a model of sales in terms of price, one that exhibits the expected behaviour. Figure 8.4.1 is probably more representative of a typical demand function.

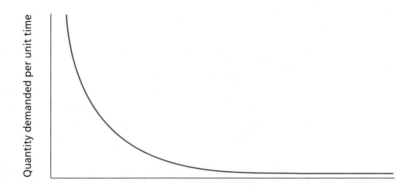

Figure 8.4.1 **A typical non-linear demand function.**

Figure 8.4.1 shows a non-linear function (i.e. curve), which, instead of crossing either axis, almost becomes the axes at extreme values (i.e. when price is almost zero sales become very large or when price is very large sales become almost zero). We consider such functions in Chapter 9.

In general, there are several appropriate mathematical functions that we could use as models for a particular dataset. We could initially consider all of them and then use a criterion (e.g. MAE or MSE) to select the most suitable function.

Exercises 8.4

1 In Question 1 of Exercises 8.1, we used a linear function to model the behaviour of demand in terms of price. Discuss why at extreme values (i.e. the x and y intercepts) such a linear model is not applicable to the whole range of demands and prices, and identify a valid domain for the linear function in this case. Do the same for Question 3 of Exercises 8.1.

2 If, in Question 1 of Exercises 8.3, sales of 595 were later observed for a sales area having 60 customers, what might you conclude?

3 For Questions 1, 2 and 3 of Exercises 8.3, calculate the coefficient of determination and the correlation coefficient, and use the Chi-squared distribution to comment on the appropriateness of using a linear function as a model in each case.

4 What values would you expect for the coefficient of determination and the correlation coefficient for the supply and demand functions found in Question 3 of Exercises 8.2?

This chapter introduced the concept of using mathematical functions to model behaviour observed in business and management. These are sometimes referred to as 'causal' models. They provide information for managers and decision-makers by analysing the relationships between the dependent and independent variables of the model. For example, such models can predict what might happen between or beyond the set of data from which the model was constructed. In Chapter 10 we shall show how these models can be analysed to provide information for managers and decision-makers.

In this chapter we considered the simplest mathematical function (i.e. the linear function) and its typical applications in Business and Management (e.g. Economics, Operations Management and Marketing). In some cases, it is possible to construct a linear model without using mathematics, whereas in others it is necessary to solve a system of equations or use least-squares regression to find the appropriate linear function. Sometimes there may be more than one mathematical function that could be used as a model, and by using common sense and quantitative criteria we can identify the most suitable model. In Chapter 9 we shall consider other kinds of mathematical function (e.g. non-linear and multivariate functions) and in Chapter 11 other models in which the independent variable is time (i.e. 'time-series').

Non-linear and multivariate relationships

Introduction

In Chapter 8 we used linear functions to model relationships between variables. However, linear models are not always appropriate: for example, instead of expecting sales of any product to increase linearly for ever, we would expect them to gradually level off as the market becomes saturated. In such cases a graph of sales over time would be a curve rather than a straight line. We saw in Chapter 6 that continuous probability distributions are curves. Therefore we might want to use non-linear functions as models. So far we have only considered relationships between one dependent and one independent variable (e.g. the profit resulting from the sales of a single product). In general, a firm's profits depend on the sales of all its products. In this chapter we look at non-linear functions, and functions with more than one independent variable.

Chapter objectives

- To recognise quadratic, polynomial, hyperbolic and exponential functions
- To recognise multivariate functions
- To appreciate non-linear and multivariate modelling techniques
- To appreciate the applications of non-linear and multivariate models in management

Chapter contents

Quadratic functions

In this section we look at one of the most common non-linear functions used in business and management, particularly in Economics, the **quadratic function**. It has extremely useful properties, and is often used to model the revenue and profit functions of firms.

The prerequisites of this section are:
- What is Quantitative Methods? (Section 1.1);
- From numbers to symbols (Chapter 2);
- Presenting and describing small datasets (Section 4.3);
- Modelling relationships (Chapter 8).

The quadratic function

The general quadratic function has the equation:

$$y = ax^2 + bx + c \qquad (9.1.1)$$

where a, b and c determine the shape and position of the graph. The y-axis (vertical) intercept is c, and a and b determine the curvature of the graph.

The graph of a quadratic function is called a **parabola**, and it has some very useful properties. A quadratic function always contains a squared independent variable, and its parabola is a symmetrical curve. The line of symmetry is located at what we call the **turning point**, which can be a **maximum** or a **minimum**. The graph may or may not cross the horizontal axis; if it does, it is said to have **real roots**. A quadratic function can have **no real roots** (i.e. it does not cross the horizontal axis); **two coincidental real roots**, **which appear as one real root** (i.e. it sits on the horizontal axis); or **two distinct real roots** (i.e. it crosses the horizontal axis). Figure 9.1.1 shows some typical parabolas and their features.

The quadratic function arises naturally in microeconomics, when calculating the revenue obtained from a linear sales function (Example 9.1.1).

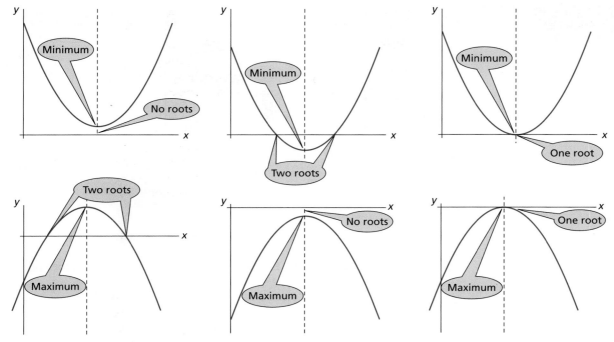

Figure 9.1.1 **Some typical parabolas (the line of symmetry is shown dashed).**

We can see from Figure 9.1.1 that the **turning point of any parabola is always located midway between the roots (if they exist)** (because of a parabola's symmetry).

Example **9.1.1**

Q In Example 8.1.1 the linear function $s = -20p + 1,200$ was used to model the sales (s) of a product in terms of unit price (p). Find an expression for revenue in terms of price, and comment on its features.

A Revenue is income gained from the quantity of products sold at a particular price:

Revenue = Quantity sold * Price   *(9.1.2)*

Table 9.1.1 shows the revenue calculations over a range of prices for the sales function $s = -20p + 1,200$.

Table 9.1.1 **Sales and revenue at various prices for Example 9.1.1.**

Price	Sales ($s = -20p + 1,200$)	Revenue (= Sales * Price)
0	1,200	0
5	1,100	5,500
10	1,000	10,000
15	900	13,500
20	800	16,000
25	700	17,500
30	600	18,000
35	500	17,500
40	400	16,000
45	300	13,500
50	200	10,000
55	100	5,500
60	0	0

9.1

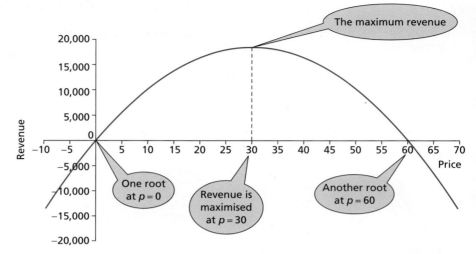

Figure 9.1.2 **A revenue curve for Example 9.1.1, showing its roots and turning point.**

Figure 9.1.2 shows a graph (in this case a parabola) of revenue against price.

The highest point on the curve (i.e. the turning point where revenue is maximised) is exactly halfway between the roots, at a price of £30. We look at this form of analysis in greater detail in Chapter 10. By studying the parabola in Figure 9.1.2, we can find an equation for revenue in terms of price. Let us start with the sales function:

Sales $= -20p + 1{,}200$

and from equation (9.1.2) we know that
Revenue = (Number of units sold) $*$ (Unit price), so:

$$\text{Revenue} = (-20p + 1{,}200) * p$$
$$= -20p^2 + 1{,}200p$$
$$\text{or} \quad R = -20p^2 + 1{,}200p \qquad\qquad (9.1.3)$$

This is a quadratic function and, as we have seen, its graph is a parabola.

Fitting quadratic functions

In Example 9.1.1 we saw how quadratic functions arise in microeconomics when we calculate revenue from a linear sales function. Sometimes we want to fit a quadratic function to a scattergram, as we did with linear functions in Chapter 8. Example 9.1.2 illustrates how we can fit a quadratic function exactly through a set of datapoints, and Example 9.1.3 illustrates how we can find a best-fit quadratic function using least-squares regression.

Example 9.1.2

Q   Table 9.1.2 shows the profits and output levels of a firm over 3 years. Find a profit function in terms of output to support production planning.

Table 9.1.2 **Profit and production output over 3 years for Example 9.1.2.**

Year	Production output (1,000 units)	Profit (£1,000s)
1	30	500
2	40	800
3	50	900

A Let us start by drawing a scattergram as we did in Section 8.2, shown by Figure 9.1.3.

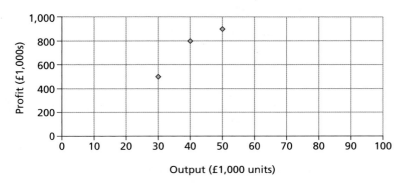

Figure 9.1.3 **A scattergram of profit against output for Table 9.1.2.**

We can see from Figure 9.1.3 that the three scatterpoints do not lie on a line. Furthermore, a linear relationship between profit and output would suggest that profit could be increased indefinitely by increasing output. This is unlikely because of diminishing returns to scale, which can be seen in Figure 9.1.3, and means that there is a point where the costs of increased output outweigh the revenue gained. So we would expect a profit function to have a turning point (i.e. maximum) and a point beyond which it is no longer profitable to increase output (i.e. there would be a root). A non-linear function (i.e. curve) would be appropriate to model profit in terms of output, and the simplest curve with these properties is a parabola.

As there are only three scatterpoints in Figure 9.1.3, we may be able to draw a parabola that passes through them exactly. To see whether this is possible, we can take the general quadratic equation (equation 9.1.1), substitute the three datapoints, and try to solve the resulting system of equations, as we did with the linear function in Example 8.2.3.

In Economics, the π (pi) symbol is often used to denote profit, and quantity is denoted by q, so our quadratic model becomes:

$$\pi = aq^2 + bq + c \tag{9.1.4}$$

As the data in Table 9.1.2 are in 1,000s, we shall use 1,000s throughout, to make life easy. Putting the three datapoints into equation (9.1.4) gives the following system of equations:

$$500 = a * 30^2 + b * 30 + c \quad \text{i.e.} \quad 900a + 30b + c = 500$$

$$800 = a * 40^2 + b * 40 + c \quad \text{i.e.} \quad 1{,}600a + 40b + c = 800$$

$$900 = a * 50^2 + b * 50 + c \quad \text{i.e.} \quad 2{,}500a + 50b + c = 900$$

As we have seen, if such a system of equations can be solved, we can use any of the methods from Sections 2.2 or 3.5. This system can be solved, and gives the solution:

$$a = -1, b = 100 \text{ and } c = -1,600$$

Therefore our exact-fitting quadratic model for the data in Table 9.1.2 is:

$$\pi = -q^2 + 100q - 1,600 \qquad\qquad (9.1.5)$$

We can now plot a graph of equation (9.1.5) for production planning (Figure 9.1.4):

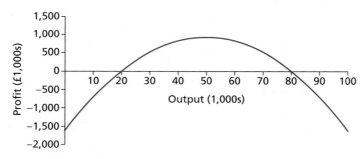

Figure 9.1.4 **An exact-fitting quadratic profit function for Example 9.1.2.**

Figure 9.1.4 shows that profits are made only when production is in the range $20,000 < q < 80,000$, and that production output of $q = 50,000$ maximises profit. We look at this form of analysis in greater detail in Chapter 10.

Best-fit quadratic functions

In Example 9.1.2 we were able to find a quadratic function that passed through all the data points because we had only three scatterpoints, and because the general quadratic function (i.e. equation 9.1.1) has only three coefficients (a, b and c). So we were able to solve a system of equations to find the coefficients. In other cases we can find a best-fit quadratic, and we can use least-squares regression to do so. Unlike linear functions, there are no standard off-the-shelf formulae for the coefficients of the best-fit quadratic, although it is quite possible to derive them. However, many spreadsheets and statistical packages (e.g. Minitab and the Statistical Package for the Social Sciences [SPSS]) can perform non-linear, least-squares regression, as shown in Example 9.1.3.

Example | **9.1.3**

Q   Table 9.1.3 shows the monthly output and profit figures for a product. Find a quadratic model of profits in terms of output to support production planning.

A   Using non-linear, least-squares regression the best-fit quadratic function is:

$$\pi = -1.01q^2 + 101q - 1,018 \qquad\qquad (9.1.6)$$

Figure 9.1.5 shows a graph of equation (9.1.6) superimposed on the scattergram drawn from Table 9.1.3:

Table 9.1.3 **Monthly output and profits for Example 9.1.3.**

Month	Output	Profit
1	40	1,190
2	50	1,500
3	45	1,390
4	60	1,250
5	55	1,450
6	40	1,600
7	55	1,410
8	60	1,420
9	55	1,560
10	45	1,610
11	50	1,490
12	60	1,550

9.2

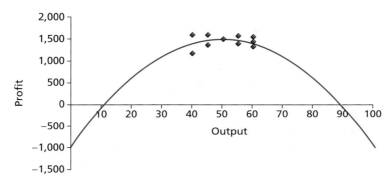

Figure 9.1.5 **Best-fit quadratic model of profit for Example 9.1.3.**

Figure 9.1.5 shows that profits are made only when production is in the range $10 < q < 90$, and that production output of $q = 50$ maximises profit. We look at this form of analysis in greater detail in Chapter 10.

Exercises 9.1

1 Multiply out the brackets in the expression below to obtain an equation:

$$y = (x - 1)(x - 3)$$

Calculate y for $x = 0, 1, 2, 3$ and 4, and from the data draw a scattergram, joining up the scatterpoints to form a graph. What is this graph called, and where does it cross the x-axis? How could you find where the graph crosses the horizontal axis from the expression above? Where does the graph cross the y-axis, and how could you find this from your equation?

2 For each of the functions below construct a data table, draw a scattergram, and join up the points to form graphs. What do they show?
(a) $y = x^2$ (b) $y^2 = -x$
(c) $y = -x^2 + 3x - 2$ (d) $y = x^2 - 3x + 10$.

3 For Questions 2 and 4 of Exercises 8.2, assume that demand and price are linearly related and that production is exactly geared to demand. Calculate the revenue (i.e. price * quantity) at demands ranging from 0 to 1,200 in steps of 100, and draw scattergrams of revenue at these points. Write down the equations for revenue as a function of output.

4 A monopolist has a fixed cost of £500 and a unit production cost of £3 for one of its products and is faced with the linear weekly demand function, Demand = $1,500 - 200 *$ Price. Write down equations for cost, revenue and profit as functions of production level q (where Profit = Revenue − Cost). How would you describe the cost, revenue and profit functions?

5 Fit a quadratic function $q = ap^2 + bp + c$ to the demands and prices below:

Price	Demand
3	120
4	90
5	70

Draw a scattergram and graph and comment on the features and applicability of the quadratic function.

6 **(This can only be done using a spreadsheet.)** The costs of producing a product over the last 12 months are:

Month	Jan.	Feb.	Mar.	Apr.	May	Jun.	Jul.	Aug.	Sept.	Oct.	Nov.	Dec.
Output (1,000s)	80	60	120	90	150	135	95	110	125	130	90	75
Cost (1,000s)	80	132	69	85	48	56	79	60	58	64	80	98

Find an equation to model costs in terms of output, and use it to forecast the cost of producing 100 units.

9.2   Polynomial functions

If we look at the general equation for a quadratic function (Section 9.1) and a linear function (Chapter 8) we can see that they are part of a greater family of functions. In this section we consider this greater family, their properties and where we might encounter them.

The prerequisites of this section are:
- What is Quantitative Methods? (Section 1.1);
- From numbers to symbols (Chapter 2);
- Modelling relationships (Chapter 8).
- Quadratic functions (Section 9.1).

Linear and quadratic functions

By studying the general equations for and the properties of linear and quadratic functions, we can see a pattern (Table 9.2.1).

Table 9.2.1 **Linear and quadratic functions.**

Function name	General equation	Coefficients	Roots	Turning points
			Possible number of	
Linear	$y = ax + b$	2	1	0
Quadratic	$y = ax^2 + bx + c$	3	2	1

A linear function has two coefficients, one root and no turning point, whereas a quadratic can have three coefficients, at most two roots and one turning point. Furthermore, a quadratic can be thought of as a linear function with an extra squared component.

Polynomial functions

Let us extend Table 9.2.1 by introducing the **cubic function**, which has a cubed independent variable, four coefficients, three roots and two turning points. Such a function is a member of the family of **polynomial functions**, which includes functions with any power and any number of coefficients, roots and turning points. In general, we can say that a linear function is a polynomial of degree (i.e. power) 1, a quadratic is a polynomial of degree 2, and so on (Table 9.2.2).

Table 9.2.2 **Part of the polynomial family of functions.**

| Function name | General equation | Degree of polynomial | Possible number of | | |
			Coefficients	Roots	Turning points
Linear	$y = ax + b$	1	2	1	0
Quadratic	$y = ax^2 + bx + c$	2	3	2	1
Cubic	$y = ax^3 + bx^2 + cx + d$	3	4	3	2
Quartic	$y = ax^4 + bx^3 + cx^2 + dx + e$	4	5	4	3
etc.	etc.	etc.	etc.	etc.	etc.

With polynomials of degree 25 or higher, we run out of labels for the coefficients, so we often use a more general notation, using subscripts. If we denote coefficients of a general polynomial function using subscripts, a_0 is the constant, a_1 is the coefficient of x, a_2 the coefficient of x^2 and so on. So:

Linear function: $\quad y = a_1 x + a_0$
Quadratic function: $y = a_2 x^2 + a_1 x + a_0$

In general, we can write a polynomial of degree n as:

$$y = a_n x^n + a_{n-1} x^{n-1} + \ldots + a_2 x^2 + a_1 x + a_0 \qquad (9.2.1)$$

Recall from Section 2.4 that any number raised to the power of zero is unity (i.e. 1); so, using sigma notation, we can abbreviate equation (9.2.1) to:

$$y = \sum_{i=0}^{n} a_i x^i \qquad (9.2.2)$$

We use polynomial functions to model situations where we expect to have turning points (with the exception of linear models). However, not all turning points are maxima or minima; sometimes we find a point of inflexion at which the graph of the function turns but continues in the same direction (Figure 9.2.1, and see Chapter 10). When using polynomials as models, we always use the simplest polynomial function that will satisfactorily represent the data. As with quadratic functions, to find the equation of a polynomial function to fit a dataset on a scattergram requires solving a system of equations or the use of a spreadsheet to undertake non-linear least-squares regression (see the further reading at the end of the book).

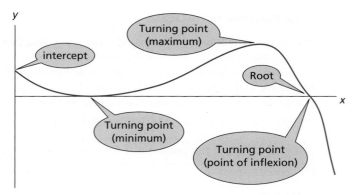

Figure 9.2.1 **The graph and features of a polynomial function.**

Exercises 9.2

1 Multiply out the brackets in the expression below to obtain an equation:

$$y = (x - 1)(x - 3)(x - 5)$$

Create a data table for $x = 0, 1, 2, 3, 5$ and 6, draw a scattergram, and join up the points to form a graph. Where does the graph cross the x-axis, and what are these values usually called? How could you find these values from the expression above? Where does the graph cross the y-axis, and how could you find this from your equation? Where are the turning points?

2 What is the highest-order polynomial function that could be exactly fitted through:
(a) 4   (b) 5 and   (c) 6 points on a scattergram?

How many points are required to exactly fit an nth degree polynomial? What is the maximum number of turning points and roots that a polynomial of degree n can have?

3 **(This can only be done using a spreadsheet.)** For the data below, find the best-fit polynomials of degrees 1 to 6. Which appear to best represent the data?

x	115	395	235	11	235	355	35	75	315	27	155	195
y	355	1,995	1,795	135	2,195	1,395	595	1,195	1,195	475	195	275

9.3 Hyperbolic functions

In the previous section we saw that polynomial functions constitute a family of functions with common properties and features. In this section we consider another family of functions often encountered in business and management, called the **hyperbolic** family.

The prerequisites of this section are:
- What is Quantitative Methods? (Section 1.1);
- From numbers to symbols (Chapter 2);
- Presenting and describing small datasets (Section 4.3);
- Modelling relationships (Chapter 8).

The basic rectangular hyperbola

The simplest hyperbolic function is the basic rectangular hyperbola:

$$y = \frac{1}{x} \tag{9.3.1}$$

Figure 9.3.1 shows a graph of equation (9.3.1), which is a symmetrical curve (the dashed line is the line of symmetry). The curve approaches the horizontal axis when x is very large and approaches the vertical axis when x is very small (either positive or negative). These features are called **asymptotes**, and the curve is said to exhibit asymptotic properties. So the asymptotes of the hyperbola given by equation (9.3.1) are $y = 0$ and $x = 0$. We can identify these asymptotes explicitly by considering what happens to the function at extreme values, when x gets very large (i.e. as x approaches either positive or negative infinity) (see Section 10.1).

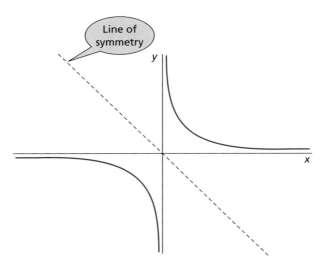

Figure 9.3.1 **The graph of a simple rectangular hyperbola.**

Rectangular hyperbolae

The asymptotes of a rectangular hyperbola do not have to be the horizontal or vertical axes as shown in Figure 9.3.2 for the hyperbola given by equation (9.3.2):

$$y = 10 + \frac{2}{(x + 1)} \tag{9.3.2}$$

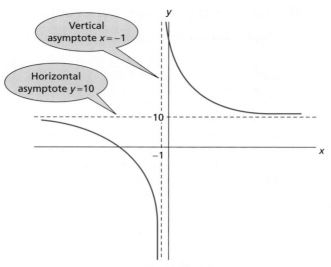

Figure 9.3.2 **Graph of equation (9.3.2).**

It can also appear in a different orientation (Figure 9.3.3) by drawing a graph of equation (9.3.3):

$$y = 10 - \frac{2}{(x + 1)}$$

(9.3.3)

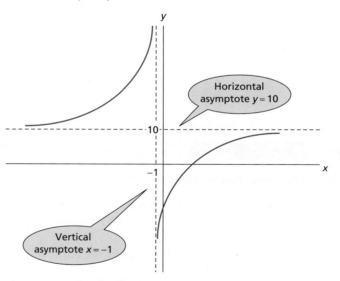

Figure 9.3.3 **Graph of equation (9.3.3).**

A general rectangular hyperbola

A more general rectangular hyperbola is given by equation (9.3.4):

$$y = a + \frac{b}{(x + c)}$$

(9.3.4)

where a, b and c are coefficients that affect the position and shape of the graph. Coefficient a determines the position of the horizontal asymptote and coefficient c the position of the vertical asymptote. Coefficient b determines the curvature and orientation of the curve.

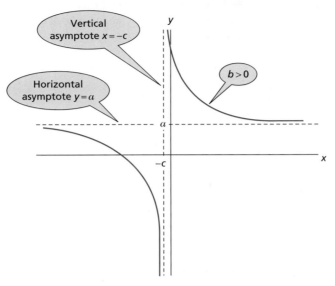

Figure 9.3.4 **A general rectangular hyperbola.**

Applications of rectangular hyperbolae

Hyperbolic functions are widely used in business and management (though often only part of them is used in modelling). They arise naturally in Economics, Production and Operations Management as a result of making assumptions about behaviour, particularly in relation to costs. Example 9.3.1 shows how a hyperbolic model arises from a linear total cost function. In Section 8.4 we saw a curve was more appropriate than a linear function as a model of demand in terms of price. So hyperbolic functions are often used as demand functions in Economics because they exhibit unit elasticity (Section 10.3). They are also used as sales functions (Example 9.3.2), and to model 'learning' curves (Example 9.3.3).

Example **9.3.1**

Q Find the average cost function per metre for the total cost function in Example 8.4.2:

$$\text{Total cost} = 10x + 5{,}000 \qquad (9.3.5)$$

where x is the number of metres of plastic pipe produced.

A Average cost is total cost divided by quantity produced:

$$\text{Average cost} = \frac{\text{Total cost}}{\text{Quantity}} \qquad (9.3.6)$$

Therefore we have:

$$\text{Average cost} = \frac{10x + 5{,}000}{x} \qquad (9.3.7)$$

Divide the numerator (i.e. $10x + 5{,}000$) by the denominator (i.e. x) and we get:

$$\text{Average cost} = 10 + \frac{5{,}000}{x} \qquad (9.3.8)$$

Equation (9.3.8) is a hyperbolic function whose graph over the valid range ($x > 0$) is shown in Figure 9.3.5 having a horizontal asymptote $y = 10$ and vertical asymptote $x = 0$:

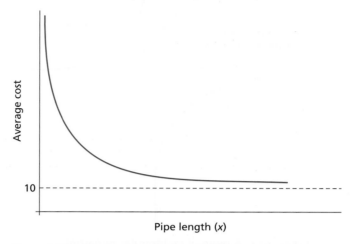

Figure 9.3.5 **Average costs per unit for Example 9.3.1.**

Example 9.3.2

Q A firm's sales for a product over 3 months are shown in Table 9.3.1. Find a suitable hyperbolic function to model sales over time.

Table 9.3.1 **Sales over 3 months.**

Time (months)	Sales (£s)
1	4,000
2	6,000
3	7,000

A We use the same approach as in Sections 8.2 and 9.1. As there are three data points, we choose a function with three coefficients so we can solve the appropriate system of equations. If we denote sales by S and time by t in equation (9.3.4), then we want a model of the form:

$$S = a + \frac{b}{(t + c)} \qquad (9.3.9)$$

Inserting the three data points into equation (9.3.9) gives this system of equations:

$$4{,}000 = a + \frac{b}{(1 + c)} \qquad (9.3.10)$$

$$6{,}000 = a + \frac{b}{(2 + c)} \qquad (9.3.11)$$

$$7{,}000 = a + \frac{b}{(3 + c)} \qquad (9.3.12)$$

We solve this system of equations by eliminating variables (see section 2.2). First, we subtract pairs of equations to eliminate coefficient a.

Subtracting equation (9.3.10) from equation (9.3.11) gives:

$$2{,}000 = \frac{b}{(2+c)} - \frac{b}{(1+c)} \qquad (9.3.13)$$

Subtracting equation (9.3.11) from (9.3.12) gives:

$$1{,}000 = \frac{b}{(3+c)} - \frac{b}{(2+c)} \qquad (9.3.14)$$

We now have two equations with two unknowns, but we cannot simply subtract them to eliminate one of the unknown coefficients. As it is better not to have fractions, we multiply each equation by the denominators. Equation (9.3.13) gives:

$$2{,}000(2+c)(1+c) = b(1+c) - b(2+c) \qquad (9.3.15)$$

Equation (9.3.14) gives:

$$1{,}000(3+c)(2+c) = b(2+c) - b(3+c) \qquad (9.3.16)$$

By multiplying out the RHS of equation (9.3.15) we get:

$$2{,}000(2+c)(1+c) = b(1+c) - b(2+c) = -b \qquad (9.3.17)$$

and if we multiply out the RHS of equation (9.3.16) we get:

$$1{,}000(3+c)(2+c) = b(2+c) - b(3+c) = -b \qquad (9.3.18)$$

Note that equations (9.3.17) and (9.3.18) are both equal to $-b$. So the two equations must be equal:

$$2{,}000(2+c)(1+c) = 1{,}000(3+c)(2+c) \qquad (9.3.19)$$

Dividing both sides of equation (9.3.19) by 1,000 and also by $(2+c)$ assuming that $c \neq -2$ then we find:

$$2(1+c) = (3+c)$$

i.e. $\quad 2 + 2c = 3 + c$

giving: $\quad c = 1$

As $c = 1$, we substitute this into either equation (9.3.17) or (9.3.18) to find a value for b. Substituting $c = 1$ into equation (9.3.17) gives:

$$2{,}000(2+1)(1+1) = -b$$

and so: $\quad b = -12{,}000$

Having found two of the coefficients, we substitute their values (i.e. $c = 1$ and $b = -12{,}000$) into equations (9.3.10), (9.3.11) or (9.3.12) to find a value for a:

Equation (9.3.10) gives: $\quad 4{,}000 = a + \dfrac{-12{,}000}{(1+1)}$

i.e. $\quad 4{,}000 = a - 6{,}000$

and so: $\quad a = 10{,}000$

So the hyperbolic function that passes through the three data points in Table 9.3.1 is:

$$S = 10,000 - \frac{12,000}{(t + 1)} \qquad (9.3.20)$$

Figure 9.3.6 shows a graph of equation (9.3.20) over 12 months:

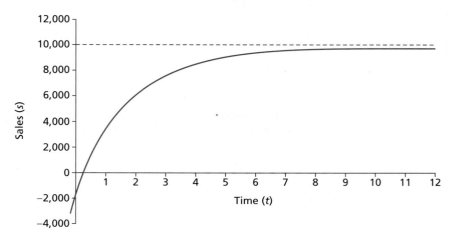

Figure 9.3.6 **Sales forecasts over 12 months for Example 9.3.2.**

The firm can use equation (9.3.20) or the graph in Figure 9.3.6 to forecast future sales. For example, in the next 2 months, when $t = 4$ and $t = 5$, equation (9.3.20) gives $S = 7,600$ and $S = 8,000$, respectively.

Best-fit hyperbolic function

In Example 9.3.2 we found a hyperbolic function to fit through three data points. In general, we might want to find the best-fit hyperbolic function to any number of points on a scattergram, but, as with quadratic and polynomial functions, there are no simple off-the-shelf formulae for the coefficients of the best-fit hyperbola, nor any inbuilt spreadsheet formulae available. However, we can find a best-fit a rectangular hyperbola with two coefficients to a scattergram by using the least-squares linear regression formulae of Section 8.3 (see Example 9.3.3).

In general, for most hyperbolic functions we have to guess a hyperbolic equation, compute MAE or MSE, and use trial and error to improve our guess (Section 8.3).

Example 9.3.3

Q At the end of an IT training course, students take a timed test. The course provider thinks the duration of the course can be reduced without significantly affecting performance in the timed tests. The course runs for 10 days, and, instead of taking the test at the end of the course, the students were given it at the end of each day (their average completion times are shown in Table 9.3.2). Model the relationship between average test completion time and the number of days of training.

Table 9.3.2 **Student times for word-processing test.**

Number of days training	1	2	3	4	5	6	7	8	9	10
Average test completion (min)	19.0	18.0	11.0	11.6	12.2	11.0	10.4	9.8	11.8	9.0

A First, we can draw a scattergram (Figure 9.3.7):

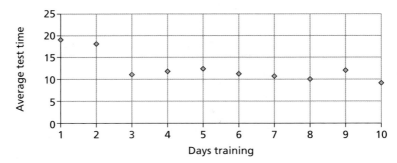

Figure 9.3.7 **Scattergram of test times for Example 9.3.3.**

Figure 9.3.7 shows that the average test time falls as more days are spent training, but eventually levels off. As linear and polynomial models seem inappropriate, we shall try a hyperbolic model of the form:

$$y = a + \frac{b}{t} \qquad (9.3.21)$$

where t is the number of days training and y the average test completion time. To best-fit the hyperbolic functions in equation (9.3.21), we make a simple transformation allowing use of the least-squares linear regression formula of Section 8.3.

By putting $x = 1/t$ equation (9.3.21) becomes:

$$y = a + bx \qquad (9.3.22)$$

As equation (9.3.22) is now a linear function of x, we can find the best-fit least-squares regression line for y as a linear function of x, as we did in Section 8.3. However, we must calculate $x = 1/t$ for each of the days before we apply equations (8.3.5) and (8.3.6).

We lay the calculations out as we did for Example 8.3.3 but include an extra column to calculate $x_i = 1/t_i$ (Table 9.3.3):

Table 9.3.3 **Least-squares regression calculations for Example 9.3.3.**

i	t_i	$x_i = 1/t_i$	y_i	x_i^2	$x_i y_i$
1	1	1.00	19.00	1.00	19.00
2	2	0.50	18.00	0.25	9.00
3	3	0.33	11.00	0.11	3.67
4	4	0.25	11.60	0.06	2.90
5	5	0.20	12.20	0.04	2.44
6	6	0.17	11.00	0.03	1.83
7	7	0.14	10.40	0.02	1.49
8	8	0.13	9.80	0.02	1.23
9	9	0.11	11.80	0.01	1.31
10	10	0.10	9.00	0.01	0.90
		Sums = 2.93	123.80	1.55	43.76

Entering the 'sums' in equations (8.3.5) and (8.3.6) we get:

$$\text{Slope} = \frac{10*43.76 - 2.93*123.8}{10*1.55 - 2.93*2.93} = 10.84$$

$$\text{Intercept} = \frac{123.8}{10} - 10.84*\frac{2.93}{10} = 9.2$$

So the equation of the best-fit line is:

$$y = 10.84x + 9.2 \tag{9.3.23}$$

and therefore the equation of the best-fit hyperbola is:

$$y = \frac{10.84}{t} + 9.2 \tag{9.3.24}$$

The graph in Figure 9.3.8 shows the best-fit hyperbola (i.e. equation 9.3.24) superimposed on a scattergram for the data in Example 9.3.3.

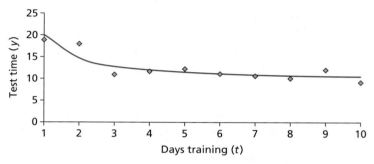

Figure 9.3.8 **Scattergram and hyperbolic function for Example 9.3.3.**

Figure 9.3.8 shows the model to be a good fit to the data, which can be confirmed by calculating the correlation coefficient. Figure 9.3.4 also shows that, after 4 days' training, test completion times improve only slightly.

Exercises 9.3

1 An economist has proposed the following model for the demand of a particular product in terms of its price:

$$\text{Demand} = \frac{1,000}{\text{Price}} \text{ (where price is in £'s)}$$

Create a data table for prices £10, £20, ..., £100, draw a scattergram, and join up the scatterpoints to produce a graph. What demand does the model predict as prices: (a) become infinitely high and (b) approach zero? Would it make any difference to the graph if price was plotted on the vertical axis? Assuming that a manufacturer can meet the demand, write down expressions for revenue in terms of: (i) price only and (ii) quantity only. If market research shows that, no matter how high the price, there is always a demand of at least 10 units for the product, how would the original model be affected?

2 A monopolist is faced with a fixed cost of £500 and a unit cost of £3 for a product. Write down an expression for average costs in terms of production quantity, and sketch a graph.

3 Sales, S, of a product are thought to be a function of advertising expenditure, x, having the following properties:
(a) Sales are 100 if no expenditure is made on advertising.
(b) Sales are 200 if advertising expenditure is £100.
(c) Very large advertising expenditure pushes sales towards a ceiling of 500, but this level is never exceeded however much is spent on advertising.

Find a function of the form: $S = a + b/(x + c)$ and identify its features.

4 Students on a psychology course were given a memory recall test, and on average it was found that after 30 minutes only 60% of the material learned was recalled, and after 60 minutes only 40% of the material was recalled. Suggest a suitable hyperbolic model of memory over time (in minutes). What percentage of learned material is held in long-term memory?

5 The following data were collected by the manufacturer of a particular model of barbecue at ten different stores last week.

Store	1	2	3	4	5	6	7	8	9	10
Price	20	22	38	28	22	33	38	29	25	28
Sales	58	56	37	50	54	39	36	45	48	47

Use these data to find a demand function for the barbecue manufacturer.

6 The demand curve for a particular product passes through the following points:

Price	Demand
3	500
4	350
5	250

(a) Find a quadratic function of the form: $q = ap^2 + bp + c$

(b) Find a hyperbolic function of the form: $q = a + \dfrac{b}{(p + c)}$

Comment on these functions as models of quantity demanded in terms of price.

9.4 Exponential functions

Exponential functions are another family of functions that are often used as models in business and management. We encountered the exponential function in Section 6.4 for calculating probabilities for the exponential distribution. Unlike polynomial and hyperbolic functions, exponential functions can exhibit very different features, and they offer a wide scope for use as models.

The prerequisites of this section are:
- What is Quantitative Methods? (Section 1.1);
- From numbers to symbols (Chapter 2);
- Counting, factorials, permutations and combinations (Section 2.6);
- Presenting and describing small datasets (Section 4.3);
- Modelling relationships (Chapter 8);
- Hyperbolic functions (Section 9.3).

A simple exponential function

In Section 1.2 we looked at counting in binary, and in Section 1.5 we encountered exponents (powers). In an exponential function the independent variable is an exponent of a base, say a, as shown in equation (9.4.1):

$$y = a^x \qquad\qquad (9.4.1)$$

A simple exponential function is shown in Example 9.4.1.

Example 9.4.1

Q A company sells lingerie through its agents via 'parties'. At these 'parties', agents are recruited, and on past evidence two further agents per month are recruited. How many agents are recruited after 1, 2, 3 and 4 months?

A Let us start by using the counting approach of Section 2.6 (see Figure 9.4.1):

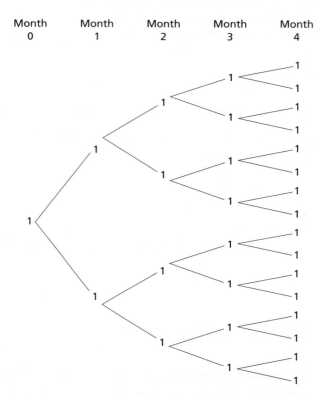

| Month 0 | Month 1 | Month 2 | Month 3 | Month 4 |

Figure 9.4.1 **The growth in the number of agents over time.**

Figure 9.4.1 shows that the number of agents grows monthly by powers of 2, as set out in Table 9.4.1:

Table 9.4.1 **Number of agents per month.**

Month	0	1	2	3	4	... etc ...	t
Number of agents	1	2	4	8	16		
i.e.	2^0	2^1	2^2	2^3	2^4	... etc ...	2^t

The relationship between number of agents (A) and time in months (t) is given by:

$$A = 2^t \tag{9.4.2}$$

Equation (9.4.2) is an example of a simple exponential function with base $a = 2$.

Features of the simple exponential function

Figure 9.4.2 shows how features of exponential functions are determined by the value of the base. Note that simple exponential functions always cross the vertical axis at $y = 1$ because any number raised to the power zero is unity.

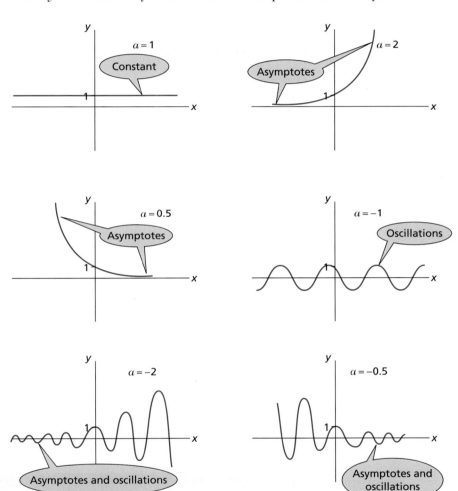

Figure 9.4.2 **Features of a simple exponential function.**

A standard form for exponential functions

As we saw in Section 1.5, although exponential functions can have any base, we often use the natural base e = 2.718 (to 3 d.p.):

$$y = e^x \tag{9.4.3}$$

9.6

The graph of equation (9.4.3) is shown in Figure 9.4.3:

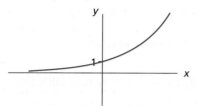

Figure 9.4.3 **Graph of a simple exponential function.**

The exponential function shown in Figure 9.4.3 has asymptotic properties, similar to those of the hyperbolic function but without symmetry.

The exponential family

Other members of the exponential family of functions that we often encounter in business and management include:

$$y = a + e^x \tag{9.4.4}$$

$$y = ae^x \tag{9.4.5}$$

$$y = e^{ax} \tag{9.4.6}$$

$$y = a + be^x \tag{9.4.7}$$

$$y = a + e^{bx} \tag{9.4.8}$$

$$y = ae^{bx} \tag{9.4.9}$$

$$y = a + be^{cx} \tag{9.4.10}$$

where a, b and c are coefficients that affect the position and shape of the graph.

Applications of exponential functions

As exponential functions have such diverse features, they are widely used as models. As we have seen in previous sections, in some cases we might be able to solve a system of equations to find the coefficients, and in other cases we might find best-fit exponential functions. Some typical applications are presented in Examples 9.4.2, 9.4.3 and 9.4.4.

Example | **9.4.2**

Q Sales of a product at the end of each of the last 3 months are shown in Table 9.4.2. Find a suitable exponential function to model sales over time.

Table 9.4.2 **Sales over time.**

Time (months)	Sales (£s)
1	4,000
2	6,000
3	7,000

A With a small number of data points, we might be able to find a function that passes through them all. An exact-fitting function must have the same number of coefficients as data points, so that we can solve the resulting system of equations. So we want an exponential function with three coefficients, such as that given by equation (9.4.10). We can write it as:

$$S = a + be^{ct} \qquad (9.4.11)$$

where S is sales and t is time in months. As we saw in Examples 8.2.3, 9.1.2 and 9.3.2, we first put the three data points into the appropriate function (in this case equation 9.4.11) to obtain the system of equations:

$$4{,}000 = a + be^{c} \qquad (9.4.12)$$

$$6{,}000 = a + be^{2c} \qquad (9.4.13)$$

$$7{,}000 = a + be^{3c} \qquad (9.4.14)$$

To solve this system of equations, we subtract pairs of equations to eliminate a. Subtracting equation (9.4.12) from equation (9.4.13) gives:

$$2{,}000 = be^{2c} - be^{c} \qquad (9.4.15)$$

and subtracting equation (9.4.13) from equation (9.4.12) gives:

$$1{,}000 = be^{3c} - be^{2c} \qquad (9.4.16)$$

Here, we cannot subtract equations to eliminate b or c, but we note that equation (9.4.15) is twice equation (9.4.16):

$$be^{2c} - be^{c} = 2(be^{3c} - b^{2c}) \qquad (9.4.17)$$

We can now eliminate c by dividing both sides of equation (9.4.17) by the common factor b:

$$e^{2c} - e^{c} = 2(e^{3c} - e^{2c}) \qquad (9.4.18)$$

We now simplify equation (9.4.18) by dividing by the common factor e^{c}:

$$e^{c} - 1 = 2(e^{2c} - e^{c}) \qquad (9.4.19)$$

We can also simplify equation (9.4.19) by taking the common factor e^{c} outside the bracket on the RHS of the equation:

$$e^{c} - 1 = 2e^{c}(e^{c} - 1) \qquad (9.4.20)$$

Finally, divide both sides of equation (9.4.20) by the common factor $(e^{c} - 1)$, assuming that $e^{c} \neq 1$:

$$1 = 2e^{c} \qquad (9.4.21)$$

Therefore we have:

$$e^{c} = 1/2 = 0.5 \qquad (9.4.22)$$

To find the value of an exponent, we use logarithms. The definition of a logarithm gives the value of c:

$$c = \ln(0.5) = -0.693 \text{ (to 3 d.p.)} \qquad (9.4.23)$$

We can now substitute c into equation (9.4.15) or (9.4.16) to find b, and using (9.4.15) gives:

$$2{,}000 = 0.25b - 0.5b = -0.25b$$

and so: $\qquad b = 2{,}000/-0.25 = -8{,}000$

To find a, we substitute $c = -0.693$ and $b = -8{,}000$ into equation (9.4.12), (9.4.13) or (9.4.14), which gives $a = 8{,}000$. So the exponential model is:

$$S = 8{,}000 - 8{,}000e^{-0.693t} \qquad (9.4.24)$$

19

Equation (9.4.23) can be used to forecast future sales. For example, putting $t = 6$ into equation (9.4.23) gives a sales forecast of $8,000 - 8,000\mathrm{e}^{-0.693*6} = 7,875$, as shown in Figure 9.4.4.

9.6

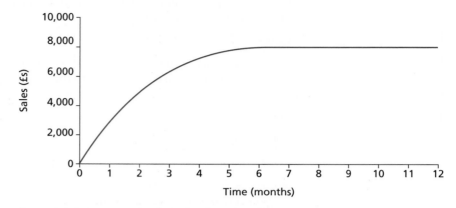

Figure 9.4.4 **An exponential sales function for Example 9.4.2.**

Best-fit exponential functions

In Example 9.3.3 we used least-squares linear regression formulae to find a best-fit hyperbola by making a simple calculation before calculating the slope and intercept. We use a similar approach in Example 9.4.3.

Example 9.4.3

Q Find a best-fit exponential function for the relationship between average test completion times and number of days' training for the data in Example 9.3.3.

A Using an approach similar to that in Example 9.3.3, we choose an exponential function having two coefficients so that we can apply least-squares linear regression such as that given by equation (9.4.7). We can write it as:

$$y = a + b\mathrm{e}^{-t} \tag{9.4.25}$$

First, as with Example 9.3.3, to transform equation (9.4.24) into a linear equation so that we can apply least-squares linear regression we need to make a substitution of the form:

$$x = \mathrm{e}^{-t} \tag{9.4.26}$$

which gives:

$$y = a + bx \tag{9.4.27}$$

Equation (9.4.26) is a linear function of x, and therefore we can find the best-fit least-squares regression line for y as a function of x as we did in Sections 8.3 and 9.3. We lay the calculations out in a table as we did for Example 9.3.3, including an extra column to calculate $x_i = \mathrm{e}_i^{-t}$ for each day, as shown in Table 9.4.3.

Now we can put the 'sums' in equations (8.3.5) and 8.3.6) to get:

$$\text{Slope} = \frac{10*10.30997 - 0.58195*123.8}{10*0.156518 - 0.58195*0.58195} = 25.31919$$

$$\text{Intercept} = \frac{123.8}{10} - 25.31919*\frac{0.5895}{10} = 10.90655$$

9.7

Table 9.4.3 **Least-squares regression calculations for Example 9.4.3.**

i	t_i	$x_i = e^{-t}$	y_i	x_i^2	$x_i y_i$
1	1	0.367879	19.00	0.135335	6.989709
2	2	0.135335	18.00	0.018316	2.436035
3	3	0.049787	11.00	0.002479	0.547658
4	4	0.018316	11.60	0.000335	0.212461
5	5	0.006738	12.20	4.54E − 05	0.082203
6	6	0.002479	11.00	6.14E − 06	0.027266
7	7	0.000912	10.40	8.32E − 07	0.009484
8	8	0.000335	9.80	1.13E − 07	0.003288
9	9	0.000123	11.80	1.52E − 08	0.001456
$n = 10$	10	4.54E − 05	9.00	2.06E − 09	0.000409
		Sums = 0.58195	123.80	0.156518	10.30997

So the equation of the best-fit line is:

$$y = 25.31919x + 10.90655 \qquad (9.4.28)$$

and therefore the equation of the best-fit exponential is:

$$y = 25.31919e^{-t} + 10.90655 \qquad (9.4.29)$$

Figure 9.4.5 shows the graph of the best-fit exponential function superimposed on the scattergram of the data in Example 9.4.3.

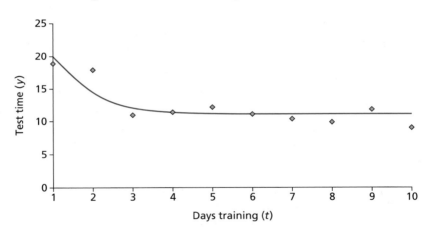

Figure 9.4.5 **An exponential model for Example 9.4.3.**

From Figure 9.4.5 we can see that the model seems a reasonably good fit to the data, and this could be confirmed by calculating the correlation coefficient. From Figure 9.4.5 we can see that after 4 days' training only minor improvements in test completion times are being made. Both the hyperbolic model found in Example 9.3.3 and the exponential model appear to be good fits to the data. We could use MAE and MSE to decide which of the two models to use.

Other exponential functions

In Example 9.4.3 we used least-squares regression to find a best-fit exponential function having two coefficients using equation (9.4.7). There are many other two-coefficient exponential models, but we cannot fit them to a dataset in the same way. Example 9.4.4 illustrates how we can fit an exponential function of the form given by equation (9.4.9).

Chapter 9 Non-linear and multivariate relationships

Example 9.4.4

Q Three years ago the Gross National Product (GNP) of an economy was £80 billion, and now it is £85 billion. A macroeconomist believes that a simple exponential model for GNP over time can be used to forecast the GNP over the next two years, and also to determine when the GNP will have grown to £100 billion. Find a suitable exponential model for GNP over time.

A We shall use equation (9.4.9). Once again we can make a substitution to transform the exponential equation so that we can use the least-squares linear regression equations for the slope and intercept, but this requires us to take logarithms. However, many spreadsheets and most statistical packages (e.g. Minitab and SPSS) have included this as an inbuilt facility within their least-squares linear regression function.

9.7

As there are only two data points, we could instead solve an appropriate system of equations, as we did in Example 9.4.2. Whichever method is used, we find that the exponential equation relating GNP over time t is:

$$GNP = 80e^{0.0202t} \tag{9.4.30}$$

Figure 9.4.6 shows the graph of equation (9.4.29):

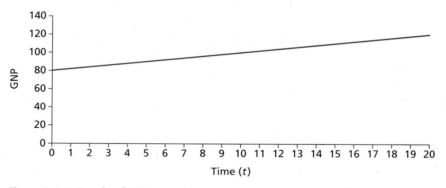

Figure 9.4.6 **Graph of GNP over time.**

We can now use this model to forecast GNP for the next two years simply by putting $t = 4$ and $t = 5$ into equation (9.4.30), giving GNP = 86.7 and GNP = 88.5 respectively. To find out when GNP has grown to £100 billion we substitute GNP = £100 in equation (9.4.30) and solve for t, i.e.:

$$80e^{0.0202t} = 100$$

Therefore: $e^{0.02t} = 100/80 = 1.25$

Using logarithms gives: $0.0202t = \ln(1.25) = 0.22314$

Therefore: $t = 0.22314/0.0202$
  $= 11$ years (i.e. 8 years from now).

Notice how the graph is almost linear, which suggests that perhaps a simpler linear model could have been used in this case.

9.4

1 For the exponential function $y = a^x$:
   (a) Let $a = 2$ and produce a data table of y against x for $-10 < x < 10$ in steps of 1, and then sketch a graph of y against x.
   (b) Repeat part (a) with the following values: $a = 10$, $a = 0.5$, $a = -2$ and $a = -10$ (hint: use a spreadsheet).
   (c) Find out what happens to the graph when $a > 1$, $0 < a < 1$ and $a < 0$.

2 Use a spreadsheet or calculator to complete the following table:

$x =$	1	2	5	10	100	1,000	10,000	100,000
$(1 + 1/x)^x =$								

What happens to the function $(1 + 1/x)^x$ when x tends to infinity?

3 Use a calculator or spreadsheet to complete the following table:

$x =$	−4	−3	−2	−1	0	1	2	3	4
$y = e^x$									
$x = \ln(y)$									

Plot graphs of these on the same set of axes, and comment on them.

4 The proportion of people P responding to an advert about a product that has been on the market for t days is given by $P = 1 - e^{-0.2t}$. There are 10,000,000 potential customers, and each response yields 0.70 pence profit (exclusive of advertising expenses). The advert costs £30,000 to produce and £5,000 for each day it runs. Express advertising costs over time, and hence net profits over time. What are net profits after 10 days?

5 Using data from Question 6 of Exercise 9.3, find models for demand in terms of price (p) of the form (a) demand $= ae^{bp}$ and (b) demand $= a + be^p$. Which is more appropriate?

6 Expenditure has been varied in three similar geographical areas to test the effectiveness of a firm's marketing. The resulting levels of sales are:

Sales area	Marketing expenditure	Sales volume
A	1	400
B	2	600
C	3	700

Find polynomial, hyperbolic and exponential functions to fit these data by solving systems of equations and by using least-squares regression. Compare these functions at, between and outside the given values, and calculate the correlation coefficients, MAD and MSE. Which gives the best model for sales in terms of advertising expenditure?

9.5 ## Multivariate models

So far we have considered functions with only one independent variable, of the form $y = f(x)$, and these are called **univariate** functions: for example, we modelled a firm's profits in terms of a single product. In Economics and Production Management we often deal with several independent variables: for example, we might want to model the entire profits of a firm in terms of all its products. To allow for any number of independent variables, we use **multivariate** functions. In this section we extend our modelling approaches to include them.

The prerequisites of this section are:
- From numbers to symbols (Chapter 2);
- Presenting and describing small datasets (Section 4.3);
- Modelling relationships (Chapter 8);
- Quadratic functions (Section 9.1).

Multivariate functions

Multivariate functions can have any number of independent variables, i.e. $x_1, x_2, x_3, ..., x_n$:

$$y = f(x_1, x_2, x_3, ..., x_n) \qquad (9.5.1)$$

It is difficult to visualise multivariate functions, and usually we cannot draw graphs of them. But this does not mean they do not exist, nor that they cannot be useful. Some multivariate functions are given specific names. For example, when $n = 2$ they are called **bivariate** functions, which sometimes can be visualised.

The applications of multivariate functions and their use as models in business and management are similar to those of the univariate functions used in Section 8.3 and previous sections of this chapter. Although the notation, algebra and arithmetic become far more laborious, with care and attention we can formulate and apply multivariate models to practical situations.

Linear multivariate functions

A general linear multivariate function is given by equation (9.5.2):

$$y = \sum_{t=1}^{n} a_i x_i + b \qquad (9.5.2)$$

where the coefficients a_i can be interpreted as the slope of a flat surface (but not of a line) and constant b has the same interpretation we gave it in Section 8.2 (i.e. the intercept of the y axis). Figure 9.5.1 shows part of a bivariate linear function given by equation (9.5.3):

$$y = a_1 x_1 + a_2 x_2 + b \qquad (9.5.3)$$

Example 9.5.1 illustrates how a multivariate linear function can arise.

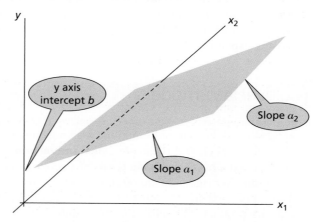

Figure 9.5.1 **Part of a bivariate linear function.**

Example 9.5.1

Q Five products have the same set-up costs of £4,000 but different unit production costs (Table 9.5.1). Find a total cost function.

Table 9.5.1 **Unit production costs for five products.**

Product	1	2	3	4	5
Unit costs (£s)	150	80	200	180	120

A In Section 8.2 we calculated Total costs = Fixed costs + Variable costs (equation 8.2.4). Let the production quantities of the five products be q_1, q_2, q_3, q_4, q_5 so the variable costs are $150q_1, 80q_2, 200q_3, 180q_4, 120q_5$. Therefore the total cost function is:

$$\text{Total cost} = 4,000 + 150q_1 + 80q_2 + 200q_3 + 180q_4 + 120q_5 \qquad (9.5.3)$$

We could write this in a more compact form using sigma notation:

$$\text{Total cost} = c_0 + \sum_{i=1}^{5} c_i q_i \qquad (9.5.4)$$

where $c_0 = 4,000$, $c_1 = 150$, $c_2 = 80$, $c_3 = 200$, $c_4 = 180$, $c_5 = 120$. Alternatively, we could write this in matrix form:

$$\text{Total cost} = (4,000 \quad 150 \quad 80 \quad 200 \quad 180 \quad 120) * \begin{pmatrix} 1 \\ q_1 \\ q_2 \\ q_3 \\ q_4 \\ q_5 \end{pmatrix}$$

Non-linear multivariate functions

Like univariate quadratic functions (Section 9.1), multivariate quadratic functions arise naturally in economics, as illustrated in Example 9.5.2.

Example 9.5.2

Q A firm finds the following demand functions for each of its two products in terms of price:

Product #1 $\qquad D_1 = -5p_1 + 100 \qquad (9.5.5)$

Product #2 $\qquad D_2 = -10p_2 + 200 \qquad (9.5.6)$

Find a total revenue function in terms of the prices of the two products.

A Because revenue is simply Quantity sold * Unit price (equation 9.1.2), we can write down equations for revenue from selling each product in terms of price:

$$R_1 = D_1 * p_1 = (-5p_1 + 100) * p_1 = -5p_1^2 + 100p_1 \qquad (9.5.7)$$

$$R_2 = D_2 * p_2 = (-10p_2 + 200) * p_2 = -10p_2^2 + 200p_2 \qquad (9.5.8)$$

where R_1 and R_2 represent revenue for each product. As total revenue is the sum of the revenues, we simply add equation (9.5.7) and (9.5.8):

$$\text{Total revenue} = R_1 + R_2 = -5p_1^2 + 100p_1 - 10p_2^2 + 200p_2$$
$$= -5p_1^2 - 10p_2^2 + 100p_1 + 200p_2 \qquad (9.5.9)$$

Equation (9.5.9) is a bivariate quadratic because it has two squared independent variables p_1 and p_2.

Although we cannot draw a graph of equation (9.5.9), we can visualise this graph as a three-dimensional parabola (Figure 9.5.2).

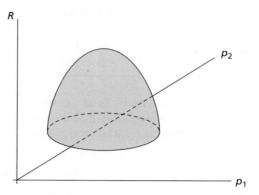

Figure 9.5.2 **A sketch of $R = -5p_1^2 - 10p_2^2 + 100p_1 + 200p_2$.**

Multivariate quadratic functions

Example 9.5.2 resulted in a multivariate quadratic having a 'hill'-shaped graph (Figure 9.5.2): that is, a bivariate function with maxima along both independent variables. In other multivariate quadratics it is possible that minima can occur along both independent variables (Figure 9.5.3).

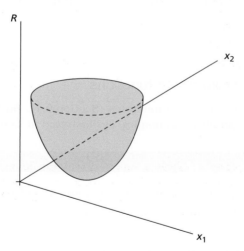

Figure 9.5.3 **Bivariate quadratic with minima in both variables.**

It is also possible that along some independent variables there may be a minimum while along others there may be a maximum, in which case we say the function has a **saddle point** (Figure 9.5.4).

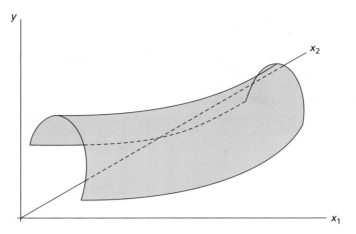

Figure 9.5.4 **A bivariate quadratic having a saddle.**

| Exercises | 9.5 |

1 A manufacturing process for four products has set-up costs of £1,500 and unit costs for each product of £100, £120, £150 and £200 respectively. Write down a total cost function for producing any quantity of all four products.

2 Sales at various prices of two substitute products (such as butter and margarine) over three weeks provide the following data:

		Week 1	Week 2	Week 3
Product 1	Price	2	3	1
	Sales	144	141	144
Product 2	Price	2	3	4
	Sales	94	91	91

Find appropriate linear demand functions of the form $q_i = a_i + b_i p_i + c_i p_i$.

3 A firm sells many products, each with demand functions:

$$D_i = a_i + b_i p_i$$

and cost functions:

$$C_i = f_i + v_i q_i$$

where i is the product reference number, D_i is the demand of the ith product, p_i is the price of the ith product, C_i is the total cost of the ith product, and a_i, b_i, f_i, v_i are the appropriate coefficients. Find expressions for the total cost, total revenue and total profit functions of the firm.

| 9.6 | ## Chapter review |

This chapter considered typical non-linear mathematical functions, namely quadratic, polynomial, hyperbolic and exponential functions, which are commonly used as models in business and management. It also introduced multivariate models and simple multivariate linear and bivariate quadratic models. In some cases it was possible to write down an appropriate equation to model a relationship without doing any mathematics, whereas in others we solved a system of equations or used least-squares regression to find the appropriate functions. Sometimes more than one mathematical function could be used as a model, and common sense and quantitative criteria (e.g. MAE and MSE) can be used to identify the most suitable model.

Generally, we should always use the simplest mathematical function that appears to fit the data. For example, the reason why the graph in Figure 9.4.6 does not appear to be an exponential function (it is almost linear) is that only a small range of values has been considered. As equation (9.4.30) will probably be used only over the limited range of values shown in Figure 9.4.6, and the data have probably been rounded, it might have been simpler to use a linear model over a small range, say 5 to 10 years.

Chapter 10

Analysing models

Introduction

In Chapters 8 and 9 we employed mathematical functions as models in business and management. The next stage is to analyse the model to provide information for managers. In Section 10.1 we look at graphical analysis in more detail; other forms of analysis (e.g. marginal analysis) are presented in subsequent sections.

Chapter objectives

- To appreciate the need for analysing models to provide information

- To recognise the range of methods of analysis available

- To identify and interpret the key graphical features of models

- To appreciate how differentiation and integration can provide information

- To differentiate and integrate typical functions employed as models

- To appreciate the concepts of arc and point elasticity

Chapter contents

10.1 Graphical and numerical analysis

Graphical analysis is one way of analysing models to provide information. But reliance on graphical analysis requires that graphs be drawn correctly and with sufficient accuracy for the degree of precision needed.

The prerequisites of this section are:
- An introduction to Quantitative Methods (Chapter 1);
- From numbers to symbols (Chapter 2);
- Presenting and describing small datasets (Section 4.3);
- Modelling relationships (Chapter 8);
- Non-linear and multivariate relationships (Chapter 9).

The key features that can be identified from a graph are (see Figure 10.1.1):

Trend Is part or all of a function increasing (i.e. upward or positive sloping) or decreasing (i.e. downward or negative sloping)?

Predictions What does the function predict at values within and outside the data points?

Intercepts Does the graph cross the vertical (y) axis (i.e. does it have an intercept), and where is the intercept?

Roots Does the graph cross the horizontal (x) axis (i.e. does it have roots) and, if so, where?

Turning points Does the graph have turning points (i.e. change direction) and, if so, what type of turning points are they (e.g. maximum, minimum, point of inflexion) and where are they?

Optima If a graph has several high points (i.e. local maxima) or several low points (i.e. local minima) what are the highest (i.e. absolute maximum) and lowest (i.e. absolute minimum) points on a graph, and where are they?

Asymptotes Does the graph have horizontal or vertical asymptotes (i.e. tend to some limiting values), for example, is there a ceiling or floor?

Sometimes it is not possible or it is too difficult to draw accurate graphs, so we may use them just to provide ballpark estimates of their features, which we then refine through some other form of analysis. For example, if we have the original data from which a graph was drawn, we may be able to examine them to provide further or more detailed information. Or, if we know the mathematical function being used as the model, we might obtain more information by undertaking other forms of mathematical or numerical analysis. We now look at the key features that we can identify by graphical or numerical analysis; later we shall look at more sophisticated forms of mathematical analysis, such as marginal analysis.

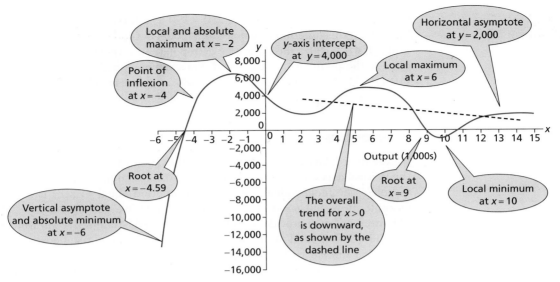

Figure 10.1.1 **Typical features of a graph.**

Trend

Overall trend can be seen from the horizontal axis (i.e. independent variable). It may exhibit an upward (increasing) trend or a downward (decreasing) trend, or be relatively constant. For example, in Figure 10.1.1 the graph has a downward trend (shown by the dashed line) for increases in positive values of the independent variable.

Predictions

Through **interpolation** we estimate values between observations, whereas through **extrapolation** we estimate values outside the observations. More generally, we talk about **forecasting**. Armed with an explicit mathematical function relating dependent and independent variables, we can use it to make forecasts or predictions (Example 10.1.1).

Example

10.1.1

Q Make predictions if the costs of manufacturing q items have been modelled by the function:

$$C = 20q + 250 \text{ for } 0 \leqslant q \leqslant 100 \qquad (10.1.1)$$

A If equation (10.1.1) holds as a model for output costs at all points in the range $0 \leqslant q \leqslant 100$, we can interpolate (i.e. forecast) costs at any point between the points we have plotted (see Figure 10.1.2): for example, putting $q = 12$ into equa-

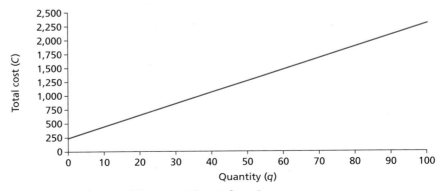

Figure 10.1.2 **Graph of linear total cost function.**

tion (10.1.1) gives $C = 20 * 12 + 250 = 490$ as a forecast for cost when output is 12 units. If this function also holds as a model beyond the dataset (i.e. outside the range $0 \leqslant q \leqslant 100$), then we can extrapolate (i.e. forecast) cost at any point outside the points we have plotted. For example, putting $q = 110$ into equation (10.1.1) gives $C = 20 * 110 + 250 = 2,450$ as a forecast for cost when output is 110 units.

Intercepts

We can approximate the intercept of a graph simply by looking at where it crosses the vertical axis (e.g. $y = 4,000$ in Figure 10.1.1). To find the intercept precisely, we make the independent variable of a function equal to zero (i.e. $x = 0$). For example, if we put $q = 0$ into equation (10.1.1), we get $C = 20 * 0 + 250 = 250$. The intercept may provide useful information. For example, recall from Sections 8.1 and 8.2 that total production costs were made up of fixed costs and variable costs. In Example 10.1.1 the intercept represents fixed cost, because $q = 0$ (i.e. there is no production and so no unit costs are incurred). Examples 10.1.2 and 10.1.3 illustrate the intercepts of other (non-linear) functions.

Roots

We can approximate the roots simply by looking at where the graph crosses the horizontal axis (e.g. $x = 9$ in Figure 10.1.1). To calculate roots precisely, we make the dependent variable of a function equal to zero (i.e. $y = 0$). For simple functions (e.g. linear functions) we can algebraically rearrange the equation to find the root. Example 10.1.2 illustrates how we can find the intercepts and roots of a hyperbolic function.

Example	**10.1.2**

Q Find the intercept and root of the sales function S in terms of advertising expenditure x below:

$$S = 100 - \frac{400}{(x + 1)} \qquad (10.1.2)$$

A We can find the intercept by putting $x = 0$ in equation (10.1.2):

$$S = 100 - 400 = -300$$

To calculate the root precisely, put $S = 0$ in equation (10.1.2) and solve for x:

i.e. $$0 = 100 - \frac{400}{(x + 1)}$$

i.e. $$100 = \frac{400}{(x + 1)}$$

i.e. $$100(x + 1) = 400$$

i.e. $$(x + 1) = 4$$

i.e. $$x = 4 - 1 = 3$$

The intercept implies sales of −300 units with no expenditure on advertising. This is clearly meaningless in this context. However, the root implies that 3 units of advertising expenditure have to be incurred before any sales are made, which is useful information. The graph of equation (10.1.2) is shown in Figure 10.1.3.

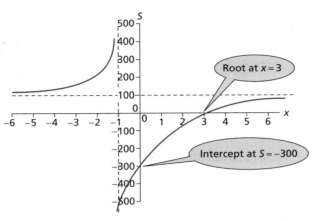

Figure 10.1.3 **Intercept and roots of a rectangular hyperbola.**

There are several ways of finding the **roots of quadratic functions** (e.g. drawing a graph and factorisation), but the most foolproof is to use the formula:

$$\text{Roots of quadratic} = \frac{-b \pm \sqrt{(b^2 - 4\,ac)}}{2a} \qquad (10.1.3)$$

where a, b and c are the coefficients in the general quadratic:

$$y = ax^2 + bx + c \qquad (10.1.4)$$

Note that quadratics can have two roots, one from adding and the other from subtracting the expression in the square root sign in equation (10.1.3). If $b^2 - ac$ is negative (i.e. $b^2 - ac < 0$), there are **no real roots** (i.e. the parabola does not cross the horizontal axis). This formula is easily implemented on a spreadsheet, and is illustrated in Example 10.1.3. The derivation of equation (10.1.3) can found on the CD and on the associated website **www.mcgraw-hill.co.uk/textbooks/ dewhurst**.

Example | **10.1.3**

Q Find the intercept and roots of the quadratic profit function:

$$\pi = -q^2 + 100q - 1{,}600 \qquad (10.1.5)$$

A If we put $q = 0$ into equation (10.1.5), the intercept is $-1{,}600$, representing the profit when output is zero (i.e. $q = 0$); because this is negative, it represents a loss.

To find the roots we apply equation (10.1.3), but first we need to put the quadratic in its general form (equation 10.1.4) to identify coefficients a, b and c. In general form, equation (10.1.5) is:

$$\pi = -1q^2 + 100q - 1{,}600$$

Therefore the coefficients are:

$$a = -1,\ b = 100 \text{ and } c = -1{,}600$$

We can now apply equation (10.1.3):

$$\text{The first root} = \frac{-100 + \sqrt{(100^2 - 4*-1*-1{,}600)}}{2*-1} = 20$$

$$\text{The second root} = \frac{-100 - \sqrt{(100^2 - 4*-1*-1{,}600)}}{2*-1} = 80$$

Figure 10.1.4 shows the location of these roots on a graph of the function.

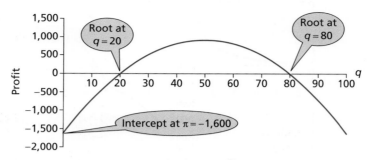

Figure 10.1.4 **Intercept and roots of a quadratic.**

So the firm makes a profit if it produces in the range $20 < q < 80$, whereas, outside this range, it makes a loss.

For other types of function (e.g. general polynomials) whose exact roots cannot be computed, we can refine an initial graphical estimate using some form of search or numerical method (Example 10.1.4).

Example

10.1.4

Q Find the roots in the interval $x_1 = 0$ to $x_2 = 10$ of the cubic:

$$y = x^3 - 5x^2 - 5x + 10 \qquad (10.1.6)$$

A First, graph the cubic in the range $0 \leqslant x \leqslant 10$ (Figure 10.1.5):

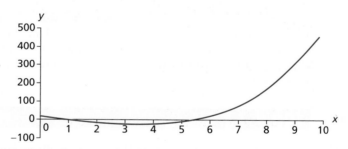

Figure 10.1.5 **Roots of a cubic.**

In Figure 10.1.5 we can see two roots, one near $x = 1$ and the other near $x = 5.5$. If this is accurate enough, we simply stop and accept these values for the roots. However, we can find roots more precisely. Let us try to find the root near $x = 5$ to 2 d.p. We know that on one side of a root the function is positive and on the other it is negative (because at the root it is zero), so we can test each side of the interval to see whether the sign of variable y changes, in which case the interval contains a root. We begin by investigating the interval $x_1 = 5$ to $x_2 = 6$, which have y-values $y_1 = -15$ and $y_2 = 16$ respectively. The sign has changed, confirming that there is indeed a root between these values, so we shall now halve this interval to see which half the root is in and then choose its new interval. By repeating this process, we reach the desired accuracy. The results of applying this process to equation (10.1.6) are shown in Table 10.1.1, from which we find that the root is $x = 5.58$ to 2 d.p.

Table 10.1.1 **Finding a root in the interval $5 < x < 6$.**

x_1	x_2	y_1	y_2	Root here
5	6	−15	16	Yes
5	5.5	−15	−2.375	No
5.5	5.6	−2.375	16	Yes
5.5	5.75	−2.375	6.046875	Yes
5.5	5.625	−2.375	1.650391	Yes
5.5625	5.625	−0.40796	1.650391	Yes
5.59375	5.625	0.609711	1.650391	No
5.5625	5.59375	−0.40796	0.609711	Yes
5.5625	5.578125	−0.40796	0.098011	Yes
5.570313	5.578125	−0.15569	0.098011	Yes

This numerical approach to finding a root to a particular degree of accuracy is called the method of **bisection**.

Finding turning points

When a quadratic has roots (i.e. crosses the horizontal axis), we know, because of symmetry, that the turning point lies exactly halfway between them. For example, in Example 10.1.3, having found the roots of the quadratic profit function we can locate the position of the turning point at $(20 + 80)/2 = 50$, and, from Figure 10.1.4, we see this is the output level that maximises profits. For some other functions (e.g. cubic functions or higher-order polynomials), other analytical methods are needed to locate and identify turning points. One is differentiation (see Section 10.2). Numerical analysis could also be used,. and we could modify the method of bisection to refine the location of turning points from an initial graphical estimate.

Finding asymptotes

We can identify asymptotes from a graph (see Figure 10.1.1), and also by considering what happens when variables in the function become extremely large (i.e. infinite) or extremely small (Example 10.1.5).

Example

10.1.5

Q Identify the asymptotes and appropriateness of the model of sales S (units) in terms of price p (£'s) given by:

$$S = 1,000 + \frac{400}{(p-1)}$$

(10.1.7)

A First, we investigate what happens to equation (10.1.7) as price becomes very large and positive (i.e. $p \rightarrow +\infty$). As $p \rightarrow +\infty$, then $(p-1)$ is still very large and positive (i.e. $+\infty$).

Therefore $400/(p-1)$ is very small (i.e. $400/(p-1) \rightarrow 0$), and hence $S \rightarrow 1,000$.

When price gets very large and negative (i.e. $p \rightarrow -\infty$) then $(p-1)$ is still very large and negative (i.e. $-\infty$). Therefore, again $400/(p-1) \rightarrow 0$ and $S \rightarrow 1,000$. So the sales function given by equation (10.1.7) has a horizontal asymptote at $S = 1,000$ (see Figure 10.1.6).

Equation (10.1.7) shows that $400/(p-1)$ will become infinitely large when p tends towards +1 (i.e. when $p \rightarrow +1$). So, as p falls to +1, then $(p-1)$ tends towards zero from the positive side and $400/(p-1) \rightarrow \infty$ and $S \rightarrow +\infty$. Similarly, as p increases to $+1$, then $(p-1)$ tends towards zero from the negative side and $400/(p-1) \rightarrow -\infty$ and $S \rightarrow -\infty$. So the sales function given by equation (10.1.7) has a vertical asymptote at $p = 1$ (Figure 10.1.6):

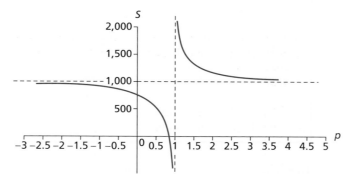

Figure 10.1.6 **The asymptotes of equation (10.1.7).**

Only part of equation (10.1.7) is a realistic model of how we might expect demand to behave in terms of price. First, we would not expect negative prices, so therefore we should have $p > 0$. Furthermore, from Figure 10.1.6 we can see that the function models the expected behaviour of a downward-sloping demand function realistically only for $p > 1$. Consequently, equation (10.1.7) is appropriate only for prices above £1.

Finding optima

Except for quadratic functions (Section 9.1), where a turning point is not only a local maximum or minimum but also an absolute maximum or minimum (i.e. largest or smallest point on a graph), there is no simple means of finding the absolute maximum or minimum of a function. In general, we need to find and compare all local turning points and asymptotes. For example, for the polynomial function graphed in Figure 10.1.1 we can see that the absolute maximum occurs at the turning point at $x = -2$ (i.e. the largest of all turning points and vertical asymptotes) and the absolute minimum at the vertical asymptote at $x = -6$ (i.e. the smallest of all the turning points and vertical asymptotes).

Multivariate functions

In general we cannot draw multivariate functions, and if we want to visualise them we usually consider only one aspect (i.e. point of view) at a time. For instance, we might consider what the function looks like along the y and x_1 axes while treating the other variables (i.e. x_2, x_3, ..., x_n) as constants, or what the function looks like along the y and x_2 axes while treating x_1, x_3, ..., x_n as constants, and so on. This idea is used extensively in economics for analysing multivariate functions, and is known as **partial analysis**. In partial analysis we investigate the function one variable at a time while holding all the others constant (i.e. *ceteris paribus*, 'other things being equal'). Another way to visualise a multivariate function is to look at two independent variables (or axes) from above as if viewing the contour lines on a map (Example 10.1.6).

Example | **10.1.6**

Q Investigate the total revenue R from selling two products at prices p_1 and p_2, which has been modelled by the bivariate quadratic function:

$$R = -5p_1^2 - 10p_2^2 + 100p_1 + 200p_2 \qquad (10.1.8)$$

A To visualise this quadratic, first hold p_2 constant (e.g. we could set $p_2 = 1$ or, indeed, any other number) and look at the graph of R in terms of p_1 (Figure 10.1.7):

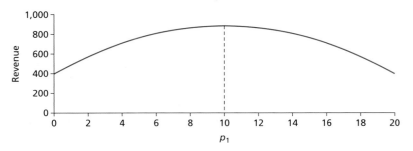

Figure 10.1.7 **Graph of $-5p_1^2 - 10p_2^2 + 100p_1 + 200p_2$ holding p_2 constant.**

Figure 10.1.7 indicates a maximum at $p_1 = 10$ when p_2 is held constant.

Next, hold p_1 constant and look at the graph of R in terms of p_2 (Figure 10.1.8):

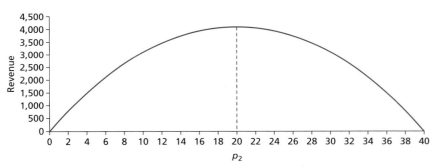

Figure 10.1.8 **Graph of $-5p_1^2 - 10p_2^2 + 100p_1 + 200p_2$ holding p_1 constant.**

Figure 10.1.8 indicates a maximum at $p_2 = 20$ when p_1 is held constant.

Looking from above the R axis, we see the contours of a hill, as on a map (Figure 10.1.9):

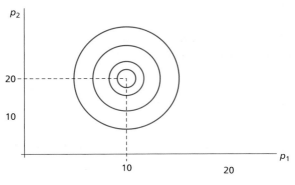

Figure 10.1.9 **The contours of $R = -5p_1^2 - 10p_2^2 + 100p_1 + 200p_2$.**

So we can see that the total revenue function has a graph similar to that shown in Figure 10.1.10:

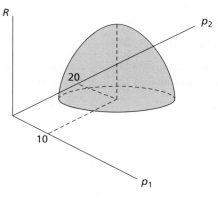

Figure 10.1.10 **Part of the graph of $R = -5p_1^2 - 10p_2^2 + 100p_1 + 200p_2$.**

Exercises   **10.1**

1   These functions have been fitted to a set dataset to relate sales to price:
(a) $S = -0.2p + 100$ (b) $S = 100e^{-0.003p}$ (c) $S = 30 + 3,000/p$
(d) $S = 45 + 135e^{-0.02p}$ (e) $S = 0.0012p^2 - 0.6p + 115$

Graph the functions for prices in the range 0 to 500 in steps of 50, identify their features, and comment on which function seems the most appropriate model for sales at different prices.

2   Graph the following functions and find the asymptotes:

(a) $y = \dfrac{1}{x}$ (b) $y = \dfrac{-1}{x}$ (c) $y = \dfrac{1}{(x-1)}$

(d) $y = \dfrac{1}{(x+1)}$ (e) $y = 1 + \dfrac{1}{(x-1)}$ (f) $y = 1 - \dfrac{1}{(x-1)}$

3   Sales S over time t has been modelled by:

$$S = 10,000 - \frac{12,000}{(t+1)}$$

What is the expected market size that the firm could ever hope to achieve?

4   The annual profit function for a particular product is:

$$AP(t) = 10,000 + 25,000(\tfrac{1}{4})^{0.5t}$$

where t is the number of years the product has been on the market. Graph the function, estimate the profit for $t = 1, 2, 3, 4$ and 5 years, and comment on the underlying trend in profits.

5   Sales S of a product over time t (years) follow the logistics curve:

$$S = \frac{10,000}{1 + 100e^{-t}}$$

Graph this curve over 10 years and identify where sales growth (a) is increasing, (b) is decreasing, and (c) has reached a maximum.

6   Break-even point is when Total Revenue = Total Cost. Faced with a total cost function of $C = 500 + 3q$, show that, for any price p, the break-even point quantity $= 500/(p - 3)$. Graph this quantity for £0, £1, £2, £3, £4 and £5. What is the break-even point quantity when price is infinitely high, and what happens as price falls towards £3?

7 Profit π in terms of output q has been modelled by the function:

$$\pi = -1.01q^2 + 101q - 1{,}018$$

Graph the profit function over the interval $0 \leqslant q \leqslant 100$ in steps of 10, and estimate the range of output that generates profit and the output level that maximises profits. Confirm them by finding the roots of the quadratic.

8 Graph the cubic $y = -x^3 - 5x^2 - 20x + 1{,}000$ over the range $-10 \leqslant x \leqslant 10$ and identify its features.

9 Consider the two functions $z = x + y$ and $z = xy$. For each function:
(a) hold y constant and sketch a graph of z against x
(b) hold x constant and sketch a graph of z against y
(c) sketch a three-dimensional picture.

10 An economy's production P has been modelled in terms of capital C and labour L by the (Cobb–Douglas) function:

$$P = 100C^{1/3}L^{2/3}$$

Sketch the three-dimensional graph of this function, and consider how P changes with C when L is fixed and with L when C is fixed.

10.2 Marginal analysis and differentiation

In Section 10.1 we saw how we could analyse functions graphically to provide information. For example, for a quadratic model of profits in terms of output, we identified the roots, so gaining information about the range of output that generates profit and the output level that maximises profit. However, managers may want further information, such as the effects on profit of changing output. Economists use marginal analysis to provide such information.

The prerequisites of this section are:
■ An introduction to Quantitative Methods (Chapter 1);
■ From numbers to symbols (Chapter 2);
■ Presenting and describing small datasets (Section 4.3);
■ Modelling relationships (Chapter 8);
■ Non-linear and multivariate relationships (Chapter 9);
■ Graphical and numerical analysis (Section 10.1).

Marginal analysis

Marginal analysis considers the effect on a dependent variable of changes to an independent variable. To calculate such marginal quantities (e.g. marginal profit), we take the ratio of a change in the dependent variable and divide it by the corresponding change in the independent variable. For example, marginal profit is the change in profit resulting from a one-unit change in output:

$$\text{Marginal} = \frac{\text{Change in dependent variable}}{\text{Change in independent variable}} \qquad (10.2.1)$$

Economists use the Greek capital letter delta (Δ) to denote 'change in', and so, for a function $y = f(x)$, we write equation (10.2.1) as:

$$\text{Marginal} = \frac{\text{Change in } y}{\text{Change in } x} = \frac{\Delta y}{\Delta x}$$

Let us denote the marginal by My:

$$My = \frac{\Delta y}{\Delta x} \tag{10.2.2}$$

To calculate the marginal of a function at any point, we make changes to the independent variable and apply equation (10.2.2) (see Example 10.2.1).

Example 10.2.1

Q Find marginal profits between $q = 0$ and $q = 100$, in steps of 10 units of output, for:

$$\pi = -q^2 + 100q - 1{,}600 \tag{10.2.3}$$

A We can perform the calculations in a table.

Table 10.2.1 **Marginal profits.**

q	π	Δq	$\Delta \pi$	$M\pi = \dfrac{\Delta \pi}{\Delta q}$
0	−1,600			
		10	900	90
10	−700			
		10	700	70
20	0			
		10	500	50
30	500			
		10	300	30
40	800			
		10	100	10
50	900			
		10	−100	−10
60	800			
		10	−300	−30
70	500			
		10	−500	−50
80	0			
		10	−700	−70
90	−700			
		10	−900	−90
100	−1,600			

Table 10.2.1 shows that marginal profit between $q = 0$ and $q = 10$ is 90, between $q = 10$ and $q = 20$ it is 70, between $q = 20$ and $q = 30$ it is 50, and so on. This suggests that the firm would increase profits more by increasing output from 10 to 20 units than from 20 to 30 units. Marginal profit decreases as output increases, and once maximum profits are achieved (at $q = 50$), marginal profit becomes negative (i.e. profits reduce as output rises). The relationship between marginal profit and output is shown more clearly in Figure 10.2.1. Note that marginal profits have been assumed to occur at the midpoint of the intervals on the graph (e.g. marginal profit between $q = 0$ and $q = 10$ occurs at $q = 5$, etc.).

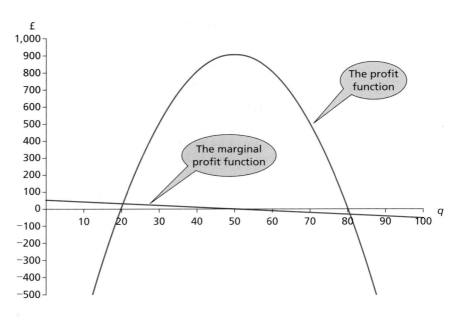

Figure 10.2.1 **Profit and marginal profit.**

Figure 10.2.1 shows that in this case marginal profit is linear, so we can determine an equation for marginal profit in terms of output by taking any pair of values (e.g. when $q = 5$, $M\pi = 90$ and when $q = 15$, $M\pi = 70$). Solving these simultaneous equations gives:

$$M\pi = -2q + 100 \tag{10.2.4}$$

We can now use equation (10.2.4) to calculate marginal profit at any level of output. This equation and the graph also show that, when $q = 50$, marginal profit is zero and profit is maximised. To see why this is so, we can interpret marginal profit as the **slope** (or **gradient**) of the profit function and think of the graph of the quadratic profit function (equation 10.2.3) as a hill. Note that at the foot of a hill the slope is much steeper than at the top (i.e. marginal profit is greater near the bottom than the top). At the very top of this hill (the maximum of this quadratic function) you stand on level ground (i.e. a slope of zero), and so marginal profit is zero. We return to this in Section 10.4, but for now you need to understand that marginal analysis is essentially concerned with finding the slope of a function.

There is another interpretation for the marginal, or what we have now seen is the slope, of a function. We can also say that equation (10.2.2) tells us that the function is changing at the rate of Δy for every unit change in x (i.e. for $\Delta x = 1$). So we can also interpret the margin (or slope) of a function as the rate of change of the function. For example, marginal profit is the rate of change of profit.

Derivatives

Let us now look at the process of finding marginals and slopes in more detail. In Example 10.2.1 we considered changes in the profit function $\pi = q^2 + 100q - 1{,}600$ and obtained $M\pi = -2q + 100$ for the margin and slope of the function. Because we are dealing with differences (i.e. changes) mathematicians call this process **differentiation**, and its results (i.e. slope, margin, gradient, rate of change) are called **derivatives** (in particular, the **first derivative** of the original function). The process we have just undertaken is called **numerical differentiation**, where we found the first derivative by calculating specific changes in a function and then deduced an expression for the first derivative (i.e. slope, margin, gradient, rate of change) from our calculations.

Differentiation and differential calculus

Mathematicians usually refer to marginal analysis as **differential calculus**. They have developed formal analytical methods for finding derivatives because numerical differentiation does not always give a true picture of the slope (margin, gradient or derivative) of a particular function. We were able to undertake the numerical differentiation that obtained an expression for the derivative of a quadratic function (e.g. Example 10.2.1) because we knew what the curve looked like, and because the size of the changes we considered was large enough for us to capture anything that might happen. In more complex functions we might need to consider very small changes in a function. Figure 10.2.2 shows a case in which, if we applied numerical differentiation with one-unit changes in x, we would miss the turning point at $x = 0.5$.

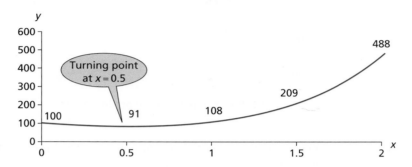

Figure 10.2.2 **A function with a turning point between two integers.**

To capture all possible features in a function, we need to make the changes as small as possible (i.e. so small that they are almost zero). In general, for any function $y = f(x)$ we define the first derivative as the expression obtained from the limiting behaviour of the change in y divided by the change in x as x tends towards zero. As we are no longer dealing with discrete intervals, instead of the notation $\dfrac{\Delta y}{\Delta x}$, we use $\dfrac{dy}{dx}$ to denote the first derivative of the function y with respect to x (pronounced 'dee why by dee eks'). More formally, we define $\dfrac{dy}{dx}$ to be the value that $\dfrac{\Delta y}{\Delta x}$ tends to (i.e. the limiting value) when we let Δx get very small (i.e. almost zero) and denote this by:

$$\frac{dy}{dx} = \underset{\Delta x \to 0}{\text{Limit}} \left\{ \frac{\Delta y}{\Delta x} \right\} \qquad\qquad (10.2.5)$$

Differentiation from first principles

The process used to obtain the first derivative (i.e. margin, slope, gradients) is known as **differentiation from first principles**, and is illustrated in Example 10.2.2.

Example

10.2.2

Q Find, from first principles, the first derivative of the function $y = -x^2 + 100x - 1,600$.

A   Consider a small change in x, say Δx, which results in a small change in y, say Δy (Figure 10.2.3):

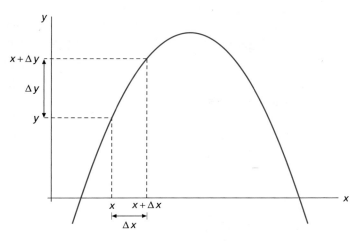

Figure 10.2.3 **Small changes.**

Let us consider these two points on our graph. At coordinate (x, y), we have:

$$y = -x^2 + 100x - 1{,}600 \qquad\qquad (10.2.6)$$

and at coordinate $(x + \Delta x, y + \Delta y)$, we have:

$$y + \Delta y = -(x + \Delta x)^2 + 100(x + \Delta x) - 1{,}600 \qquad\qquad (10.2.7)$$

First, we multiply out equation (10.2.7):

$$y + \Delta y = -x^2 - 2x\Delta x - \Delta x^2 + 100x + 100\Delta x - 1{,}600 \qquad\qquad (10.2.8)$$

We find the change in Δy by subtracting equation (10.2.6) from (10.2.28):

$$\Delta y = (y + \Delta y) - y = -2x\Delta x - \Delta x^2 + 100\Delta x \qquad\qquad (10.2.9)$$

To find the slope, we divide Δy by Δx:

$$\frac{\Delta y}{\Delta x} = \frac{-2x\Delta x - \Delta x^2 + 100\Delta x}{\Delta x} = -2x - \Delta x + 100 \qquad\qquad (10.2.10)$$

We now explore what happens to the slope as we let Δx get very small (i.e. $\Delta x \rightarrow 0$). Putting $\Delta x = 0$ in equation (10.2.10) gives:

$$\frac{\Delta y}{\Delta x} = -2x + 100 \qquad\qquad (10.2.11)$$

More formally, we examine what happens to the slope in the limit as $\Delta x \rightarrow 0$ and write:

$$\frac{dy}{dx} = \underset{\Delta x \rightarrow 0}{\text{Limit}} \{-2x - \Delta x + 100\} = -2x + 100 \qquad\qquad (10.2.12)$$

Notice that this is exactly the same expression we obtained from performing numerical differentiation in Example 10.2.1.

Rules of differentiation

Although differentiation is useful because it gives us another tool of analysis, the processes of numerical differentiation and differentiation from first principles are tedious. However, mathematicians have devised simple rules for finding derivatives of most functions that we use in business and management.

The first rule is known as the **Power Rule** and is easily derived from Example 10.2.2 by comparing the original function and its derivative:

Function $\quad y = -x^2 + 100x - 1,600$

Derivative $\quad \dfrac{dy}{dx} = -2x + 100$

By writing these expressions in full standard form, including x^0 (recall from Section 1.5 that $x^0 = 1$), one below the other, we can see how the Power Rule operates:

$$y = -x^2 + 100x^1 - 1,600x^0$$

$$\frac{dy}{dx} = -2x^1 + 100x^0 - 0$$

Compare each term in the original function and the corresponding term in the derivative:

$-x^2 \qquad$ has become $-2x^1$

$+100x^1 \qquad$ has become $+100x^0$

$-1,600x^0 \quad$ has become -0

So the rule is that the power of the variable in the original function becomes a multiple of the variable in the derivative, and the power of the variable in the original function is reduced by one. The formal derivation of this Power Rule and other rules of differentiation can be found on the CD and on the associated website **www.mcgraw-hill.co.uk/textbooks/dewhurst**.

The Power Rule

We have seen that the Power Rule applies to functions consisting of powers of an independent variable (e.g. polynomial functions).

For $y = ax^n$ for any power n and any coefficient a	(10.2.13)
$\dfrac{dy}{dx} = nax^{n-1}$	(10.2.14)

Until you get used to applying the Power Rule, write the original function in full standard form with x written as x^1 and constants written as multiples of x^0 and apply the rule to each term, as shown in Example 10.2.3.

Example | **10.2.3**

Q Find the first derivatives of the following functions:

(a) $y = 5x^{10}$

(b) $C = 2q^2 - 26q + 80$

(c) $y = 4x^{1/4} + 2x^3 - 100$

(d) $S = 100 - \dfrac{200}{p}$

(e) $y = \dfrac{10}{\sqrt{x}} + 500x.$

A   (a) $y = 5x^{10}$ is already in full standard from:

Applying the Power Rule: $\dfrac{dy}{dx} = 10 * 5x^{10-1}$

i.e. $\dfrac{dy}{dx} = 50x^9$

(b) First, put $C = 2q^2 - 26q + 80$ in full standard form:

$$C = 2q^2 - 26q^1 + 80q^0$$

Applying the Power Rule: $\dfrac{dC}{dq} = 2 * 2q^{2-1} - 1 * 26q^{1-1} + 0 * 80q^{0-1}$

i.e. $\dfrac{dC}{dq} = 4q^1 - 26q^0 + 0$

i.e. $\dfrac{dC}{dq} = 4q - 26$

(c) Putting $y = 4x^{1/4} + 2x^3 - 100$ in full standard form:

$$y = 4x^{0.25} + 2x^3 - 100x^0$$

Applying the Power Rule: $\dfrac{dy}{dx} = 0.25 * 4x^{0.25-1} + 3 * 2x^{3-1} - 0 * 100x^{0-1}$

i.e. $\dfrac{dy}{dx} = 1x^{-0.75} + 6x^2 - 0$

i.e. $\dfrac{dy}{dx} = x^{-0.75} + 6x^2$

or: $\dfrac{dy}{dx} = x^{-3/4} + 6x^2$

(d) Putting $S = 100 - \dfrac{200}{p}$ in full standard form:

$$S = 100p^0 - 200p^{-1} \text{ (remember that } 1/p = p^{-1})$$

Applying the Power Rule: $\dfrac{dy}{dx} = 0 * 100p^{0-1} + 1 * 200p^{-1-1}$

i.e. $\dfrac{dy}{dx} = 200p^{-2}$

i.e. $\dfrac{dy}{dx} = \dfrac{200}{p^2}$

(e) Putting $y = \dfrac{10}{\sqrt{x}} + 500x$ in full standard form:

$$y = 10x^{-0.5} + 500x^1 \text{ (remember that } \sqrt{x} = x^{0.5})$$

Applying the Power Rule: $\dfrac{dy}{dx} = -0.5 * 10x^{-0.5-1} + 1 * 500x^{1-1}$

i.e. $\dfrac{dy}{dx} = -5x^{-1.5} + 500$

i.e. $\dfrac{dy}{dx} = \dfrac{-5}{x^{1.5}} + 500$

The Exponential Rule

The Exponential Rule applies to exponential functions:

For $y = e^{nx}$ for any constant n (10.2.15)

$$\frac{dy}{dx} = ne^{nx}$$ (10.2.16)

BE CAREFUL not to confuse the Power Rule and Exponential Rule.

Example 10.2.4

Q Find the first derivatives of:

(a) $y = 5e^{4x}$ (b) $y = 2e^{-3x}$ (c) $y = x^4 - 3e^{-2x}$.

A (a) Applying the Exponential Rule to $y = 5^{4x}$:

$$\frac{dy}{dx} = 4 * 5e^{4x}$$

i.e. $\dfrac{dy}{dx} = 20^{4x}$

(b) Applying the Exponential Rule to $y = 2e^{-3x}$:

$$\frac{dy}{dx} = -3 * 2e^{-3x}$$

i.e. $\dfrac{dy}{dx} = -6e^{-3x}$

(c) As $y = x^4 - 3e^{-2x}$ contains powers of x and an exponential component, we apply both the Power and Exponential Rules:

$$\frac{dy}{dx} = 4x^{4-1} - 2 * -3e^{-2x}$$

i.e. $\dfrac{dy}{dx} = 4x^3 + 6e^{-2x}$

The Product Rule

The Product Rule applies to functions that are the product of two or more functions. For the product of two functions $u(x)$ and $v(x)$, we differentiate each separately to obtain their derivatives $\dfrac{du}{dx}$ and $\dfrac{dv}{dx}$ and then combine them to obtain the total derivative of the product.

For $y = u(x)v(x)$ (10.2.17)

$$\frac{dy}{dx} = v(x)\frac{du}{dx} + u(x)\frac{dv}{dx}$$ (10.2.18)

Example | **10.2.5**

Q Find the first derivatives of:

(a) $y = (3x^2 + 4)x^8$ (b) $y = 5e^{3x}x^{10}$.

A (a) There are two ways of finding the derivative of $y = (3x^2 + 4)x^8$.

First, we could use the Product Rule to identify the two functions being multiplied together:

$$u(x) = (3x^2 + 4) \text{ and } v(x) = x^8$$

Differentiate these two functions separately using the Power Rule:

$$\frac{du}{dx} = 6x \quad \text{and} \quad \frac{dv}{dx} = 8x^7$$

Now, use the Product Rule to find the total derivative:

$$\frac{dy}{dx} = (3x^2 + 4) * 8x^7 + x^8 * 6x$$

i.e. $\quad \dfrac{dy}{dx} = 8x^7(3x^2 + 4) + 6x * x^8$

i.e. $\quad \dfrac{dy}{dx} = 8x^7(3x^2 + 4) + 6x^9$

We could leave the result in this form or, better still, multiply out the bracket:

i.e. $\quad \dfrac{dy}{dx} = 24x^9 + 32x^7 + 6x^9$

i.e. $\quad \dfrac{dy}{dx} = 30x^9 + 32x^7$

If we take out the common factor $2x^7$ we get:

$$\frac{dy}{dx} = 2x^7(15x^7 + 16)$$

Alternatively, as both functions in the product are powers of x, we could simply multiply them out at the beginning and then use the Power Rule. Let us do this to check our results:

multiply out $\quad y = (3x^2 + 4)x^8$

to get $\quad y = 3x^2 * x^8 + 4 * x^8$

i.e. $\quad y = 3x^{10} + 4x^8$

We can now use the Power Rule to find the first derivative:

$$\frac{dy}{dx} = 3 * 10x^{10-1} + 8 * 4x^{8-1}$$

i.e. $\quad \dfrac{dy}{dx} = 30x^9 + 32x^7$

which is the same as when we used the Product Rule.

On this occasion, it was easier to multiply out the bracket and apply the Power Rule, rather than apply the Product Rule. However, there are occasions when we cannot multiply out an expression to apply the Power Rule, as we see in part (b).

(b) As function $y = 5e^{3x}x^{10}$ cannot be simplified or multiplied out to apply the Power Rule, we must use the Product Rule. As before, we identify the two functions making up the product:

$$u(x) = 5e^{3x} \text{ and } v(x) = x^{10}$$

On this occasion, apply the Exponential Rule to find the derivative of $u(x)$:

$$\frac{du}{dx} = 3 * 5e^{3x}$$

i.e. $\quad \dfrac{du}{dx} = 15e^{3x}$

To find the derivative of $v(x)$, we apply the Power Rule:

$$\frac{dv}{dx} = 10x^{10-1}$$

i.e. $\quad \dfrac{dv}{dx} = 10x^9$

Now apply the Product Rule to find the total derivative:

$$\frac{dy}{dx} = 5e^{3x} * 10x^9 + x^{10} * 15e^{3x}$$

i.e. $\quad \dfrac{dy}{dx} = 50x^9 e^{3x} + 15x^{10} e^{3x}$

We could leave this as it is or simplify the expression by taking out the common factors of $5x^9 e^{3x}$:

$$\frac{dy}{dx} = 5x^9 e^{3x}(10 + 3x)$$

The Quotient Rule

The Quotient Rule applies to cases where one function is divided by another. For the quotient of two functions $u(x)$ and $v(x)$ $\left(\text{i.e. } \dfrac{u(x)}{v(x)} \right)$, we differentiate each separately to obtain their derivatives $\dfrac{du}{dx}$ and $\dfrac{dv}{dx}$ and then combine them to obtain the total derivative of the quotient.

For $y = \dfrac{u(x)}{v(x)}$ $\hspace{4cm}$ (10.2.19)

$$\frac{dy}{dx} = \frac{v(x)\dfrac{du}{dx} - u(x)\dfrac{dv}{dx}}{v(x)^2} \hspace{2cm} (10.2.20)$$

Example **10.2.6**

Q Find the derivatives of:

(a) $\quad y = \dfrac{15x^9 + x^4}{5x^2}$ $\quad$ (b) $\quad y = \dfrac{x^2}{5x^3 + 2x^2 + 10}$ $\quad$ (c) $\quad y = \dfrac{e^{3x}}{x^2}$

A   (a) To apply the Quotient Rule, we need to identify the numerator and denominator of the quotient:

$$u(x) = 15x^9 + x^4 \text{ and } v(x) = 5x^2$$

Apply the Power Rule to find their derivatives:

$$\frac{du}{dx} = 9 * 15x^{9-1} + 4 * x^{4-1} = 135x^8 + 4x^3$$

$$\text{and } \frac{dv}{dx} = 2 * 5x^{2-1} = 10x^1 = 10x$$

We find the total derivative by applying the Quotient Rule:

$$\frac{dy}{dx} = \frac{5x^2 * (135x^8 + 4x^3) - (15x^9 + x^4) * 10x}{(5x^2)^2}$$

We could leave the result in this form, or better still we can multiply out the brackets in the numerator:

$$\frac{dy}{dx} = \frac{675x^{10} + 20x^5 - 150x^{10} - 10x^5}{25x^4} = \frac{525x^{10} + 10x^5}{25x^4}$$

Dividing by the denominator gives:

$$\frac{dy}{dx} = 21x^6 + 0.4x$$

Alternatively, we could use algebra to simplify the original equation and then apply the Power Rule:

$$y = \frac{15x^9 + x^4}{5x^2} = \frac{15x^9}{5x^2} + \frac{x^4}{5x^2} = 3x^7 + 0.2x^2$$

Applying the Power Rule gives:

$$\frac{dy}{dx} = 7 * 3x^{7-1} + 2 * 0.2x^{2-1}$$

i.e. $$\frac{dy}{dx} = 21x^6 + 0.4x$$

Again we have seen, in this case, that it was easier to apply algebra first to enable us to use the Power Rule than to apply the Quotient Rule. However, this is not always possible, as shown below.

(b) The function $y = \dfrac{x^2}{5x^3 + 2x^2 + 10}$ cannot be simplified to enable use of the Power Rule.

The two components of the quotient are:

$$u(x) = x^2 \text{ and } v(x) = 5x^3 + 2x^2 + 10$$

Applying the Power Rule to find the derivatives of each function gives:

$$\frac{du}{dx} = 2x^{2-1} = 2x \text{ and } \frac{dv}{dx} = 3 * 5x^{3-1} + 2 * 2x^{2-1} + 0 = 15x^2 + 4x$$

Now applying the Quotient Rule gives:

$$\frac{dy}{dx} = \frac{(5x^3 + 2x^2 + 10) * 2x - x^2 * (15x^2 + 4x)}{(5x^3 + 2x^2 + 10)^2}$$

We could leave the result in this form or better still we could multiply out the brackets in the numerator:

$$\frac{dy}{dx} = \frac{(10x^4 + 4x^3 + 20x) - (15x^4 + 4x^3)}{(5x^3 + 2x^2 + 10)^2}$$

i.e. $\quad \dfrac{dy}{dx} = \dfrac{-5x^4 + 20x}{(5x^3 + 2x^2 + 10)^2}$

Taking out the common factor of $5x$ gives:

$$\frac{dy}{dx} = \frac{5x(-x^3 + 4)}{(5x^3 + 2x^2 + 10)^2}$$

(c) Once again the function $y = \dfrac{e^{3x}}{x^2}$ cannot be simplified to enable us to use the Power Rule. In this case:

$$u(x) = e^{3x} \text{ and } v(x) = x^2$$

We find the derivatives by applying the Exponential and Power Rules, respectively:

$$\frac{du}{dx} = 3e^{3x} \text{ and } \frac{dv}{dx} = 2x^{2-1} = 2x$$

Applying the Quotient Rule gives:

$$\frac{dy}{dx} = \frac{x^2 * 3e^{3x} - e^{3x} * 2x}{(x^2)^2}$$

i.e. $\quad \dfrac{dy}{dx} = \dfrac{3x^2 e^{3x} - 2x e^{3x}}{(x^4)}$

We can simplify by taking out the common factor xe^{3x} in the numerator, giving:

$$\frac{dy}{dx} = \frac{xe^{3x}(3x - 2)}{(x^4)} = \frac{e^{3x}(3x - 2)}{x^3}$$

The Chain Rule

The Chain Rule applies to functions where y is a function of another function of x, i.e. a chain of two functions $y = f(z)$ and $z = f(x)$. We differentiate each function separately to obtain their derivatives $\dfrac{dy}{dz}$ and $\dfrac{dz}{dx}$ and then combine them to obtain the total derivative. The result is usually expressed in terms of the independent variable (e.g. x).

For $y = f(z)$ where $z = f(x)$	(10.2.21)
$\dfrac{dy}{dx} = \dfrac{dy}{dz}\dfrac{dz}{dx}$	(10.2.22)

Example   **10.2.7**

Q   Find the derivatives of:

(a) $\quad y = \dfrac{1}{(x - 6)^4}$ (b) $\quad y = (2x^2 - 2x + 6)^3$ (c) $\quad y = e^{3x + 2}$.

A (a) As we have already seen, we could differentiate $y = \dfrac{1}{(x-6)^4}$ by using the Quotient Rule but, to do so, we need to multiply out the denominator [i.e. $(x-6)^4$]. It is easier to differentiate this function using the Chain Rule by identifying the two functions:

$$z = (x-6) \quad \text{and} \quad y = \frac{1}{z^4} = z^{-4}$$

Differentiating these two components using the Power Rule gives:

$$\frac{dz}{dx} = 1 \quad \text{and} \quad \frac{dy}{dz} = -4z^{-4-1} = -4z^{-5}$$

Applying the Chain Rule gives:

$$\frac{dy}{dx} = 1 * -4z^{-5} = -4z^{-5}$$

Finally, substituting $z = (x-6)$ gives:

$$\frac{dy}{dx} = -4(x-6)^{-5} = \frac{-4}{(x-6)^5}$$

(b) We could differentiate $y = (2x^2 - 2x + 6)^3$ using the Product Rule or multiply out the brackets and apply the Power Rule but these require a lot of effort. Once again, it is easier to apply the Chain Rule, in which we identify:

$$z = (2x^2 - 2x + 6) \text{ and } y = z^3$$

Differentiating each using the Power Rule gives:

$$\frac{dz}{dx} = (4x - 2) \text{ and } \frac{dy}{dz} = 3z^2$$

and applying the Chain Rule gives:

$$\frac{dy}{dx} = (4x-2) * 3z^2 = 3(4x-2)(2x^2 - 2x + 6)^2$$

(c) There is no alternative but to apply the Chain Rule to $y = e^{3x+2}$ and identify $z = 3x + 2$ and $y = e^z$. Differentiating by the Power and Exponential rules gives:

$$\frac{dz}{dx} = 3 \quad \text{and} \quad \frac{dy}{dz} = e^z$$

Applying the Chain Rule gives:

$$\frac{dy}{dx} = 3e^z = 3e^{3x+2}$$

Exercises 10.2

1 What is the slope of the linear cost function $C = 0.05q + 50$? Find its first derivative and interpret its meaning.

2 Find the first derivatives of:

(a) $y = -12x^4 + 2x^2$ (b) $y = x^2 + 3x - 4$ (c) $y = 1/x^4$
(d) $y = 1/(x^2 - 1)$ (e) $y = (3x^2 + 2)(x + 3)$ (f) $y = 2x/(3x - 2)$
(g) $y = (x^3 + 10)^2$ (h) $y = (4x + 10)^4$ (i) $y = (1 + x)/(2x^2 + 1)$
(j) $y = 5xe^{2x}$.

3 Find the marginal cost at production levels of 10, 20, 50 and 100 units for:
(a) $C = 3q^2 - 8q + 50$ (b) $C = q^2 - 3q + 9$ (c) $C = 2q^2 - 4q + 65$.

4 Differentiate the quadratic $y = -0.01x^2 + 10x - 2{,}000$. What sort of function is the derivative, and what is its meaning in terms of the quadratic? Sketch a graph of the quadratic and of the derivative over the range $x = 0$ to $x = 1{,}000$ in steps of 100. What happens to these graphs at $x = 500$? If x is quantity and y is the profit resulting from sales, what economic interpretation would the derivative have?

Elasticity

Economists use the concept of elasticity to measure the responsiveness of a function to changes in an independent variable, particularly for demand functions in terms of price. In this section we consider definitions and applications of elasticity, and the relationship between it and the derivative.

The prerequisites for this section are:
- What is Quantitative Methods? (Section 1.1);
- Modelling relationships (Chapter 8);
- Graphical and numerical analysis (Section 10.1);
- Marginal analysis and differentiation (Section 10.2).

In Section 1.7 the price elasticity of demand (the elasticity of demand with respect to price) was defined as:

$$\text{Elasticity} = \frac{\text{Percentage change in quantity demanded}}{\text{Percentage change in price}} \qquad (10.3.1)$$

Let us see how we can apply this concept to any change along any demand function of the form $D = f(p)$. First, we shall consider elasticity at a specific change in price. A specific change over a particular interval of a demand function is called **Arc Elasticity**.

Arc Elasticity

To obtain a formula for Arc Elasticity, we consider a change in the price Δp, resulting in a change in demand ΔD. So:

$$\text{Arc Elasticity} = \frac{100\% * \dfrac{\Delta D}{D}}{100\% * \dfrac{\Delta p}{p}} \qquad (10.3.2)$$

Let us simplify this by undertaking a little algebra. First, we can divide both numerator and denominator by 100% giving:

$$\text{Arc Elasticity} = \frac{\dfrac{\Delta D}{D}}{\dfrac{\Delta p}{p}}$$

Rewriting gives:

$$\text{Arc Elasticity} = \frac{\Delta D}{D} * \frac{p}{\Delta p}$$

i.e.:

$$\text{Arc Elasticity} = \frac{\Delta D}{\Delta p} * \frac{p}{D}$$

(10.3.3)

Example 10.3.1

Q Calculate Arc Elasticity between $p = 4$ and $p = 6$ for the demand function:

$$D = 50 + \frac{100}{(p-2)}$$

(10.3.4)

A First, calculate the demand at both prices. At $p = 4$, equation (10.3.4) gives $D = 100$, and at $p = 6$, it gives $D = 75$. So the change in price is $\Delta p = 6 - 4 = 2$, and the corresponding change in demand is $\Delta D = 75 - 100 = -25$. (Note that we expect ΔD to be negative for an increase in price with a downward-sloping demand curve.)

Before we can apply equation (10.3.3), we need to decide on values for price and demand. Let us take the average of the two prices $\left(\text{i.e. } p = \frac{4+6}{2} = 5\right)$ and the average of the two corresponding demand values $\left(\text{i.e. } D = \frac{100 + 75}{2} \quad 87.5\right)$:

$$\text{Arc Elasticity} = \frac{-25}{2} * \frac{5}{87.5} = -0.7143$$

So Arc Elasticity between prices 4 and 6 for our demand function is −0.7143 (i.e. it is inelastic). Therefore price increases between these prices result in a 71.43% reduction in demand. We can see why equation (10.3.3) is called Arc Elasticity by looking at the graph for the demand function (Figure 10.3.1):

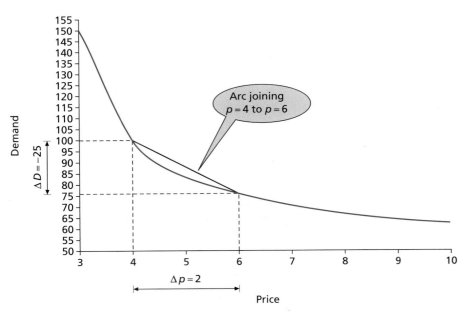

Figure 10.3.1 **Arc Price Elasticity of demand.**

Point Elasticity

Figure 10.3.1 shows that the arc is significantly distant from the curve of the demand function, and so arc elasticity represents only an approximation to the true elasticity along the demand curve. With a smaller change in price the approximation improves, because the arc gets closer to the demand curve. Let us make the change in price very small, tending towards zero (i.e. $\Delta p \to 0$). In this case the arc becomes a point on the demand curve, and we call this **Point Elasticity**.

Let us consider Point Elasticity and see what happens to equation (10.3.3) as price tends towards zero. We are interested in what happens to $\dfrac{\Delta D}{\Delta p}$ as we let the change in price tend towards zero (i.e. $\Delta p \to 0$). We came across this issue in Section 10.2 when we encountered the first derivative, which in this case we define as:

$$\frac{\mathrm{d}D}{\mathrm{d}p} = \underset{\Delta p \to 0}{\text{Limit}} \left\{ \frac{\Delta D}{\Delta p} \right\}$$

So we can define **Point Elasticity** to be:

$$\text{Point Elasticity} = \frac{\mathrm{d}D}{\mathrm{d}p} * \frac{p}{D} \qquad (10.3.5)$$

Example 10.3.2 illustrates the use of equation (10.3.5) to calculate Point Price Elasticity of demand.

Example 10.3.2

Q Find an expression for the Point Price Elasticity of demand for the demand function:

$$D = 50 + \frac{100}{(p-2)}$$

and calculate Point Elasticity at a price of $p = 6$. What price gives unit Point Elasticity?

A First, we find the first derivative of the demand function. Using the Power and Chain or the Quotient rules (Section 10.2) we get:

$$\frac{\mathrm{d}D}{\mathrm{d}p} = -\frac{100}{(p-2)^2}$$

Applying equation (10.3.5) gives:

$$\text{Point Elasticity} = \frac{-100}{(p-2)^2} * \frac{p}{D}$$

We can also represent Point Elasticity as a function of price p by substituting in the demand function:

$$\text{Point Elasticity} = \frac{-100}{(p-2)^2} * \frac{p}{\left(50 + \frac{100}{(p-2)}\right)}$$

$$= \frac{-100p}{50(p-2)^2 + 100(p-2)}$$

$$= \frac{-100p}{50(p-2)(p-2+2)}$$

$$= \frac{-100p}{50(p-2)p}$$

$$= \frac{-2}{(p-2)} \qquad (10.3.6)$$

Having found an expression for Point Elasticity in terms of price, we can now calculate Point Elasticity at any price:

$$\text{At } p = 6 \text{ Point Elasticity} = \frac{-2}{(6-2)} = -0.5$$

To find the price at which Point Elasticity is **unity**, we set equation (10.3.6) equal to -1 (we use -1 for unity because the demand function is downward sloping):

$$\text{At unit Point Elasticity} = \frac{-2}{(p-2)} = -1$$

Algebraically rearranging this expression we find:

$$2 - p = -2$$
$$\text{i.e. } p = 2 + 2 = 4$$

So we can see that, at price $p = 4$, the demand function exhibits unit Point Elasticity.

10.8

| Exercises | **10.3** |

1 If the quantity demanded q is related to price p by:

$$q = -40 + 1{,}000p^{-1} - 960p^{-2}$$

find the demand q at prices of $p = 4$, $p = 6$ and $p = 8$ per unit and the revenue obtained. Hence show that Arc Elasticity between $p = 4$ and $p = 6$ is unity and find an expression for Point Elasticity at p. What is the Point Elasticity at $p = 4$ and $p = 6$? At what price is revenue maximised? Relate these results to a graph of the demand curve. Find another arc where Arc Elasticity is unity when one end of the arc is at $p = 5$. Comment on the relationship between Point and Arc Elasticity.

2 Investigate Point Elasticity along the following demand curves:

(a) $q = 25 + \dfrac{200}{(p+2)}$ \qquad (b) $q = 25 + \dfrac{200}{(p-2)}$

(c) $q = -25 + \dfrac{200}{(p+2)}$ \qquad (d) $q = -25 + \dfrac{200}{(p-2)}$

Which demand functions have points with unit elasticity?

3 Show for the demand curve $D = \dfrac{k}{\text{price}}$, where k is a constant, that Point Elasticity is unity at every point. Find an appropriate expression for a demand curve that has a Point Elasticity of -1.5 at every point.

4 Show for any cost function $C = f(q)$ that Point Elasticity of average cost with respect to quantity is defined in the usual way as follows: $\dfrac{q}{A}\dfrac{dA}{dq}$ is related to marginal cost MC by $\dfrac{q}{A}\dfrac{dA}{dq} = \dfrac{MC - A}{A}$.

10.4	**Turning points**

In Section 10.1 we considered different types of turning point (maximum, minimum or point of inflexion). Finding such turning points graphically is tedious, and may only result in an approximation (depending upon the accuracy of the graph). We can use derivatives to find and identify the type of turning point.

The prerequisites for this section are:
- Presenting and describing small datasets (Section 4.3);
- Non-linear and multivariate relationships (Chapter 9);
- Graphical and numerical analysis (Section 10.1);
- Marginal analysis and differentiation (Section 10.2).

Locating turning points

Recall from Section 10.2 that the first derivative is the slope of a function. At a turning point the slope of a function is zero (e.g. at the top of a local maximum or bottom of a local minimum), as we can see in Figure 10.4.1.

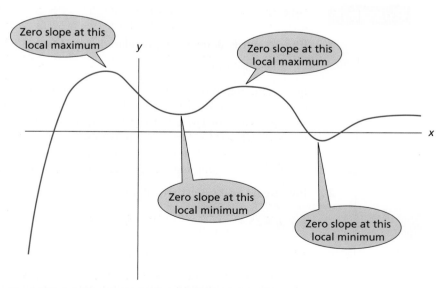

Figure 10.4.1 **The slope is zero at a turning point.**

So, to locate a turning point, we need only find out when the slope is zero. As the first derivative is the slope of a function, this is equivalent to equating the first derivative of a function to zero, i.e.:

$$\frac{dy}{dx} = 0 \qquad\qquad (10.4.1)$$

Example | **10.4.1**

Q Find the position of the turning points of the function:

$$y = x^3 - 21x^2 + 120x + 100 \qquad\qquad (10.4.2)$$

A First, we find the first derivative by applying the Power Rule:

$$\frac{dy}{dx} = 3x^2 - 42x + 120$$

and equate this to zero, i.e.

$$\frac{dy}{dx} = 3x^2 - 42x + 120 = 0 \qquad\qquad (10.4.3)$$

As equation (10.4.3) is a quadratic, asking what values of x make it zero is equivalent to finding its roots (see Section 10.1). So we can apply equation (10.1.3), which gives two roots at:

$$x = 4 \text{ and } x = 10$$

Therefore equation (10.4.2) has two turning points, one at $x = 4$ and another at $x = 10$.

The type of turning point

Although the first derivative locates a turning point, we do not know what type of turning point it is (i.e. maximum, minimum or point of inflexion), unless we draw a graph. However, we can extend the use of derivatives to tell us about the type of turning point at a particular location. We need to find the second derivative (i.e. differentiate the first derivative) to identify the type of turning point.

In fact, we can repeat differentiation over and over again. Further derivatives are denoted by superscripts:

$\dfrac{dy}{dx}$ is the first derivative of $y = f(x)$

$\dfrac{d^2y}{dx^2}$ is the second derivative of $y = f(x)$, found by differentiating $\dfrac{dy}{dx}$

$\dfrac{d^3y}{dx^3}$ is the third derivative of $y = f(x)$, found by differentiating $\dfrac{d^2y}{dx^2}$

and so on.

To see how higher-order derivatives help us to identify turning points, consider what happens at a local maximum. Think of a local maximum as a hill. When we start to walk up a hill, we find a steep positive (upward) slope, but as we approach the top of a hill the slope decreases to zero. On going down a hill the slope becomes negative, and increasingly steeper and more negative at the foot of the hill. This is equivalent to saying that the first derivative has a negative slope (or the slope of the original function is negative), as shown in Figure 10.4.2:

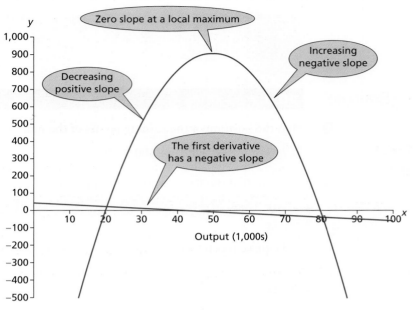

Figure 10.4.2 **The slope around a maximum.**

So if the slope of the first derivative (i.e. the slope of the slope of the original function) is negative, the graph has a local maximum. We know from Section 10.2 that a derivative is the slope of a function, so the slope of the first derivative (i.e. the slope of the slope of the original function) is the second derivative. So we know a turning point is a local maximum if the second derivative is negative. Similarly, we know a turning point is a local minimum if the second derivative is positive, as shown in Figure 10.4.3:

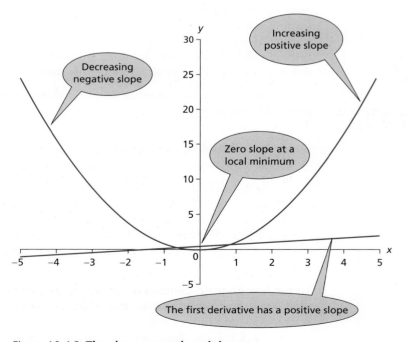

Figure 10.4.3 **The slope around a minimum.**

Finally, as a point of inflexion is neither a local minimum nor a local maximum, we expect the second derivative and possibly higher-order derivatives to be zero. So we have three conditions for identifying a local turning point:

At a local maximum	$\dfrac{d^2y}{dx^2} < 0$ (i.e. negative)	(10.4.4)
At a local minimum	$\dfrac{d^2y}{dx^2} > 0$ (i.e. positive)	(10.4.5)
At a local point of inflexion	$\dfrac{d^2y}{dx^2} = 0$ (i.e. zero)	(10.4.6)

10.9

Some spreadsheets have inbuilt tools for finding turning points.

Example

10.4.2

Q In Example 10.4.1 we found that $y = x^3 - 21x^2 + 120x + 100$ has two turning points (at $x = 4$ and $x = 10$). Identify the type of turning point at each location.

A To find the second derivative, we differentiate the first derivative. The first derivative was:

$$\frac{dy}{dx} = 3x^2 - 42x + 120$$

Applying the Power Rule gives:

$$\frac{d^2y}{dx^2} = 6x - 42$$

We now calculate the second derivative at the two turning points.

At $x = 4$ we have: $\dfrac{d^2y}{dx^2} = 6*4 - 42 = -18 < 0$

From equation (10.4.4) this is a local maximum.

At $x = 10$ we have: $\dfrac{d^2y}{dx^2} = 6*10 - 42 = 18 > 0$

10.9

From equation (10.4.5) this is a local minimum.

Exercises

10.4

1 Consider the following functions in terms of output level q:
(a) Profit $= q^2 + 12q - 20$ (b) Cost $= q^2 - 12q + 100$
(c) Profit $= -q^3 + 6q^2 + 36q - 120$ (d) Cost $= q^3 - 6q^2 + 36q + 240$

In each case, find: (i) an expression for the margin in terms of output (e.g. marginal profit); (ii) the output levels that make the expressions in (i) zero; (iii) an expression for the margin of the margin (i.e. the second derivative); and (iv) the value of the second derivative in (iii) at the output level(s) in (ii).

For each function, sketch graphs of the original function and the expressions for the first and second derivatives on one set of axes. In each case, relate the graphs of the original function to the graphs of the derivatives.

2 Differentiate these functions:
   (a) $R = -100p^3 - 200p^2 + 1,800p$ (Revenue function)
   (b) $P = -100p^3 - 250p^2 + 1,900p - 150$ (Profit function)

   In each case, find the values of p (price) that make the derivatives zero. Without drawing graphs, explain what happens to the original functions at these points. What are the economic interpretations of the first and second derivatives of both functions?

3 Find the absolute (largest) maximum and absolute (smallest) minimum of $y = x^3 - 3x^2 + 10$ in the interval $1 < x < 4$, and sketch the graph of the function.

4 Find the location and nature of the turning points of the functions (a) $y = x^3 + 1$ and (b) $y = (x - 1)^2(x + 2)^3$.

5 Total weekly costs C associated with weekly production of quantity q are given by $C = 400 + 2q + 0.01q^2$. Find expressions for marginal and average costs in terms of q. Sketch graphs of marginal and average costs and show that the minimum value of average cost occurs when average cost is equal to marginal cost. Consider (a) $C = 400 + 2q - 0.01q^2$ and (b) $C = 400 + 2q$. Can similar statements be made relating average to marginal cost?

6 Consider the demand function Demand $= -p^3 + 30p^2 - 300p + 2,000$ in terms of price p. Show that this function has a point of inflexion, and determine the price level at this point. Is this function suitable as a model of demand in terms of price over the range $p = 0$ to $p = 20$?

10.5   Integration

In Sections 10.2 and 10.3 we looked at differentiation (differential calculus). In this section we look at the reverse process, **integration** or **integral calculus**, which takes two forms: **indefinite integration** and **definite integration**.

The prerequisites for this section are:
- Presenting and describing small datasets (Section 4.3);
- Non-linear and multivariate relationships (Chapter 9);
- Graphical and numerical analysis (Section 10.1);
- Marginal analysis and differentiation (Section 10.2).

Indefinite integration

This is essentially the reverse of differentiation, and so we reverse the rules we encountered in Section 10.2 but use different notation. We are still dealing with small changes, so we again refer to the notation used in Section 10.2. We denote the integral y of a function $f(x)$ as:

$$y = \int f(x)\,dx \qquad\qquad (10.5.1)$$

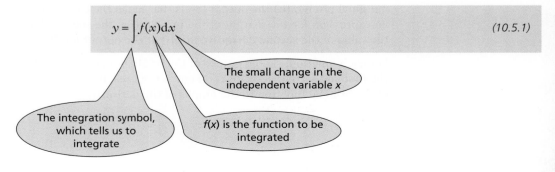

The integration symbol, which tells us to integrate

$f(x)$ is the function to be integrated

The small change in the independent variable x

Example 10.5.1

Q Marginal profit from producing q units of a product is:

$$M\pi = -2q + 12 \qquad\qquad (10.5.2)$$

What is the profit function for this product?

A As marginal profit results from differentiating a profit function (Section 10.2), we write it as:

$$\frac{\mathrm{d}\pi}{\mathrm{d}q} = -2q + 12$$

We now apply the reverse of differentiation (i.e. integrate marginal profit) to find the profit function, which we write as:

$$\pi = \int (-2q + 12)\mathrm{d}q \qquad\qquad (10.5.3)$$

We know from Section 10.2 that a linear marginal profit function results from applying the Power Rule of differentiation. So to reverse the process of differentiation, we need to reverse the Power Rule of differentiation.

The Power Rule of integration

For $y = ax^n$ the Power Rule of differentiation gives $\dfrac{\mathrm{d}y}{\mathrm{d}x} = nax^{n-1}$

When we apply the Power Rule of differentiation, we multiply by the power of x and reduce the power of x by 1. So the reverse of this process must be to increase the power of x by 1 and divide by this new power:

For $y = ax^n$ when $n \neq 1$ integrating gives:

$$\int y\mathrm{d}x = \int (ax^n)\mathrm{d}x = \frac{ax^{n+1}}{(n+1)} + K \qquad\qquad (10.5.4)$$

K represents any number, because the derivative of a number is zero, and is called the **constant of integration**. In some cases we might be able to identify the constant of integration. Let us return to Example 10.5.1.

Example 10.5.1 (revisited)

Before applying equation (10.5.4) to the marginal profit function, we need to write it in full standard form:

$$\pi = \int (-2q^1 + 12q^0)\, \mathrm{d}q \qquad\qquad (10.5.5)$$

Now apply the rule for integration, i.e. equation (10.5.4), to each part of equation (10.5.5) and include the constant of integration K:

$$\pi = \int (-2q^1 + 12q^0)\, \mathrm{d}q$$

$$= \frac{2q^{1+1}}{(1+1)} + \frac{12q^{0+1}}{(0+1)} + K$$

i.e. $\pi = \dfrac{-2q^2}{2} + \dfrac{12q^1}{1} + K$

i.e. $\pi = -q^2 + 12q + K \qquad\qquad (10.5.6)$

We can check we have the correct integral by differentiating this profit function to obtain the marginal profit function we started with (i.e. equation 10.5.2). Without additional information, we cannot say what K is. However, if the manufacturer had fixed costs of £20 for this product, then because profit = revenue – cost we would have $K = -20$.

Definite integration

Definite integration has specific values for the independent variable, and can be interpreted as the area under a graph between two values of the independent variable. Example 10.5.2 illustrates this interpretation.

Example | 10.5.2

Q   All gas suppliers to a market are faced with the same profit function in terms of output q:

$$\text{Profit} = -q^2 + 12q - 20 \qquad (10.5.7)$$

There are many suppliers, and each operates at a different level of output. What are the total profits for this gas market?

A   Our approach is to look at the profits obtained by each supplier. First we graph the profit function that all the suppliers face, and consider their profits at any level of output:

Figure 10.5.1 shows that the profitable range of output for all suppliers is $2 \leqslant q \leqslant 10$ (alternatively, we could calculate the roots of the profit function). To calculate the total profits achievable in this market, we calculate the profit at all possible levels of output (i.e. the area under the graph between $q = 2$ and $q = 10$). To approximate the area under the curve of Figure 10.5.1, we could calculate the area of each trapezium (i.e. a rectangle with a triangle on top) shown in Figure 10.5.2, and the relevant calculations are set out in Table 10.5.1.

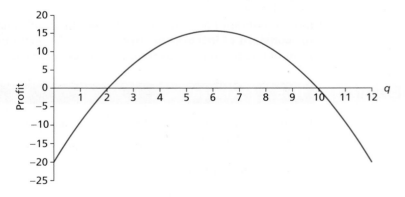

Figure 10.5.1 **The profit function of all gas suppliers.**

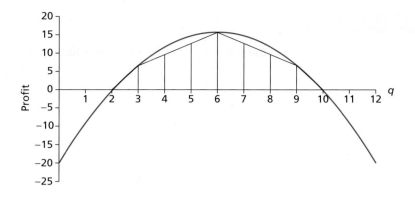

Figure 10.5.2 **The approximate area under the curve.**

Table 10.5.1 **Approximate area under a curve.**

Interval	Area
2 to 3	0.5 * 7 * 1 = 3.5
3 to 4	7 * 1 + 0.5 * 1 * 5 = 9.5
4 to 5	12 * 1 + 0.5 * 1 * 3 = 13.5
5 to 6	15 * 1 + 0.5 * 1 * 1 = 15.5
6 to 7	15 * 1 + 0.5 * 1 * 1 = 15.5
7 to 8	12 * 1 + 0.5 * 1 * 3 = 13.5
8 to 9	7 * 1 + 0.5 * 1 * 5 = 9.5
9 to 10	0.5 * 7 * 1 = 3.5
	Total = 84

However, this gives us only an approximation, because in Figure 10.5.2 the trapezia are only an approximation to the curve. By making the intervals smaller (i.e. letting their width tend to zero) we get a better approximation. Definite integration does this, and so the integral sign represents the summation of all the very thin trapezia. The area between two values ($x = a$ and $x = b$, where $a < b$) can be found by calculating the area up to $x = b$ and subtracting from it the area up to $x = a$.

Let us now calculate the definite integral for Example 10.5.2:

$$\text{Area} = \int_2^{10} (-q^2 + 12q - 20)\,dq \qquad (10.5.8)$$

First we apply equation (10.5.4) and use square brackets and super/subscripts to denote the range of integration:

$$\text{Area} = \left[-\frac{q^3}{3} + 6q^2 - 20q + K \right]_2^{10} \qquad (10.5.9)$$

Now we evaluate the equation in the square brackets at $q = 10$ and $q = 2$, and then subtract to get the area under the curve between $q = 2$ and $q = 10$:

$$\text{Area} = \left[-\frac{10^3}{3} + 6*10^2 - 20*10 + K \right] - \left[-\frac{2^3}{3} + 6*2^2 - 20*2 + K \right]$$

$$\text{Area} = 85.333$$

The true area, and therefore the potential total profit to be made in this gas market, is 85.33.

1 Evaluate the following indefinite integrals (don't forget the constants of integration):

(a) $\int x^3\,dx$

(b) $\int v^{-2}\,dv$

(c) $\int w^{1/2}\,dw$

(d) $\int (x^2 + 8x + 2)\,dx$

(e) $\int (3v^2 - v + 7)\,dv$

(f) $\int \left(2 - \frac{6}{y^3}\right)dv.$

2 Evaluate the definite integral:

$$\int_{10}^{20} (3x^2 + 6x - 10)\,dx$$

Sketch a graph of the function $3x^2 + 6x - 10$ for $x = 0$ to $x = 30$ in steps of 1, indicating the results of integration. How can you approximate these results from the graph?

3 A toy's marginal cost of production is $MC = 2q^2 - 3q - 500$ (where q is the quantity produced).
(a) With fixed production costs of £1,700, find the total cost function C.
(b) If marginal revenue is $MR = 2q^2 - 5q$, find the revenue function R.

4 A graph of marginal cost MC as a function of output q is:

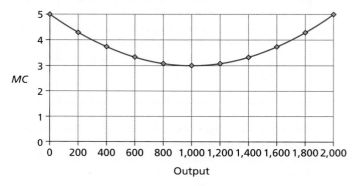

Assuming the graph is a parabola, find an expression for marginal cost as a function of q. If fixed costs are £4,000 per week, find an equation for total costs as a function of q. What is the cost of producing 2,000 units per week?

5 Sales of a product at the start of the year were 100 units. After 2 months they were 400 units, and after a further 2 months they were 600 units.
(a) Find an exponential model for sales quantity in terms of time (months), and sketch the graph.
(b) What are the sales forecasts for the first half of the year and the end of the year?
(c) What is the expected ceiling on sales?
(d) Find an expression for the rate of sales over time, and sketch the graph. What is the rate of sales after 1 year?
(e) What are total sales during the first 6 months and in the first year?

10.6 | Partial differentiation and applications

In Section 9.5 we saw how multivariate functions can be used as models, and in Section 10.1 we saw it was almost impossible to analyse such models graphically. However, by extending the ideas of marginal analysis and differentiation (Section 10.2), we can analyse such multivariate models.

The prerequisites of this section are:
- Presenting and describing small datasets (Section 4.3);
- Non-linear and multivariate relationships (Chapter 9);
- Graphical and numerical analysis (Section 10.1);
- Marginal analysis and differentiation (Section 10.2);
- Elasticity (Section 10.3).

Partial differentiation

When attempting to visualise multivariate functions in Section 10.1, we saw that we can take only a partial view by considering the function one variable at a time, while holding all the others constant (i.e. *ceteris paribus*, 'other things being equal'). We take the same approach when considering marginal analysis and differentiation of multivariate functions. Hence we refer to **partial derivatives** and **partial differentiation**. In partial marginal analysis we investigate the derivatives of one independent variable while holding the others constant (as we did when graphically analysing multivariate functions in Section 10.1). So, when undertaking partial differentiation, we MUST remember to treat these variables being held constant as if they were numbers.

To indicate that we are finding only partial derivatives, we use a slightly different notation. As we are viewing a multivariate function in terms of each independent variable, there may be many possible derivatives to consider, and we MUST remember we are taking a partial view.

In general, for the multivariate function

$$y = f(x_1, x_2, x_3 \dots, x_n) \qquad (10.6.1)$$

we define these **first-order partial derivatives**:

$\dfrac{\partial y}{\partial x_1}$ is the first-order partial derivative of y with respect to x_1, holding ALL other variables (i.e. $x_2, x_3, \dots, x_n$) constant

$\dfrac{\partial y}{\partial x_2}$ is the first-order partial derivative of y with respect to x_2, holding ALL other variables (i.e. $x_1, x_3, \dots, x_n$) constant

$\dfrac{\partial y}{\partial x_3}$ is the first-order partial derivative of y with respect to x_3, holding ALL other variables (i.e. $x_1, x_2, \dots, x_n$) constant

$\vdots$

$\dfrac{\partial y}{\partial x_n}$ is the first-order partial derivative of y with respect to x_n, holding ALL other variables (i.e. $x_1, x_2, \dots, x_{n-1}$) constant

In general, we define the first-order partial derivative of the multivariate function $y = f(x_1, x_2, x_3, ..., x_n)$ **with respect to the ith independent variable**, while holding all other independent variables (i.e. $x_1, x_2, x_3, ..., x_n$) constant, to be:

$$\frac{\partial y}{\partial x_i} \qquad (10.6.2)$$

We may also want to consider second-order derivatives (as we did in Section 10.4 for univariate functions). This leads to complex notation and the concept of **cross-derivatives**.

In general we can have these **second-order partial derivatives** from $\partial y/\partial x_1$:

$\dfrac{\partial^2 y}{\partial x_1 \partial x_1}$ is the second-order partial derivative of y with respect to x_1, holding ALL other variables constant

$\dfrac{\partial^2 y}{\partial x_1 \partial x_2}$ is the second-order cross partial derivative of y with respect to x_1 for the first derivative and x_2 for the second derivative, holding ALL other variables constant

$\dfrac{\partial^2 y}{\partial x_1 \partial x_3}$ is the first-order partial derivative of y with respect to x_1 for the first derivative and x_3 for the second derivative, holding ALL other variables constant

$\vdots$

$\dfrac{\partial^2 y}{\partial x_1 \partial x_n}$ is the first-order partial derivative of y with respect to x_1 for the first derivative and x_n for the second derivative, holding ALL other variables constant

Similarly, we find the cross-derivatives from:

$$\frac{\partial y}{\partial x_2}, \frac{\partial y}{\partial x_3}, ..., \frac{\partial y}{\partial x_n}$$

and in general denote them by:

$$\frac{\partial^2 y}{\partial x_i \partial x_j} \qquad (10.6.3)$$

for all possible pairs of independent variables i and j (see Example 10.6.1).

Example

10.6.1

Q A firm sells two products and has modelled total revenue in terms of their price by:

$$R = -5p_1^2 - 10p_2^2 + 100p_1 + 200p_2 \qquad (10.6.4)$$

Find the marginal revenue of each product when $p_1 = £2$ and $p_2 = £4$.

A   As there are two independent variables, p_1 and p_2, we find two expressions for partial marginal revenue:

$$\frac{\partial R}{\partial p_1} \text{ (marginal revenue with respect to } p_1 \text{, holding } p_2 \text{ constant)}$$

$$\text{and } \frac{\partial R}{\partial p_2} \text{ (marginal revenue with respect to } p_2 \text{, holding } p_1 \text{ constant)}$$

As equation (10.6.4) is a bivariate quadratic, we can use the Power Rule to obtain the derivatives. Let us write the function in full standard form, as we did in Section 10.2:

$$R = -5p_1^2 p_2^0 - 10p_1^0 p_2^2 + 100p_1^1 p_2^0 + 200p_1^0 p_2^1 \qquad (10.6.5)$$

To find $\dfrac{\partial R}{\partial p_1}$, we treat p_2 as a number and apply the Power Rule to p_1:

$$\frac{\partial R}{\partial p_1} = -2 * 5p_1^{2-1} p_2^0 - 0 * 10p_1^{0-1} p_2^2 + 1 * 100p_1^{1-1} p_2^0 + 0 * 200p_1^{0-1} p_2^1$$

i.e. $\dfrac{\partial R}{\partial p_1} = -10p_1^1 - 0 + 100p_1^0 p_2^0 + 0$

i.e. $\dfrac{\partial R}{\partial p_1} = -10p_1 + 100 \qquad (10.6.6)$

This is the marginal revenue of p_1, holding p_2 constant.

To find $\dfrac{\partial R}{\partial p_2}$, we treat p_1 as a number and apply the Power Rule to p_2:

$$\frac{\partial R}{\partial p_2} = 0 * 5p_1^2 p_2^{0-1} - 2 * 10p_1^0 p_2^{2-1} + 0 * 100p_1^1 p_2^{0-1} + 1 * 200p_1^0 p_2^{1-1}$$

i.e. $\dfrac{\partial R}{\partial p_2} = 0 - 20p_1^0 p_2^1 + 0 + 200p_1^0 p_2^0$

i.e. $\dfrac{\partial R}{\partial p_2} = -20p_2 + 200 \qquad (10.6.7)$

This is the marginal revenue of p_2, holding p_1 constant.

We can now calculate marginal revenue at any price by substituting the relevant prices into the two partial derivatives. At $p_1 = £2$ and $p_2 = £4$, the marginal revenues are:

$$\frac{\partial R}{\partial p_1} = -10 * 2 + 100 = 80 \text{ and } \frac{\partial R}{\partial p_2} = -20 * 4 + 200 = 120.$$

Approximating the total derivative

With a univariate function, we interpreted the first derivative as the margin, slope or rate of change of the function. However, with multivariate functions, we can only interpret derivatives in a partial way. We interpret first-order partial derivatives as the slope or rate of change of the function in terms of one independent variable while keeping all other independent variables constant. In general, for the ith independent variable, the first-order partial derivative $\dfrac{\partial y}{\partial x_i}$ is the margin, slope or rate of change of the function, while all other variables (i.e. $x_1, x_2, ..., x_n$) are held constant. So $\frac{\partial y}{\partial x_i}$ is the margin, slope or rate of change of the function looking from the x_i axis.

Although we cannot get a complete picture of how a multivariate function changes owing to changes in the independent variables (i.e. the total derivative), we can approximate this by adding together all the individual changes of each independent variable multiplied by their rates of change:

$$\Delta y \approx \Delta x_1 \frac{\partial y}{\partial x_1} + \Delta x_2 \frac{\partial y}{\partial x_2} + \Delta x_3 \frac{\partial y}{\partial x_3} ... \Delta x_n \frac{\partial y}{\partial x_n}$$

i.e.:

$$\Delta y \approx \sum_{i=1}^{n} \Delta x_i \frac{\partial y}{\partial x_i} \tag{10.6.8}$$

The use of equation (10.6.8) is illustrated in Example 10.6.2.

Example 10.6.2

Q What is the effect on revenue of a 20% increase in p_1 and a 10% decrease in p_2 from the current price levels for the revenue function:

$$R = -5p_1^2 - 10p_2^2 + 100p_1 + 200p_2$$

A In Example 10.6.1 we found the two partial first-order derivatives (equations (10.6.6) and (10.6.7)):

$$\frac{\partial R}{\partial p_1} = -10p_1 + 100$$

$$\frac{\partial R}{\partial p_2} = -20p_2 + 200$$

Let us approximate the change in revenue (i.e. ΔR) from changes in the two prices (i.e. Δp_1 and Δp_2) by using the appropriate version of equation (10.6.8):

$$\Delta R \approx \Delta p_1 \frac{\partial R}{\partial p_1} + \Delta p_2 \frac{\partial R}{\partial p_2} \tag{10.6.9}$$

Substituting equations (10.6.6) and (10.6.7) into equation (10.6.9) gives:

$$\Delta R \approx \Delta p_1(-10p_1 + 100) + \Delta p_2(-20p_2 + 200) \tag{10.6.10}$$

We can now evaluate equation (10.6.10) for $p_1 = 2$, $p_2 = 4$, $\Delta p_1 = 0.2$ (i.e. 20% increase) and $\Delta p_2 = -0.1$ (i.e. 10% decrease):

$$\Delta R \approx 0.2 * (-10 * 2 + 100) - 0.1 * (-20 * 4 + 200) = 4$$

So a 20% increase in $p_1 = 2$ and a 10% decrease in $p_2 = 4$ increases revenue by approximately £4.

Partial Point elasticity

In Section 10.3 we used derivatives to find Point elasticity, and, similarly, we use partial derivatives for **Partial Point elasticity** (economists also call this **Cross** and **Own Point elasticity**). In general, for any set of goods with demands $D_1, D_2, D_3, ..., D_n$, which are functions of prices $p_1, p_2, p_3, ..., p_n$:

$$D_j = f(p_1, p_2, p_3, ..., p_n) \tag{10.6.11}$$

Let us define the following Partial Point elasticities:

$$\text{Own elasticity} = \frac{\partial D_i}{\partial p_i}\frac{p_i}{D_i} \qquad (10.6.12)$$

Equation (10.6.12) is the Point elasticity of demand for the ith good with respect to its own price, while holding the prices of all other goods constant.

$$\text{Cross elasticity} = \frac{\partial D_i}{\partial p_j}\frac{p_j}{D_i} \qquad (10.6.13)$$

Equation (10.6.13) is the Point elasticity of demand for the ith good with respect to the price of the jth good, while holding the prices of all other goods constant (see Example 10.6.3).

Example 10.6.3

Q The demand (D_1) for a product depends on its price and that of a substitute:

$$D_1 = \frac{5p_2}{p_1} + \frac{10p_1}{p_2} \qquad (10.6.14)$$

Find expressions for and hence calculate the partial elasticities of demand at $p_1 = 2$ and $p_2 = 4$.

A First, we find the first-order partial derivatives of demand at both prices:

$$\frac{\partial D_1}{\partial p_1} = \frac{10}{p_2} - \frac{5p_2}{p_1^2} \qquad (10.6.15)$$

$$\frac{\partial D_1}{\partial p_2} = \frac{5}{p_1} - \frac{10p_1}{p_2^2} \qquad (10.6.16)$$

We can now find expressions for the Own and Cross elasticities of demand using equations (10.6.12) and (10.6.13):

Own elasticity $\quad \dfrac{\partial D_1}{\partial p_1}\dfrac{p_1}{D_1} = \left(\dfrac{10}{p_2} - \dfrac{5p_2}{p_1^2}\right) * \dfrac{p_1}{D_1}$

Cross elasticity $\quad \dfrac{\partial D_1}{\partial p_2}\dfrac{p_2}{D_1} = \left(\dfrac{5}{p_1} - \dfrac{10p_1}{p_2^2}\right) * \dfrac{p_2}{D_1}$

At prices $p_1 = 2$ and $p_2 = 4$, $D_1 = (5*4)/2 + (10*2)/4 = 15$, and the elasticities are:

Own elasticity $\quad \left(\dfrac{10}{4} - \dfrac{5*4}{4}\right) * \dfrac{2}{15} = -\dfrac{1}{3} = -0.333$

Cross elasticity $\quad \left(\dfrac{5}{2} - \dfrac{10*2}{16}\right) * \dfrac{4}{15} = \dfrac{1}{3} = 0.333$

Stationary points

In Section 10.4 we used the first derivative of a function to find turning points (by finding the roots of the first derivative) and the second derivatives to identify the type of turning point (i.e. local maximum, local minimum or point of inflexion). We use partial derivatives in a similar way but refer to such points as **stationary points** because, strictly speaking, we are analysing functions with regard to whether their partial derivatives are zero (i.e. their slopes are stationary and unchanging).

To find these stationary points, we use the same approach as in Section 10.4, except we set ALL partial first-order derivatives to zero:

$$\frac{\partial y_i}{\partial x_i} = 0 \text{ for ALL independent variables } i \qquad (10.6.17)$$

However, the conditions on the second derivatives are complex and apply only in a few cases. For example, for a bivariate function, these conditions are:

If $\frac{\partial^2 y}{\partial x_1^2} > 0$ and $\left(\frac{\partial^2 y}{\partial x_1^2}\right) * \left(\frac{\partial^2 y}{\partial x_2^2}\right) > \left(\frac{\partial^2 y}{\partial x_1 x_2}\right) * \left(\frac{\partial^2 y}{\partial x_2 \partial x_1}\right)$

the function has a local minimum $\qquad (10.6.18)$

If $\frac{\partial^2 y}{\partial x_1^2} < 0$ and $\left(\frac{\partial^2 y}{\partial x_1^2}\right) * \left(\frac{\partial^2 y}{\partial x_2^2}\right) > \left(\frac{\partial^2 y}{\partial x_1 \partial x_2}\right) * \left(\frac{\partial^2 y}{\partial x_2 \partial x_1}\right)$

the function has a local maximum $\qquad (10.6.19)$

If $\left(\frac{\partial^2 y}{\partial x_1^2}\right) * \left(\frac{\partial^2 y}{\partial x_2^2}\right) < \left(\frac{\partial^2 y}{\partial x_1 \partial x_2}\right) * \left(\frac{\partial^2 y}{\partial x_2 \partial x_1}\right)$

there is a local saddle point (Section 10.1) $\qquad (10.6.20)$

If $\left(\frac{\partial^2 y}{\partial x_1^2}\right) * \left(\frac{\partial^2 y}{\partial x_2^2}\right) = \left(\frac{\partial^2 y}{\partial x_1 \partial x_2}\right) * \left(\frac{\partial^2 y}{\partial x_2 \partial x_1}\right)$

the function needs further investigation $\qquad (10.6.21)$

Example 10.6.4

Q Find the location and identify any stationary points for the function:

$$y = -2x_1^2 - x_2^2 - 2x_1 x_2 + 1{,}000x_1 + 800x_2$$

A First, we find the first-order partial derivatives:

$\frac{\partial y}{\partial x_1} = -4x_1 - 2x_2 + 1{,}000$ (differentiating with respect to x_1 holding x_2 constant)

$\frac{\partial y}{\partial x_2} = -2x_2 - 2x_1 + 800$ (differentiating with respect to x_2 holding x_1 constant)

To locate the stationary points, we put both first-order partial derivatives equal to zero:

$$\frac{\partial y}{\partial x_1} = -4x_1 - 2x_2 + 1{,}000 = 0 \qquad (10.6.22)$$

$$\frac{\partial y}{\partial x_2} = -2x_1 - 2x_2 + 800 = 0 \qquad (10.6.23)$$

We now solve this system of equations (Section 2.2), and in this case we can simply subtract the equations giving the location of the stationary points:

$$x_1 = 100 \text{ and } x_2 = 300$$

To identify the type of stationary point, we test to see which of the appropriate conditions, i.e. equations (10.6.18) to (10.6.21), apply. To do this we need to find the second-order partial derivatives:

$$\frac{\partial^2 y}{\partial x_1^2} = -4 \text{ (i.e. partially differentiate (10.6.22) with respect to } x_1)$$

$$\frac{\partial^2 y}{\partial x_2^2} = -2 \text{ (i.e. partially differentiate (10.6.23) with respect to } x_2)$$

$$\frac{\partial^2 y}{\partial x_1 \partial x_2} = -2 \text{ (i.e. partially differentiate (10.6.22) with respect to } x_2)$$

$$\frac{\partial^2 y}{\partial x_2 \partial x_1} = -2 \text{ (i.e. partially differentiate (10.6.23) with respect to } x_1)$$

Since

$$\frac{\partial^2 y}{\partial x_1^2} = -4 < 0 \text{ and } (-4)*(-2) > (-2)*(-2)$$

then the function has a local maximum at $x_1 = 100$ and $x_2 = 300$.

Exercises 10.6

1 For the Cobb–Douglas production function in Question 10 of Exercises 10.1, find values for:

$$P, \frac{\partial P}{\partial C} \text{ and } \frac{\partial P}{\partial L} \text{ at } \quad C = 8 \text{ and } L = 27$$

and interpret the partial derivatives in economic terms.

2 Find the two partial elasticities of demand at $p_A = 10$ and $p_B = 5$ for the demand function $q_A = 60 - 5p_A + 10p_B$.

3 Consider two products, A and B, having:

$$q_A = p_A^{-1.3} p_B^{0.4} \text{ and } q_B = p_A^{0.3} p_B^{0.1}$$

Find expressions for the four possible partial elasticities and show that these are all constants.

4 Consider the function $z = 6x + 3y + xy - x^2 - y^2 + 3$.
   (a) Find expressions for the two first-order partial derivatives.
   (b) Evaluate z and the derivatives at $x = 2$ and $y = 2$, and hence find the approximate value of z at $x = 2.01$ and $y = 2.01$.
   (c) Show that at $x = 3$ and $y = 3$, $\frac{\partial z}{\partial y} = 0$. What does this mean?
   (d) Show that at $x = 5$ and $y = 4$ both partial derivatives are zero. What does this mean in terms of the function z?

5 Using the approximation for the total derivative, show for a general demand function $q_A = f(P_A, P_B)$ that:

$$
\begin{pmatrix} \% \\ \text{increase} \\ \text{in demand} \\ \text{for } A \end{pmatrix} \approx \begin{pmatrix} \text{Partial elasticity} \\ \text{of demand for } A \\ \text{with respect to} \\ \text{price of } A \end{pmatrix} * \begin{pmatrix} \% \\ \text{increase} \\ \text{in price} \\ \text{of A} \end{pmatrix} + \begin{pmatrix} \text{Partial elasticity} \\ \text{of demand for } A \\ \text{with respect to} \\ \text{price of } B \end{pmatrix} * \begin{pmatrix} \% \\ \text{increase} \\ \text{in price} \\ \text{of B} \end{pmatrix}
$$

6   Use the result from Question 5 and the demand functions from Question 3 to do the following:

(a)   Find the % changes in demand for A and B caused by a 2% increase in the price of A and a 5% decrease in the price of B.

(b)   If the price of A increases by 5%, what is the largest % increase in the price of B that would **not** decrease demand for B?

7   Find the derivatives and stationary points for

(a) $z = x^3 + xy + y^2$

(b) $z = x^2 - 2xy^2 + 4xy + 1$.

10.7 Chapter review

In this chapter we considered some approaches for analysing models encountered in business, management and economics. The simplest form of analysis interpreted the features of the graphs of the functions used as models (Section 10.1). We also considered a simple method of numerical analysis (the method of bisection), which can be used for refining initial estimates from graphs. Numerical methods can be extended to other forms of analysis, but they are beyond the scope of this book.

In general, graphical and numerical analyses provide only approximate results. In subsequent sections of this chapter we saw how marginal analysis (i.e. differentiation) can be used to analyse some functions without the need to draw a graph. Marginal analysis is often used in Economics and in Operations and Production Management.

However, in some cases such forms of analysis are too cumbersome or inappropriate for complex models (e.g. multivariate models), and then we might have to rely on graphical or numerical analysis. In Part C we see how these concepts can be applied to solving decision problems.

Chapter 11

An introduction to time series

Introduction

A time series is a dataset that relates to one or more variables over time. They are important in management and economics, where they are analysed to develop models that forecast values of variables into the future. Time-series analysis and forecasting are used at the micro level for planning operations (e.g. production) and business strategies (e.g. marketing), and at the macro level by governments for planning national economic strategies. In this chapter we consider the concepts of time-series analysis and forecasting.

Chapter objectives

- To introduce the concept and components of time series
- To introduce methods of time-series analysis and forecasting
- To introduce the method of exponential smoothing.

Chapter contents

Classical time-series analysis

The traditional or classical view of a time series is that it comprises four basic components:

- **Trend**
- **Seasonal variation**
- **Cyclical variation**
- **Irregular variation**

In this section we consider these basic components.

The prerequisites of this section are:

- Relationships, functions and equations (Section 8.1);
- Linear functions (Section 8.2);
- Non-linear and multivariate relationships (Chapter 9);
- Graphical and numerical analysis (Section 10.1).

Trend

A scattergram or graph of a time series often exhibits an underlying **trend**: for example, the graph may appear to be increasing, decreasing or constant over time. To identify the trend of a time series we can consider the mathematical functions we encountered in Chapters 8 and 9. For example, Figure 11.1.1 has a constant trend, Figure 11.1.2 has a linear trend whereas Figure 11.1.3 has a non-linear trend (e.g. hyperbolic or exponential), and Figure 11.1.4 appears to oscillate but might have a very small upward trend. However, we cannot always, and may not want to, model trend by a mathematical function (e.g. Figures 11.1.1 and 11.1.4).

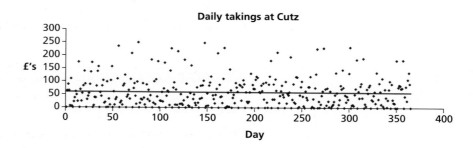

Figure 11.1.1 **Time series with constant trend.**

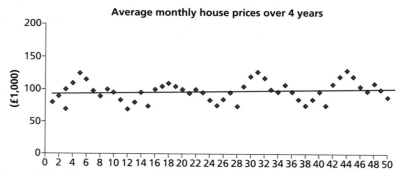

Figure 11.1.2 **Linear upward-sloping (increasing) trend.**

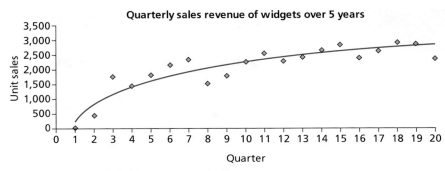

Figure 11.1.3 **Non-linear asymptotic trend.**

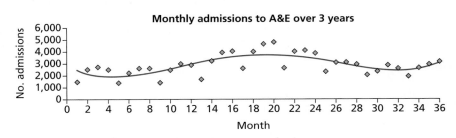

Figure 11.1.4 **Oscillating and little or no apparent trend.**

Seasonal variation

Seasonal variation is a regular, repeating pattern around the trend. For example, the same pattern may occur every week in a daily time series. There may be weekly, monthly or quarterly patterns: for example, more customers may arrive at a bank on Fridays than on other days of the week, perhaps to withdraw money for the weekend; or more customers may visit a bank at the start and end of each month because bills and wages are paid at that time.

Seasonal variation is an inherent characteristic of the time series being studied: for example, more customers turning up at a bank on Fridays might be because it is closed over the weekend. However, not all seasonal variations can be explained in this way.

Figure 11.1.2 shows seasonal variation around a trend line, and this can be seen more clearly by joining up the scatterpoints and drawing vertical lines at regular intervals (e.g. each year). Figure 11.1.5 shows the same repetitive pattern for each year, which is related to the same months each year: some months have peaks above the trend and others troughs below the trend. A time series might have several seasonal patterns. Figure 11.1.6 also has a repetitive pattern, and the underlying oscillations might be the result of another, but there are insufficient data to be certain.

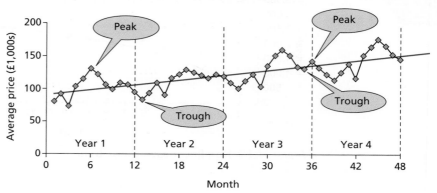

Figure 11.1.5 **Seasonal variation.**

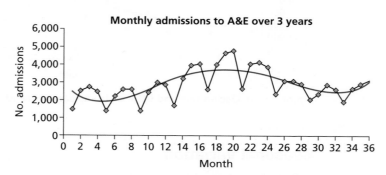

Figure 11.1.6 **Seasonal variation.**

Cyclical variation

Cyclical variation is similar to seasonal variation but relates only to long periods of time. Furthermore, it is often associated with external factors that are outside the domain of the time series. For example, over a 10-year period, we might find a decline in the number of bank customers in the 4th and 8th years of a longitudinal study, and that this decline coincided with a recession. Figure 11.1.5 seems to show cyclical variation – the central peak in Year 2 is not as pronounced as those in Years 1, 3 and 4 – and investigation may reveal that Year 2 saw a down-turn in the economic cycle (e.g. a recession). The apparent underlying oscillations in Figure 11.1.6 might also be cyclical variation (perhaps related to weather cycles).

Irregular variation

Irregular variation cannot be accounted for, or exhibits no recognisable pattern. It is also called **random noise** or **random error**, and might result from sampling error (such as those in Section 4.2). Taking larger samples might reduce irregular variation. The seasonal variation in Figure 11.1.5 is not the same in Years 1, 3, and 4, and might be considered to be irregular variation.

Visual inspection

As we have seen, a close visual inspection of the graph of a time series plays a key role in identifying the underlying components and in prompting further investigation (e.g. possible explanations), and this should be the first stage of a time-series analysis.

95

11.1.1

Q Table 11.1.1 shows the monthly sales of tyres over the last 5 years. Visually analyse the time series.

Table 11.1.1 **Monthly tyre sales over 5 years.**

Month	Year				
	1	2	3	4	5
January	19	27	29	33	36
February	20	26	28	32	34
March	20	30	37	41	43
April	22	30	39	44	47
May	27	35	40	50	49
June	27	32	35	52	51
July	24	26	23	44	40
August	30	30	35	45	43
September	32	35	40	53	49
October	36	39	49	63	57
November	37	38	46	54	55
December	42	47	56	71	66

A First, we number the months 0, 1, 2, etc up to 59 to create the horizontal scale, and then draw a graph of sales over time (Figure 11.1.7). We then draw vertical lines between repeating peaks (or troughs) to help identify patterns, and use judgement to identify any trend.

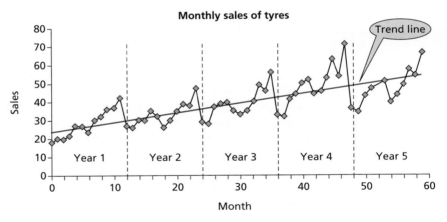

Figure 11.1.7 **Graph for Example 11.1.1.**

A visual inspection shows an upward trend and a seasonal variation each year. January and February appear to be have the lowest sales, while December has the highest. Peaks also appear in Spring followed by a trough. There are insufficient data to comment on whether there is any cyclical component.

11.1

1 Annual sales of UK healthcare insurance over the last 14 years are tabulated below. Plot the data on a scattergram and identify the trend. What can you conclude about future sales?

Year	1	2	3	4	5	6	7
Sales	23,489	25,276	30,827	36,375	45,635	47,648	51,678
Year	8	9	10	11	12	13	14
Sales	52,883	55,016	56,998	64,267	74,012	83,485	89,658

2 The table below shows the number of UK children found in possession of hard drugs over the last 16 years. Plot a graph of these data and identify and comment on the trend.

Year	1	2	3	4	5	6	7	8
No. children	427	465	516	486	567	621	686	759
Year	9	10	11	12	13	14	15	16
No. children	848	1,025	1,141	1,220	1,331	1,507	1,745	2,342

3 Monthly wine production (thousands of litres) over the last 5 years is tabulated below. Analyse the data graphically and identify the features.

	Year 1	Year 2	Year 3	Year 4	Year 5
January	3.3	3.8	2.7	3.4	7.4
February	2.7	3.4	3.0	3.0	2.6
March	2.5	2.9	3.4	3.1	2.6
April	2.1	2.4	2.2	3.7	2.3
May	2.6	2.4	1.8	3.2	3.0
June	1.7	1.8	1.9	2.5	2.3
July	1.1	2.1	0.8	1.5	1.5
August	6.1	3.0	3.1	3.9	9.6
September	59.7	45.4	59.1	49.5	72.9
October	86.9	108.7	95.2	113.6	88.4
November	14.8	21.8	13.3	36.0	17.9
December	5.7	4.8	6.7	9.5	8.3

11.2 Classical time-series models

There are different views about how the trend, seasonal, cyclical and irregular variation interact in producing a time series. In order to construct a model we need to find values for the components of a time series. In this section we consider how we calculate these basic components.

The prerequisites of this section are:
- Measures of location (Section 5.1);
- Index numbers (Section 5.4);
- Least-squares linear regression (Section 8.3).

Time-series models

To model the interaction of these components, let us introduce some notation:

t = A point in time (i.e. a value on the horizontal axis)

TS_t = A value of the time series (i.e. a value on the vertical axis)

T_t = The value of the trend component at time period t

S_t = The value of the seasonal component at time period t

C_t = The value of the cyclical component at time period t

I_t = The value of the irregular component at time period t

The simplest form of interaction between these basic components can be modelled by an **additive model**:

$$TS_t = T_t + S_t + C_t + I_t \qquad\qquad (11.2.1)$$

However, **multiplicative models** are generally considered better at representing these interactions:

$$TS_t = T_t * S_t * C_t * I_t \qquad\qquad (11.2.2)$$

If it were true that a time series comprised four basic components, combined in some way (e.g. by a multiplicative model), then time-series analysis would be an exact science. Unfortunately, these ideas are assumptions, and we do not know whether they are true, either generally or for a particular time series. Economists disagree about the number of basic components. For example, some macroeconomists think trend and cyclical components are produced by the same underlying forces, whereas some microeconomists make no distinction between seasonal and cyclical components. Furthermore, many statisticians question whether the components are separable and, even if they are, whether they interact in an additive or multiplicative manner. Some would argue that even in the multiplicative model we should simply add rather than multiply the irregular component.

Calculating values of the components

Having identified the existence of any components, we can then calculate their values. We begin by removing any cyclical and seasonal components so that we can find any trend and irregular components. If there are sufficient data, a simple approach would be to ignore the data relating to a cyclical component (e.g. omit the data for the 2nd year in Figure 11.1.5); however, this is not always possible or desirable. To calculate seasonal components we can **use moving averages**.

Moving averages

A **moving average (MA)** can be thought of as a window spanning consecutive items of data over a number of periods over which we calculate the mean. To calculate a moving average, we specify the number of periods (i.e. the size of the window or subset) from which to calculate the mean. For example, a window spanning two consecutive items of data is called a 2-period moving average and denoted MA(2); one spanning 12 consecutive items of data has a 12-period moving average and is denoted MA(12). To determine the size of our moving-average window, we identify the seasonal variations by studying a graph of the time series. For example, if in a daily time series we see a repeating seasonal pattern every week, we might choose to calculate a 7-period moving average. Some spreadsheets have tools for calculating a moving average.

11.3

Having decided on the size of the moving-average window, we move it along the dataset one period at a time and calculate the mean. Figure 11.2.1 shows how a 3-period moving average is calculated.

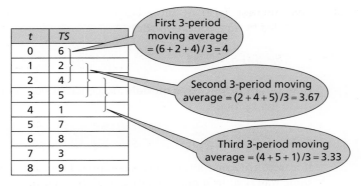

Figure 11.2.1 **Constructing a 3-period moving average.**

We place moving-average values in a column adjacent to the original time series data and in the centre of the time window (Table 11.2.1):

Table 11.2.1 **A 3-period moving average.**

t	TS	MA(3)
0	6	
1	2	4.00
2	4	3.67
3	5	3.33
4	1	4.33
5	7	5.33
6	8	6.00
7	3	6.67
8	9	

Note that a moving average results in fewer numbers than we started with. With an odd number of periods in the moving-average window, we put the moving average at its centre. However, this is not possible with an even number of periods, and we have to make adjustments in such cases (see Example 11.2.2).

Example **11.2.2**

Q Calculate a 12-period moving average for the time series in Example 11.1.1, and compare it with the original time series.

A Table 11.2.2 shows the 12-period moving average and the adjustments made to deal with an even number of periods. With an even number of periods in the moving-average window, we cannot directly relate the moving-average value to a period in the time series. Here, the first moving average needs to be placed midway between June and July. So we take a 2-period moving average of the 12-period moving average and put the first of these values at July of the first year. Figure 11.2.2 shows the graph of the original time series and the 12-period moving average and how the 12-period (monthly) moving average has smoothed out the seasonal variation in the time series. The graph of the moving average indicates the trend and other variations (e.g. cyclical and irregular) in the time series.

Table 11.2.2 **A 12-period moving average for Example 11.1.1.**

Year	Month	Sales	MA(12)	Adjusted MA(12)	Year	Month	Sales	MA(12)	Adjusted MA(12)
1	January	19			4	January	33	43.50	43.04
	February	20				February	32	44.33	43.92
	March	20				March	41	45.42	44.88
	April	22				April	44	46.58	46.00
	May	27				May	50	47.25	46.92
	June	27	28.00			June	52	48.50	47.88
	July	24	28.67	28.33		July	44	48.75	48.63
	August	30	29.17	28.92		August	45	48.92	48.83
	September	32	30.00	29.58		September	53	49.08	49.00
	October	36	30.67	30.33		October	63	49.33	49.21
	November	37	31.33	31.00		November	54	49.25	49.29
	December	42	31.75	31.54		December	71	49.17	49.21
2	January	27	31.92	31.83	5	January	36	48.83	49.00
	February	26	31.92	31.92		February	34	48.67	48.75
	March	30	32.17	32.04		March	43	48.33	48.00
	April	30	32.42	32.29		April	47	47.83	48.08
	May	35	32.50	32.46		May	49	47.92	47.88
	June	32	32.92	32.71		June	51	47.50	47.71
	July	26	33.08	33.00		July	40		
	August	30	33.25	33.17		August	43		
	September	35	33.83	33.54		September	49		
	October	39	34.58	34.21		October	57		
	November	38	35.00	34.79		November	55		
	December	47	35.25	35.13		December	66		
3	January	29	35.83	35.54					
	February	28	36.25	36.04					
	March	37	36.67	36.46					
	April	39	37.50	37.08					
	May	40	38.17	37.83					
	June	35	38.92	38.54					
	July	33	39.25	39.08					
	August	35	39.58	39.42					
	September	40	39.92	39.75					
	October	49	40.33	40.13					
	November	46	41.17	40.75					
	December	56	42.58	41.88					

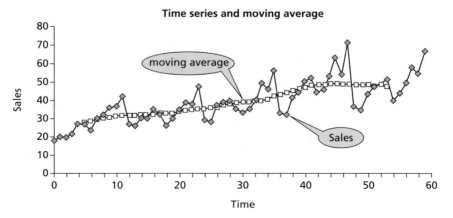

Figure 11.2.2 **The smoothing effect of a moving average.**

Calculating seasonal components

We have seen how a moving average can smooth out the seasonal variation of a time series. Therefore the moving-average values represent the trend, cyclical and irregular components of a time series. If we remove the moving-average values from the time series we are then left with the seasonal component. In the additive model (equation (11.2.1) we would need to subtract the moving averages, whereas in the multiplicative model (11.2.2) we would need to divide by the moving averages. Once we have removed the moving averages (i.e. trend, cyclical and irregular components) from a time series we can then calculate the values of the seasonal components by taking a representative value (e.g. mean or median). Example 11.2.3 illustrates this process for the data in Example 1.1.1, assuming that a multiplicative model (equation 11.2.2) best describes the interactions of the components.

Example

11.2.3

Q Calculate seasonal indices for each month of the first 3 years of the time series in Example 11.1.1.

Table 11.2.3 **Ratio of actual data to moving averages.**

Month	t	Sales	MA(12)	Adjusted MA(12)	Ratio
January	0	19			
February	1	20		24/28.33 = 0.85	
March	2	20			
April	3	22			
May	4	27			
June	5	27	28.00		
July	6	24	28.67	28.33	0.85
August	7	30	29.17	28.92	1.04
September	8	32	30.00	29.58	1.08
October	9	36	30.67	30.33	1.19
November	10	37	31.33	31.00	1.19
December	11	42	31.75	31.54	1.33
January	12	27	31.92	31.83	0.85
February	13	26	31.92	31.92	0.81
March	14	30	32.17	32.04	0.94
April	15	30	32.42	32.29	0.93
May	16	35	32.50	32.46	1.08
June	17	32	32.92	32.71	0.98
July	18	26	33.08	33.00	0.79
August	19	30	33.25	33.17	0.90
September	20	35	33.83	33.54	1.04
October	21	39	34.58	34.21	1.14
November	22	38	35.00	34.79	1.09
December	23	47	35.25	35.13	1.34
January	24	29	35.83	35.54	0.82
February	25	28	36.25	36.04	0.78
March	26	37	36.67	36.46	1.01
April	27	39	37.50	37.08	1.05
May	28	40	38.17	37.83	1.06
June	29	35	38.92	38.54	0.91
July	30	33			
August	31	35			
September	32	40			
October	33	49			
November	34	46			
December	35	56			

A Table 11.2.3 is the same as Table 11.2.2 with an extra column containing the ratios of the original time series to the adjusted 12-period moving-average values. From these ratios, we calculate seasonal indices by taking representative values. Such calculations are best performed using a spreadsheet.

We now calculate values for each month by taking a representative value (e.g. mean or median) across the three years. In Table 11.2.4 the median has been calculated.

Table 11.2.4 **Ratio to MA seasonal indices for Example 11.2.3**

Month	Year 1 ratio	Year 2 ratio	Year 3 ratio	Median
January		0.85	0.82	0.83
February		0.81	0.78	0.80
March		0.94	1.01	0.98
April		0.93	1.05	0.99
May		1.08	1.06	1.07
June		0.98	0.91	0.94
July	0.85	0.79		0.82
August	1.04	0.90		0.97
September	1.08	1.04		1.06
October	1.19	1.14		1.16
November	1.19	1.09		1.14
December	1.33	1.34		1.33
				Total = 12.10

We would expect the sum of the medians in Table 11.2.5 to be 12 (if there was no difference in the months, then the index for each month would be 1). However, as we can see, the sum of the medians is not as expected, and so we calculate the seasonal indices by multiplying the medians by the expected sum and dividing by their actual sum. For example:

$$\text{Index for February} = \frac{12 * 0.80}{12.10} = 0.79$$

Table 11.2.5 shows the monthly indices for Example 11.2.3.

11.4

Table 11.2.5 **Seasonal indices for Example 11.2.3.**

Month	Year 1 ratio	Year 2 ratio	Year 3 ratio	Median	Index
January		0.85	0.82	0.83	0.83
February		0.81	0.78	0.80	0.79
March		0.94	1.01	0.98	0.97
April		0.93	1.05	0.99	0.98
May		1.08	1.06	1.07	1.06
June		0.98	0.91	0.94	0.94
July	0.85	0.79		0.82	0.81
August	1.04	0.90		0.97	0.96
September	1.08	1.04		1.06	1.05
October	1.19	1.14		1.16	1.15
November	1.19	1.09		1.14	1.13
December	1.33	1.34		1.33	1.32
			Total = 12.10		12.00

Calculating the trend, cyclical and irregular components

When we have found the seasonal indices we can focus attention on the remaining components. To identify the remaining components we **deseasonalise** the time series and draw a graph, as illustrated in Example 11.2.4.

Example

11.2.4

Q Assuming a multiplicative model, deseasonalise the time series in Example 11.2.3.

A To deseasonalise multiplicative-modelled time series we simply divide the original data by the seasonal indices, as shown in Table 11.2.6. A graph of this deseasonalised time series is shown in Figure 11.2.3.

Table 11.2.6 **Deseasonalised data for Example 11.2.3.**

Month	t	Sales	Index	Deseasonalised data
January	0	19	0.83	22.89
February	1	20	0.79	25.32
March	2	20	0.97	20.62
April	3	22	0.98	22.45
May	4	27	1.06	25.47
June	5	27	0.94	28.72
July	6	24	0.81	29.63
August	7	30	0.96	31.25
September	8	32	1.05	30.48
October	9	36	1.15	31.30
November	10	37	1.13	32.74
December	11	421	1.32	31.82
January	12	27	0.83	32.53
February	13	26	0.79	32.91
March	14	30	0.97	30.93
April	15	301	0.98	30.61
May	16	35	1.06	33.02
June	17	32	0.94	34.04
July	18	26	0.81	32.10
August	19	30	0.96	31.25
September	20	35	1.05	33.33
October	21	39	1.15	33.91
November	22	38	1.13	33.63
December	23	47	1.32	35.61
January	24	29	0.83	34.94
February	25	28	0.79	35.44
March	26	37	0.97	38.14
April	27	39	0.98	39.80
May	28	40	1.06	37.74
June	29	35	0.94	37.23
July	30	33	0.81	40.74
August	31	35	0.96	36.46
September	32	40	1.05	38.10
October	33	49	1.15	42.61
November	34	46	1.13	40.71
December	35	56	1.32	42.42

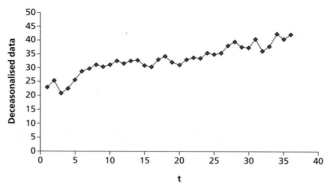

Figure 11.2.3 **Graph of deseasonalised data.**

Figure 11.2.3 indicates a clear upward trend in the deseasonalised data, the minor fluctuations are the irregular components and there would appear to be no cyclical component.

Modelling the trend

Having deseasonalised the data we are left with the trend, cyclical and irregular components. If we have not already removed the cyclical component (e.g. by omitting data from the sample) we could attempt to find an index for the cyclical component by using other moving averages, or we might be able to use information about the cycle to estimate an index (e.g. published data on the economy). We do not know the irregular component, and we could assume it is a random variable drawn from a theoretical probability distribution (e.g. the Normal distribution). To model trend we might use a mathematical function, and this could be obtained through finding the best-fit function to model the underlying trend by using least-squares regression (Example 11.2.5).

Example

11.2.5

Q Find the best-fit linear model for the deseasonalised data in Example 11.2.4.

A We apply least-squares regression to find the slope and intercept of the best-fit line for the deseasonalised data, and then draw in the line of best fit (Figure 11.2.4). These calculations are best done on a spreadsheet or by using the inbuilt functions in Excel.

The slope of the best-fit line is 0.47 and the intercept is 24.35, therefore an equation for the trend line is:

$$T_t = 0.47t + 24.35 \tag{11.2.3}$$

The value of the correlation coefficient is $r = 0.93$, which suggests a good fit to the data.

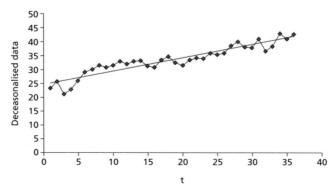

Figure 11.2.4 **The trend in the deseasonalised data.**

182

220

222

1 Analyse the time series in Questions 1, 2 and 3 of Exercises 11.1

2 The table below shows the retail sales of rubber gloves in a supermarket. Analyse the data using a spreadsheet

	Year									
	1	2	3	4	5	6	7	8	9	10
January	310	341	359	367	347	361	371	399	427	466
February	283	278	322	324	315	312	321	365	367	428
March	347	394	455	383	457	418	421	487	433	544
April	406	420	417	526	401	496	474	449	538	604
May	422	425	461	436	434	463	452	492	496	563
June	381	358	410	406	405	407	413	454	456	532
July	338	334	356	370	358	368	383	418	440	492
August	390	373	378	394	399	414	438	451	443	524
September	398	418	428	443	438	455	439	482	496	571
October	434	457	471	467	462	468	463	530	553	596
November	448	451	451	464	483	513	499	522	602	614
December	701	744	776	749	770	801	817	895	992	979

3 The table below shows admissions to a hospital A&E department over three years. Analyse the data and comment on the key components.

Month	Admissions Year 1	Year 2	Year 3
Jan	1,476	1,688	2,327
Feb	2,518	3,226	3,092
Mar	2,731	3,935	3,107
Apr	2,491	4,043	2,930
May	1,393	2,597	2,051
Jun	2,212	4,011	2,344
Jul	2,602	4,646	2,854
Aug	2,595	4,797	2,587
Sep	1,405	2,644	1,932
Oct	2,455	4,026	2,637
Nov	2,988	4,113	2,925
Dec	2,870	3,859	3,152

11.3   Classical time-series forecasting

In the previous sections we identified four basic components of a time series and briefly considered how these can be calculated. In this section we use these components to build classical time-series forecasting models.

The prerequisites of this section are:
- Modelling relationships (Chapter 8);
- Non-linear and multivariate relationships (Chapter 9);
- Non-parametric tests (Section 7.3);
- Classical time-series models (Section 11.2).

Forecasting

One of the purposes of analysing a time series and identifying the components is to extrapolate their values into the future to provide forecasts. This of course assumes that in the future these components will behave as they did in the past, and this might not be true. Therefore any underlying explanatory reasons for the existence of these components should be identified and documented as assumptions underpinning the forecasts.

Once we have identified appropriate values of the components, we can use them to calculate future values of a time series. Using the additive model (equation 11.2.1), we extrapolate the trend into the future, and then add or subtract the seasonal, cyclical and irregular components to represent the peaks and troughs. In the multiplicative model (equation 11.2.2) we also extrapolate the trend, but we then multiply the trend values by seasonal and cyclical factors or indices and including the irregular component. The irregular component might be estimated by random numbers drawn from a theoretical or empirical probability distribution. In Section 11.2 we saw how we might use a mathematical equation to model the trend, which we can easily extrapolate into the future by choosing values for the time variable beyond the dataset.

Testing and validating forecasts

As we have seen, there are two basic models (additive and multiplicative) that we could use to create forecasts, and in some cases there might be several suitable mathematical functions for modelling the underlying trend. So we need some way of choosing the best forecasting model. Therefore we need to validate our models through testing before we begin forecasting, so that we can ensure that we employ the model that is likely to provide the best forecasts.

There are essentially two approaches to testing forecast models, and, if possible, both should be employed. The first is to test the model on some known data, and the second is to produce some forecasts and wait and see what happens in the future. In the former case, where we test our models on some existing data, we should ensure that we do not use the same data from which we constructed our models. Therefore, when building and testing forecasting models from a dataset, we should divide the dataset into at least two parts: the first part is used to construct the model (e.g. find the seasonal components and the trend equation) and the second part should be used for testing the model against. Some statisticians recommend dividing a dataset into three parts: the first two parts are for constructing and testing, and the third part is used for refining the model. However, the size of a dataset will limit the extent to which this can be done.

Having constructed a forecasting model, how do we test it against a set of existing or future data? We can simply compare graphs of forecasts against the actual data and/or we can measure the differences between the forecasts and the actual data using the measures of MAE and MSE (Section 8.3). We can also test our models using hypothesis tests (e.g. Chi-squared) as in Section 7.3.

221

206

| Example | **11.3.1** |

Q Build a forecasting model using the first 3 years of data in Example 11.1.1 and test the model against the data in year 4.

A We know from Example 11.2.5 that the underlying trend can be modelled by $T_t = 0.47t + 24.35$.

From Example 11.2.4 we have the seasonal indices from each month, i.e.

Table 11.3.1 **Seasonal indices for Example 13.3.1.**

Month	index
January	0.83
February	0.79
March	0.97
April	0.98
May	1.06
June	0.94
July	0.81
August	0.96
September	1.05
October	1.15
November	1.13
December	1.32

The analysis of the time series in the previous section suggested that there was no cyclical component, and we shall initially ignore any irregular component. The forecasts for year 4 based on a multiplicative model $F_t = T_t * S_t$ are shown in Table 11.3.2. The forecasts have been rounded because the original data were integers.

Table 11.3.2 **Forecasts for year 4.**

Month	t	T_t	S_t	F_t
January	36	41.27	0.83	34
February	37	41.74	0.79	33
March	38	42.21	0.97	41
April	39	42.68	0.98	42
May	40	43.15	1.06	46
June	41	43.62	0.94	41
July	42	44.09	0.81	36
August	43	44.56	0.96	43
September	44	45.03	1.05	47
October	45	45.50	1.15	53
November	46	45.97	1.13	52
December	47	46.44	1.32	61

Figure 11.3.1 shows how the forecasts compare with the actual data.

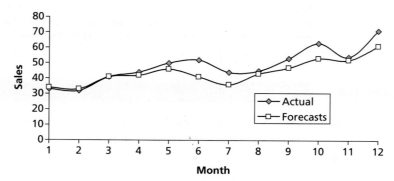

Figure 11.3.1 **Year 4 forecasts and actuals.**

We can see from Figure 11.3.1 that the forecasts, are quite close to the actual data. We can also calculate the forecast error using MAE or MSE, as shown in Table 11.3.3 giving MAE = 4.75 and MSE = 37.58.

Table 11.3.3 **Forecast error.**

Month	Forecast (F_t)	Actual (A_t)	Absolute error	Squared error
January	34	33	1	1
February	33	32	1	1
March	41	41	0	0
April	42	44	2	4
May	46	50	4	16
June	41	52	11	121
July	36	44	8	64
August	43	45	2	4
September	47	53	6	36
October	53	63	10	100
November	52	54	2	4
December	61	71	10	100
			SUM = 57	SUM = 451

We can also test our forecasts using a Chi-squared test (see Section 7.3), as shown in Table 11.3.4.

Table 11.3.4 **Chi-squared test.**

Month	Forecast (F_t)	Actual (A_t)	$(A_t - F_t)^2 / F_t$
January	34	33	0.03
February	33	32	0.03
March	41	41	0.00
April	42	44	0.10
May	46	50	0.35
June	41	52	2.95
July	36	44	1.78
August	43	45	0.09
September	47	53	0.77
October	53	63	1.89
November	52	54	0.08
December	61	71	1.64
		Sum =	9.69
	At 5% significance Chi-squared = 19.68		

The Chi-squared test confirms the hypothesis that the forecasts are acceptable.

We could now experiment with the trend and seasonal indices to see whether we can improve the forecasts, and we could test any new forecasts against the data in year 5.

1 Use the first 4 years of data in Question 3 of Exercises 11.1 to develop a multiplicative forecasting model. Use the data in year 5 to validate your model.

2 Use the first 7 years of the data in Question 2 of Exercises 11.2 to produce a multiplicative forecasting model. Test your model on the data for years 8 and 9, and comment on the validity of your model.

3 Develop and test a forecasting model for the data in Question 3 of Exercises 11.2.

4 Use a spreadsheet to undertake the calculations in Question 2 above, and experiment with the trend and seasonal components to improve the forecast accuracy. Use the data for year 10 to test your revised model.

5 Repeat Question 1 but use the mean rather than the median to calculate the seasonal components. Compare the forecasts using these with those obtained earlier.

6 Use least-squares regression on the first 3 years of the data in Example 11.1.1 to find a best-fit line. Calculate the values of this best-fit line for the first 36 months, and divide them into the actual values for each month. From these ratios calculate a seasonal index for each month, taking the median of the three ratios. This is known as the ratio to trend method. Use the best-fit line and the indices to develop a multiplicative forecasting model, and use the data for years 4 and 5 to test and compare the model with that produced in Example 11.3.1. Which is the better model and why?

11.4 Exponential smoothing

In the previous section we used moving averages to smooth a time series in order to identify the underlying trend and other components (e.g. cyclicals). To calculate moving averages we need a reasonably long time series (i.e. a large sample) and therefore a lot of historical data. A smoothing method that can place less emphasis on the distant past and more on the recent past is **exponential smoothing**. This is often used to make frequent forecasts on the aggregation of many time series over relatively short periods of time, for example, the daily sales of the full range of products in a retail store. In this section, we consider just two forms of exponential smoothing, although there are many other variants used in practice.

The prerequisites of this section are:
- Relationships, functions and equations (Section 8.1);
- Linear functions (Section 8.2);
- Classical time-series models (Section 11.2);
- Classical time-series forecasting (Section 11.3).

The Simple Exponential Smoothing (SES) model

The simple exponential smoothing model is used when a time series has no recognisable trend, seasonal or cyclical components. So it only recognises irregular variation around a constant mean level. It works on the principle that any forecast can be based on a previous forecast but updated to reflect any errors or differences in the earlier forecast. Exponential smoothing takes a previous forecast and adds a proportion of the errors found between the actual and forecast values of the previous period:

Forecast for next period = Last forecast + Proportion of errors in the last forecast

We can write this as a simple equation. Assume we want a forecast for the current time period t, denoted by F_t, and that, in the immediately preceding time period $(t-1)$, we recorded the actual time series TS_{t-1} and its forecast F_{t-1}. Let us denote the proportion of error in the last forecast to be included in this as α, where $0 < \alpha < 1$:

$$F_t = F_{t-1} + \alpha(TS_{t-1} - F_{t-1}) \qquad (11.4.1)$$

α is called the **smoothing constant**. Exponential smoothing is related to moving averages (Section 11.2), as it takes a weighted average at each period. We can see this by rearranging equation (11.4.1). First, multiply the bracket by the smoothing constant:

$$F_t = F_{t-1} + \alpha TS_{t-1} - \alpha F_{t-1} \qquad (11.4.2)$$

Now, take the common factor $F_t - 1$ outside a bracket:

$$F_t = \alpha TS_{t-1} + (1 - \alpha)F_{t-1} \qquad (11.4.3)$$

So F_t is a weighted average of TS_{t-1} and F_{t-1} in which the weights are α and $(1 - \alpha)$, The latter weight, i.e. $(1 - \alpha)$, is called the **damping factor**.

Equation (11.4.3) shows that high values of the damping factor (or, equivalently, low values of the smoothing factor) place more emphasis on previous forecasts, which are based on earlier forecasts and, therefore, more distant history. So, to place more emphasis on the recent past, we should choose high values for α.

When we first use the exponential smoothing equation we have no forecast for the initial period F_0. We can either guess or use a forecasting method, such as classical time-series analysis, to estimate it (see Example 11.4.1).

As with classical time-series analysis, calculations are best done on a spreadsheet. Some spreadsheets have a tool for implementing exponential smoothing, using equation (11.4.3), for a specified damping factor. However, it is just as easy to enter either equation (11.4.1) or (11.4.3) into the cells of a spreadsheet.

 11.7

Example

11.4.1

Q Monthly sales of A4 copy paper have been recorded over the last 22 months (Table 11.4.1). Plot a graph of actual sales and compare it with forecasts using exponential smoothing with smoothing factors of (a) $\alpha = 0.2$ and (b) $\alpha = 0.5$. Comment on the effects of using different smoothing factors.

Table 11.4.1 **Sales data for Example 11.4.1.**

Month	Reams
January	1,704
February	1,740
March	1,858
April	1,800
May	1,827
June	2,008
July	1,735
August	1,580
September	1,753
October	1,956
November	1,841
December	1,852
January	1,534
February	1,936
March	2,032
April	2,050
May	2,078
June	1,988
July	2,101
August	1,640
September	2,099
October	2,175
November	1,905
December	2,187

A   To apply equation (11.4.1) or (11.4.3), we shall estimate F_0 at 1,700. Table 11.4.2 shows calculations for the two values of α and for the MSE so that we can quantitatively compare the two exponential smoothing models (Figure 11.4.1).

Table 11.4.2 **Exponential smoothing for Example 11.4.1.**

Month	Period (t)	Reams	Smoothing factor $\alpha = 0.2$ F_t	$\alpha = 0.5$ F_t	Squared error (when $\alpha = 0.2$)	(when $\alpha = 0.5$)
January	0	1,704	1,700	1,700	16.00	16.00
February	1	1,740	1,701	1,702	1,536.64	1,444.00
March	2	1,858	1,709	1,721	22,308.41	18,769.00
April	3	1,800	1,739	1,790	3,780.77	110.25
May	4	1,827	1,751	1,795	5,804.98	1,040.06
June	5	2,008	1,766	1,811	58,540.93	38,858.27
July	6	1,735	1,814	1,909	6,310.42	30,428.44
August	7	1,580	1,799	1,822	47,764.33	58,669.92
September	8	1,753	1,755	1,701	3.39	2,692.64
October	9	1,956	1,754	1,727	40,613.40	52,415.96
November	10	1,841	1,795	1,842	2,136.49	0.28
December	11	1,852	1,804	1,841	2,301.86	115.27
January	12	1,534	1,814	1,847	78,186.13	97,738.66
February	13	1,936	1,758	1,690	31,792.93	60,360.67
March	14	2,032	1,793	1,813	56,951.24	47,891.84
April	15	2,050	1,841	1,923	43,645.76	16,236.12
May	16	2,078	1,883	1,986	38,076.71	8,410.82
June	17	1,988	1,922	2,032	4,370.01	1,948.76
July	18	2,101	1,935	2,010	27,517.77	8,267.83
August	19	1,640	1,968	2,056	107,775.73	172,670.32
September	20	2,099	1,903	1,848	38,559.72	63,117.47
October	21	2,175	1,942	1,973	54,332.36	40,648.99
November	22	1,905	1,989	2,074	6,976.52	28,625.94
December	23	2,187	1,972	1,990	46,302.23	38,968.33
					MSE = 30,233.53	32,893.58

When $\alpha = 0.2$, the original time series is smoothed, revealing the underlying trend. However, when $\alpha = 0.5$, the graph is very similar to the original times series, lagging behind it by one period (i.e. the peaks and troughs of the original time series appear one period before those from exponential smoothing). Figure 11.3.1 shows the actual time series and the forecasts from exponential smoothing. The MSE is lower when $\alpha = 0.2$, indicating that it gives a better forecast than when $\alpha = 0.5$.

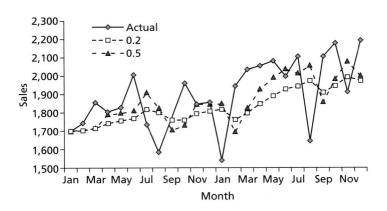

Figure 11.4.1 **Actual sales and exponential smoothing for Example 11.4.1.**

Choosing the smoothing factor

Example 11.4.1 shows that the choice of smoothing factor is important. When the time series is thought to be stationary, we use a low value of α, and if it has variations, we use a higher value. Generally, values of around $\alpha = 0.2$ are chosen for the simple exponential smoothing model, and values of $\alpha > 0.5$ are not used. If values of $\alpha > 0.5$ give better forecasts then we use other exponential smoothing models, such as the one below.

The Holt–Winters exponential smoothing model

The simple exponential smoothing model does not take into account seasonal variation and is unable to deal with non-constant trends. Several extensions of SES have been devised including Holt's Linear Growth Model, which consists of two smoothing equations: one for the mean level (the same as equation 11.4.1) and a second for a linear trend component. Winters devised extensions for including seasonal components into the SES model, which we now consider, and this is called the Holt–Winters multiplicative model. This model consists of three smoothing equations. The first is essentially the same as equation (11.4.1), and considers the mean level of the time series, ignoring trend and seasonal variation. The second updates the trend component, and the third updates the seasonal component, which consists of several indices depending on the nature of seasonal variation (e.g. four indices for quarterly variations, 12 indices for monthly variations, etc.). So we need to know how many seasonal indices Y make up the seasonal component (i.e. $Y = 12$ if we have 12 seasonal indices). We also need three smoothing factors, one for each equation (i.e. mean level, trend and seasonal components), and a further equation to represent the interaction of these components to produce the forecasts.

To write the equations, we extend the notation we used in previous sections:

t	= a particular period for which we want a forecast
$t-1$	= the previous period, which we have already forecast
T_{t-1}	= the value of the trend component at period $t-1$
TS_{t-1}	= the actual value of the time series at period $t-1$
L_{t-1}	= the mean level of the time series at period $t-1$
S_{t-Y}	= the decimal value of the seasonal index at period $t-Y$
F_t	= the forecast at period t
α	= the smoothing constant for the mean level
β	= the smoothing constant for the trend component
γ	= the smoothing constant for the seasonal component

Initial estimates for the mean level, the trend component and all the seasonal indices can be made from informed guesses or by using the methods from Section 11.2. For example, the mean level can be estimated from the mean of the sample data, the trend component can be estimated from the slope of a least-squares linear regression model, and seasonal indices can be estimated from the ratio to trend or ratio to moving averages methods. Once we have calculated the initial values of the mean level, trend and seasonal indices, we can then forecast their future values using:

$$\text{Mean level value } L_t = \alpha \frac{TS_t}{S_{t-Y}} + (1-\alpha)(L_{t-1} + T_{t-1}) \qquad (11.4.4)$$

$$\text{Trend value } T_t = \beta(L_t - L_{t-1}) + (1-\beta)T_{t-1} \qquad (11.4.5)$$

$$\text{Seasonal value } S_t = \gamma\left(\frac{TS_t}{L_t}\right) + (1-\gamma)S_{t-Y} \qquad (11.4.6)$$

$$\text{Forecast } F_t = (F_{t-1} + T_{t-1})S_{t-Y} \tag{11.4.7}$$

Equation (11.4.4) calculates (updates) the mean level by taking a weighted average of (the previous actual time series value divided by the relevant seasonal index) and (the previous mean level plus previous trend). Equation (11.4.5) updates the trend by taking a weighted average of (the difference between the updated and previous mean levels) and the previous trend. Equation (11.4.6) updates the seasonal index by taking a weighted average of (the new actual divided by the updated mean level) and the previous appropriate seasonal index. Finally, equation (11.4.7) produces a forecast by multiplying the previous mean level and trend by the previous appropriate seasonal index. Although daunting, these equations are very easily implemented on a spreadsheet. Example 11.4.2 illustrates their use.

Example **11.4.2**

Q Use the first three years of data from Example 11.1.1 to calculate initial estimates of the mean level, trend and seasonal indices to:

(a) forecast sales of tyres in January of the 4th year using equation (11.4.7);
(b) update the mean level and trend using equations (11.4.4) and (11.4.5) with $\alpha = 0.3$ and $\alpha = 0.1$ to produce a forecast for February of the 4th year;
(c) update the mean level, trend and seasonal indices with $\alpha = 0.3$, $\beta = 0.1$ and $\alpha = 0.2$ to produce monthly forecasts for the 4th and 5th years, and comment on their accuracy.

A We shall initially estimate the mean level by taking the mean of the first three years of sales (i.e. mean level = 33.28) and estimate the initial trend from the slope of the best-fit least-squares regression line on the data (i.e. trend = 0.60). The initial values for the seasonal indices have been calculated using the ratio to trend method (see Question 6 of Exercises 11.3).

(a) If we denote January of the 1st year by $t = 0$, then we denote the required forecast for January of the 4th year (i.e. $t = 36$) by F_{36}, and the initial estimates are denoted as follows:

Table 11.4.3 **Initial estimates.**

Month	Initial values
	Mean level $L_{35} = 33.28$
	Trend $T_{35} = 0.60$
	Seasonal index
January	$S_{24} = 0.84$
February	$S_{25} = 0.86$
March	$S_{26} = 0.98$
April	$S_{27} = 0.96$
May	$S_{28} = 1.09$
June	$S_{29} = 0.98$
July	$S_{30} = 0.82$
August	$S_{31} = 0.89$
September	$S_{32} = 1.02$
October	$S_{33} = 1.17$
November	$S_{34} = 1.08$
December	$S_{35} = 1.30$

11.8

We can now apply equation (11.4.7) to calculate the forecast for January of the 4th year:

$$F_{36} = (L_{35} + T_{35})S_{24} = (33.28 + 0.60) * 0.84 = 28.46$$

(b) Using equation (11.4.4), we obtain the updated mean level:

$$L_{36} = \alpha \frac{TS_{36}}{S_{24}} + (1 - \alpha)(L_{35} + T_{35})$$

$$= 0.3 * \frac{33}{0.84} + (1 - 0.3) * (33.28 + 0.60) = 35.50$$

Using equation (11.4.5), we obtain the updated trend:

$$T_{36} = \beta(L_{36} - L_{35}) + (1 - \beta)T_{35}$$
$$= 0.1 * (35.50 - 33.28) + (1 - 0.1) * 0.60 = 0.76$$

We can now apply equation (11.4.7) to forecast February of the 4th year:

$$F_{37} = (L_{36} + T_{36})S_{25} = (35.50 + 0.76) * 0.86 = 31.19$$

(c) The calculations are best undertaken on a spreadsheet.

Figure 11.4.2 shows a graph of actual sales against forecasts.

Compare these with the forecasts found in Question 6 of Exercises 11.3 and Example 11.3.1.

Table 11.4.4 **Forecasts (rounded to the nearest integer) for years 4 and 5.**

Period (t)	L	T	S	F
36	35.50	0.76	0.86	28
37	36.55	0.79	0.86	31
38	38.69	0.93	1.00	37
39	41.48	1.11	0.98	38
40	43.58	1.21	1.10	46
41	47.27	1.46	1.00	44
42	50.21	1.61	0.83	40
43	51.44	1.57	0.89	46
44	52.69	1.54	1.02	54
45	54.12	1.53	1.17	63
46	53.95	1.36	1.06	60
47	55.10	1.34	1.30	72
48	52.09	0.90	0.82	48
49	48.91	0.49	0.83	46
50	47.54	0.31	0.98	49
51	47.88	0.31	0.98	47
52	47.08	0.20	1.09	54
53	48.33	0.30	1.01	47
54	48.48	0.29	0.83	40
55	48.68	0.28	0.89	43
56	48.73	0.26	1.01	50
57	48.92	0.25	1.17	57
58	49.92	0.33	1.07	52
59	50.43	0.34	1.30	65

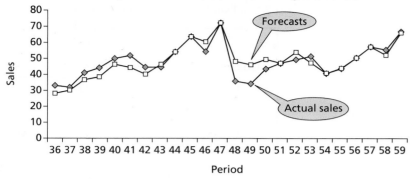

Figure 11.4.2 **Actual versus forecasts for years 4 and 5.**

Forecasting many periods ahead from the current period

All forms of Exponential Smoothing forecast only one period ahead. However, we can modify equation (11.4.7) to forecast any number of periods beyond our current period. If we denote the number of periods beyond our current period by B, then if $B < Y$ we can write equation (11.4.7) as:

$$F_{t+B} = (L_t + BT_t)S_{t-Y+B} \qquad (11.4.8)$$

If $B > Y$, then the forecasts will be less accurate, and we need a further modification to equation (11.4.8), which is beyond the scope of this introductory text (see the further reading at the end of the book).

| Example | **11.4.3** |

Q Use the Holt–Winters exponential smoothing model to forecast the sales of tyres in Example 11.1.1 in March of the 4th year from the initial estimates (i.e. without updating the mean level, trend and seasonal components) calculated in Example 11.4.2.

A To forecast sales in March of the 4th year, because $B < 12$ we can apply equation (11.4.8) with $t = 35$ and $B = 3$, giving:

$$F_{35+3} = (L_{35} + 3 * T_{35})S_{35-12+3}$$
$$F_{38} = (33.28 + 3 * 0.60) * 0.98 = 34 \text{ rounded to the nearest integer)}$$

This forecast is not as good as that obtained in Example 11.4.2.

| Exercises | **11.4** |

1 Use the Simple Exponential Smoothing model to produce one-period-ahead forecasts for the following time series:

Month	1	2	3	4	5	6	7	8
Demand	356	360	312	300	324	316	308	264

2 Use the Simple Exponential Smoothing model with smoothing factors of $\alpha = 0.1$, $\alpha = 0.2$, $\alpha = 0.5$, $\alpha = 0.8$ for the time series in Questions 1 and 2 of Exercises 11.1 and comment on the effects of the different smoothing factors.

3 (a) Apply the Simple Exponential Smoothing model with an initial forecast of 670 and smoothing constant of 0.2 to the data below.

Quarter	Year 1	Year 2	Year 3	Year 4
1	672	744	828	936
2	636	700	800	860
3	680	756	840	944
4	704	784	880	972

(b) Apply the Holt–Winters model with mean level = 752, trend = 20.14, seasonal indices of 1.03, 0.96, 1.00 and 1.00 and $\alpha = 0.3$, $\beta = 0.1$ to the data in part (a) and compare your forecasts.

4 Use the first year of the data below to initialise the Holt–Winters exponential smoothing model with $\alpha = 0.3$, $\beta = 0.1$ and $\gamma = 0.25$. Calculate the mean level, trend and seasonal indices for every month in the last four years, and compare one-period-after forecasts with the actual data in the last two years.

	Year 1	Year 2	Year 3	Year 4	Year 5
January	1,446	1,741	1,819	2,068	2,170
February	1,385	1,567	1,741	2,129	2,193
March	1,682	2,049	2,171	2,656	2,655
April	1,605	1,925	2,027	2,465	2,470
May	1,628	1,914	2,094	2,534	2,509
June	1,764	1,925	2,200	2,530	2,618
July	1,763	2,116	2,366	2,726	2,751
August	1,883	2,158	2,531	2,816	2,905
September	1,532	1,638	1,964	2,153	2,274
October	1,649	1,773	2,101	2,308	2,473
November	1,556	1,651	1,987	2,293	2,322
December	1,560	1,942	2,212	2,293	2,347

11.5 ## Chapter review

This chapter has looked at time-series forecasting. The classical approach is to identify four key components: trend, seasonal, cyclical and irregular. Although this traditional approach can provide accurate forecasts, it is considered a static approach because it assumes that the future is based on the average of a long period of history. In some cases we might have little history, or the past might not be indicative of the future (e.g. in rapidly changing markets or new technology), and we should then consider using Exponential Smoothing methods because they can place more emphasis on the recent past and take greater account of sudden changes. Both the classical approach and Exponential Smoothing are easily implemented on a spreadsheet and are readily adopted by managers. However, there are more sophisticated approaches available for time-series forecasting such as ARMA (Auto-regressive Moving Averages) and ARIMA (Auto-regressive Integrated Moving Averages) devised by Box and Jenkins, which, although superior in many respects, are not easily implemented without using specialist packages, which are beyond the scope of this introductory book (see the further reading at the end of the book).

Chapter 12

Models for finance and accounting

Introduction

This chapter introduces mathematics and models used in Finance and Accounting, and illustrates methods of building and using these models. Although all institutions use the same basic concepts, they often apply them in slightly different ways. For example, when you borrow money, some institutions might charge you an arrangement fee, some might require you to take out insurance, and others might have no 'hidden' charges at all. As we cannot always apply a standard set of formulae, it is important to understand the basic concepts. So, unlike most other chapters, here we derive some basic formulae to help you understand how and when the basic concepts arise, which you can then modify as necessary.

Chapter objectives

- To introduce the concepts of simple and compound growth

- To introduce the concepts of multiple and continuous compounding, AER and APR

- To introduce the concept of discounting

- To introduce the concepts of endowments, sinking funds, mortgages and annuities

Chapter contents

12.1 Simple interest and compound growth

In Chapter 1 we saw that interest is the reward received for investing with, or the cost of borrowing money from, a financial institution. Usually it is calculated as a percentage mark-up on the amount invested or borrowed. This section considers the principles that institutions apply when calculating interest or growth.

The prerequisites of this section are:
- Basic arithmetic (Section 1.4);
- Powers, roots and logarithms (Section 1.5);
- Operator precedence (Section 1.6);
- Fractions, ratios and percentages (Section 1.7).

Interest and growth

The amount invested or borrowed is called the **principal** and the mark-up the **interest rate**. With investments, we also refer to the interest rate as the **growth rate**. The two basic forms, **simple interest** and **compound interest**, are calculated on a specified time basis (e.g. at the end of each year), using the abbreviation p.a. for per annum (i.e. annually). The rate of interest or growth can be expressed as a percentage or a decimal. We shall let R denote a general percentage of interest or growth and r the decimal equivalent (e.g. if $R = 10\%$ p.a., then $r = 10/100 = 0.1$ p.a.).

Simple interest

Simple interest is encountered only in a few special cases, such as government bonds. However, understanding it will help in understanding compound interest. Simple interest occurs when the investment reward cannot be left to accumulate with the principal (Example 12.1.1).

Example 12.1.1

Q Five-year government bonds cost £1,000 per unit and offer 3% p.a. simple interest at the end of each year. What interest is paid each year and in total if 8 units are purchased?

A At the end of each year, interest of $8 * 1,000 * \dfrac{3}{100} = £240$ is paid. As these bonds can be purchased only in units of £1,000, the £240 interest cannot be used to purchase further bonds.

At the end of 5 years a total of $5 * 240 = £1,200$ in interest is paid and the principal of £8,000 is returned.

The simple interest formula

We can derive a formula to calculate the total accumulated value at any point in time from the number of time periods (days, weeks, months, years, etc.) that have elapsed since starting the investment. We denote the rate of growth by r, the number of time periods by t, the principal invested at time zero (i.e. $t = 0$) by F_0, and the future value (i.e. after t periods of time) by F_t. We call F_0 the **present value** (PV) and F_t the **future value** (FV) of the initial investment. The relationship between F_t and the other variables (F_0, r and t) can be found by drawing a timescale showing how the value of money changes over time. So, at time period $t = 0$, an initial investment of F_0 (i.e. principal) is made, and at the end of the first period the future value will be the principal plus the interest. At the end of the second period the future value will be the principal and two amounts of interest. We can calculate the future value after any number of periods, as shown in Figure 12.1.1.

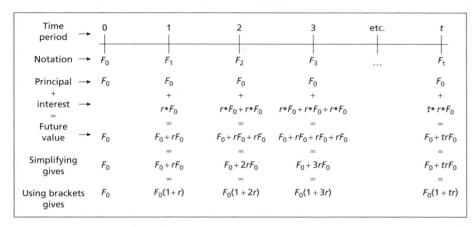

Figure 12.1.1 **Value of money over time for simple interest.**

The last column of Figure 12.1.1 shows the simple interest or simple growth formula:

$$F_t = F_0(1 + tr) \tag{12.1.1}$$

Example 12.1.2

Q Calculate the future value after 5 periods from investing £8,000 at a simple interest rate of 3% per period.

A Putting $r = 0.03$, $t = 5$ and $F_0 = £8,000$ in equation (12.1.1) gives:

$$F_5 = 8,000 * (1 + 5 * 0.03) = 9,200$$

where £8,000 is the principal and £1,200 is the interest after 5 periods.

12.1

Compound interest and growth

Most institutions use compound interest (growth), in which interest received can be left to accumulate with the principal and therefore also gain interest (Example 12.1.3).

Example 12.1.3

Q A sum of £8,000 is invested in a long-term fixed rate savings account at 3% p.a. interest, which leaves interest in the account to accumulate. At the end of the 5th year, how much is in the account and how much interest has been earned?

A After the 1st year £8,000 + 0.03 * 8,000 = £8,240 is in the account. At the start of the second year £8,240 is in the account, and at the end of the year interest is added to give 8,240 + 0.03 * 8,240 = £8,487.2 in the account. The end-of-year balance for each of the five years is shown in Figure 12.1.2.

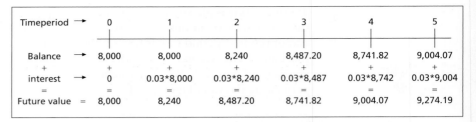

Figure 12.1.2 **The value of money over time for Example 12.1.3.**

After 5 years there is £9,274.19 in the account, of which £1,274.19 is the total interest.

The basic compound growth formula

We saw how easy it was to find a formula for the future value resulting from applying simple interest, and similarly we can derive a formula for the future value resulting from investing any amount over any number of periods with compound interest. Using the same notation that we used for simple interest, then we find that, after one period, the present amount F_0 has grown through the addition of interest to a future value of: $F_1 = F_0 + r * F_0 = F_0(1 + r)$. So at the start of the second period we have $F_1 = F_0(1 + r)$, and at the end of the second period we receive interest on this of rF_1, giving a future value of $F_2 = F_1(1 + r)$. Because $F_1 = F_0(1 + r)$ then $F_2 = F_1(1 + r) = F_0(1 + r) * (1 + r) = F_0(1 + r)^2$. Continuing this process we can calculate the future value after $t = 3$ periods, $t = 4$ periods and so on, as shown in Figure 12.1.3.

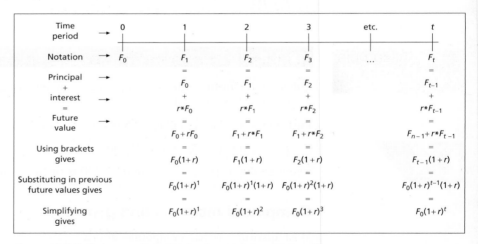

Figure 12.1.3 **Future values for basic compound growth.**

12.2

So a formula for the future value from basic compound growth is:

$$F_t = F_0(1 + r)^t \qquad (12.1.2)$$

Example

12.1.4

Q Calculate the future value after five periods of investing £8,000 at a compound interest rate of 3% per period.

A Putting $r = 0.03$, $t = 5$ and $F_0 = £8{,}000$ into equation (12.1.2) gives:

$$F_5 = £8{,}000 * (1 + 0.03)^5 = £9{,}274.19$$

where £8,000 is the principal and £1,274.19 is the accumulated interest. By comparing the answers in Examples 12.1.1 and 12.1.4, we see that the investor is better off with compound growth.

12.2

Exercises **12.1**

1 Assuming simple growth, calculate the future values of:
   (a) £20,000 invested for 6 years at 18% p.a.
   (b) £50.00 invested for 20 years at 12% p.a.
   (c) £10.00 invested for 15 years at 9.75% p.a.

2 With compound growth, calculate the future values of:
   (a) £20,000 invested for 6 years at 18% p.a.
   (b) £50.00 invested for 20 years at 12% p.a.
   (c) £10.00 invested for 15 years at 9.75% p.a.

3 With compound growth, find the future values of:
   (a) £100 invested for 36 months at 3% per month.
   (b) £50 invested for 5 years with interest of 1.5% added at the end of each month.
   (c) The debt owed on a 5-year loan of £100 with interest added at 5% per year.
   (d) The debt after 1 year on a loan of £2,000 with interest of 1% per week charged.

4 A sum of £5,000 is invested in a building society account, which pays 8% p.a. compound. After 3 years the building society changes the growth rate to 0.5% per month compound. How much is in the account after 5 years?

12.2 Multiple compounding, AER and continuous compounding

So far we have calculated interest at the end of a given time period (e.g. annually). Some institutions calculate interest more frequently than once per year, and this is called multiple compounding. For example, interest on loans and mortgages is often calculated on a monthly basis, and credit card loan interest is often calculated daily. When borrowing money, interest rates are usually higher and calculated more frequently than when we deposit money, with the difference providing revenues for the financial institutions. Because the various institutions calculate interest at different points in time, it is difficult to make comparisons. In 1977 the UK government introduced the **Annual Percentage Rate** (APR) and more recently the **Annual Equivalent Rate** (AER) to make it possible to compare the costs of borrowing and saving at different institutions. APR includes any fees charged by the institution for borrowing or saving, whereas AER is simply the equivalent annual rate of interest being applied.

In this section we shall look at how the AER is calculated.

The prerequisites of this section are:
- Basic arithmetic (Section 1.4);
- Powers, roots and logarithms (Section 1.5);
- Operator precedence (Section 1.6);
- Fractions, ratios and percentages (Section 1.7);
- Simple interest and compound growth (Section 12.1).

Monthly compounding

To see how we can extend the formula for basic compound growth (equation (12.1.2)) to deal with multiple compounding, consider the case of calculating interest at the end of each month. Interest stated on an annual basis is called the **Nominal Annual Interest Rate**. Monthly compounding is based on 1/12th of the Nominal Annual Interest Rate, and is called the **Nominal Monthly Interest Rate**.

12.2.1

Q If the Nominal Annual Interest Rate is 6%, what is the equivalent Nominal Monthly Interest Rate?

A The Nominal Annual Rate = 0.06, so the Nominal Monthly Rate = 0.06/12 = 0.005 (i.e. $\frac{1}{2}$% per month).

The monthly compounding formula

We can derive a formula for the future value resulting from monthly compounding as we did for basic compound growth. With monthly compounding, we must remember to use the appropriate Nominal Monthly Interest Rate, denoted by $i/12$, where i is the Nominal Annual Interest Rate in decimal form. Figure 12.2.1 shows the value of money over the first 12 months using the basic compound growth formula (i.e. equation 12.1.2).

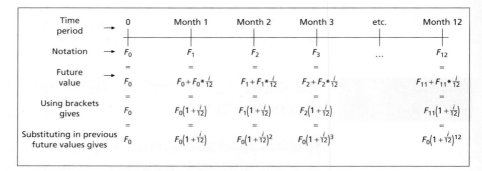

Figure 12.2.1 **Monthly compounding for 1 year.**

Extending the timescale over any number of years, say Y, we can calculate future values at the end of each year (Figure 12.2.3):

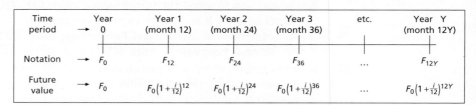

Figure 12.2.2 **Monthly compounding over Y years.**

The last column of Figure 12.2.2 gives a formula for the future value resulting from monthly compounding a nominal annual interest rate i for Y years:

$$F_Y = F_0 \left(1 + \frac{i}{12}\right)^{12Y}$$

(12.2.1)

Multiple compounding

We can extend equation (12.2.1) to calculate the future value resulting from any compounding frequency (weekly, daily, etc.). In general, if we have c compoundings per year of a nominal annual rate of interest i, the future value after Y years will be:

$$F_Y = F_0 \left(1 + \frac{i}{c}\right)^{cY} \qquad (12.2.2)$$

Example **12.2.2**

Q A firm takes out a 3-year business loan of £5,000 on which a Nominal Annual Rate of interest of 12% p.a. is charged at the end of each quarter, but with an agreement that it makes no repayments until the end of the 3 years. What is the Nominal Quarterly Rate of interest, and how much will the firm pay back at the end of the agreement?

A To calculate the Nominal Quarterly Rate of interest, we divide the Nominal Annual Rate of interest by the number of compoundings per year (i.e. $c = 4$) to get $12/4 = 3\%$ per quarter. To calculate total debt after 3 years, we put $Y = 3$, $c = 4$, $i = 0.12$ and $F_0 = 5{,}000$ into equation (12.2.2):

$$
\begin{aligned}
F_3 &= 5{,}000\left(1 + \frac{0.12}{4}\right)^{4*3} \\
&= 5{,}000(1 + 0.03)^{12} \\
&= 5{,}000 * 1.03^{12} \\
&= 5{,}000 * 1.4258 \\
&= 7{,}129
\end{aligned}
$$

 12.3

Therefore the firm will have to pay back £7,129.

The Annual Equivalent Rate

The **annual equivalent rate** is the annual rate of growth if we compound only once at the end of each year. It depends on the number of compounding periods per year, and is the same as the Nominal Annual Rate of interest if only one compounding is undertaken at the end of each year (Example 12.2.3).

Example **12.2.3**

Q What is the equivalent rate of growth if a Nominal Annual Rate of growth of 24% is compounded (a) annually, (b) monthly, (c) weekly and (d) daily?

A Here we have $i = 0.24$, and as we are dealing with multiple compounding for (a) $c = 1$, (b) $c = 12$, (c) $c = 52$ and (d) $c = 365$, we use equation (12.2.2). We need to consider only one year ($Y = 1$), and for ease of calculations we consider $F_0 = 1$.

(a) With annual compounding $c = 1$, equation (12.2.2) gives:

$$F_1 = 1 * (1 + 0.24)^1 = 1.24$$

The equivalent annual rate of growth is 0.24 because $1.24 = (1 + 0.24)$, and this is the same as the nominal annual growth rate (i.e. 24% p.a.).

(b) With monthly compounding $c = 12$, equation (12.2.2) gives:

$$F_1 = 1 * \left(1 + \frac{0.24}{12}\right)^{12*1} = 1.268$$

Although the nominal annual rate of 24% is equivalent to a nominal monthly rate of 2% (i.e. $24/12 = 2$), the future value is greater because of the number of compoundings. For the equivalent annual growth rate, we need to find the equivalent annual rate of interest if only one compounding was undertaken at the end of the year, i.e. what value of x gives:

$$F_1 = 1 * (1 + x)^1 = 1.268$$

Clearly, $x = 0.268$ and the effective annual growth rate is 26.8% p.a.

(c) With weekly compounding $c = 52$, so equation (12.2.2) gives:

$$F_1 = 1 * \left(1 + \frac{0.24}{52}\right)^{52*1} = 1.2706$$

Although the nominal annual rate of 24% is equivalent to a nominal weekly rate of 0.46% (i.e. $24/52 = 0.46$), again its future value is higher because of the higher number of compoundings. For the equivalent annual growth rate we need to find the annual rate of interest compounded once at the end of the year that yields £1.2706, i.e. what value of x gives:

$$F_1 = 1 * (1 + x)^1 = 1.2706$$

Clearly, $x = 0.2706$ and the equivalent annual growth rate is 27.06%.

(d) With $c = 365$, equation (12.2.2) gives:

$$F_1 = 1 * \left(1 + \frac{0.24}{365}\right)^{365*1} = 1.2712$$

The nominal annual rate of 24% is equivalent to a nominal daily rate of 0.066%, and the equivalent annual growth rate is 27.12%.

All UK financial institutions must state the AER so that interest rates can be compared on a like-for-like basis. From Example 12.2.3 we can derive a formula for calculating the AER. Instead of calling the unknown equivalent annual rate of interest x, we call this the AER. In equation (12.2.2) we put $Y = 1$ and $F_0 = 1$ to get:

$$1 * (1 + \text{AER})^1 = 1 * \left(1 + \frac{i}{c}\right)^{c*1}$$

i.e. $(1 + \text{AER}) = \left(1 + \frac{i}{c}\right)^c$

Rearranging, we get:

12.4

$$\text{AER} = \left(1 + \frac{i}{c}\right)^c - 1 \qquad (12.2.3)$$

Example 12.2.4 illustrates the use of equation (12.2.3).

Example 12.2.4

Q Use equation (12.2.3) to find the AER for the cases in Example 12.2.3:

A (a) $i = 0.24$, $c = 1$ gives AER = $\left(1 + \dfrac{0.24}{1}\right)^{1} - 1 = 0.24$

 (b) $i = 0.24$, $c = 12$ gives AER = $\left(1 + \dfrac{0.24}{12}\right)^{12} - 1 = 0.268$

 (c) $i = 0.24$, $c = 52$ gives AER = $\left(1 + \dfrac{0.24}{52}\right)^{52} - 1 = 0.2706$

 (d) $i = 0.24$, $c = 365$ gives AER = $\left(1 + \dfrac{0.24}{365}\right)^{356} - 1 = 0.2712$

The Annual Percentage Rate (APR)

The **Annual Percentage Rate (APR)** is the equivalent annual rate of interest irrespective of the number of compounding periods per year, and it also includes all costs charged by the financial institution. To calculate the APR we add all fees and charges to the principal at the appropriate point of time. For example, a set-up fee will be added to the initial amount borrowed, and will be subject to interest charges, but a completion fee will be added at the end and will not be subject to interest. When there are no fees or charges then the APR and AER are the same.

Continuous compounding

With long investment periods and many compounding periods per year (i.e. when c is very large), institutions use another formula called the **continuous compounding** formula. For a present value of F_0 and a nominal annual rate of interest i, then the future value after Y years is given by:

12.5

20

$$F_Y = F_0 e^{iY} \qquad\qquad (12.2.4)$$

where e = 2.718 is the exponential constant (see Section 1.5). This equation is used only for large values of c and Y and gives only approximate results because interest is being calculated and added continuously. Example 12.2.5 illustrates the difference between applying continuous and the previous discrete multiple compounding formulae. The derivation of this formula can be found on the CD and on the associated website **www.mcgraw-hill.co.uk/textbooks/dewhurst**.

Example 12.2.5

Q What is the difference between daily and continuous compounding of £10 at a nominal annual rate of growth of 12% for 5 years?

A First, apply the discrete multiple compounding formula (i.e. equation 12.2.2):

$$F_5 = 10\left(1 + \frac{0.12}{365}\right)^{5*365} = 18.2194$$

Next, apply the continuous compounding formula (i.e. equation 12.2.4):

$$F_5 = 10e^{0.12*5} = 18.2212$$

The small difference is due to the fact that daily compounding is not continuous.

12.2

1 If interest is added to an account at the end of each quarter at 10% p.a., what is the future value of £20 after 2 years?

2 If interest is added every half year rather than once per year, verify that the future value F_t of a present amount F_0, compounded at I% p.a. over Y years, is given by:

$$F_Y = F_0 \left(1 + \frac{I\%}{200}\right)^{2Y}$$

3 Calculate the future value of £100 invested at a nominal rate of 18% p.a. compounded quarterly, and calculate the AER. What is the AER if compounding is (a) monthly, (b) weekly and (c) daily?

4 What is the future value of £5 if continuously compounded at 5% p.a. for 10 years?

5 Compare the future value of continuously compounding £100 at 6% p.a. for 4 years with discrete compounding on a (a) monthly, (b) weekly, (c) daily, (d) hourly and (e) minute basis.

6 Calculate the future value of £1 for 1 year using discrete compounding at the rate of 100% every second, and show that this gives the same result as continuous compounding. What is this number called?

12.3 Discounting and other related applications of compound growth

In Section 12.1 we derived the basic compound growth formula to calculate the future value of an investment left to grow over a number of periods of time. Sometimes we invest money for a particular purpose (e.g. to buy something in the future). To make sure we get a particular future value, we need to know how much to invest now and for how long. Likewise, in business and management we may need to forecast future costs, revenues or profits and enter their current value in this year's accounts or, conversely, calculate the present value of a future value given a constant rate of interest. When comparing different investment opportunities, we may want to do so in terms of their growth rates. In this section we consider how we can use the concept of compound growth to address such issues.

The prerequisites of this section are:
■ Basic arithmetic (Section 1.4);
■ Powers, roots and logarithms (Section 1.5);
■ Operator precedence (Section 1.6);
■ Fractions, ratios and percentages (Section 1.7);
■ Simple interest and compound growth (Section 12.1).

Discounting

When compiling end-of-year accounts, many companies include the present or current value of their investments or assets. Often the monetary equivalent of these investments or assets cannot be realised (i.e. cashed in), but they need to be included in the accounts. In such cases we use **discounting** to represent future values of present values. This occurs when we want to make a one-off investment for a particular future purpose and need to know how much to invest now (i.e. the present value) to realise a particular future value. For present values it is easy to rearrange the basic compound growth formula (equation 12.1.2) used in Section 12.1:

$$F_t = F_0(1 + r)^t \qquad (12.1.2)$$

Dividing both sides of equation (12.1.2) by $(1 + r)^t$, we get:

$$\frac{F_t}{(1 + r)^t} = F_0$$

that is:

$$F_0 = \frac{F_t}{(1 + r)^t} \qquad (12.3.1)$$

Equation (12.3.1) calculates the present value F_0 given a known future value F_t received after t periods, and is referred to as the **discounting formula**. r is called the **discounting rate** (see Example 12.3.1).

Example | **12.3.1**

Q A grandparent wants to invest a lump sum on the birth of a grandchild that will give the child £5,000 for its education at the age of 18. If an investment trust offers a guaranteed rate of growth of 4% p.a., how much should be invested now?

A We know the future value ($F_{18} = 5,000$), the rate of growth ($r = 0.04$ p.a.) and the investment horizon ($t = 18$ years), but not the present value (F_0). Applying equation (12.3.1) gives:

$$F_0 = \frac{5,000}{(1 + 0.04)^{18}} = £2,468.14$$

So £2,468.14 should be invested now to provide £5,000 in 18 years' time.

Calculating the growth/discounting horizon and growth/discounting rates

Just as we can rearrange equation (12.1.2) to determine F_0 if we know F_t, r and t, we can similarly rearrange it algebraically to calculate t if we know F_t, r and F_0, and r if we know F_t, t and F_0. This gives us the following formulae for calculating the investment or discounting horizons and growth/discounting rates:

$$\text{Investment/discounting horizon } t = \frac{\log\left(\dfrac{F_t}{F_0}\right)}{\log(1 + r)} \qquad (12.3.2)$$

$$\text{Growth/discounting rate } r = \left(\frac{F_t}{F_0}\right)^{\frac{1}{t}} - 1 \qquad (12.3.3)$$

Derivations of these formulae can be found on the CD and on the associated website **www.mcgraw-hill.co.uk/textbooks/dewhurst**. Some spreadsheets have inbuilt functions that can be used to calculate them (Example 12.3.2).

12.3.2

Q A company's sales have doubled in 5 years. What is the annual growth rate of sales? If sales continue to grow at the same rate, how long will it take for sales to treble?

A To find the annual growth rate r (we already know $t = 5$), we assume that sales 5 years ago were £1 (i.e. $F_0 = 1$). So they must now be £2 (i.e. $F_5 = 2$). We can now apply equation (12.3.3):

$$r = \left(\frac{2}{1}\right)^{1/5} - 1 = 2^{0.2} - 1 = 1.1487 - 1 = 0.1487$$

So the annual growth rate of sales is 14.87%. To find out how long it will take for sales to treble from their current value (i.e. $F_5 = 2$), we need to calculate t for $F_t = 6$. We can now apply equation (12.3.2):

$$t = \frac{\log\left(\frac{6}{2}\right)}{\log(1 + 0.147)} = \frac{\log(3)}{\log(1.1487)} = \frac{0.4771}{0.0602} = 7.925$$

So sales will take almost a further 8 years to treble.

Reducing-balance depreciation

End-of-year accounts include the current book value of a business's assets (e.g. equipment). These may have been purchased several years ago, and owing to wear and tear (i.e. depreciation) would not realise their original purchase price if sold. Accountants use several mechanisms to calculate the reduction in the book value of assets (e.g. straight-line depreciation). One popular method, **reducing-balance depreciation**, operates like compound growth, except that present values (i.e. original price or value) are reduced (i.e. marked down) rather than increased (i.e. marked up) by a particular percentage each period to give the future (i.e. current book) value of an asset.

By replacing the '+' sign with a '−' sign in the compound growth formula, we reduce rather than increase value over time:

12.8

$$\text{Current book value} = F_t = F_0(1 - r)^t \tag{12.3.4}$$

where F_0 is the original purchase price or value, r is now called the **rate of depreciation**, and t is the number of periods over which the asset is depreciated.

12.3.3

Q A computer purchased 3 years ago for £1,500 is subject to 30% depreciation each year for accounting and tax purposes. What is its current book value?

A Applying equation (12.3.4) gives the current book value = £1,500$(1 - 0.3)^3$ = £514.5.

12.3

1 Calculate the following:
(a) The sum to be set aside now that would yield £15,000 in 5 years if the interest rate remains constant at 8% p.a.
(b) The present value of an investment expected to yield £500 in 2 years' time, assuming a discounting rate of 12% p.a.

(c) In 2000 a company's sales were £150,000, and growth is expected to be 15% p.a. When will sales be doubled?

(d) Over 7 years a company's sales have increased by one third. What was the compound rate of growth?

(e) If sales of the company in (d) continue to grow at the same rate, how many years will it take for sales to double?

(f) How long will it take for a country to increase its GNP by 50% if the GNP is growing at 2.5% p.a.?

2 How much should be invested now to get £10,000 in 15 years if interest is added monthly at a rate of 1.5% per month?

3 Find to 2 d.p., for each pair of values below, the annual compound rate of growth operating for $N = 1, 2, 3$ and 4 years:

Present value	Future value
20	25
100	150
1,500	2,000

For each pair of present and future values plot graphs of interest rate against number of years, so you have three graphs on the same set of axes. What can you deduce from these graphs? What happens to these graphs for large N and r?

4 A company buys equipment for £10,000, which is expected to last five years. If it depreciates on a reducing balance basis at 20% p.a., what is its eventual value? What annual rate of depreciation would reduce its value by 50% after 3 years?

12.4   Savings, endowments and sinking funds

Having considered problems involving a single amount of money, let us now turn to problems involving investing a stream of money to 'save up' for a future purchase. In this section we extend the basic concept of compound growth to situations in which we save regular amounts over a period of time.

The prerequisites of this section are:
- Basic arithmetic (Section 1.4);
- Powers, roots and logarithms (Section 1.5);
- Operator precedence (Section 1.6);
- Fractions, ratios and percentages (Section 1.7);
- Simple interest and compound growth (Section 12.1).

Saving schemes

With personal investment schemes we often talk about regular savings or **endowment schemes** (e.g. to purchase a house or car). When a business makes regular savings (e.g. to expand or purchase equipment) we talk about **sinking funds**. Essentially, they are the same thing and involve saving a regular, equal amount of money over a period of time, with each individual amount and the running total attracting compound interest. With endowment schemes, the future value is called the **maturity value**.

To show the changes in the value of money over time we use a timescale as we did when deriving the formulae for compound growth, as shown in Example 12.4.1.

Example 12.4.1

Q A company plans to replace its production line in 5 years' time and sets aside £5,000 from its end-of-year profits to create a sinking fund towards the purchase of the new equipment. It can get a guaranteed 8% p.a. from its bank. How much will the company have available in 5 years' time to put towards the new production line?

A Payments into the sinking fund attract interest, except for the final payment. To calculate the future value of each payment plus interest we apply the basic compound growth formula (i.e. equation 12.1.2). To find the total amount saved with interest we sum the future values. Figure 12.4.1 shows the calculations, and the arrows indicate how each payment grows by applying equation (12.1.2).

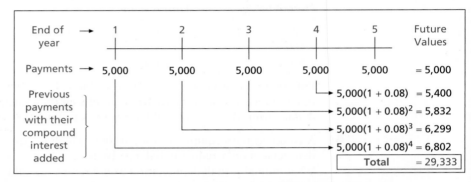

Figure 12.4.1 **The future values for payments made in Example 12.4.1.**

So the company will have £29,333 to put towards its new production line.

The future value of saving schemes

The approach used in Example 12.4.1 can be applied to any savings scheme in which payments into the scheme are made at the end of each period. Let A denote equal-size payments at the end of each period, FV the future value, t the number of periods and r the compound growth rate per period. Using these variables, we can generalise Figure 12.4.1 as shown in Figure 12.4.2:

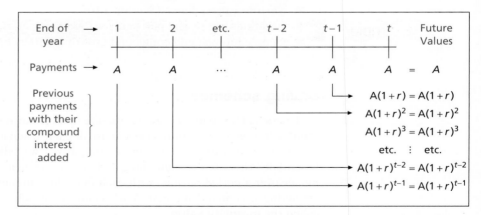

Figure 12.4.2 **The future values for payments made at the end of each period into a saving scheme.**

We can calculate the future value of the savings scheme by summing the future values of all payments with their interest:

$$FV = A + A(1+r)^1 + A(1+r)^2 + \cdots + A(1+r)^{t-2} + A(1+r)^{t-1} \qquad (12.4.1)$$

 12.9

Some spreadsheets have an inbuilt function for calculating equation (12.4.1).

Calculating the future value of a savings scheme as a geometric series

Instead of a spreadsheet, we can use a shortcut formula to calculate future value of a savings scheme. This takes advantage of the fact that equation (12.4.1) is a well-known mathematical series called a **geometric series**, which in general takes the form:

$$\text{Geometric series} = F + FC + FC^2 + FC^3 + \cdots + FC^{n-1} \qquad (12.4.2)$$

where F is the first term of the series and C is called the common ratio. Note how C increases in power by 1 as we move up the terms of the series. The second, third and all higher terms in the series are made up of the product of the first term and C raised to a power. This is the pattern that defines a geometric series. Such series have been well studied, and a formula derived for the sum of the first n terms of the series S_n is:

$$S_n = F * \frac{(1 - C^n)}{(1 - C)} \qquad (12.4.3)$$

The derivation of equation (12.4.3) can be found on the CD and on the associated website **www.mcgraw-hill.co.uk/textbooks/dewhurst**, and its use is illustrated in Example 12.4.2.

By comparing equations (12.4.1) and (12.4.2) we can see that the series for the future value of a savings scheme has a first term A and common ratio $(1 + r)$, so we can write equation (12.4.1) as:

 12.9

$$FV = A \frac{1 - (1+r)^t}{1 - (1+r)} = A \frac{(1+r)^t - 1}{r} \qquad (12.4.4)$$

Example	**12.4.2**

Q Use equations (12.4.1), (12.4.3) and (12.4.4) to calculate the future value of the sinking fund in Example 12.4.1.

A We put $A = 5,000$, $r = 0.08$ and $t = 5$ into equation (12.4.1) to get:

$$FV = 5,000 + 5,000(1 + 0.08)^1 + 5,000(1 + 0.08)^2 + 5,000(1 + 0.08)^3$$
$$\qquad + 5,000(1 + 0.08)^4$$
$$= 5,000 + 5,000(1.08)^1 + 5,000(1.08)^2 + 5,000(1.08)^3 + 5,000(1.08)^4$$
$$= 29,333 \text{ as we saw in Figure 12.4.1}$$

As this is a geometric series with $F = 5,000$ and $C = 1.08$, we can use equation (12.4.3):

$$S_5 = 5,000 * \frac{(1 - 1.08^5)}{(1 - 1.08)}$$

$$= 5,000 * \frac{(1 - 1.469328)}{(1 - 1.08)}$$

$$= 5,000 * \frac{(0.469328)}{(0.08)}$$

$$= 29,333.$$

Using equation (12.4.4) we get: $FV = 5,000 * \dfrac{[(1 + 0.08)^5 - 1]}{0.08} = 29,333$

Saving schemes with payments at the start of a period

With endowment and sinking funds or similar savings schemes, payments are sometimes made at the start, rather than the end, of a period, with interest still added at the end of the period. Clearly, this affects the calculations because, unlike in Example 12.4.1, the last payment will attract interest: it will have been in the savings scheme for a year, as shown by Example 12.4.3.

Example | **12.4.3**

Q A sum of £5,000 is invested at the start of each year in an endowment policy offering a guaranteed 8% p.a. growth over 5 years. What is the maturity value of the endowment policy?

A As interest on the balance in the savings scheme is calculated at the end of each year, our timescale needs to reflect this. To allow for payments being made at the start of each year, we introduce a Year 0, and the end of Year 0 is the start of Year 1, as shown in Figure 12.4.3:

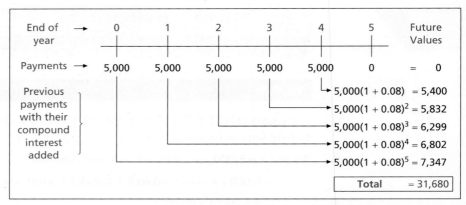

Figure 12.4.3 **The future values for payments made in Example 12.4.3.**

Figure 12.4.3 shows the maturity value will be £31,680.

The future value of savings with payments at the start of a period

After Example 12.4.1 we generalised the calculation of the future value of any savings scheme in which equal end of year payments A are made over t periods for a rate of growth r per period, and we can do likewise for payments made at the start of a period, as shown in Figure 12.4.4:

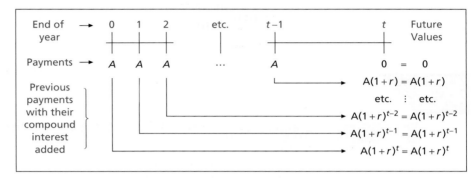

Figure 12.4.4 **The future values for payments made at the start of a period into a savings scheme.**

In general, the future value of such a savings scheme is:

$$FV = A(1+r)^1 + A(1+r)^2 + \cdots + A(1+r)^{t-1} + A(1+r)^t \qquad (12.4.5)$$

Once again we can use the inbuilt function of a spreadsheet to calculate equation (12.4.5), or, because it is also a geometric series, we can also use equation (12.4.3). This time the first term of the geometric series is $F = A(1+r)$ and the common ratio is $C = (1+r)$, so we get:

$$FV = A(1+r)\frac{1-(1+r)^t}{1-(1+r)} = A(1+r)\frac{(1+r)^t - 1}{r} \qquad (12.4.6)$$

Example 12.4.4

Q Use equations (12.4.5), (12.4.3) and (12.4.6) to calculate the future value of the endowment scheme in Example 12.4.3.

A Put $A = 5{,}000$, $r = 0.08$ and $t = 5$ into equation (12.4.5):

$$FV = 5{,}000(1 + 0.08)^1 + 5{,}000(1 + 0.08)^2 + 5{,}000(1 + 0.08)^3$$
$$+ 5{,}000(1 + 0.08)^4 + 5{,}000(1 + 0.08)^5$$
$$= 5{,}000(1.08)^1 + 5{,}000(1.08)^2 + 5{,}000(1.08)^3 + 5{,}000(1.08)^4$$
$$+ 5{,}000(1.08)^5$$
$$= 31{,}680 \text{ as we saw in Figure 12.4.3}$$

As this is a geometric series, we again use equation (12.4.3) with $F = 5,000(1.08)$ and $C = 1.08$:

$$S_5 = 5,000(1.08) * \frac{(1 - 1.08^5)}{(1 - 1.08)}$$

$$= 5,400 * \frac{(1 - 1.469328)}{(1 - 1.08)}$$

$$= 5,400 * \frac{(0.469328)}{(0.08)}$$

$$= 31,680$$

Using equation (12.4.6) gives $FV = 5,000(1.08) * \dfrac{(1 + 0.08)^5 - 1}{0.08} = 31,680$

 12.9

Exercises **12.4**

1 A company sets aside £3,000 each year out of its end-of-year profits as a reserve fund, invested at 10% p.a. What is its value after 10 years?

2 Sixty regular monthly instalments of £100 are invested in a 5-year endowment policy at the end of each month. With a compound rate of growth of 8% p.a. and interest added at the end of each month, what will be the policy's eventual maturity value?

3 To save for their daughter's university education, her parents invest a sum of £50 a month in a scheme paying 0.4% p.a. compounded monthly. If the child is 3 when savings begin, what is the eventual value when she is 18?

4 A homeowner takes out an endowment policy to pay off a mortgage loan of £150,000 in 20 years' time. Growth rates on endowment schemes are currently at 4% p.a.:
(a) What are the annual instalments paid at the end of each year?
(b) What are the annual instalments if payments are made at the start of each year?
(c) What are the instalments if payments are made at the end of each month and the interest is compounded monthly?

12.5 ## Loans, mortgages and annuities

In the previous sections we looked at how investment schemes operate. Let us now look at how institutions apply compound growth to calculate loans and mortgages. The same concept can also be used to calculate a certain type of pension scheme known as an annuity.

When arranging loans, mortgages and annuities, the borrower or annuity buyer sometimes pays an arrangement or administrative fee to the financial institution, the amount of which varies from institution to institution (some institutions do not charge them). So it is not possible to find general formulae for any type of loan, mortgage or annuity. The basic principles of these financial products are explained in this section, but in practice additional costs or calculations might need to be considered.

The prerequisites of this section are:
■ Basic arithmetic (Section 1.4);
■ Powers, roots and logarithms (Section 1.5);

- ■ Operator precedence (Section 1.6);
- ■ Fractions, ratios and percentages (Section 1.7);
- ■ Simple interest and compound growth (Section 12.1);
- ■ Multiple compounding, AER and continuous compounding (Section 12.2);
- ■ Savings, endowments and sinking funds (Section 12.4).

Loans and mortgages

Mathematically, a mortgage is just a long-term loan, usually taken out to purchase a house or business. Although several types of mortgage are sold by financial institutions, essentially there are just three: **interest only**, **repayment** and **endowment**. All other types of mortgage are variants of these. For example, a pension mortgage is a type of endowment mortgage that provides a pension and pays off the mortgage with interest. The most common form is the repayment mortgage, and we shall see that these are related to the savings schemes in Section 12.4.

Interest-only loans and mortgages

An interest-only loan or mortgage is exactly that: the borrower pays interest monthly, and at the end of the agreement repays the amount borrowed (see Example 12.5.1).

Example	**12.5.1**

Q A speculative builder has bought a plot of land and takes out an interest-only loan of £10,000 over 3 years. His bank offers him a rate of 12% p.a. with interest paid monthly. The bank also charges an arrangement fee of 5%, which is paid on completion. What are the AER, the monthly payments to the bank and the total paid?

A Although the interest rate is annual (i.e. 12% p.a. nominal), it is actually being calculated and charged monthly (i.e. 1% per month nominal) with an AER of 12.68%. So annually the interest is $10,000 * 0.1268 = £1,268$ and monthly it is $1,268/12 = £105.67$. The total amount paid is therefore:

Interest over 3 years	$3 * 1,268$	$= £3,804$
The original loan	$10,000$	$= £10,000$
The arrangement fee	$0.05 * 10,000$	$= £500$
	Total	$= £14,304.$

Repayment loans and mortgages

Repayment mortgages are paid off by equal, regular payments. Compound interest is calculated by the lender and added to the loan at the end of each compounding period before any payment is deducted. At the end of each compounding period it is possible to calculate the outstanding debt owed by the borrower. At the end of the agreed loan period the entire loan and interest will have been paid off (Example 12.5.2).

12.5.2

Q A motorist, buying a car costing £5,000, is offered a 3-year repayment loan at 15% p.a. compounded annually, to be paid by equal end-of-year payments. What are the three payments?

A Let us call the equal end-of-year payments A. We can write down mathematical expressions for the outstanding debt at the end of each year, as shown in Figure 12.5.1:

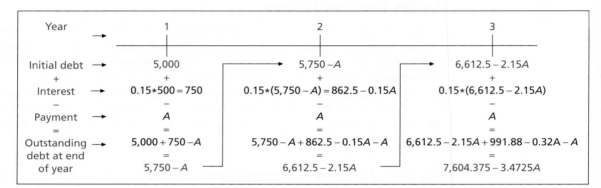

Figure 12.5.1 **The end-of-year outstanding debt for Example 12.5.1.**

To pay off all the outstanding debt, we must have:

$$7,604.375 - 3.4725A = 0$$

Therefore $A = 7,604.375/3.4725 = 2,189.885$

So the motorist pays £2,189.89 each year for 3 years.

Formulae for repayment loans and mortgages

The calculations in Example 12.5.1 were tedious, and get worse for longer-term loans (e.g. 20 or more years). We can derive a formula to calculate the regular instalments, given that we know the amount borrowed, the rate of interest and the period of time. To do so, let us denote the amount borrowed by L, the compound rate of interest charged on the outstanding debt at the end of each period by r, the number of periods by t, and the equal, regular payments made at the end of each period by A. To derive a formula we replace the numbers in Figure 12.5.1 with these general variables (Figure 12.5.2).

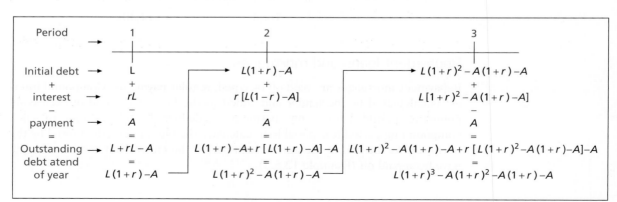

Figure 12.5.2 **The outstanding debt at the end of each period.**

If we look at the outstanding debt at the end of each period, we can see a pattern and infer the general result for any number of periods t:

Outstanding debt after t periods

$$L(1+r)^t - A(1+r)^{t-1} - \cdots - A(1+r)^3 - A(1+r)^2 - A(1+r)^1 - A$$

Now, as before, after t periods the outstanding debt is 0, so we have:

$$L(1+r)^t - A(1+r)^{t-1} - \cdots - A(1+r)^3 - A(1+r)^2 - A(1+r)^1 - A = 0$$

Therefore:

$$L(1+r)^t = A(1+r)^{t-1} + \cdots + A(1+r)^3 + A(1+r)^2 + A(1+r)^1 + A \qquad (12.5.1)$$

Let us rearrange equation (12.5.1) to calculate the annual payments A. First we take out the common factor of A on the right-hand side:

$$L(1+r)^t = A\{(1+r)^{t-1+} + \cdots + (1+r)^3 + (1+r)^2 + (1+r)^1 + 1\} \qquad (12.5.2)$$

Next, we divide both sides of equation (12.5.2) by $\{(1+r)^{t-1} + \cdots + (1+r)^2 + (1+r)^1 + 1\}$:

$$A = \frac{L(1+r)^t}{(1+r)^{t-1} + (1+r)^{t-2} + \cdots + (1+r)^3 + (1+r)^2 + (1+r) + 1} \qquad (12.5.3)$$

In equation (12.5.3) we see that the **denominator** is a geometric series based on compound growth similar to the one in Section 12.4 when we were calculating the future value of saving schemes. So we can use equation (12.4.3) with first term $F = 1$ and common ratio $C = (1 + r)$ to save work in calculating long-term loans and mortgages, as shown in Example 12.5.3. Spreadsheets have inbuilt functions to calculate these annual payments.

12.10

If we know how much we can afford to pay, we can also calculate how much we can borrow. That is, we can calculate L if we know A, r and t by dividing both sides of equation (12.5.2) by $(1 + r)^t$:

$$L = \frac{A\{(1+r)^{t-1} + (1+r)^{t-2} + \cdots + (1+r)^3 + (1+r)^2 + (1+r) + 1\}}{(1+r)^t} \qquad (12.5.4)$$

This time the **numerator** is a geometric series, so again we can use equation (12.4.3) to perform the calculation when we have large numbers of periods.

It is also possible to represent equations (12.5.3) and (12.5.4) in the form of a geometric series based on discounting. For example, if we undertake the division in equation (12.5.4) we get:

$$L = A\{(1+r)^{-1} + (1+r)^{-2} + \cdots + (1+r)^{3-t} + (1+r)^{2-t} + (1+r)^{1-t} + (1+r)^{-t}\} (12.5.5)$$

i.e.

$$L = A\left\{\frac{1}{(1+r)} + \frac{1}{(1+r)^2} + \cdots + \frac{1}{(1+r)^{t-3}} + \frac{1}{(1+r)^{t-2}} + \frac{1}{(1+r)^{t-1}} + \frac{1}{(1+r)^t}\right\} \qquad (12.5.6)$$

In equation (12.5.6) the first term and common ratio of the geometric series are $\frac{1}{(1+r)}$, and using equation (12.4.3) we get:

$$L = A\left[\frac{1}{(1+r)} * \frac{1 - \frac{1}{(1+r)^t}}{1 - \frac{1}{(1+r)}}\right] = \frac{A}{(1+r)}\frac{1 - \frac{1}{(1+r)^t}}{1 - \frac{1}{(1+r)}} \qquad (12.5.7)$$

We can easily rearrange equation (12.5.7) to give an equation for A in terms of L, r and t.

Although we considered savings schemes in which payments were made at the start of a period in Section 12.4, this rarely happens with loans and mortgages and so is not considered here. However, you should now be capable of deriving the appropriate formulae.

Example | 12.5.3

Q Use equations (12.5.3) and (12.4.3) to calculate the annual payments that the motorist makes in Example 12.5.2.

A The loan $L = 5,000$ has to be repaid over $t = 3$ years with interest of $r = 0.15$ per period. Applying equation (12.5.3) gives:

$$A = \frac{5,000(1 + 0.15)^3}{(1 + 0.15)^2 + (1 + 0.15) + 1}$$

$$= \frac{5,000(1.15)^3}{(1.15)^2 + (1.15) + 1}$$

$$= \frac{5,000 * 1.521}{1.3225 + 1.15 + 1}$$

$$= \frac{7,605}{3.4725}$$

$$= £2,189.89$$

Once again, we can save work by using equation (12.4.3) with first term $F = 1$ and common ratio $C = 1.15$ to calculate the denominator:

$$S_3 = 1 * \frac{(1 - 1.15^3)}{(1 - 1.15)} = 3.4725.$$

12.10

Rip-off charges

Some financial institutions try to rip you off by including additional charges (e.g. arrangement fees) or by calculating loan payments in such a way that they benefit from your ignorance. For example, they may calculate monthly repayments on a loan by dividing the annual payment by 12 rather than using the monthly periods in equation (12.5.3) (see Example 12.5.4). Some institutions add charges or fees to the amount you borrow so you start with a higher debt than you originally intended.

Example | **12.5.4**

Q Calculate the monthly repayments on a loan of £10,000 over 5 years when a Nominal Annual Rate of interest of 10% p.a. is charged on the outstanding debt.

A Let us assume that all calculations are made at the end of each year, and use equation (12.5.3) with $L = 10,000$, $t = 5$, and $r = 0.1$. This gives an annual payment of:

$$A = \frac{10,000(1+0.1)^5}{(1+0.1)^4 + (1+0.1)^3 + (1+0.1)^2 + (1+0.1) + 1} = 2,637.98$$

This is equivalent to paying $2,637.98/12 = 219.83$ monthly. However, instead of paying these monthly amounts into the account, the lender will invest them to gain interest, then pay just £2,637.98 into the account at the end of the year, keeping for itself the interest made on each monthly payment.

Now, let us assume that all calculations are made at the end of each month and this time use equation (12.5.3) with $L = 10,000$, $t = 60$ and $r = 0.1/12 = 0.008333$. This gives a monthly repayment of:

$$A = \frac{10,000(1+0.1/12)^{60}}{(1+0.1/12)^{59} + (1+0.1/12)^{58} + \cdots + (1+0.1/12)^2 + (1+0.1/12) + 1}$$

In this case, it is better to use equation (12.4.3) to calculate the denominator:

$$S_{60} = 1 * \frac{(1 - 1.008333^{60})}{(1 - 1.008333)} = 77.4$$

$$\text{Therefore } A = \frac{10,000 * (1 + 0.008333)^{60}}{77.4} = 212.56$$

So not only are the payments less by over £7 per month but also the lender is not making additional profits from investing the monthly payments.

Endowment loans and mortgages

Endowment loans and mortgages operate differently from interest-only and repayment loans. Although once quite popular, they have since become less so as they depend on both growth rates and interest rates. They are based on the borrower paying interest on the loan (as with an interest-only loan) and also taking out an endowment or other savings scheme to pay off the loan at the end of the period. In some cases this savings scheme may provide other benefits, for example an additional amount in excess of the original loan to be used for a specific purpose (e.g. to purchase a pension, in which case it is referred to as a pension mortgage). In these types of loans and mortgages the borrower will pay instalments made up of interest on the loan and the payments into the savings scheme. Example 12.5.5 contrasts endowment and repayment mortgages.

Example | **12.5.5**

Q A couple approach their building society for a mortgage of £100,000 to put towards the purchase of their new home. The building society offers them two choices: (a) a repayment mortgage with an interest rate of 12% p.a. compounded annually; and (b) an endowment mortgage with an interest rate of 12% p.a. compounded annually on the loan and an endowment scheme with a guaranteed maturity value of at least £100,000 at a growth rate of 10% p.a. In both cases, annual compounding takes place over 20 years. Which option has the lowest cost to the couple?

A Let us calculate the monthly instalments on both types of mortgage.

(a) For a repayment mortgage, we use equation (12.5.3):

$$A = \frac{100,000(1 + 0.12)^{20}}{(1 + 0.12)^{19} + (1 + 0.12)^{18} + \cdots + (1 + 0.12)^2 + (1 + 0.12) + 1}$$

Once again, we use equation (12.4.3) to ease the calculations:

$$S_{20} = 1 * \frac{(1 - 1.12^{20})}{(1 - 1.12)} = 72.05 \text{ therefore } A = \frac{100,000 * (1.12)^{20}}{72.05} = \£13,388.$$

(b) To calculate the total cost of the endowment mortgage, we calculate the interest and then the endowment scheme instalments. The interest paid per year is simply $100,000 * 0.12 = \£12,000$. In Section 12.4, we calculated the future value of an endowment scheme using equation (12.4.1). Here, we want the future value to pay off the loan after $t = 20$. As the growth rate is $r = 0.1$, we need the value of A that satisfies:

$$100,000 = A + A(1.1)^1 + A(1.1)^2 + \cdots + A(1.1)^{19} \qquad (12.5.8)$$

Taking the common factor A in equation (12.5.8) outside a bracket:

$$100,000 = A\{1 + (1.1)^1 + (1.1)^2 + \cdots + (1.1)^{19}\} \qquad (12.5.9)$$

We can now divide both sides of equation (12.5.9) by $\{1 + (1.1)^1 + (1.1)^2 + \cdots + (1.1)^{19}\}$ to get:

$$A = \frac{100,000}{(1 + 0.1)^{19} + \cdots + (1 + 0.1)^2 + (1 + 0.1) + 1}$$

Once again, we can use equation (12.4.3):

$$S_{20} = 1 * \frac{(1 - 1.1^{20})}{(1 - 1.1)} = 57.275 \text{ therefore } A = \frac{100,000}{57.275} = \£1,745.96$$

So the annual cost of the endowment mortgage is:

$$12,000 + 1,745.96 = \£13,745.96$$

The repayment mortgage has lower annual costs than the endowment mortgage.

Annuities

Annuities give a guaranteed income for a specified period of time (e.g. for life when purchased to provide a pension). Mathematically, an annuity is the same as a repayment mortgage in which the annuity's purchase price equals the amount borrowed and income equals the payments made to pay off the loan (Example 12.5.4). Spreadsheets have inbuilt functions to calculate the purchase price of an annuity.

12.10

Example | **12.5.6**

Q What is the purchase price of an annuity that guarantees an annual end-of-year income of $\£2,000$ over 10 years if the annuity rate is 10% p.a.?

A We use the formula for a repayment loan (i.e. equation 12.5.4) but replace the loan value by the annuity purchase price and annual payments by income received. So we put $r = 0.1$, $t = 10$ years and $A = 2,000$ into equation (12.5.4):

12.10

$$L = \frac{2,000\{(1.1)^9 + (1.1)^8 + \cdots + (1.1)^3 + (1.1)^2 + (1.1) + 1\}}{(1.1)^{10}} = 12,289.13$$

The annuity would cost $\£12,289.13$.

1 A loan of £10,000 is taken out over 5 years with interest of 12% p.a. charged on the outstanding debt. Monthly repayments are based on 1/12th of the annual instalment. What monthly instalments are payable for:
(a) an interest-only loan;   (b) a repayment loan;
(c) an endowment loan with growth rate of 8% p.a. with end-of-year payments.

2 On a mortgage of £40,000 over 20 years, a building society offers a choice of two types of mortgage, both subject to an annual interest charge on outstanding debts of 15% at the end of each year. The first is a repayment mortgage in which both capital and interest are paid off by equal annual instalments. The second is an endowment mortgage, which has an expected maturity value equal to the loan and an expected annual growth rate of 1% p.a. below the mortgage interest rate. The endowment policy requires payments to be made at the start of each year. Which mortgage minimises annual instalments, and how does a change in interest rates affect the choice of mortgage?

3 Ms Z is 40 and is planning for her retirement. When she retires she wants a fixed monthly income for 25 years. Assume she will retire at 60 and can afford to invest £100 per month in a plan offering 6% p.a. compounded monthly. What will monthly income on retirement be, if annuity rates are expected to be 4% p.a. in 20 years' time?

4 Calculate the following:
(a) the annual instalments on a 10-year repayment loan of £5,000 with interest of 6% p.a. charged on the outstanding debt at the end of each year;
(b) the repayment loan that can be paid off by 20 equal end-of-year instalments of £2,000 with interest of 5% p.a. charged on the outstanding debt at the end of each year;
(c) the regular annual income from a 10-year annuity costing £5,000 with an annuity rate of 6% p.a.;
(d) the purchase price of a 20-year annuity that offers end-of-year income of £2,000 with an annuity rate of 5% p.a.

5 A homebuyer has just paid the 3rd annual instalment on a 20-year repayment mortgage of £20,000 on which interest is charged at 12% p.a. at the year-end. The building society then reduces the interest rate to 11% and offers the homebuyer a choice of reducing his annual instalments over the remaining years, or reducing the payback period while paying the same annual instalments. What figures did the building society provide, and which option pays the lowest gross sum to the building society?

12.6 Chapter review

This chapter looked at how mathematics can model situations in finance and accounting, and how financial institutions use the concept of compound growth in savings and lending agreements. Financial institutions vary in how they undertake compound growth calculations, and we looked at the most frequently used approaches. Because of these variations, we stressed the importance of understanding the underlying concepts so that the basic formulae can be adapted as required. Most spreadsheets have inbuilt functions to perform the basic compound growth calculations, but again it is important to understand the concept and choose the appropriate function.

The concept of compound growth can also assist managers in decision-making, for example by providing information about different investment alternatives. We look at these applications in Part C of this book.

Closing comments

We have now completed the second part of this book, which considered how Quantitative Methods can be of use in providing information to support managers in their decision-making processes. In the next part of this book we go one step further and consider how we can also employ Quantitative Methods to model and analyse the decision-making problems faced by managers.

There are three mini-case studies at the end of this part of the book to reinforce the basic concepts in a business and management context. Although these mini-case studies can be undertaken manually or by using a calculator, they would in practice be undertaken using a spreadsheet. These mini-cases are based on the chapters as shown below.

Case	Required reading
Case B1: NHTBeds	Chapters 5, 6, 7
Case B2: Techno Ltd	Chapters 7, 8, 10, 11
Case B3: Mr and Mrs Lean	Chapter 12

Where we have few or no quantitative data, we can instead use 'qualitative' or 'judgemental' approaches for modelling, and the interested reader is referred to the further reading at the end of the book.

Case B1

NHT Beds

The amount of time for which a patient occupies a hospital bed is called the length of stay (LOS), and is widely used for allocating hospital resources. The Northern Hospital Trust (NHT) believe that new initiatives introduced last year should have reduced their previous LOS figures, which were 5 days on average.

NHT have surveyed the LOS of 200 patients over the last 2 months and have observed the following:

5	10	1	4	5	3	5	6	3	2
2	2	4	4	2	6	6	1	2	4
4	3	2	9	3	6	9	5	3	2
2	3	5	9	6	3	9	3	2	4
10	4	1	1	9	3	9	5	1	6
4	2	3	9	6	3	22	6	4	2
3	5	3	11	2	1	17	4	4	4
2	4	6	21	3	6	9	3	2	4
5	3	3	2	11	1	2	4	4	17
6	4	3	7	3	14	6	4	4	3
14	6	4	3	7	6	4	4	3	3
8	4	2	1	1	3	4	5	2	2
2	2	2	8	4	1	1	3	4	5
3	10	3	9	1	3	1	2	1	5
3	16	2	5	1	1	2	1	8	3
8	3	3	17	2	5	1	1	1	2
5	1	2	1	3	1	9	3	10	3
4	1	10	1	3	9	9	5	6	1
4	2	1	6	6	2	4	4	2	2
2	3	6	5	3	5	4	1	10	5

Does the evidence support their belief?

Case B2

Techno Ltd

Techno Ltd is a small electronics company, which launched a new DVD recorder with digital receiver and integral hard disk to replace consumer VHS recorders. Each month the number of units sold has been recorded as shown below. The company believes that sales are increasing, and it needs to plan production facilities for the next 5 years. Devise and test a forecasting model, and advise Techno Ltd accordingly.

	Year				
Month	2001	2002	2003	2004	2005
January	19	27	29	33	36
February	20	26	28	32	34
March	20	30	37	41	43
April	22	30	39	44	47
May	27	35	40	50	49
June	27	32	35	52	51
July	24	26	33	44	40
August	30	30	35	45	43
September	32	35	40	53	49
October	36	39	49	63	57
November	37	38	46	54	55
December	42	47	56	71	66

Case B3   Mr and Mrs Lean

(a) Mr and Mrs Lean wish to take out a 20-year mortgage for £150,000.

Their local building society offers the following mortgage options:

1 A standard repayment mortgage with an annual variable interest rate of 6% with no set-up fees.
2 An endowment mortgage with a growth rate of 2% below the mortgage rate with no set-up fees but a redemption charge of £500 when the endowment policy matures.
3 A fixed-rate mortgage at 4%, which reverts to the standard variable rate after 5 years with a set-up fee of £500 and a penalty charge of 1% on the outstanding debt if the mortgage is transferred or paid off in the first 5 years.
4 A discounted rate mortgage at 4% for 2 years with a set-up fee of £1,000 and a transfer fee of £200 to any mortgage after the discount period.
5 A lifetime tracker mortgage which tracks the base rate +1%, with a set-up fee of £500 and no transfer fees.

Currently the base rate is 4.8%, and it is expected to fall by at least 0.5% each year for the next two years.

Advise Mr and Mrs Lean on their choice of mortgage.

(b) To save for his daughter's university education Mr Lean sets aside £50 each month in a scheme paying 10% p.a. compounded monthly. If he begins saving when his daughter is 3 years old, how much will he have saved by the time his daughter is 18?

(c) Mrs Lean is 40 on her daughter's third birthday and decides that she needs to plan for her retirement. When she retires she wants a fixed monthly income for 25 years. Assuming that Mrs Lean will retire at 65 and can afford to save £100 per month in a retirement plan offering 6% p.a. compounded monthly, what will her monthly income be on retirement?

Modelling and analysing decisions

We are all faced by decisions: for example, which course or career path to choose or which product to buy. Therefore it is not surprising that a key role of managers is to make informed and successful decisions. Typical management decision problems include planning how and when to invest in new opportunities, market new products, manufacture products, or employ staff.

Although scientific and mathematical concepts have always been employed in supporting decisions, they became formalised and recognised in the middle of the last century for supporting military decisions during, and for redeveloping the devastated economies after, World War II. Many systematic management philosophies (e.g. Total Quality Management) utilising these concepts were also developed at this time. Quantitative Methods in this context are often called Decision Analysis and sometimes Management Science. If the decision problems are concerned with operations then we talk of Operational Research, whereas if the decision problems involve probabilities we talk of Statistical Decision Theory.

The models and techniques of analysing decisions, although based on the concepts introduced in Part B, are usually taught in specialised courses, and use specialised textbooks such as those listed in the further reading at the end of this book. Therefore this part of the book will serve only as a very basic introduction to Decision Analysis.

To reinforce your understanding of the notation and concepts, you should undertake the end-of-section exercises and attempt the mini-cases at the end of this part of the book.

Part contents

Chapter 13

An introduction to decision analysis

Introduction

In Part B we applied scientific methodology to model and analyse business situations. In this chapter we extend this to modelling and analysing business decisions.

Chapter objectives

- To identify decision-making problems faced by business and management
- To recognise different classifications of decision-making problems
- To model and analyse decisions under uncertainty
- To model and analyse decision problems under risk

Chapter contents

Decisions under certainty, uncertainty and risk

Before modelling the decision-making process, we need to understand what we mean by decision-making. In this section we look at different decision problems and the terminology and notation used by decision analysts.

The prerequisites of this section are:
- Scalars, vectors, matrices and arrays (Section 2.3);
- Subscripted variables and sigma notation (Section 2.4);
- An introduction to probability (Section 6.1).

Decision-making

Any decision-making situation has a number of common characteristics:
- a **decision-maker** who is responsible for making the decisions;
- a number of **alternatives** or **actions** from which the decision-maker chooses;
- a set of **events** that can occur;
- a set of **outcomes** or **pay-offs** resulting from the alternatives and events;
- an **objective** for the decision-maker (e.g. to select the alternative that maximises profit);
- **criteria** for selecting the best alternative.

For example, as a student you have to choose which elective modules or course units (i.e. alternatives) to follow to complete your programme of study. In this case you are the decision-maker, and you identify the alternatives (i.e. elective modules or course units) from the programme prospectus or handbook. The events might be whether you pass or fail or the marks you achieve on the module or unit, and the outcomes might be the choice of further modules or units in future years of your studies, your future career or job options, the titles on your certificates, or the marks at the end of your programme of study. Your objective might be to maximise your future earnings potential on completing your studies.

Problem maps

Problem maps (Figure 13.1.1) represent the structure of a decision problem and help to clarify and identify its important features.

Figure 13.1.1 **Problem map for a student of business studies.**

Figure 13.1.1 shows that only the elective in accounting can lead to professional training, whereas all electives lead to further study or a job. Although such maps help identify interactions and clarify issues (e.g. alternatives, events and outcomes), they do not help us in making decisions.

Modelling decision problems

To model decision problems we need a more formal approach. In particular, we need to identify the alternatives (actions), events, outcomes (pay-offs) and objective(s) for the decision problem, and we need to have some method of selecting between alternatives. We can model decision problems using **pay-off matrices, decision trees** or mathematical equations, and we can devise **criteria** for selecting between alternatives. In many cases the objectives relate to measures of business performance such as profit or revenue (to be maximised) or costs (to be minimised).

Pay-off matrices

There can be any number of actions and events. With m actions and n events, we have $m * n$ pay-offs, and we can represent them as a **pay-off matrix**. We denote the pay-off matrix by O and the elements of the individual pay-offs by o_{ij} when action i is taken and event j occurs (Figure 13.1.2):

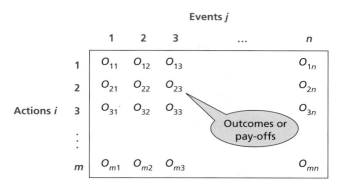

Figure 13.1.2 **A general pay-off matrix.**

Types of decision problem

Decision analysts often identify three basic categories of decision problem:

- decision-making under certainty;
- decision-making under uncertainty;
- decision-making under risk.

Each of these is briefly defined and illustrated below.

Decision-making under certainty

In some decision problems events are known, or are assumed to be known, with **certainty**. Although nothing in life is certain, history, experience, forecasts, etc. might tell us an event is extremely likely to happen and so can be considered certain: we call this a case of **decision-making under certainty** (as illustrated by Example 13.1.1). We can use the modelling concepts encountered in Part B to develop mathematical models of such decision problems, and employ mathematical techniques to solve them. In Chapters 14, 15 and 16 we consider some simple decision problems under certainty.

Example **13.1.1**

Q A company, facing increasing demand, has allocated £100,000 for investment. Three alternatives have been identified: expand existing production facilities, which is expected to generate annual revenues of £300,000; outsource production, which is expected to generate annual revenue of £200,000; or leave funds on deposit at 5% p.a. and defer the decision.

A To address this problem we list the three alternatives and events together with their outcomes. We assume the objective of the firm is to maximise end-of-year gain from its investment, so there is only one event (gain from investment), and we can calculate the pay-offs that would result from each alternative. To determine the pay-offs we calculate the expected profits from expansion and outsourcing by subtracting the costs from the revenues, and calculate the gain from deposits by calculating the interest, as shown in the pay-off matrix in Figure 13.1.3:

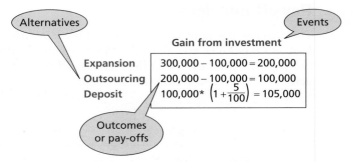

Figure 13.1.3 **Pay-off matrix for Example 13.1.1.**

The pay-off matrix shows that expansion maximises end-of-year gains.

Decisions under uncertainty

In some decision problems we cannot identify all the possible events, or, even when we can, they might not be measurable. We call this **decision-making under strict uncertainty**. Example 13.1.2 illustrates such a case, and Section 13.2 considers methods for dealing with such decision-making problems.

Example **13.1.2**

Q A company is considering retailing through the Internet and whether to advertise this service in the press, on TV or both for 1 month. Although the chances of success of Internet retailing are unknown, the costs of advertising and setting up the web service are known. Setting up the website costs £50,000, a month's advertising on TV costs £330,000, and a month's advertising in the press costs £180,000. Based on the introduction of a successful telephone shopping service 20 years ago, the company thinks it might achieve revenues of at most £450,000 in the first month. Construct a pay-off matrix for the alternative courses of action.

A This case has four alternatives: advertising on TV, advertising in the press, advertising on both, and no advertising at all. We could identify many possible events, but shall only consider the two extremes: achieving first-month revenues of at most £450,000 (success), and achieving no sales and no revenue at all in the first month (failure). We can calculate expected profits by subtracting costs from revenues (Figure 13.1.4).

Alternatives — Events — Pay-off

	Success	Failure
Advertising on TV	450 – 50 – 330 = 70	–50 – 330 = –380
Advertising in press	450 – 50 – 180 = 220	–50 – 180 = –230
Advertising on both	450 – 50 – 330 – 180 = – 110	–50 – 330 – 180 = –560
No advertising	450 – 50 = 400	–50

Figure 13.1.4 **Pay-off matrix for Example 13.1.2 (all figures are multiples of £1,000).**

The matrix shows that no advertising in the press or on TV yields the maximum profit if the service is successful and the minimum loss if unsuccessful, whereas advertising in the press and on TV results in a loss irrespective of whether the service is successful.

Decisions under risk

Sometimes we can identify the likelihood of an event occurring and assign a probability to it. We call this **decision-making under risk** (Example 13.1.3).

Example **13.1.3**

Q A store is considering whether to sell pies, sandwiches, or an equal mixture of both as part of its takeaway service. Sales depend on the weather, and daily profits have been estimated over the last 50 days (see Table 13.1.1). Write down a pay-off matrix and identify the probabilities of each event.

Table 13.1.1 **Daily profits over 50 days.**

		Profits (£) on:		
Weather	No. days	Pies	Sandwiches	Both
Good	20	2,000	3,600	1,000
Average	15	3,000	2,000	4,000
Poor	15	3,200	–1,000	2,000

154

A We can estimate the probability of each type of weather by calculating its relative frequency of occurrence:

$$P(\text{good weather}) = 20/50 = 0.4$$

$$P(\text{average weather}) = 15/50 = 0.3$$

$$P(\text{poor weather}) = 15/50 = 0.3$$

Figure 13.1.5 shows the pay-off matrix and the probability of each event:

		Event		
		Good weather ($P=0.4$)	**Average weather ($P=0.3$)**	**Poor weather ($P=0.3$)**
Alternative	Pies	2,000	3,000	3,200
	Sandwiches	3,600	2,000	−1,000
	Both	1,000	4,000	2,000

Figure 13.1.5 **Pay-off matrix and probabilities for Example 13.1.3.**

Constrained decisions

In most decision problems we are limited in what we can choose. Our imagination, time, budgets, etc. will limit the alternatives that we can consider and restrict the list of actions and possible events. In Example 13.1.2 we limited the events to the two extreme cases of success and failure. However, in complex problems, such limitations can often be modelled mathematically by equations called **constraints**. When dealing with constrained decision problems under certainty, we can often write down mathematical expressions for the objective and constraints, and can represent the entire decision problem in mathematical form. One approach to modelling constrained decision problems under certainty is Linear Programming (see Chapter 14).

Sequential decision problems

So far we have considered only single-stage decision problems in which a single decision is to be made. But in many problems one decision leads to a sequence of other decisions: for example, when you leave school you may consider a degree programme in Business or Mathematics. For the Business degree you will have to choose from a selection of electives in each year (e.g. Marketing, Operations, Human Resources, Quantitative Methods, Accounting), and your choices will lead to further decisions about a career. For the Mathematics degree you will have different choices (e.g. Pure Mathematics, Statistics, Mechanics), leading to different career decisions. Your choices of electives and careers will also be affected by exam performance. These problems are called **sequential** or **multi-stage** decision problems and can be represented by **decision trees**, which model a sequence of decisions over time (the timescale goes from left to right). Decisions and events are represented by **branches**, and the points at which decisions are made and events happen are represented by **nodes**. There are three types of node: those representing decisions or choices, represented by boxes; those where the decision-maker has no control (i.e. chance or environmental events), represented by circles; and terminal nodes showing outcomes, represented by vertical bars. Figure 13.1.6 illustrates part of an 'A' level maths student's decision tree.

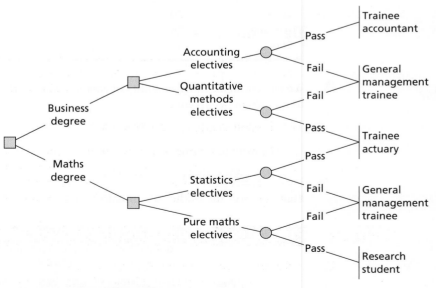

Figure 13.1.6 **Part of a student's decision tree.**

13.1

1   Identify the six components of a decision situation.

2   Identify the three broad categories of decision problem.

3   How are problem maps, pay-off matrices and decision trees used to model decision problems?

4   An order for 5,000 widgets can be produced on any of three machines. Each machine has different set-up and unit production costs (shown below). Identify the decision problem.

	Set-up cost (£)	Unit costs (£)
Machine 1	1,200	1.50
Machine 2	1,000	2.00
Machine 3	2,000	1.10

5   A trader can buy stocks, bonds or both. In the short term the stock market can rise, fall or remain stable. If the trader can estimate the outcomes of each decision under each market condition, how would you describe the decision problem? How would you describe the problem if the probabilities of a rise, fall or stability in the market were 0.5, 0.2 and 0.3, respectively?

13.2   Decisions under uncertainty

In the previous section we identified problems in which we could not identify or measure all the events. In this section we consider these problems in greater detail and describe methods for addressing them.

The prerequisites of this section are:
- Decisions under certainty, uncertainty and risk (Section 13.1);
- Measures of location (Section 5.1).

Decision criteria

Having identified the alternatives (actions), events and outcomes (pay-offs), we now want to select the 'best' alternative. We shall now define and illustrate several alternative **decision criteria**, applicable to decisions under uncertainty.

The Laplace decision criterion

As it is not possible to say which event is more likely to occur than any other, Laplace suggests we treat them as equally likely and calculate the mean pay-off for each alternative. We can then choose the best according to the objective (e.g. maximise profits or minimise costs) (see Example 13.2.1).

Example   **13.2.1**

Q   A day trader can buy shares, bonds or both, and estimates the daily profits under different market conditions (Table 13.2.1). Identify the decision problem and use the Laplace criterion to advise the day trader.

Table 13.2.1 **Daily profits for day trading.**

	Market condition		
	Rising	Stable	Falling
Shares	10,000	0	−15,000
Bonds	2,000	1,000	2,000
Both	6,000	2,000	−5,000

A   The average pay-offs are calculated in Table 13.2.2:

Table 13.2.2 **Average pay-offs for Example 13.2.1.**

	Market condition			
	Rising	Stable	Falling	Mean pay-off
Shares	10,000	0	−15,000	$(10,000 + 0 − 15,000)/3 = −5,000/3$
Bonds	2,000	1,000	2,000	$(2,000 + 1,000 + 2,000)/3 = 5,000/3$
Both	6,000	2,000	−5,000	$(6,000 + 2,000 − 5,000)/3 = 3,000/3$

13.1

So by the Laplace criterion the highest mean pay-off is to trade in bonds only.

The Wald (maximin) criterion

Most decision-makers cannot afford large losses and hence are cautious. So Wald suggests we find the event with the worst outcome (e.g. minimum profit) for each alternative and select the best (i.e. maximum) among them. This is called the **maximin** criterion (see Example 13.2.2).

Example   **13.2.2**

Q   Apply the maximin criterion to the problem in Example 13.2.1 and advise the day trader.

A   The minimum for each alternative (i.e. row) has been boxed in Table 13.2.3:

13.2

Table 13.2.3 **Row minima for Table 13.2.1.**

	Market condition		
	Rising	Stable	Falling
Share	10,000	0	−15,000
Bonds	2,000	1,000	2,000
Both	6,000	2,000	−5,000

From the boxed alternatives (i.e. −15,000, 1,000, −5,000), we see the maximum is 1,000, and on the Wald criterion we would advise investing in bonds only.

The Savage (minimax regret) decision criterion

Sometimes we make decisions not on how well we did but on how well we could do. For example, a student achieving 65% in an exam might be judged as getting 35% below the maximum. This difference between what is actually achieved and what could have been achieved is called the **regret**: for example, the student with 65% has a regret of 100% − 65% = 35%. Savage proposed that maximum regret be minimised by finding the best possible pay-off for each event (i.e. for each column of the pay-off matrix) and then calculating the regret for each alternative of each event to create a 'regret matrix'. Once the regret matrix has been calculated, we find the largest regret in each row and then choose the minimum (i.e. **minimax**): see Example 13.2.3.

Example 13.2.3

Q Apply Savage's regret criterion to the data in Example 13.2.1 and advise the day trader.

A The best outcome for each event is shown boxed in Table 13.2.4:

Table 13.2.4 **Column maxima for Table 13.2.1.**

	Market condition		
	Rising	Stable	Falling
Shares	10,000	0	−15,000
Bonds	2,000	1,000	2,000
Both	6,000	2,000	−5,000

13.3

Subtracting each column entry from the maximum in each column yields the regret matrix (Table 13.2.5). The largest regret in each row is shown boxed.

Table 13.2.5 **Regret matrix for Table 13.2.4.**

	Market condition		
	Rising	Stable	Falling
Shares	10,000 − 10,000 = 0	2,000 − 0 = 2,000	2,000 − (−15,000) = 17,000
Bonds	10,000 − 2,000 = 8,000	2,000 − 1,000 = 1,000	2,000 − 2,000 = 0
Both	10,000 − 6,000 = 4,000	2,000 − 2,000 = 0	2,000 − (−5,000) = 7,000

The lowest regret of 7,000 occurs when both shares and bonds are traded.

Which criterion?

Often, different criteria recommend the same alternative. However, there is no guarantee that they will: for example, in Example 13.2.1 both the Laplace and Wald criteria suggested investing only in bonds, whereas the Savage criterion suggested investing in both shares and bonds. If you are to be held responsible for the decision, the most cautious approach is Savage's regret criterion. If high losses cannot be risked (e.g. in a small company), Wald's maximin criterion might be preferable. Alternatively, when there is no reason to distinguish between events, we might use Laplace's mean pay-off criterion. The Wald and Savage criteria base the decision on a single outcome, and therefore a decision might be affected by an atypical outcome. People in their everyday purchase decisions might employ a maximax criterion. Sometimes none of these criteria is suitable, but there are many others. For example, some weighted average of the best and the worst outcome may be selected. This concept is considered in the next section, where we use probabilities as weights for the outcomes.

Exercises 13.2

1 Apply the Laplace, Wald and Savage decision criteria to Example 13.1.2. Which alternative do you recommend and why?

2 Apply the mean pay-off, maximin, minimax, maximax and regret criteria to the decision problem below. Which alternative do you recommend and why?

Alternative	Event 1	2	3
1	280	440	120
2	380	360	240
3	240	340	300

3 The PCfone Co. is being sued for patent infringements for its newly designed small mobile computer phone by a mobile phone company and a laptop PC manufacturer. If PCfone loses either or both lawsuits then it will have to buy in the relevant components. PCfone Co. wants to begin manufacturing and has identified the set-up costs of all possible alternatives resulting from any patent infringements: these are shown in the table below. Advise the PCfone Co. on a suitable course of action. What features can you observe from the data to reduce the calculations?

	Costs (£m) Win both cases	Lose both cases	Win phone case only	Win computer case only
Computer PCB	1.4	0.775	0.825	1.425
Phone PCB	1.1	0.8	0.85	1
Combined PCB	1.45	0.4	0.7	1.3
Neither	1.1	0.81	0.85	1

13.3 Decisions under risk

In the previous section we considered decisions under uncertainty, in which events could occur but we did not know the likelihood of each event occurring. In this section we consider how to incorporate probabilities of events in decision-making criteria.

The prerequisites of this section are:
- Decisions under certainty, uncertainty and risk (Section 13.1);
- Decisions under uncertainty (Section 13.2);
- An introduction to probability (Section 6.1);
- Scalars, vectors, matrices and arrays (Section 2.3);
- Subscripted variables and sigma notation (Section 2.4);
- Measures of location (Section 5.1);
- Modelling relationships (Chapter 8)*;
- Non-linear and multivariate relationships (Chapter 9)*.

* The sections marked with an asterisk are optional and required only for the last subsection.

Incorporating probabilities

154

When dealing with decisions under risk, every event has an associated probability, which can be labelled $p_1, p_2, p_3, ..., p_n$ (Section 7.1).

Expected values

123

In Section 5.1 we discussed the concept of a weighted mean, in which observations are multiplied by appropriate weights and summed, and this sum is then divided by the total weight (equation 5.1.7). By treating pay-offs as observations and their probabilities as weights, the ith alternative has weighted mean given by:

$$\frac{o_{i1}P_1 + o_{i2}P_2 + \cdots + o_{in}P_n}{P_1 + P_2 + \cdots + P_n} = \frac{\sum_{j=1}^{n} o_{ij}P_j}{\sum_{j=1}^{n} P_j} \qquad (13.3.1)$$

155

As event probabilities for any alternative must sum to 1 (i.e. $\sum_{j=1}^{n} p_j = 1$), we can simplify equation (13.3.1). This gives what is known as the expected value (EV) of the ith alternative:

$$EV_i = o_{i1}P_1 + o_{i2}P_2 + o_{i3}P_3 + o_{in}P_n = \sum_{j=1}^{n} o_{ij}P_j \qquad (13.3.2)$$

Using matrix notation (Section 2.3) and denoting the vector of event probabilities by P and the pay-off matrix by O, we can write the vector of expected values in matrix form:

75

$$EV = PO^{T} \qquad (13.3.3)$$

where O^{T} is the transpose of the pay-off matrix O (Section 3.4).

Example 13.3.1

Q An investor is considering four investment opportunities, each having three possible outcomes dependent on three possible states of the economy – growth, stability, recession. The probability of growth is 0.3, that of stability 0.5, and of a recession 0.2. The estimated annual returns of each investment opportunity under each event are given in Table 13.3.1. Which investment do you recommend?

Table 13.3.1 **Estimated annual returns (£) for Example 13.3.1.**

Investment	Economic state		
	Growth	Stability	Recession
1	200	140	100
2	60	400	40
3	60	80	220
4	160	80	40

A In this case the probabilities are:

$$p_i = 0.3, p_2 = 0.5, p_3 = 0.2$$

and the pay-off matrix is:

$$
O = \begin{array}{c@{\quad}c@{\quad}c@{\quad}c}
 & 1 & 2 & 3 \\
\begin{array}{c} 1 \\ 2 \\ 3 \\ 4 \end{array} &
\begin{array}{|ccc|}
\hline
200 & 140 & 100 \\
60 & 400 & 40 \\
60 & 80 & 220 \\
160 & 80 & 40 \\
\hline
\end{array}
\end{array}
$$

Using equation 13.3.2, we calculate the expected values for each alternative:

$$EV_1 = 200*0.3 + 140*0.5 + 100*0.2 = 150$$
$$EV_2 = 60*0.3 + 400*0.5 + 40*0.2 = 226$$
$$EV_3 = 60*0.3 + 80*0.5 + 220*0.2 = 102$$
$$EV_4 = 160*0.3 + 80*0.5 + 40*0.2 = 96$$

 13.4

So alternative 2 has the maximum expected value of $EV_2 = £226$.

Sequential decisions under risk

In Section 13.1 we saw that a multi-stage decision problem can be represented by a decision tree. Some of its branches will represent events to which we can assign probabilities so that, as we follow a sequence of branches, the expected value can be calculated at any node. We can then decide which branches to follow from a node, based on maximising (or minimising) expected value. When calculating the expected value at nodes along the tree, we work backwards from right to left (see Example 13.3.2).

Example | **13.3.2**

 Q A furniture manufacturer is considering increasing its productive capacity. It has two options: either expand its production facilities, or buy out another company, which could be either a nearby competitor or a dining furniture manufacturer with similar production facilities. Expansion brings with it a 60% chance that revenue will increase by £100m and a 40% chance of a £30m increase (which is unlikely to cover the costs of expansion). Chances of a successful acquisition are 70%. The competitor's accounts suggest there is a 50% chance of increasing revenue by either £72m or £86m following a takeover, and the dining furniture manufacturer's accounts suggest an 80% chance of increasing revenue by £90m or a 20% chance of a £70 m increase. At worst, acquisition would increase revenue by £60m. What strategy should the firm consider?

A The decision tree in Figure 13.3.1 shows the nodes and branches of this two-stage decision problem and the probabilities of each event:

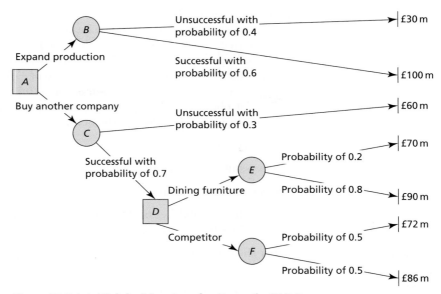

Figure 13.3.1 **Initial decision tree for Example 13.3.2.**

We calculate the expected value at each node (shown in Table 13.3.2) by working backwards (i.e. from right to left), identifying the best sequence of decisions (i.e. branches) through the decision tree.

Table 13.3.2 **Expected values for Example 13.3.2.**

Node	Expected value (£m)
F	$72 * 0.5 + 86 * 0.5 = 79$
E	$70 * 0.2 + 90 * 0.8 = 86$
D	Maximum $\{79, 86\} = 86$
C	$60 * 0.3 + 86 * 0.7 = 78.2$
B	$30 * 0.4 + 100 * 0.6 = 72$
A	Maximum $\{78.2, 72\} = 78.2$

Figure 13.3.2 shows the complete decision tree with the expected values from Table 13.3.2 placed on the nodes.

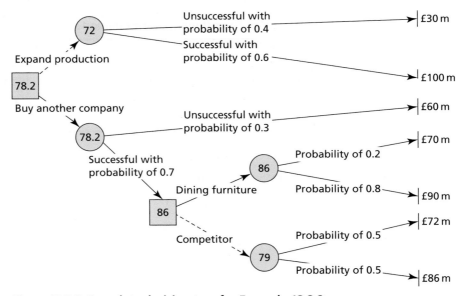

Figure 13.3.2 **Complete decision tree for Example 13.3.2.**

In Figure 13.3.2 those branches that do not maximise expected values at nodes D and A are shown dotted and would not be considered as desirable paths through the decision tree. The expected value of the optimum strategy is £78.2m, as shown at the leftmost node in Figure 13.3.2. As the probability of a successful acquisition of a competitor is 0.7 and of obtaining a revenue of £70m is 0.2, the probability of obtaining £70m from buying the competitor is $0.7 * 0.2 = 0.14$. Similarly, the probability of obtaining £90m from buying the competitor is $0.7 * 0.8 = 0.56$. So there are three events following the decision to buy a company:

Unsuccessful, with probability = 0.3

Successful, with revenue of £70m with probability = 0.14

Successful, with revenue of £90m with probability = 0.56

Notice how the probabilities of these three events must sum to 1 (i.e. $0.3 + 0.14 + 0.56 = 1$).

Therefore the expected value of the optimum strategy is:

Expected value = $60 * 0.3 + 70 * 0.7 * 0.2 + 90 * 0.7 * 0.8 = 78.2$.

Misleading expected values

Expected value is essentially a weighted mean in which probabilities are the weights. But these are not always appropriate. We have seen that the mean is not always representative of reality (Section 5.1), and it assumes our sample is representative (i.e. it assumes we are repeating the decision many times over). When decisions are taken only once, expected values can be misleading (Example 13.3.3).

Example **13.3.3**

Q Internet business is risky, and the probability of success (i.e. making a profit) in the first year is thought to be 0.1. An investor has £20,000 to start up an Internet business that has the potential to generate sales revenue of £500,000 in the first year. What action would you recommend?

A The pay-off matrix is shown in Table 13.3.3:

Table 13.3.3 **Pay-off matrix for Example 13.3.3.**

Alternative	Event	
	Success ($p = 0.1$)	Failure ($p = 0.9$)
1 Invest	500,000	−20,000
2 Do not invest	0	0

The expected values are:

$EV_1 = 0.1 * 500,000 - 0.9 * 20,000 = 32,000$

$EV_2 = 0.1 * 0 + 0.9 * 0 = 0$

The expected values suggest making the investment, despite there being a greater chance of failure than of success.

Other decision criteria and utility theory*

* You might want to skip this section if you have not read Chapters 8 and 9.

Several other criteria employ the concept of expected value. For example, if we calculate the pay-off under certainty and subtract the expected value of the best alternative, we have the **expected value of perfect information** (EVPI). When dealing with investment decision problems we encounter the **return to risk ratio** – the expected value of an alternative divided by its standard deviation. When the cost of a wrong decision is known, we can calculate the **expected opportunity cost** of each alternative (EOC).

Additional information is sometimes available, usually at a cost, and may be in the form of conditional probabilities. For example, in Example 13.3.1 the probabilities for each future state of the economy might be conditional on the current state of the economy. In Section 6.1 we used Bayes' theorem to update initial probabilities, but we shall need to subtract the cost of this additional information from the updated expected values.

Another way of viewing a weighted mean is to think of it as a multivariate linear function in which the probabilities are the coefficients and the outcomes are the variables. As linear functions may not be appropriate models of behaviour (Chapters 8 and 9), sometimes we model the value of a set of outcomes by non-linear functions called **utility functions**, which model the utility that decision-makers derive from the outcomes. Figure 13.3.3 shows a typical **utility curve** for a single decision-maker:

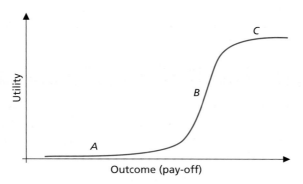

Figure 13.3.3 **A typical utility curve.**

The utility curve in Figure 13.3.3 has three distinct regions. At the bottom (region A), a decision-maker has little utility, and lower pay-offs would be of little consequence. However, gaining utility would be important, and decision-makers who would be prepared to take risks are called **risk takers**. At the top (region C), a decision-maker has much utility, so gaining more is of little consequence but losing utility is of concern. These decision-makers are not likely to take risks and are said to be **risk averse**. The centre (region B) is almost linear and similar to the behaviour assumed when calculating expected value. Although important, utilities are difficult to define as each person has a different view about the value of outcomes and therefore will work on different utility functions from each other. Further discussion of utility theory is beyond the scope of this book, but can be found in the further reading at the end of the book).

1 Norgas drills for gas in the North Sea and categorises gas fields into small, normal and large. It has to decide whether to develop a find quickly, which is costly but has a competitive advantage, or more slowly, which is less costly but subject to more competition. There is a 30% chance of a small find and a 20% chance of a large find. Advise Norgas on a development strategy for the expected profits shown below:

	Find (£m)		
	Small	Normal	Large
Fast development	100	130	180
Slow development	80	150	210

2 A logistics firm has to tender for transporting beer from a brewery to isolated pubs. Because of uncertainty in beer sales, it has to decide whether to make a low, average or high tender. Past indications show a 40% chance that beer sales will decrease, a 30% chance they will stay the same, and a 30% chance they will increase. Profits for the logistics firm for each scenario are shown in the table. Recommend a tendering strategy for the logistics firm.

	Beer sales (£)		
Tender	Decrease	Stay same	Increase
Low	10,000	15,000	16,000
Average	5,000	20,000	10,000
High	18,000	10,000	−5,000

3 A travel agent is required to pay an advance deposit of £300 per booking to a hotel. If a reservation is confirmed, the agent makes £500. If more than five reservations are made, the hotel reimburses the deposit and pays a fixed gratuity fee of £1,500 to the travel agent. From past experience, the agent identifies the probabilities of confirmed reservations as $P(0) = 0.15$, $P(1) = 0.1$, $P(2) = 0.2$, $P(3) = 0.3$, $P(4) = 0.15$, $P(5$ or more$) = 0.1$. Construct a pay-off matrix and advise the travel agent on the number of reservations to make with the hotel.

4 A printed circuit board (PCB) manufacturer has invited tenders from three suppliers of robots: Bordrobo, Cirkit and Eman. The Bordrobo robot produces 2,600 high-quality PCBs a day with a unit profit of £6 or 3,200 standard-quality PCBs a day with a unit profit of £5. The Cirkit robot produces much better quality PCBs with a unit profit of £10 but is less reliable. It claims a daily production rate of 1,400 with probability of 0.4 or 2,000 with probability of 0.6. The PCB manufacturer already has an Eman robot, and knows reliability depends on how it is set up and that unit profits are much lower at £4. Its current Eman robot produces daily 2,000 with a probability of 0.1, 4,000 with a probability of 0.7 or 6,000 with a probability of 0.2. When output exceeds 4,000 units a day the excess can be sold on the spot market, with a 60% chance of increasing profit by 50% but a 40% chance of selling for 40% less profit. Advise the PCB manufacturer on the purchase decision.

13.4　Chapter review

In this chapter we considered different kinds of decision problem, how they can be modelled, and how to analyse them in order to support the decision-making process. In most cases models are simplifications of a particular decision-making problem based on a set of assumptions. So results from any analysis should clearly state the assumptions made, and should not be regarded as the definitive 'answer' to a problem.

When dealing with uncertainty and risk, we considered different criteria and approaches to help identify the best alternatives from all those available. With large, complex decision problems it might be too difficult or impossible to identify all the alternatives, because we have limited resources (e.g. time), and so we might be able to explore only a part of the decision problem. In some situations, even having identified the alternatives, the analysis may be too complex or time consuming. In such cases we use computers to perform the calculations and explore the alternatives.

Simulation is another approach for exploring alternatives, in which we design experiments to consider outcomes. These approaches are beyond the scope of this introductory book, but references to simulation can be found in the further reading at the end of the book.

Chapter 14

An introduction to linear programming

Introduction

In Chapter 13 we classified decision problems into three basic types: decisions under certainty, uncertainty and risk. In most decision problems we must also consider any limitations (constraints) on the alternatives. For example, limited resources, such as money, will only allow certain actions. In this chapter we consider a method for modelling some types of constrained decision problems under certainty.

Chapter objectives

- To introduce the concept of linear programming
- To introduce graphical methods for solving linear programs
- To introduce the use of Excel for solving linear programs

Chapter contents

In Section 13.1 we saw that one component of a decision problem is the objective of the decision-maker. In some decision-making situations we can model (i.e. represent) the objective and the constraints of a decision problem by mathematical equations. If these mathematical equations are linear (see Chapter 8), we say the model is a **linear program**.

The prerequisites of this section are:
- Decisions under certainty, uncertainty and risk (Section 13.1);
- Relationships, functions and equations (Section 8.1);
- Linear functions (Section 8.2).

Linear programming

Linear programming is a method that begins by representing (i.e. modelling) the objective and any constraints on the alternatives of a decision problem under certainty as linear equations and/or inequalities, which we can then solve and analyse to provide information for the decision-maker. The complete model of such a decision problem is called a **linear program**. When creating the linear program we say we are **formulating** it, and this will often involve detailed discussions with the decision-maker in order to obtain all the relevant data relating to the problem. Having completed the formulation we **solve** the model, and two methods are presented in Sections 14.2 and 14.3. We might then also consider how 'sensitive' this solution is to changes in the parameters of the problem (i.e. the data used in the formulation), and this is known as **sensitivity analysis**. We might also investigate how any underlying assumptions made during the formulation process might have contributed to the solution and how changes in these assumptions can alter the solution, which might involve reformulating and/or further solving. Having analysed the model, we then **interpret** the solution in the light of the original decision problem. Interpretation involves considering the assumptions made in building the model, the values of the decision variables, and the limited resources available to the decision-maker in the solution. Finally, we **report back** to the decision-maker with our conclusions and recommendations, stating the assumptions made during the formulation and analysis stages. This methodology is summarised in Figure 14.1.1.

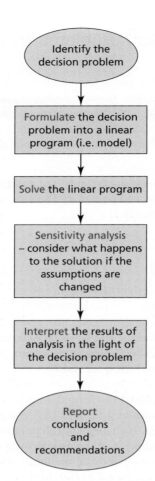

Figure 14.1.1 **Linear programming methodology.**

Formulating linear programs

To formulate a decision problem as a linear program, we follow a three-stage procedure:

1 Identify the alternatives and represent them as **decision variables**. For example, in an investment problem the alternatives might be how much to invest in different investment opportunities.

2 Represent the objective as a linear equation (see Sections 8.1 and 8.2) in terms of the decision variables. This equation is called the **objective function**. In some linear programs we want to maximise the objective function and, in others, to minimise it. For example, we might want to maximise the annual returns from a portfolio of investment opportunities or minimise the total costs of production.

3 Represent the **constraints** (i.e. limitations) on the alternatives or actions as linear equations and/or inequalities in terms of the decision variables. For example, in an investment decision problem one constraint will be the total funds (i.e. budget) available. We do not want decision variables to be negative, and this gives rise to non-negativity constraints on the decision variables. For example, we cannot spend a negative amount of money.

A basic standard form for linear programs

Having identified the decision variables, objective function and the constraints, we write the linear program in a **basic standard form** (see Examples 14.1.1 and 14.1.2):

Maximise or minimise: The objective function

Subject to: A set of constraints
Non-negativity constraints

Example

14.1.1

Q A firm makes two types of wrought-iron chair – the Roundback, with a back made from round steel bar, and the Flatback, with a back made from flat steel strip. The seats of both chairs are made from flat steel strip. To make one Flatback chair requires 2 kg of round steel bar and 3 kg flat steel strip, whereas one Roundback chair requires 4 kg of round steel bar and 2 kg of flat steel strip. Each Flatback chair makes £10 profit and each Roundback chair makes £15 profit. Today, the firm only has 12 kg of round steel bar and 10 kg of flat steel strip available. Write in basic standard form the linear program for this decision problem.

A First we must identify the decision variables of the problem. Without further information, we shall assume that the firm has to decide how many of each type of chair to make today. So the decision variables are the production quantities of Flatback chairs and Roundback chairs, which we shall define as:

F = the production quantity of Flatback chairs today

R = the production quantity of Roundback chairs today

Because we cannot have negative production quantities, we can write the non-negativity constraints $F \geqslant 0$ and $R \geqslant 0$.

Having defined the decision variables we can now write down the objective function. We know the unit profit for each type of chair, and therefore we can construct an objective function for the total profit from producing both types of chair. The profit from producing F flatback chairs is $10 * F$ and the profit from producing R roundback chairs is $15 * R$, and therefore:

Total profit (£) = $10F + 15R$ *(14.1.1)*

Organisations usually want to maximise their profits, so we need to maximise this objective function.

The firm is limited (constrained) by having only 12 kg of round steel bar and 10 kg of flat steel strip available today. A Flatback chair requires 2 kg of round steel bar and a Roundback chair 4 kg. So producing F Flatback chairs require $(2 * F)$ kg of round steel bar and producing R Roundback chairs require $(4 * R)$ kg of round steel bar, giving a total requirement of $(2 * F + 4 * R)$ kg, but this total cannot exceed 12 kg. We can represent this constraint as an inequality:

$2F + 4R \leqslant 12$ kg of round steel bar   *(14.1.2)*

Similarly, a Flatback chair requires 3 kg of flat steel strip and a Roundback chair 2 kg. So producing F Flatback chairs requires $(3 * F)$ kg of flat steel strip and producing R Roundback chairs will require $(2 * R)$ kg of flat steel strip, giving a total flat steel strip requirement of $(3 * F + 2 * R)$ kg, but this total cannot exceed 10 kg. We also represent this constraint as an inequality:

$3F + 2R \leqslant 10$ kg of flat steel strip   *(14.1.3)*

In basic standard form, the linear program is:

Maximise: $10F + 15R$ = Total profit   (i.e. the objective function)

Subject to: $2F + 4R \leqslant 12$ (i.e. round steel bar constraint)

            $3F + 2R \leqslant 10$ (i.e. flat steel strip constraint)

            $F \geqslant 0$ (i.e. non-negative decision variable)

            $R \geqslant 0$ (i.e. non-negative decision variable)

14.1.2

Q A council has involved the local community, business and other agencies in its inner-city development plan. Housing associations want at least 4,000 hectares set aside for housing; the business community wants at least 5,000 hectares for industrial use. Environmental and governmental agencies want at least 10,000 hectares to be reclaimed. To reclaim derelict land costs £400 per hectare for housing and £300 per hectare for industrial use. How can the council satisfy all these requirements?

A In this case, the amounts of land to be allocated for housing and for business are the two decision variables:

H = the number of hectares for housing development

I = the number of hectares for industrial development

Once again, non-negativity constraints $H \geq 0$ and $I \geq 0$ apply because we cannot have negative quantities of land.

As the costs of reclaiming land for housing and for business development are £400 and £300 per hectare respectively, we can write down a total cost function:

Total land reclamation cost (£) = $400H + 300I$ (14.1.4)

We would expect that the council wants to minimise this total cost function.

As the housing associations require at least 4,000 hectares, one constraint is:

$H \geq 4,000$ (14.1.5)

Similarly, as the business community requires at least 5,000 hectares, a second constraint is:

$I \geq 5,000$ (14.1.6)

Finally, as environmental and governmental agencies require at least 10,000 hectares, another constraint is:

$H + I \geq 10,000$ (14.1.7)

So in basic standard form the linear program is:

Minimise:	$400H + 300I$ = Total cost	(i.e. the objective function)
Subject to:	$H \geq 4,000$	(i.e. housing action associations constraint)
	$I \geq 5,000$	(i.e. business community constraint)
	$H + I \geq 10,000$	(i.e. environment/ government constraint)
	$H \geq 0$	(i.e. non-negative decision variable)
	$I \geq 0$	(i.e. non-negative decision variable)

Note that the non-negativity constraints are satisfied by the housing and business constraints, because $4,000 \geq 0$ and $5,000 \geq 0$. Constraints made ineffective by other constraints are said to be **redundant**, but we still write them down in the basic standard form.

Slack and surplus variables

Examples 14.1.1 and 14.1.2 showed that the constraints of a linear program often take the form of inequalities (i.e. less than or equal to, '$\leq$', or greater than or equal to, '⩾'). We can convert inequalities to equalities by inserting extra variables that take up the difference between the left-hand and right-hand sides of the constraints. To convert '⩽' constraints to equality constraints we **add slack variables** to the left-hand side of the constraint, and to convert '⩾' constraints to equality constraints we **subtract surplus variables** from the left-hand side of the constraint. As with decision variables, these slack and surplus variables cannot have negative values (i.e. they are ⩾ 0). They represent the extent to which the constraints are satisfied in a solution of a linear program, and represent how much we under-utilise or over-utilise the constraints. Clearly, we do not convert the non-negativity constraints of our original decision variables in this way.

Inserting slack and surplus variables into a linear program gives us an **enhanced standard form** (see Example 14.1.3).

Example	**14.1.3**

Q Find the enhanced standard forms of the linear programs in Examples 14.1.1 and 14.1.2.

A In Example 14.1.1 the linear program was:

Minimise:	$10F + 15R$ = Total profit	(i.e. the objective function)
Subject to:	$2F + 4R ⩽ 12$	(i.e. round steel bar constraint)
	$3F + 2R ⩽ 10$	(i.e. flat steel strip constraint)
	$F ⩾ 0$	(i.e. non-negativity constraint)
	$R ⩾ 0$	(i.e. non-negativity constraint)

In this case we have two '⩽' constraints on the availability of round steel bar and flat steel strip, which may or may not be fully utilised. So we introduce two slack variables, say B to represent under-utilisation of the round steel bar and S the under-utilisation of the flat steel strip where, $B ⩾ 0$ and $S ⩾ 0$. Adding these slack variables into the left-hand sides of the constraint gives:

$$2F + 4R + B = 12 \tag{14.1.8}$$
$$3F + 2R + S = 10 \tag{14.1.9}$$

So the enhanced standard form of the linear program is:

Maximise:	$10F + 15R$ = Total profit	(i.e. the objective function)
Subject to:	$2F + 4R + B = 12$	(i.e. round steel bar equality constraint)
	$3F + 2R + S = 10$	(i.e. flat steel strip equality constraint)
	$F ⩾ 0$	(i.e. non-negative decision variable)
	$R ⩾ 0$	(i.e. non-negative decision variable)
	$B ⩾ 0$	(i.e. non-negative slack variable)
	$S ⩾ 0$	(i.e. non-negative slack variable)

In Example 14.1.2 the linear program was:

Minimise: $400H + 300I$ = Total cost   (i.e. the objective function)

Subject to: $H \geqslant 4,000$ (i.e. housing associations constraint)

$I \geqslant 5,000$ (i.e. business community constraint)

$H + I \geqslant 10,000$ (i.e. environment/ government constraint)

$H \geqslant 0$ (i.e. non-negative decision variable)

$I \geqslant 0$ (i.e. non-negative decision variable)

In this case we have three '$\geqslant$' constraints, because the council may allocate more land than the minimum required by the housing associations, the business community and the environmental/governmental agencies. To write the constraints as equalities we subtract surplus variables from the left-hand sides: say A for the excess land allocated to housing associations, B for the excess land allocated to the business community, and E for the excess land allocated to the environmental and governmental agencies. Including these surplus variables into the constraints gives:

$$H - A = 4,000 \qquad (14.1.10)$$
$$I - B = 5,000 \qquad (14.1.11)$$
$$H + I - E = 10,000 \qquad (14.1.12)$$

The enhanced standard form is therefore:

Minimise: $400H + 300I$ = Total cost   (i.e. the objective function)

Subject to: $H - A = 4,000$ (i.e. housing associations constraint)

$I - B = 5,000$ (i.e. business community constraint)

$H + I - E = 10,000$ (i.e. environment/government constraint)

$H \geqslant 0$ (i.e. non-negative decision variable)

$I \geqslant 0$ (i.e. non-negative decision variable)

$A \geqslant 0$ (i.e. non-negative surplus variable)

$B \geqslant 0$ (i.e. non-negative surplus variable)

$E \geqslant 0$ (i.e. non-negative surplus variable)

The linear equations

The enhanced standard form shows that the objective function and the constraints (except the non-negativity constraints) are linear equations with variables having coefficients (numbers) on the left-hand side and only a single number on the right-hand side of the equation. This is why we call such models linear programs. The only mathematical difference between the linear equations of the constraints and that of the objective function is that the constraints have a known number on the right-hand side whereas the objective function has no known value. In Example 14.1.1 the objective function measured total profit, whereas in Example 14.1.2 it measured total cost. In general we **optimise** (i.e. maximise or minimise) the objective function whatever the objective of the decision problem. As the value of the objective function is generally unknown, we simply denote it by a variable Z (the objective variable). So, in Example 14.1.1, we write the objective function as:

$$Z = 10F + 15R \qquad (14.1.13)$$

Similarly, we write the objective function in Example 14.1.2 as:

$$Z = 400H + 300I \qquad (14.1.14)$$

General notation for linear programs*

* This subsection can be omitted if you have not read Sections 2.4 and 9.5.

Although the linear programs in Examples 14.1.1 and 14.1.2 had only two decision variables, in general a linear program can have any number. For example, a company with 3,000 different products wanting to model its entire production decision problem might use 3,000 different decision variables to represent the production quantities of each product.

We can use subscripts to allow for any number of variables (see Section 2.4). Let us denote n decision variables as:

$$x_1, x_2, x_3, ..., x_n$$

As the objective function is a linear function of these decision variables, we denote their coefficients (e.g. unit profits or unit costs) by:

$$c_1, c_2, c_3, ..., c_n$$

So, in general, we optimise the multivariate (see Section 9.5) linear objective function:

$$Z = \sum_{j=1}^{n} c_j x_j = c_1 x_1 + c_2 x_2 + c_3 x_3 + \cdots + c_n x_n \qquad (14.1.15)$$

Likewise, we can have any number of constraints in a linear program. Some may be equalities (e.g. an entire budget must be spent) and others inequalities. Each decision variable in each constraint is multiplied by a coefficient to form a linear combination of the decision variables. For the ith constraint, we denote the coefficient of the jth decision variable by a_{ij} and the right-hand side by R_i. Equation (14.1.16) illustrates the general notation for a 'less than or equal to' inequality constraint.

$$\sum_{j=1}^{n} a_{ij} x_j = a_{i1} x_1 + a_{i2} x_2 + a_{i3} x_3 + \cdots + a_{in} x_n \leqslant R_i \qquad (14.1.16)$$

So a more general basic standard form for a linear program is:

Maximise or minimise:	$\sum_{j=1}^{n} c_j x_j = Z$	(the objective function)
Subject to:	$\sum_{j=1}^{n} a_{ij} x_j \begin{Bmatrix} \leqslant \\ \geqslant \\ = \end{Bmatrix} R_i$	for $i = 1, 2, 3, ..., m$ (the set of m constraints)
	$x_1, x_2, x_3, ..., x_n \geqslant 0$	(non-negative decision variables)

To convert inequality constraints to equalities, we insert slack and surplus variables $S_1, S_2, S_3, ..., S_m$ and write the linear program in a general enhanced standard form:

Maximise or minimise:	$\sum_{j=1}^{n} c_j x_j = Z$	(the objective function)
Subject to:	$\sum_{j=1}^{n} a_{ij} x_j \pm S_i = R_i$	for $i = 1, 2, 3, ..., m$ (the set of m constraints)
	$x_1, x_2, x_3, ..., x_n \geqslant 0$	(non-negative decision variables)
	$S_1, S_2, S_3, ..., S_n \geqslant 0$	(non-negative slack/surplus variables)

Note that the enhanced standard form is a system of linear equations and can be represented in matrix form (Section 3.5).

Exercises 14.1

1   A firm makes two products X and Y, each requiring capital and labour for which the firm has £2,000 and 1,000 hours available each week for their production. To produce one unit of X requires £1 and 1 hour of processing, whereas one unit of Y requires £2 and 1 hour of processing. Product X sells for £3 and product Y sells for £5.
  (a) Formulate the problem of determining the weekly production quantities of the two products to maximise revenue.
  (b) How would the formulation differ if the weekly output of product Y was limited to 600 units?

2   A company produces kitchen and dining chairs with unit profits of £4 and £6, respectively. Each kitchen chair requires 1 hour's production time and 3m^2 of timber, and each dining chair requires 2 hours' production time and 2.5m^2 of timber. The company must produce at least 20 chairs each week, has stocks of 75m^2 of timber, and operates a 40-hour week.
  (a) Identify the decision variables, the objective function and the constraints, and formulate the problem as a linear program.
  (b) Put appropriate slack and surplus variables in the constraints. What interpretation do the slack and surplus variables have in this problem?

3   The costs of manufacture, assembly time and retail price of a firm's electrical goods are:

Product	Cost of parts (£)	Assembly time (hours)	Retail price (£)
TV	160	20	230
DVD recorder	20	10	70
Radio	7	5	22
DAB radio	35	8	73
Personal CD player	10	2	20

Unit assembly costs are £1 per hour, and total assembly time available each week is 1,000 hours. Market research indicates that sales of DAB radios will exceed sales of personal CD players by at least 10 units each week. Formulate the production planning problem as a linear program.

4   A supermarket opens 24 hours a day and employs staff on 8-hour shifts. It has identified the following minimum daily staffing requirements:

Time (24 hour clock)	Minimum staff required
02–06	20
06–10	50
10–14	80
14–18	100
18–22	40
22–02	30

Formulate as a linear program the problem of determining how many staff should start work at the beginning of each 4-hour slot.

14.2 Solving small linear programs

In Section 14.1 we looked at the methodology of linear programming, but only to the stage of formulating decision problems as linear program models. The next stages involve solving these models, interpreting the solution, and reporting back with some conclusions and recommendations. When there are only two decision variables we can use graphs to solve linear programs. In this section we also consider how to interpret results from a graph to provide recommendations for decision-makers.

The prerequisites of this section are:
■ Formulating decision problems as linear programs (Section 14.1);
■ Linear functions (Section 8.2);
■ Graphical and numerical analysis (Section 10.1).

The graphical method

To solve simple linear programs graphically (i.e. those with only two decision variables), we draw a graph of the constraint equations to identify the alternatives permitted by all the constraints. The area of the graph that shows the permitted alternatives is called the **feasible region**. We then find the best alternative(s) that optimise the objective function within the feasible region.

The feasible region

The graph of a linear program contains only non-negative values because both variables are non-negative, so we only need show the positive quadrant. Initially we treat each constraint as an equality so that we can draw a line on a graph. As we need only two points on a graph to draw a line (Section 8.2), for each constraint we can simply plot two points and join them together with a line. The smallest value any decision variable can take is 0 (owing to the non-negativity constraints), so we can set one decision variable to zero and calculate the other to find one point on the line, and then set the other decision variable to zero to find the second point. When we have drawn all the constraint lines, we identify the area below all the '≤' constraints and the area above all the '≥' constraints, and this is the **feasible region** (see Example 14.2.1).

Example 14.2.1

Q Draw the feasible region for the linear program in Example 14.1.1.

A The constraints of the linear program in Example 14.1.1 are:

$2F + 4R \leqslant 12$ (i.e. round steel bar constraint) *(14.2.1)*

$3F + 2R \leqslant 10$ (i.e. flat steel strip constraint)   *(14.2.2)*

$F \geqslant 0$ (i.e. non-negative decision variable)   *(14.2.3)*

$R \geqslant 0$ (i.e. non-negative decision variable)   *(14.2.4)*

First, we construct a graph showing the positive quadrant for the two decision variables F and R so that non-negativity constraints (14.2.3) and (14.2.4) are satisfied, as shown in Figure 14.2.1. It does not matter which of the two decision variables is placed on the vertical axis and which on the horizontal axis.

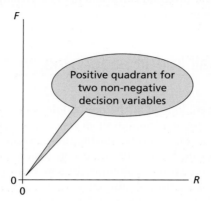

Figure 14.2.1 **Non-negativity of two decision variables.**

Next, we consider the remaining constraints. We shall start with equation (14.2.1) (i.e. $2F + 4R \leqslant 12$). Making $F = 0$ and treating the inequality as an equality, we get $4R = 12$. So $R = 12/4 = 3$, and one point on the constraint line is the coordinate (3, 0). Making $R = 0$, we get $2F = 12$. So $F = 12/2 = 6$, and a second point on the constraint line is the coordinate (0, 6). Now we have two points, we can draw the line; however, we need a scale on the axes. Before constructing the scale and drawing the lines, it is best to calculate the two coordinates for all the constraint lines. So we shall consider the next constraint given by equation (14.2.2) (i.e. $3F + 2R \leqslant 10$). Once again, making $F = 0$ and treating it as an equality, we get $2R = 10$, so, $R = 10/2 = 5$, giving the coordinate (5, 0); then making $R = 0$, we get $3F = 10$, so $F = 10/3 = 3.33$, giving the coordinate (0, 3.33).

Having calculated two points for every constraint of the linear program, we construct a suitable scale and draw in the constraint lines (Figure 14.2.2). The feasible region is the area that satisfies every constraint (shown shaded in Figure 14.2.2).

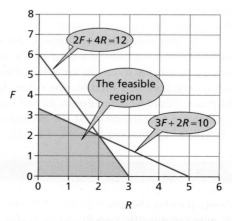

Figure 14.2.2 **The feasible region for Example 14.1.1.**

The objective function

Having identified the feasible region, we need a way to find the points in the feasible region that maximise or minimise the objective function. As the objective function is simply a linear function whose right-hand side is unknown, one way is to guess possible values for its right-hand side (i.e. Z) and see where the line appears on the graph, as illustrated in Example 14.2.2.

| Example | **14.2.2** |

Q For the objective function given by equation (14.1.3) (i.e. $Z = 10F + 15R$), show on the graph of the feasible region where the line appears for: (a) $Z = 30$, (b) $Z = 60$ and (c) $Z = 50$. Which point appears to maximise the objective function? Interpret your findings (i.e. comment on your result) in relation to the original decision problem given in Example 14.1.1.

A
(a) When $Z = 30$, the objective function is $10F + 15R = 30$, and we plot this as we did for the constraints. When $F = 0$, $R = 30/15 = 2$, and when $R = 0$, $F = 30/10 = 3$, giving the coordinates $(2, 0)$ and $(0, 3)$, respectively. The line joining these two coordinates is shown dashed in Figure 14.2.3.

(b) When $Z = 60$, the objective function is $10F + 15R = 60$. When $F = 0$, $R = 60/15 = 4$, and when $R = 0$, $F = 60/10 = 6$, giving the coordinates $(4, 0)$ and $(0, 6)$, respectively. The line joining them is shown dashed in Figure 14.2.3.

(c) When $Z = 50$, the objective function is $10F + 15R = 50$. When $F = 0$, $R = 50/15 = 3.33$, and when $R = 0$, $F = 50/10 = 5$, giving the coordinates $(3.33, 0)$ and $(0, 5)$, respectively. The line joining them is shown solid in Figure 14.2.3.

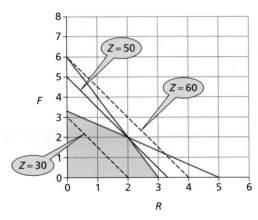

Figure 14.2.3 **The objective function for different values of Z.**

Note that, when $Z = 30$, the objective function line is well within the shaded (feasible) region, but not at its highest position within the feasible region. Increasing Z to $Z = 60$ moves the line up and outside the shaded feasible region. Notice that when $Z = 60$ the line is parallel to the line when $Z = 30$. The highest possible value for Z is when the line touches the upper boundary of the feasible region, and this occurs when $Z = 50$ and is at the point $R = 2$ and $F = 2$. So the solution to the linear program is where: $R = 2$, $F = 2$ and $Z = 50$.

Interpreting this solution for the original decision problem, we can say that the firm needs to manufacture 2 units of Roundback and 2 units of Flatback chairs each week to achieve a maximum profit of £50, given the available resources. We can see what quantities of resources (i.e. round steel bar and flat steel strip) are used in the optimum solution by calculating the values of the slack variables in the enhanced standard form of the constraints. From Example 14.1.3, we have:

$$2F + 4R + B = 12 \qquad\qquad (14.2.5)$$

where B represents the amount of unused round steel bar.

We also have:

$$3F + 2R + S = 10 \qquad\qquad (14.2.6)$$

where S represents the amount of unused flat steel strip.

When $F = 2$ and $R = 2$, we see from equation (14.2.5) that $B = 12 - 2 * 2 - 4 * 2 = 0$ and from equation (14.2.6) that $S = 10 - 3 * 2 - 2 * 2 = 0$. So all resources have been consumed, with none left unused. Figure 14.2.3 also shows this because the optimum point on the graph (i.e. $F = 2$ and $R = 2$) lies on both constraint lines (i.e. when both constraints are equalities and fully satisfied).

The vertices of the feasible region

To solve a linear program we have so far used a tedious approach that involves either drawing the objective function many times or drawing an extremely accurate graph to find its optimum position. Instead, we can calculate the optimum solution by making a few observations. First, notice that when we increase the value of Z, the objective function line moves upwards, whereas if we decrease it the line moves downwards. As the solution to a linear program lies in the feasible region, the optimum must lie on its boundary. Second, notice that the boundary of the feasible region is made up of lines (from drawing the constraints as equalities). As any straight line can be drawn from two points, the lines of the boundary of the feasible region can be constructed from the **vertices** (corner points) of the feasible region. So an optimum solution must lie at a vertex or on a line joining two vertices of the feasible region. To find an optimum solution to a linear program, all we need do is find all the vertices of the feasible region, calculate the objective function at these vertices, and select those that maximise or minimise the objective function. We can find the vertices of the feasible region by drawing an accurate graph or by noting that a vertex is where two lines cross, which can be found by solving simultaneous equations (see Section 2.2), as illustrated by Example 14.2.3.

Example	**14.2.3**

Q Calculate the vertices of the feasible region for Example 14.1.1 and find the optimum solution to the linear program.

A Figure 14.2.2 shows the vertices of the feasible region at $(0, 0)$, $(0, 3.33)$, $(2, 2)$ and $(3, 0)$. Vertex $(0, 3.33)$ is found by putting $R = 0$ into equation (14.2.2), vertex $(3, 0)$ by putting $F = 0$ into equation (14.2.1), and vertex $(2, 2)$ by solving the simultaneous equations:

$$2F + 4R = 12$$
$$3F + 2R = 10$$

Table 14.2.1 shows these vertices and the corresponding value of the objective function. We see that the maximum is achieved at vertex $(2, 2)$.

Table 14.2.1 **Evaluating the objective function at the vertices.**

Vertex	Objective function value
(0, 0)	$Z = 10 * 0 + 15 * 0 = 0$
(3.33, 0)	$Z = 10 * 3.33 + 15 * 0 = 33.33$
(2, 2)	$Z = 10 * 2 + 15 * 2 = 50$
(0, 3)	$Z = 10 * 0 + 15 * 3 = 45$

38

14.1

Types of feasible region

We have just seen how we can use the vertices of the feasible region to calculate a solution to a linear program. Some linear programs have many solutions. For example, if the objective function is parallel to one of the constraints, then it passes through two vertices, and any combination of the vertices is also a solution. However, not all linear programs have a solution. If there is no feasible region, then there is no solution to the problem. If in a maximisation problem the feasible region is **unbounded above**, then the decision variables could be infinite, and again there is no solution to the problem. However, sometimes we can solve a minimisation problem if the feasible region is unbounded. These issues are illustrated in Example 14.2.4 and in the exercises at the end of this section.

Example

14.2.4

Q Find and interpret the solution to the linear program formulated in Example 14.1.2. How would the solution be affected if (a) we wanted to maximise the objective, (b) the additional constraint $H + I \leqslant 8,000$ was introduced, (c) at least 5,000 hectares were required for housing, or (d) the cost of land reclamation was the same for both industrial use and housing?

A The linear program from Example 14.1.2 is:

Minimise: $Z = 400H + 300I$

Subject to: $H \geqslant 4,000$

$I \geqslant 5,000$

$H + I \geqslant 10,000$

$H \geqslant 0, I \geqslant 0$

First, we draw a graph showing the feasible region (shown shaded in Figure 14.2.4):

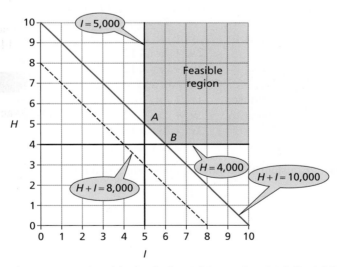

Figure 14.2.4 **Graphical solution of Example 14.1.2 (in 1,000s acres).**

The graph shows that the minimum must occur on the lower boundary of the feasible region. Although the feasible region is unbounded, we can find a solution to the minimisation problem. Either reading from the graph or solving simultaneous equations, we find the vertices are A at (5, 5) and B at (6, 4). At vertex A, the objective function has the value $Z = 400 * 5 + 300 * 5 = 2,000 + 1,500 = 3,500$, and at vertex B, $Z = 400 * 6 + 300 * 4 = 2,400 + 1,200 = 3,600$. So vertex A minimises the objective function, and the council should allocate 5,000 hectares to both industry and housing.

(a) As the feasible region is unbounded above, we cannot maximise the objective because we could infinitely increase it by choosing infinite values for the decision variables.

(b) If $H + I \leqslant 8{,}000$ were introduced (shown dotted in Figure 14.2.4), there would be no feasible region and so no solution to the problem.

(c) If at least 5,000 hectares were required for housing, the first constraint would become $H \geqslant 5{,}000$ and, on the graph, the constraint line would move up so that the only vertex was A and the solution would not change.

(d) If the cost of reclamation was the same for any use, the coefficients of both decision variables in the objective function would be the same, and the slope would be the same as the environment/government constraint line (i.e. $H + I = 10{,}000$). Both vertices A and B would yield the same cost, so any combination of these would minimise costs and there would be an infinite number of solutions.

Exercises 14.2

1 Solve and interpret the solutions to the linear programs formulated in Questions 1 and 2 of Exercises 14.1.

2 An advertising agency buys local radio and TV slots for its client and wants to maximise the total audience exposure for all clients. Its client has a maximum budget of £1 million per month. Each radio slot reaches 1,000 customers and each TV slot reaches 3,000 different customers. Radio slots cost £4,000, provided at least 100 slots are taken in any month, and TV slots cost £20,000, with no restrictions on the number of slots. Each radio slot requires 20 hours and each TV slot 50 hours of the agency's executive time out of a total of 4,000 hours available each month. Formulate and solve the decision problem faced by the advertising agency as a linear program.

3 Comment on the solutions to each of the linear programs below

(a) Maximise: $5x_1 + 7x_2$
    subject to: $x_1 + x_2 \geqslant 2$
                  $2x_1 + 3x_2 \leqslant 12$
                  $3x_1 + 2x_2 \leqslant 12$
                  $x_1 \geqslant 0, x_2 \geqslant 0$

(b) Maximise: $3x_1 + x_2$
    subject to: $x_1 + x_2 \leqslant 5$
                  $6x_1 + 2x_2 \leqslant 18$
                  $x_1 \geqslant 0, x_2 \geqslant 0$

(c) Maximise: $4x_1 + 3x_2$
    subject to: $x_1 + x_2 \leqslant 2$
                  $3x_1 + 5x_2 \geqslant 15$
                  $x_1 \geqslant 0, x_2 \geqslant 0$

(d) Maximise: $x_1 + 2x_2$
    subject to: $4x_1 + 5x_2 \geqslant 20$
                  $x_1 \leqslant 10$
                  $x_1 \geqslant 0, x_2 \geqslant 0$

4 Consider the following constraints of a linear program:

$$2x_1 + 3x_2 \leqslant 24$$
$$3x_1 + 2x_2 \leqslant 30$$
$$2x_1 + x_2 \leqslant 12$$
$$x_2 \leqslant 6$$
$$x_1 + x_2 \geqslant 4$$
$$x_1 \geqslant 0$$
$$x_2 \geqslant 0$$

(a) Draw an accurate graph showing the constraints, the feasible region, and the vertices of the feasible region.

(b) Put appropriate slack/surplus variables into the constraints.

(c) Find the optimum values of the decision variables, the objective function and slack/surplus variables for the following objectives:
(i) maximise: $9x_1 + 9x_2$ (ii) maximise: $10x_1 + 2x_2$ (iii) minimise: $x_1 + x_2$

(d) How would the solutions in part (c) be affected if the fourth constraint was $x_2 \leqslant 4$?

(e) How would the solutions in part (c) be affected if the fifth constraint was $x_1 + x_2 \geqslant 10$?

14.3 Solving large linear programs

In Section 14.2 we solved simple linear programs graphically, but most realistic linear programs cannot be solved in this way. There are numerous methods available for solving large linear programs. One popular method is the Simplex Method, which is based on using matrices to solve systems of equations (Section 3.5) to find the vertices of the feasible region; details of this can be found on the CD and on the associated website **www.mcgraw-hill.co.uk/textbooks/dewhurst**. In this section we consider using the Solver tool available in Microsoft Excel™, which implements the Simplex Method for us. There are several ways in which we can lay out an Excel spreadsheet so that we can use the Solver tool. Two ways are shown below: the first offers the most basic approach, whereas the second is a little more general and allows you to see the effects of changing the data (e.g. the co-efficients of the objective function or right-hand sides of the constraints).

The prerequisites of this section are:
- Formulating decision problems as linear programs (Section 14.1);
- Solving small linear programs (Section 14.2);
- Using Microsoft Excel Solver™ (preface).

A note on installing Solver

The Excel Solver tool may or may not have been installed on your version of Excel. To check whether it has been installed, launch Excel, select **Tools** and see whether **Solver...** appears in the drop-down menu. If not then you will need to install it from your Microsoft Office installation disk, as shown on the CD and on the associated website, **www.mcgraw-hill.co.uk/textbooks/dewhurst**.

Entering a linear program into Excel – a very basic approach

To use Excel Solver we need to allocate one spreadsheet cell for each decision variable and in other cells we enter equations that reference the decision variable cells for the objective function and each constraint. Therefore we need one cell for each decision variable, one cell for the objective function, and one cell for each constraint. In the previous section we saw how we could solve linear programs by calculating the value of the objective function at each of the vertices of the feasible region in the positive quadrant of a graph. The Simplex method, which Solver uses, is based on this idea, and works systematically round all the vertices of the feasible region in the positive quadrant, starting at the origin, where all the decision variables are zero, until it finds the vertex (or vertices) that optimise(s) the objective function. Therefore we initially set the values of the cells representing the decision variables to zero, and when we execute Solver we obtain the values of the decision variables that optimise the objective function in these cells. This very basic approach is illustrated in Example 14.3.1.

14.3.1

Q Create an Excel spreadsheet to represent the decision variables, objective function and constraints for the linear program in Example 14.1.1.

A The linear program in standard form is:

Maximise: $10F + 15R = Z$ (the profit objective function)

Subject to: $2F + 4R \leqslant 12$ (round steel bar constraint)

$3F + 2R \leqslant 10$ (flat steel strip constraint)

$F \geqslant 0$ (non-negative decision variable)

$R \geqslant 0$ (non-negative decision variable)

We need five cells: two cells to contain the values of the decision variables (i.e. the values of F and R); one cell for the objective function (i.e. $10F + 15R$); and two more cells for each of the constraints (i.e. $2F + 4R$ and $3F + 2R$). Remember that when we enter a formula into a cell of a spreadsheet we must prefix the formula by an equals sign, otherwise we are just entering text. Remember also that we must include the '$*$' symbol when multiplying, and we must use cell names to refer to the decision variables. An illustrative spreadsheet is shown in Figure 14.3.1, where the initial values (i.e. zero) for the decision variables have been entered in cells A1 and A2; the formula for the objective function (i.e. $=10*A1 + 15*A2$) has been entered in cell A3; and the two constraint formulae (i.e. $=2*A1 + 4*A2$ and $=3*A1 + 2*A2$) have been entered in cells A4 and A5 respectively.

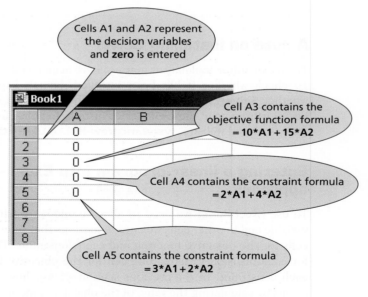

Figure 14.3.1 **Entering a linear program into Excel.**

Using Excel Solver – a very basic approach

To execute (run) Solver in the simplest way, follow the following procedure:

1 Ensure that:
   - all the decision variables have been assigned to different cells, each containing zero
   - one cell contains a formula for the objective function
   - each constraint formula has been entered into different cells.

2 Click on the cell containing the formula for the objective function
3 Click **Tools** and select **Solver...** from the pull down menu to obtain the **Solver Parameters** dialogue box:

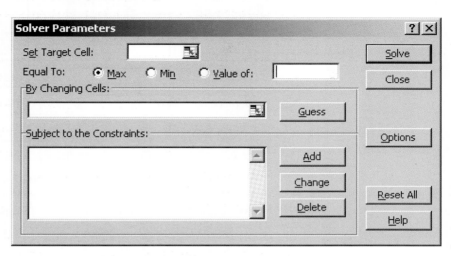

4 Ensure that the **Set Target Cell** field contains the cell reference for the objective function formula.

If not, you can enter the cell reference by typing at the keyboard or by clicking  to obtain:

then click on the cell containing the objective function formula and click ⊡.

5 Click either the **Max** or **Min** field to indicate whether the objective function is to be maximised or minimised.

6 Type the range of cells containing the decision variables into the **By Changing Cells** field or click ⬛, select the range of cells containing the decision variables (as in step 4), and then click ⊡.

7 The constraints are entered one at a time by clicking the **Add** button to open the **Add Constraint** dialogue box:

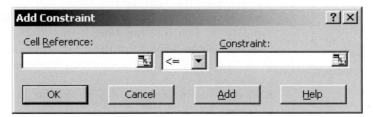

For each constraint enter the cell containing the constraint formula in the **Cell Reference** field, select the appropriate inequality, enter the right hand side (RHS) value in the **Constraint** field, and click the **OK** button. Repeat this step for each constraint.

8 Click the **Options** button to obtain the Solver Options dialogue box:

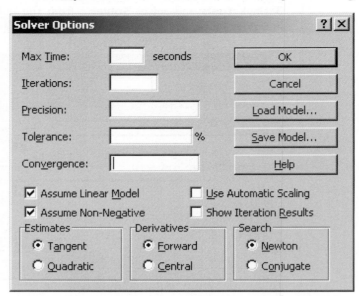

Ensure that both the **Assume Linear Model** and **Assume Non-Negative** boxes are checked and click **OK** to return to the Solver Parameters dialogue box.

9 When you have entered the linear program click the **Solve** button to obtain the Solver Results dialogue box:

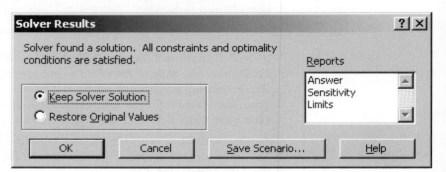

The optimum decision variable values will appear in the cells containing the decision variables, and the objective function cell will contain the optimum value for the objective function.

Checking **Keep Solver Solution** will leave the optimum values in the cells of the worksheet, whereas checking **Restore Original Values** will put the worksheet values back to zero. If you click and highlight items in the **Reports** field then new worksheets containing the chosen reports will appear in the workbook.

10 Click **OK** to complete the process.

Example 14.3.2 illustrates the use of Solver.

Example 14.3.2

Q Use Solver to find the optimum values for the decision variables and objective function entered into the spreadsheet in Example 14.3.1.

A The results of applying steps 1 to 8 are shown in Figure 14.3.2, and the results from applying step 9 to obtain the solution are shown in Figure 14.3.3.

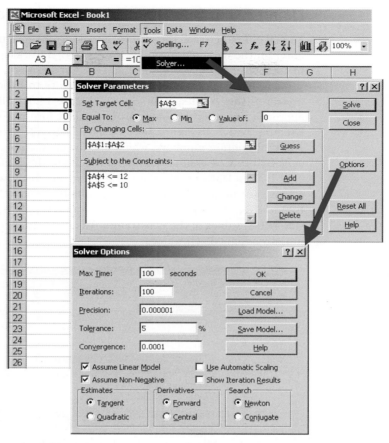

Figure 14.3.2 **Applying steps 1 to 8 of the basic Solver approach.**

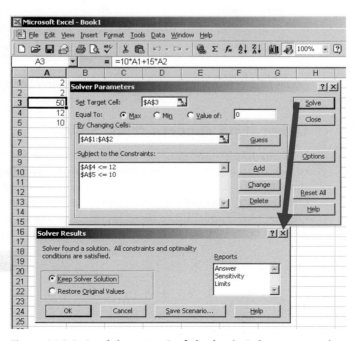

Figure 14.3.3 **Applying step 9 of the basic Solver approach.**

Using Excel Solver – a more general approach

To make it easy to see the effects of making changes to a linear program, we can enter all the data and formulae into cells of a worksheet and refer to these cells in the Solver Parameters dialogue box. Furthermore, we can enter the decision variable labels and names for the constraints to make it easier to identify and interpret the results from Solver. Figure 14.3.4 illustrates a more general approach for entering linear program data into a worksheet and Solver, using Example 14.1.1. In Figure 14.3.4 cells A21 to A25 simply contain text; cells B22 and C22 contain numbers, which are the coefficients of the objective function; cells B23 to C24 contain numbers, which are the coefficients of the constraints; cells D22 to D24 contain the formula for the objective function and constraints relative to the decision variables in cells B25 and C25 and coefficients in cells B22 to C24; and cells E23 and E24 contain numbers, which are the right-hand side (RHS) values of the constraints. The decision variable cells B25 and C25 are initially assigned zero values.

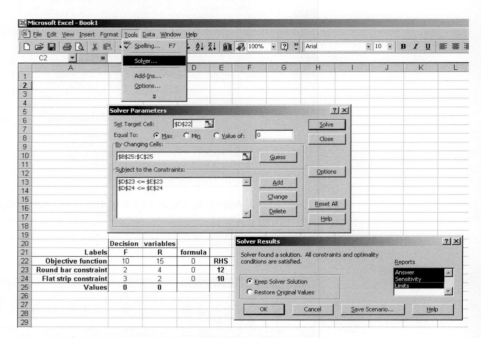

Figure 14.3.4 **A more general approach for using Solver.**

Generating reports from Solver

It is possible to generate up to three reports from Solver by highlighting the required reports in the **Solver Results** dialogue box **Reports** field before clicking the **OK** button. Each report is placed into a different worksheet, which can be obtained by clicking on the appropriate worksheet tab, as illustrated in Figures 14.3.5 and 14.3.6: these reports give the solution, and how sensitive the solution is to changes (e.g. to the RHS values of the constraints).

Microsoft Excel Answer Report

Target Cell (Max)

Cell	Name	Original Value	Final Value
$D$22	Objective function formula	50	50

Adjustable Cells

Cell	Name	Original Value	Final Value
$B$25	Values F	2	2
$C$25	Values R	2	2

Constraints

Cell	Name	Cell Value	Formula	Status	Slack
$D$23	Round bar constraint formula	12	$D$23<=$E$23	Binding	0
$D$24	Flat strip constraint formula	10	$D$24<=$E$24	Binding	0

Figure 14.3.5 **A solver answer report for Example 14.1.1.**

From Figure 14.3.5 we see from the entries under **Target Cell** that the optimum value of the objective function is 50 (**Final Value**); from the entries under **Adjustable Cells** that the decision variable values at the optimum vertex are $F = 2$ and $R = 2$ (**Final Value**); and from the entries under **Constraints** that the two slack variables are zero (**Slack**) at the optimum vertex.

Microsoft Excel Sensitivity Report

Adjustable Cells

Cell	Name	Final Value	Reduced Price	Objective Coefficient	Allowable Increase	Allowable Decrease
$B$25	Values F	2	0	10	12.5	2.5
$C$25	Values R	2	0	15	5	8.333

Constraints

Cell	Name	Final Value	Shadow Price	Constraint R.H side	Allowable Increase	Allowable Decrease
$D$23	Round bar constraint formula	12	3.125	12	8	5.333
$D$24	Flat strip constraint formula	10	1.25	10	8	4

Figure 14.3.6 **A solver sensitivity report for Example 14.1.1.**

From Figure 14.3.6 we see from the entries under **Adjustable Cells** that the decision variable F can be increased by at most 12.5 (**Allowable Increase**) or decreased by at most 2.5 (**Allowable Decrease**) without affecting the optimum vertex of the feasible region (i.e. $F = 2$ and $R = 2$). Similarly the decision variable R can be increased by at most 5 or decreased by at most 8.33 without affecting the optimum vertex of the feasible region (i.e. $F = 2$ and $R = 2$). From the entries under **Constraints** we can also see the ranges of changes that can be made to the right-hand sides of the two constraints.

Further information about the use of Excel Solver and the reports can be found in Excel Help.

14.3

1 Use the Excel Solver to solve Question 1 of Exercises 14.1.

2 Widgets and wodgets are processed through two production cells. Each widget requires 12 hours' processing in cell 1 and 4 hours in cell 2, whereas each wodget requires 4 hours in cell 1 and 8 hours in cell 2. The two production cells are used for other product lines, and in any given week only 60 hours of cell 1 and 40 hours of cell 2 are available. Each widget contributes £1,000 towards profits and each wodget £600. Formulate and solve the problem both graphically and by using Solver.

3 Use the Excel Solver to solve Questions 2, 3 and 4 of Exercises 14.1

4 Solve the problem below using the Excel Solver:

Maximise: $8x_1 + 7x_2 + 6x_3$

Subject to: $3x_1 + 4x_2 + 5x_3 \leqslant 500$

$x_1 + x_2 \leqslant 100$

$x_1 \leqslant 50$

$x_1 \geqslant 0, x_2 \geqslant 0, x_3 \geqslant 0.$

14.4 ## Chapter review

In this chapter we considered some typical constrained decision problems under certainty and how they can be modelled. When such problems can be entirely modelled by linear functions, we can formulate them as linear programs. However, only the simplest linear programs can be solved graphically. There are several ways of solving linear programs, the most popular being the Simplex Method. The calculations required to implement the Simplex method manually are extremely tedious, and are based on the Gauss–Jordan pivoting method for solving systems of equations. A detailed explanation of the basic Simplex method and Gauss–Jordan pivoting can be found on the CD and on the associated website **www.mcgraw-hill.co.uk/ textbooks/dewhurst**. There are many variants of the Simplex method, but they are beyond the scope of this book (see the further reading at the end of the book). Instead of undertaking the Simplex Method manually we employed the Microsoft Excel Solver tool, which undertakes the calculations of the Simplex method for us. However, Excel Solver can solve linear programs only up to 200 variables with 200 constraints, and if larger problems are to be solved then other Excel add-ons or entirely different linear programming software tools can be purchased (e.g. Front Line Systems Premium Solver, **http://www.solver.com** or Lindo, **http://www.lindo. com**). Some decision problems cannot be modelled by linear equations, and we then formulate them as non-linear programs; some non-linear decision problems are described and solved in Chapter 15.

An introduction to non-linear and other decision models

Introduction

In Chapter 14 we saw how, in some business decision problems, the objective of the decision-maker(s) and constraints on the alternatives could be modelled by the linear equations encountered in Chapter 8, resulting in linear programs. In Chapter 14 we also saw how linear programs can be solved by using graphical methods or as systems of linear equations. However, in Chapters 9 and 12 we saw that some measures of performance are non-linear, and consequently in such cases we need to employ other methods of analysis, which we encountered in Chapters 10 and 12. In this chapter we consider some common decision problems found in business, management and economics.

Chapter objectives

- To appreciate the use of non-linear functions for supporting management decisions

- To introduce the use of mathematical analysis to support inventory management decisions

- To introduce the use of statistical methods to support quality management decisions

- To introduce concepts of Discounted Cash Flow, Net Present Value, Internal Rate of Return and Payback period

Chapter contents

15.1 Decisions in business economics and operations management

In Chapter 9 we saw how some typical economic measures of business performance (e.g. costs, revenues and profits) could be modelled by non-linear functions. In Chapter 10 we saw how non-linear models could be analysed (e.g. by graphical and marginal analysis) to provide information. In this section we extend these ideas to some management decision problems typically found in the areas of business economics and operations management.

The prerequisites of this section are:
■ Decisions under certainty, uncertainty and risk (Section 13.1);
■ Formulating decision problems as linear programs (Section 14.1);
■ Non-linear and multivariate relationships (Chapter 9);
■ Analysing models (Chapter 10).

Optimising non-linear objectives

In Chapter 14 we encountered the concept of finding the values of decision variables that optimised a decision-maker's objective function subject to constraints, in which all the equations were linear. We start this section by considering unconstrained decision problems having a non-linear objective. Examples 15.1.1 and 15.1.2 illustrate decision problems from business economics and operations management.

Example

15.1.1

Q A manufacturing firm has found that the monthly sales volume of a particular product is related to the unit price (p) (see Chapter 8) by equation (15.1.1). In manufacturing this particular product the firm has fixed costs of £3,500 and unit production costs of £20. Find the firm's optimum level of production if it wants to: (a) maximise revenue and (b) maximise profits.

$$\text{Sales volume} = 1{,}200 - 20p \qquad (15.1.1)$$

A First we find expressions for revenue and profit in terms of production level, and then we find their absolute maxima (see Chapter 10). We shall denote the firm's production level (output) for this product by q and assume that the firm can gear production to meet any level of demand.

Revenue from the sales of this product is found from calculating: **sales volume * unit price**, so the firm's revenue function for this product can be represented by:

$$R = qp \qquad (15.1.2)$$

As profit is the difference between revenue from sales and cost of making these sales (i.e. **revenue – cost**) then total costs (variable + fixed costs) are $20q + 3{,}500$, and the firm's profit function for this product will be:

$$\Pi = qp - 20q - 3{,}500 \qquad (15.1.3)$$

However, we want the revenue and profit objectives in terms of only a single decision variable (production level, q) and under our assumptions we can equate sales to production, i.e.:

$$q = 1{,}200 - 20p \qquad (15.1.4)$$

262

We can now rearrange equation (15.1.4) to represent p as a function of q so that we can make an appropriate substitution in equations (15.1.2) and (15.1.3). From equation (15.1.4) we have:

$$q + 20p = 1{,}200 \qquad\qquad (15.1.5)$$

Therefore,

$$20p = 1{,}200 - q$$

So:

$$p = \frac{1{,}200 - q}{20} = 60 - 0.05q \qquad\qquad (15.1.6)$$

We can now substitute equation (15.1.6) into equations (15.1.2) and (15.1.3), giving:

(a) $R = q(60 - 0.05q) = 60q - 0.05q^2$ $\qquad\qquad (15.1.7)$

and

(b) $\pi = 60q - 0.05q^2 - 20q - 3{,}500$
$\qquad = -0.05q^2 + 40q - 3{,}500$ $\qquad\qquad (15.1.8)$

From a graph of revenue and profit against production level (Figure 15.1.1) we see that both are quadratic functions and have absolute maxima at their turning points. The locations of these maxima can be found from the graph or, more accurately, from differentiation (Section 10.2), as shown below.

(a) Marginal revenue = $dR/dq = -0.1q + 60$, and setting to zero gives $q = 600$ for the optimum production level to maximum revenue.
(b) Marginal profit = $d\pi/dq = -0.1q + 40$, and setting to zero gives $q = 400$ for the optimum production level to maximise profit.

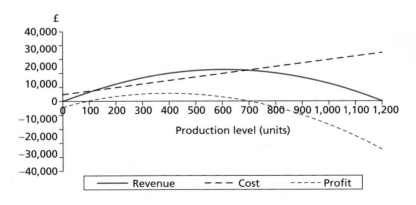

Figure 15.1.1 **Cost, revenue and profit for Example 15.1.1.**

Example | **15.1.2**

Q A company sells two products in quantities q_1 and q_2, for which annual profits are modelled by the function:

$$\pi = -2q_1^2 - q_2^2 - 2q_1q_2 + 1{,}000q_1 + 800q_2 \qquad\qquad (15.1.9)$$

Can the company maximise profits and, if so, what are the optimum sales levels of the two products?

288

A   Again we first find expressions for marginal profit with respect to each product, but this time by partial differentiation, and set them to zero (Section 10.4) to locate the stationary points:

$$M\pi = \frac{\partial \pi}{\partial q_1} = -4q_1 - 2q_2 + 1{,}000 = 0 \qquad\qquad (15.1.10)$$

$$M\pi = \frac{\partial \pi}{\partial q_2} = -2q_2 - 2q_1 + 800 = 0 \qquad\qquad (15.1.11)$$

We now solve this system of equations (see Section 2.2), and in this case we can simply subtract the equations, giving:

$$q_1 = 100 \text{ and } q_2 = 300$$

So we can say that the profit function has stationary points at $q_1 = 100$ and $q_2 = 300$.

To identify the type of stationary point, we test to see which of the appropriate conditions, i.e. equations (10.4.4) to (10.4.6), apply. To do this we need to find the second-order partial derivatives:

$$\frac{\partial^2 \pi}{\partial q_1^2} = -4 \text{ (i.e. partially differentiate (15.1.10) with respect to } q_1)$$

$$\frac{\partial^2 \pi}{\partial q_2^2} = -2 \text{ (i.e. partially differentiate (15.1.10) with respect to } q_2)$$

$$\frac{\partial^2 \pi}{\partial q_1 q_2} = -2 \text{ (i.e. partially differentiate (15.1.11) with respect to } q_2)$$

$$\frac{\partial^2 \pi}{\partial q_2 q_1} = -2 \text{ (i.e. partially differentiate (15.1.11) with respect to } q_1)$$

Testing the conditions in Section 10.4 we find:

$$\frac{\partial^2 \pi}{\partial q_1^2} = -4 < 0 \text{ and } (-4) * (-2) > (-2) * (-2)$$

So the function has a local maximum at $q_1 = 100$ and $q_2 = 300$, and these are the sales levels of the two products that maximise profits.

An inventory problem

As with linear programs, non-linear decision problems are not restricted to maximising objective functions. A common minimisation non-linear problem encountered in most organisations is that of managing inventory (stock). Example 15.1.3 illustrates a simple case, which is often called the Economic Order Quantity (EOQ) or Wilson's Lot Size problem. In this example we also see how a constraint can be introduced into non-linear problems.

Example   **15.1.3**

Q   Consumption of A4 paper has been monitored over 3 years and amounts to 1,000 boxes per year. Each box costs £10, and any quantity ordered can be delivered within 4 hours of receiving an order (each delivery costs £5). The cost of storing the boxes is estimated at 10% of its value per year. When should the office place orders for paper, and how many boxes should be in each order? Write down the general result for an annual demand of D boxes purchased for £UC with a delivery charge of £OC and a unit annual storage cost of £HC.

A This is a typical inventory or stock control problem in which we want to minimise total annual costs of operating an inventory (i.e. stock control) system. Over a year, boxes of paper will be purchased, delivered and placed into stock, and therefore we can write the objective (to be minimised) as:

Total annual costs	=	Annual purchase costs	+ Annual delivery costs	+ Annual storage costs

(15.1.12)

The decisions are the number of orders to be made each year and the size of each order, so we define two decision variables:

N = the number of orders made per year

q = the size of each order (i.e. number of boxes of paper ordered)

Figure 15.1.2 shows the behaviour of stocks over time:

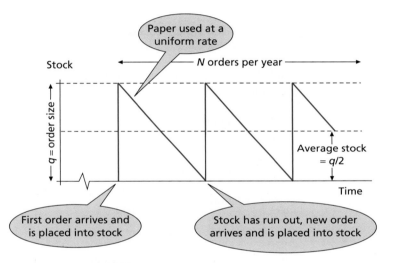

Figure 15.1.2 **Graph of stock over time.**

As the costs of paper, delivery and storage are known, we can construct a total annual cost function in terms of the decision variables by considering each component of total annual costs in equation (15.1.12):

Annual purchase costs = (Unit purchase cost) * (Number of units purchased per year)

$$= 10 * 100 = 1{,}000$$

Annual delivery costs = (Delivery cost) * (Number of deliveries per year)
$$= 5N$$

However, in any year 1,000 boxes are purchased through making N orders of size q.

So $q * N = 1{,}000$, and therefore $N = 1{,}000/q$, so

$$\text{Annual delivery costs} = 5 * \frac{1{,}000}{q} = \frac{5{,}000}{q}$$

Figure 15.1.2 shows that half the time there is no stock, so the average stock level is $q/2$, and therefore:

$$\text{Annual storage cost} = 0.1 * \frac{10q}{2} = \frac{q}{2}$$

Therefore we can write the total annual cost (TAC) equation (15.1.12) as:

$$TAC = 1,000 + \frac{5,000}{q} + \frac{q}{2}$$

(15.1.13)

Equation (15.1.13) is a non-linear, function (see Section 9.3) of q, as shown by Figure 15.1.3.

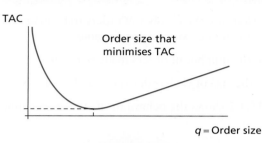

Figure 15.1.3 **Total annual cost of stocks.**

To find the stock (i.e. order level) that minimises equation (15.1.3), we find an expression for marginal cost and set it equal to zero, i.e.

$$\frac{dTAC}{dq} = \frac{-5,000}{q^2} + \frac{1}{2} = 0$$

(15.1.14)

Rearranging equation (15.1.14) gives:

$$q = \sqrt{\frac{2*5,000}{1}} = \sqrt{10,000} = 100$$

(15.1.15)

So the office should order 100 boxes at a time and do so $N = \frac{1,000}{q} = \frac{1,000}{100} = 10$ times per year.

We can generalise equation (15.1.13), where UC represents unit costs, OC represents the cost of an order, D represents demand per unit time (e.g. annually), and HC represents the cost of holding one unit in stock per period of time (e.g. annually):

$$TAC = UC*D + \frac{OC*D}{q} + \frac{q*HC}{2}$$

(15.1.16)

and the general optimum order quantity is:

$$q = \sqrt{\frac{2*OC*D}{HC}}$$

(15.1.17)

Note that equation (15.1.17) is a key formula in inventory control.

Constrained non-linear problems

There are many ways of dealing with constraints in non-linear problems. Some basic approaches are illustrated in Examples 15.1.4, 15.1.5 and 15.1.6 below.

Example 15.1.4

Q How would the solution to the inventory problem in Example 15.1.3 be affected if the office store could hold (a) only 80 boxes or (b) 120 boxes of paper?

A Figure 15.1.4 illustrates the two constraints (a) $q \leqslant 80$ and (b) $q \leqslant 120$. The unconstrained optimum is $q = 100$, so in the first case (a) the solution would change to ordering 80 boxes $1{,}000/80 = 12.5$ times per year, which we might round down to 12 orders per year. In case (b) the solution would not change.

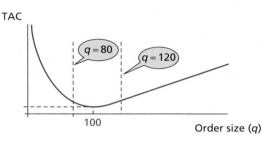

Figure 15.1.4 **Total annual cost of stocks with a capacity constraint.**

Example 15.1.5

Q A chocolate manufacturer produces a chocolate bar with a unit material cost of £1, a unit labour cost of £2, and a production function:

$$P = 4ML + L^2 \qquad (15.1.18)$$

What levels of materials (M) and labour (L) maximise output for a budget of £105?

A To maximise output it is obvious that the entire budget should be used, therefore:

$$M + 2L = 105 \qquad (15.1.19)$$

Rearranging equation (15.1.19) gives a relationship between the decision variables:

$$M = 105 - 2L \qquad (15.1.20)$$

We can substitute equation (15.1.20) into the production function (equation (15.1.18)) to give:

$$\begin{aligned} P &= 4(105 - 2L)L + L^2 \\ &= 420L - 8L^2 + L^2 \\ &= 420L - 7L^2 \qquad (15.1.21) \end{aligned}$$

Equation (15.1.21) is a quadratic and has a maximum, which we can locate by finding marginal production and setting it to zero, i.e.

$$\frac{dP}{dL} = 420 - 7L \text{ so } L = \frac{420}{14} = 30$$

We can find the optimum value of M from equation (15.1.20),
i.e. $M = 105 - 2 * 30 = 45$. So the firm should employ 30 units of labour and 45 units of materials to maximise output.

A general non-linear program and the Lagrangian*

* This subsection can be omitted if you have not read Sections 2.4 and 9.5.

When we have more than two decision variables and a single constraint we cannot make substitutions as we did in Example 15.1.5. As with linear programs it is possible to write down a general form of a non-linear program containing an objective and a constraint (see Section 14.1). If we denote n decision variables by $x_1, x_2, ..., x_n$, the non-linear objective function by $f(x_1, x_2, ..., x_n)$ and the constraint by $g(x_1, x_2, ..., x_n)$, then the general single constraint non-linear program has the standard form:

Maximise or minimise: $\quad f(x_1, x_2, ..., x_n) \qquad$ (the objective function)

Subject to: $\qquad g(x_1, x_2, ..., x_n) \begin{Bmatrix} \leq \\ = \\ \geq \end{Bmatrix} R \quad$ (the constraint)

$$x_1 \geq 0, x_2 \geq 0, ..., x_n \geq 0 \quad \text{(non-negativity constraints)}$$

To solve such problems we define a new function (called the Lagrangian function L) made up of the objective function and a multiple (called the Lagrange multiplier θ) of the constraint:

$$L(x_1, x_2, ..., x_n, \theta) = f(x_1, x_2, ..., x_n) + \theta\{R - g(x_1, x_2, ..., x_n)\} \qquad (15.1.22)$$

We then find all the partial derivatives of the Lagrangian function $L(x_1, x_2, ..., x_n, \theta)$ and set them to zero, giving rise to a system of equations to find the optimum values of $x_1, x_2, ..., x_n$ and θ. Sometimes it is not possible to solve the system of equations and we might have to use trial and error methods instead, as illustrated by Example 15.1.6.

Example 15.1.6

Q Generalise the inventory problem of Example 15.1.3 to order any number, say n, of products for a firm with limited storage capacity. Solve the problem for the three products using the data given in Table 15.1.1 and a limited store capacity of 1,000 m^3.

Table 15.1.1 **Data for a three-product inventory problem.**

Product	Delivery charge (£)	Annual demand	Unit price (£)	Annual storage cost (£)	Unit space requirement (m³)
1	50	1,000	10	1	1
2	25	500	20	2	4
3	30	1,000	15	0.5	2

A Let us denote the decision variables (i.e. order quantity) of the n products by $q_1, q_2, q_3, ..., q_n$ so that q_i denotes the order quantity of the ith product. For the ith product, we know:

The delivery charge $\qquad OC_i$

The annual demand $\qquad D_i$

The unit purchase price $\qquad UC_i$

The annual unit storage cost HC_i

The unit storage requirements a_i

The total available storage capacity A

From equation (15.1.16) in Example 15.1.1, we know the total annual cost of the ith product is:

$$\text{TAC for } i\text{th product} = UC_i * D_i + \frac{OC_i * D_i}{q} + \frac{q * HC_i}{2} \qquad (15.1.23)$$

The total annual cost function is the sum of the annual cost functions for all products:

$$\text{TAC} = \sum_{i=1}^{n} \frac{OC_i D_i}{q_i} + \sum_{i=1}^{n} UC_i D_i + \frac{1}{2} \sum_{i=1}^{n} HC_i q_i \qquad (15.1.24)$$

We want to minimise equation (15.1.24) subject to the constraint:

$$a_1 q_1 + a_2 q_2 + \cdots + a_n q_n = \sum_{i=1}^{n} a_i q_i = A \qquad (15.1.25)$$

Using equation (15.1.23), we can form the Lagrangian function from equations (15.1.24) and (15.1.25):

$$L(q_1, q_2, \ldots q_n, \theta) = \sum_{i=1}^{n} \frac{OC_i D_i}{q_i} + \sum_{i=1}^{n} UC_i D_i + \frac{1}{2} \sum_{i=1}^{n} HC_i q_i + \theta \left(A - \sum_{i=1}^{n} a_i q_i \right) \qquad (15.1.26)$$

Partially differentiating equation (15.1.26) and setting the derivatives to zero gives the system of equations:

$$q_1 = \sqrt{\frac{2OC_1 D_1}{HC_1 - 2\theta a_1}}$$

$$q_2 = \sqrt{\frac{2OC_2 D_2}{HC_2 - 2\theta a_2}}$$

$$\vdots$$

$$q_n = \sqrt{\frac{2OC_n D_n}{HC_n - 2\theta a_n}}$$

$$\text{and } \sum_{i=1}^{n} a_i q_i = A. \qquad (15.1.27)$$

Putting the data from Table 15.1.1 into equations (15.1.27) gives the system of equations:

$$q_1 = \sqrt{\frac{2 * 50 * 1{,}000}{1 - 2\theta}} = \sqrt{\frac{100{,}000}{1 - 2\theta}}$$

$$q_2 = \sqrt{\frac{2 * 25 * 500}{2 - 2 * 4\theta}} = \sqrt{\frac{25{,}000}{2 - 8\theta}}$$

$$q_3 = \sqrt{\frac{2 * 30 * 1{,}000}{0.5 - 2 * 2\theta}} = \sqrt{\frac{60{,}000}{0.5 - 4\theta}}$$

$$\text{and } q_1 + 4q_2 + 2q_3 = 1{,}000. \qquad (15.1.28)$$

However, we cannot solve the system of equations (15.1.25), and instead we use trial and error or the method of bisection (Section 10.1) to find a value for θ that satisfies all the equations, as shown in Table 15.1.2:

Table 15.1.2 **Calculating the optimum values for the decision variables in Example 15.1.6.**

θ	q_1	q_2	q_3	$\Sigma\, a_i q_i$
0.0000	316.23	111.80	346.41	1,456.26
−0.1000	288.68	94.49	258.20	1,183.04
−0.2000	267.26	83.33	214.83	1,030.26
−0.3000	250.00	75.38	187.87	927.25
−0.2500	258.20	79.06	200.00	974.43
−0.2250	262.61	81.11	207.02	1,001.10
−0.2260	262.43	81.03	206.72	999.98

Therefore the optimum order quantities are $q_1 = 262$, $q_2 = 81$ and $q_3 = 206$ approximately.

Excel solver can be used to find local optima for unconstrained and constrained non-linear problems.

15.1

Exercises   **15.1**

1   The total cost of producing q tons per week of a product is £$(3,600 + 18q + 0.01q^2)$. Within the practicable range of prices, demand is $3,000 − 50p$ tons per week (where p is price). Find expressions, in terms of q, for weekly revenue, weekly profit, marginal revenue, marginal cost, marginal profit, and the average cost per ton. Find those values of q that (a) maximise revenue, (b) maximise profit, and (c) minimise average costs.

2   Consider the demand function Demand $= -p^3 + 30p^2 − 300p + 2,000$ in terms of price p. Find an expression for revenue and determine the price level that maximises it.

3   A toy's marginal cost of production is $MC = 2q^2 − 3q − 500$ (where q is the quantity produced). If fixed costs of production are £1,700 and marginal revenue is $MR = 2q^2 − 5q$, find an expression for profit and hence the optimum production quantity to maximise profit.

4   Given a cost function $C = 30(q − 10)^2 + 5qv + (v − 50)^2 + 700$, where q is the production level in thousands of units and v is the number of varieties, determine the firm's optimum strategy if it wants to minimise costs.

5   A firm is to locate a warehouse to supply four shops. The relative locations of the shops are designated S1, S2, etc. on the diagram below:

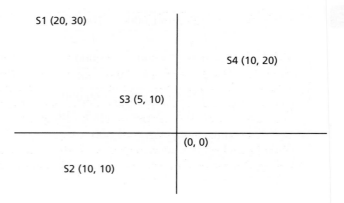

Using partial differentiation, determine the location of the warehouse that minimises the sum of squared distances from each shop to the warehouse.

6 An MP's consultants, aware of the legal constraints on the use of campaign funds, have proposed a model for the number of votes V expressed in terms of the amounts spent on broadcasting X and other forms of publicity Y:

$$V = KYX^{0.5} \text{ where } K \text{ is a constant}$$

(a) Find expressions for the two partial derivatives and interpret their meaning.
(b) Given a budget of £500,000, how should it be allocated to broadcasting and other forms of publicity to maximise the votes for the MP?

7 A manager of a retail store has to decide on how much of and when to order a particular product for which there is an annual demand of 2,000 units. Each time the manager places an order with the supplier it costs £20 for delivery and administrative overheads, and the unit purchase costs per item are £10. If stockholding costs are estimated to be £2 per year per item, determine the optimum order quantity that minimises total costs. What would be the order size if the maximum storage capacity was limited to (a) 100 units (b) 200 units?

8 Footsie Shoe Stores Ltd has studied sales for its most popular brand of shoe over the last 10 weeks, and has observed the following data:

Week no.	1	2	3	4	5	6	7	8	9	10
Sales (pairs)	200	195	203	210	200	204	198	190	200	200

Assume that demand is uniform at the average sales level, stockholding costs are costed at £2 per pair per year, and the shop operates a 50-week year. Determine the optimum number of pairs to be ordered and the number of orders per year, together with the total cost if the shop purchases shoes at £10 per pair and incurs ordering/delivery costs of £9 per order.

9 In Question 8 assume that the shop operates 6 days per week over the 50-week year, and that there is a lead-time of 3 days between placing the order and its arrival at the shop. What is the re-order level (i.e. the stock level when the next order is placed)?

10 A company stocks three products having the following details:

Product code	Order cost	Annual demand	Storage cost	Purchase price	Storage area
1	10	2	0.3	1	1
2	5	4	0.1	1	1
3	15	4	0.2	1	1

Find an optimum inventory policy if (a) there is unlimited storage capacity and (b) storage capacity is limited to 25 units.

15.2 Quality management decisions

Although we might make our purchase decisions for products and services based on price, we do so based on expectations. Quality is a measure of the extent to which these expectations are met. We expect a product or service to be of a standard or minimum quality, and might pay more if this level is exceeded. Given the extent of global competition and the reduction of costs, many businesses now compete on quality rather than solely on price. Therefore a key issue in management is the continual improvement of products and services, and the processes and systems through which they are created and flow within an organisation. These concepts are embodied in the systematic management approaches known as **Total Quality Management (TQM)** and more recently **Six Sigma**, which employ a wide variety of statistical tools. One key tool is that of **Shewart Control Charts**, used to monitor and identify areas for improvement, under the heading of **Statistical Process Control (SPC)**.

The prerequisites of this section are:
■ Elementary statistics (Chapter 4);
■ Summary statistics (Chapter 5);
■ The Normal distribution (Section 6.5);
■ Estimating and confidence intervals (Section 7.1);
■ Analysing models (Chapter 10);
■ An introduction to time series (Chapter 11).

Control charts

A **control chart** is a graph is similar to that of a time series (Section 11.1), in that the horizontal axis represents time, but the vertical axis represents a variable measuring the characteristics of a process relating to a product or service. Control chart characteristic variables can be of various data types (Section 4.1): continuous (e.g. the waiting time for a hospital appointment, connection to a service call operator, arrival of a repairman); discrete (e.g. the number of people complaining about a product or service, or the number of failed products on a production line); or ordinal (e.g. customer satisfaction with a product or service). A control chart can be used to display past and present performance to enable managers to make informed decisions about a process, particularly for improvement.

Because we live in a random world we cannot expect our measurements to be exact, and when analysing time series we recognise this as irregular variation or random noise. A control chart displays the variation in the characteristics of a process over time, and if the variation is due only to random noise then we say the process has a common cause of variation and is in control. However, sometimes a control chart might indicate otherwise, in which case we say that the process has special or assignable causes of variation and is out of control.

As well as displaying a variable over time, a control chart also has a centre line to represent the typical attributes of a characteristic (e.g. mean weight of a can of baked beans) and an Upper Control Limit (UCL) and Lower Control Limit (LCL), which are set to be the upper and lower values of the variable when the process in control. In addition to being based on the ideas we encountered in time series (Chapter 11), control charts are also based on the ideas that we encountered in Chapter 7 for calculating the upper and lower control limits. As with time series, we use historical data to initially construct a control chart (i.e. to calculate the centre line and control limits) but then insert current data to monitor a process. Figures 15.2.1, 15.2.2 and 15.2.3 illustrate three types of control chart.

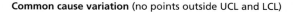

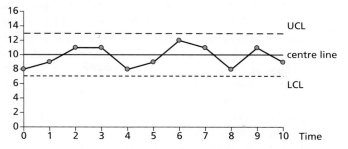

Figure 15.2.1 **A process that appears to be in control.**

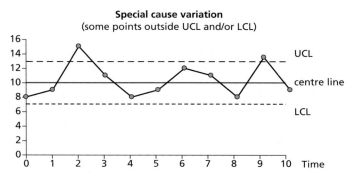

Figure 15.2.2 **A process possibly out of control.**

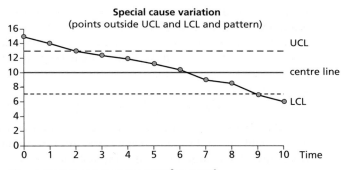

Figure 15.2.3 **A process out of control.**

Using control charts to support decisions

The distinction between common and special causes of variation is very important. If a control chart exhibits common causes of variation (i.e. the process is in control) then management need to decide whether the amount of common cause variation is small enough to meet customer expectations, and, if not, when and how the process can be improved.

Special causes of variation might appear as sudden or large variations beyond that of a process in control, or as a pattern or trend (see Section 11.1) occurring over time, see Figures 15.2.2 and 15.2.3. In either case managers need to consider what corrective action is required (e.g. a sudden increase in variation might be due to equipment failure, necessitating immediate repair or replacement; or a gradually increasing variation over time might indicate a problem with a supplier).

If points on a control chart behave in any non-random way (e.g. exhibit a pattern or a trend), even within the upper and lower control limits, then managers should be concerned. We saw, in Chapters 8 and 11, how we could identify and model trend. However, many control charts are not assessed by managers but by computers, which need to be given rules. These rules, which are usually based on looking at consecutive data points on a control chart, often differ for different types of business process and even between different companies. The most recent and sophisticated rules include the use of the time series modelling methods encountered in Chapter 11. Typical rules include:

- One or more points outside the control limits.
- A run of eight consecutive data points on one side of the centre line.
- Six data points in a row increasing or decreasing.
- Fourteen points in a row alternating up and down.
- One or more points near a control limit.

In addition to informing managers to support decisions, control charts can prevent managers from making erroneous decisions. There are two types of error, which relate to those of hypothesis testing (Section 7.2). The first type of error occurs where a manager believes that he/she has observed special cause variation, when in fact it was due to common cause, and consequently tampers with or over-adjusts a process and increases variation. The second type of error occurs where special cause variation is treated as if it were common cause variation, and either corrective actions are not taken or process improvements are made to an out-of-control process, also resulting in increased variation.

Calculating the centre line and the control limits

Recall from Section 5.1 that a typical value for a variable or set of data can be obtained from a measure of central location, the most easily calculated and statistically useful being the mean, denoted by an overbar (e.g. $\overline{x}$). Therefore we often use the mean as the centre line of a control chart. Recall also from Section 5.3 that variability in a set of data is often measured by calculating the standard deviation, which we denote by σ (sigma), which is the square root of variance (σ^2).

In Section 6.5 we encountered the Normal distribution, which is a good model of the distribution of many observed phenomena that we measure using continuous variables. We saw, even when we have discrete variables, that the Normal distribution could be used to approximate the discrete Binomial and Poisson distributions. If we look carefully at any graph of the Standard Normal distribution (e.g. Figure 6.5.3 or Figure 15.2.4 below) then we can see that three standard deviations on either side of the mean covers almost the entire range of the distribution. Alternatively, look at a Standard Normal table (e.g. Table 4 at the end of this book) and you can see that when z = 3 the Standard Normal table has a value of 0.9987 (i.e. 99.87% of the distribution falls within 3 standard deviations on either side of the mean). This is almost true for many other distributions. Indeed, a famous statistician, Chebyshev, showed for any distribution that at least 88.9% of all observations fall within 3 standard deviations of the mean, and for bell-shaped distributions (e.g. Normal and Binomial) that at least 99.7% do so.

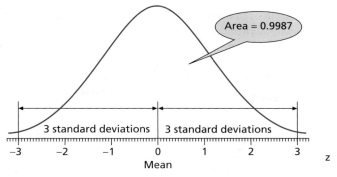

Figure 15.2.4 **Six Sigma area under the Standard Normal distribution.**

Therefore we often set the upper and lower control limits to be within 3 standard deviations on either side of the mean, as shown in equation (15.2.1). Since 3 standard deviations on either side of the mean amount to 6 standard deviations overall, then we sometimes talk about using a Six Sigma management approach.

$$UCL = \bar{x} + 3\sigma$$
$$LCL = \bar{x} - 3\sigma$$

(15.2.1)

Note that lower control limits (LCL) cannot be negative, because none of the measurements could be zero. If equation 15.2.1 results in a negative number then we set the LCL = 0.

Sometimes other limits are set at 1 or 2 standard deviations, often to serve as warnings so rules for identifying patterns or trends might include runs of data points between 1 or 2 standard deviations but below the control limits. Chebyshev and others have also shown for bell-shaped distributions that 68% and 95% of all observations fall within one and two standard deviations of the mean. The relationship between the areas under a bell-shaped distribution and these control limits is shown in Figure 15.2.5.

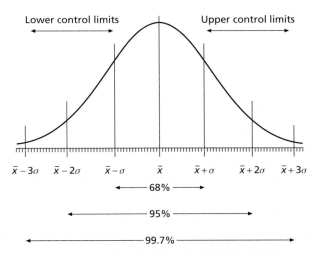

Figure 15.2.5 **Areas under a bell-shaped distribution within different control limits.**

Example

15.2.1

Q In a canning process, samples of 50 cans are weighed every hour. Over the last five years, when the process was in control, the mean and standard deviation were observed to be 450g and 6g respectively. Recently the process was stopped following a fire but has just begun operating again, and the following 20 samples have just been taken. Construct a control chart for the mean, and comment on the process.

Sample	Mean	Sample	Mean
1	447.80	11	451.36
2	451.56	12	450.08
3	450.12	13	451.64
4	448.68	14	447.60
5	450.56	15	449.12
6	449.20	16	450.96
7	451.76	17	448.20
8	449.64	18	450.16
9	450.24	19	447.48
10	451.40	20	451.12

A We have the mean and standard deviation, and we know from the Central Limit Theorem in Section 7.1 that the standard error of the mean is

$\dfrac{\sigma}{\sqrt{n}} = \dfrac{6}{\sqrt{50}} = \dfrac{6}{7.07} = 0.85$ to 2 d.p., so we can calculate the upper and lower control limits from equation (15.1.1) by: UCL $= 450 + 3 * 0.85 = 452.55$

LCL $= 450 - 3 * 0.85 = 447.45$

The control chart is shown in Figure 15.2.6.

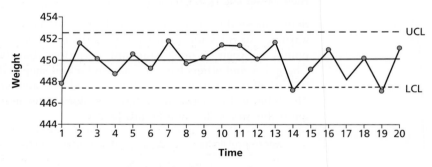

Control chart for mean can weights

Figure 15.2.6 **A control chart for Example 15.2.1.**

Two samples (14 and 19) are just outside the LCL so the process might not yet be in control

Types of control chart

Many different types of control chart are used, and they can be categorised by type of variable being measured (e.g. continuous or discrete) and sometimes by the control limits being set (usually 3 standard deviations but sometimes also 2 or 1 standard deviations). The four most popular control charts are:

■ *Control charts for continuous variables*. These are used when the quality characteristic is measured by a continuous variable (e.g. time, size, weight). Typical control charts in this category use the mean and range (i.e. $\overline{X}$**-Charts** and **R-Charts**) and assume that the Central Limit theorem applies so that we can employ the Normal distribution. R-Charts are used only when the sample size is 10 or less, which is frequently the case in most modern processes; otherwise we use a Standard Deviation Chart (**σ-Chart**).

■ *Control chart for attributes*. These are used when a number cannot easily represent a quality characteristic (e.g. for ordinal data), and items are classified as 'conforming' or 'non-conforming' to specifications of the characteristic being examined. These charts look similar to control charts for variables, but are often based on the Binomial distribution instead of the Normal distribution. Two of the most common attribute control charts are for proportions of 'non-conforming' and defects, and include **p-Charts** and **c-Charts**.

■ *Cumulative sum control charts.* A disadvantage of control charts for variables and attributes is that they use data only from the most recent measurement to draw conclusions about a process. This makes them quite insensitive to monitoring variability of 1.5 standard deviations or less. The cumulative sum control chart (**Cusum-Chart**) is a more sensitive control chart that uses information from an entire set of data points to draw conclusions about a process and shows the cumulative sum of measurement deviations from an average. Therefore, if an abnormal amount of measurements fall on only one side of the average this sum will grow and indicate an out of control condition.

■ *Exponentially weighted moving average control chart.* These (**EWMA-Charts**) charts are similar to the Cusum-Chart but use the ideas of exponential smoothing encountered in Chapter 11, whereby instead of weighting each measurement the same, recent measurements are given more influence.

Below we consider some control charts for continuous variables, and we illustrate their use in Example 15.2.2. The other types of control chart described above are beyond the scope of this introduction, but can be found in the Further Reading at the end of the book.

Control charts for small samples of continuous variables

When considering continuous variables (e.g. weight, time, volume) we often use two charts, one to measure the process mean and another to measure the process variation.

In Example 15.1.1 we were told the mean and standard deviation when the process was in control, but this is rare. In practice we usually have to estimate them by taking a large number of preliminary samples when the process is thought to be in control. We often write the mean of all these preliminary samples as $\bar{\bar{x}}$ (x double-bar) because we are estimating from the mean of the preliminary sample means, and from this we construct an $\bar{X}$-Chart.

For small sample sizes (10 or less) we usually estimate process variation by taking the mean of the ranges of the preliminary samples, which we denote by $\bar{R}$, and calculate an R-Chart. Recall that range is the difference between the largest (x_{max}) and smallest (x_{min}) observations, i.e. $R = x_{max} - x_{min}$: see equation (5.3.1) in Section 5.3.

The R-Chart for measuring variation is constructed and examined first, because if it indicates that process variation is out of control then the $\bar{X}$-Chart for the mean will be misleading. If the process range is in control then the amount of process variation is consistent over time, and the results obtained from the R-Chart can be used to develop the control limits for the $\bar{X}$-Chart.

To develop control limits for the range we see from equation (15.2.1) that we need to estimate the mean and standard deviation of the range.

The mean of the range is estimated from:

$$\bar{R} = \frac{\sum_{i=1}^{k} R_i}{k} \qquad \text{(where } k \text{ is the number of samples)} \tag{15.2.2}$$

The standard deviation of the range is estimated from:

$$\bar{R}\frac{d_3}{d_2} \qquad (15.2.3)$$

where d_2 represents the relationship between the standard deviation and the range for varying sample sizes, and d_3 represents the relationship between the standard deviation and the standard error of the range for varying sample sizes. These values (often called 'd sub 2' and 'd sub 3' have been obtained from numerous studies of the relationship between the range and standard deviation for small sample sizes of testing materials, and are available from tables such as that shown below in Table 15.2.1.

Table 15.2.1 **Control chart factors.**

Sample size (n)	d_2	d_3
2	1.128	0.853
3	1.693	0.888
4	2.059	0.880
5	2.326	0.864
6	2.534	0.848
7	2.704	0.833
8	2.847	0.820
9	2.970	0.808
10	3.078	0.797

To develop control limits for the mean we see from equation (15.2.1) that we need to estimate the mean and standard deviation of the mean.

The mean of the mean is estimated from:

$$\bar{\bar{X}} = \frac{\sum_{i=1}^{k}\bar{X}_i}{k} \quad \text{(where } k \text{ is the number of samples)} \qquad (15.2.4)$$

The standard deviation of the mean is estimated from:

$$\frac{\bar{R}}{d_2\sqrt{n}} \quad \text{(where } n \text{ is the sample size)} \qquad (15.2.5)$$

Again d_2 is obtained from Table 15.2.1 and represents the relationship between the standard deviation and the range for varying sample sizes.

Example **15.2.2**

Q Five service times in minutes at a call centre sampled on 10 days two weeks ago are shown in Table 15.2.2 below. Calculate the UCL and LCL for an R-Chart and $\bar{X}$-Chart to monitor the call centre process.

Table 15.2.2 **Service times for call centre in Example 15.2.2.**

Day	Service times (minutes)					Mean	Range
1	6.70	11.70	9.70	7.50	7.80	8.68	5.00
2	7.60	11.40	9.00	8.40	9.20	9.12	3.80
3	9.50	8.90	9.90	8.70	10.70	9.54	2.00
4	9.80	13.20	6.90	9.30	9.40	9.72	6.30
5	11.00	9.90	11.30	11.60	8.50	10.46	3.10
6	8.30	8.40	9.70	9.80	7.10	8.66	2.70
7	9.40	9.30	8.20	7.10	6.10	8.02	3.30
8	11.20	9.80	10.50	9.00	9.70	10.04	2.20
9	10.00	10.70	9.00	8.20	11.00	9.78	2.80
10	8.60	5.80	8.70	9.50	11.40	8.80	5.60
					Sum (Σ) =	92.82	36.80

A First we calculate the mean and range for each sample, as shown in Figure 15.2.2.

We start by considering the variation in the range.

From equation (15.2.2) we calculate the centre line: $\bar{R} = \dfrac{\sum_{i=1}^{k} R_i}{k} = \dfrac{36.80}{10} = 3.68$

On each day five samples were taken, so $n = 5$, and from Table 15.2.1 we have $d_2 = 2.326$ and $d_3 = 0.864$.

Therefore, using equation (15.2.3), we estimate the standard deviation of the range by:

$\bar{R}\dfrac{d_3}{d_2} = 3.68 * \dfrac{0.864}{2.326} = 1.367$

From equation (15.2.1) we have the control limits:

UCL $= 3.68 + 3 * 1.367 = 7.781$

LCL $= 3.68 - 3 * 1.367 = -0.421$

The LCL for the range is negative, and therefore we shall make it zero, so the control limits are:

UCL $= 7.781$ and LCL $= 0$

Having calculated the control limits for the range we can now calculate them for the process mean.

From equation (15.2.4) we calculate the centre line: $\bar{\bar{X}} = \dfrac{\sum_{i=1}^{k} 92.82}{10} = 9.282$

The standard deviation of the mean is estimated from: $\dfrac{3.68}{2.326 * \sqrt{5}} = 0.708$

From equation (15.2.1) we have the control limits:

UCL $= 9.282 + 3 * 0.708 = 11.406$

LCL $= 9.282 - 3 * 0.708 = 7.158$

Example **15.2.3**

Q Use the results from Example 15.2.2 to construct an R-Chart and $\bar{X}$-Chart for this week's call centre samples, given in Table 15.2.3 below, and comment on the process.

Table 15.2.3 **Service times for call centre in Example 15.2.3.**

Day	Service times (minutes)					Mean	Range
11	10.70	8.60	9.10	10.90	8.60	9.58	2.30
12	10.80	8.30	10.60	10.30	10.00	10.00	2.50
13	9.50	10.50	7.00	8.60	10.10	9.14	3.50
14	12.90	8.90	8.10	9.00	7.60	9.30	5.30
15	7.80	9.00	12.20	9.10	11.70	9.96	4.40

A The R-Chart is plotted first, and the data for both Example 15.2.2 and Example 15.2.3 are shown below in Figure 15.2.7. Note that the horizontal axis has been drawn at a range value of −1 for illustrative purposes only to show that the LCL = 0.

From Figure 15.2.7 we can see that the range is in control, and therefore there is no concern about the variability of the process and we can be reasonably confident about any interpretation of the $\bar{X}$-Chart shown in Figure 15.2.8.

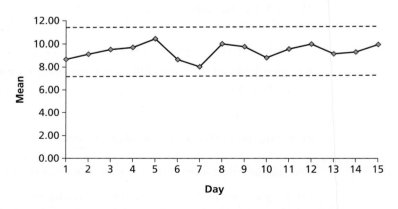

Figure 15.2.7 **R-Chart for the data in Examples 15.2.2 and 15.2.3.**

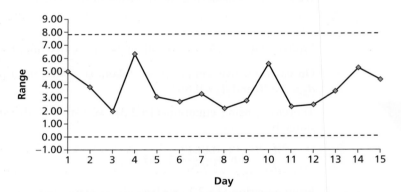

Figure 15.2.8 **$\bar{X}$-Chart for the data in Examples 15.2.2 and 15.2.3.**

From Figure 18.2.8 we can see that the process is in control, both for the two weeks on which the control limits were calculated and for this week.

Exercises 15.2

1 A widget manufacturing process in control produces widgets with a mean size of 500 mm and a standard deviation of 5 mm. For the last 10 days samples of 100 widgets were taken, as shown below. Construct a control chart for the mean, and comment on the process.

Day	Mean
1	499.65
2	480.20
3	515.56
4	520.29
5	505.41
6	473.98
7	502.14
8	506.87
9	511.34
10	498.73

2 The following data have become available for the call centre in Example 15.2.3:

Day	Service times (minutes)				
16	10.69	9.60	7.89	11.90	8.60
17	11.82	9.30	10.56	9.30	10.02
18	9.89	11.51	7.56	8.65	11.10
19	12.90	13.91	14.10	9.00	5.60
20	7.95	11.00	11.12	11.10	11.70

Extend the control charts in Example 15.2.3 and discuss your observations.

3 The following summary data are for samples of size 4 over a 10-day period:

Day	Mean	Range	Day	Mean	Range
1	15.2	4.6	6	13.9	2.9
2	11.8	3.7	7	17.3	4.5
3	12.6	2.6	8	12.9	4.8
4	12.6	3.8	9	14.3	4.1
5	15.3	5.0	10	13.6	3.5

(a) Calculate control limits for the range, and comment on the process.
(b) Calculate control limits for the mean, and comment on the process.

4 Customer service times at a Post Office counter between 1 and 2 pm on Saturday lunchtimes are sampled every 15 minutes. The data for the last 10 weeks are shown below:

Time	Day									
	1	2	3	4	5	6	7	8	9	10
13.00	2.6	4.6	4.9	7.1	7.1	6.7	5.5	4.9	7.2	6.1
13.15	3.9	2.7	6.2	6.3	5.8	6.9	6.3	5.1	8.0	3.4
13.30	5.2	6.3	7.8	8.2	6.9	7.0	3.2	3.2	4.1	7.2
13.45	4.8	3.4	8.7	5.5	7.0	9.4	4.9	7.6	5.9	5.9

Calculate appropriate control charts and comment on your findings

Investment decisions

In this section we use the concept of compound growth and the related concept of discounting future values that we encountered in Chapter 12 to model simple financial decision problems. We begin by considering how compound growth can be used as a criterion to evaluate investment opportunities, and then see how the related concept of discounting can be used instead, giving rise to the concepts of Discounted Cash Flow (DCF), Net Present Value (NPV), Internal Rate of Return (IRR) and Payback Period (PB).

The prerequisites of this section are:
- Simple interest and compound growth (Section 12.1);
- Multiple compounding, AER and continuous compounding (Section 12.2);
- Decisions under certainty, uncertainty and risk (Section 13.1).

When making investment decisions we are faced with many choices between alternative investment opportunities, as illustrated by Example 15.3.1.

Example   **15.3.1**

Q   A manufacturing firm has £40,000 on deposit, from which it receives 3% p.a. compound growth. Currently it sells all output, and customers have agreed to buy any additional output over the next 5 years. To increase capacity to meet this demand the firm is considering a new machine costing £40,000, which would generate profits of £7,000 at the end of the first year, increasing by £1,000 at the end of each subsequent year. Identify the investment decision problem and the alternatives.

A   The firm has two alternatives: leave the £40,000 on deposit or purchase a new machine. Before we can address this decision problem, we need to define some terminology.

Cash flow, inflow and outflow

Streams of money into and out of a business over time are called **cash flow**. The stream of money in Example 15.3.1, including the initial cost, end of first year profits, end of second year profit (i.e. £40,000, £7,000, £8,000) etc., is the **cash flow** of the machine. The first amount is expenditure (e.g. the purchase price of the machine), and because it flows out of the firm we call it **outflow**. The other amounts are **inflows** (e.g. profits from sales). Let us denote outflow as negative and inflow as positive. So, in Example 15.3.1, we write the outflow as −£40,000 and the inflows as +£7,000, +£8,000, etc. Figure 15.3.1 shows a timescale illustrating the cash flow for the purchase of the machine.

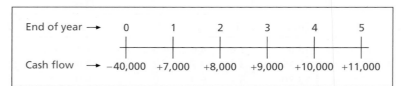

Figure 15.3.1 **The cash flow for Example 15.3.1.**

Future values

We can model investment decision problems by considering the value of the investment at certain points in time, using compound growth. In Chapter 12 we calculated the future value of saving schemes using a timescale. We can do the same for investment opportunities by calculating the future values of all possible investment alternatives and then selecting the investment with the largest future value over a particular period of time (i.e. the **investment horizon**) (see Example 15.3.2).

| Example | **15.3.2** |

Q By considering the future values at the end of 5 years, should the firm in Example 15.3.1 buy the machine or leave its money on deposit?

A In Section 12.1 we calculated future values using equation (12.1.2):

$$F_t = F_0(1 + r)^t$$

For the first alternative, the future value of leaving the money on deposit using equation (12.1.2) is:

$$F_5 = 40,000(1 + 0.03)^5$$
$$= £46,370.96$$

So the money left on deposit will be worth £46,370.96 in 5 years' time.

The other alternative gives the firm cash inflows of £7,000, £8,000, etc. at the end of each year. For a fair comparison, let us assume the firm puts its end-of-year cash inflows (i.e. £7,000, £8,000, £9,000, etc.) in the bank to grow. In Figure 15.3.2 the arrows show the growth after applying equation (12.1.2) to the cash flow:

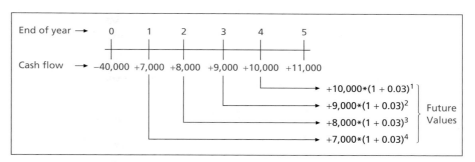

Figure 15.3.2 **Future values for machine investment after 5 years.**

So, calculating their future values gives:

$$11,000 + 10,000(1 + 0.03)^1 + 9,000(1 + 0.03)^2 +$$
$$8,000(1 + 0.03)^3 + 7,000(1 + 0.03)^4 = £47,468.48$$

Having calculated the future values, we can now compare them using a pay-off matrix (Table 15.3.1):

Table 15.3.1 **Future values for Example 15.3.2**

Alternative	Total future value (£)
Leave money on deposit	46,370.96
Purchase machine	47,468.48

Table 15.3.1 shows that purchasing the machine results in a higher future value than leaving the money on deposit. The firm is better off by:

$$£47,468.48 - £46,370.96 = £1,097.52 \text{ in 5 years' time}$$

Of course, we are assuming that future cash inflows are precisely known, and that the interest rate on deposits remains constant over the 5-year investment horizon.

Discounted Cash Flow (DCF) and Net Present Value (NPV)

Just as accountants prefer to work with present values rather than future values (Section 12.2), we do likewise when comparing investment alternatives. We convert future values to present values by applying the discounting formula (equation 12.2.1):

$$\text{Present value} = F_0 \frac{F_t}{(1+r)^t}$$

We can then compare investment alternatives on the basis of present values by discounting the future values using equation (12.2.1). This is known as **Discounted Cash Flow (DCF)**. Summing the individual discounted future cash flows to calculate a total present value of a stream of cash flows and including the initial outflow is known as **Net Present Value (NPV)**: see Example 15.3.3.

Example	15.3.3

Q   Evaluate the investment alternatives in Example 15.3.1 using the criteria of Discounted Cash Flow and Net Present Value.

A   As we are now working in present values, we need only consider discounting the future cash flows of the machine (Figure 15.3.3):

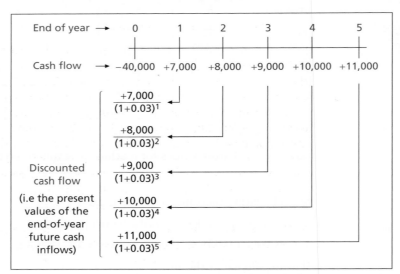

Figure 15.3.3 **Discounted cash flow for Example 15.3.3.**

By summing these discounted cash flows, we get:

$$\frac{7,000}{(1+0.03)^1} + \frac{8,000}{(1+0.03)^2} + \frac{9,000}{(1+0.03)^3} + \frac{10,000}{(1+0.03)^4} + \frac{11,000}{(1+0.03)^5}$$
$$= 6,796.12 + 7,540.77 + 8,236.28 + 8,884.87 + 9,488.70$$
$$= 40,946.73$$

As the machine costs £40,000 to purchase, the Net Present Value is:

$$\text{NPV} = 40,946.73 - 40,000 = £946.73$$

The Net Present Value of £946.73 represents the total present value of investing in the machine over the 5-year investment horizon (the amount by which the firm is better off than leaving the money on deposit). Note that this is the same as the future value we calculated in Example 15.3.2, because $946.73 * (1 + 0.03)^5 = 1,097.52$.

Calculating Net Present Value

Let us write down the general formula for NPV for an investment:

$$\text{NPV} = \text{Capital outlay} + \text{Discounted future cash inflows} \qquad (15.3.1)$$

If we denote **capital outlay** (i.e. purchase price) by F_0, future cash flows by F_1, F_2, F_3, ..., F_t, and the rate of discounting by r, then NPV over t periods is given by:

$$\text{NPV} = F_0 + \frac{F_1}{(1+r)^1} + \frac{F_2}{(1+r)^2} + \frac{F_3}{(1+r)^3} + \cdots + \frac{F_n}{(1+r)^t} \qquad (15.3.2)$$

Here F_0 = capital outlay is a cash outflow and is negative, whereas F_1, F_2, F_3, ..., F_t are cash inflows and are positive. Recall from Section 1.5 that anything to the power of 0 is unity, so $(1+r)^0 = 1$ and therefore the concepts of NPV and DCF are the same from a mathematical perspective, i.e.:

$$\text{NPV} = \frac{F_0}{(1+r)^0} + \frac{F_1}{(1+r)^1} + \frac{F_2}{(1+r)^2} + \frac{F_3}{(1+r)^3} + \cdots + \frac{F_t}{(1+r)^t}$$

Using subscripted notation, we can also write this as:

$$\text{NPV} = \sum_{i=0}^{t} \frac{F_i}{(1+r)^i} \qquad (15.3.3)$$

Spreadsheets and some calculators have inbuilt functions for calculating NPV.

For investment opportunities in which a capital outflow (a negative quantity) yields cash inflows (positive quantities), we can make general statements about their worth. For example, when the **NPV is positive** (i.e. NPV > 0), the discounted positive cash flows exceed the negative capital outlay and the investment is worth while (i.e. better than depositing the cash at the bank at the interest rate used for discounting). Conversely, if the **NPV is negative** (i.e. NPV < 0), the negative capital outlay exceeds the discounted positive cash flows and the investment is not worth while (i.e. it is worse than depositing the cash at the bank at the interest rate used for discounting). However, if the **NPV is zero** (i.e. NPV = 0), the negative capital outlay equals the discounted cash flow, and the investment is neither better nor worse than the bank deposit.

NPV and DCF can also be used to compare cash flows that do not have a capital outlay (e.g. costs over a particular period of time). In such cases we compare one set of NPVs with those of alternatives, and choose on the basis of one being larger or smaller (see Exercises 15.3).

Internal Rate of Return (IRR)

We have just seen how some financial decision problems can be modelled and analysed by calculating their Net Present Value (NPV) through the use of Discounted Cash Flow (DCF). This approach required us to identify an appropriate discounting rate. In some cases an organisation may have a standard discounting rate that might be based on internal investment opportunities or on what it can get from depositing money in financial institutions and markets. However, in other cases there may be no suitable discounting rate available, or we might be choosing between two or more alternatives that exclude leaving money on deposit or elsewhere. Usually an investment opportunity will have a negative capital outlay (i.e. F_0) producing positive future cash flows (i.e. $F_1, F_2, F_3, ..., F_n$). For such investment problems we can calculate the discounting rate that makes NPV zero (i.e. the sum of the discounted future cash flows equals the capital outlay). Therefore we can calculate the effective annual percentage rate of return on the capital outlay. This is called the **Internal Rate of Return (IRR)** of an investment, and we now consider methods of calculating it.

Calculating the Internal Rate of Return

It is NOT possible to derive a formula to calculate the IRR, but we can use a number of methods:
(a) trial and error guesses;
(b) bisection (Section 10.1);
(c) a graph of NPV against discounting rate;
(d) a spreadsheet or some other computer program.

Example

15.3.4

Q Calculate the IRR for the machine investment in Example 15.3.1.

A (a) Using trial and error, we could guess a low value (e.g. 1%) and compute the NPV. At a discounting rate of 1%, NPV = 3,584.30. Next we try a higher value (e.g. 10%) and compute the NPV again. At a discounting rate of 10%, NPV = −6,602.70. The IRR must fall between these two rates, because the NPV has changed from positive to negative. It must be nearer to 1% than 10% because 3,584.30 is nearer to zero than −6,602.70. So we might approximate the IRR to be 5%.

(b) Using the method of bisection, we take the initial interval, after trial and error, and keep halving and checking it to find the IRR to the required precision. It is approximately 3.8% (see Table 15.3.2):

Table 15.3.2 **Method of bisection for Example 15.3.4.**

Discounting rate (%)	NPV (£)
1	3,548.81
10	−6,002.45
5.5	−1,918.62
3.25	614.10
4.375	−698.61
3.8125	−54.31

(c) To sketch a graph, guess two different discounting rates and compute the NPV by trial and error. Then sketch a linear graph to approximate a graph of NPV against discounting rate between these two values (Figure 15.3.4). Note that NPV is not actually a linear function of discounting rate, but a shallow hyperbolic curve (see Section 9.3 for further details). From the graphs, we see the line crosses the horizontal axis at 3.8% approximately.

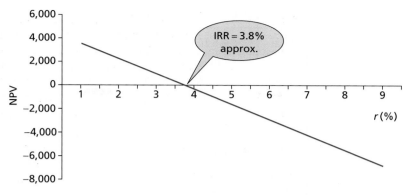

Figure 15.3.4 **Graph of NPV against discounting rate for Example 15.3.4.**

(d) Using Excel's inbuilt IRR function, we find the IRR is 3.77% to 2 d.p.

Payback period (PB)

We began this section by looking at how some financial decision problems could be modelled and analysed by calculating their NPV. To calculate NPV we need to know the planning or investment horizon over which we are discounting future values, and also the discounting rate. We have just seen how we can use IRR to evaluate investment alternatives when the discounting rate is unknown and the planning horizon is known. Sometimes we know what discounting to apply, but not the planning horizon: for example, a firm may operate a machine for 5, 10, 15 or more years. In such situations, we need some other criteria to evaluate and compare alternatives: for example, by calculating how long it takes for discounted future returns to pay back the initial capital outlay. This is called the **Payback period (PB)**.

Calculating the payback period

As with the IRR, it is not possible to derive a formula for the payback period, and there are no inbuilt spreadsheet functions to do so. Therefore we either (a) calculate a running total of NPV over time to find out when the investment breaks even (i.e. pays off the initial capital outlay), or (b) sketch a graph of the NPV over time and see where this graph crosses the horizontal axis. The payback period depends on what assumptions we make about the discounting rate to apply to future cash inflows (Example 15.3.5).

Example	**15.3.5**

Q Calculate the payback period for the machine in Example 15.3.1 (i) assuming a 20% discounting rate is applied to future returns and (ii) assuming that future returns are not discounted.

A (a) When using a running total, it is best to lay the calculations out in a table. The calculations for (i) are shown in Table 15.3.3 and those for (ii) in Table 15.3.4:

Table 15.3.3 **Calculating the payback period at 20% discounting.**

Year	Cash flow (£)	DCF (£)	NPV (£)
0	−40,000.00	−40,000.00	−40,000.00
1	7,000.00	5,833.33	−34,166.67
2	8,000.00	5,555.55	−28,611.11
3	9,000.00	5,208.33	−23,402.78
4	10,000.00	4,822.53	−18,580.25
5	11,000.00	4,420.65	−14,159.59
6	12,000.00	4,018.78	−10,140.82
7	13,000.00	3,628.06	−6,512.76
8	14,000.00	3,255.95	−3,256.80
9	15,000.00	2,907.10	−349.70
10	16,000.00	2,584.09	+2,234.39
11	17,000.00	2,288.00	+4,522.38
12	18,000.00	2,018.82	+6,541.20

Table 15.3.3 shows a payback period of just over 9 years (i.e. the machine breaks even by the tenth year, when the discounting rate is 20%).

Table 15.3.4 **Calculating the payback period with no discounting.**

Year	Cash flow (£)	NPV (£)
0	−40,000	−40,000
1	7,000	−33,000
2	8,000	−25,000
3	9,000	−16,000
4	10,000	−6,000
5	11,000	+5,000

Table 15.3.4 shows the payback period is about $4\frac{1}{2}$ years when no discounting is applied.

(b) The graphical method uses the same approach employed earlier to graph NPV against discount rate, but this time we graph NPV against time. Though it is non-linear, the NPV graph has only a very shallow curve and so can be assumed to be linear over a small interval of time. Figures 15.3.5 and 15.3.6 show the graphs of NPV over time (i) applying a discounting rate of 20%, and (ii) applying no discounting rate to the future returns.

(i) At a discounting rate of 20%, after one year NPV = −34,166.67 and after ten years NPV = 2,234.39.

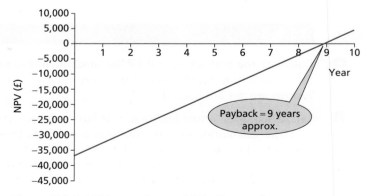

Figure 15.3.5 **NPV over time at 20% discounting.**

(ii) With no discounting, after one year NPV = −33,000 and after five years NPV = 5,000.

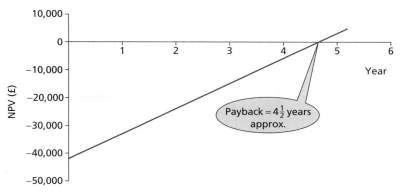

Figure 15.3.6 **NPV over time with no discounting.**

Exercises | **15.3**

1 Find the NPV of an investment requiring an outlay of £5,000 and yielding net annual revenues of £2,000, £2,000, £1,000, £1,000 and £1,000 for the ends of the next 5 years, assuming a discounting rate of 12% p.a.

2 A company can buy a machine that would yield net revenues of £50,000 p.a. for 2 years and £40,000 p.a. for a further 2 years, and can then be sold for scrap at £10,000. Using NPV at a discounting rate of 10% p.a., find the maximum price the company should pay for such a machine.

3 Show that, mathematically, repayment loans and annuities are the same and can be considered as special cases of NPV. Hence find the following:
  (a) The Net Present Value of an investment of £10,000, which yields £2,000 p.a. for 8 years at a discounting rate of 12% p.a. What difference does it make if the discounting rate is 11% p.a.?
  (b) The time taken for an investment of £5,000, yielding net benefits of £1,000, to be recouped at a discounting rate of 15% p.a.
  (c) The discounting rate, if an investment yields net returns of £1,000 p.a. over 10 years for an outlay of £5,000.

4 A firm has to choose between two machines whose operating costs fall at the **beginning** of each year:

Year	Machine 1	Machine 2
1	1,000	1,600
2	200	100
3	400	200
4	–	300
5	–	400
6	–	500

After 3 years, Machine 1 will have no scrap value and will be replaced by an identical machine with the same costs. In each case, the first year cost includes purchase, installation and running costs. In subsequent years, maintenance and running costs are included. Over a 6 year period at a 10% p.a. discounting rate, show that Machine 1 is a better buy and, using a graph, show how the discounting rate affects the decision about which machine to choose.

5 By investing £10,000 now in a machine with a life expectancy of 3 years, a company estimates it will generate returns of £5,000, £4,000 and £3,000 at the end of each year. After 3 years, the machine has no scrap value.
  (a) Find the NPV if the discounting rate is 10% p.a.

(b) Find the NPV at other discounting rates.

(c) Plot a graph of NPV against discounting rate to find the IRR.

6 A machine costs £10,000 and yields £2,000 for each year of its life. It has no scrap value at any stage. Find the IRR to the nearest $\frac{1}{2}$% if the machine lasts for 10 years. What would the IRR be if the machine lasted only 6 years? For lifetimes of 5, 10, 15, 20, etc. years, determine the IRR and plot a graph of IRR against lifetime. Explain what happens to this graph.

7 Machine *X* costs £50,000 and will yield end-of-year net revenues of £18,000 p.a. over 4 years, after which it has no scrap value. An alternative, Machine *Y*, costs £30,000 but would yield end-of-year net revenues of only £11,000 p.a. over 4 years. It also has no scrap value. Find the IRR of both machines and state which machine is the better option on the basis of IRR. Plot graphs of NPV for both machines against discounting rates of 10% to 20% in steps of 1%. What are your conclusions now? How do the results differ if machine *X* has a scrap value of £2,000 at the end of its life?

8 A machine costing £200,000 is expected to produce net profits of £10,000, £20,000, £40,000, £70,000, £95,000 and £100,000 at the end of each year. Calculate the payback period at discounting rates of 0%, 5%, 10%, 15% and 20% p.a.

9 A machine costing £10,000 is expected to produce net annual end-of-year returns of £1,800. Find the payback period at discounting rates of 0% to 16%, and draw a graph to show how it varies with discounting rate. What happens to this graph at high discounting rates? Use your graph, or otherwise, to find:

(a) the payback period if the discounting rate is 12%;

(b) the IRR of the investment if the machine has a lifetime of 7 years and no scrap value.

10 A firm faces the choice of buying either Machine 1, costing £120,000, which is expected to generate end-of-year profits of £30,000, or Machine 2, which costs £200,000 and is expected to generate end-of-year profits of £45,000. If no discounting rate is applied, which machine would you recommend? If future values are discounted at 10%, which machine would you recommend?

15.4 Chapter review

In this chapter we extended the modelling and analysis of decision problems to those in which the functions are non-linear. As the models become more realistic then the analysis becomes more complex. We have focused on only a few common non-linear decision problems, and others can be found in the further reading listed at the end of this book.

In constructing our models, we made several assumptions. In particular, we assumed that all the information was known with certainty (e.g. discounting rates and future cash flows). Most models can be extended to deal with uncertainty by introducing probabilities (see Chapter 6). For example, if future cash flows are uncertain, then as long as we know the probabilities of each cash flow occurring, we can use expected values (Section 14.3) and calculate expected NPV. However, this and similar extensions to other decision problems are beyond the scope of this book.

In Chapter 14 we saw how we could use Excel Solver to solve linear programs, and we can also use Solver to solve many non-linear problems, such as those considered in Section 15.1. Such problems are often referred to as non-linear programming problems.

For investment decision problems we have seen that there are useful inbuilt Excel functions for calculating NPV and IRR.

Chapter 16

An introduction to decision problem network models

Introduction

In Chapter 13 we saw how business decision problems could be modelled and in Chapter 14 how linear programs could address some decision problems. Linear programming is a generic approach, and although many decision problems can be formulated and solved as linear programs, there are alternative approaches available. For some decision problems alternative approaches provide deeper insights into the problem and consequently offer simpler and more easily understood and implemented solution methods. In such cases it is easier for managers to interpret the results of these solution methods and communicate them to others (e.g. people who will implement the decisions). In this chapter we look at one such alternative approach.

Chapter objectives

- To introduce the use of network diagrams to represent decision problems

- To introduce methods for solving simple network optimisation problems

- To introduce Critical Path Analysis

Chapter contents

We all use networks: for example, people network socially or at work, we use telephone and computer networks to communicate, and we use transportation networks (roads, rail, etc.) to travel. We can represent the entities that form a network (e.g. people, computers, towns) by means of a diagram. Many decision problems can be modelled as networks and represented through network diagrams similar to those that we saw in Chapter 13 (e.g. problem maps and decision trees). In this section we consider the components and notation used for drawing network diagrams. In subsequent sections we look at some specific decision problems and see how we can model the problem by means of a network and consider problem specific solution methods for such problems.

The prerequisites of this section are:
■ An introduction to decision analysis (Chapter 13);
■ An introduction to linear programming (Chapter 14);
■ Scalars, vectors, matrices and arrays (Section 2.3);
■ Subscripted variables and sigma notation (Section 2.4).

Network optimisation problems

In Chapter 13 we saw that, to formulate a decision problem as a linear program, we had to identify the objective of the decision-maker(s) and any constraints on the alternatives, and we do likewise when modelling decision problems with networks. There is a very close relationship between network models and linear programs for many decision problems, and such network models are often collectively called **network optimisation problems**. Indeed, so close is the relationship between network models and linear programs that we can formulate or convert most network optimisation problems into linear programs. However, this is beyond the scope of this introductory text, and the interested reader is referred to the further reading at the end of the book.

Nodes, arcs and conventions

A network diagram is made up of two basic components, **nodes** and **arcs**, which represent different types of entity in a decision problem. We **label** nodes and arcs so that we can see from the diagram what the entities are and how they are related. Therefore a network diagram can provide a clear picture of a decision problem, and is in itself a useful communication tool.

There are no agreed symbols or conventions for drawing network diagrams, although there have been many attempts at doing so, such as that of the ISO (International Standards Organisation). The simplest approach is to use **circles** to represent nodes (although some people use squares) and **lines** to represent arcs, which connect nodes together. Arcs can have **arrows** on them to indicate the direction of possible movement between a pair of nodes, and these are called **directed arcs**, but in some cases direction of movement is not relevant, in which case we have **undirected arcs**. Figure 16.1.1 illustrates how we draw parts of a network diagram. Directed arcs pointing left to right or top to bottom (e.g. A) are called **forward arcs**, those pointing from right to left or bottom to top are called **reverse arcs**, and some arcs can be forward and reverse (e.g. E). Arcs can be referred to either by their own label or by the pair of nodes that they connect. For example, arc A could be referred to as the 'arc connecting node 1 to node 2' or simply as (1, 2).

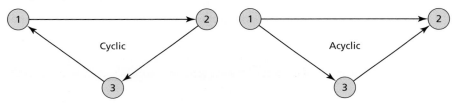

Figure 16.1.1 **Nodes connected by directed and undirected arcs.**

Network types

Networks, or more precisely network diagrams, are often classified according to the features of their arcs and nodes. For example, if all arcs are directed then we say that we have a **directed network**, and if all arcs are undirected then we have an **undirected network**. If every pair of nodes in a network is connected together then we have a **completely connected network**. In some networks it is possible to start from one node and follow some arrowed arcs, pass through some nodes and return to the same node from which we started (i.e. the network contains a loop). Such networks are said to be **cyclic**. If a network does not contain any loops then it is said to be **acyclic**. Figure 16.1.2 illustrates cyclic and acyclic completely connected directed networks.

Figure 16.1.2 **Cyclic and acyclic networks.**

Arc values (capacities)

Arcs can have values assigned to them relating to data of the entity that the arcs represent, for example the time taken to travel between two locations (nodes). In some cases the value might be the maximum that an entity can handle, for example the maximum data transmission speed on a computer network or the volume of traffic that a road, pipe or cable can handle per hour, and in such cases we refer to this as the **arc capacity**. Often the value or capacity of an arc connecting node i to node j (i.e. arc (i, j)) is denoted by using subscripted variables (Section 2.4), for example $v_{i,j}$.

Example **16.1.1**

Q A truck has to make deliveries from a depot to three retail outlets. The average travelling times between each location are given below.

From	To	Average time (mins)
Depot	Store A	45
Depot	Store B	25
Depot	Store C	50
Store A	Store B	20
Store A	Store C	30
Store B	Store A	25
Store B	Store C	15
Store C	Store A	25
Store C	Store B	20

Represent the problem by a network and describe the type of network.

A We shall represent the locations by nodes labelled 1 for the depot, 2 for store A, 3 for store B, 4 for store C, and travelling times by arc values, with $v(1, 2) = 45$, $v(2, 3) = 20$, etc., i.e.

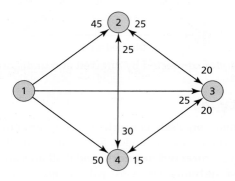

This is a directed cyclic network, but it is not completely connected (e.g. nodes 3 and 4 are not connected to node 1).

Matrix representation

Any network diagram, such as that shown in Figure 16.1.1, can be represented by a matrix (Section 2.3), in which the rows and columns are node reference numbers and the matrix elements are the corresponding arc values, as illustrated in Example 16.1.2.

| Example | **16.1.2** |

Q Write the network in Example 16.1.1 in matrix form.

A There are no reverse or return arcs from the stores to the depot, and we might assign these arcs large values (i.e. ∞). As there is no time taken in not moving (i.e. staying at a node) then we might assign the diagonal elements zero.

		To node			
		1	2	3	4
	1	0	45	25	50
From node	2	∞	0	20	30
	3	∞	25	0	15
	4	∞	25	20	0

If we denote the arc values $v(i, j)$ then we would label this matrix V.

Node values (capacities)

As with arcs, we might assign values to nodes, and sometimes nodes might have a capacity. For example, in a computer network computers represented by nodes might have a maximum data processing speed, and the cables connecting the computers will have a maximum data transmission speed. In such cases we might extend our notation for nodes so that the nodes show not only node reference numbers but also their value or capacity. Indeed we might also include in our node notation the results of calculations, see section 16.3.

Source and target nodes

In some network optimisation problems we might specify one or more nodes from which we wish to start and other nodes where we want to end. For example, in Example 16.1.1 the truck starts from the depot. Nodes from which we start are often called **source** nodes, and nodes at which we wish to end are called **target** or **destination** nodes.

Paths and chains

A **path** is a sequence of arcs or nodes from the source node to the destination node in a network. The **length** of a path is the sum of arc values of those arcs in the path: see Example 16.1.3. A **chain** is similar to a path but is just a sequence of arcs between any two nodes.

16.1.3

Q The nodes in Figure 16.1.3 represent towns on a map, and the arcs represent Sunday bus routes (some only being one way), whose values are the average times in minutes that a bus takes to travel between towns. This Sunday someone at town 2 wishes to go to town 5.

(a) Identify the source and destination nodes.
(b) Find all possible paths from the source to the destination and calculate their lengths.
(c) Find the shortest path from those in part (b).
(d) Find the longest path from those in part (b).
(e) How would your answer to (d) differ if the arc between node 1 and node 3 was reversed?

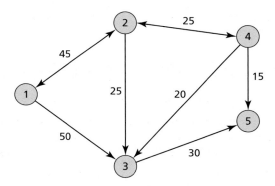

Figure 16.1.3 **Bus routes for Example 16.1.3.**

A (a) The source is node 2 and the destination is node 5.

(b) All possible paths are:

Path	Length
2, 1, 3, 5	$45 + 50 + 30 = 125$
2, 3, 5	$25 + 30 = 55$
2, 4, 5	$25 + 15 = 40$
2, 4, 3, 5	$25 + 20 + 30 = 75$

(c) The shortest path is 2, 4, 5 with length 40
(d) The longest path is 2, 1, 3, 5 with length 125
(e) The longest path would be infinite due to the loop 2, 3, 1, 2

1 The costs of linking 12 computer sites are shown below. Describe the network.

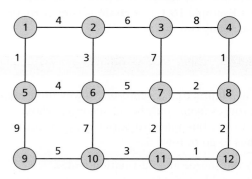

2 A parcel delivery van has to deliver to seven addresses. The road distances between all the addresses are shown below. Represent these data as a network.

From	To	Miles	From	To	Miles
A	B	15	D	E	4
A	C	10	D	G	5
B	A	13	E	C	4
B	C	3	E	D	4
B	D	6	E	F	2
B	G	17	F	E	2
C	A	10	F	G	6
C	B	3	G	B	17
C	E	4	G	D	5
D	B	6	G	F	6

3 Parcel Flight Limited (PFL) provides a mail and parcel service using available airline services between international airports. Mail and parcels are placed in containers for each destination. Having contacted several airlines PFL has identified the connecting services that it can use today and these are shown below, where the delivery times include loading, flight and unloading.

Flights		Delivery
From	To	Time
London	Sydney	40
London	Adelaide	36
Sydney	Adelaide	5
Adelaide	Sydney	7
Sydney	Toronto	21
Sydney	Rio	24
New York	Delhi	47
Toronto	Rio	11
Rio	Toronto	9
Rio	Delhi	38
Sydney	New York	28
Adelaide	New York	15
Toronto	New York	7
New York	Toronto	3
Toronto	Delhi	38

(a) Represent the data as a network.

(b) Identify the source and destination nodes if PFL wants to know the quickest way to deliver from London to Rio. Find a path from the source to destination and calculate its length.

4 Represent the networks in questions 1, 2 and 3 by matrices.

Communication and distribution decisions

In the previous section we saw how data pertaining to delivery problems could be represented by a network. In this section we consider some typical network problems and methods of finding their solution.

The prerequisites of this section are:
- Algorithms, variables and algebra (Section 2.1);
- Set notation, set properties and Venn diagrams (Section 2.5);
- Counting, factorials, permutations and combinations (Section 2.6);
- An introduction to decision analysis (Chapter 13);
- Networks and network diagrams (Section 16.1).

The minimum spanning tree problem (MSTP)

This is the one of the simplest network optimisation problems. The objective is to find a set of arcs to join all the nodes of an undirected network so that the sum of the arc values is minimised. These problems arise when we want to find the minimum quantity of some material to connect things together: for example, pipe to connect buildings to a supply (e.g. water or gas); cable to supply electricity, phone, TV services or to network computers; concrete, tarmac, track to provide roads or rail. Example 16.2.1 illustrates a typical minimum spanning tree problem.

Example

16.2.1

Q A college campus contains six buildings, which are to be connected by underground high-speed fibre optics cable. Not all pairs of buildings can be connected because of obstacles (e.g. a swimming pool). For those pairs of buildings that can be connected the costs (£10,000's) of doing so have been calculated as shown in the network below. What is the minimum cost of connecting all six buildings, and where should the cable be laid?

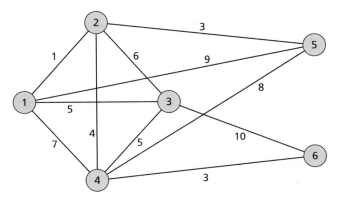

Figure 16.2.1 **The MSTP network for Example 16.2.1.**

A We could simply list all the possible combinations (Section 2.6), calculate the sums of their arc values, and pick the set of arcs with the smallest sum. For example, one possible tree (Figure 16.2.2) would be the set of arcs $(1, 2)$, $(2, 3)$, $(3, 4)$, $(4, 5)$, $(4, 6)$ with value $1 + 6 + 5 + 8 + 3 = 23$, i.e.

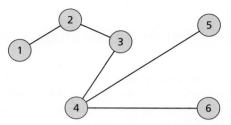

Figure 16.2.2 **A tree for Example 16.2.1.**

Another tree (Figure 16.2.3) would be defined by the arcs $(1, 2)$, $(2, 3)$, $(3, 4)$, $(4, 5)$, $(3, 6)$ with value $1 + 6 + 5 + 8 + 10 = 30$, i.e.

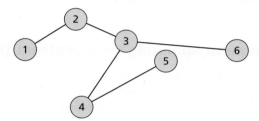

Figure 16.2.3 **A tree for Example 16.2.1.**

However, until we have listed all possible sets and compared their sums we shall not know which is the optimum (least cost) solution.

Prim's algorithm for the MSTP

If we think carefully, we can see that the solution must involve finding arcs having the smallest value. Therefore, if we look at any node, we want to connect it to its nearest/cheapest neighbour (i.e. to a node using an arc having the smallest value). For example, in Figure 16.2.1 we must connect node 6 to either node 3 or node 5 because these are the only possibilities, and as arc $(6, 4)$ has a lower value than arc $(6, 3)$ then node 3 is the cheapest/nearest node to and from node 6. Therefore, in general, we can simply pick any node and find its nearest/cheapest neighbouring node by looking at all the arc values from that node. However, we want to ensure that we connect each node only once, because it would be pointless and more expensive to connect a node to two or more others (think about the practical applications of cabling and pipe laying). The solution procedure is iterative (Section 2.2): at each iteration we need to keep a record of which nodes we have connected, and we shall call this the connected set (Section 2.5), which we shall denote by S. We also need to keep a record of the total value of the connected arcs, and we shall call this T. In Prim's algorithm we shall connect a node (i.e. put it in set S) by looking for the nearest unconnected node at each iteration and add its value $v_{i,x}$ to the total so far. It does not matter where we start, because we want to connect all nodes; when we have all nodes in set S we can stop the algorithm.

Algorithm A4 (Prim)

Step	Instructions and comments
0	Initialise the procedure by setting $S = \{1\}$ and setting $T = 0$
1	For all nodes in S find the nearest connected node and call this node x with arc value $v_{i,x}$
2	Record the arcs (i, x) Let $S = S \cup \{x\}$ Let $T = T + v_{i,x}$
3	If all nodes are in S stop, otherwise go to step 1

Example

16.2.2

Q Use algorithm A4 to find the solution to the MSTP in Example 16.2.1.

A Applying algorithm A4:

Iteration	Step	Instructions and comments
Initialise	0	$S = \{1\}$ and $T = 0$
	1	$v_{1,2} = 1$, $v_{1,3} = 5$, $v_{1,4} = 7$, $v_{1,5} = 9$, so $x = 2$
	2	$(1, 2)$ $S = \{1\} \cup \{2\} = \{1, 2\}$ $T = 0 + 1$
	3	Go to step 1
2	1	$v_{1,3} = 5$, $v_{1,4} = 7$, $v_{2,3} = 6$, $v_{2,4} = 4$, $v_{2,5} = 3$, so $x = 5$
	2	$(2, 5)$ $S = \{1, 2\} \cup \{5\} = \{1, 2, 5\}$ $T = 1 + 3 = 4$
	3	Go to step 1
3	1	$v_{1,3} = 5$, $v_{1,4} = 7$, $v_{2,3} = 6$, $v_{2,4} = 4$, $v_{5,4} = 8$, so $x = 4$
	2	$(2, 4)$ $S = \{1, 2, 5\} \cup \{4\} = \{1, 2, 4, 5\}$ $T = 4 + 4 = 8$
	3	Go to step 1
4	1	$v_{1,3} = 5$, $v_{2,3} = 6$, $v_{4,3} = 5$, $v_{4,6} = 3$, so $x = 6$
	2	$(4, 6)$ $S = \{1, 2, 4, 5\} \cup \{6\} = \{1, 2, 4, 5, 6\}$ $T = 8 + 3 = 11$
	3	Go to step 1
5	1	$v_{1,3} = 5$, $v_{2,3} = 6$, $v_{4,3} = 5$, $v_{6,3} = 10$, so $x = 3$
	2	$(1, 3)$ and $(4, 3)$ $S = \{1, 2, 4, 5, 6\} \cup \{3\} = \{1, 2, 3, 4, 5, 6\}$ $T = 11 + 5 = 16$
	3	STOP

There are two possible solutions:
(1, 2), (2, 5), (2, 4) (4, 6), (1, 3) or (1, 2), (2, 5), (2, 4) (4, 6), (4, 3), both having total cost = 16

Laying out the MSTP calculations in a matrix

It is much easier to perform the calculations by working on the matrix representation. At each iteration, we can simply tick a row and cross out a column when we connect a node (i.e. put it in set S), and to find the next nearest node we look along all the ticked rows (ignoring the crossed-out columns) for the smallest number. Example 16.2.3 illustrates the matrix calculations. When all rows have been ticked (or all columns crossed out) then we stop.

Example 16.2.3

Q Apply algorithm A4 to the matrix form of the MSTP in Example 16.2.1

A The crossed-out columns are shown shaded and the minimum arc values in the ticked rows are shown bold. We can read from the bold elements those arcs that connect the nodes to give the solution.

Iteration 0 (initialise)

		1	2	3	4	5	6
√	1	–	1	5	7	9	∞
	2	1	–	6	4	3	∞
	3	5	6	–	5	∞	10
	4	7	4	5	–	8	3
	5	9	3	∞	8	–	∞
	6	∞	∞	10	3	∞	–

$T = 0$

Iteration 1

		1	2	3	4	5	6
√	1	–	1	5	7	9	∞
√	2	1	–	6	4	3	∞
	3	5	6	–	5	∞	10
	4	7	4	5	–	8	3
	5	9	3	∞	8	–	∞
	6	∞	∞	10	3	∞	–

$T = 0 + 1 = 1$

Iteration 2

		1	2	3	4	5	6
√	1	–	1	5	7	9	∞
√	2	1	–	6	4	3	∞
	3	5	6	–	5	∞	10
	4	7	4	5	–	8	3
√	5	9	3	∞	8	–	∞
	6	∞	∞	10	3	∞	–

$T = 1 + 3 = 4$

Iteration 3

		1	2	3	4	5	6
√	1	–	1	5	7	9	∞
√	2	1	–	6	4	3	∞
	3	5	6	–	5	∞	10
√	4	7	4	5	–	8	3
√	5	9	3	∞	8	–	∞
	6	∞	∞	10	3	∞	–

$T = 4 + 4 = 8$

Iteration 4

		1	2	3	4	5	6
√	1	–	1	5	7	9	∞
√	2	1	–	6	4	3	∞
	3	5	6	–	5	∞	10
√	4	7	4	5	–	8	3
√	5	9	3	∞	8	–	∞
√	6	∞	∞	10	3	∞	–

$T = 8 + 3 = 11$

Iteration 5

		1	2	3	4	5	6
√	1	–	1	5*	7	9	∞
√	2	1	–	6	4	3	∞
√	3	5	6	–	5	∞	10
√	4	7	4	5*	–	8	3
√	5	9	3	∞	8	–	∞
√	6	∞	∞	10	3	∞	–

$T = 11 + 5 = 16$
The * denotes alternative solutions

The shortest path problem and Dijkstra's algorithm

This is perhaps one of the most frequently occurring problems in the world today and has the objective of finding the shortest path between a source and destination in a network. In Example 16.1.3 we saw a typical application of the shortest path problem, but the most common application is in sending emails from one computer to another. Other typical applications include mail and parcel systems, and these problems have become increasingly common as a result of Internet shopping. In Example 16.1.3 we found the shortest path in a network by complete enumeration (i.e. listing all paths, calculating their lengths and finding the smallest). In all but the simplest problems this could be extremely tedious and time consuming. An efficient method of solving this problem was devised by Dijkstra, and it is his algorithm that is used in all email systems. Dijkstra's algorithm finds the shortest path in a network having non-negative arc values between a source and a specified destination, and can also find the shortest path from a source to all other nodes in the network. There are numerous ways of implementing Dijkstra's method. We consider a method based on entering the data (i.e. arc values) into the columns of a table after sorting them into increasing order. We then extend the ideas used in algorithm A4 by looking for the next nearest neighbour to the source node at each iteration. At each iteration we find a shortest path to a node in the network and cross out all the arcs ending at that node. Once we reach the destination we stop. This tabular version of Dijkstra's algorithm (algorithm A5) is illustrated in Example 16.2.4.

Algorithm A5

Step	Instructions and comments
0	Initialise the procedure by creating a table with columns labelled by node numbers.
	In each column enter the arcs (with their values) that start at the column number and put them in increasing order of value.
	At the bottom of the table create a row labelled 'shortest path' and below this a row labelled 'length.'
	In the source column enter a dash in the 'shortest path' and 0 (zero) in the 'length'.
	Cross out all arcs ending at the source node.
1	Stop if the 'shortest path' and 'length' are completed in the destination column.
2	For all columns with an entry in the 'shortest path' row, take the smallest uncrossed arc in the column and add it to the 'length'. Find the smallest of all these calculations and put the arcs and the results of the calculation in the 'shortest path' and 'length' rows in the column at the end of the chain.
3	Cross out all arcs ending at the column node in step 2.
4	Go to step 1.

Example 16.2.4

Q Use algorithm A5 to find the shortest path in the network below.

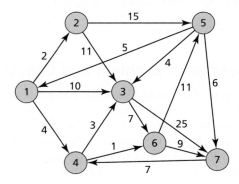

A Initialising the table:

	From node						
	1	2	3	4	5	6	7
	(1, 2) 2	(2, 3) 11	(3, 6) 7	(4, 6) 1	(5, 3) 4	(6, 7) 9	(7, 4) 7
	(1, 4) 4	(2, 5) 15	(3, 7) 25	(4, 3) 3	(5, 1) 5	(6, 5) 11	
	(1, 3) 10				(5, 7) 6		
Shortest path	–						
Length	0						

Iteration 1

The only column with an entry in the bottom rows is column 1.

The smallest uncrossed arc is $(1, 2)$

Adding the arc value to the 'length' row gives $0 + 2 = 2$ which we enter in column 2

We now cross out all arcs ending at node 2

				From node			
	1	2	3	4	5	6	7
	~~(1, 2)~~ 2	(2, 3) 11	(3, 6) 7	(4, 6) 1	(5, 3) 4	(6, 7) 9	(7, 4) 7
	(1, 4) 4	(2, 5) 15	(3, 7) 25	(4, 3) 3	~~(5, 1)~~ 5	(6, 5) 11	
	(1, 3) 10				(5, 7) 6		
Shortest path	–	(1, 2)					
Length	0	2					

Iteration 2

Columns 1 and 2 have entries in the bottom rows of the table.

Taking the smallest value uncrossed arcs and adding the value to the 'length' gives the chains:

$(1, 4)$ with $0 + 4 = 4$ and $(1, 2)$, $(2, 3)$ with $2 + 11 = 13$.

The smallest of these is $(1, 4)$, which we enter in column 4.

We now cross out all arcs ending at node 4.

				From node			
	1	2	3	4	5	6	7
	~~(1, 2)~~ 2	(2, 3) 11	(3, 6) 7	(4, 6) 1	(5, 3) 4	(6, 7) 9	~~(7, 4)~~ 7
	~~(1, 4)~~ 4	(2, 5) 15	(3, 7) 25	(4, 3) 3	~~(5, 1)~~ 5	(6, 5) 11	
	(1, 3) 10				(5, 7) 6		
Shortest path	–	(1, 2)		(1, 4)			
Length	0	0 + 2 = 2		0 + 4 = 4			

Iteration 3

Columns 1, 2 and 4 have entries in the bottom rows of the table.

Taking the smallest-value uncrossed arcs and adding the value to the 'length' gives the chains:

$(1, 3)$ with $0 + 10 = 10$; $(1, 2)$, $(2, 3)$ with $2 + 11 = 13$ and $(1, 4)$, $(4, 6)$ with $1 + 4 = 5$

The smallest of these is $(1, 4)$, $(4, 6)$ which we enter in column 6.

We now cross out all arcs ending at node 6.

				From node			
	1	2	3	4	5	6	7
	~~(1, 2)~~ 2	(2, 3) 11	~~(3, 6)~~ 7	~~(4, 6)~~ 1	(5, 3) 4	(6, 7) 9	~~(7, 4)~~ 7
	~~(1, 4)~~ 4	(2, 5) 15	(3, 7) 25	(4, 3) 3	~~(5, 1)~~ 5	(6, 5) 11	
	(1, 3) 10				(5, 7) 6		
Shortest path	–	(1, 2)		(1, 4)		(1, 4),(4, 6)	
Length	0	0 + 2 = 2		0 + 4 = 4		1 + 4 = 5	

Iteration 4

Columns 1, 2, 4 and 6 have entries in the bottom rows of the table.

Taking the smallest value uncrossed arcs and adding the value to the 'length' gives the chains:

(1, 3) with $0 + 10 = 10$; (1, 2), (2, 3) with $2 + 11 = 13$; (1, 4), (4, 3) with $4 + 3 = 7$

and (1, 4), (4, 6), (6, 7) with $5 + 9 = 14$

The smallest of these is (1, 4), (4, 3), which we enter in column 3.

We now cross out all arcs ending at node 3.

	From node						
	1	2	3	4	5	6	7
	~~(1, 2) 2~~	~~(2, 3) 11~~	~~(3, 6) 7~~	~~(4, 6) 1~~	~~(5, 3) 4~~	(6, 7) 9	~~(7, 4) 7~~
	~~(1, 4) 4~~	(2, 5) 15	(3, 7) 25	~~(4, 3) 3~~	~~(5, 1) 5~~	(6, 5) 11	
	~~(1, 3) 10~~				(5, 7) 6		
Shortest path	–	(1, 2)	(1, 4), (4, 3)	(1, 4)		(1, 4), (4, 6)	
Length	0	$0 + 2 = 2$	$4 + 3 = 7$	$0 + 4 = 4$		$1 + 4 = 5$	

Iteration 5

Columns 1, 2, 3, 4 and 6 have entries in the bottom rows of the table.

Taking the smallest value uncrossed arcs and adding the value to the 'length' gives the chains:

(1, 2), (2, 5) with $2 + 15 = 17$; (1, 4), (4, 3), (3, 7) with $7 + 25 = 32$; and (1, 4), (4, 6), (6, 7) with $5 + 9 = 14$

Note that all arcs in column 1 have been crossed out.

The smallest of these is (1, 4), (4, 6), (6, 7) which we enter in column 7.

We now cross out all arcs ending at node 7.

	From node						
	1	2	3	4	5	6	7
	~~(1, 2) 2~~	~~(2, 3) 11~~	~~(3, 6) 7~~	~~(4, 6) 1~~	~~(5, 3) 4~~	~~(6, 7) 9~~	~~(7, 4) 7~~
	~~(1, 4) 4~~	(2, 5) 15	~~(3, 7) 25~~	~~(4, 3) 3~~	~~(5, 1) 5~~	(6, 5) 11	
	~~(1, 3) 10~~				~~(5, 7) 6~~		
Shortest path	–	(1, 2)	(1, 4), (4, 3)	(1, 4)		(1, 4), (4, 6)	(1, 4), (4, 6) and (6, 7)
Length	0	$0 + 2 = 2$	$4 + 3 = 7$	$0 + 4 = 4$		$1 + 4 = 5$	$5 + 9 = 14$

Iteration 6

16.2

We now have an entry in the destination column so we stop.

The shortest path from node 1 to node 7 is (1, 4), (4, 6), (6, 7) with length 14

NOTE: We have also found the shortest paths from node 1 to nodes 2, 3, 4 and 6.

We could find the shortest paths to all remaining nodes (in this case node 5) by continuing with the algorithm until all columns are completed.

444

Exercises   **16.2**

1   Find the minimum cost solution to the MSTP in Question 1 Exercises 16.1

2   A cable TV company wishes to connect seven distribution points to a central transmitter using the minimum length of cable. The table below gives the distances (in miles) between each location.

		TO						
		1	2	3	4	5	6	7	8
	1	–	2	3	4	∞	∞	∞	∞
	2	2	–	0.5	∞	∞	3	∞	∞
	3	3	0.5	–	1.6	1.2	1.5	1	∞
FROM	4	4	∞	1.6	–	1	∞	∞	4
	5	∞	∞	1.2	1	–	∞	0.5	3
	6	∞	3	1.5	∞	∞	–	1	2
	7	∞	∞	1	∞	0.5	1	–	2.5
	8	∞	∞	∞	4	3	2	2.5	–

(a)   Find a solution to the problem if the transmitter is located at node 1.
(b)   Would the solution differ if the transmitter was to be located at node 3?

3   Find the shortest routes from node 1 to all other nodes in the network below:

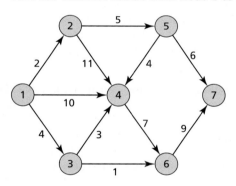

4   The distances between seven locations are given below:

		TO					
		1	2	3	4	5	6	7
	1	–	15	10	∞	∞	∞	∞
	2	15	–	3	6	∞	∞	17
	3	10	3	–	∞	4	∞	∞
FROM	4	∞	6	∞	–	4	∞	5
	5	∞	∞	4	4	–	2	∞
	6	∞	∞	∞	∞	2	–	6
	7	∞	17	∞	5	∞	6	–

(a)   Find the shortest routes from node 1 to all other nodes.
(b)   Determine the shortest routes from every node to all other nodes by applying algorithm A5 repeatedly.

5   For Question 3 of Exercises 16.1 find the shortest paths from London to all other cities.

Project planning decisions

In the previous section we saw how some common communication and distribution problems could be represented by a network and solved by minimising an objective. In this section we consider another very common decision problem that can be represented by a network model, that of project scheduling.

The prerequisites of this section are:
- An introduction to decision analysis (Chapter 13);
- Formulating decision problems as linear programs (Section 14.1);
- Networks and network diagrams (Section 16.1);
- Communication and distribution decisions (Section 16.2).

Projects and project scheduling

We all undertake **projects**, for example finding a job after graduation, and we regularly encounter them in business and management. Projects are the fundamental commodities of construction industries such as building (e.g. office blocks, power stations, manufacturing plants) and engineering (e.g. ships, aircraft, defence systems). We also encounter projects in all aspects of business and management: for example, launching a new product; analysing, designing and implementing a new computer system; undertaking a continuous improvement programme (CI). All projects have an element of uniqueness, so a mass-produced commodity (e.g. a car) is not a project, although the prototype will be.

A project comprises **activities** (e.g. jobs), all of which have to be completed in a specific order before the project can be completed. For example, a new house project might involve: finding a plot of land; employing an architect to design the house; applying for planning consent; buying the plot of land; finding and employing builders; levelling and digging the ground for foundations and services; building walls; building the roof; etc. The specific order in which activities have to be done are known as **precedence constraints**, and these are usually stated as 'activity A precedes activity B' or 'activity B depends on activity A'. It is these precedence constraints that we represent by a network model.

The main **objective** of project scheduling is to find the time when all the activities should be started and completed to get the entire project completed as quickly as possible.

A methodology

In Section 14.1 we encountered a scientific methodology for linear programming, and we follow a similar methodology for project scheduling problems. To model and solve a project-scheduling problem we need a list of all activities constituting the project, the relationship between them (i.e. precedence constraints), and the time (**duration**) that each activity requires. These data are usually obtained through a discussion with the project manager/team and with those who will undertake the activities. Having collected these data we then draw a network (see below) and present this to the project team to validate the model. At this stage we might have to redraw the network if activities are missing or precedence constraints were incorrect. It is not as easy to validate the durations of each activity, as it is possible that some activities might not have been done before. Issues concerning the estimation of activity durations and their uncertainty are beyond this introduction but can be found in the further reading at the end of this book. Once the network has been validated we can then undertake an analysis (see below) to find the earliest completion date for the project and the necessary start and completion times of each activity. As in linear programming we can undertake sensitivity analysis (e.g. consider the effect of changes to the data), and one form is called 'crashing'. However, this too is beyond the scope of this introductory text, and again can be found in the further reading at the end of the book.

Drawing project networks

There are two ways of drawing project activity networks, representing activities by nodes (activity on node) or by arcs (activity on arc). We shall use **activity on arc** networks, in which each activity is represented by a directed arc joining two nodes, one node representing the start of the activity and the other representing the end of the activity. To draw a project network we need a complete list of activities and what activities, if any, they depend on. We represent the precedence constraints by joining the start and end nodes of the activity arcs with '**dummy**' arcs, which are drawn as dotted arrowed lines to distinguish them from activity arcs. As we shall see later, we can remove many, but not all, of these dummy arcs. There are some basic rules that we must follow when drawing project scheduling networks, and we shall see later why these rules are necessary. These rules are:

- Each activity is represented by one directed arc having a start node and end node.
- Precedence constraints are represented by dummy directed arcs drawn with dotted lines.
- The entire project must start with a single node and end with a single node.
- A project network cannot have loops (i.e. it must be **acyclic**).

To draw an 'activity on arc network' we start by drawing arcs for activities having no predecessors (the initial activities) and then draw arcs for the activities that depend on these initial activities. As we draw the network we move from the left-hand side of the page to the right-hand side. When two or more activities can occur at the same time we draw their arcs below or above each other. The process of drawing arcs only when we have drawn their predecessors is continued until we have drawn arcs to represent all the activities. We can then draw dummy arcs between the end node of a predecessor and start node of an activity that depends on it. The length of the arrowed lines does not matter, so you should draw them as conveniently as possible. This procedure for drawing activity networks is illustrated in Example 16.3.1.

| Example | **16.3.1** |

Q   In a student flat, three students always share cooking and another washes up after. They have bought potatoes, baked beans and sausages for their evening meal. To peel and chop the potatoes takes one student 10 minutes; they then have to be boiled for 15 minutes before being mashed, which takes 2 minutes. The sausages take only 15 minutes to grill, and the baked beans take only 10 minutes to heat in a pan. Represent the meal as a project network, and calculate how long it takes from unwrapping the ingredients (1 minute) to eating the meal.

A First we draw up a list of activities with their precedence and duration data, and label the activities to avoid having to write the full name or description of each activity on the network.

Activity label	Activity description	Preceding activities (i.e. depends on)	Duration (time) in minutes
A	Unwrap and open ingredients	none	1
B	Peel and chop potatoes	A	10
C	Boil potatoes	B	15
D	Mash potatoes	C	3
E	Grill sausages	A	15
F	Heat baked beans	A	10
G	Serve meal on plates	D, E and F	1

To draw the network we look down the 'preceding activities' column to find those activities having no predecessors (i.e. A). The start of activity A is represented by the first node in the network and its end by a different node:

We now draw an arc to the right of activity arc A to represent activity B:

We now draw an arc to the right of activity arc A to represent activity B:

Similarly we can draw arcs for activities C and D:

Activities E and F both depend upon A and can be done at the same time as each other and at the same time as activities B, C and D:

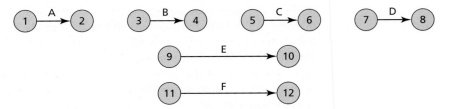

The only remaining activity is G, and this must be the last activity in our network, so we draw it as far to the right as possible:

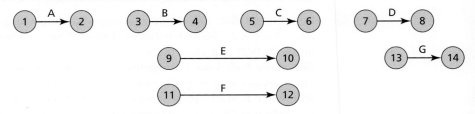

Having drawn in all the activities we can now represent their precedence constraints by drawing in dummy arcs. Activities B, E and F all depend on the completion of activity A, so we use dummy arcs to connect the end node of activity A (node 2) to the start nodes of activities B, E and F (nodes 3, 9 and 11). Activity C depends on activity B, so we draw a dummy arc from node 4 to node 5, and similarly we draw a dummy arc from node 6 to node 7. Activity G depends on the completion of activities D, E and F, so we also draw dummy arcs from nodes 8, 10 and 12 to node 13. The complete network for the project is shown in Figure 16.3.1.

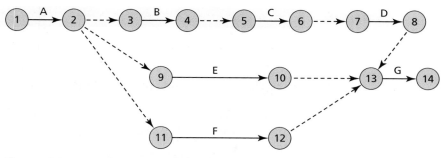

Figure 16.3.1 **A project network for Example 16.3.1.**

The dummy arcs only represent the precedence constraints and indicate that when one activity is completed another can start, so they do not take any time, and therefore dummy arcs have a zero value or duration.

From Figure 16.3.1 we can see that the path of activities A, B, C, D, G takes $1 + 10 + 15 + 3 + 1 = 30$ minutes; the path of activities A, E, G takes $1 + 20 + 1 = 22$ minutes; and the path of activities A, F, G takes $1 + 10 + 1 = 12$ minutes. Therefore it will be 30 minutes from starting the meal to sitting down and eating it, and this is the earliest time in which the project can be completed. This earliest project completion time is the longest path from the first node in the network (node 1) to the last node in the network (node 14), so when solving project scheduling problems we are finding the **longest path** in a network. This issue, and a more systematic way of calculating the longest path, are discussed in more detail below.

Simplifying project network diagrams

A useful feature of a project network diagram is that it serves as a means of communication with the project team. People involved in individual activities can see immediately how their activities are affected by preceding activities. However, this feature is useful only if the network diagram is clear and simple. When arcs cross, or where there are unnecessary dummy arcs, then network diagrams can be confusing. Therefore it pays to simplify network diagrams wherever possible.

We have seen how dummy arcs are inserted to help construct a project network. In many cases we can remove these without affecting the validity of a network model, and after some practice you will find that you can draw project networks without inserting these unnecessary dummy arcs. However, some dummy arcs are essential for representing the precedence constraints, and cannot be removed: see Example 16.3.3. There are several situations where we can remove unnecessary dummy arcs, including:

■ Where a single activity arc can be extended forwards or backwards through a dummy arc;
■ Where two or more activities have the exact same predecessors then they can start at the same node
■ If a loop is created when a dummy arc is reversed then it is unnecessary and can be removed

Examples 16.3.2 and 16.3.3 illustrate how we can simplify project network diagrams.

Example **16.3.2**

Q Remove all the unnecessary dummy arcs in Figure 16.3.1 to simplify the network diagram.

A In the chain of arcs from node 2 to node 4 we can extend the single activity B backwards without affecting the constraint that it depends on activity A. So we can remove the dummy arc from node 2 to node 3 and remove node 3 so that activity B starts at node 2. We can apply the same arguments to activities C, D, E and F:

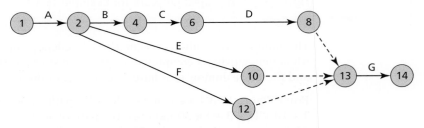

Figure 16.3.2 **A reduced project network for Example 16.3.1.**

We can also extend the single activity arc D forward through the dummy connecting node 8 to node 9 and remove node 8. Similarly we can extend activity arcs E and F through the dummy arcs leading into node 13, as shown in Figure 16.3.3.

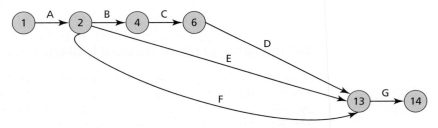

Figure 16.3.3 **A project network for Example 16.3.1 with no dummy arcs.**

Having removed unnecessary arcs and nodes we would then re-number the nodes in the network diagram.

Example **16.3.3**

Q Construct and simplify an activity network to represent the following data:

Activity label	Depends on	Duration (days)
A	–	1
B	–	2
C	A	3
D	A	4
E	B, C	2
F	B, C	1
G	E, F	2
H	E, D	3
I	E, D	2
J	G, H	7

A An initial attempt at drawing a network diagram is shown in Figure 16.3.4.

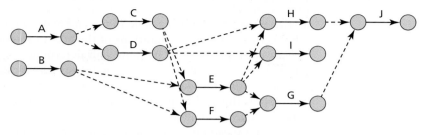

Figure 16.3.4 **Initial network for Example 16.3.3.**

The network in Figure 16.3.4 can be simplified by re-drawing. As activities E and F have the exact same predecessors then they can both start at the same node, and likewise for activities H and I. Furthermore, if we move the chain starting with activity B above that starting with activity A we can prevent dummy arcs crossing; likewise for activities E and F, and also for activities G and H, as shown in Figure 16.3.5.

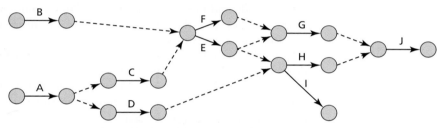

Figure 16.3.5 **Revised network for Example 16.3.3.**

Figure 16.3.5 is much easier to read than Figure 16.3.4, but it does not have a unique starting node, nor does it have a unique end node, so it is not clear where the project starts or ends. As activities A and B have no predecessors then they can both start at the same node. Similarly, as there are no activities that have activities I and J as predecessors then we can assume that both I and J finish at the end of the project, so they can both finish at the same node. Furthermore, we can remove many, but not all, of the dummy arcs (e.g. those on either side of activity C) to simplify the network diagram further. Figure 16.3.6 shows a further revised project network that satisfies all the requirements.

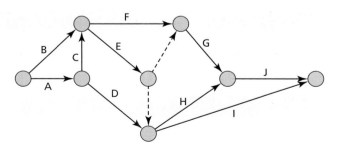

Figure 16.3.6 **A simplified network diagram for Example 16.3.2.**

NOTE: Having simplified a network diagram you should check that it still corresponds to the original problem precedence data. You can do this by reading from the diagram and checking against the original data table. We cannot remove the remaining dummy arcs in Figure 16.3.6 without contravening the precedence constraints.

Critical activities and the critical path

In Example 16.3.1 we found the earliest completion time of the project by finding all the paths from the start node to the end node of the project, calculating their lengths by summing the durations of the arcs in the paths and then finding the longest path. This longest path not only determines the earliest completion time for the project; it is also critical, in that if any activity along this path takes longer than the estimated duration then it will have an adverse effect on the project completion time. Therefore we often refer to these activities as **critical activities**, and they form a longest path in a network, which we call the **critical path**. In general we cannot list all paths because this will be extremely tedious, particularly for large networks found in the real world (e.g. a construction project might comprise millions of activities). Therefore we need a systematic method of finding the critical or longest path in a network.

The forward pass and earliest times

To find the longest path we can start at the beginning of the project network and find the longest chain to the nearest node. Then we can move forwards to the next nearest node and find the longest chain, and so on, until we reach the last node in the network (i.e. the end of the project). In other words we find the earliest time that we can be at any node in the network to ensure that all preceding activities have been completed. This process is called a **forward pass** through the network; it finds the **earliest times** at any node, and these are the earliest times activities that begin at these nodes can start (i.e. the **earliest start time of an activity**). We need to record these earliest times at each node so that we can undertake our calculations. There are many ways of recording these calculations at each node; one approach is to extend the notation used for the nodes. We shall split the circles that represent the nodes into three parts, as shown in Figure 16.3.7.

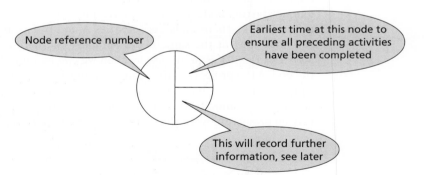

Figure 16.3.7 **An extended node notation.**

Example

16.3.4

Q Enter the activity durations onto the arcs of the network in Figure 16.3.6 and undertake a forward pass to find the earliest times at each node and the earliest completion time (days) for the project.

A We shall use the extended node notation (Figure 16.3.7) to record our calculations, and we shall assume that we can start the project immediately, so we set the earliest time at node 1 to be zero, as shown in Figure 16.3.8.

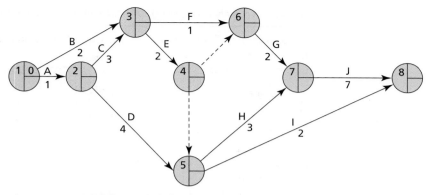

Figure 16.3.8 **Initial network for the forward pass.**

Starting from node 1, the nearest node is node 2 because activity A has a duration of 1 day whereas activity B has a duration of 2 days. Therefore the earliest that we can be at node 2 is after 1 day, as shown in Figure 16.3.9.

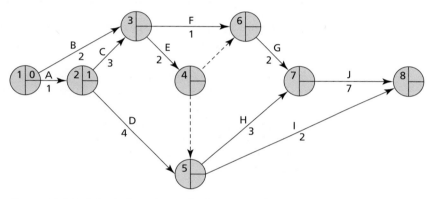

Figure 16.3.9 **Calculating the early time at node 2.**

The next nearest node is node 3, but we can arrive at node 3 by going either from node 1 along activity arc B (in which case we would arrive at node 3 after $0 + 2 = 2$ days) or from node 2 along activity arc C (in which case we would arrive at node 3 after $1 + 3 = 4$ days). Node 3 is the start of activities E and F, both of which depend upon the completion of activities B and C. To ensure that we have completed both B and C, then the earliest we can be at node 3 is after 4 days (i.e. the longest path from node 1 to node 3). Therefore, when we calculate the earliest time at any node, we look at all incoming arcs (for each incoming arc we take the earliest start time and add the duration) and then take the largest (maximum) of these calculations. The calculations for each of the nodes in Figure 16.3.9 are shown in Table 16.3.1, and the earliest times are shown on Figure 16.3.10.

Table 16.3.1 **Calculations for earliest times at each node.**

Node	Incoming arcs	Time (days)	Earliest time (day)
1	none	0	0
2	A	0 + 1 = 1	1
3	B	0 + 2 = 2	
	C	1 + 3 = 4	4
4	E	4 + 2 = 6	6
5	D	1 + 4 = 5	
	dummy	6 + 0 = 6	6
6	F	4 + 1 = 5	
	dummy	6 + 0 = 6	6
7	G	6 + 2 = 8	
	H	6 + 3 = 9	9
8	I	6 + 2 = 8	
	J	9 + 7 = 16	16

From Figure 16.3.10 we can see that the earliest we can get to node 8 is after 16 days.

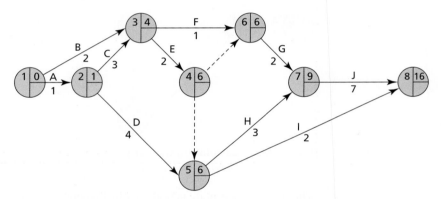

Figure 16.3.10 **The completed forward pass for Example 16.3.4.**

Therefore the earliest completion time for the project is after 16 days.

The backward pass and latest times

We have already seen that the earliest completion time of a project results from the longest (critical) path in a network, and that the activities that form this path are critical to ensuring that the project ends by its earliest completion time. We can identify these critical activities by working backwards through the network after we have found the earliest project completion time. For example, in Figure 16.3.10 we can see that the project completion time of 16 came from activity J (i.e. 9 + 7 = 16), and so J must be a critical activity, because if activity J finished later than 16 then so too would the project. Therefore we can work backwards to calculate the latest time that we can be at each node by subtracting arc durations from the latest time at their end node. For example, in Figure 16.3.10 the latest time at node 8 is 16, and by subtraction the latest time at node 7 is 16 − 7 = 9. However, the latest time at node 5 is found from either 16 − 2 = 14 (working back along arc I) or 9 − 3 = 6 (working back along arc H). Clearly the latest time at node 5 must be 6 (i.e. the smallest of the alternatives), otherwise the project would not complete by 16 days. Therefore, when calculating the latest times at a node, we work backwards, subtracting durations from latest times and taking the minimum when we have two or more alternatives. This is the opposite of the forward pass calculations, and we can put the results in the lower-right portion of the extended node notation (see Figure 16.3.7), as shown in Example 16.3.5. These latest node times are also the latest finish or completion times for activities that end at these nodes.

Example 16.3.5

Q Calculate the latest times at each node in Figure 16.3.10.

A By working backwards from node 8 to node 1 we undertake the calculations shown in Table 16.3.2, and the results are shown in Figure 16.3.11.

Table 16.3.2 **Calculations for latest times at each node.**

Node	Outgoing arcs	Time (days)	Latest time (day)
8	None	16	16
7	J	16 − 7 = 9	9
6	G	9 − 2 = 7	7
5	H	9 − 3 = 6	
	I	16 − 2 = 14	6
4	Dummy (4, 6)	7 − 0 = 7	
	Dummy (4, 5)	6 − 0 = 6	6
3	E	6 − 2 = 4	
	F	7 − 1 = 6	4
2	C	4 − 3 = 1	
	D	6 − 4 = 2	1
1	A	1 − 1 = 0	
	B	4 − 2 = 2	0

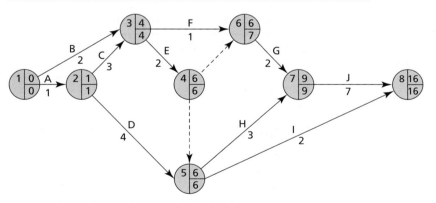

Figure 16.3.11 **The earliest and latest times at each node.**

NOTE: Had any of the latest times been lower than an earliest time, or had we not found the latest time at the starting node to be zero, then we must have made an error.

Critical path analysis

Having undertaken a forward pass to find the earliest times at each node and a backward pass to find the latest times at each node we can use these results to provide the project manager and team with useful information. The earliest times at each node are also the earliest start times for activities leading out of these nodes, and the latest times at each node are also the latest finish or completion times for activities ending at these nodes. By examining these earliest and latest times we can see that some activities must start at their earliest start time and finish at their latest finish time to ensure that the project is completed as quickly as possible. For example, from Figure 16.3.11 we can see that activity H must start at 6 and finish at 9, otherwise the project would not complete in 16 days. For activity H, the time available between the latest finish and earliest start time is $9 - 6 = 3$, which is exactly the same as its duration. However, this is not the case for all activities: for example, activity G can start as early as 6 and finish as late as 9, which gives $9 - 6 = 3$ days, but its duration is only 2 days. Therefore activity G could start 1 day late without affecting the 16-day project completion time. The difference between the time available and the duration for an activity is called the **Total Float** or **Total Slack**

For an activity: Total Float = Latest Finish – Earliest Start – duration   *(16.3.1)*

Activities that have a Total Float of zero, such as H, are those on the longest (critical) path and are critical activities, whereas those such as G are said to be non-critical and have non-zero Total Float. When undertaking a **critical path analysis** we usually list the activities, their Early Start times, their Latest Finish times and their Total Floats. Example 16.3.6 shows the results of the critical path analysis of Example 16.3.3. An examination of this information will allow the project manager or team to see what effects any changes to the activity durations will have on the project completion time. However, this is beyond the scope of this introduction, but can be found in the further reading at the end of the book.

Example **16.3.6**

Q Undertake a critical path analysis for the data in Example 16.3.3.

A The results from the forward and backward pass and equation (16.3.1) are tabulated below. The critical path is: A, C, E, H, J with an earliest project completion time of 16 days.

Table 16.3.3 **The results from a critical path analysis of Example 16.3.3.**

16.3

Activity label	Earliest start	Latest finish	Total Float	Critical
A	0	1	1 – 1 = 0	YES
B	0	4	4 – 0 – 2 = 2	NO
C	1	4	4 – 1 – 3 = 0	YES
D	1	6	6 – 1 – 4 = 1	NO
E	4	6	6 – 4 – 2 = 0	YES
F	4	7	7 – 4 – 1 = 2	NO
G	6	9	9 – 6 – 2 = 1	NO
H	6	9	9 – 6 – 3 = 0	YES
I	6	16	16 – 6 – 2 = 8	NO
J	9	16	16 – 9 – 7 = 0	YES

Exercises **16.3**

1 For the following project find the earliest completion date and critical path.

Activity	A	B	C	D	E	F	G	H
Depends on	–	–	A	A, B	B	D, E	E	C, F, G
Duration	3	2	5	4	3	4	3	1

2 Denote the earliest start time for an activity by ES and the latest finish time by LF; then we can also calculate the early finish time (EF) for an activity from ES plus duration, and a late start time (LS) for an activity from LF minus duration. For the following project find the ES, EF, LS and LF dates and the critical path.

Activity	A	B	C	D	E	F	G	H
Depends on	–	–	–	A, C	B	C	A, E	D, F, G
Duration	2	1	4	4	2	3	2	1

How can the Total Float be calculated from ES and LS or EF and LF times?

3 A firm is modifying its warehouse operation with the installation of an automated stock-handling system. Specific activities include redesigning the warehouse layout, installing new equipment, and testing the new equipment. The project management network is shown below.

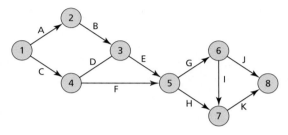

Activity	Expected time (weeks)
A	3
B	2
C	8
D	0
E	6
F	4
G	0
H	5
I	0
J	5
K	6

What is the critical path and expected completion time?

4 The Choo-Chew Restaurants group converts old railway carriages into restaurants. The activities involved in a conversion are:

Label	Activity description	Depends on	Duration
A	Purchase and renovate coaches	–	10
B	Purchase restaurant equipment	–	3
C	Hire personnel	–	1
D	Select and purchase site	–	2
E	Obtain licences	D	7
F	Prepare site	E	3
G	Move coaches to site	A, F	5
H	Install gas, water, electricity	G	4
I	Install equipment	B, H	4
J	Decorate	B, H	3
K	Stock bar and kitchen	I, J	6
L	Advertise	G	3
M	Train personnel	C, I	4
N	Undertake pilot study	K, L	7
O	Start operating fully	M, N	0

Undertake a critical path analysis to find the critical path and the earliest opening date.

5 A small project consists of 16 activities with the following details:

Activity	Depends on	Durations (days)
A	B	8
B	F	5
C	–	5
D	F, P	6
E	O	7
F	K	8
G	F	9
H	C	7
I	J	7
J	P	5
K	C	6
L	A	2
M	B, D, E, G	8
N	I, L, M	6
O	P	2
P	H	4

Undertake a critical path analysis and tabulate the ES, LF, EF, LS and Total Float for each activity.

16.4 # Chapter review

In this chapter we have seen how network diagrams can be used to represent or model some typical decision problems. Such problems are known as network optimisation problems. We have only considered three simple but frequently occurring network optimisation problems, but there are many more. For example, if we want to find the maximum quantity of material (e.g. gas, water, data, commuters) that can be sent between two locations (e.g. towns) then the network optimisation problem is known as the maximum flow problem. Another extremely common decision problem is finding the shortest circular path that starts and ends at the same node but which passes through all other nodes only once (a tour). This latter problem is called the travelling salesperson problem (TSP) and occurs when sales representatives visit their customers; when vehicles deliver to several customers (e.g. supermarket retail outlets) and return to a central depot; and for bus routes. These problems are beyond the scope of this introduction, but can be found in the further reading at the end of this book.

We have now completed the last part of this book, and laid the foundations for the more specialised areas of Decision Analysis, Operational Research and Decision Theory. This and earlier parts of the book have been limited in scope, and can serve only as a very basic introduction to Quantitative Methods for Business and Management, because the breadth and depth of the area have only been touched upon. This book has focused on what might be considered as 'traditional' or 'classical' mathematical and statistical approaches, which require many assumptions. However, the results from such approaches are often used as a starting point for more sophisticated approaches. At the other extreme, where few if any assumptions are made, and consequently traditional mathematics and statistics cannot be used, then we move into the realm of so called 'soft' analysis. One common form of 'soft' analysis is simulation, in which models are built from experience and then tested and experimented on. For example, model prototype vehicles or bridges might be built to experiment on for the effects of weather conditions, while in business and management logical computer models might be constructed to experiment with different business or economic conditions.

There are three mini-case studies at the end of this part of the book to reinforce the basic concepts in a business and management context. Although these mini-case studies can be undertaken manually or by using a calculator, they would in practice be undertaken using a spreadsheet. These mini-cases are based on the chapters as shown below.

Case	Required reading
Case C1: Firmecon	Chapter 14
Case C2: Pandbe Co.	Chapter 14
Case C3: Makit Ltd	Chapter 15
Case C4: PrintsRus	Chapter 15

When we present the results of decision analysis to decision-makers we must explain any of the assumptions that we have made so that any recommendations are qualified. Decision-makers might require further analysis to consider the effects of changes to the assumptions, and this is often called 'what if' analysis (i.e. what are the effects of changing one or more of the assumptions). Such analysis is beyond the scope of this book, and often requires the use of computer software (e.g. spreadsheets).

Case C1 — **Firmecon**

Firmecon has monitored and recorded the monthly sales of its major product line over the last 2 years, together with unit price charged. The marketing manager of Firmecon has tried different pricing strategies over this period. The fixed costs of production for this product line are £660, and the unit costs of production are £20.

Month	Price	Sales
1	25	400
2	25	410
3	25	420
4	25	400
5	25	400
6	25	415
7	30	315
8	30	300
9	30	300
10	30	320
11	30	310
12	30	300
13	27	360
14	27	370
15	27	370
16	27	360
17	27	355
18	27	375
19	28	350
20	28	340
21	28	340
22	28	350
23	28	350
24	28	340

Analyse the pricing policy and comment on possible production policies if the firm is interested in:

(a) minimising costs,

(b) maximising revenue,

(c) maximising profit.

Pandbe Co.

Pandbe Co. (a book publishing company) is about to produce a new book called *All you ever wanted to know about QM ... and were afraid to ask*. The book is to be produced in both hardback and softback editions, and Pandbe believes that it will sell all its production if it prices the hardback at £25 and the softback at £15. The softback edition is aimed at students, and includes additional worked exercises, whereas the hardback edition is aimed at teachers and libraries. Book production is undertaken in batches, and the Pandbe production department has allocated £24,000 to production of the first batch. The unit costs of production are £20 for the hardback and £12 for the softback. Pandbe produces a wide range of textbooks, and is therefore limited in the printing and binding departments. The printing department can allocate only 4,800 hours and the binding department can allocate 6,000 hours to the first batch of this book. Each softback requires 6 hours of printing and 5 hours of binding, whereas each hardback requires only 4 hours of printing but 10 hours of binding.

How should Pandbe plan production of the first batch? What advice would you give to the production, printing and binding departments?

A competitor book is similarly priced for the softback but has a higher price for the hardback, and so Pandbe decides to increase the price of the hardback by 10% on the second production run. How does this affect its production plan? Pandbe is also considering producing a softback student workbook in future production runs. How would this affect your modelling approach, and what information would you need to construct a suitable model?

Makit Ltd

Makit Ltd manufactures parts for the automobile industry. To meet the requirements of the automobile industry, it needs to reinvest in new plant and equipment on a regular basis. In order to fund replacement equipment, Makit Ltd operates a sinking fund using net end-of-year profits (after costs, tax, share dividends, etc. have been paid) through its bank. The bank offers interest on the sinking fund at 1% above the base rate, compounded at the end of each year. Six years ago Makit Ltd had £20,000 in the sinking fund and had spent 90% on replacement equipment and left the rest in the account.

Over the last 6 years the net end-of-year profits were:

Years ago	0	1	2	3	4	5
Profit (£)	200	400	500	800	1,000	900

Over the last 6 years the base rate was:

Years ago	0	1	2	3	4	5
Base rate	9	9	9	10	10	11

This year Makit Ltd has evaluated the equipment replacement options and has identified that one particular machine will not be able to cope with the expected demand over the next 6 years. Makit Ltd purchased this machine some 3 years ago at a cost of £2,200. As a result of negotiating with the suppliers of this particular machine, it has identified three possible options: (1) purchase a second identical machine for £3,000 and run the two in parallel; (2) sell its existing machine; and (3) either buy a new, higher productive capacity machine costing £8,000, or rent an equivalent machine from a leasing company. If a new machine is bought, then the company will also take out annual maintenance. Annual maintenance contracts cost £730 per machine, payable at the beginning of each year. The rental of a machine will cost £2,640 p.a. at the end of each year. Machines of this type are usually scrapped with no residual value after 6 years, but prior to that they are depreciated at 12% p.a. on a reducing balance basis. Support Makit Ltd in its equipment replacement decisions.

Case C4 — PrintsRus

PrintsRus is a high-street shop producing high-quality prints on A4 glossy photo quality paper from customer's film, digital cameras or original prints and drawings. PrintsRus purchases the A4 glossy photo quality paper in reams from a photo paper manufacturer at a unit price of £3 per ream, and the paper manufacturer will deliver any order quantity for £12. Based on past experience, PrintsRus uses 1,200 reams of this particular paper uniformly throughout the year (i.e. 100 per month). PrintsRus has a special storage room for such paper, requiring constant temperature and humidity, which costs £4 per ream per year. PrintsRus sells each A4 print at £5, and each ream of glossy photo quality paper contains 150 sheets. Advise PrintsRus on a purchasing policy.

PrintsRus has just installed a new machine for printing glossy photos on A3 paper, which it can purchase from the same photo paper manufacturer. Although the delivery charges are the same, the purchase price is £5 per ream, and owing to the increased size PrintsRus estimates storage costs at £6 per ream. Based on customer enquiries PrintsRus estimates that it will use 900 reams of A3 paper per year. How does this affect its purchasing policy?

PrintsRus is considering further expansion by way of up to 10 different sizes of paper. Each paper size will have different purchase prices, storage costs and, in general, different delivery charges (as some paper will be purchased from different sources) and a different demand. How would your model of its purchasing problem be affected?

Further reading

[1]   *Improve Your Maths: A Refresher Course*
       J. Curwin and R. Slater, 1999
       International Thomson Business Press

[2]   *Basic Business Statistics: Concepts and Applications*
       D. M. Levine, T. C. Krehbiel and M. L. Berenson,
       Tenth edition, 2005
       Prentice Hall, Upper Saddle River, New Jersey

[3]   *Model Building in Mathematical Programming*
       H. P. Williams
       Fourth edition, 1999
       John Wiley & Sons, Chichester

[4]   *Statistical Tables for Students of Science, Engineering,*
       Business, Management, Finance
       J. Murdoch and J. A. Barnes
       Fourth edition, 1998
       Macmillan, Basingstoke

[5]   *Forecasting: Methods and Applications*
       S. Makridakis, S. C. Wheelwright and R. J. Hyndman
       Third edition, 1998
       John Wiley & Sons, New York

[6]   *Operational Research: An Introduction*
       H. A. Taha
       Seventh edition, 2002
       Prentice-Hall International Editions, Upper Saddle
       River, New Jersey

[7]   *An Introduction to Management Science: Quantitative*
       Approaches to Decision Making
       D. R. Anderson, D. J. Sweeney and T. A. Williams
       Eleventh edition, 2004
       Thomson/South-Western, Mason, Ohio

[8]   *The Science of Decision Making: A Problem-based*
       Approach Using Excel
       E. V. Denardo
       2001
       John Wiley & Sons, Chichester

[9]   *Statistics for Business and Economics*
       P. G. Benson, T. Sincich and J. T. McClave
       Ninth edition, 2004
       Pearson Prentice Hall, Upper Saddle River,
       New Jersey

[10]   *Business Statistics in Practice*
       Bruce L Bowerman and Richard T O'Connell
       Fourth Edition, 2006
       McGraw-Hill Education, New York

[11]   *Introduction to Operations Research*
       Frederick S. Hillier and Gerald J. Lieberman
       Eighth Edition, 2005
       McGraw-Hill Education, New York

[12]   *Introduction to Management Science*
       Frederick S. Hillier and Mark S. Hillier
       Second edition, 2003
       McGraw-Hill Education, New York

[13]   *Statistical Techniques in Business and Economics*
       Douglas A. Lind, William G Marchal,
       Samuel A. Wathen
       Twelfth edition, 2005
       McGraw-Hill Education, New York

[14]   *O'Leary Series: Microsoft Excel 2002 Complete*
       Timothy J O'Leary and Linda I O'Leary
       2003
       McGraw-Hill Education, New York

[15]   *SPSS Survival Manual Version 12*
       Julie Pallant
       2004
       Open University Press/McGraw-Hill Education
       Europe, Maidenhead

[16]   *Using Statistics in Economics*
       Leighton Thomas
       2004
       McGraw-Hill Education Europe, Maidenhead

[17]   *Business Forecasting*
       J. Holton Wilson, Barry Keating and John Galt
       Fourth edtion, 2006
       McGraw-Hill Education, New York

Table 1

Binomial distribution

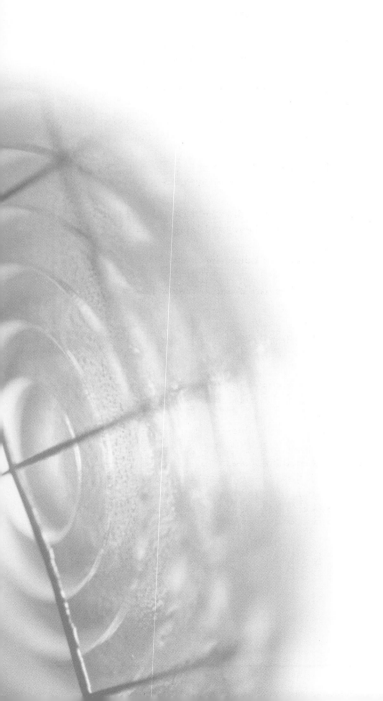

Probabilities for the Binomial distribution

n	x							Probability of success P =							
		0.01	0.02	0.03	0.04	0.05	0.1	0.15	0.2	0.25	0.3	0.35	0.4	0.45	0.5
1	0	0.9900	0.9800	0.9700	0.9600	0.9500	0.9000	0.8500	0.8000	0.7500	0.7000	0.6500	0.6000	0.5500	0.5000
1	1	0.0100	0.0200	0.0300	0.0400	0.0500	0.1000	0.1500	0.2000	0.2500	0.3000	0.3500	0.4000	0.4500	0.5000
2	0	0.9801	0.9604	0.9409	0.9216	0.9025	0.8100	0.7225	0.6400	0.5625	0.4900	0.4225	0.3600	0.3025	0.2500
2	1	0.0198	0.0392	0.0582	0.0768	0.0950	0.1800	0.2550	0.3200	0.3750	0.4200	0.4550	0.4800	0.4950	0.5000
2	2	0.0001	0.0004	0.0009	0.0016	0.0025	0.0100	0.0225	0.0400	0.0625	0.0900	0.1225	0.1600	0.2025	0.2500
3	0	0.9703	0.9412	0.9127	0.8847	0.8574	0.7290	0.6141	0.5120	0.4219	0.3430	0.2746	0.2160	0.1664	0.1250
3	1	0.0294	0.0576	0.0847	0.1106	0.1354	0.2430	0.3251	0.3840	0.4219	0.4410	0.4436	0.4320	0.4084	0.3750
3	2	0.0003	0.0012	0.0026	0.0046	0.0071	0.0270	0.0574	0.0960	0.1406	0.1890	0.2389	0.2880	0.3341	0.3750
3	3	0.0000	0.0000	0.0000	0.0001	0.0001	0.0010	0.0034	0.0080	0.0156	0.0270	0.0429	0.0640	0.0911	0.1250
		1.0000	1.0000	1.0000	1.0000	1.0000	1.0000	1.0000	1.0000	1.0000	1.0000	1.0000	1.0000	1.0000	1.0000
4	0	0.9606	0.9224	0.8853	0.8493	0.8145	0.6561	0.5220	0.4096	0.3164	0.2401	0.1785	0.1296	0.0915	0.0625
4	1	0.0388	0.0753	0.1095	0.1416	0.1715	0.2916	0.3685	0.4096	0.4219	0.4116	0.3845	0.3456	0.2995	0.2500
4	2	0.0006	0.0023	0.0051	0.0088	0.0135	0.0486	0.0975	0.1536	0.2109	0.2646	0.3105	0.3456	0.3675	0.3750
4	3	0.0000	0.0000	0.0001	0.0002	0.0005	0.0036	0.0115	0.0256	0.0469	0.0756	0.1115	0.1536	0.2005	0.2500
4	4	0.0000	0.0000	0.0000	0.0000	0.0000	0.0001	0.0005	0.0016	0.0039	0.0081	0.0150	0.0256	0.0410	0.0625
5	0	0.9510	0.9039	0.8587	0.8154	0.7738	0.5905	0.4437	0.3277	0.2373	0.1681	0.1160	0.0778	0.0503	0.0313
5	1	0.0480	0.0922	0.1328	0.1699	0.2036	0.3281	0.3915	0.4096	0.3955	0.3602	0.3124	0.2592	0.2059	0.1563
5	2	0.0010	0.0038	0.0082	0.0142	0.0214	0.0729	0.1382	0.2048	0.2637	0.3087	0.3364	0.3456	0.3369	0.3125
5	3	0.0000	0.0001	0.0003	0.0006	0.0011	0.0081	0.0244	0.0512	0.0879	0.1323	0.1811	0.2304	0.2757	0.3125
5	4	0.0000	0.0000	0.0000	0.0000	0.0000	0.0005	0.0022	0.0064	0.0146	0.0284	0.0488	0.0768	0.1128	0.1563
5	5	0.0000	0.0000	0.0000	0.0000	0.0000	0.0000	0.0001	0.0003	0.0010	0.0024	0.0053	0.0102	0.0185	0.0313
6	0	0.9415	0.8858	0.8330	0.7828	0.7351	0.5314	0.3771	0.2621	0.1780	0.1176	0.0754	0.0467	0.0277	0.0156
6	1	0.0571	0.1085	0.1546	0.1957	0.2321	0.3543	0.3993	0.3932	0.3560	0.3025	0.2437	0.1866	0.1359	0.0938
6	2	0.0014	0.0055	0.0120	0.0204	0.0305	0.0984	0.1762	0.2458	0.2966	0.3241	0.3280	0.3110	0.2780	0.2344
6	3	0.0000	0.0002	0.0005	0.0011	0.0021	0.0146	0.0415	0.0819	0.1318	0.1852	0.2355	0.2765	0.3032	0.3125
6	4	0.0000	0.0000	0.0000	0.0000	0.0001	0.0012	0.0055	0.0154	0.0330	0.0595	0.0951	0.1382	0.1861	0.2344
6	5	0.0000	0.0000	0.0000	0.0000	0.0000	0.0001	0.0004	0.0015	0.0044	0.0102	0.0205	0.0369	0.0609	0.0938
6	6	0.0000	0.0000	0.0000	0.0000	0.0000	0.0000	0.0000	0.0001	0.0002	0.0007	0.0018	0.0041	0.0083	0.0156
7	0	0.9321	0.8681	0.8080	0.7514	0.6983	0.4783	0.3206	0.2097	0.1335	0.0824	0.0490	0.0280	0.0152	0.0078
7	1	0.0659	0.1240	0.1749	0.2192	0.2573	0.3720	0.3960	0.3670	0.3115	0.2471	0.1848	0.1306	0.0872	0.0547
7	2	0.0020	0.0076	0.0162	0.0274	0.0406	0.1240	0.2097	0.2753	0.3115	0.3177	0.2985	0.2613	0.2140	0.1641
7	3	0.0000	0.0003	0.0008	0.0019	0.0036	0.0230	0.0617	0.1147	0.1730	0.2269	0.2679	0.2903	0.2918	0.2734
7	4	0.0000	0.0000	0.0000	0.0001	0.0002	0.0026	0.0109	0.0287	0.0577	0.0972	0.1442	0.1935	0.2388	0.2734
7	5	0.0000	0.0000	0.0000	0.0000	0.0000	0.0002	0.0012	0.0043	0.0115	0.0250	0.0466	0.0774	0.1172	0.1641
7	6	0.0000	0.0000	0.0000	0.0000	0.0000	0.0000	0.0001	0.0004	0.0013	0.0036	0.0084	0.0172	0.0320	0.0547
7	7	0.0000	0.0000	0.0000	0.0000	0.0000	0.0000	0.0000	0.0000	0.0001	0.0002	0.0006	0.0016	0.0037	0.0078

n	x														
8	0	0.0039	0.0084	0.0168	0.0319	0.0576	0.1001	0.1678	0.2725	0.4305	0.6634	0.7214	0.7837	0.8508	0.9227
8	1	0.0313	0.0548	0.0896	0.1373	0.1977	0.2670	0.3355	0.3847	0.3826	0.2793	0.2405	0.1939	0.1389	0.0746
8	2	0.1094	0.1569	0.2090	0.2587	0.2965	0.3115	0.2936	0.2376	0.1488	0.0515	0.0351	0.0210	0.0099	0.0026
8	3	0.2188	0.2568	0.2787	0.2786	0.2541	0.2076	0.1468	0.0839	0.0331	0.0054	0.0029	0.0013	0.0004	0.0001
8	4	0.2734	0.2627	0.2322	0.1875	0.1361	0.0865	0.0459	0.0185	0.0046	0.0004	0.0002	0.0001	0.0000	0.0000
8	5	0.2188	0.1719	0.1239	0.0808	0.0467	0.0231	0.0092	0.0026	0.0004	0.0000	0.0000	0.0000	0.0000	0.0000
8	6	0.1094	0.0703	0.0413	0.0217	0.0100	0.0038	0.0011	0.0002	0.0000	0.0000	0.0000	0.0000	0.0000	0.0000
8	7	0.0313	0.0164	0.0079	0.0033	0.0012	0.0004	0.0001	0.0000	0.0000	0.0000	0.0000	0.0000	0.0000	0.0000
8	8	0.0039	0.0017	0.0007	0.0002	0.0001	0.0000	0.0000	0.0000	0.0000	0.0000	0.0000	0.0000	0.0000	0.0000
9	0	0.0020	0.0046	0.0101	0.0207	0.0404	0.0751	0.1342	0.2316	0.3874	0.6302	0.6925	0.7602	0.8337	0.9135
9	1	0.0176	0.0339	0.0605	0.1004	0.1556	0.2253	0.3020	0.3679	0.3874	0.2985	0.2597	0.2116	0.1531	0.0830
9	2	0.0703	0.1110	0.1612	0.2162	0.2668	0.3003	0.3020	0.2597	0.1722	0.0629	0.0433	0.0262	0.0125	0.0034
9	3	0.1641	0.2119	0.2508	0.2716	0.2668	0.2336	0.1762	0.1069	0.0446	0.0077	0.0042	0.0019	0.0006	0.0001
9	4	0.2461	0.2600	0.2508	0.2194	0.1715	0.1168	0.0661	0.0283	0.0074	0.0006	0.0003	0.0001	0.0000	0.0000
9	5	0.2461	0.2128	0.1672	0.1181	0.0735	0.0389	0.0165	0.0050	0.0008	0.0000	0.0000	0.0000	0.0000	0.0000
9	6	0.1641	0.1160	0.0743	0.0424	0.0210	0.0087	0.0028	0.0006	0.0001	0.0000	0.0000	0.0000	0.0000	0.0000
9	7	0.0703	0.0407	0.0212	0.0098	0.0039	0.0012	0.0003	0.0000	0.0000	0.0000	0.0000	0.0000	0.0000	0.0000
9	8	0.0176	0.0083	0.0035	0.0013	0.0004	0.0001	0.0000	0.0000	0.0000	0.0000	0.0000	0.0000	0.0000	0.0000
9	9	0.0020	0.0008	0.0003	0.0001	0.0000	0.0000	0.0000	0.0000	0.0000	0.0000	0.0000	0.0000	0.0000	0.0000
10	0	0.0010	0.0025	0.0060	0.0135	0.0282	0.0563	0.1074	0.1969	0.3487	0.5987	0.6648	0.7374	0.8171	0.9044
10	1	0.0098	0.0207	0.0403	0.0725	0.1211	0.1877	0.2684	0.3474	0.3874	0.3151	0.2770	0.2281	0.1667	0.0914
10	2	0.0439	0.0763	0.1209	0.1757	0.2335	0.2816	0.3020	0.2759	0.1937	0.0746	0.0519	0.0317	0.0153	0.0042
10	3	0.1172	0.1665	0.2150	0.2522	0.2668	0.2503	0.2013	0.1298	0.0574	0.0105	0.0058	0.0026	0.0008	0.0001
10	4	0.2051	0.2384	0.2508	0.2377	0.2001	0.1460	0.0881	0.0401	0.0112	0.0010	0.0004	0.0001	0.0000	0.0000
10	5	0.2461	0.2340	0.2007	0.1536	0.1029	0.0584	0.0264	0.0085	0.0015	0.0001	0.0000	0.0000	0.0000	0.0000
10	6	0.2051	0.1596	0.1115	0.0689	0.0368	0.0162	0.0055	0.0012	0.0001	0.0000	0.0000	0.0000	0.0000	0.0000
10	7	0.1172	0.0746	0.0425	0.0212	0.0090	0.0031	0.0008	0.0001	0.0000	0.0000	0.0000	0.0000	0.0000	0.0000
10	8	0.0439	0.0229	0.0106	0.0043	0.0014	0.0004	0.0001	0.0000	0.0000	0.0000	0.0000	0.0000	0.0000	0.0000
10	9	0.0098	0.0042	0.0016	0.0005	0.0001	0.0000	0.0000	0.0000	0.0000	0.0000	0.0000	0.0000	0.0000	0.0000
10	10	0.0010	0.0003	0.0001	0.0000	0.0000	0.0000	0.0000	0.0000	0.0000	0.0000	0.0000	0.0000	0.0000	0.0000
11	0	0.0005	0.0014	0.0036	0.0088	0.0198	0.0422	0.0859	0.1673	0.3138	0.5688	0.6382	0.7153	0.8007	0.8953
11	1	0.0054	0.0125	0.0266	0.0518	0.0932	0.1549	0.2362	0.3248	0.3835	0.3293	0.2925	0.2433	0.1798	0.0995
11	2	0.0269	0.0513	0.0887	0.1395	0.1998	0.2581	0.2953	0.2866	0.2131	0.0867	0.0609	0.0376	0.0183	0.0050
11	3	0.0806	0.1259	0.1774	0.2254	0.2568	0.2581	0.2215	0.1517	0.0710	0.0137	0.0076	0.0035	0.0011	0.0002
11	4	0.1611	0.2060	0.2365	0.2428	0.2201	0.1721	0.1107	0.0536	0.0158	0.0014	0.0006	0.0002	0.0000	0.0000
11	5	0.2256	0.2360	0.2207	0.1830	0.1321	0.0803	0.0388	0.0132	0.0025	0.0001	0.0000	0.0000	0.0000	0.0000
11	6	0.2256	0.1931	0.1471	0.0985	0.0566	0.0268	0.0097	0.0023	0.0003	0.0000	0.0000	0.0000	0.0000	0.0000
11	7	0.1611	0.1128	0.0701	0.0379	0.0173	0.0064	0.0017	0.0003	0.0000	0.0000	0.0000	0.0000	0.0000	0.0000
11	8	0.0806	0.0462	0.0234	0.0102	0.0037	0.0011	0.0002	0.0000	0.0000	0.0000	0.0000	0.0000	0.0000	0.0000
11	9	0.0269	0.0126	0.0052	0.0018	0.0005	0.0001	0.0000	0.0000	0.0000	0.0000	0.0000	0.0000	0.0000	0.0000
11	10	0.0054	0.0021	0.0007	0.0002	0.0000	0.0000	0.0000	0.0000	0.0000	0.0000	0.0000	0.0000	0.0000	0.0000
11	11	0.0005	0.0002	0.0000	0.0000	0.0000	0.0000	0.0000	0.0000	0.0000	0.0000	0.0000	0.0000	0.0000	0.0000

(continued)

Probabilities for the Binomial distribution (cont.)

Probability of success $P =$

n	x	0.01	0.02	0.03	0.04	0.05	0.1	0.15	0.2	0.25	0.3	0.35	0.4	0.45	0.5
12	0	0.8864	0.7847	0.6938	0.6127	0.5404	0.2824	0.1422	0.0687	0.0317	0.0138	0.0057	0.0022	0.0008	0.0002
12	1	0.1074	0.1922	0.2575	0.3064	0.3413	0.3766	0.3012	0.2062	0.1267	0.0712	0.0368	0.0174	0.0075	0.0029
12	2	0.0060	0.0216	0.0438	0.0702	0.0988	0.2301	0.2924	0.2835	0.2323	0.1678	0.1088	0.0639	0.0339	0.0161
12	3	0.0002	0.0015	0.0045	0.0098	0.0173	0.0852	0.1720	0.2362	0.2581	0.2397	0.1954	0.1419	0.0923	0.0537
12	4	0.0000	0.0001	0.0003	0.0009	0.0021	0.0213	0.0683	0.1329	0.1936	0.2311	0.2367	0.2128	0.1700	0.1208
12	5	0.0000	0.0000	0.0000	0.0001	0.0002	0.0038	0.0193	0.0532	0.1032	0.1585	0.2039	0.2270	0.2225	0.1934
12	6	0.0000	0.0000	0.0000	0.0000	0.0000	0.0005	0.0040	0.0155	0.0401	0.0792	0.1281	0.1766	0.2124	0.2256
12	7	0.0000	0.0000	0.0000	0.0000	0.0000	0.0000	0.0006	0.0033	0.0115	0.0291	0.0591	0.1009	0.1489	0.1934
12	8	0.0000	0.0000	0.0000	0.0000	0.0000	0.0000	0.0001	0.0005	0.0024	0.0078	0.0199	0.0420	0.0762	0.1208
12	9	0.0000	0.0000	0.0000	0.0000	0.0000	0.0000	0.0000	0.0001	0.0004	0.0015	0.0048	0.0125	0.0277	0.0537
12	10	0.0000	0.0000	0.0000	0.0000	0.0000	0.0000	0.0000	0.0000	0.0000	0.0002	0.0008	0.0025	0.0068	0.0161
12	11	0.0000	0.0000	0.0000	0.0000	0.0000	0.0000	0.0000	0.0000	0.0000	0.0000	0.0001	0.0003	0.0010	0.0029
12	12	0.0000	0.0000	0.0000	0.0000	0.0000	0.0000	0.0000	0.0000	0.0000	0.0000	0.0000	0.0000	0.0001	0.0002
13	0	0.8775	0.7690	0.6730	0.5882	0.5133	0.2542	0.1209	0.0550	0.0238	0.0097	0.0037	0.0013	0.0004	0.0001
13	1	0.1152	0.2040	0.2706	0.3186	0.3512	0.3672	0.2774	0.1787	0.1029	0.0540	0.0259	0.0113	0.0045	0.0016
13	2	0.0070	0.0250	0.0502	0.0797	0.1109	0.2448	0.2937	0.2680	0.2059	0.1388	0.0836	0.0453	0.0220	0.0095
13	3	0.0003	0.0019	0.0057	0.0122	0.0214	0.0997	0.1900	0.2457	0.2517	0.2181	0.1651	0.1107	0.0660	0.0349
13	4	0.0000	0.0001	0.0004	0.0013	0.0028	0.0277	0.0838	0.1535	0.2097	0.2337	0.2222	0.1845	0.1350	0.0873
13	5	0.0000	0.0000	0.0000	0.0001	0.0003	0.0055	0.0266	0.0691	0.1258	0.1803	0.2154	0.2214	0.1989	0.1571
13	6	0.0000	0.0000	0.0000	0.0000	0.0000	0.0008	0.0063	0.0230	0.0559	0.1030	0.1546	0.1968	0.2169	0.2095
13	7	0.0000	0.0000	0.0000	0.0000	0.0000	0.0001	0.0011	0.0058	0.0186	0.0442	0.0833	0.1312	0.1775	0.2095
13	8	0.0000	0.0000	0.0000	0.0000	0.0000	0.0000	0.0001	0.0011	0.0047	0.0142	0.0336	0.0656	0.1089	0.1571
13	9	0.0000	0.0000	0.0000	0.0000	0.0000	0.0000	0.0000	0.0001	0.0009	0.0034	0.0101	0.0243	0.0495	0.0873
13	10	0.0000	0.0000	0.0000	0.0000	0.0000	0.0000	0.0000	0.0000	0.0001	0.0006	0.0022	0.0065	0.0162	0.0349
13	11	0.0000	0.0000	0.0000	0.0000	0.0000	0.0000	0.0000	0.0000	0.0000	0.0001	0.0003	0.0012	0.0036	0.0095
13	12	0.0000	0.0000	0.0000	0.0000	0.0000	0.0000	0.0000	0.0000	0.0000	0.0000	0.0000	0.0001	0.0005	0.0016
13	13	0.0000	0.0000	0.0000	0.0000	0.0000	0.0000	0.0000	0.0000	0.0000	0.0000	0.0000	0.0000	0.0000	0.0001
14	0	0.8687	0.7536	0.6528	0.5647	0.4877	0.2288	0.1028	0.0440	0.0178	0.0068	0.0024	0.0008	0.0002	0.0001
14	1	0.1229	0.2153	0.2827	0.3294	0.3593	0.3559	0.2539	0.1539	0.0832	0.0407	0.0181	0.0073	0.0027	0.0009
14	2	0.0081	0.0286	0.0568	0.0892	0.1229	0.2570	0.2912	0.2501	0.1802	0.1134	0.0634	0.0317	0.0141	0.0056
14	3	0.0003	0.0023	0.0070	0.0149	0.0259	0.1142	0.2056	0.2501	0.2402	0.1943	0.1366	0.0845	0.0462	0.0222
14	4	0.0000	0.0001	0.0006	0.0017	0.0037	0.0349	0.0998	0.1720	0.2202	0.2290	0.2022	0.1549	0.1040	0.0611
14	5	0.0000	0.0000	0.0000	0.0001	0.0004	0.0078	0.0352	0.0860	0.1468	0.1963	0.2178	0.2066	0.1701	0.1222
14	6	0.0000	0.0000	0.0000	0.0000	0.0000	0.0013	0.0093	0.0322	0.0734	0.1262	0.1759	0.2066	0.2088	0.1833
14	7	0.0000	0.0000	0.0000	0.0000	0.0000	0.0002	0.0019	0.0092	0.0280	0.0618	0.1082	0.1574	0.1952	0.2095
14	8	0.0000	0.0000	0.0000	0.0000	0.0000	0.0000	0.0003	0.0020	0.0082	0.0232	0.0510	0.0918	0.1398	0.1833
14	9	0.0000	0.0000	0.0000	0.0000	0.0000	0.0000	0.0000	0.0003	0.0018	0.0066	0.0183	0.0408	0.0762	0.1222
14	10	0.0000	0.0000	0.0000	0.0000	0.0000	0.0000	0.0000	0.0000	0.0003	0.0014	0.0049	0.0136	0.0312	0.0611
14	11	0.0000	0.0000	0.0000	0.0000	0.0000	0.0000	0.0000	0.0000	0.0000	0.0002	0.0010	0.0033	0.0093	0.0222
14	12	0.0000	0.0000	0.0000	0.0000	0.0000	0.0000	0.0000	0.0000	0.0000	0.0000	0.0001	0.0005	0.0019	0.0056
14	13	0.0000	0.0000	0.0000	0.0000	0.0000	0.0000	0.0000	0.0000	0.0000	0.0000	0.0000	0.0001	0.0002	0.0009

n	x	0.01	0.02	0.03	0.04	0.05	0.10	0.15	0.20	0.25	0.30	0.35	0.40	0.45	0.50
14	14	0.0000	0.0000	0.0000	0.0000	0.0000	0.0000	0.0000	0.0000	0.0000	0.0000	0.0000	0.0000	0.0000	0.0001
15	0	0.8601	0.7386	0.6333	0.5421	0.4633	0.2059	0.0874	0.0352	0.0134	0.0047	0.0016	0.0005	0.0001	0.0000
15	1	0.1303	0.2261	0.2938	0.3388	0.3658	0.3432	0.2312	0.1319	0.0668	0.0305	0.0126	0.0047	0.0016	0.0005
15	2	0.0092	0.0323	0.0636	0.0988	0.1348	0.2669	0.2856	0.2309	0.1559	0.0916	0.0476	0.0219	0.0090	0.0032
15	3	0.0004	0.0029	0.0085	0.0178	0.0307	0.1285	0.2184	0.2501	0.2252	0.1700	0.1110	0.0634	0.0318	0.0139
15	4	0.0000	0.0002	0.0008	0.0022	0.0049	0.0428	0.1156	0.1876	0.2252	0.2186	0.1792	0.1268	0.0780	0.0417
15	5	0.0000	0.0000	0.0001	0.0002	0.0006	0.0105	0.0449	0.1032	0.1651	0.2061	0.2123	0.1859	0.1404	0.0916
15	6	0.0000	0.0000	0.0000	0.0000	0.0000	0.0019	0.0132	0.0430	0.0917	0.1472	0.1906	0.2066	0.1914	0.1527
15	7	0.0000	0.0000	0.0000	0.0000	0.0000	0.0003	0.0030	0.0138	0.0393	0.0811	0.1319	0.1771	0.2013	0.1964
15	8	0.0000	0.0000	0.0000	0.0000	0.0000	0.0000	0.0005	0.0035	0.0131	0.0348	0.0710	0.1181	0.1647	0.1964
15	9	0.0000	0.0000	0.0000	0.0000	0.0000	0.0000	0.0001	0.0007	0.0034	0.0116	0.0298	0.0612	0.1048	0.1527
15	10	0.0000	0.0000	0.0000	0.0000	0.0000	0.0000	0.0000	0.0001	0.0007	0.0030	0.0096	0.0245	0.0515	0.0916
15	11	0.0000	0.0000	0.0000	0.0000	0.0000	0.0000	0.0000	0.0000	0.0001	0.0006	0.0024	0.0074	0.0191	0.0417
15	12	0.0000	0.0000	0.0000	0.0000	0.0000	0.0000	0.0000	0.0000	0.0000	0.0001	0.0004	0.0016	0.0052	0.0139
15	13	0.0000	0.0000	0.0000	0.0000	0.0000	0.0000	0.0000	0.0000	0.0000	0.0000	0.0001	0.0003	0.0010	0.0032
15	14	0.0000	0.0000	0.0000	0.0000	0.0000	0.0000	0.0000	0.0000	0.0000	0.0000	0.0000	0.0000	0.0001	0.0005
15	15	0.0000	0.0000	0.0000	0.0000	0.0000	0.0000	0.0000	0.0000	0.0000	0.0000	0.0000	0.0000	0.0000	0.0000
16	0	0.8515	0.7238	0.6143	0.5204	0.4401	0.1853	0.0743	0.0281	0.0100	0.0033	0.0010	0.0003	0.0001	0.0000
16	1	0.1376	0.2363	0.3040	0.3469	0.3706	0.3294	0.2097	0.1126	0.0535	0.0228	0.0087	0.0030	0.0009	0.0002
16	2	0.0104	0.0362	0.0705	0.1084	0.1463	0.2745	0.2775	0.2111	0.1336	0.0732	0.0353	0.0150	0.0056	0.0018
16	3	0.0005	0.0034	0.0102	0.0211	0.0359	0.1423	0.2285	0.2463	0.2079	0.1465	0.0888	0.0468	0.0215	0.0085
16	4	0.0000	0.0002	0.0010	0.0029	0.0061	0.0514	0.1311	0.2001	0.2252	0.2040	0.1553	0.1014	0.0572	0.0278
16	5	0.0000	0.0000	0.0001	0.0003	0.0008	0.0137	0.0555	0.1201	0.1802	0.2099	0.2008	0.1623	0.1123	0.0667
16	6	0.0000	0.0000	0.0000	0.0000	0.0001	0.0028	0.0180	0.0550	0.1101	0.1649	0.1982	0.1983	0.1684	0.1222
16	7	0.0000	0.0000	0.0000	0.0000	0.0000	0.0004	0.0045	0.0197	0.0524	0.1010	0.1524	0.1889	0.1969	0.1746
16	8	0.0000	0.0000	0.0000	0.0000	0.0000	0.0001	0.0009	0.0055	0.0197	0.0487	0.0923	0.1417	0.1812	0.1964
16	9	0.0000	0.0000	0.0000	0.0000	0.0000	0.0000	0.0001	0.0012	0.0058	0.0185	0.0442	0.0840	0.1318	0.1746
16	10	0.0000	0.0000	0.0000	0.0000	0.0000	0.0000	0.0000	0.0002	0.0014	0.0056	0.0167	0.0392	0.0755	0.1222
16	11	0.0000	0.0000	0.0000	0.0000	0.0000	0.0000	0.0000	0.0000	0.0002	0.0013	0.0049	0.0142	0.0337	0.0667
16	12	0.0000	0.0000	0.0000	0.0000	0.0000	0.0000	0.0000	0.0000	0.0000	0.0002	0.0011	0.0040	0.0115	0.0278
16	13	0.0000	0.0000	0.0000	0.0000	0.0000	0.0000	0.0000	0.0000	0.0000	0.0000	0.0002	0.0008	0.0029	0.0085
16	14	0.0000	0.0000	0.0000	0.0000	0.0000	0.0000	0.0000	0.0000	0.0000	0.0000	0.0000	0.0001	0.0005	0.0018
16	15	0.0000	0.0000	0.0000	0.0000	0.0000	0.0000	0.0000	0.0000	0.0000	0.0000	0.0000	0.0000	0.0001	0.0002
16	16	0.0000	0.0000	0.0000	0.0000	0.0000	0.0000	0.0000	0.0000	0.0000	0.0000	0.0000	0.0000	0.0000	0.0000
17	0	0.8429	0.7093	0.5958	0.4996	0.4181	0.1668	0.0631	0.0225	0.0075	0.0023	0.0007	0.0002	0.0000	0.0000
17	1	0.1447	0.2461	0.3133	0.3539	0.3741	0.3150	0.1893	0.0957	0.0426	0.0169	0.0060	0.0019	0.0005	0.0001
17	2	0.0117	0.0402	0.0775	0.1180	0.1575	0.2800	0.2673	0.1914	0.1136	0.0581	0.0260	0.0102	0.0035	0.0010
17	3	0.0006	0.0041	0.0120	0.0246	0.0415	0.1556	0.2359	0.2393	0.1893	0.1245	0.0701	0.0341	0.0144	0.0052
17	4	0.0000	0.0003	0.0013	0.0036	0.0076	0.0605	0.1457	0.2093	0.2209	0.1868	0.1320	0.0796	0.0411	0.0182
17	5	0.0000	0.0000	0.0001	0.0004	0.0010	0.0175	0.0668	0.1361	0.1914	0.2081	0.1849	0.1379	0.0875	0.0472
17	6	0.0000	0.0000	0.0000	0.0000	0.0001	0.0039	0.0236	0.0680	0.1276	0.1784	0.1991	0.1839	0.1432	0.0944
17	7	0.0000	0.0000	0.0000	0.0000	0.0000	0.0007	0.0065	0.0267	0.0668	0.1201	0.1685	0.1927	0.1841	0.1484
17	8	0.0000	0.0000	0.0000	0.0000	0.0000	0.0001	0.0014	0.0084	0.0279	0.0644	0.1134	0.1606	0.1883	0.1855

(continued)

Probabilities for the Binomial distribution (cont.)

Probability of success P =

n	x	0.01	0.02	0.03	0.04	0.05	0.1	0.15	0.2	0.25	0.3	0.35	0.4	0.45	0.5
17	9	0.0000	0.0000	0.0000	0.0000	0.0000	0.0000	0.0003	0.0021	0.0093	0.0276	0.0611	0.1070	0.1540	0.1855
17	10	0.0000	0.0000	0.0000	0.0000	0.0000	0.0000	0.0000	0.0004	0.0025	0.0095	0.0263	0.0571	0.1008	0.1484
17	11	0.0000	0.0000	0.0000	0.0000	0.0000	0.0000	0.0000	0.0001	0.0005	0.0026	0.0090	0.0242	0.0525	0.0944
17	12	0.0000	0.0000	0.0000	0.0000	0.0000	0.0000	0.0000	0.0000	0.0001	0.0006	0.0024	0.0081	0.0215	0.0472
17	13	0.0000	0.0000	0.0000	0.0000	0.0000	0.0000	0.0000	0.0000	0.0000	0.0001	0.0005	0.0021	0.0068	0.0182
17	14	0.0000	0.0000	0.0000	0.0000	0.0000	0.0000	0.0000	0.0000	0.0000	0.0000	0.0001	0.0004	0.0016	0.0052
17	15	0.0000	0.0000	0.0000	0.0000	0.0000	0.0000	0.0000	0.0000	0.0000	0.0000	0.0000	0.0001	0.0003	0.0010
17	16	0.0000	0.0000	0.0000	0.0000	0.0000	0.0000	0.0000	0.0000	0.0000	0.0000	0.0000	0.0000	0.0000	0.0001
17	17	0.0000	0.0000	0.0000	0.0000	0.0000	0.0000	0.0000	0.0000	0.0000	0.0000	0.0000	0.0000	0.0000	0.0000
18	0	0.8345	0.6951	0.5780	0.4796	0.3972	0.1501	0.0536	0.0180	0.0056	0.0016	0.0004	0.0001	0.0000	0.0000
18	1	0.1517	0.2554	0.3217	0.3597	0.3763	0.3002	0.1704	0.0811	0.0338	0.0126	0.0042	0.0012	0.0003	0.0001
18	2	0.0130	0.0443	0.0846	0.1274	0.1683	0.2835	0.2556	0.1723	0.0958	0.0458	0.0190	0.0069	0.0022	0.0006
18	3	0.0007	0.0048	0.0140	0.0283	0.0473	0.1680	0.2406	0.2297	0.1704	0.1046	0.0547	0.0246	0.0095	0.0031
18	4	0.0000	0.0004	0.0016	0.0044	0.0093	0.0700	0.1592	0.2153	0.2130	0.1681	0.1104	0.0614	0.0291	0.0117
18	5	0.0000	0.0000	0.0001	0.0005	0.0014	0.0218	0.0787	0.1507	0.1988	0.2017	0.1664	0.1146	0.0666	0.0327
18	6	0.0000	0.0000	0.0000	0.0000	0.0002	0.0052	0.0301	0.0816	0.1436	0.1873	0.1941	0.1655	0.1181	0.0708
18	7	0.0000	0.0000	0.0000	0.0000	0.0000	0.0010	0.0091	0.0350	0.0820	0.1376	0.1792	0.1892	0.1657	0.1214
18	8	0.0000	0.0000	0.0000	0.0000	0.0000	0.0002	0.0022	0.0120	0.0376	0.0811	0.1327	0.1734	0.1864	0.1669
18	9	0.0000	0.0000	0.0000	0.0000	0.0000	0.0000	0.0004	0.0033	0.0139	0.0386	0.0794	0.1284	0.1694	0.1855
18	10	0.0000	0.0000	0.0000	0.0000	0.0000	0.0000	0.0001	0.0008	0.0042	0.0149	0.0385	0.0771	0.1248	0.1669
18	11	0.0000	0.0000	0.0000	0.0000	0.0000	0.0000	0.0000	0.0001	0.0010	0.0046	0.0151	0.0374	0.0742	0.1214
18	12	0.0000	0.0000	0.0000	0.0000	0.0000	0.0000	0.0000	0.0000	0.0002	0.0012	0.0047	0.0145	0.0354	0.0708
18	13	0.0000	0.0000	0.0000	0.0000	0.0000	0.0000	0.0000	0.0000	0.0000	0.0002	0.0012	0.0045	0.0134	0.0327
18	14	0.0000	0.0000	0.0000	0.0000	0.0000	0.0000	0.0000	0.0000	0.0000	0.0000	0.0002	0.0011	0.0039	0.0117
18	15	0.0000	0.0000	0.0000	0.0000	0.0000	0.0000	0.0000	0.0000	0.0000	0.0000	0.0000	0.0002	0.0009	0.0031
18	16	0.0000	0.0000	0.0000	0.0000	0.0000	0.0000	0.0000	0.0000	0.0000	0.0000	0.0000	0.0000	0.0001	0.0006
18	17	0.0000	0.0000	0.0000	0.0000	0.0000	0.0000	0.0000	0.0000	0.0000	0.0000	0.0000	0.0000	0.0000	0.0001
18	18	0.0000	0.0000	0.0000	0.0000	0.0000	0.0000	0.0000	0.0000	0.0000	0.0000	0.0000	0.0000	0.0000	0.0000
19	0	0.8262	0.6812	0.5606	0.4604	0.3774	0.1351	0.0456	0.0144	0.0042	0.0011	0.0003	0.0001	0.0000	0.0000
19	1	0.1586	0.2642	0.3294	0.3645	0.3774	0.2852	0.1529	0.0685	0.0268	0.0093	0.0029	0.0008	0.0002	0.0000
19	2	0.0144	0.0485	0.0917	0.1367	0.1787	0.2852	0.2428	0.1540	0.0803	0.0358	0.0138	0.0046	0.0013	0.0003
19	3	0.0008	0.0056	0.0161	0.0323	0.0533	0.1796	0.2428	0.2182	0.1517	0.0869	0.0422	0.0175	0.0062	0.0018
19	4	0.0000	0.0005	0.0020	0.0054	0.0112	0.0798	0.1714	0.2182	0.2023	0.1491	0.0909	0.0467	0.0203	0.0074
19	5	0.0000	0.0000	0.0002	0.0007	0.0018	0.0266	0.0907	0.1636	0.2023	0.1916	0.1468	0.0933	0.0497	0.0222
19	6	0.0000	0.0000	0.0000	0.0001	0.0002	0.0069	0.0374	0.0955	0.1574	0.1916	0.1844	0.1451	0.0949	0.0518
19	7	0.0000	0.0000	0.0000	0.0000	0.0000	0.0014	0.0122	0.0443	0.0974	0.1525	0.1844	0.1797	0.1443	0.0961
19	8	0.0000	0.0000	0.0000	0.0000	0.0000	0.0002	0.0032	0.0166	0.0487	0.0981	0.1489	0.1797	0.1771	0.1442
19	9	0.0000	0.0000	0.0000	0.0000	0.0000	0.0000	0.0007	0.0051	0.0198	0.0514	0.0980	0.1464	0.1771	0.1762
19	10	0.0000	0.0000	0.0000	0.0000	0.0000	0.0000	0.0001	0.0013	0.0066	0.0220	0.0528	0.0976	0.1449	0.1762
19	11	0.0000	0.0000	0.0000	0.0000	0.0000	0.0000	0.0000	0.0003	0.0018	0.0077	0.0233	0.0532	0.0970	0.1442
19	12	0.0000	0.0000	0.0000	0.0000	0.0000	0.0000	0.0000	0.0000	0.0004	0.0022	0.0083	0.0237	0.0529	0.0961

n	x														
19	13	0.0000	0.0000	0.0000	0.0000	0.0000	0.0000	0.0000	0.0000	0.0001	0.0005	0.0024	0.0085	0.0233	0.0518
19	14	0.0000	0.0000	0.0000	0.0000	0.0000	0.0000	0.0000	0.0000	0.0000	0.0001	0.0006	0.0024	0.0082	0.0222
19	15	0.0000	0.0000	0.0000	0.0000	0.0000	0.0000	0.0000	0.0000	0.0000	0.0000	0.0001	0.0005	0.0022	0.0074
19	16	0.0000	0.0000	0.0000	0.0000	0.0000	0.0000	0.0000	0.0000	0.0000	0.0000	0.0000	0.0001	0.0005	0.0018
19	17	0.0000	0.0000	0.0000	0.0000	0.0000	0.0000	0.0000	0.0000	0.0000	0.0000	0.0000	0.0000	0.0001	0.0003
19	18	0.0000	0.0000	0.0000	0.0000	0.0000	0.0000	0.0000	0.0000	0.0000	0.0000	0.0000	0.0000	0.0000	0.0000
19	19	0.0000	0.0000	0.0000	0.0000	0.0000	0.0000	0.0000	0.0000	0.0000	0.0000	0.0000	0.0000	0.0000	0.0000
20	0	0.8179	0.6676	0.5438	0.4420	0.3585	0.1216	0.0388	0.0115	0.0032	0.0008	0.0002	0.0000	0.0000	0.0000
20	1	0.1652	0.2725	0.3364	0.3683	0.3774	0.2702	0.1368	0.0576	0.0211	0.0068	0.0020	0.0005	0.0001	0.0000
20	2	0.0159	0.0528	0.0988	0.1458	0.1887	0.2852	0.2293	0.1369	0.0669	0.0278	0.0100	0.0031	0.0008	0.0002
20	3	0.0010	0.0065	0.0183	0.0364	0.0596	0.1901	0.2428	0.2054	0.1339	0.0716	0.0323	0.0123	0.0040	0.0011
20	4	0.0000	0.0006	0.0024	0.0065	0.0133	0.0898	0.1821	0.2182	0.1897	0.1304	0.0738	0.0350	0.0139	0.0046
20	5	0.0000	0.0000	0.0002	0.0009	0.0022	0.0319	0.1028	0.1746	0.2023	0.1789	0.1272	0.0746	0.0365	0.0148
20	6	0.0000	0.0000	0.0000	0.0001	0.0003	0.0089	0.0454	0.1091	0.1686	0.1916	0.1712	0.1244	0.0746	0.0370
20	7	0.0000	0.0000	0.0000	0.0000	0.0000	0.0020	0.0160	0.0545	0.1124	0.1643	0.1844	0.1659	0.1221	0.0739
20	8	0.0000	0.0000	0.0000	0.0000	0.0000	0.0004	0.0046	0.0222	0.0609	0.1144	0.1614	0.1797	0.1623	0.1201
20	9	0.0000	0.0000	0.0000	0.0000	0.0000	0.0001	0.0011	0.0074	0.0271	0.0654	0.1158	0.1597	0.1771	0.1602
20	10	0.0000	0.0000	0.0000	0.0000	0.0000	0.0000	0.0002	0.0020	0.0099	0.0308	0.0686	0.1171	0.1593	0.1762
20	11	0.0000	0.0000	0.0000	0.0000	0.0000	0.0000	0.0000	0.0005	0.0030	0.0120	0.0336	0.0710	0.1185	0.1602
20	12	0.0000	0.0000	0.0000	0.0000	0.0000	0.0000	0.0000	0.0001	0.0008	0.0039	0.0136	0.0355	0.0727	0.1201
20	13	0.0000	0.0000	0.0000	0.0000	0.0000	0.0000	0.0000	0.0000	0.0002	0.0010	0.0045	0.0146	0.0366	0.0739
20	14	0.0000	0.0000	0.0000	0.0000	0.0000	0.0000	0.0000	0.0000	0.0000	0.0002	0.0012	0.0049	0.0150	0.0370
20	15	0.0000	0.0000	0.0000	0.0000	0.0000	0.0000	0.0000	0.0000	0.0000	0.0000	0.0003	0.0013	0.0049	0.0148
20	16	0.0000	0.0000	0.0000	0.0000	0.0000	0.0000	0.0000	0.0000	0.0000	0.0000	0.0000	0.0003	0.0013	0.0046
20	17	0.0000	0.0000	0.0000	0.0000	0.0000	0.0000	0.0000	0.0000	0.0000	0.0000	0.0000	0.0000	0.0002	0.0011
20	18	0.0000	0.0000	0.0000	0.0000	0.0000	0.0000	0.0000	0.0000	0.0000	0.0000	0.0000	0.0000	0.0000	0.0002
20	19	0.0000	0.0000	0.0000	0.0000	0.0000	0.0000	0.0000	0.0000	0.0000	0.0000	0.0000	0.0000	0.0000	0.0000
20	20	0.0000	0.0000	0.0000	0.0000	0.0000	0.0000	0.0000	0.0000	0.0000	0.0000	0.0000	0.0000	0.0000	0.0000

Cumulative probabilities for the Binomial distribution

n	x	Probability of success $P =$													
		0.01	0.02	0.03	0.04	0.05	0.1	0.15	0.2	0.25	0.3	0.35	0.4	0.45	0.5
1	0	0.9900	0.9800	0.9700	0.9600	0.9500	0.9000	0.8500	0.8000	0.7500	0.7000	0.6500	0.6000	0.5500	0.5000
1	1	1.0000	1.0000	1.0000	1.0000	1.0000	1.0000	1.0000	1.0000	1.0000	1.0000	1.0000	1.0000	1.0000	1.0000
2	0	0.9801	0.9604	0.9409	0.9216	0.9025	0.8100	0.7225	0.6400	0.5625	0.4900	0.4225	0.3600	0.3025	0.2500
2	1	0.9999	0.9996	0.9991	0.9984	0.9975	0.9900	0.9775	0.9600	0.9375	0.9100	0.8775	0.8400	0.7975	0.7500
2	2	1.0000	1.0000	1.0000	1.0000	1.0000	1.0000	1.0000	1.0000	1.0000	1.0000	1.0000	1.0000	1.0000	1.0000
3	0	0.9703	0.9412	0.9127	0.8847	0.8574	0.7290	0.6141	0.5120	0.4219	0.3430	0.2746	0.2160	0.1664	0.1250
3	1	0.9997	0.9988	0.9974	0.9953	0.9928	0.9720	0.9393	0.8960	0.8438	0.7840	0.7183	0.6480	0.5748	0.5000
3	2	1.0000	1.0000	1.0000	0.9999	0.9999	0.9990	0.9966	0.9920	0.9844	0.9730	0.9571	0.9360	0.9089	0.8750
3	3	1.0000	1.0000	1.0000	1.0000	1.0000	1.0000	1.0000	1.0000	1.0000	1.0000	1.0000	1.0000	1.0000	1.0000
4	0	0.9606	0.9224	0.8853	0.8493	0.8145	0.6561	0.5220	0.4096	0.3164	0.2401	0.1785	0.1296	0.0915	0.0625
4	1	0.9994	0.9977	0.9948	0.9909	0.9860	0.9477	0.8905	0.8192	0.7383	0.6517	0.5630	0.4752	0.3910	0.3125
4	2	1.0000	1.0000	0.9999	0.9998	0.9995	0.9963	0.9880	0.9728	0.9492	0.9163	0.8735	0.8208	0.7585	0.6875
4	3	1.0000	1.0000	1.0000	1.0000	1.0000	0.9999	0.9995	0.9984	0.9961	0.9919	0.9850	0.9744	0.9590	0.9375
4	4	1.0000	1.0000	1.0000	1.0000	1.0000	1.0000	1.0000	1.0000	1.0000	1.0000	1.0000	1.0000	1.0000	1.0000
5	0	0.9510	0.9039	0.8587	0.8154	0.7738	0.5905	0.4437	0.3277	0.2373	0.1681	0.1160	0.0778	0.0503	0.0313
5	1	0.9990	0.9962	0.9915	0.9852	0.9774	0.9185	0.8352	0.7373	0.6328	0.5282	0.4284	0.3370	0.2562	0.1875
5	2	1.0000	0.9999	0.9997	0.9994	0.9988	0.9914	0.9734	0.9421	0.8965	0.8369	0.7648	0.6826	0.5931	0.5000
5	3	1.0000	1.0000	1.0000	1.0000	1.0000	0.9995	0.9978	0.9933	0.9844	0.9692	0.9460	0.9130	0.8688	0.8125
5	4	1.0000	1.0000	1.0000	1.0000	1.0000	0.9999	0.9999	0.9997	0.9990	0.9976	0.9947	0.9898	0.9815	0.9688
5	5	1.0000	1.0000	1.0000	1.0000	1.0000	1.0000	1.0000	1.0000	1.0000	1.0000	1.0000	1.0000	1.0000	1.0000
6	0	0.9415	0.8858	0.8330	0.7828	0.7351	0.5314	0.3771	0.2621	0.1780	0.1176	0.0754	0.0467	0.0277	0.0156
6	1	0.9985	0.9943	0.9875	0.9784	0.9672	0.8857	0.7765	0.6554	0.5339	0.4202	0.3191	0.2333	0.1636	0.1094
6	2	1.0000	0.9998	0.9995	0.9988	0.9978	0.9842	0.9527	0.9011	0.8306	0.7443	0.6471	0.5443	0.4415	0.3438
6	3	1.0000	1.0000	1.0000	1.0000	0.9999	0.9987	0.9941	0.9830	0.9624	0.9295	0.8826	0.8208	0.7447	0.6563
6	4	1.0000	1.0000	1.0000	1.0000	1.0000	0.9999	0.9996	0.9984	0.9954	0.9891	0.9777	0.9590	0.9308	0.8906
6	5	1.0000	1.0000	1.0000	1.0000	1.0000	1.0000	1.0000	0.9999	0.9998	0.9993	0.9982	0.9959	0.9917	0.9844
6	6	1.0000	1.0000	1.0000	1.0000	1.0000	1.0000	1.0000	1.0000	1.0000	1.0000	1.0000	1.0000	1.0000	1.0000
7	0	0.9321	0.8681	0.8080	0.7514	0.6983	0.4783	0.3206	0.2097	0.1335	0.0824	0.0490	0.0280	0.0152	0.0078
7	1	0.9980	0.9921	0.9829	0.9706	0.9556	0.8503	0.7166	0.5767	0.4449	0.3294	0.2338	0.1586	0.1024	0.0625
7	2	1.0000	0.9997	0.9991	0.9980	0.9962	0.9743	0.9262	0.8520	0.7564	0.6471	0.5323	0.4199	0.3164	0.2266
7	3	1.0000	1.0000	1.0000	0.9999	0.9998	0.9973	0.9879	0.9667	0.9294	0.8740	0.8002	0.7102	0.6083	0.5000
7	4	1.0000	1.0000	1.0000	1.0000	1.0000	0.9998	0.9988	0.9953	0.9871	0.9712	0.9444	0.9037	0.8471	0.7734
7	5	1.0000	1.0000	1.0000	1.0000	1.0000	1.0000	0.9999	0.9996	0.9987	0.9962	0.9910	0.9812	0.9643	0.9375
7	6	1.0000	1.0000	1.0000	1.0000	1.0000	1.0000	1.0000	1.0000	0.9999	0.9998	0.9994	0.9984	0.9963	0.9922
7	7	1.0000	1.0000	1.0000	1.0000	1.0000	1.0000	1.0000	1.0000	1.0000	1.0000	1.0000	1.0000	1.0000	1.0000
8	0	0.9227	0.8508	0.7837	0.7214	0.6634	0.4305	0.2725	0.1678	0.1001	0.0576	0.0319	0.0168	0.0084	0.0039
8	1	0.9973	0.9897	0.9777	0.9619	0.9428	0.8131	0.6572	0.5033	0.3671	0.2553	0.1691	0.1064	0.0632	0.0352

n	x														
8	2	0.1445	0.2201	0.3154	0.4278	0.5518	0.6785	0.7969	0.8948	0.9619	0.9942	0.9969	0.9987	0.9996	0.9999
8	3	0.3633	0.4770	0.5941	0.7064	0.8059	0.8862	0.9437	0.9786	0.9950	0.9996	0.9998	0.9999	1.0000	1.0000
8	4	0.6367	0.7396	0.8263	0.8939	0.9420	0.9727	0.9896	0.9971	0.9996	1.0000	1.0000	1.0000	1.0000	1.0000
8	5	0.8555	0.9115	0.9502	0.9747	0.9887	0.9958	0.9988	0.9998	1.0000	1.0000	1.0000	1.0000	1.0000	1.0000
8	6	0.9648	0.9819	0.9915	0.9964	0.9987	0.9996	0.9999	1.0000	1.0000	1.0000	1.0000	1.0000	1.0000	1.0000
8	7	0.9961	0.9983	0.9993	0.9998	0.9999	1.0000	1.0000	1.0000	1.0000	1.0000	1.0000	1.0000	1.0000	1.0000
8	8	1.0000	1.0000	1.0000	1.0000	1.0000	1.0000	1.0000	1.0000	1.0000	1.0000	1.0000	1.0000	1.0000	1.0000
9	0	0.0020	0.0046	0.0101	0.0207	0.0404	0.0751	0.1342	0.2316	0.3874	0.6302	0.6925	0.7602	0.8337	0.9135
9	1	0.0195	0.0385	0.0705	0.1211	0.1960	0.3003	0.4362	0.5995	0.7748	0.9288	0.9522	0.9718	0.9869	0.9966
9	2	0.0898	0.1495	0.2318	0.3373	0.4628	0.6007	0.7382	0.8591	0.9470	0.9916	0.9955	0.9980	0.9994	0.9999
9	3	0.2539	0.3614	0.4826	0.6089	0.7297	0.8343	0.9144	0.9661	0.9917	0.9994	0.9997	0.9999	1.0000	1.0000
9	4	0.5000	0.6214	0.7334	0.8283	0.9012	0.9511	0.9804	0.9944	0.9991	1.0000	1.0000	1.0000	1.0000	1.0000
9	5	0.7461	0.8342	0.9006	0.9464	0.9747	0.9900	0.9969	0.9994	0.9999	1.0000	1.0000	1.0000	1.0000	1.0000
9	6	0.9102	0.9502	0.9750	0.9888	0.9957	0.9987	0.9997	1.0000	1.0000	1.0000	1.0000	1.0000	1.0000	1.0000
9	7	0.9805	0.9909	0.9962	0.9986	0.9996	0.9999	1.0000	1.0000	1.0000	1.0000	1.0000	1.0000	1.0000	1.0000
9	8	0.9980	0.9992	0.9997	0.9999	1.0000	1.0000	1.0000	1.0000	1.0000	1.0000	1.0000	1.0000	1.0000	1.0000
9	9	1.0000	1.0000	1.0000	1.0000	1.0000	1.0000	1.0000	1.0000	1.0000	1.0000	1.0000	1.0000	1.0000	1.0000
10	0	0.0010	0.0025	0.0060	0.0135	0.0282	0.0563	0.1074	0.1969	0.3487	0.5987	0.6648	0.7374	0.8171	0.9044
10	1	0.0107	0.0233	0.0464	0.0860	0.1493	0.2440	0.3758	0.5443	0.7361	0.9139	0.9418	0.9655	0.9838	0.9957
10	2	0.0547	0.0996	0.1673	0.2616	0.3828	0.5256	0.6778	0.8202	0.9298	0.9885	0.9938	0.9972	0.9991	0.9999
10	3	0.1719	0.2660	0.3823	0.5138	0.6496	0.7759	0.8791	0.9500	0.9872	0.9990	0.9996	0.9999	1.0000	1.0000
10	4	0.3770	0.5044	0.6331	0.7515	0.8497	0.9219	0.9672	0.9901	0.9984	0.9999	1.0000	1.0000	1.0000	1.0000
10	5	0.6230	0.7384	0.8338	0.9051	0.9527	0.9803	0.9936	0.9986	0.9999	1.0000	1.0000	1.0000	1.0000	1.0000
10	6	0.8281	0.8980	0.9452	0.9740	0.9894	0.9965	0.9991	0.9999	1.0000	1.0000	1.0000	1.0000	1.0000	1.0000
10	7	0.9453	0.9726	0.9877	0.9952	0.9984	0.9996	0.9999	1.0000	1.0000	1.0000	1.0000	1.0000	1.0000	1.0000
10	8	0.9893	0.9955	0.9983	0.9995	0.9999	1.0000	1.0000	1.0000	1.0000	1.0000	1.0000	1.0000	1.0000	1.0000
10	9	0.9990	0.9997	0.9999	1.0000	1.0000	1.0000	1.0000	1.0000	1.0000	1.0000	1.0000	1.0000	1.0000	1.0000
10	10	1.0000	1.0000	1.0000	1.0000	1.0000	1.0000	1.0000	1.0000	1.0000	1.0000	1.0000	1.0000	1.0000	1.0000
11	0	0.0005	0.0014	0.0036	0.0088	0.0198	0.0422	0.0859	0.1673	0.3138	0.5688	0.6382	0.7153	0.8007	0.8953
11	1	0.0059	0.0139	0.0302	0.0606	0.1130	0.1971	0.3221	0.4922	0.6974	0.8981	0.9308	0.9587	0.9805	0.9948
11	2	0.0327	0.0652	0.1189	0.2001	0.3127	0.4552	0.6174	0.7788	0.9104	0.9848	0.9917	0.9963	0.9988	0.9998
11	3	0.1133	0.1911	0.2963	0.4256	0.5696	0.7133	0.8389	0.9306	0.9815	0.9984	0.9993	0.9998	1.0000	1.0000
11	4	0.2744	0.3971	0.5328	0.6683	0.7897	0.8854	0.9496	0.9841	0.9972	0.9999	1.0000	1.0000	1.0000	1.0000
11	5	0.5000	0.6331	0.7535	0.8513	0.9218	0.9657	0.9883	0.9973	0.9997	1.0000	1.0000	1.0000	1.0000	1.0000
11	6	0.7256	0.8262	0.9006	0.9499	0.9784	0.9924	0.9980	0.9997	1.0000	1.0000	1.0000	1.0000	1.0000	1.0000
11	7	0.8867	0.9390	0.9707	0.9878	0.9957	0.9988	0.9998	1.0000	1.0000	1.0000	1.0000	1.0000	1.0000	1.0000
11	8	0.9673	0.9852	0.9941	0.9980	0.9994	0.9999	1.0000	1.0000	1.0000	1.0000	1.0000	1.0000	1.0000	1.0000
11	9	0.9941	0.9978	0.9993	0.9998	1.0000	1.0000	1.0000	1.0000	1.0000	1.0000	1.0000	1.0000	1.0000	1.0000
11	10	0.9995	0.9998	1.0000	1.0000	1.0000	1.0000	1.0000	1.0000	1.0000	1.0000	1.0000	1.0000	1.0000	1.0000
11	11	1.0000	1.0000	1.0000	1.0000	1.0000	1.0000	1.0000	1.0000	1.0000	1.0000	1.0000	1.0000	1.0000	1.0000
12	0	0.0002	0.0008	0.0022	0.0057	0.0138	0.0317	0.0687	0.1422	0.2824	0.5404	0.6127	0.6938	0.7847	0.8864
12	1	0.0032	0.0083	0.0196	0.0424	0.0850	0.1584	0.2749	0.4435	0.6590	0.8816	0.9191	0.9514	0.9769	0.9938
12	2	0.0193	0.0421	0.0834	0.1513	0.2528	0.3907	0.5583	0.7358	0.8891	0.9804	0.9893	0.9952	0.9985	0.9998

(continued)

Cumulative probabilities for the Binomial distribution (cont.)

Probability of success $P =$

n	x	0.01	0.02	0.03	0.04	0.05	0.1	0.15	0.2	0.25	0.3	0.35	0.4	0.45	0.5
12	3	1.0000	0.9999	0.9997	0.9990	0.9978	0.9744	0.9078	0.7946	0.6488	0.4925	0.3467	0.2253	0.1345	0.0730
12	4	1.0000	1.0000	1.0000	0.9999	0.9998	0.9957	0.9761	0.9274	0.8424	0.7237	0.5833	0.4382	0.3044	0.1938
12	5	1.0000	1.0000	1.0000	1.0000	1.0000	0.9995	0.9954	0.9806	0.9456	0.8822	0.7873	0.6652	0.5269	0.3872
12	6	1.0000	1.0000	1.0000	1.0000	1.0000	0.9999	0.9993	0.9961	0.9857	0.9614	0.9154	0.8418	0.7393	0.6128
12	7	1.0000	1.0000	1.0000	1.0000	1.0000	1.0000	0.9999	0.9994	0.9972	0.9905	0.9745	0.9427	0.8883	0.8062
12	8	1.0000	1.0000	1.0000	1.0000	1.0000	1.0000	1.0000	0.9999	0.9996	0.9983	0.9944	0.9847	0.9644	0.9270
12	9	1.0000	1.0000	1.0000	1.0000	1.0000	1.0000	1.0000	1.0000	1.0000	0.9998	0.9992	0.9972	0.9921	0.9807
12	10	1.0000	1.0000	1.0000	1.0000	1.0000	1.0000	1.0000	1.0000	1.0000	1.0000	0.9999	0.9997	0.9989	0.9968
12	11	1.0000	1.0000	1.0000	1.0000	1.0000	1.0000	1.0000	1.0000	1.0000	1.0000	1.0000	1.0000	0.9999	0.9998
12	12	1.0000	1.0000	1.0000	1.0000	1.0000	1.0000	1.0000	1.0000	1.0000	1.0000	1.0000	1.0000	1.0000	1.0000
13	0	0.8775	0.7690	0.6730	0.5882	0.5133	0.2542	0.1209	0.0550	0.0238	0.0097	0.0037	0.0013	0.0004	0.0001
13	1	0.9928	0.9730	0.9436	0.9068	0.8646	0.6213	0.3983	0.2336	0.1267	0.0637	0.0296	0.0126	0.0049	0.0017
13	2	0.9997	0.9980	0.9938	0.9865	0.9755	0.8661	0.6920	0.5017	0.3326	0.2025	0.1132	0.0579	0.0269	0.0112
13	3	1.0000	0.9999	0.9995	0.9986	0.9969	0.9658	0.8820	0.7473	0.5843	0.4206	0.2783	0.1686	0.0929	0.0461
13	4	1.0000	1.0000	1.0000	0.9999	0.9997	0.9935	0.9658	0.9009	0.7940	0.6543	0.5005	0.3530	0.2279	0.1334
13	5	1.0000	1.0000	1.0000	1.0000	1.0000	0.9991	0.9925	0.9700	0.9198	0.8346	0.7159	0.5744	0.4268	0.2905
13	6	1.0000	1.0000	1.0000	1.0000	1.0000	0.9999	0.9987	0.9930	0.9757	0.9376	0.8705	0.7712	0.6437	0.5000
13	7	1.0000	1.0000	1.0000	1.0000	1.0000	1.0000	0.9998	0.9988	0.9944	0.9818	0.9538	0.9023	0.8212	0.7095
13	8	1.0000	1.0000	1.0000	1.0000	1.0000	1.0000	1.0000	0.9998	0.9990	0.9960	0.9874	0.9679	0.9302	0.8666
13	9	1.0000	1.0000	1.0000	1.0000	1.0000	1.0000	1.0000	1.0000	0.9999	0.9993	0.9975	0.9922	0.9797	0.9539
13	10	1.0000	1.0000	1.0000	1.0000	1.0000	1.0000	1.0000	1.0000	1.0000	0.9999	0.9997	0.9987	0.9959	0.9888
13	11	1.0000	1.0000	1.0000	1.0000	1.0000	1.0000	1.0000	1.0000	1.0000	1.0000	1.0000	0.9999	0.9995	0.9983
13	12	1.0000	1.0000	1.0000	1.0000	1.0000	1.0000	1.0000	1.0000	1.0000	1.0000	1.0000	1.0000	1.0000	0.9999
13	13	1.0000	1.0000	1.0000	1.0000	1.0000	1.0000	1.0000	1.0000	1.0000	1.0000	1.0000	1.0000	1.0000	1.0000
14	0	0.8687	0.7536	0.6528	0.5647	0.4877	0.2288	0.1028	0.0440	0.0178	0.0068	0.0024	0.0008	0.0002	0.0001
14	1	0.9916	0.9690	0.9355	0.8941	0.8470	0.5846	0.3567	0.1979	0.1010	0.0475	0.0205	0.0081	0.0029	0.0009
14	2	0.9997	0.9975	0.9923	0.9833	0.9699	0.8416	0.6479	0.4481	0.2811	0.1608	0.0839	0.0398	0.0170	0.0065
14	3	1.0000	0.9999	0.9994	0.9981	0.9958	0.9559	0.8535	0.6982	0.5213	0.3552	0.2205	0.1243	0.0632	0.0287
14	4	1.0000	1.0000	1.0000	0.9998	0.9996	0.9908	0.9533	0.8702	0.7415	0.5842	0.4227	0.2793	0.1672	0.0898
14	5	1.0000	1.0000	1.0000	1.0000	1.0000	0.9985	0.9885	0.9561	0.8883	0.7805	0.6405	0.4859	0.3373	0.2120
14	6	1.0000	1.0000	1.0000	1.0000	1.0000	0.9998	0.9978	0.9884	0.9617	0.9067	0.8164	0.6925	0.5461	0.3953
14	7	1.0000	1.0000	1.0000	1.0000	1.0000	1.0000	0.9997	0.9976	0.9897	0.9685	0.9247	0.8499	0.7414	0.6047
14	8	1.0000	1.0000	1.0000	1.0000	1.0000	1.0000	1.0000	0.9996	0.9978	0.9917	0.9757	0.9417	0.8811	0.7880
14	9	1.0000	1.0000	1.0000	1.0000	1.0000	1.0000	1.0000	1.0000	0.9997	0.9983	0.9940	0.9825	0.9574	0.9102
14	10	1.0000	1.0000	1.0000	1.0000	1.0000	1.0000	1.0000	1.0000	1.0000	0.9998	0.9989	0.9961	0.9886	0.9713
14	11	1.0000	1.0000	1.0000	1.0000	1.0000	1.0000	1.0000	1.0000	1.0000	1.0000	0.9999	0.9994	0.9978	0.9935
14	12	1.0000	1.0000	1.0000	1.0000	1.0000	1.0000	1.0000	1.0000	1.0000	1.0000	1.0000	0.9999	0.9997	0.9991
14	13	1.0000	1.0000	1.0000	1.0000	1.0000	1.0000	1.0000	1.0000	1.0000	1.0000	1.0000	1.0000	1.0000	0.9999
14	14	1.0000	1.0000	1.0000	1.0000	1.0000	1.0000	1.0000	1.0000	1.0000	1.0000	1.0000	1.0000	1.0000	1.0000
15	0	0.8601	0.7386	0.6333	0.5421	0.4633	0.2059	0.0874	0.0352	0.0134	0.0047	0.0016	0.0005	0.0001	0.0000
15	1	0.9904	0.9647	0.9270	0.8809	0.8290	0.5490	0.3186	0.1671	0.0802	0.0353	0.0142	0.0052	0.0017	0.0005

n	x														
15	2	0.0037	0.0107	0.0271	0.0617	0.1268	0.2361	0.3980	0.6042	0.8159	0.9638	0.9797	0.9906	0.9970	0.9996
15	3	0.0176	0.0424	0.0905	0.1727	0.2969	0.4613	0.6482	0.8227	0.9444	0.9945	0.9976	0.9992	0.9998	1.0000
15	4	0.0592	0.1204	0.2173	0.3519	0.5155	0.6865	0.8358	0.9383	0.9873	0.9994	0.9998	0.9999	1.0000	1.0000
15	5	0.1509	0.2608	0.4032	0.5643	0.7216	0.8516	0.9389	0.9832	0.9978	0.9999	1.0000	1.0000	1.0000	1.0000
15	6	0.3036	0.4522	0.6098	0.7548	0.8689	0.9434	0.9819	0.9964	0.9997	1.0000	1.0000	1.0000	1.0000	1.0000
15	7	0.5000	0.6535	0.7869	0.8868	0.9500	0.9827	0.9958	0.9994	1.0000	1.0000	1.0000	1.0000	1.0000	1.0000
15	8	0.6964	0.8182	0.9050	0.9578	0.9848	0.9958	0.9992	0.9999	1.0000	1.0000	1.0000	1.0000	1.0000	1.0000
15	9	0.8491	0.9231	0.9662	0.9876	0.9963	0.9992	0.9999	1.0000	1.0000	1.0000	1.0000	1.0000	1.0000	1.0000
15	10	0.9408	0.9745	0.9907	0.9972	0.9993	0.9999	1.0000	1.0000	1.0000	1.0000	1.0000	1.0000	1.0000	1.0000
15	11	0.9824	0.9937	0.9981	0.9995	0.9999	1.0000	1.0000	1.0000	1.0000	1.0000	1.0000	1.0000	1.0000	1.0000
15	12	0.9963	0.9989	0.9997	0.9999	1.0000	1.0000	1.0000	1.0000	1.0000	1.0000	1.0000	1.0000	1.0000	1.0000
15	13	0.9995	0.9999	1.0000	1.0000	1.0000	1.0000	1.0000	1.0000	1.0000	1.0000	1.0000	1.0000	1.0000	1.0000
15	14	1.0000	1.0000	1.0000	1.0000	1.0000	1.0000	1.0000	1.0000	1.0000	1.0000	1.0000	1.0000	1.0000	1.0000
15	15	1.0000	1.0000	1.0000	1.0000	1.0000	1.0000	1.0000	1.0000	1.0000	1.0000	1.0000	1.0000	1.0000	1.0000
16	0	0.0000	0.0001	0.0003	0.0010	0.0033	0.0100	0.0281	0.0743	0.1853	0.4401	0.5204	0.6143	0.7238	0.8515
16	1	0.0003	0.0010	0.0033	0.0098	0.0261	0.0635	0.1407	0.2839	0.5147	0.8108	0.8673	0.9182	0.9601	0.9891
16	2	0.0021	0.0066	0.0183	0.0451	0.0994	0.1971	0.3518	0.5614	0.7892	0.9571	0.9758	0.9887	0.9963	0.9995
16	3	0.0106	0.0281	0.0651	0.1339	0.2459	0.4050	0.5981	0.7899	0.9316	0.9930	0.9968	0.9989	0.9998	1.0000
16	4	0.0384	0.0853	0.1666	0.2892	0.4499	0.6302	0.7982	0.9209	0.9830	0.9991	0.9997	0.9999	1.0000	1.0000
16	5	0.1051	0.1976	0.3288	0.4900	0.6598	0.8103	0.9183	0.9765	0.9967	0.9999	1.0000	1.0000	1.0000	1.0000
16	6	0.2272	0.3660	0.5272	0.6881	0.8247	0.9204	0.9733	0.9944	0.9995	1.0000	1.0000	1.0000	1.0000	1.0000
16	7	0.4018	0.5629	0.7161	0.8406	0.9256	0.9729	0.9930	0.9989	0.9999	1.0000	1.0000	1.0000	1.0000	1.0000
16	8	0.5982	0.7441	0.8577	0.9329	0.9743	0.9925	0.9985	0.9998	1.0000	1.0000	1.0000	1.0000	1.0000	1.0000
16	9	0.7728	0.8759	0.9417	0.9771	0.9929	0.9984	0.9998	1.0000	1.0000	1.0000	1.0000	1.0000	1.0000	1.0000
16	10	0.8949	0.9514	0.9809	0.9938	0.9984	0.9997	1.0000	1.0000	1.0000	1.0000	1.0000	1.0000	1.0000	1.0000
16	11	0.9616	0.9851	0.9951	0.9987	0.9997	1.0000	1.0000	1.0000	1.0000	1.0000	1.0000	1.0000	1.0000	1.0000
16	12	0.9894	0.9965	0.9991	0.9998	1.0000	1.0000	1.0000	1.0000	1.0000	1.0000	1.0000	1.0000	1.0000	1.0000
16	13	0.9979	0.9994	0.9999	1.0000	1.0000	1.0000	1.0000	1.0000	1.0000	1.0000	1.0000	1.0000	1.0000	1.0000
16	14	0.9997	0.9999	1.0000	1.0000	1.0000	1.0000	1.0000	1.0000	1.0000	1.0000	1.0000	1.0000	1.0000	1.0000
16	15	1.0000	1.0000	1.0000	1.0000	1.0000	1.0000	1.0000	1.0000	1.0000	1.0000	1.0000	1.0000	1.0000	1.0000
16	16	1.0000	1.0000	1.0000	1.0000	1.0000	1.0000	1.0000	1.0000	1.0000	1.0000	1.0000	1.0000	1.0000	1.0000
17	0	0.0000	0.0000	0.0002	0.0007	0.0023	0.0075	0.0225	0.0631	0.1668	0.4181	0.4996	0.5958	0.7093	0.8429
17	1	0.0001	0.0006	0.0021	0.0067	0.0193	0.0501	0.1182	0.2525	0.4818	0.7922	0.8535	0.9091	0.9554	0.9877
17	2	0.0012	0.0041	0.0123	0.0327	0.0774	0.1637	0.3096	0.5198	0.7618	0.9497	0.9714	0.9866	0.9956	0.9994
17	3	0.0064	0.0184	0.0464	0.1028	0.2019	0.3530	0.5489	0.7556	0.9174	0.9912	0.9960	0.9986	0.9997	1.0000
17	4	0.0245	0.0596	0.1260	0.2348	0.3887	0.5739	0.7582	0.9013	0.9779	0.9988	0.9996	0.9999	1.0000	1.0000
17	5	0.0717	0.1471	0.2639	0.4197	0.5968	0.7653	0.8943	0.9681	0.9953	0.9999	1.0000	1.0000	1.0000	1.0000
17	6	0.1662	0.2902	0.4478	0.6188	0.7752	0.8929	0.9623	0.9917	0.9992	1.0000	1.0000	1.0000	1.0000	1.0000
17	7	0.3145	0.4743	0.6405	0.7872	0.8954	0.9598	0.9891	0.9983	0.9999	1.0000	1.0000	1.0000	1.0000	1.0000
17	8	0.5000	0.6626	0.8011	0.9006	0.9597	0.9876	0.9974	0.9997	1.0000	1.0000	1.0000	1.0000	1.0000	1.0000
17	9	0.6855	0.8166	0.9081	0.9617	0.9873	0.9969	0.9995	1.0000	1.0000	1.0000	1.0000	1.0000	1.0000	1.0000
17	10	0.8338	0.9174	0.9652	0.9880	0.9968	0.9994	0.9999	1.0000	1.0000	1.0000	1.0000	1.0000	1.0000	1.0000
17	11	0.9283	0.9699	0.9894	0.9970	0.9993	0.9999	1.0000	1.0000	1.0000	1.0000	1.0000	1.0000	1.0000	1.0000

(continued)

Cumulative probabilities for the Binomial distribution (cont.)

Probability of success $P =$

n	x	0.01	0.02	0.03	0.04	0.05	0.1	0.15	0.2	0.25	0.3	0.35	0.4	0.45	0.5
17	12	1.0000	1.0000	1.0000	1.0000	1.0000	1.0000	1.0000	1.0000	1.0000	0.9999	0.9994	0.9975	0.9914	0.9755
17	13	1.0000	1.0000	1.0000	1.0000	1.0000	1.0000	1.0000	1.0000	1.0000	1.0000	0.9999	0.9995	0.9981	0.9936
17	14	1.0000	1.0000	1.0000	1.0000	1.0000	1.0000	1.0000	1.0000	1.0000	1.0000	1.0000	0.9999	0.9997	0.9988
17	15	1.0000	1.0000	1.0000	1.0000	1.0000	1.0000	1.0000	1.0000	1.0000	1.0000	1.0000	1.0000	1.0000	0.9999
17	16	1.0000	1.0000	1.0000	1.0000	1.0000	1.0000	1.0000	1.0000	1.0000	1.0000	1.0000	1.0000	1.0000	1.0000
17	17	1.0000	1.0000	1.0000	1.0000	1.0000	1.0000	1.0000	1.0000	1.0000	1.0000	1.0000	1.0000	1.0000	1.0000
18	0	0.8345	0.6951	0.5780	0.4796	0.3972	0.1501	0.0536	0.0180	0.0056	0.0016	0.0004	0.0001	0.0000	0.0000
18	1	0.9862	0.9505	0.8997	0.8393	0.7735	0.4503	0.2241	0.0991	0.0395	0.0142	0.0046	0.0013	0.0003	0.0001
18	2	0.9993	0.9948	0.9843	0.9667	0.9419	0.7338	0.4797	0.2713	0.1353	0.0600	0.0236	0.0082	0.0025	0.0007
18	3	1.0000	0.9996	0.9982	0.9950	0.9891	0.9018	0.7202	0.5010	0.3057	0.1646	0.0783	0.0328	0.0120	0.0038
18	4	1.0000	1.0000	0.9998	0.9994	0.9985	0.9718	0.8794	0.7164	0.5187	0.3327	0.1886	0.0942	0.0411	0.0154
18	5	1.0000	1.0000	1.0000	0.9999	0.9998	0.9936	0.9581	0.8671	0.7175	0.5344	0.3550	0.2088	0.1077	0.0481
18	6	1.0000	1.0000	1.0000	1.0000	1.0000	0.9988	0.9882	0.9487	0.8610	0.7217	0.5491	0.3743	0.2258	0.1189
18	7	1.0000	1.0000	1.0000	1.0000	1.0000	0.9998	0.9973	0.9837	0.9431	0.8593	0.7283	0.5634	0.3915	0.2403
18	8	1.0000	1.0000	1.0000	1.0000	1.0000	1.0000	0.9995	0.9957	0.9807	0.9404	0.8609	0.7368	0.5778	0.4073
18	9	1.0000	1.0000	1.0000	1.0000	1.0000	1.0000	0.9999	0.9991	0.9946	0.9790	0.9403	0.8653	0.7473	0.5927
18	10	1.0000	1.0000	1.0000	1.0000	1.0000	1.0000	1.0000	0.9998	0.9988	0.9939	0.9788	0.9424	0.8720	0.7597
18	11	1.0000	1.0000	1.0000	1.0000	1.0000	1.0000	1.0000	1.0000	0.9998	0.9986	0.9938	0.9797	0.9463	0.8811
18	12	1.0000	1.0000	1.0000	1.0000	1.0000	1.0000	1.0000	1.0000	1.0000	0.9997	0.9986	0.9942	0.9817	0.9519
18	13	1.0000	1.0000	1.0000	1.0000	1.0000	1.0000	1.0000	1.0000	1.0000	1.0000	0.9997	0.9987	0.9951	0.9846
18	14	1.0000	1.0000	1.0000	1.0000	1.0000	1.0000	1.0000	1.0000	1.0000	1.0000	1.0000	0.9998	0.9990	0.9962
18	15	1.0000	1.0000	1.0000	1.0000	1.0000	1.0000	1.0000	1.0000	1.0000	1.0000	1.0000	1.0000	0.9999	0.9993
18	16	1.0000	1.0000	1.0000	1.0000	1.0000	1.0000	1.0000	1.0000	1.0000	1.0000	1.0000	1.0000	1.0000	0.9999
18	17	1.0000	1.0000	1.0000	1.0000	1.0000	1.0000	1.0000	1.0000	1.0000	1.0000	1.0000	1.0000	1.0000	1.0000
18	18	1.0000	1.0000	1.0000	1.0000	1.0000	1.0000	1.0000	1.0000	1.0000	1.0000	1.0000	1.0000	1.0000	1.0000
19	0	0.8262	0.6812	0.5606	0.4604	0.3774	0.1351	0.0456	0.0144	0.0042	0.0011	0.0003	0.0001	0.0000	0.0000
19	1	0.9847	0.9454	0.8900	0.8249	0.7547	0.4203	0.1985	0.0829	0.0310	0.0104	0.0031	0.0008	0.0002	0.0000
19	2	0.9991	0.9939	0.9817	0.9616	0.9335	0.7054	0.4413	0.2369	0.1113	0.0462	0.0170	0.0055	0.0015	0.0004
19	3	1.0000	0.9995	0.9978	0.9939	0.9868	0.8850	0.6841	0.4551	0.2631	0.1332	0.0591	0.0230	0.0077	0.0022
19	4	1.0000	1.0000	0.9998	0.9993	0.9980	0.9648	0.8556	0.6733	0.4654	0.2822	0.1500	0.0696	0.0280	0.0096
19	5	1.0000	1.0000	1.0000	0.9999	0.9998	0.9914	0.9463	0.8369	0.6678	0.4739	0.2968	0.1629	0.0777	0.0318
19	6	1.0000	1.0000	1.0000	1.0000	1.0000	0.9983	0.9837	0.9324	0.8251	0.6655	0.4812	0.3081	0.1727	0.0835
19	7	1.0000	1.0000	1.0000	1.0000	1.0000	0.9997	0.9959	0.9767	0.9225	0.8180	0.6656	0.4878	0.3169	0.1796
19	8	1.0000	1.0000	1.0000	1.0000	1.0000	1.0000	0.9992	0.9933	0.9713	0.9161	0.8145	0.6675	0.4940	0.3238
19	9	1.0000	1.0000	1.0000	1.0000	1.0000	1.0000	0.9999	0.9984	0.9911	0.9674	0.9125	0.8139	0.6710	0.5000
19	10	1.0000	1.0000	1.0000	1.0000	1.0000	1.0000	1.0000	0.9997	0.9977	0.9895	0.9653	0.9115	0.8159	0.6762
19	11	1.0000	1.0000	1.0000	1.0000	1.0000	1.0000	1.0000	1.0000	0.9995	0.9972	0.9886	0.9648	0.9129	0.8204
19	12	1.0000	1.0000	1.0000	1.0000	1.0000	1.0000	1.0000	1.0000	0.9999	0.9994	0.9969	0.9884	0.9658	0.9165
19	13	1.0000	1.0000	1.0000	1.0000	1.0000	1.0000	1.0000	1.0000	1.0000	0.9999	0.9993	0.9969	0.9891	0.9682
19	14	1.0000	1.0000	1.0000	1.0000	1.0000	1.0000	1.0000	1.0000	1.0000	1.0000	0.9999	0.9994	0.9972	0.9904
19	15	1.0000	1.0000	1.0000	1.0000	1.0000	1.0000	1.0000	1.0000	1.0000	1.0000	1.0000	0.9999	0.9995	0.9978

n	x													
19	16	0.9996	0.9999	1.0000	1.0000	1.0000	1.0000	1.0000	1.0000	1.0000	1.0000	1.0000	1.0000	1.0000	1.0000
19	17	1.0000	1.0000	1.0000	1.0000	1.0000	1.0000	1.0000	1.0000	1.0000	1.0000	1.0000	1.0000	1.0000	1.0000
19	18	1.0000	1.0000	1.0000	1.0000	1.0000	1.0000	1.0000	1.0000	1.0000	1.0000	1.0000	1.0000	1.0000	1.0000
19	19	1.0000	1.0000	1.0000	1.0000	1.0000	1.0000	1.0000	1.0000	1.0000	1.0000	1.0000	1.0000	1.0000	1.0000
20	0	0.0000	0.0000	0.0000	0.0002	0.0008	0.0032	0.0115	0.0388	0.1216	0.3585	0.4420	0.5438	0.6676	0.8179
20	1	0.0000	0.0001	0.0005	0.0021	0.0076	0.0243	0.0692	0.1756	0.3917	0.7358	0.8103	0.8802	0.9401	0.9831
20	2	0.0002	0.0009	0.0036	0.0121	0.0355	0.0913	0.2061	0.4049	0.6769	0.9245	0.9561	0.9790	0.9929	0.9990
20	3	0.0013	0.0049	0.0160	0.0444	0.1071	0.2252	0.4114	0.6477	0.8670	0.9841	0.9926	0.9973	0.9994	1.0000
20	4	0.0059	0.0189	0.0510	0.1182	0.2375	0.4148	0.6296	0.8298	0.9568	0.9974	0.9990	0.9997	1.0000	1.0000
20	5	0.0207	0.0553	0.1256	0.2454	0.4164	0.6172	0.8042	0.9327	0.9887	0.9997	0.9999	1.0000	1.0000	1.0000
20	6	0.0577	0.1299	0.2500	0.4166	0.6080	0.7858	0.9133	0.9781	0.9976	1.0000	1.0000	1.0000	1.0000	1.0000
20	7	0.1316	0.2520	0.4159	0.6010	0.7723	0.8982	0.9679	0.9941	0.9996	1.0000	1.0000	1.0000	1.0000	1.0000
20	8	0.2517	0.4143	0.5956	0.7624	0.8867	0.9591	0.9900	0.9987	0.9999	1.0000	1.0000	1.0000	1.0000	1.0000
20	9	0.4119	0.5914	0.7553	0.8782	0.9520	0.9861	0.9974	0.9998	1.0000	1.0000	1.0000	1.0000	1.0000	1.0000
20	10	0.5881	0.7507	0.8725	0.9468	0.9829	0.9961	0.9994	1.0000	1.0000	1.0000	1.0000	1.0000	1.0000	1.0000
20	11	0.7483	0.8692	0.9435	0.9804	0.9949	0.9991	0.9999	1.0000	1.0000	1.0000	1.0000	1.0000	1.0000	1.0000
20	12	0.8684	0.9420	0.9790	0.9940	0.9987	0.9998	1.0000	1.0000	1.0000	1.0000	1.0000	1.0000	1.0000	1.0000
20	13	0.9423	0.9786	0.9935	0.9985	0.9997	1.0000	1.0000	1.0000	1.0000	1.0000	1.0000	1.0000	1.0000	1.0000
20	14	0.9793	0.9936	0.9984	0.9997	1.0000	1.0000	1.0000	1.0000	1.0000	1.0000	1.0000	1.0000	1.0000	1.0000
20	15	0.9941	0.9985	0.9997	1.0000	1.0000	1.0000	1.0000	1.0000	1.0000	1.0000	1.0000	1.0000	1.0000	1.0000
20	16	0.9987	0.9997	1.0000	1.0000	1.0000	1.0000	1.0000	1.0000	1.0000	1.0000	1.0000	1.0000	1.0000	1.0000
20	17	0.9998	1.0000	1.0000	1.0000	1.0000	1.0000	1.0000	1.0000	1.0000	1.0000	1.0000	1.0000	1.0000	1.0000
20	18	1.0000	1.0000	1.0000	1.0000	1.0000	1.0000	1.0000	1.0000	1.0000	1.0000	1.0000	1.0000	1.0000	1.0000
20	19	1.0000	1.0000	1.0000	1.0000	1.0000	1.0000	1.0000	1.0000	1.0000	1.0000	1.0000	1.0000	1.0000	1.0000
20	20	1.0000	1.0000	1.0000	1.0000	1.0000	1.0000	1.0000	1.0000	1.0000	1.0000	1.0000	1.0000	1.0000	1.0000

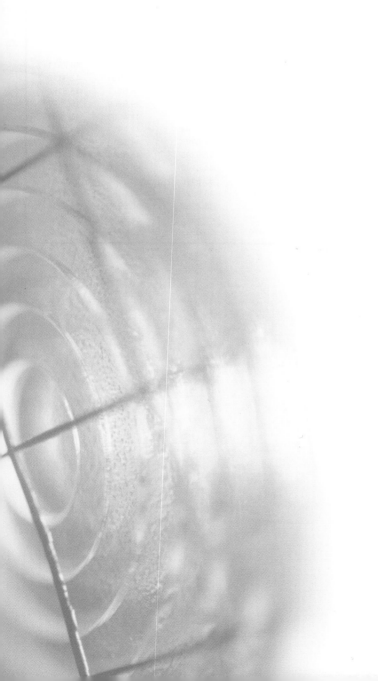

Table 2

Chi-squared distribution

Critical values for the Chi-squared distribution

Significance (parameter)		Level of significance						
		25.00% 0.25	10.00% 0.1	5.00% 0.05	2.50% 0.025	1.00% 0.01	0.50% 0.005	0.10% 0.001
	1	1.3233	2.7055	3.8415	5.0239	6.6349	7.8794	10.8274
	2	2.7726	4.6052	5.9915	7.3778	9.21041	0.5965	13.8150
	3	4.1083	6.2514	7.8147	9.3484	11.3449	12.8381	16.2660
	4	5.3853	7.7794	9.4877	11.1433	13.2767	14.8602	18.4662
	5	6.6257	9.2363	11.0705	12.8325	15.0863	16.7496	20.5147
Degree of freedom	6	7.8408	10.6446	12.5916	14.4494	16.8119	18.5475	22.4575
	7	9.0371	12.0170	14.0671	16.0128	18.4753	20.2777	24.3213
	8	10.2189	13.3616	15.5073	17.5345	20.0902	21.9549	26.1239
	9	11.3887	14.6837	16.9190	19.0228	21.6660	23.5893	27.8767
	10	12.5489	15.9872	18.3070	20.4832	23.2093	25.1881	29.5879
	11	13.7007	17.2750	19.6752	21.9200	24.7250	26.7569	31.2635
	12	14.8454	18.5493	21.0261	23.3367	26.2170	28.2997	32.9092
	13	15.9839	19.8119	22.3620	24.7356	27.6882	29.8193	34.5274
	14	17.1169	21.0641	23.6848	26.1189	29.1412	31.3194	36.1239
	15	18.2451	22.3071	24.9958	27.4884	30.5780	32.8015	37.6978
	16	19.3689	23.5418	26.2962	28.8453	31.9999	34.2671	39.2518
	17	20.4887	24.7690	27.5871	30.1910	33.4087	35.7184	40.7911
	18	21.6049	25.9894	28.8693	31.5264	34.8052	37.1564	42.3119
	19	22.7178	27.2036	30.1435	32.8523	36.1908	38.5821	43.8194
	20	23.8277	28.4120	31.4104	34.1696	37.5663	39.9969	45.3142
	21	24.9348	29.6151	32.6706	35.4789	38.9322	41.4009	46.7963
	22	26.0393	30.8133	33.9245	36.7807	40.2894	42.7957	48.2676
	23	27.1413	32.0069	35.1725	38.0756	41.6383	44.1814	49.7276
	24	28.2412	33.1962	36.4150	39.3641	42.9798	45.5584	51.1790
	25	29.3388	34.3816	37.6525	40.6465	44.3140	46.9280	52.6187
	26	30.4346	35.5632	38.8851	41.9231	45.6416	48.2898	54.0511
	27	31.5284	36.7412	40.1133	43.1945	46.9628	49.6450	55.4751
	28	32.6205	37.9159	41.3372	44.4608	48.2782	50.9936	56.8918
	29	33.7109	39.0875	42.5569	45.7223	49.5878	52.3355	58.3006
	30	34.7997	40.2560	43.7730	46.9792	50.8922	53.6719	59.7022

Table 3

Poisson distribution

Probabilities for the Poisson distribution

Probability of success $x =$

λ	0	1	2	3	4	5	6	7	8	9	10	11	12	13	14	15	16	17	18	19	20	21	22	23	24	25
0.01	0.9900	0.0099	0.0000	0.0000	0.0000	0.0000	0.0000	0.0000	0.0000	0.0000	0.0000	0.0000	0.0000	0.0000	0.0000	0.0000	0.0000	0.0000	0.0000	0.0000	0.0000	0.0000	0.0000	0.0000	0.0000	0.0000
0.02	0.9802	0.0196	0.0002	0.0000	0.0000	0.0000	0.0000	0.0000	0.0000	0.0000	0.0000	0.0000	0.0000	0.0000	0.0000	0.0000	0.0000	0.0000	0.0000	0.0000	0.0000	0.0000	0.0000	0.0000	0.0000	0.0000
0.03	0.9704	0.0291	0.0004	0.0000	0.0000	0.0000	0.0000	0.0000	0.0000	0.0000	0.0000	0.0000	0.0000	0.0000	0.0000	0.0000	0.0000	0.0000	0.0000	0.0000	0.0000	0.0000	0.0000	0.0000	0.0000	0.0000
0.04	0.9608	0.0384	0.0008	0.0000	0.0000	0.0000	0.0000	0.0000	0.0000	0.0000	0.0000	0.0000	0.0000	0.0000	0.0000	0.0000	0.0000	0.0000	0.0000	0.0000	0.0000	0.0000	0.0000	0.0000	0.0000	0.0000
0.05	0.9512	0.0476	0.0012	0.0000	0.0000	0.0000	0.0000	0.0000	0.0000	0.0000	0.0000	0.0000	0.0000	0.0000	0.0000	0.0000	0.0000	0.0000	0.0000	0.0000	0.0000	0.0000	0.0000	0.0000	0.0000	0.0000
0.06	0.9418	0.0565	0.0017	0.0000	0.0000	0.0000	0.0000	0.0000	0.0000	0.0000	0.0000	0.0000	0.0000	0.0000	0.0000	0.0000	0.0000	0.0000	0.0000	0.0000	0.0000	0.0000	0.0000	0.0000	0.0000	0.0000
0.07	0.9324	0.0653	0.0023	0.0001	0.0000	0.0000	0.0000	0.0000	0.0000	0.0000	0.0000	0.0000	0.0000	0.0000	0.0000	0.0000	0.0000	0.0000	0.0000	0.0000	0.0000	0.0000	0.0000	0.0000	0.0000	0.0000
0.08	0.9231	0.0738	0.0030	0.0001	0.0000	0.0000	0.0000	0.0000	0.0000	0.0000	0.0000	0.0000	0.0000	0.0000	0.0000	0.0000	0.0000	0.0000	0.0000	0.0000	0.0000	0.0000	0.0000	0.0000	0.0000	0.0000
0.09	0.9139	0.0823	0.0037	0.0001	0.0000	0.0000	0.0000	0.0000	0.0000	0.0000	0.0000	0.0000	0.0000	0.0000	0.0000	0.0000	0.0000	0.0000	0.0000	0.0000	0.0000	0.0000	0.0000	0.0000	0.0000	0.0000
0.1	0.9048	0.0905	0.0045	0.0002	0.0000	0.0000	0.0000	0.0000	0.0000	0.0000	0.0000	0.0000	0.0000	0.0000	0.0000	0.0000	0.0000	0.0000	0.0000	0.0000	0.0000	0.0000	0.0000	0.0000	0.0000	0.0000
0.2	0.8187	0.1637	0.0164	0.0011	0.0001	0.0000	0.0000	0.0000	0.0000	0.0000	0.0000	0.0000	0.0000	0.0000	0.0000	0.0000	0.0000	0.0000	0.0000	0.0000	0.0000	0.0000	0.0000	0.0000	0.0000	0.0000
0.3	0.7408	0.2222	0.0333	0.0033	0.0003	0.0000	0.0000	0.0000	0.0000	0.0000	0.0000	0.0000	0.0000	0.0000	0.0000	0.0000	0.0000	0.0000	0.0000	0.0000	0.0000	0.0000	0.0000	0.0000	0.0000	0.0000
0.4	0.6703	0.2681	0.0536	0.0072	0.0007	0.0001	0.0000	0.0000	0.0000	0.0000	0.0000	0.0000	0.0000	0.0000	0.0000	0.0000	0.0000	0.0000	0.0000	0.0000	0.0000	0.0000	0.0000	0.0000	0.0000	0.0000
0.5	0.6065	0.3033	0.0758	0.0126	0.0016	0.0002	0.0000	0.0000	0.0000	0.0000	0.0000	0.0000	0.0000	0.0000	0.0000	0.0000	0.0000	0.0000	0.0000	0.0000	0.0000	0.0000	0.0000	0.0000	0.0000	0.0000
0.6	0.5488	0.3293	0.0988	0.0198	0.0030	0.0004	0.0000	0.0000	0.0000	0.0000	0.0000	0.0000	0.0000	0.0000	0.0000	0.0000	0.0000	0.0000	0.0000	0.0000	0.0000	0.0000	0.0000	0.0000	0.0000	0.0000
0.7	0.4966	0.3476	0.1217	0.0284	0.0050	0.0007	0.0001	0.0000	0.0000	0.0000	0.0000	0.0000	0.0000	0.0000	0.0000	0.0000	0.0000	0.0000	0.0000	0.0000	0.0000	0.0000	0.0000	0.0000	0.0000	0.0000
0.8	0.4493	0.3595	0.1438	0.0383	0.0077	0.0012	0.0002	0.0000	0.0000	0.0000	0.0000	0.0000	0.0000	0.0000	0.0000	0.0000	0.0000	0.0000	0.0000	0.0000	0.0000	0.0000	0.0000	0.0000	0.0000	0.0000
0.9	0.4066	0.3659	0.1647	0.0494	0.0111	0.0020	0.0003	0.0000	0.0000	0.0000	0.0000	0.0000	0.0000	0.0000	0.0000	0.0000	0.0000	0.0000	0.0000	0.0000	0.0000	0.0000	0.0000	0.0000	0.0000	0.0000
1	0.3679	0.3679	0.1839	0.0613	0.0153	0.0031	0.0005	0.0001	0.0000	0.0000	0.0000	0.0000	0.0000	0.0000	0.0000	0.0000	0.0000	0.0000	0.0000	0.0000	0.0000	0.0000	0.0000	0.0000	0.0000	0.0000
1.1	0.3329	0.3662	0.2014	0.0738	0.0203	0.0045	0.0008	0.0001	0.0000	0.0000	0.0000	0.0000	0.0000	0.0000	0.0000	0.0000	0.0000	0.0000	0.0000	0.0000	0.0000	0.0000	0.0000	0.0000	0.0000	0.0000
1.2	0.3012	0.3614	0.2169	0.0867	0.0260	0.0062	0.0012	0.0002	0.0000	0.0000	0.0000	0.0000	0.0000	0.0000	0.0000	0.0000	0.0000	0.0000	0.0000	0.0000	0.0000	0.0000	0.0000	0.0000	0.0000	0.0000
1.3	0.2725	0.3543	0.2303	0.0998	0.0324	0.0084	0.0018	0.0003	0.0001	0.0000	0.0000	0.0000	0.0000	0.0000	0.0000	0.0000	0.0000	0.0000	0.0000	0.0000	0.0000	0.0000	0.0000	0.0000	0.0000	0.0000
1.4	0.2466	0.3452	0.2417	0.1128	0.0395	0.0111	0.0026	0.0005	0.0001	0.0000	0.0000	0.0000	0.0000	0.0000	0.0000	0.0000	0.0000	0.0000	0.0000	0.0000	0.0000	0.0000	0.0000	0.0000	0.0000	0.0000
1.5	0.2231	0.3347	0.2510	0.1255	0.0471	0.0141	0.0035	0.0008	0.0001	0.0000	0.0000	0.0000	0.0000	0.0000	0.0000	0.0000	0.0000	0.0000	0.0000	0.0000	0.0000	0.0000	0.0000	0.0000	0.0000	0.0000
1.6	0.2019	0.3230	0.2584	0.1378	0.0551	0.0176	0.0047	0.0011	0.0002	0.0000	0.0000	0.0000	0.0000	0.0000	0.0000	0.0000	0.0000	0.0000	0.0000	0.0000	0.0000	0.0000	0.0000	0.0000	0.0000	0.0000
1.7	0.1827	0.3106	0.2640	0.1496	0.0636	0.0216	0.0061	0.0015	0.0003	0.0001	0.0000	0.0000	0.0000	0.0000	0.0000	0.0000	0.0000	0.0000	0.0000	0.0000	0.0000	0.0000	0.0000	0.0000	0.0000	0.0000
1.8	0.1653	0.2975	0.2678	0.1607	0.0723	0.0260	0.0078	0.0020	0.0005	0.0001	0.0000	0.0000	0.0000	0.0000	0.0000	0.0000	0.0000	0.0000	0.0000	0.0000	0.0000	0.0000	0.0000	0.0000	0.0000	0.0000
1.9	0.1496	0.2842	0.2700	0.1710	0.0812	0.0309	0.0098	0.0027	0.0006	0.0001	0.0000	0.0000	0.0000	0.0000	0.0000	0.0000	0.0000	0.0000	0.0000	0.0000	0.0000	0.0000	0.0000	0.0000	0.0000	0.0000
2	0.1353	0.2707	0.2707	0.1804	0.0902	0.0361	0.0120	0.0034	0.0009	0.0002	0.0000	0.0000	0.0000	0.0000	0.0000	0.0000	0.0000	0.0000	0.0000	0.0000	0.0000	0.0000	0.0000	0.0000	0.0000	0.0000
2.1	0.1225	0.2572	0.2700	0.1890	0.0992	0.0417	0.0146	0.0044	0.0011	0.0003	0.0001	0.0000	0.0000	0.0000	0.0000	0.0000	0.0000	0.0000	0.0000	0.0000	0.0000	0.0000	0.0000	0.0000	0.0000	0.0000
2.2	0.1108	0.2438	0.2681	0.1966	0.1082	0.0476	0.0174	0.0055	0.0015	0.0004	0.0001	0.0000	0.0000	0.0000	0.0000	0.0000	0.0000	0.0000	0.0000	0.0000	0.0000	0.0000	0.0000	0.0000	0.0000	0.0000
2.3	0.1003	0.2306	0.2652	0.2033	0.1169	0.0538	0.0206	0.0068	0.0019	0.0005	0.0001	0.0000	0.0000	0.0000	0.0000	0.0000	0.0000	0.0000	0.0000	0.0000	0.0000	0.0000	0.0000	0.0000	0.0000	0.0000
2.4	0.0907	0.2177	0.2613	0.2090	0.1254	0.0602	0.0241	0.0083	0.0025	0.0007	0.0002	0.0000	0.0000	0.0000	0.0000	0.0000	0.0000	0.0000	0.0000	0.0000	0.0000	0.0000	0.0000	0.0000	0.0000	0.0000
2.5	0.0821	0.2052	0.2565	0.2138	0.1336	0.0668	0.0278	0.0099	0.0031	0.0009	0.0002	0.0000	0.0000	0.0000	0.0000	0.0000	0.0000	0.0000	0.0000	0.0000	0.0000	0.0000	0.0000	0.0000	0.0000	0.0000
2.6	0.0743	0.1931	0.2510	0.2176	0.1414	0.0735	0.0319	0.0118	0.0038	0.0011	0.0003	0.0001	0.0000	0.0000	0.0000	0.0000	0.0000	0.0000	0.0000	0.0000	0.0000	0.0000	0.0000	0.0000	0.0000	0.0000
2.7	0.0672	0.1815	0.2450	0.2205	0.1488	0.0804	0.0362	0.0139	0.0047	0.0014	0.0004	0.0001	0.0000	0.0000	0.0000	0.0000	0.0000	0.0000	0.0000	0.0000	0.0000	0.0000	0.0000	0.0000	0.0000	0.0000
2.8	0.0608	0.1703	0.2384	0.2225	0.1557	0.0872	0.0407	0.0163	0.0057	0.0018	0.0005	0.0001	0.0000	0.0000	0.0000	0.0000	0.0000	0.0000	0.0000	0.0000	0.0000	0.0000	0.0000	0.0000	0.0000	0.0000
2.9	0.0550	0.1596	0.2314	0.2237	0.1622	0.0940	0.0455	0.0188	0.0068	0.0022	0.0006	0.0002	0.0000	0.0000	0.0000	0.0000	0.0000	0.0000	0.0000	0.0000	0.0000	0.0000	0.0000	0.0000	0.0000	0.0000
3	0.0498	0.1494	0.2240	0.2240	0.1680	0.1008	0.0504	0.0216	0.0081	0.0027	0.0008	0.0002	0.0001	0.0000	0.0000	0.0000	0.0000	0.0000	0.0000	0.0000	0.0000	0.0000	0.0000	0.0000	0.0000	0.0000
3.1	0.0450	0.1397	0.2165	0.2237	0.1733	0.1075	0.0555	0.0246	0.0095	0.0033	0.0010	0.0003	0.0001	0.0000	0.0000	0.0000	0.0000	0.0000	0.0000	0.0000	0.0000	0.0000	0.0000	0.0000	0.0000	0.0000
3.2	0.0408	0.1304	0.2087	0.2226	0.1781	0.1140	0.0608	0.0278	0.0111	0.0040	0.0013	0.0004	0.0001	0.0000	0.0000	0.0000	0.0000	0.0000	0.0000	0.0000	0.0000	0.0000	0.0000	0.0000	0.0000	0.0000
3.3	0.0369	0.1217	0.2008	0.2209	0.1823	0.1203	0.0662	0.0312	0.0129	0.0047	0.0016	0.0005	0.0001	0.0000	0.0000	0.0000	0.0000	0.0000	0.0000	0.0000	0.0000	0.0000	0.0000	0.0000	0.0000	0.0000
3.4	0.0334	0.1135	0.1929	0.2186	0.1858	0.1264	0.0716	0.0348	0.0148	0.0056	0.0019	0.0006	0.0002	0.0000	0.0000	0.0000	0.0000	0.0000	0.0000	0.0000	0.0000	0.0000	0.0000	0.0000	0.0000	0.0000
3.5	0.0302	0.1057	0.1850	0.2158	0.1888	0.1322	0.0771	0.0385	0.0169	0.0066	0.0023	0.0007	0.0002	0.0001	0.0000	0.0000	0.0000	0.0000	0.0000	0.0000	0.0000	0.0000	0.0000	0.0000	0.0000	0.0000
3.6	0.0273	0.0984	0.1771	0.2125	0.1912	0.1377	0.0826	0.0425	0.0191	0.0076	0.0028	0.0009	0.0003	0.0001	0.0000	0.0000	0.0000	0.0000	0.0000	0.0000	0.0000	0.0000	0.0000	0.0000	0.0000	0.0000
3.7	0.0247	0.0915	0.1692	0.2087	0.1931	0.1429	0.0881	0.0466	0.0215	0.0089	0.0033	0.0011	0.0003	0.0001	0.0000	0.0000	0.0000	0.0000	0.0000	0.0000	0.0000	0.0000	0.0000	0.0000	0.0000	0.0000
3.8	0.0224	0.0850	0.1615	0.2046	0.1944	0.1477	0.0936	0.0508	0.0241	0.0102	0.0039	0.0013	0.0004	0.0001	0.0000	0.0000	0.0000	0.0000	0.0000	0.0000	0.0000	0.0000	0.0000	0.0000	0.0000	0.0000
3.9	0.0202	0.0789	0.1539	0.2001	0.1951	0.1522	0.0989	0.0551	0.0269	0.0116	0.0045	0.0016	0.0005	0.0002	0.0000	0.0000	0.0000	0.0000	0.0000	0.0000	0.0000	0.0000	0.0000	0.0000	0.0000	0.0000

Poisson probability table (continued)

μ	0	1	2	3	4	5	6	7	8	9	10	11	12	13	14	15	16	17	18	19	20	21	22	23	24
4	0.0183	0.0733	0.1465	0.1954	0.1954	0.1563	0.1042	0.0595	0.0298	0.0132	0.0053	0.0019	0.0006	0.0002	0.0001	0.0000	0.0000	0.0000	0.0000	0.0000	0.0000	0.0000	0.0000	0.0000	0.0000
4.1	0.0166	0.0679	0.1393	0.1904	0.1951	0.1600	0.1093	0.0640	0.0328	0.0150	0.0061	0.0023	0.0008	0.0002	0.0001	0.0000	0.0000	0.0000	0.0000	0.0000	0.0000	0.0000	0.0000	0.0000	0.0000
4.2	0.0150	0.0630	0.1323	0.1852	0.1944	0.1633	0.1143	0.0686	0.0360	0.0168	0.0071	0.0027	0.0009	0.0003	0.0001	0.0000	0.0000	0.0000	0.0000	0.0000	0.0000	0.0000	0.0000	0.0000	0.0000
4.3	0.0136	0.0583	0.1254	0.1798	0.1933	0.1662	0.1191	0.0732	0.0393	0.0188	0.0081	0.0032	0.0011	0.0004	0.0001	0.0000	0.0000	0.0000	0.0000	0.0000	0.0000	0.0000	0.0000	0.0000	0.0000
4.4	0.0123	0.0540	0.1188	0.1743	0.1917	0.1687	0.1237	0.0778	0.0428	0.0209	0.0092	0.0037	0.0013	0.0005	0.0002	0.0000	0.0000	0.0000	0.0000	0.0000	0.0000	0.0000	0.0000	0.0000	0.0000
4.5	0.0111	0.0500	0.1125	0.1687	0.1898	0.1708	0.1281	0.0824	0.0463	0.0232	0.0104	0.0043	0.0016	0.0006	0.0002	0.0001	0.0000	0.0000	0.0000	0.0000	0.0000	0.0000	0.0000	0.0000	0.0000
4.6	0.0101	0.0462	0.1063	0.1631	0.1875	0.1725	0.1323	0.0869	0.0500	0.0255	0.0118	0.0049	0.0019	0.0007	0.0002	0.0001	0.0000	0.0000	0.0000	0.0000	0.0000	0.0000	0.0000	0.0000	0.0000
4.7	0.0091	0.0427	0.1005	0.1574	0.1849	0.1738	0.1362	0.0914	0.0537	0.0281	0.0132	0.0056	0.0022	0.0008	0.0003	0.0001	0.0000	0.0000	0.0000	0.0000	0.0000	0.0000	0.0000	0.0000	0.0000
4.8	0.0082	0.0395	0.0948	0.1517	0.1820	0.1747	0.1398	0.0959	0.0575	0.0307	0.0147	0.0064	0.0026	0.0009	0.0003	0.0001	0.0000	0.0000	0.0000	0.0000	0.0000	0.0000	0.0000	0.0000	0.0000
4.9	0.0074	0.0365	0.0894	0.1460	0.1789	0.1753	0.1432	0.1002	0.0614	0.0334	0.0164	0.0073	0.0030	0.0011	0.0004	0.0001	0.0000	0.0000	0.0000	0.0000	0.0000	0.0000	0.0000	0.0000	0.0000
5	0.0067	0.0337	0.0842	0.1404	0.1755	0.1755	0.1462	0.1044	0.0653	0.0363	0.0181	0.0082	0.0034	0.0013	0.0005	0.0002	0.0000	0.0000	0.0000	0.0000	0.0000	0.0000	0.0000	0.0000	0.0000
5.1	0.0061	0.0311	0.0793	0.1348	0.1719	0.1753	0.1490	0.1086	0.0692	0.0392	0.0200	0.0093	0.0039	0.0015	0.0006	0.0002	0.0001	0.0000	0.0000	0.0000	0.0000	0.0000	0.0000	0.0000	0.0000
5.2	0.0055	0.0287	0.0746	0.1293	0.1681	0.1748	0.1515	0.1125	0.0731	0.0423	0.0220	0.0104	0.0045	0.0018	0.0007	0.0002	0.0001	0.0000	0.0000	0.0000	0.0000	0.0000	0.0000	0.0000	0.0000
5.3	0.0050	0.0265	0.0701	0.1239	0.1641	0.1740	0.1537	0.1163	0.0771	0.0454	0.0241	0.0116	0.0051	0.0021	0.0008	0.0003	0.0001	0.0000	0.0000	0.0000	0.0000	0.0000	0.0000	0.0000	0.0000
5.4	0.0045	0.0244	0.0659	0.1185	0.1600	0.1728	0.1555	0.1200	0.0810	0.0486	0.0262	0.0129	0.0058	0.0024	0.0009	0.0003	0.0001	0.0000	0.0000	0.0000	0.0000	0.0000	0.0000	0.0000	0.0000
5.5	0.0041	0.0225	0.0618	0.1133	0.1558	0.1714	0.1571	0.1234	0.0849	0.0519	0.0285	0.0143	0.0065	0.0028	0.0011	0.0004	0.0001	0.0000	0.0000	0.0000	0.0000	0.0000	0.0000	0.0000	0.0000
5.6	0.0037	0.0207	0.0580	0.1082	0.1515	0.1697	0.1584	0.1267	0.0887	0.0552	0.0309	0.0157	0.0073	0.0032	0.0013	0.0005	0.0002	0.0001	0.0000	0.0000	0.0000	0.0000	0.0000	0.0000	0.0000
5.7	0.0033	0.0191	0.0544	0.1033	0.1472	0.1678	0.1594	0.1298	0.0925	0.0586	0.0334	0.0173	0.0082	0.0036	0.0015	0.0006	0.0002	0.0001	0.0000	0.0000	0.0000	0.0000	0.0000	0.0000	0.0000
5.8	0.0030	0.0176	0.0509	0.0985	0.1428	0.1656	0.1601	0.1326	0.0962	0.0620	0.0359	0.0190	0.0092	0.0041	0.0017	0.0007	0.0002	0.0001	0.0000	0.0000	0.0000	0.0000	0.0000	0.0000	0.0000
5.9	0.0027	0.0162	0.0477	0.0938	0.1383	0.1632	0.1605	0.1353	0.0998	0.0654	0.0386	0.0207	0.0102	0.0046	0.0019	0.0008	0.0003	0.0001	0.0000	0.0000	0.0000	0.0000	0.0000	0.0000	0.0000
6	0.0025	0.0149	0.0446	0.0892	0.1339	0.1606	0.1606	0.1377	0.1033	0.0688	0.0413	0.0225	0.0113	0.0052	0.0022	0.0009	0.0003	0.0001	0.0000	0.0000	0.0000	0.0000	0.0000	0.0000	0.0000
6.1	0.0022	0.0137	0.0417	0.0848	0.1294	0.1579	0.1605	0.1399	0.1066	0.0723	0.0441	0.0244	0.0124	0.0058	0.0025	0.0010	0.0004	0.0001	0.0000	0.0000	0.0000	0.0000	0.0000	0.0000	0.0000
6.2	0.0020	0.0126	0.0390	0.0806	0.1249	0.1549	0.1601	0.1418	0.1099	0.0757	0.0469	0.0265	0.0137	0.0065	0.0029	0.0012	0.0005	0.0002	0.0001	0.0000	0.0000	0.0000	0.0000	0.0000	0.0000
6.3	0.0018	0.0116	0.0364	0.0765	0.1205	0.1519	0.1595	0.1435	0.1130	0.0791	0.0498	0.0285	0.0150	0.0073	0.0033	0.0014	0.0005	0.0002	0.0001	0.0000	0.0000	0.0000	0.0000	0.0000	0.0000
6.4	0.0017	0.0106	0.0340	0.0726	0.1162	0.1487	0.1586	0.1450	0.1160	0.0825	0.0528	0.0307	0.0164	0.0081	0.0037	0.0016	0.0006	0.0002	0.0001	0.0000	0.0000	0.0000	0.0000	0.0000	0.0000
6.5	0.0015	0.0098	0.0318	0.0688	0.1118	0.1454	0.1575	0.1462	0.1188	0.0858	0.0558	0.0330	0.0179	0.0089	0.0041	0.0018	0.0007	0.0003	0.0001	0.0000	0.0000	0.0000	0.0000	0.0000	0.0000
6.6	0.0014	0.0090	0.0296	0.0652	0.1076	0.1420	0.1562	0.1472	0.1215	0.0891	0.0588	0.0353	0.0194	0.0099	0.0046	0.0020	0.0008	0.0003	0.0001	0.0000	0.0000	0.0000	0.0000	0.0000	0.0000
6.7	0.0012	0.0082	0.0276	0.0617	0.1034	0.1385	0.1546	0.1480	0.1240	0.0923	0.0618	0.0377	0.0210	0.0108	0.0052	0.0023	0.0010	0.0004	0.0001	0.0001	0.0000	0.0000	0.0000	0.0000	0.0000
6.8	0.0011	0.0076	0.0258	0.0584	0.0992	0.1349	0.1529	0.1486	0.1263	0.0954	0.0649	0.0401	0.0227	0.0119	0.0058	0.0026	0.0011	0.0004	0.0002	0.0001	0.0000	0.0000	0.0000	0.0000	0.0000
6.9	0.0010	0.0070	0.0240	0.0552	0.0952	0.1314	0.1511	0.1489	0.1284	0.0985	0.0679	0.0426	0.0245	0.0130	0.0064	0.0029	0.0013	0.0005	0.0002	0.0001	0.0000	0.0000	0.0000	0.0000	0.0000
7	0.0009	0.0064	0.0223	0.0521	0.0912	0.1277	0.1490	0.1490	0.1304	0.1014	0.0710	0.0452	0.0263	0.0142	0.0071	0.0033	0.0014	0.0006	0.0002	0.0001	0.0000	0.0000	0.0000	0.0000	0.0000
7.1	0.0008	0.0059	0.0208	0.0492	0.0874	0.1241	0.1468	0.1489	0.1321	0.1042	0.0740	0.0478	0.0283	0.0154	0.0078	0.0037	0.0016	0.0007	0.0003	0.0001	0.0000	0.0000	0.0000	0.0000	0.0000
7.2	0.0007	0.0054	0.0194	0.0464	0.0836	0.1204	0.1445	0.1486	0.1337	0.1070	0.0770	0.0504	0.0303	0.0168	0.0086	0.0041	0.0019	0.0008	0.0003	0.0001	0.0000	0.0000	0.0000	0.0000	0.0000
7.3	0.0007	0.0049	0.0180	0.0438	0.0799	0.1167	0.1420	0.1481	0.1351	0.1096	0.0800	0.0531	0.0323	0.0181	0.0095	0.0046	0.0021	0.0009	0.0004	0.0001	0.0001	0.0000	0.0000	0.0000	0.0000
7.4	0.0006	0.0045	0.0167	0.0413	0.0764	0.1130	0.1394	0.1474	0.1363	0.1121	0.0829	0.0558	0.0344	0.0196	0.0104	0.0051	0.0024	0.0010	0.0004	0.0002	0.0001	0.0000	0.0000	0.0000	0.0000
7.5	0.0006	0.0041	0.0156	0.0389	0.0729	0.1094	0.1367	0.1465	0.1373	0.1144	0.0858	0.0585	0.0366	0.0211	0.0113	0.0057	0.0026	0.0012	0.0005	0.0002	0.0001	0.0000	0.0000	0.0000	0.0000
7.6	0.0005	0.0038	0.0145	0.0366	0.0696	0.1057	0.1339	0.1454	0.1381	0.1167	0.0887	0.0613	0.0388	0.0227	0.0123	0.0062	0.0030	0.0013	0.0006	0.0002	0.0001	0.0000	0.0000	0.0000	0.0000
7.7	0.0005	0.0035	0.0134	0.0345	0.0663	0.1021	0.1311	0.1442	0.1388	0.1187	0.0914	0.0640	0.0411	0.0243	0.0134	0.0069	0.0033	0.0015	0.0006	0.0003	0.0001	0.0000	0.0000	0.0000	0.0000
7.8	0.0004	0.0032	0.0125	0.0324	0.0632	0.0986	0.1282	0.1428	0.1392	0.1207	0.0941	0.0667	0.0434	0.0260	0.0145	0.0075	0.0037	0.0017	0.0007	0.0003	0.0001	0.0000	0.0000	0.0000	0.0000
7.9	0.0004	0.0029	0.0116	0.0305	0.0602	0.0951	0.1252	0.1413	0.1395	0.1224	0.0967	0.0695	0.0457	0.0278	0.0157	0.0083	0.0041	0.0019	0.0008	0.0003	0.0001	0.0001	0.0000	0.0000	0.0000
8	0.0003	0.0027	0.0107	0.0286	0.0573	0.0916	0.1221	0.1396	0.1396	0.1241	0.0993	0.0722	0.0481	0.0296	0.0169	0.0090	0.0045	0.0021	0.0009	0.0004	0.0002	0.0001	0.0000	0.0000	0.0000
8.1	0.0003	0.0025	0.0100	0.0269	0.0544	0.0882	0.1191	0.1378	0.1395	0.1256	0.1017	0.0749	0.0505	0.0315	0.0182	0.0098	0.0050	0.0024	0.0011	0.0005	0.0002	0.0001	0.0000	0.0000	0.0000
8.2	0.0003	0.0023	0.0092	0.0252	0.0517	0.0849	0.1160	0.1358	0.1392	0.1269	0.1040	0.0776	0.0530	0.0334	0.0196	0.0107	0.0055	0.0026	0.0012	0.0005	0.0002	0.0001	0.0000	0.0000	0.0000
8.3	0.0002	0.0021	0.0086	0.0237	0.0491	0.0816	0.1128	0.1338	0.1388	0.1280	0.1063	0.0802	0.0555	0.0354	0.0210	0.0116	0.0060	0.0029	0.0014	0.0006	0.0002	0.0001	0.0000	0.0000	0.0000
8.4	0.0002	0.0019	0.0079	0.0222	0.0466	0.0784	0.1097	0.1317	0.1382	0.1290	0.1084	0.0828	0.0579	0.0374	0.0225	0.0126	0.0066	0.0033	0.0015	0.0007	0.0003	0.0001	0.0000	0.0000	0.0000
8.5	0.0002	0.0017	0.0074	0.0208	0.0443	0.0752	0.1066	0.1294	0.1375	0.1299	0.1104	0.0853	0.0604	0.0395	0.0240	0.0136	0.0072	0.0036	0.0017	0.0008	0.0003	0.0001	0.0001	0.0000	0.0000
8.6	0.0002	0.0016	0.0068	0.0195	0.0420	0.0722	0.1034	0.1271	0.1366	0.1306	0.1123	0.0878	0.0629	0.0416	0.0256	0.0147	0.0079	0.0040	0.0019	0.0009	0.0004	0.0002	0.0001	0.0000	0.0000
8.7	0.0002	0.0014	0.0063	0.0183	0.0398	0.0692	0.1003	0.1247	0.1356	0.1311	0.1140	0.0902	0.0654	0.0438	0.0272	0.0158	0.0086	0.0044	0.0021	0.0010	0.0004	0.0002	0.0001	0.0000	0.0000
8.8	0.0002	0.0013	0.0058	0.0171	0.0377	0.0663	0.0972	0.1222	0.1344	0.1315	0.1157	0.0925	0.0679	0.0459	0.0289	0.0169	0.0093	0.0048	0.0024	0.0011	0.0005	0.0002	0.0001	0.0000	0.0000
8.9	0.0001	0.0012	0.0054	0.0160	0.0357	0.0635	0.0941	0.1197	0.1332	0.1317	0.1172	0.0948	0.0703	0.0481	0.0306	0.0181	0.0101	0.0053	0.0026	0.0012	0.0005	0.0002	0.0001	0.0000	0.0000
9	0.0001	0.0011	0.0050	0.0150	0.0337	0.0607	0.0911	0.1171	0.1318	0.1318	0.1186	0.0970	0.0728	0.0504	0.0324	0.0194	0.0109	0.0058	0.0029	0.0014	0.0006	0.0003	0.0001	0.0000	0.0000
9.1	0.0001	0.0010	0.0046	0.0140	0.0319	0.0581	0.0881	0.1145	0.1302	0.1317	0.1198	0.0991	0.0752	0.0526	0.0342	0.0208	0.0118	0.0063	0.0032	0.0015	0.0007	0.0003	0.0001	0.0000	0.0000
9.2	0.0001	0.0009	0.0043	0.0131	0.0302	0.0555	0.0851	0.1118	0.1286	0.1315	0.1210	0.1012	0.0776	0.0549	0.0361	0.0221	0.0127	0.0069	0.0035	0.0017	0.0008	0.0003	0.0001	0.0001	0.0000

(continued)

Probabilities for the Poisson distribution (cont.)

Probability of success $x =$

	0	1	2	3	4	5	6	7	8	9	10	11	12	13	14	15	16	17	18	19	20	21	22	23	24	25
9.3	0.0001	0.0009	0.0040	0.0123	0.0285	0.0530	0.0822	0.1091	0.1269	0.1311	0.1219	0.1031	0.0799	0.0572	0.0380	0.0235	0.0137	0.0075	0.0039	0.0019	0.0009	0.0004	0.0002	0.0001	0.0000	0.0000
9.4	0.0001	0.0008	0.0037	0.0115	0.0269	0.0506	0.0793	0.1064	0.1251	0.1306	0.1228	0.1049	0.0822	0.0594	0.0399	0.0250	0.0147	0.0081	0.0042	0.0021	0.0010	0.0004	0.0002	0.0001	0.0000	0.0000
9.5	0.0001	0.0007	0.0034	0.0107	0.0254	0.0483	0.0764	0.1037	0.1232	0.1300	0.1235	0.1067	0.0844	0.0617	0.0419	0.0265	0.0157	0.0088	0.0046	0.0023	0.0011	0.0005	0.0002	0.0001	0.0000	0.0000
9.6	0.0001	0.0007	0.0031	0.0100	0.0240	0.0460	0.0736	0.1010	0.1212	0.1293	0.1241	0.1083	0.0866	0.0640	0.0439	0.0281	0.0168	0.0095	0.0051	0.0026	0.0012	0.0006	0.0002	0.0001	0.0000	0.0000
9.7	0.0001	0.0006	0.0029	0.0093	0.0226	0.0439	0.0709	0.0982	0.1191	0.1284	0.1245	0.1098	0.0888	0.0662	0.0459	0.0297	0.0180	0.0103	0.0055	0.0028	0.0014	0.0006	0.0003	0.0001	0.0000	0.0000
9.8	0.0001	0.0005	0.0027	0.0087	0.0213	0.0418	0.0682	0.0955	0.1170	0.1274	0.1249	0.1112	0.0908	0.0685	0.0479	0.0313	0.0192	0.0111	0.0060	0.0031	0.0015	0.0007	0.0003	0.0001	0.0001	0.0000
9.9	0.0001	0.0005	0.0025	0.0081	0.0201	0.0398	0.0656	0.0928	0.1148	0.1263	0.1250	0.1125	0.0928	0.0707	0.0500	0.0330	0.0204	0.0119	0.0065	0.0034	0.0017	0.0008	0.0004	0.0002	0.0001	0.0000
10	0.0000	0.0005	0.0023	0.0076	0.0189	0.0378	0.0631	0.0901	0.1126	0.1251	0.1251	0.1137	0.0948	0.0729	0.0521	0.0347	0.0217	0.0128	0.0071	0.0037	0.0019	0.0009	0.0004	0.0002	0.0001	0.0000
10.1	0.0000	0.0004	0.0021	0.0071	0.0178	0.0360	0.0606	0.0874	0.1103	0.1238	0.1250	0.1148	0.0966	0.0751	0.0542	0.0365	0.0230	0.0137	0.0077	0.0041	0.0021	0.0010	0.0005	0.0002	0.0001	0.0000
10.2	0.0000	0.0004	0.0019	0.0066	0.0168	0.0342	0.0581	0.0847	0.1080	0.1224	0.1249	0.1158	0.0984	0.0772	0.0563	0.0383	0.0244	0.0146	0.0083	0.0045	0.0023	0.0011	0.0005	0.0002	0.0001	0.0000
10.3	0.0000	0.0003	0.0018	0.0061	0.0158	0.0325	0.0558	0.0821	0.1057	0.1209	0.1246	0.1166	0.1001	0.0793	0.0584	0.0401	0.0258	0.0156	0.0089	0.0048	0.0025	0.0012	0.0006	0.0003	0.0001	0.0000
10.4	0.0000	0.0003	0.0016	0.0057	0.0148	0.0309	0.0535	0.0795	0.1033	0.1194	0.1241	0.1174	0.1017	0.0814	0.0604	0.0419	0.0272	0.0167	0.0096	0.0053	0.0027	0.0014	0.0006	0.0003	0.0001	0.0001
10.5	0.0000	0.0003	0.0015	0.0053	0.0139	0.0293	0.0513	0.0769	0.1009	0.1177	0.1236	0.1180	0.1032	0.0834	0.0625	0.0438	0.0287	0.0177	0.0104	0.0057	0.0030	0.0015	0.0007	0.0003	0.0002	0.0001
10.6	0.0000	0.0003	0.0014	0.0049	0.0131	0.0278	0.0491	0.0743	0.0985	0.1160	0.1230	0.1185	0.1047	0.0853	0.0646	0.0457	0.0303	0.0189	0.0111	0.0062	0.0033	0.0017	0.0008	0.0004	0.0002	0.0001
10.7	0.0000	0.0002	0.0013	0.0046	0.0123	0.0264	0.0470	0.0718	0.0961	0.1142	0.1222	0.1189	0.1060	0.0872	0.0667	0.0476	0.0318	0.0200	0.0119	0.0067	0.0036	0.0018	0.0009	0.0004	0.0002	0.0001
10.8	0.0000	0.0002	0.0012	0.0043	0.0116	0.0250	0.0450	0.0694	0.0936	0.1124	0.1214	0.1192	0.1072	0.0891	0.0687	0.0495	0.0334	0.0212	0.0127	0.0072	0.0039	0.0020	0.0010	0.0005	0.0002	0.0001
10.9	0.0000	0.0002	0.0011	0.0040	0.0109	0.0237	0.0430	0.0669	0.0912	0.1105	0.1204	0.1193	0.1084	0.0909	0.0708	0.0514	0.0350	0.0225	0.0136	0.0078	0.0043	0.0022	0.0011	0.0005	0.0002	0.0001
11	0.0000	0.0002	0.0010	0.0037	0.0102	0.0224	0.0411	0.0646	0.0888	0.1085	0.1194	0.1194	0.1094	0.0926	0.0728	0.0534	0.0367	0.0237	0.0145	0.0084	0.0046	0.0024	0.0012	0.0006	0.0003	0.0001
11.1	0.0000	0.0002	0.0009	0.0034	0.0096	0.0212	0.0393	0.0623	0.0864	0.1065	0.1182	0.1193	0.1104	0.0942	0.0747	0.0553	0.0384	0.0250	0.0154	0.0090	0.0050	0.0026	0.0013	0.0007	0.0003	0.0001
11.2	0.0000	0.0002	0.0009	0.0032	0.0090	0.0201	0.0375	0.0600	0.0840	0.1045	0.1170	0.1192	0.1112	0.0958	0.0767	0.0572	0.0401	0.0264	0.0164	0.0097	0.0054	0.0029	0.0015	0.0007	0.0003	0.0001
11.3	0.0000	0.0001	0.0008	0.0030	0.0084	0.0190	0.0358	0.0578	0.0816	0.1024	0.1157	0.1189	0.1120	0.0973	0.0786	0.0592	0.0418	0.0278	0.0174	0.0104	0.0059	0.0032	0.0016	0.0008	0.0004	0.0002
11.4	0.0000	0.0001	0.0008	0.0028	0.0079	0.0180	0.0341	0.0556	0.0792	0.1003	0.1144	0.1185	0.1126	0.0987	0.0804	0.0611	0.0435	0.0292	0.0185	0.0111	0.0063	0.0034	0.0018	0.0009	0.0004	0.0002
11.5	0.0000	0.0001	0.0007	0.0026	0.0074	0.0170	0.0325	0.0535	0.0769	0.0982	0.1129	0.1181	0.1131	0.1001	0.0822	0.0630	0.0453	0.0306	0.0196	0.0119	0.0068	0.0037	0.0020	0.0010	0.0005	0.0002
11.6	0.0000	0.0001	0.0006	0.0024	0.0069	0.0160	0.0310	0.0514	0.0745	0.0961	0.1114	0.1175	0.1136	0.1014	0.0840	0.0649	0.0471	0.0321	0.0207	0.0126	0.0073	0.0041	0.0021	0.0011	0.0005	0.0002
11.7	0.0000	0.0001	0.0006	0.0022	0.0065	0.0152	0.0295	0.0494	0.0722	0.0939	0.1099	0.1169	0.1139	0.1025	0.0857	0.0668	0.0489	0.0336	0.0219	0.0135	0.0079	0.0044	0.0023	0.0012	0.0006	0.0003
11.8	0.0000	0.0001	0.0005	0.0021	0.0061	0.0143	0.0281	0.0474	0.0700	0.0917	0.1082	0.1161	0.1142	0.1036	0.0874	0.0687	0.0507	0.0352	0.0231	0.0143	0.0084	0.0047	0.0025	0.0013	0.0006	0.0003
11.9	0.0000	0.0001	0.0005	0.0019	0.0057	0.0135	0.0268	0.0455	0.0677	0.0895	0.1066	0.1153	0.1143	0.1046	0.0889	0.0706	0.0525	0.0367	0.0243	0.0152	0.0091	0.0051	0.0028	0.0014	0.0007	0.0003
12	0.0000	0.0001	0.0004	0.0018	0.0053	0.0127	0.0255	0.0437	0.0655	0.0874	0.1048	0.1144	0.1144	0.1056	0.0905	0.0724	0.0543	0.0383	0.0255	0.0161	0.0097	0.0055	0.0030	0.0016	0.0008	0.0004
12.1	0.0000	0.0001	0.0004	0.0016	0.0050	0.0120	0.0242	0.0419	0.0634	0.0852	0.1031	0.1134	0.1143	0.1064	0.0920	0.0742	0.0561	0.0399	0.0268	0.0171	0.0103	0.0060	0.0033	0.0017	0.0009	0.0004
12.2	0.0000	0.0001	0.0004	0.0015	0.0046	0.0113	0.0230	0.0402	0.0612	0.0830	0.1013	0.1123	0.1142	0.1072	0.0934	0.0759	0.0579	0.0416	0.0282	0.0181	0.0110	0.0064	0.0036	0.0019	0.0010	0.0005
12.3	0.0000	0.0001	0.0003	0.0014	0.0043	0.0107	0.0219	0.0385	0.0591	0.0808	0.0994	0.1112	0.1139	0.1078	0.0947	0.0777	0.0597	0.0432	0.0295	0.0191	0.0118	0.0069	0.0038	0.0021	0.0011	0.0005
12.4	0.0000	0.0001	0.0003	0.0013	0.0041	0.0101	0.0208	0.0368	0.0571	0.0787	0.0975	0.1100	0.1136	0.1084	0.0960	0.0794	0.0615	0.0449	0.0309	0.0202	0.0125	0.0074	0.0042	0.0022	0.0012	0.0006
12.5	0.0000	0.0000	0.0003	0.0012	0.0038	0.0095	0.0197	0.0353	0.0551	0.0765	0.0956	0.1087	0.1132	0.1089	0.0972	0.0810	0.0633	0.0465	0.0323	0.0213	0.0133	0.0079	0.0045	0.0024	0.0013	0.0006
12.6	0.0000	0.0000	0.0003	0.0011	0.0035	0.0089	0.0187	0.0337	0.0531	0.0744	0.0937	0.1074	0.1127	0.1093	0.0983	0.0826	0.0650	0.0482	0.0337	0.0224	0.0141	0.0085	0.0048	0.0027	0.0014	0.0007
12.7	0.0000	0.0000	0.0002	0.0011	0.0033	0.0084	0.0178	0.0323	0.0512	0.0723	0.0918	0.1060	0.1121	0.1096	0.0994	0.0841	0.0668	0.0499	0.0352	0.0235	0.0149	0.0090	0.0052	0.0029	0.0015	0.0008
12.8	0.0000	0.0000	0.0002	0.0010	0.0031	0.0079	0.0169	0.0308	0.0493	0.0702	0.0898	0.1045	0.1115	0.1098	0.1004	0.0856	0.0685	0.0516	0.0367	0.0247	0.0158	0.0096	0.0056	0.0031	0.0017	0.0009
12.9	0.0000	0.0000	0.0002	0.0009	0.0029	0.0074	0.0160	0.0295	0.0475	0.0681	0.0878	0.1030	0.1107	0.1099	0.1013	0.0871	0.0702	0.0533	0.0382	0.0259	0.0167	0.0103	0.0060	0.0034	0.0018	0.0009
13	0.0000	0.0000	0.0002	0.0008	0.0027	0.0070	0.0152	0.0281	0.0457	0.0661	0.0859	0.1015	0.1099	0.1099	0.1021	0.0885	0.0719	0.0550	0.0397	0.0272	0.0177	0.0109	0.0065	0.0037	0.0020	0.0010
13.1	0.0000	0.0000	0.0002	0.0008	0.0025	0.0066	0.0144	0.0269	0.0440	0.0640	0.0839	0.0999	0.1091	0.1099	0.1028	0.0898	0.0735	0.0567	0.0412	0.0284	0.0186	0.0116	0.0069	0.0039	0.0022	0.0011
13.2	0.0000	0.0000	0.0002	0.0007	0.0023	0.0062	0.0136	0.0256	0.0423	0.0620	0.0819	0.0983	0.1081	0.1098	0.1035	0.0911	0.0751	0.0583	0.0428	0.0297	0.0196	0.0123	0.0074	0.0042	0.0023	0.0012
13.3	0.0000	0.0000	0.0001	0.0007	0.0022	0.0058	0.0129	0.0245	0.0407	0.0601	0.0799	0.0966	0.1071	0.1096	0.1041	0.0923	0.0767	0.0600	0.0443	0.0310	0.0206	0.0131	0.0079	0.0046	0.0025	0.0013
13.4	0.0000	0.0000	0.0001	0.0006	0.0020	0.0055	0.0122	0.0233	0.0391	0.0582	0.0779	0.0949	0.1060	0.1093	0.1046	0.0934	0.0783	0.0617	0.0459	0.0324	0.0217	0.0138	0.0084	0.0049	0.0027	0.0015
13.5	0.0000	0.0000	0.0001	0.0006	0.0019	0.0051	0.0115	0.0222	0.0375	0.0563	0.0760	0.0932	0.1049	0.1089	0.1050	0.0945	0.0798	0.0633	0.0475	0.0337	0.0228	0.0146	0.0090	0.0053	0.0030	0.0016
13.6	0.0000	0.0000	0.0001	0.0005	0.0018	0.0048	0.0109	0.0212	0.0360	0.0544	0.0740	0.0915	0.1037	0.1085	0.1054	0.0955	0.0812	0.0650	0.0491	0.0351	0.0239	0.0155	0.0096	0.0057	0.0032	0.0017
13.7	0.0000	0.0000	0.0001	0.0005	0.0016	0.0045	0.0103	0.0202	0.0345	0.0526	0.0720	0.0897	0.1024	0.1080	0.1056	0.0965	0.0826	0.0666	0.0507	0.0365	0.0250	0.0163	0.0102	0.0061	0.0035	0.0019
13.8	0.0000	0.0000	0.0001	0.0004	0.0015	0.0042	0.0097	0.0192	0.0331	0.0508	0.0701	0.0880	0.1011	0.1074	0.1058	0.0974	0.0840	0.0682	0.0523	0.0380	0.0262	0.0172	0.0108	0.0065	0.0037	0.0021
13.9	0.0000	0.0000	0.0001	0.0004	0.0014	0.0040	0.0092	0.0183	0.0318	0.0491	0.0682	0.0862	0.0998	0.1067	0.1060	0.0982	0.0853	0.0697	0.0539	0.0394	0.0274	0.0181	0.0115	0.0069	0.0040	0.0022
14	0.0000	0.0000	0.0001	0.0004	0.0013	0.0037	0.0087	0.0174	0.0304	0.0473	0.0663	0.0844	0.0984	0.1060	0.1060	0.0989	0.0866	0.0713	0.0554	0.0409	0.0286	0.0191	0.0121	0.0074	0.0043	0.0024
14.1	0.0000	0.0000	0.0001	0.0004	0.0012	0.0035	0.0082	0.0165	0.0292	0.0457	0.0644	0.0825	0.0970	0.1052	0.1060	0.0996	0.0878	0.0728	0.0570	0.0423	0.0298	0.0200	0.0128	0.0079	0.0046	0.0026

14.2	0.0028	0.0050	0.0084	0.0136	0.0210	0.0311	0.0438	0.0586	0.0743	0.0889	0.1002	0.1058	0.1043	0.0955	0.0807	0.0625	0.0440	0.0279	0.0157	0.0078	0.0033	0.0012	0.0003	0.0001	0.0000	0.0000	0.0000
14.3	0.0030	0.0053	0.0089	0.0143	0.0220	0.0324	0.0453	0.0602	0.0757	0.0900	0.1007	0.1057	0.1034	0.0940	0.0789	0.0607	0.0424	0.0267	0.0149	0.0073	0.0031	0.0011	0.0003	0.0001	0.0000	0.0000	0.0000
14.4	0.0033	0.0057	0.0095	0.0151	0.0231	0.0337	0.0468	0.0617	0.0771	0.0911	0.1012	0.1054	0.1025	0.0925	0.0771	0.0589	0.0409	0.0256	0.0142	0.0069	0.0029	0.0010	0.0003	0.0001	0.0000	0.0000	0.0000
14.5	0.0035	0.0061	0.0100	0.0159	0.0242	0.0350	0.0483	0.0632	0.0785	0.0920	0.1016	0.1051	0.1014	0.0910	0.0753	0.0571	0.0394	0.0244	0.0135	0.0065	0.0027	0.0009	0.0003	0.0001	0.0000	0.0000	0.0000
14.6	0.0038	0.0065	0.0106	0.0168	0.0253	0.0363	0.0498	0.0648	0.0798	0.0930	0.1019	0.1047	0.1004	0.0894	0.0735	0.0553	0.0379	0.0234	0.0128	0.0061	0.0025	0.0009	0.0002	0.0001	0.0000	0.0000	0.0000
14.7	0.0041	0.0069	0.0113	0.0176	0.0264	0.0377	0.0513	0.0663	0.0811	0.0938	0.1021	0.1042	0.0992	0.0878	0.0716	0.0536	0.0365	0.0223	0.0122	0.0058	0.0024	0.0008	0.0002	0.0001	0.0000	0.0000	0.0000
14.8	0.0043	0.0073	0.0119	0.0185	0.0275	0.0390	0.0528	0.0677	0.0824	0.0946	0.1023	0.1037	0.0981	0.0861	0.0698	0.0519	0.0351	0.0213	0.0115	0.0055	0.0022	0.0007	0.0002	0.0001	0.0000	0.0000	0.0000
14.9	0.0047	0.0078	0.0126	0.0194	0.0287	0.0404	0.0543	0.0692	0.0836	0.0954	0.1024	0.1031	0.0969	0.0845	0.0681	0.0502	0.0337	0.0204	0.0109	0.0051	0.0021	0.0007	0.0002	0.0001	0.0000	0.0000	0.0000
15	0.0050	0.0083	0.0133	0.0204	0.0299	0.0418	0.0557	0.0706	0.0847	0.0960	0.1024	0.1024	0.0956	0.0829	0.0663	0.0486	0.0324	0.0194	0.0104	0.0048	0.0019	0.0006	0.0002	0.0001	0.0000	0.0000	0.0000
15.1	0.0053	0.0088	0.0140	0.0213	0.0311	0.0432	0.0572	0.0720	0.0858	0.0966	0.1024	0.1017	0.0943	0.0812	0.0645	0.0470	0.0311	0.0186	0.0098	0.0046	0.0018	0.0006	0.0002	0.0001	0.0000	0.0000	0.0000
15.2	0.0057	0.0093	0.0147	0.0223	0.0323	0.0446	0.0587	0.0734	0.0869	0.0972	0.1023	0.1010	0.0930	0.0795	0.0628	0.0454	0.0299	0.0177	0.0093	0.0043	0.0017	0.0006	0.0002	0.0001	0.0000	0.0000	0.0000
15.3	0.0061	0.0099	0.0155	0.0233	0.0335	0.0460	0.0602	0.0747	0.0879	0.0977	0.1021	0.1001	0.0916	0.0778	0.0611	0.0439	0.0287	0.0169	0.0088	0.0040	0.0016	0.0005	0.0002	0.0001	0.0000	0.0000	0.0000
15.4	0.0064	0.0105	0.0163	0.0244	0.0348	0.0474	0.0616	0.0760	0.0888	0.0981	0.1019	0.0992	0.0902	0.0762	0.0594	0.0424	0.0275	0.0161	0.0084	0.0038	0.0015	0.0005	0.0002	0.0001	0.0000	0.0000	0.0000
15.5	0.0069	0.0111	0.0171	0.0254	0.0361	0.0489	0.0630	0.0773	0.0897	0.0984	0.1016	0.0983	0.0888	0.0745	0.0577	0.0409	0.0264	0.0153	0.0079	0.0036	0.0014	0.0005	0.0002	0.0001	0.0000	0.0000	0.0000
15.6	0.0073	0.0117	0.0180	0.0265	0.0373	0.0503	0.0645	0.0785	0.0906	0.0987	0.1012	0.0974	0.0874	0.0728	0.0560	0.0395	0.0253	0.0146	0.0075	0.0034	0.0013	0.0004	0.0001	0.0001	0.0000	0.0000	0.0000
15.7	0.0077	0.0123	0.0188	0.0276	0.0386	0.0517	0.0659	0.0797	0.0914	0.0989	0.1008	0.0963	0.0859	0.0711	0.0544	0.0381	0.0243	0.0139	0.0071	0.0032	0.0012	0.0004	0.0001	0.0001	0.0000	0.0000	0.0000
15.8	0.0082	0.0130	0.0197	0.0287	0.0400	0.0531	0.0672	0.0808	0.0921	0.0991	0.1003	0.0953	0.0844	0.0695	0.0527	0.0367	0.0232	0.0132	0.0067	0.0030	0.0011	0.0004	0.0001	0.0001	0.0000	0.0000	0.0000
15.9	0.0087	0.0137	0.0206	0.0298	0.0413	0.0545	0.0686	0.0819	0.0928	0.0992	0.0998	0.0942	0.0829	0.0678	0.0512	0.0354	0.0223	0.0126	0.0063	0.0028	0.0011	0.0003	0.0001	0.0001	0.0000	0.0000	0.0000
16	0.0092	0.0144	0.0216	0.0310	0.0426	0.0559	0.0699	0.0830	0.0934	0.0992	0.0992	0.0930	0.0814	0.0661	0.0496	0.0341	0.0213	0.0120	0.0060	0.0026	0.0010	0.0003	0.0001	0.0001	0.0000	0.0000	0.0000
16.1	0.0097	0.0151	0.0225	0.0322	0.0439	0.0573	0.0712	0.0840	0.0939	0.0992	0.0986	0.0918	0.0799	0.0645	0.0481	0.0328	0.0204	0.0114	0.0057	0.0025	0.0009	0.0003	0.0001	0.0001	0.0000	0.0000	0.0000
16.2	0.0103	0.0159	0.0235	0.0333	0.0453	0.0587	0.0725	0.0850	0.0944	0.0991	0.0979	0.0906	0.0783	0.0628	0.0466	0.0316	0.0195	0.0108	0.0054	0.0023	0.0009	0.0003	0.0001	0.0001	0.0000	0.0000	0.0000
16.3	0.0108	0.0166	0.0245	0.0345	0.0466	0.0601	0.0737	0.0859	0.0949	0.0989	0.0971	0.0894	0.0768	0.0612	0.0451	0.0304	0.0187	0.0103	0.0051	0.0022	0.0008	0.0003	0.0001	0.0001	0.0000	0.0000	0.0000
16.4	0.0114	0.0174	0.0255	0.0358	0.0480	0.0614	0.0749	0.0868	0.0952	0.0987	0.0963	0.0881	0.0752	0.0596	0.0436	0.0293	0.0178	0.0098	0.0048	0.0020	0.0008	0.0002	0.0001	0.0000	0.0000	0.0000	0.0000
16.5	0.0120	0.0182	0.0265	0.0370	0.0493	0.0628	0.0761	0.0876	0.0956	0.0985	0.0955	0.0868	0.0736	0.0580	0.0422	0.0281	0.0171	0.0093	0.0045	0.0019	0.0007	0.0002	0.0001	0.0000	0.0000	0.0000	0.0000
16.6	0.0127	0.0191	0.0276	0.0382	0.0507	0.0641	0.0772	0.0884	0.0958	0.0981	0.0946	0.0855	0.0721	0.0565	0.0408	0.0270	0.0163	0.0088	0.0043	0.0018	0.0006	0.0002	0.0001	0.0000	0.0000	0.0000	0.0000
16.7	0.0133	0.0199	0.0287	0.0395	0.0520	0.0654	0.0783	0.0891	0.0960	0.0978	0.0937	0.0841	0.0705	0.0549	0.0394	0.0260	0.0156	0.0084	0.0040	0.0017	0.0006	0.0002	0.0001	0.0000	0.0000	0.0000	0.0000
16.8	0.0140	0.0208	0.0297	0.0407	0.0533	0.0667	0.0794	0.0898	0.0962	0.0973	0.0927	0.0828	0.0690	0.0534	0.0381	0.0250	0.0149	0.0080	0.0038	0.0016	0.0006	0.0002	0.0001	0.0000	0.0000	0.0000	0.0000
16.9	0.0147	0.0217	0.0309	0.0420	0.0547	0.0679	0.0804	0.0904	0.0963	0.0968	0.0917	0.0814	0.0674	0.0518	0.0368	0.0240	0.0142	0.0076	0.0036	0.0015	0.0005	0.0002	0.0001	0.0000	0.0000	0.0000	0.0000
17	0.0154	0.0226	0.0320	0.0433	0.0560	0.0692	0.0814	0.0909	0.0963	0.0963	0.0906	0.0800	0.0658	0.0504	0.0355	0.0230	0.0135	0.0072	0.0034	0.0014	0.0005	0.0002	0.0001	0.0000	0.0000	0.0000	0.0000
17.1	0.0161	0.0236	0.0331	0.0445	0.0573	0.0704	0.0823	0.0914	0.0966	0.0957	0.0895	0.0785	0.0643	0.0489	0.0343	0.0221	0.0129	0.0068	0.0032	0.0013	0.0005	0.0002	0.0001	0.0000	0.0000	0.0000	0.0000
17.2	0.0169	0.0246	0.0343	0.0458	0.0586	0.0715	0.0832	0.0919	0.0972	0.0951	0.0884	0.0771	0.0628	0.0474	0.0331	0.0212	0.0123	0.0064	0.0030	0.0012	0.0004	0.0002	0.0001	0.0000	0.0000	0.0000	0.0000
17.3	0.0177	0.0255	0.0354	0.0471	0.0596	0.0727	0.0840	0.0923	0.0977	0.0944	0.0873	0.0757	0.0612	0.0460	0.0319	0.0203	0.0117	0.0061	0.0028	0.0011	0.0004	0.0001	0.0001	0.0000	0.0000	0.0000	0.0000
17.4	0.0185	0.0265	0.0366	0.0484	0.0608	0.0738	0.0848	0.0926	0.0981	0.0936	0.0861	0.0742	0.0597	0.0446	0.0308	0.0195	0.0112	0.0058	0.0027	0.0011	0.0004	0.0001	0.0001	0.0000	0.0000	0.0000	0.0000
17.5	0.0193	0.0275	0.0378	0.0496	0.0620	0.0749	0.0856	0.0929	0.0981	0.0929	0.0849	0.0728	0.0583	0.0432	0.0297	0.0186	0.0107	0.0055	0.0025	0.0010	0.0004	0.0001	0.0001	0.0000	0.0000	0.0000	0.0000
17.6	0.0201	0.0286	0.0390	0.0509	0.0632	0.0760	0.0863	0.0932	0.0984	0.0920	0.0837	0.0713	0.0567	0.0419	0.0286	0.0179	0.0101	0.0052	0.0024	0.0009	0.0003	0.0001	0.0001	0.0000	0.0000	0.0000	0.0000
17.7	0.0210	0.0296	0.0402	0.0522	0.0643	0.0770	0.0870	0.0934	0.0987	0.0912	0.0824	0.0699	0.0553	0.0406	0.0275	0.0171	0.0097	0.0049	0.0022	0.0009	0.0003	0.0001	0.0001	0.0000	0.0000	0.0000	0.0000
17.8	0.0218	0.0307	0.0414	0.0535	0.0655	0.0780	0.0876	0.0935	0.0989	0.0903	0.0812	0.0684	0.0538	0.0393	0.0265	0.0164	0.0092	0.0046	0.0021	0.0008	0.0003	0.0001	0.0000	0.0000	0.0000	0.0000	0.0000
17.9	0.0227	0.0318	0.0426	0.0547	0.0666	0.0789	0.0882	0.0936	0.0992	0.0894	0.0799	0.0669	0.0524	0.0380	0.0255	0.0157	0.0088	0.0044	0.0020	0.0008	0.0003	0.0001	0.0000	0.0000	0.0000	0.0000	0.0000
18	0.02371	0.0328	0.0438	0.0560	0.0676	0.0798	0.0887	0.0936	0.0992	0.0884	0.0786	0.0655	0.0509	0.0368	0.0245	0.0150	0.0083	0.0042	0.0019	0.0007	0.0002	0.0001	0.0000	0.0000	0.0000	0.0000	0.0000
18.1	0.02461	0.0340	0.0450	0.0572	0.0687	0.0807	0.0891	0.0936	0.0992	0.0874	0.0773	0.0640	0.0495	0.0356	0.0236	0.0143	0.0079	0.0039	0.0017	0.0007	0.0002	0.0001	0.0000	0.0000	0.0000	0.0000	0.0000
18.2	0.02551	0.0351	0.0462	0.0584	0.0697	0.0815	0.0896	0.0935	0.0991	0.0864	0.0759	0.0626	0.0481	0.0344	0.0227	0.0137	0.0075	0.0037	0.0016	0.0007	0.0002	0.0001	0.0000	0.0000	0.0000	0.0000	0.0000
18.3	0.02651	0.0362	0.0475	0.0596	0.0706	0.0823	0.0899	0.0934	0.0989	0.0853	0.0746	0.0611	0.0468	0.0332	0.0218	0.0131	0.0072	0.0035	0.0015	0.0006	0.0002	0.0001	0.0000	0.0000	0.0000	0.0000	0.0000
18.4	0.02751	0.0373	0.0487	0.0608	0.0717	0.0830	0.0902	0.0932	0.0987	0.0842	0.0732	0.0597	0.0454	0.0321	0.0209	0.0125	0.0068	0.0033	0.0014	0.0006	0.0002	0.0001	0.0000	0.0000	0.0000	0.0000	0.0000
18.5	0.02851	0.0385	0.0499	0.0620	0.0727	0.0837	0.0905	0.0930	0.0985	0.0831	0.0719	0.0583	0.0441	0.0310	0.0201	0.0120	0.0065	0.0031	0.0014	0.0005	0.0002	0.0001	0.0000	0.0000	0.0000	0.0000	0.0000
18.6	0.02951	0.0396	0.0511	0.0632	0.0738	0.0844	0.0907	0.0927	0.0981	0.0820	0.0705	0.0569	0.0428	0.0299	0.0193	0.0114	0.0061	0.0030	0.0013	0.0005	0.0002	0.0001	0.0000	0.0000	0.0000	0.0000	0.0000
18.7	0.03051	0.0408	0.0523	0.0643	0.0747	0.0850	0.0909	0.0924	0.0978	0.0808	0.0692	0.0555	0.0415	0.0289	0.0185	0.0109	0.0058	0.0028	0.0012	0.0004	0.0001	0.0000	0.0000	0.0000	0.0000	0.0000	0.0000
18.8	0.03151	0.0419	0.0535	0.0655	0.0757	0.0856	0.0910	0.0920	0.0973	0.0796	0.0678	0.0541	0.0403	0.0278	0.0178	0.0104	0.0055	0.0026	0.0011	0.0004	0.0001	0.0000	0.0000	0.0000	0.0000	0.0000	0.0000
18.9	0.0326	0.0431	0.0547	0.0666	0.0766	0.0861	0.0911	0.0916	0.0968	0.0785	0.0664	0.0527	0.0390	0.0269	0.0171	0.0099	0.0053	0.0025	0.0011	0.0004	0.0001	0.0000	0.0000	0.0000	0.0000	0.0000	0.0000
19	0.0336	0.0442	0.0559	0.0676	0.0772	0.0866	0.0911	0.0911	0.0963	0.0772	0.0650	0.0514	0.0378	0.0259	0.0164	0.0095	0.0050	0.0024	0.0010	0.0004	0.0001	0.0000	0.0000	0.0000	0.0000	0.0000	0.0000
19.1	0.0347	0.0454	0.0570	0.0687	0.0760	0.0870	0.0911	0.0906	0.0957	0.0760	0.0637	0.0500	0.0367	0.0249	0.0157	0.0090	0.0047	0.0022	0.0009	0.0003	0.0001	0.0000	0.0000	0.0000	0.0000	0.0000	0.0000
19.2	0.0358	0.0466	0.0582	0.0697	0.0748	0.0874	0.0910	0.0901	0.0951	0.0748	0.0623	0.0487	0.0355	0.0240	0.0150	0.0086	0.0045	0.0021	0.0009	0.0003	0.0001	0.0000	0.0000	0.0000	0.0000	0.0000	0.0000
19.3	0.0368	0.0477	0.0594	0.0707	0.0735	0.0877	0.0909	0.0895	0.0944	0.0735	0.0610	0.0474	0.0344	0.0231	0.0144	0.0082	0.0042	0.0020	0.0008	0.0003	0.0001	0.0000	0.0000	0.0000	0.0000	0.0000	0.0000

(continued)

Probabilities for the Poisson distribution (cont.)

Probability of success x =

λ	0	1	2	3	4	5	6	7	8	9	10	11	12	13	14	15	16	17	18	19	20	21	22	23	24	25
19.4	0.0000	0.0000	0.0000	0.0000	0.0000	0.0001	0.0003	0.0008	0.0019	0.0040	0.0078	0.0138	0.0223	0.0333	0.0461	0.0596	0.0723	0.0825	0.0889	0.0907	0.0880	0.0813	0.0717	0.0605	0.0489	0.0379
19.5	0.0000	0.0000	0.0000	0.0000	0.0000	0.0001	0.0003	0.0007	0.0018	0.0038	0.0074	0.0132	0.0214	0.0322	0.0448	0.0582	0.0710	0.0814	0.0882	0.0905	0.0883	0.0820	0.0727	0.0616	0.0500	0.0390
19.6	0.0000	0.0000	0.0000	0.0000	0.0000	0.0001	0.0002	0.0007	0.0017	0.0036	0.0071	0.0126	0.0206	0.0311	0.0436	0.0569	0.0697	0.0804	0.0875	0.0903	0.0885	0.0826	0.0736	0.0627	0.0512	0.0401
19.7	0.0000	0.0000	0.0000	0.0000	0.0000	0.0001	0.0002	0.0006	0.0016	0.0034	0.0067	0.0121	0.0198	0.0301	0.0423	0.0556	0.0684	0.0793	0.0868	0.0900	0.0886	0.0831	0.0745	0.0638	0.0523	0.0412
19.8	0.0000	0.0000	0.0000	0.0000	0.0000	0.0001	0.0002	0.0006	0.0015	0.0032	0.0064	0.0116	0.0191	0.0291	0.0411	0.0543	0.0671	0.0782	0.0860	0.0896	0.0887	0.0837	0.0753	0.0648	0.0535	0.0424
19.9	0.0000	0.0000	0.0000	0.0000	0.0000	0.0001	0.0002	0.0006	0.0014	0.0031	0.0061	0.0111	0.0183	0.0281	0.0399	0.0529	0.0659	0.0771	0.0852	0.0893	0.0888	0.0842	0.0761	0.0659	0.0546	0.0435
20	0.0000	0.0000	0.0000	0.0000	0.0000	0.0001	0.0002	0.0005	0.0013	0.0029	0.0058	0.0106	0.0176	0.0271	0.0387	0.0516	0.0646	0.0760	0.0844	0.0888	0.0888	0.0846	0.0769	0.0669	0.0557	0.0446
20.1	0.0000	0.0000	0.0000	0.0000	0.0000	0.0001	0.0002	0.0005	0.0012	0.0028	0.0055	0.0101	0.0169	0.0262	0.0376	0.0504	0.0633	0.0748	0.0835	0.0884	0.0888	0.0850	0.0777	0.0679	0.0568	0.0457
20.2	0.0000	0.0000	0.0000	0.0000	0.0000	0.0001	0.0002	0.0005	0.0012	0.0026	0.0053	0.0097	0.0163	0.0253	0.0365	0.0491	0.0620	0.0736	0.0826	0.0879	0.0887	0.0854	0.0784	0.0688	0.0579	0.0468
20.3	0.0000	0.0000	0.0000	0.0000	0.0000	0.0001	0.0001	0.0004	0.0011	0.0025	0.0050	0.0092	0.0156	0.0244	0.0353	0.0478	0.0607	0.0725	0.0817	0.0873	0.0886	0.0857	0.0791	0.0698	0.0590	0.0479
20.4	0.0000	0.0000	0.0000	0.0000	0.0000	0.0001	0.0001	0.0004	0.0010	0.0023	0.0048	0.0088	0.0150	0.0235	0.0343	0.0466	0.0594	0.0713	0.0808	0.0868	0.0885	0.0860	0.0797	0.0707	0.0601	0.0490
20.5	0.0000	0.0000	0.0000	0.0000	0.0000	0.0001	0.0001	0.0004	0.0010	0.0022	0.0045	0.0084	0.0144	0.0227	0.0332	0.0454	0.0581	0.0701	0.0798	0.0861	0.0883	0.0862	0.0803	0.0716	0.0611	0.0501
20.6	0.0000	0.0000	0.0000	0.0000	0.0000	0.0001	0.0001	0.0004	0.0009	0.0021	0.0043	0.0080	0.0138	0.0219	0.0322	0.0442	0.0569	0.0689	0.0789	0.0855	0.0881	0.0864	0.0809	0.0724	0.0622	0.0512
20.7	0.0000	0.0000	0.0000	0.0000	0.0000	0.0001	0.0001	0.0003	0.0009	0.0020	0.0041	0.0077	0.0132	0.0211	0.0311	0.0430	0.0556	0.0677	0.0778	0.0848	0.0878	0.0865	0.0814	0.0733	0.0632	0.0523
20.8	0.0000	0.0000	0.0000	0.0000	0.0000	0.0001	0.0001	0.0003	0.0008	0.0019	0.0039	0.0073	0.0127	0.0203	0.0301	0.0418	0.0543	0.0665	0.0768	0.0841	0.0875	0.0866	0.0819	0.0741	0.0642	0.0534
20.9	0.0000	0.0000	0.0000	0.0000	0.0000	0.0001	0.0001	0.0003	0.0008	0.0018	0.0037	0.0070	0.0122	0.0195	0.0292	0.0406	0.0531	0.0653	0.0758	0.0834	0.0871	0.0867	0.0824	0.0748	0.0652	0.0545
21	0.0000	0.0000	0.0000	0.0000	0.0000	0.0000	0.0001	0.0003	0.0007	0.0017	0.0035	0.0067	0.0116	0.0188	0.0282	0.0395	0.0518	0.0640	0.0747	0.0826	0.0867	0.0867	0.0828	0.0756	0.0661	0.0555
21.1	0.0000	0.0000	0.0000	0.0000	0.0000	0.0000	0.0001	0.0003	0.0007	0.0016	0.0033	0.0063	0.0112	0.0181	0.0273	0.0384	0.0506	0.0628	0.0736	0.0818	0.0863	0.0867	0.0831	0.0763	0.0671	0.0566
21.2	0.0000	0.0000	0.0000	0.0000	0.0000	0.0000	0.0001	0.0002	0.0006	0.0015	0.0031	0.0060	0.0107	0.0174	0.0264	0.0373	0.0494	0.0616	0.0726	0.0810	0.0858	0.0866	0.0835	0.0769	0.0680	0.0576
21.3	0.0000	0.0000	0.0000	0.0000	0.0000	0.0000	0.0001	0.0002	0.0006	0.0014	0.0030	0.0058	0.0102	0.0168	0.0255	0.0362	0.0482	0.0604	0.0715	0.0801	0.0853	0.0865	0.0838	0.0776	0.0689	0.0587
21.4	0.0000	0.0000	0.0000	0.0000	0.0000	0.0000	0.0001	0.0002	0.0006	0.0013	0.0028	0.0055	0.0098	0.0161	0.0246	0.0351	0.0470	0.0592	0.0703	0.0792	0.0848	0.0864	0.0840	0.0782	0.0697	0.0597
21.5	0.0000	0.0000	0.0000	0.0000	0.0000	0.0000	0.0001	0.0002	0.0005	0.0012	0.0027	0.0052	0.0094	0.0155	0.0238	0.0341	0.0458	0.0580	0.0692	0.0783	0.0842	0.0862	0.0842	0.0788	0.0705	0.0607
21.6	0.0000	0.0000	0.0000	0.0000	0.0000	0.0000	0.0001	0.0002	0.0005	0.0012	0.0025	0.0050	0.0090	0.0149	0.0230	0.0331	0.0447	0.0567	0.0681	0.0774	0.0836	0.0860	0.0844	0.0793	0.0714	0.0617
21.7	0.0000	0.0000	0.0000	0.0000	0.0000	0.0000	0.0001	0.0002	0.0005	0.0011	0.0024	0.0047	0.0086	0.0143	0.0222	0.0321	0.0435	0.0555	0.0669	0.0765	0.0830	0.0857	0.0846	0.0798	0.0721	0.0626
21.8	0.0000	0.0000	0.0000	0.0000	0.0000	0.0000	0.0001	0.0002	0.0004	0.0010	0.0023	0.0045	0.0082	0.0137	0.0214	0.0311	0.0424	0.0543	0.0658	0.0755	0.0823	0.0854	0.0847	0.0802	0.0729	0.0636
21.9	0.0000	0.0000	0.0000	0.0000	0.0000	0.0000	0.0001	0.0001	0.0004	0.0010	0.0022	0.0043	0.0078	0.0132	0.0206	0.0301	0.0413	0.0531	0.0647	0.0745	0.0816	0.0851	0.0847	0.0807	0.0736	0.0645
22	0.0000	0.0000	0.0000	0.0000	0.0000	0.0000	0.0001	0.0001	0.0004	0.0009	0.0020	0.0041	0.0075	0.0127	0.0199	0.0292	0.0401	0.0520	0.0635	0.0735	0.0809	0.0847	0.0847	0.0810	0.0743	0.0654
22.1	0.0000	0.0000	0.0000	0.0000	0.0000	0.0000	0.0001	0.0001	0.0004	0.0009	0.0019	0.0039	0.0072	0.0122	0.0192	0.0283	0.0391	0.0508	0.0623	0.0725	0.0801	0.0843	0.0847	0.0814	0.0750	0.0663
22.2	0.0000	0.0000	0.0000	0.0000	0.0000	0.0000	0.0001	0.0001	0.0003	0.0008	0.0018	0.0037	0.0068	0.0117	0.0185	0.0274	0.0380	0.0496	0.0612	0.0715	0.0794	0.0839	0.0847	0.0817	0.0756	0.0671
22.3	0.0000	0.0000	0.0000	0.0000	0.0000	0.0000	0.0001	0.0001	0.0003	0.0008	0.0017	0.0035	0.0065	0.0112	0.0178	0.0265	0.0369	0.0485	0.0600	0.0705	0.0786	0.0834	0.0846	0.0820	0.0762	0.0680
22.4	0.0000	0.0000	0.0000	0.0000	0.0000	0.0000	0.0000	0.0001	0.0003	0.0007	0.0016	0.0033	0.0062	0.0107	0.0172	0.0256	0.0359	0.0473	0.0589	0.0694	0.0777	0.0829	0.0844	0.0822	0.0767	0.0688
22.5	0.0000	0.0000	0.0000	0.0000	0.0000	0.0000	0.0000	0.0001	0.0003	0.0007	0.0016	0.0032	0.0059	0.0103	0.0165	0.0248	0.0349	0.0462	0.0577	0.0684	0.0769	0.0824	0.0843	0.0824	0.0773	0.0695
22.6	0.0000	0.0000	0.0000	0.0000	0.0000	0.0000	0.0000	0.0001	0.0003	0.0006	0.0015	0.0030	0.0057	0.0099	0.0159	0.0240	0.0339	0.0451	0.0566	0.0673	0.0760	0.0818	0.0841	0.0826	0.0778	0.0703
22.7	0.0000	0.0000	0.0000	0.0000	0.0000	0.0000	0.0000	0.0001	0.0002	0.0006	0.0013	0.0029	0.0054	0.0095	0.0153	0.0232	0.0329	0.0439	0.0554	0.0662	0.0751	0.0812	0.0838	0.0827	0.0782	0.0710
22.8	0.0000	0.0000	0.0000	0.0000	0.0000	0.0000	0.0000	0.0001	0.0002	0.0006	0.0013	0.0027	0.0052	0.0091	0.0147	0.0224	0.0319	0.0428	0.0543	0.0651	0.0742	0.0806	0.0835	0.0828	0.0787	0.0717
22.9	0.0000	0.0000	0.0000	0.0000	0.0000	0.0000	0.0000	0.0001	0.0002	0.0005	0.0012	0.0026	0.0049	0.0087	0.0142	0.0217	0.0310	0.0418	0.0531	0.0640	0.0733	0.0800	0.0832	0.0829	0.0791	0.0724
23	0.0000	0.0000	0.0000	0.0000	0.0000	0.0000	0.0000	0.0001	0.0002	0.0005	0.0012	0.0024	0.0047	0.0083	0.0136	0.0209	0.0301	0.0407	0.0520	0.0629	0.0724	0.0793	0.0829	0.0829	0.0794	0.0731
23.1	0.0000	0.0000	0.0000	0.0000	0.0000	0.0000	0.0000	0.0001	0.0002	0.0005	0.0011	0.0023	0.0045	0.0080	0.0131	0.0202	0.0292	0.0396	0.0509	0.0618	0.0714	0.0786	0.0825	0.0829	0.0798	0.0737
23.2	0.0000	0.0000	0.0000	0.0000	0.0000	0.0000	0.0000	0.0001	0.0002	0.0005	0.0010	0.0022	0.0043	0.0076	0.0126	0.0195	0.0283	0.0386	0.0498	0.0607	0.0705	0.0779	0.0821	0.0828	0.0801	0.0743
23.3	0.0000	0.0000	0.0000	0.0000	0.0000	0.0000	0.0000	0.0001	0.0002	0.0004	0.0010	0.0021	0.0041	0.0073	0.0121	0.0188	0.0274	0.0376	0.0486	0.0596	0.0695	0.0771	0.0817	0.0827	0.0803	0.0748
23.4	0.0000	0.0000	0.0000	0.0000	0.0000	0.0000	0.0000	0.0001	0.0002	0.0004	0.0009	0.0020	0.0039	0.0070	0.0116	0.0182	0.0266	0.0366	0.0475	0.0585	0.0685	0.0763	0.0812	0.0826	0.0805	0.0754
23.5	0.0000	0.0000	0.0000	0.0000	0.0000	0.0000	0.0000	0.0001	0.0001	0.0004	0.0009	0.0019	0.0037	0.0067	0.0112	0.0175	0.0257	0.0356	0.0464	0.0574	0.0675	0.0755	0.0807	0.0824	0.0807	0.0759
23.6	0.0000	0.0000	0.0000	0.0000	0.0000	0.0000	0.0000	0.0001	0.0001	0.0004	0.0008	0.0018	0.0035	0.0064	0.0107	0.0169	0.0249	0.0346	0.0454	0.0563	0.0665	0.0747	0.0802	0.0822	0.0809	0.0763
23.7	0.0000	0.0000	0.0000	0.0000	0.0000	0.0000	0.0000	0.0001	0.0001	0.0003	0.0008	0.0017	0.0033	0.0061	0.0103	0.0163	0.0241	0.0336	0.0443	0.0553	0.0655	0.0739	0.0796	0.0820	0.0810	0.0768
23.8	0.0000	0.0000	0.0000	0.0000	0.0000	0.0000	0.0000	0.0001	0.0001	0.0003	0.0007	0.0016	0.0032	0.0058	0.0099	0.0157	0.0234	0.0327	0.0432	0.0542	0.0644	0.0730	0.0790	0.0818	0.0811	0.0772
23.9	0.0000	0.0000	0.0000	0.0000	0.0000	0.0000	0.0000	0.0001	0.0001	0.0003	0.0007	0.0015	0.0030	0.0056	0.0095	0.0151	0.0226	0.0318	0.0422	0.0531	0.0634	0.0722	0.0784	0.0815	0.0811	0.0776
24	0.0000	0.0000	0.0000	0.0000	0.0000	0.0000	0.0000	0.0000	0.0001	0.0003	0.0007	0.0014	0.0029	0.0053	0.0091	0.0146	0.0219	0.0309	0.0412	0.0520	0.0624	0.0713	0.0778	0.0812	0.0812	0.0779
24.1	0.0000	0.0000	0.0000	0.0000	0.0000	0.0000	0.0000	0.0000	0.0001	0.0003	0.0006	0.0014	0.0027	0.0051	0.0087	0.0140	0.0211	0.0300	0.0401	0.0509	0.0613	0.0704	0.0771	0.0808	0.0811	0.0782
24.2	0.0000	0.0000	0.0000	0.0000	0.0000	0.0000	0.0000	0.0000	0.0001	0.0002	0.0006	0.0013	0.0026	0.0048	0.0084	0.0135	0.0204	0.0291	0.0391	0.0498	0.0603	0.0695	0.0764	0.0804	0.0811	0.0785
24.3	0.0000	0.0000	0.0000	0.0000	0.0000	0.0000	0.0000	0.0000	0.0001	0.0002	0.0006	0.0012	0.0025	0.0046	0.0080	0.0130	0.0198	0.0282	0.0381	0.0488	0.0592	0.0686	0.0757	0.0800	0.0810	0.0787

24.4	0.0000	0.0000	0.0000	0.0000	0.0000	0.0001	0.0002	0.0005	0.0012	0.0024	0.0044	0.0077	0.0125	0.0191	0.0274	0.0371	0.0477	0.0582	0.0676	0.0750	0.0796	0.0809	0.0789
24.5	0.0000	0.0000	0.0000	0.0000	0.0000	0.0001	0.0002	0.0005	0.0011	0.0022	0.0042	0.0074	0.0120	0.0184	0.0266	0.0362	0.0466	0.0571	0.0667	0.0742	0.0791	0.0807	0.0791
24.6	0.0000	0.0000	0.0000	0.0000	0.0000	0.0001	0.0002	0.0005	0.0010	0.0021	0.0040	0.0071	0.0116	0.0178	0.0258	0.0352	0.0456	0.0561	0.0657	0.0735	0.0786	0.0806	0.0793
24.7	0.0000	0.0000	0.0000	0.0000	0.0000	0.0001	0.0002	0.0004	0.0010	0.0020	0.0038	0.0068	0.0111	0.0172	0.0250	0.0343	0.0446	0.0550	0.0647	0.0727	0.0781	0.0803	0.0794
24.8	0.0000	0.0000	0.0000	0.0000	0.0000	0.0001	0.0002	0.0004	0.0009	0.0019	0.0037	0.0065	0.0107	0.0166	0.0242	0.0334	0.0435	0.0540	0.0638	0.0719	0.0775	0.0801	0.0795
24.9	0.0000	0.0000	0.0000	0.0000	0.0000	0.0001	0.0002	0.0004	0.0009	0.0018	0.0035	0.0062	0.0103	0.0160	0.0235	0.0325	0.0425	0.0530	0.0628	0.0711	0.0769	0.0798	0.0795
25	0.0000	0.0000	0.0000	0.0000	0.0000	0.0001	0.0001	0.0004	0.0008	0.0017	0.0033	0.0059	0.0099	0.0155	0.0227	0.0316	0.0415	0.0519	0.0618	0.0702	0.0763	0.0795	0.0795

Cumulative probabilities for the Poisson distribution

Probability of success x =

	0	1	2	3	4	5	6	7	8	9	10	11	12	13	14	15	16	17	18	19	20	21	22	23	24	25
0.01	0.9900	1.0000	1.0000	1.0000	1.0000	1.0000	1.0000	1.0000	1.0000	1.0000	1.0000	1.0000	1.0000	1.0000	1.0000	1.0000	1.0000	1.0000	1.0000	1.0000	1.0000	1.0000	1.0000	1.0000	1.0000	1.0000
0.02	0.9802	0.9998	1.0000	1.0000	1.0000	1.0000	1.0000	1.0000	1.0000	1.0000	1.0000	1.0000	1.0000	1.0000	1.0000	1.0000	1.0000	1.0000	1.0000	1.0000	1.0000	1.0000	1.0000	1.0000	1.0000	1.0000
0.03	0.9704	0.9996	1.0000	1.0000	1.0000	1.0000	1.0000	1.0000	1.0000	1.0000	1.0000	1.0000	1.0000	1.0000	1.0000	1.0000	1.0000	1.0000	1.0000	1.0000	1.0000	1.0000	1.0000	1.0000	1.0000	1.0000
0.04	0.9608	0.9992	1.0000	1.0000	1.0000	1.0000	1.0000	1.0000	1.0000	1.0000	1.0000	1.0000	1.0000	1.0000	1.0000	1.0000	1.0000	1.0000	1.0000	1.0000	1.0000	1.0000	1.0000	1.0000	1.0000	1.0000
0.05	0.9512	0.9988	1.0000	1.0000	1.0000	1.0000	1.0000	1.0000	1.0000	1.0000	1.0000	1.0000	1.0000	1.0000	1.0000	1.0000	1.0000	1.0000	1.0000	1.0000	1.0000	1.0000	1.0000	1.0000	1.0000	1.0000
0.06	0.9418	0.9983	1.0000	1.0000	1.0000	1.0000	1.0000	1.0000	1.0000	1.0000	1.0000	1.0000	1.0000	1.0000	1.0000	1.0000	1.0000	1.0000	1.0000	1.0000	1.0000	1.0000	1.0000	1.0000	1.0000	1.0000
0.07	0.9324	0.9977	0.9999	1.0000	1.0000	1.0000	1.0000	1.0000	1.0000	1.0000	1.0000	1.0000	1.0000	1.0000	1.0000	1.0000	1.0000	1.0000	1.0000	1.0000	1.0000	1.0000	1.0000	1.0000	1.0000	1.0000
0.08	0.9231	0.9970	0.9999	1.0000	1.0000	1.0000	1.0000	1.0000	1.0000	1.0000	1.0000	1.0000	1.0000	1.0000	1.0000	1.0000	1.0000	1.0000	1.0000	1.0000	1.0000	1.0000	1.0000	1.0000	1.0000	1.0000
0.09	0.9139	0.9962	0.9999	1.0000	1.0000	1.0000	1.0000	1.0000	1.0000	1.0000	1.0000	1.0000	1.0000	1.0000	1.0000	1.0000	1.0000	1.0000	1.0000	1.0000	1.0000	1.0000	1.0000	1.0000	1.0000	1.0000
0.1	0.9048	0.9953	0.9998	1.0000	1.0000	1.0000	1.0000	1.0000	1.0000	1.0000	1.0000	1.0000	1.0000	1.0000	1.0000	1.0000	1.0000	1.0000	1.0000	1.0000	1.0000	1.0000	1.0000	1.0000	1.0000	1.0000
0.2	0.8187	0.9825	0.9989	0.9999	1.0000	1.0000	1.0000	1.0000	1.0000	1.0000	1.0000	1.0000	1.0000	1.0000	1.0000	1.0000	1.0000	1.0000	1.0000	1.0000	1.0000	1.0000	1.0000	1.0000	1.0000	1.0000
0.3	0.7408	0.9631	0.9964	0.9997	1.0000	1.0000	1.0000	1.0000	1.0000	1.0000	1.0000	1.0000	1.0000	1.0000	1.0000	1.0000	1.0000	1.0000	1.0000	1.0000	1.0000	1.0000	1.0000	1.0000	1.0000	1.0000
0.4	0.6703	0.9384	0.9921	0.9992	0.9999	1.0000	1.0000	1.0000	1.0000	1.0000	1.0000	1.0000	1.0000	1.0000	1.0000	1.0000	1.0000	1.0000	1.0000	1.0000	1.0000	1.0000	1.0000	1.0000	1.0000	1.0000
0.5	0.6065	0.9098	0.9856	0.9982	0.9998	1.0000	1.0000	1.0000	1.0000	1.0000	1.0000	1.0000	1.0000	1.0000	1.0000	1.0000	1.0000	1.0000	1.0000	1.0000	1.0000	1.0000	1.0000	1.0000	1.0000	1.0000
0.6	0.5488	0.8781	0.9769	0.9966	0.9996	1.0000	1.0000	1.0000	1.0000	1.0000	1.0000	1.0000	1.0000	1.0000	1.0000	1.0000	1.0000	1.0000	1.0000	1.0000	1.0000	1.0000	1.0000	1.0000	1.0000	1.0000
0.7	0.4966	0.8442	0.9659	0.9942	0.9992	0.9999	1.0000	1.0000	1.0000	1.0000	1.0000	1.0000	1.0000	1.0000	1.0000	1.0000	1.0000	1.0000	1.0000	1.0000	1.0000	1.0000	1.0000	1.0000	1.0000	1.0000
0.8	0.4493	0.8088	0.9526	0.9909	0.9986	0.9998	1.0000	1.0000	1.0000	1.0000	1.0000	1.0000	1.0000	1.0000	1.0000	1.0000	1.0000	1.0000	1.0000	1.0000	1.0000	1.0000	1.0000	1.0000	1.0000	1.0000
0.9	0.4066	0.7725	0.9371	0.9865	0.9977	0.9997	1.0000	1.0000	1.0000	1.0000	1.0000	1.0000	1.0000	1.0000	1.0000	1.0000	1.0000	1.0000	1.0000	1.0000	1.0000	1.0000	1.0000	1.0000	1.0000	1.0000
1	0.3679	0.7358	0.9197	0.9810	0.9963	0.9994	0.9999	1.0000	1.0000	1.0000	1.0000	1.0000	1.0000	1.0000	1.0000	1.0000	1.0000	1.0000	1.0000	1.0000	1.0000	1.0000	1.0000	1.0000	1.0000	1.0000
1.1	0.3329	0.6990	0.9004	0.9743	0.9946	0.9990	0.9999	1.0000	1.0000	1.0000	1.0000	1.0000	1.0000	1.0000	1.0000	1.0000	1.0000	1.0000	1.0000	1.0000	1.0000	1.0000	1.0000	1.0000	1.0000	1.0000
1.2	0.3012	0.6626	0.8795	0.9662	0.9923	0.9985	0.9997	1.0000	1.0000	1.0000	1.0000	1.0000	1.0000	1.0000	1.0000	1.0000	1.0000	1.0000	1.0000	1.0000	1.0000	1.0000	1.0000	1.0000	1.0000	1.0000
1.3	0.2725	0.6268	0.8571	0.9569	0.9893	0.9978	0.9996	0.9999	1.0000	1.0000	1.0000	1.0000	1.0000	1.0000	1.0000	1.0000	1.0000	1.0000	1.0000	1.0000	1.0000	1.0000	1.0000	1.0000	1.0000	1.0000
1.4	0.2466	0.5918	0.8335	0.9463	0.9857	0.9968	0.9994	0.9999	1.0000	1.0000	1.0000	1.0000	1.0000	1.0000	1.0000	1.0000	1.0000	1.0000	1.0000	1.0000	1.0000	1.0000	1.0000	1.0000	1.0000	1.0000
1.5	0.2231	0.5578	0.8088	0.9344	0.9814	0.9955	0.9991	0.9998	1.0000	1.0000	1.0000	1.0000	1.0000	1.0000	1.0000	1.0000	1.0000	1.0000	1.0000	1.0000	1.0000	1.0000	1.0000	1.0000	1.0000	1.0000
1.6	0.2019	0.5249	0.7834	0.9212	0.9763	0.9940	0.9987	0.9997	1.0000	1.0000	1.0000	1.0000	1.0000	1.0000	1.0000	1.0000	1.0000	1.0000	1.0000	1.0000	1.0000	1.0000	1.0000	1.0000	1.0000	1.0000
1.7	0.1827	0.4932	0.7572	0.9068	0.9704	0.9920	0.9981	0.9996	0.9999	1.0000	1.0000	1.0000	1.0000	1.0000	1.0000	1.0000	1.0000	1.0000	1.0000	1.0000	1.0000	1.0000	1.0000	1.0000	1.0000	1.0000
1.8	0.1653	0.4628	0.7306	0.8913	0.9636	0.9896	0.9974	0.9994	0.9999	1.0000	1.0000	1.0000	1.0000	1.0000	1.0000	1.0000	1.0000	1.0000	1.0000	1.0000	1.0000	1.0000	1.0000	1.0000	1.0000	1.0000
1.9	0.1496	0.4337	0.7037	0.8747	0.9559	0.9868	0.9966	0.9992	0.9998	1.0000	1.0000	1.0000	1.0000	1.0000	1.0000	1.0000	1.0000	1.0000	1.0000	1.0000	1.0000	1.0000	1.0000	1.0000	1.0000	1.0000
2	0.1353	0.4060	0.6767	0.8571	0.9473	0.9834	0.9955	0.9989	0.9998	1.0000	1.0000	1.0000	1.0000	1.0000	1.0000	1.0000	1.0000	1.0000	1.0000	1.0000	1.0000	1.0000	1.0000	1.0000	1.0000	1.0000
2.1	0.1225	0.3796	0.6496	0.8386	0.9379	0.9796	0.9941	0.9985	0.9997	0.9999	1.0000	1.0000	1.0000	1.0000	1.0000	1.0000	1.0000	1.0000	1.0000	1.0000	1.0000	1.0000	1.0000	1.0000	1.0000	1.0000
2.2	0.1108	0.3546	0.6227	0.8194	0.9275	0.9751	0.9925	0.9980	0.9995	0.9999	1.0000	1.0000	1.0000	1.0000	1.0000	1.0000	1.0000	1.0000	1.0000	1.0000	1.0000	1.0000	1.0000	1.0000	1.0000	1.0000
2.3	0.1003	0.3309	0.5960	0.7993	0.9162	0.9700	0.9906	0.9974	0.9994	0.9999	1.0000	1.0000	1.0000	1.0000	1.0000	1.0000	1.0000	1.0000	1.0000	1.0000	1.0000	1.0000	1.0000	1.0000	1.0000	1.0000
2.4	0.0907	0.3084	0.5697	0.7787	0.9041	0.9643	0.9884	0.9967	0.9991	0.9998	1.0000	1.0000	1.0000	1.0000	1.0000	1.0000	1.0000	1.0000	1.0000	1.0000	1.0000	1.0000	1.0000	1.0000	1.0000	1.0000
2.5	0.0821	0.2873	0.5438	0.7576	0.8912	0.9580	0.9858	0.9958	0.9989	0.9997	0.9999	1.0000	1.0000	1.0000	1.0000	1.0000	1.0000	1.0000	1.0000	1.0000	1.0000	1.0000	1.0000	1.0000	1.0000	1.0000
2.6	0.0743	0.2674	0.5184	0.7360	0.8774	0.9510	0.9828	0.9947	0.9985	0.9996	0.9999	1.0000	1.0000	1.0000	1.0000	1.0000	1.0000	1.0000	1.0000	1.0000	1.0000	1.0000	1.0000	1.0000	1.0000	1.0000
2.7	0.0672	0.2487	0.4936	0.7141	0.8629	0.9433	0.9794	0.9934	0.9981	0.9995	0.9999	1.0000	1.0000	1.0000	1.0000	1.0000	1.0000	1.0000	1.0000	1.0000	1.0000	1.0000	1.0000	1.0000	1.0000	1.0000
2.8	0.0608	0.2311	0.4695	0.6919	0.8477	0.9349	0.9756	0.9919	0.9976	0.9993	0.9998	1.0000	1.0000	1.0000	1.0000	1.0000	1.0000	1.0000	1.0000	1.0000	1.0000	1.0000	1.0000	1.0000	1.0000	1.0000
2.9	0.0550	0.2146	0.4460	0.6696	0.8318	0.9258	0.9713	0.9901	0.9969	0.9991	0.9998	0.9999	1.0000	1.0000	1.0000	1.0000	1.0000	1.0000	1.0000	1.0000	1.0000	1.0000	1.0000	1.0000	1.0000	1.0000
3	0.0498	0.1991	0.4232	0.6472	0.8153	0.9161	0.9665	0.9881	0.9962	0.9989	0.9997	0.9999	1.0000	1.0000	1.0000	1.0000	1.0000	1.0000	1.0000	1.0000	1.0000	1.0000	1.0000	1.0000	1.0000	1.0000
3.1	0.0450	0.1847	0.4012	0.6248	0.7982	0.9057	0.9612	0.9858	0.9953	0.9986	0.9996	0.9999	1.0000	1.0000	1.0000	1.0000	1.0000	1.0000	1.0000	1.0000	1.0000	1.0000	1.0000	1.0000	1.0000	1.0000
3.2	0.0408	0.1712	0.3799	0.6025	0.7806	0.8946	0.9554	0.9832	0.9943	0.9982	0.9995	0.9999	1.0000	1.0000	1.0000	1.0000	1.0000	1.0000	1.0000	1.0000	1.0000	1.0000	1.0000	1.0000	1.0000	1.0000
3.3	0.0369	0.1586	0.3594	0.5803	0.7626	0.8829	0.9490	0.9802	0.9931	0.9978	0.9994	0.9998	1.0000	1.0000	1.0000	1.0000	1.0000	1.0000	1.0000	1.0000	1.0000	1.0000	1.0000	1.0000	1.0000	1.0000
3.4	0.0334	0.1468	0.3397	0.5584	0.7442	0.8705	0.9421	0.9769	0.9917	0.9973	0.9992	0.9998	1.0000	1.0000	1.0000	1.0000	1.0000	1.0000	1.0000	1.0000	1.0000	1.0000	1.0000	1.0000	1.0000	1.0000
3.5	0.0302	0.1359	0.3208	0.5366	0.7254	0.8576	0.9347	0.9733	0.9901	0.9967	0.9990	0.9997	0.9999	1.0000	1.0000	1.0000	1.0000	1.0000	1.0000	1.0000	1.0000	1.0000	1.0000	1.0000	1.0000	1.0000
3.6	0.0273	0.1257	0.3027	0.5152	0.7064	0.8441	0.9267	0.9692	0.9883	0.9960	0.9987	0.9996	0.9999	1.0000	1.0000	1.0000	1.0000	1.0000	1.0000	1.0000	1.0000	1.0000	1.0000	1.0000	1.0000	1.0000
3.7	0.0247	0.1162	0.2854	0.4942	0.6872	0.8301	0.9182	0.9648	0.9863	0.9952	0.9984	0.9995	0.9999	1.0000	1.0000	1.0000	1.0000	1.0000	1.0000	1.0000	1.0000	1.0000	1.0000	1.0000	1.0000	1.0000
3.8	0.0224	0.1074	0.2689	0.4735	0.6678	0.8156	0.9091	0.9599	0.9840	0.9942	0.9981	0.9994	0.9998	1.0000	1.0000	1.0000	1.0000	1.0000	1.0000	1.0000	1.0000	1.0000	1.0000	1.0000	1.0000	1.0000
3.9	0.0202	0.0992	0.2531	0.4532	0.6484	0.8006	0.8995	0.9546	0.9815	0.9931	0.9977	0.9993	0.9998	1.0000	1.0000	1.0000	1.0000	1.0000	1.0000	1.0000	1.0000	1.0000	1.0000	1.0000	1.0000	1.0000
4	0.0183	0.0916	0.2381	0.4335	0.6288	0.7851	0.8893	0.9489	0.9786	0.9919	0.9972	0.9991	0.9997	0.9999	1.0000	1.0000	1.0000	1.0000	1.0000	1.0000	1.0000	1.0000	1.0000	1.0000	1.0000	1.0000
4.1	0.0166	0.0845	0.2238	0.4142	0.6093	0.7693	0.8786	0.9427	0.9755	0.9905	0.9966	0.9989	0.9997	0.9999	1.0000	1.0000	1.0000	1.0000	1.0000	1.0000	1.0000	1.0000	1.0000	1.0000	1.0000	1.0000

λ	0	1	2	3	4	5	6	7	8	9	10	11	12	13	14	15	16	17	18	19	20	21	22	23	24
4.2	0.0150	0.0780	0.2102	0.3954	0.5898	0.7531	0.8675	0.9361	0.9721	0.9889	0.9959	0.9986	0.9996	0.9999	1.0000	1.0000	1.0000	1.0000	1.0000	1.0000	1.0000	1.0000	1.0000	1.0000	1.0000
4.3	0.0136	0.0719	0.1974	0.3772	0.5704	0.7367	0.8558	0.9290	0.9683	0.9871	0.9952	0.9983	0.9995	0.9998	1.0000	1.0000	1.0000	1.0000	1.0000	1.0000	1.0000	1.0000	1.0000	1.0000	1.0000
4.4	0.0123	0.0663	0.1851	0.3594	0.5512	0.7199	0.8436	0.9214	0.9642	0.9851	0.9943	0.9980	0.9993	0.9998	1.0000	1.0000	1.0000	1.0000	1.0000	1.0000	1.0000	1.0000	1.0000	1.0000	1.0000
4.5	0.0111	0.0611	0.1736	0.3423	0.5321	0.7029	0.8311	0.9134	0.9597	0.9829	0.9933	0.9976	0.9992	0.9997	0.9999	1.0000	1.0000	1.0000	1.0000	1.0000	1.0000	1.0000	1.0000	1.0000	1.0000
4.6	0.0101	0.0563	0.1626	0.3257	0.5132	0.6858	0.8180	0.9049	0.9549	0.9805	0.9922	0.9971	0.9990	0.9997	0.9999	1.0000	1.0000	1.0000	1.0000	1.0000	1.0000	1.0000	1.0000	1.0000	1.0000
4.7	0.0091	0.0518	0.1523	0.3097	0.4946	0.6684	0.8046	0.8960	0.9497	0.9778	0.9910	0.9966	0.9988	0.9996	0.9999	1.0000	1.0000	1.0000	1.0000	1.0000	1.0000	1.0000	1.0000	1.0000	1.0000
4.8	0.0082	0.0477	0.1425	0.2942	0.4763	0.6510	0.7908	0.8867	0.9442	0.9749	0.9896	0.9960	0.9986	0.9995	0.9999	1.0000	1.0000	1.0000	1.0000	1.0000	1.0000	1.0000	1.0000	1.0000	1.0000
4.9	0.0074	0.0439	0.1333	0.2793	0.4582	0.6335	0.7767	0.8769	0.9382	0.9717	0.9880	0.9953	0.9983	0.9994	0.9998	0.9999	1.0000	1.0000	1.0000	1.0000	1.0000	1.0000	1.0000	1.0000	1.0000
5	0.0067	0.0404	0.1247	0.2650	0.4405	0.6160	0.7622	0.8666	0.9319	0.9682	0.9863	0.9945	0.9980	0.9993	0.9998	0.9999	1.0000	1.0000	1.0000	1.0000	1.0000	1.0000	1.0000	1.0000	1.0000
5.1	0.0061	0.0372	0.1165	0.2513	0.4231	0.5984	0.7474	0.8560	0.9252	0.9644	0.9844	0.9937	0.9976	0.9992	0.9997	0.9999	1.0000	1.0000	1.0000	1.0000	1.0000	1.0000	1.0000	1.0000	1.0000
5.2	0.0055	0.0342	0.1088	0.2381	0.4061	0.5809	0.7324	0.8449	0.9181	0.9603	0.9823	0.9927	0.9972	0.9990	0.9997	0.9999	1.0000	1.0000	1.0000	1.0000	1.0000	1.0000	1.0000	1.0000	1.0000
5.3	0.0050	0.0314	0.1016	0.2254	0.3895	0.5635	0.7171	0.8335	0.9106	0.9559	0.9800	0.9916	0.9967	0.9988	0.9996	0.9999	1.0000	1.0000	1.0000	1.0000	1.0000	1.0000	1.0000	1.0000	1.0000
5.4	0.0045	0.0289	0.0948	0.2133	0.3733	0.5461	0.7017	0.8217	0.9027	0.9512	0.9775	0.9904	0.9962	0.9986	0.9995	0.9998	0.9999	1.0000	1.0000	1.0000	1.0000	1.0000	1.0000	1.0000	1.0000
5.5	0.0041	0.0266	0.0884	0.2017	0.3575	0.5289	0.6860	0.8095	0.8944	0.9462	0.9747	0.9890	0.9955	0.9983	0.9994	0.9998	0.9999	1.0000	1.0000	1.0000	1.0000	1.0000	1.0000	1.0000	1.0000
5.6	0.0037	0.0244	0.0824	0.1906	0.3422	0.5119	0.6703	0.7970	0.8857	0.9409	0.9718	0.9875	0.9949	0.9980	0.9993	0.9998	0.9999	1.0000	1.0000	1.0000	1.0000	1.0000	1.0000	1.0000	1.0000
5.7	0.0033	0.0224	0.0768	0.1800	0.3272	0.4950	0.6544	0.7841	0.8766	0.9352	0.9686	0.9859	0.9941	0.9977	0.9991	0.9997	0.9999	1.0000	1.0000	1.0000	1.0000	1.0000	1.0000	1.0000	1.0000
5.8	0.0030	0.0206	0.0715	0.1700	0.3127	0.4783	0.6384	0.7710	0.8672	0.9292	0.9651	0.9841	0.9932	0.9973	0.9990	0.9996	0.9999	1.0000	1.0000	1.0000	1.0000	1.0000	1.0000	1.0000	1.0000
5.9	0.0027	0.0189	0.0666	0.1604	0.2987	0.4619	0.6224	0.7576	0.8574	0.9228	0.9614	0.9821	0.9922	0.9969	0.9988	0.9996	0.9999	1.0000	1.0000	1.0000	1.0000	1.0000	1.0000	1.0000	1.0000
6	0.0025	0.0174	0.0620	0.1512	0.2851	0.4457	0.6063	0.7440	0.8472	0.9161	0.9574	0.9799	0.9912	0.9964	0.9986	0.9995	0.9998	0.9999	1.0000	1.0000	1.0000	1.0000	1.0000	1.0000	1.0000
6.1	0.0022	0.0159	0.0577	0.1425	0.2719	0.4298	0.5902	0.7301	0.8367	0.9090	0.9531	0.9776	0.9900	0.9958	0.9984	0.9994	0.9998	0.9999	1.0000	1.0000	1.0000	1.0000	1.0000	1.0000	1.0000
6.2	0.0020	0.0146	0.0536	0.1342	0.2592	0.4141	0.5742	0.7160	0.8259	0.9016	0.9486	0.9750	0.9887	0.9952	0.9981	0.9993	0.9997	0.9999	1.0000	1.0000	1.0000	1.0000	1.0000	1.0000	1.0000
6.3	0.0018	0.0134	0.0498	0.1264	0.2469	0.3988	0.5582	0.7017	0.8148	0.8939	0.9437	0.9723	0.9873	0.9945	0.9978	0.9992	0.9997	0.9999	1.0000	1.0000	1.0000	1.0000	1.0000	1.0000	1.0000
6.4	0.0017	0.0123	0.0463	0.1189	0.2351	0.3837	0.5423	0.6873	0.8033	0.8858	0.9386	0.9693	0.9857	0.9937	0.9974	0.9990	0.9996	0.9999	1.0000	1.0000	1.0000	1.0000	1.0000	1.0000	1.0000
6.5	0.0015	0.0113	0.0430	0.1118	0.2237	0.3690	0.5265	0.6728	0.7916	0.8774	0.9332	0.9661	0.9840	0.9929	0.9970	0.9988	0.9996	0.9998	0.9999	1.0000	1.0000	1.0000	1.0000	1.0000	1.0000
6.6	0.0014	0.0103	0.0400	0.1052	0.2127	0.3547	0.5108	0.6581	0.7796	0.8686	0.9274	0.9627	0.9821	0.9920	0.9966	0.9986	0.9995	0.9998	0.9999	1.0000	1.0000	1.0000	1.0000	1.0000	1.0000
6.7	0.0012	0.0095	0.0371	0.0988	0.2022	0.3406	0.4953	0.6433	0.7673	0.8596	0.9214	0.9591	0.9801	0.9909	0.9961	0.9984	0.9994	0.9998	0.9999	1.0000	1.0000	1.0000	1.0000	1.0000	1.0000
6.8	0.0011	0.0087	0.0344	0.0928	0.1920	0.3270	0.4799	0.6285	0.7548	0.8502	0.9151	0.9552	0.9779	0.9898	0.9956	0.9982	0.9993	0.9997	0.9999	1.0000	1.0000	1.0000	1.0000	1.0000	1.0000
6.9	0.0010	0.0080	0.0320	0.0871	0.1823	0.3137	0.4647	0.6136	0.7420	0.8405	0.9084	0.9510	0.9755	0.9885	0.9950	0.9979	0.9992	0.9997	0.9999	1.0000	1.0000	1.0000	1.0000	1.0000	1.0000
7	0.0009	0.0073	0.0296	0.0818	0.1730	0.3007	0.4497	0.5987	0.7291	0.8305	0.9015	0.9467	0.9730	0.9872	0.9943	0.9976	0.9990	0.9996	0.9999	1.0000	1.0000	1.0000	1.0000	1.0000	1.0000
7.1	0.0008	0.0067	0.0275	0.0767	0.1641	0.2881	0.4349	0.5838	0.7160	0.8202	0.8942	0.9420	0.9703	0.9857	0.9935	0.9972	0.9989	0.9996	0.9998	0.9999	1.0000	1.0000	1.0000	1.0000	1.0000
7.2	0.0007	0.0061	0.0255	0.0719	0.1555	0.2759	0.4204	0.5689	0.7027	0.8096	0.8867	0.9371	0.9673	0.9841	0.9927	0.9969	0.9987	0.9995	0.9998	0.9999	1.0000	1.0000	1.0000	1.0000	1.0000
7.3	0.0007	0.0056	0.0236	0.0674	0.1473	0.2640	0.4060	0.5541	0.6892	0.7988	0.8788	0.9319	0.9642	0.9824	0.9918	0.9964	0.9985	0.9994	0.9998	0.9999	1.0000	1.0000	1.0000	1.0000	1.0000
7.4	0.0006	0.0051	0.0219	0.0632	0.1395	0.2526	0.3920	0.5393	0.6757	0.7877	0.8707	0.9265	0.9609	0.9805	0.9908	0.9959	0.9983	0.9993	0.9997	0.9999	1.0000	1.0000	1.0000	1.0000	1.0000
7.5	0.0006	0.0047	0.0203	0.0591	0.1321	0.2414	0.3782	0.5246	0.6620	0.7764	0.8622	0.9208	0.9573	0.9784	0.9897	0.9954	0.9980	0.9992	0.9997	0.9999	1.0000	1.0000	1.0000	1.0000	1.0000
7.6	0.0005	0.0043	0.0188	0.0554	0.1249	0.2307	0.3646	0.5100	0.6482	0.7649	0.8535	0.9148	0.9536	0.9762	0.9886	0.9948	0.9978	0.9991	0.9996	0.9999	1.0000	1.0000	1.0000	1.0000	1.0000
7.7	0.0005	0.0039	0.0174	0.0518	0.1181	0.2203	0.3514	0.4956	0.6343	0.7531	0.8445	0.9085	0.9496	0.9739	0.9873	0.9941	0.9974	0.9989	0.9996	0.9998	0.9999	1.0000	1.0000	1.0000	1.0000
7.8	0.0004	0.0036	0.0161	0.0485	0.1117	0.2103	0.3384	0.4812	0.6204	0.7411	0.8352	0.9020	0.9454	0.9714	0.9859	0.9934	0.9971	0.9988	0.9995	0.9998	0.9999	1.0000	1.0000	1.0000	1.0000
7.9	0.0004	0.0033	0.0149	0.0453	0.1055	0.2006	0.3257	0.4670	0.6065	0.7290	0.8257	0.8952	0.9409	0.9687	0.9844	0.9926	0.9967	0.9985	0.9994	0.9998	0.9999	1.0000	1.0000	1.0000	1.0000
8	0.0003	0.0030	0.0138	0.0424	0.0996	0.1912	0.3134	0.4530	0.5925	0.7166	0.8159	0.8881	0.9362	0.9658	0.9827	0.9918	0.9963	0.9984	0.9993	0.9997	0.9999	1.0000	1.0000	1.0000	1.0000
8.1	0.0003	0.0028	0.0127	0.0396	0.0940	0.1822	0.3013	0.4391	0.5786	0.7041	0.8058	0.8807	0.9313	0.9628	0.9810	0.9908	0.9958	0.9982	0.9992	0.9997	0.9999	1.0000	1.0000	1.0000	1.0000
8.2	0.0003	0.0025	0.0118	0.0370	0.0887	0.1736	0.2896	0.4254	0.5647	0.6915	0.7955	0.8731	0.9261	0.9595	0.9791	0.9898	0.9953	0.9979	0.9991	0.9997	0.9999	1.0000	1.0000	1.0000	1.0000
8.3	0.0002	0.0023	0.0109	0.0346	0.0837	0.1653	0.2781	0.4119	0.5507	0.6788	0.7850	0.8652	0.9207	0.9561	0.9771	0.9887	0.9947	0.9977	0.9990	0.9996	0.9998	0.9999	1.0000	1.0000	1.0000
8.4	0.0002	0.0021	0.0100	0.0323	0.0789	0.1573	0.2670	0.3987	0.5369	0.6659	0.7743	0.8571	0.9150	0.9524	0.9749	0.9875	0.9941	0.9973	0.9989	0.9995	0.9998	0.9999	1.0000	1.0000	1.0000
8.5	0.0002	0.0019	0.0093	0.0301	0.0744	0.1496	0.2562	0.3856	0.5231	0.6530	0.7634	0.8487	0.9091	0.9486	0.9726	0.9862	0.9934	0.9970	0.9987	0.9995	0.9998	0.9999	1.0000	1.0000	1.0000
8.6	0.0002	0.0018	0.0086	0.0281	0.0701	0.1422	0.2457	0.3728	0.5094	0.6400	0.7522	0.8400	0.9029	0.9445	0.9701	0.9848	0.9926	0.9966	0.9985	0.9994	0.9998	0.9999	1.0000	1.0000	1.0000
8.7	0.0002	0.0016	0.0079	0.0262	0.0660	0.1352	0.2355	0.3602	0.4958	0.6269	0.7409	0.8311	0.8965	0.9403	0.9675	0.9832	0.9918	0.9962	0.9983	0.9993	0.9997	0.9999	1.0000	1.0000	1.0000
8.8	0.0002	0.0015	0.0073	0.0244	0.0621	0.1284	0.2256	0.3478	0.4823	0.6137	0.7294	0.8220	0.8898	0.9358	0.9647	0.9816	0.9909	0.9957	0.9981	0.9992	0.9997	0.9999	1.0000	1.0000	1.0000
8.9	0.0001	0.0014	0.0068	0.0228	0.0584	0.1219	0.2160	0.3357	0.4689	0.6006	0.7178	0.8126	0.8829	0.9311	0.9617	0.9798	0.9899	0.9952	0.9978	0.9991	0.9996	0.9998	0.9999	1.0000	1.0000
9	0.0001	0.0012	0.0062	0.0212	0.0550	0.1157	0.2068	0.3239	0.4557	0.5874	0.7060	0.8030	0.8758	0.9261	0.9585	0.9780	0.9889	0.9947	0.9976	0.9989	0.9996	0.9998	0.9999	1.0000	1.0000
9.1	0.0001	0.0011	0.0058	0.0198	0.0517	0.1098	0.1978	0.3123	0.4426	0.5742	0.6941	0.7932	0.8684	0.9210	0.9552	0.9760	0.9878	0.9941	0.9973	0.9988	0.9995	0.9998	0.9999	1.0000	1.0000
9.2	0.0001	0.0010	0.0053	0.0184	0.0486	0.1041	0.1892	0.3010	0.4296	0.5611	0.6820	0.7832	0.8607	0.9156	0.9517	0.9738	0.9865	0.9934	0.9969	0.9986	0.9994	0.9998	0.9999	1.0000	1.0000
9.3	0.0001	0.0009	0.0049	0.0172	0.0456	0.0986	0.1808	0.2900	0.4168	0.5479	0.6699	0.7730	0.8529	0.9100	0.9480	0.9715	0.9852	0.9927	0.9966	0.9985	0.9993	0.9997	0.9999	1.0000	1.0000
9.4	0.0001	0.0009	0.0045	0.0160	0.0429	0.0935	0.1727	0.2792	0.4042	0.5349	0.6576	0.7626	0.8448	0.9042	0.9441	0.9691	0.9838	0.9919	0.9962	0.9983	0.9992	0.9997	0.9999	1.0000	1.0000

(continued)

Cumulative probabilities for the Poisson distribution (cont.)

Probability of success x =

	0	1	2	3	4	5	6	7	8	9	10	11	12	13	14	15	16	17	18	19	20	21	22	23	24	25
9.5	0.0001	0.0008	0.0042	0.0149	0.0403	0.0885	0.1649	0.2687	0.3918	0.5218	0.6453	0.7520	0.8364	0.8981	0.9400	0.9665	0.9823	0.9911	0.9957	0.9980	0.9991	0.9996	0.9998	0.9999	1.0000	1.0000
9.6	0.0001	0.0007	0.0038	0.0138	0.0378	0.0838	0.1574	0.2584	0.3796	0.5089	0.6329	0.7412	0.8279	0.8919	0.9357	0.9638	0.9806	0.9902	0.9952	0.9978	0.9990	0.9996	0.9998	0.9999	1.0000	1.0000
9.7	0.0001	0.0007	0.0035	0.0129	0.0355	0.0793	0.1502	0.2485	0.3676	0.4960	0.6205	0.7303	0.8191	0.8853	0.9312	0.9609	0.9789	0.9892	0.9947	0.9975	0.9989	0.9995	0.9998	0.9999	1.0000	1.0000
9.8	0.0001	0.0006	0.0033	0.0120	0.0333	0.0750	0.1433	0.2388	0.3558	0.4832	0.6080	0.7193	0.8101	0.8786	0.9265	0.9579	0.9770	0.9881	0.9941	0.9972	0.9987	0.9995	0.9998	0.9999	1.0000	1.0000
9.9	0.0001	0.0005	0.0030	0.0111	0.0312	0.0710	0.1366	0.2294	0.3442	0.4705	0.5955	0.7081	0.8009	0.8716	0.9216	0.9546	0.9751	0.9870	0.9935	0.9969	0.9986	0.9994	0.9997	0.9999	1.0000	1.0000
10	0.0000	0.0005	0.0028	0.0103	0.0293	0.0671	0.1301	0.2202	0.3328	0.4579	0.5830	0.6968	0.7916	0.8645	0.9165	0.9513	0.9730	0.9857	0.9928	0.9965	0.9984	0.9993	0.9997	0.9999	1.0000	1.0000
10.1	0.0000	0.0005	0.0026	0.0096	0.0274	0.0634	0.1240	0.2113	0.3217	0.4455	0.5705	0.6853	0.7820	0.8571	0.9112	0.9477	0.9707	0.9844	0.9921	0.9962	0.9982	0.9992	0.9997	0.9999	0.9999	1.0000
10.2	0.0000	0.0004	0.0023	0.0089	0.0257	0.0599	0.1180	0.2027	0.3108	0.4332	0.5580	0.6738	0.7722	0.8494	0.9057	0.9440	0.9684	0.9830	0.9913	0.9957	0.9980	0.9991	0.9996	0.9998	0.9999	1.0000
10.3	0.0000	0.0004	0.0022	0.0083	0.0241	0.0566	0.1123	0.1944	0.3001	0.4210	0.5456	0.6622	0.7623	0.8416	0.9000	0.9400	0.9658	0.9815	0.9904	0.9953	0.9978	0.9990	0.9996	0.9998	0.9999	1.0000
10.4	0.0000	0.0003	0.0020	0.0077	0.0225	0.0534	0.1069	0.1863	0.2896	0.4090	0.5331	0.6505	0.7522	0.8336	0.8940	0.9359	0.9632	0.9799	0.9895	0.9948	0.9975	0.9989	0.9995	0.9998	0.9999	1.0000
10.5	0.0000	0.0003	0.0018	0.0071	0.0211	0.0504	0.1016	0.1785	0.2794	0.3971	0.5207	0.6387	0.7420	0.8253	0.8879	0.9317	0.9604	0.9781	0.9885	0.9942	0.9972	0.9987	0.9994	0.9998	0.9999	1.0000
10.6	0.0000	0.0003	0.0017	0.0066	0.0197	0.0475	0.0966	0.1710	0.2694	0.3854	0.5084	0.6269	0.7316	0.8169	0.8815	0.9272	0.9574	0.9763	0.9874	0.9936	0.9969	0.9986	0.9994	0.9997	0.9999	1.0000
10.7	0.0000	0.0003	0.0016	0.0062	0.0185	0.0448	0.0918	0.1636	0.2597	0.3739	0.4961	0.6150	0.7210	0.8083	0.8750	0.9225	0.9543	0.9744	0.9863	0.9930	0.9966	0.9984	0.9993	0.9997	0.9999	0.9999
10.8	0.0000	0.0002	0.0014	0.0057	0.0173	0.0423	0.0872	0.1566	0.2502	0.3626	0.4840	0.6031	0.7104	0.7995	0.8682	0.9177	0.9511	0.9723	0.9850	0.9923	0.9962	0.9982	0.9992	0.9996	0.9998	0.9999
10.9	0.0000	0.0002	0.0013	0.0053	0.0162	0.0398	0.0826	0.1498	0.2410	0.3515	0.4719	0.5912	0.6996	0.7905	0.8612	0.9126	0.9477	0.9701	0.9837	0.9915	0.9958	0.9980	0.9991	0.9996	0.9998	0.9999
11	0.0000	0.0002	0.0012	0.0049	0.0151	0.0375	0.0786	0.1432	0.2320	0.3405	0.4599	0.5793	0.6887	0.7813	0.8540	0.9074	0.9441	0.9678	0.9823	0.9907	0.9953	0.9977	0.9990	0.9995	0.9998	0.9999
11.1	0.0000	0.0002	0.0011	0.0046	0.0141	0.0353	0.0746	0.1369	0.2232	0.3298	0.4480	0.5673	0.6777	0.7719	0.8467	0.9020	0.9403	0.9654	0.9808	0.9898	0.9948	0.9975	0.9988	0.9995	0.9998	0.9999
11.2	0.0000	0.0002	0.0010	0.0042	0.0132	0.0333	0.0708	0.1307	0.2147	0.3192	0.4362	0.5554	0.6666	0.7624	0.8391	0.8963	0.9364	0.9628	0.9792	0.9889	0.9943	0.9972	0.9987	0.9994	0.9997	0.9999
11.3	0.0000	0.0002	0.0009	0.0039	0.0123	0.0313	0.0671	0.1249	0.2064	0.3089	0.4246	0.5435	0.6555	0.7528	0.8313	0.8905	0.9323	0.9601	0.9775	0.9879	0.9938	0.9969	0.9985	0.9993	0.9997	0.9999
11.4	0.0000	0.0001	0.0009	0.0036	0.0115	0.0295	0.0636	0.1192	0.1984	0.2987	0.4131	0.5316	0.6442	0.7430	0.8234	0.8845	0.9280	0.9572	0.9757	0.9868	0.9932	0.9966	0.9984	0.9992	0.9997	0.9999
11.5	0.0000	0.0001	0.0008	0.0034	0.0107	0.0277	0.0603	0.1137	0.1906	0.2888	0.4017	0.5198	0.6329	0.7330	0.8153	0.8783	0.9236	0.9542	0.9738	0.9857	0.9925	0.9962	0.9982	0.9992	0.9996	0.9998
11.6	0.0000	0.0001	0.0007	0.0031	0.0100	0.0261	0.0571	0.1085	0.1830	0.2791	0.3905	0.5080	0.6216	0.7230	0.8069	0.8719	0.9190	0.9511	0.9718	0.9845	0.9918	0.9958	0.9980	0.9991	0.9996	0.9998
11.7	0.0000	0.0001	0.0007	0.0029	0.0094	0.0245	0.0541	0.1035	0.1757	0.2696	0.3794	0.4963	0.6102	0.7128	0.7985	0.8653	0.9142	0.9478	0.9697	0.9832	0.9910	0.9954	0.9978	0.9989	0.9995	0.9998
11.8	0.0000	0.0001	0.0006	0.0027	0.0087	0.0230	0.0512	0.0986	0.1686	0.2603	0.3685	0.4847	0.5988	0.7025	0.7898	0.8585	0.9092	0.9444	0.9674	0.9818	0.9902	0.9950	0.9975	0.9988	0.9995	0.9998
11.9	0.0000	0.0001	0.0006	0.0025	0.0081	0.0217	0.0484	0.0940	0.1617	0.2512	0.3578	0.4731	0.5874	0.6920	0.7810	0.8516	0.9040	0.9408	0.9651	0.9803	0.9893	0.9945	0.9972	0.9987	0.9994	0.9997
12	0.0000	0.0001	0.0005	0.0023	0.0076	0.0203	0.0458	0.0895	0.1550	0.2424	0.3472	0.4616	0.5760	0.6815	0.7720	0.8444	0.8987	0.9370	0.9626	0.9787	0.9884	0.9939	0.9970	0.9985	0.9993	0.9997
12.1	0.0000	0.0001	0.0005	0.0021	0.0071	0.0191	0.0433	0.0852	0.1486	0.2338	0.3368	0.4502	0.5645	0.6709	0.7629	0.8371	0.8932	0.9331	0.9600	0.9771	0.9874	0.9934	0.9966	0.9984	0.9992	0.9997
12.2	0.0000	0.0001	0.0004	0.0020	0.0066	0.0179	0.0410	0.0811	0.1424	0.2254	0.3266	0.4389	0.5531	0.6603	0.7536	0.8296	0.8875	0.9290	0.9572	0.9753	0.9863	0.9927	0.9963	0.9982	0.9991	0.9996
12.3	0.0000	0.0001	0.0004	0.0018	0.0062	0.0168	0.0387	0.0772	0.1363	0.2172	0.3166	0.4278	0.5417	0.6495	0.7442	0.8219	0.8816	0.9248	0.9543	0.9734	0.9852	0.9921	0.9959	0.9980	0.9990	0.9996
12.4	0.0000	0.0001	0.0004	0.0017	0.0057	0.0158	0.0366	0.0734	0.1305	0.2092	0.3067	0.4167	0.5303	0.6387	0.7347	0.8140	0.8755	0.9204	0.9513	0.9715	0.9840	0.9914	0.9955	0.9978	0.9989	0.9995
12.5	0.0000	0.0001	0.0003	0.0016	0.0053	0.0148	0.0346	0.0698	0.1249	0.2014	0.2971	0.4058	0.5190	0.6278	0.7250	0.8060	0.8693	0.9158	0.9481	0.9694	0.9827	0.9906	0.9951	0.9975	0.9988	0.9994
12.6	0.0000	0.0001	0.0003	0.0014	0.0050	0.0139	0.0326	0.0664	0.1195	0.1939	0.2876	0.3950	0.5077	0.6169	0.7153	0.7978	0.8629	0.9111	0.9448	0.9672	0.9813	0.9898	0.9946	0.9973	0.9987	0.9994
12.7	0.0000	0.0001	0.0003	0.0013	0.0046	0.0130	0.0308	0.0631	0.1143	0.1866	0.2783	0.3843	0.4964	0.6060	0.7054	0.7895	0.8563	0.9062	0.9414	0.9649	0.9799	0.9889	0.9941	0.9970	0.9985	0.9993
12.8	0.0000	0.0001	0.0003	0.0012	0.0043	0.0122	0.0291	0.0599	0.1093	0.1794	0.2693	0.3738	0.4853	0.5950	0.6954	0.7810	0.8495	0.9011	0.9378	0.9625	0.9783	0.9880	0.9936	0.9967	0.9984	0.9992
12.9	0.0000	0.0001	0.0002	0.0011	0.0040	0.0115	0.0274	0.0569	0.1044	0.1725	0.2604	0.3634	0.4741	0.5840	0.6853	0.7724	0.8426	0.8959	0.9341	0.9600	0.9767	0.9870	0.9930	0.9964	0.9982	0.9991
13	0.0000	0.0000	0.0002	0.0011	0.0037	0.0107	0.0259	0.0540	0.0998	0.1658	0.2517	0.3532	0.4631	0.5730	0.6751	0.7636	0.8355	0.8905	0.9302	0.9573	0.9750	0.9859	0.9924	0.9960	0.9980	0.9990
13.1	0.0000	0.0000	0.0002	0.0010	0.0035	0.0101	0.0244	0.0513	0.0953	0.1593	0.2432	0.3431	0.4522	0.5621	0.6649	0.7547	0.8282	0.8849	0.9261	0.9546	0.9732	0.9848	0.9917	0.9956	0.9978	0.9989
13.2	0.0000	0.0000	0.0002	0.0009	0.0032	0.0094	0.0230	0.0487	0.0910	0.1530	0.2349	0.3332	0.4413	0.5511	0.6546	0.7456	0.8208	0.8791	0.9219	0.9516	0.9713	0.9836	0.9910	0.9952	0.9976	0.9988
13.3	0.0000	0.0000	0.0002	0.0008	0.0030	0.0088	0.0217	0.0461	0.0868	0.1469	0.2268	0.3234	0.4305	0.5401	0.6442	0.7365	0.8132	0.8732	0.9176	0.9486	0.9692	0.9823	0.9902	0.9948	0.9973	0.9987
13.4	0.0000	0.0000	0.0002	0.0008	0.0028	0.0083	0.0204	0.0438	0.0828	0.1410	0.2189	0.3139	0.4199	0.5292	0.6338	0.7272	0.8054	0.8671	0.9130	0.9454	0.9671	0.9810	0.9894	0.9943	0.9971	0.9985
13.5	0.0000	0.0000	0.0001	0.0007	0.0026	0.0077	0.0193	0.0415	0.0790	0.1353	0.2112	0.3045	0.4093	0.5182	0.6233	0.7178	0.7975	0.8609	0.9084	0.9421	0.9649	0.9796	0.9885	0.9938	0.9968	0.9984
13.6	0.0000	0.0000	0.0001	0.0007	0.0024	0.0072	0.0181	0.0393	0.0753	0.1297	0.2037	0.2952	0.3989	0.5074	0.6128	0.7083	0.7895	0.8545	0.9035	0.9387	0.9626	0.9780	0.9876	0.9933	0.9965	0.9982
13.7	0.0000	0.0000	0.0001	0.0006	0.0023	0.0067	0.0171	0.0372	0.0718	0.1244	0.1964	0.2862	0.3886	0.4966	0.6022	0.6987	0.7813	0.8479	0.8986	0.9351	0.9601	0.9765	0.9866	0.9927	0.9961	0.9980
13.8	0.0000	0.0000	0.0001	0.0006	0.0021	0.0063	0.0161	0.0353	0.0684	0.1192	0.1893	0.2773	0.3784	0.4858	0.5916	0.6890	0.7730	0.8411	0.8934	0.9314	0.9576	0.9748	0.9856	0.9921	0.9958	0.9978
13.9	0.0000	0.0000	0.0001	0.0005	0.0019	0.0059	0.0151	0.0334	0.0652	0.1142	0.1824	0.2686	0.3684	0.4751	0.5810	0.6792	0.7645	0.8343	0.8881	0.9275	0.9549	0.9730	0.9845	0.9914	0.9954	0.9976
14	0.0000	0.0000	0.0001	0.0005	0.0018	0.0055	0.0142	0.0316	0.0621	0.1094	0.1757	0.2600	0.3585	0.4644	0.5704	0.6694	0.7559	0.8272	0.8826	0.9235	0.9521	0.9712	0.9833	0.9907	0.9950	0.9974
14.1	0.0000	0.0000	0.0001	0.0004	0.0017	0.0052	0.0134	0.0299	0.0591	0.1047	0.1691	0.2517	0.3487	0.4539	0.5598	0.6594	0.7472	0.8200	0.8770	0.9193	0.9492	0.9692	0.9820	0.9899	0.9945	0.9971
14.2	0.0000	0.0000	0.0001	0.0004	0.0016	0.0048	0.0126	0.0283	0.0562	0.1003	0.1628	0.2435	0.3391	0.4434	0.5492	0.6494	0.7384	0.8126	0.8712	0.9150	0.9461	0.9671	0.9807	0.9891	0.9941	0.9969
14.3	0.0000	0.0000	0.0001	0.0004	0.0014	0.0045	0.0118	0.0268	0.0535	0.0959	0.1566	0.2355	0.3296	0.4330	0.5387	0.6394	0.7294	0.8051	0.8653	0.9106	0.9430	0.9650	0.9793	0.9882	0.9935	0.9966
14.4	0.0000	0.0000	0.0001	0.0004	0.0013	0.0042	0.0111	0.0253	0.0509	0.0918	0.1507	0.2277	0.3203	0.4227	0.5281	0.6293	0.7204	0.7975	0.8592	0.9060	0.9396	0.9627	0.9779	0.9873	0.9930	0.9963
14.5	0.0000	0.0000	0.0001	0.0003	0.0012	0.0039	0.0105	0.0239	0.0484	0.0878	0.1449	0.2201	0.3111	0.4125	0.5176	0.6192	0.7112	0.7897	0.8530	0.9012	0.9362	0.9604	0.9763	0.9863	0.9924	0.9959

(continued)

14.6	0.9956	0.9918	0.9853	0.9747	0.9579	0.9326	0.8963	0.8466	0.7818	0.7020	0.6090	0.5071	0.4024	0.3021	0.2127	0.1392	0.0839	0.0460	0.0226	0.0098	0.0037	0.0012	0.0003	0.0001	0.0000	0.0000	0.0000
14.7	0.9952	0.9911	0.9842	0.9729	0.9553	0.9289	0.8913	0.8400	0.7737	0.6926	0.5988	0.4967	0.3925	0.2932	0.2054	0.1338	0.0802	0.0437	0.0214	0.0092	0.0034	0.0011	0.0003	0.0001	0.0000	0.0000	0.0000
14.8	0.9947	0.9904	0.9831	0.9711	0.9526	0.9251	0.8861	0.8333	0.7656	0.6832	0.5886	0.4863	0.3826	0.2845	0.1984	0.1285	0.0766	0.0415	0.0202	0.0087	0.0032	0.0010	0.0002	0.0001	0.0000	0.0000	0.0000
14.9	0.9943	0.9896	0.9818	0.9692	0.9498	0.9211	0.8807	0.8265	0.7573	0.6737	0.5783	0.4759	0.3728	0.2760	0.1915	0.1234	0.0732	0.0394	0.0191	0.0081	0.0030	0.0009	0.0002	0.0001	0.0000	0.0000	0.0000
15	0.9938	0.9888	0.9805	0.9673	0.9469	0.9170	0.8752	0.8195	0.7489	0.6641	0.5681	0.4657	0.3632	0.2676	0.1848	0.1185	0.0699	0.0374	0.0180	0.0076	0.0028	0.0009	0.0002	0.0001	0.0000	0.0000	0.0000
15.1	0.9933	0.9880	0.9792	0.9652	0.9438	0.9128	0.8696	0.8123	0.7403	0.6545	0.5578	0.4554	0.3537	0.2594	0.1782	0.1137	0.0667	0.0355	0.0170	0.0072	0.0026	0.0008	0.0002	0.0001	0.0000	0.0000	0.0000
15.2	0.9928	0.9871	0.9777	0.9630	0.9407	0.9084	0.8638	0.8051	0.7317	0.6448	0.5476	0.4453	0.3444	0.2514	0.1718	0.1091	0.0636	0.0337	0.0160	0.0067	0.0024	0.0007	0.0002	0.0001	0.0000	0.0000	0.0000
15.3	0.9922	0.9861	0.9762	0.9607	0.9374	0.9039	0.8578	0.7977	0.7230	0.6351	0.5374	0.4353	0.3351	0.2435	0.1657	0.1046	0.0607	0.0320	0.0151	0.0063	0.0023	0.0006	0.0001	0.0001	0.0000	0.0000	0.0000
15.4	0.9915	0.9851	0.9746	0.9583	0.9340	0.8992	0.8517	0.7901	0.7141	0.6253	0.5272	0.4253	0.3260	0.2358	0.1596	0.1003	0.0579	0.0304	0.0143	0.0059	0.0021	0.0006	0.0001	0.0000	0.0000	0.0000	0.0000
15.5	0.9909	0.9840	0.9730	0.9558	0.9304	0.8944	0.8455	0.7825	0.7052	0.6154	0.5170	0.4154	0.3171	0.2283	0.1538	0.0961	0.0552	0.0288	0.0135	0.0055	0.0020	0.0005	0.0001	0.0000	0.0000	0.0000	0.0000
15.6	0.9902	0.9829	0.9712	0.9532	0.9268	0.8894	0.8391	0.7747	0.6962	0.6056	0.5069	0.4056	0.3083	0.2209	0.1481	0.0921	0.0526	0.0273	0.0127	0.0052	0.0018	0.0005	0.0001	0.0000	0.0000	0.0000	0.0000
15.7	0.9894	0.9817	0.9694	0.9505	0.9230	0.8843	0.8326	0.7668	0.6871	0.5957	0.4968	0.3959	0.2996	0.2137	0.1426	0.0882	0.0501	0.0259	0.0120	0.0049	0.0017	0.0005	0.0001	0.0000	0.0000	0.0000	0.0000
15.8	0.9886	0.9804	0.9674	0.9477	0.9190	0.8791	0.8260	0.7587	0.6779	0.5858	0.4867	0.3864	0.2911	0.2067	0.1372	0.0845	0.0478	0.0245	0.0113	0.0046	0.0016	0.0004	0.0001	0.0000	0.0000	0.0000	0.0000
15.9	0.9878	0.9791	0.9654	0.9448	0.9150	0.8737	0.8192	0.7506	0.6687	0.5759	0.4767	0.3769	0.2827	0.1998	0.1320	0.0809	0.0455	0.0232	0.0106	0.0043	0.0015	0.0004	0.0001	0.0000	0.0000	0.0000	0.0000
16	0.9869	0.9777	0.9633	0.9418	0.9108	0.8682	0.8122	0.7423	0.6593	0.5660	0.4667	0.3675	0.2745	0.1931	0.1270	0.0774	0.0433	0.0220	0.0100	0.0040	0.0014	0.0004	0.0001	0.0000	0.0000	0.0000	0.0000
16.1	0.9859	0.9762	0.9611	0.9386	0.9064	0.8625	0.8052	0.7340	0.6500	0.5560	0.4569	0.3583	0.2664	0.1866	0.1221	0.0740	0.0412	0.0208	0.0094	0.0038	0.0013	0.0004	0.0001	0.0000	0.0000	0.0000	0.0000
16.2	0.9849	0.9747	0.9588	0.9353	0.9020	0.8567	0.7980	0.7255	0.6406	0.5461	0.4470	0.3492	0.2585	0.1802	0.1174	0.0708	0.0392	0.0197	0.0089	0.0035	0.0012	0.0003	0.0001	0.0000	0.0000	0.0000	0.0000
16.3	0.9839	0.9730	0.9564	0.9319	0.8974	0.8508	0.7907	0.7170	0.6311	0.5362	0.4373	0.3402	0.2508	0.1740	0.1128	0.0677	0.0373	0.0186	0.0083	0.0033	0.0011	0.0003	0.0001	0.0000	0.0000	0.0000	0.0000
16.4	0.9828	0.9713	0.9539	0.9284	0.8927	0.8447	0.7833	0.7084	0.6216	0.5263	0.4276	0.3313	0.2432	0.1680	0.1084	0.0647	0.0355	0.0176	0.0079	0.0031	0.0010	0.0003	0.0001	0.0000	0.0000	0.0000	0.0000
16.5	0.9816	0.9696	0.9513	0.9248	0.8878	0.8385	0.7757	0.6996	0.6120	0.5165	0.4180	0.3225	0.2357	0.1621	0.1041	0.0619	0.0337	0.0167	0.0074	0.0029	0.0010	0.0003	0.0001	0.0000	0.0000	0.0000	0.0000
16.6	0.9804	0.9677	0.9486	0.9210	0.8828	0.8321	0.7681	0.6908	0.6025	0.5067	0.4085	0.3139	0.2285	0.1564	0.0999	0.0591	0.0321	0.0158	0.0070	0.0027	0.0009	0.0002	0.0001	0.0000	0.0000	0.0000	0.0000
16.7	0.9791	0.9657	0.9458	0.9171	0.8777	0.8257	0.7603	0.6820	0.5929	0.4969	0.3991	0.3054	0.2213	0.1508	0.0959	0.0565	0.0305	0.0149	0.0065	0.0025	0.0008	0.0002	0.0001	0.0000	0.0000	0.0000	0.0000
16.8	0.9777	0.9637	0.9429	0.9131	0.8724	0.8191	0.7524	0.6730	0.5833	0.4871	0.3898	0.2971	0.2144	0.1454	0.0920	0.0539	0.0290	0.0141	0.0061	0.0024	0.0008	0.0002	0.0001	0.0000	0.0000	0.0000	0.0000
16.9	0.9763	0.9616	0.9398	0.9090	0.8670	0.8123	0.7444	0.6640	0.5737	0.4774	0.3806	0.2889	0.2075	0.1401	0.0883	0.0515	0.0275	0.0133	0.0058	0.0022	0.0007	0.0002	0.0000	0.0000	0.0000	0.0000	0.0000
17	0.9748	0.9594	0.9367	0.9047	0.8615	0.8055	0.7363	0.6550	0.5640	0.4677	0.3715	0.2808	0.2009	0.1350	0.0847	0.0491	0.0261	0.0126	0.0054	0.0021	0.0007	0.0002	0.0000	0.0000	0.0000	0.0000	0.0000
17.1	0.9732	0.9570	0.9334	0.9003	0.8558	0.7985	0.7281	0.6458	0.5544	0.4581	0.3624	0.2729	0.1944	0.1301	0.0812	0.0469	0.0248	0.0119	0.0051	0.0019	0.0006	0.0002	0.0000	0.0000	0.0000	0.0000	0.0000
17.2	0.9715	0.9546	0.9301	0.8958	0.8500	0.7914	0.7199	0.6367	0.5448	0.4486	0.3535	0.2651	0.1880	0.1252	0.0778	0.0447	0.0235	0.0112	0.0048	0.0018	0.0005	0.0002	0.0000	0.0000	0.0000	0.0000	0.0000
17.3	0.9698	0.9521	0.9266	0.8912	0.8441	0.7842	0.7115	0.6275	0.5352	0.4391	0.3448	0.2575	0.1818	0.1206	0.0746	0.0426	0.0223	0.0106	0.0045	0.0017	0.0005	0.0001	0.0000	0.0000	0.0000	0.0000	0.0000
17.4	0.9680	0.9495	0.9230	0.8864	0.8380	0.7769	0.7031	0.6182	0.5256	0.4297	0.3361	0.2500	0.1758	0.1160	0.0714	0.0406	0.0212	0.0100	0.0042	0.0016	0.0005	0.0001	0.0000	0.0000	0.0000	0.0000	0.0000
17.5	0.9661	0.9468	0.9193	0.8815	0.8319	0.7694	0.6945	0.6089	0.5160	0.4204	0.3275	0.2426	0.1699	0.1116	0.0684	0.0387	0.0201	0.0095	0.0040	0.0015	0.0004	0.0001	0.0000	0.0000	0.0000	0.0000	0.0000
17.6	0.9641	0.9440	0.9154	0.8765	0.8255	0.7619	0.6859	0.5996	0.5065	0.4112	0.3191	0.2354	0.1641	0.1074	0.0655	0.0369	0.0191	0.0089	0.0037	0.0014	0.0004	0.0001	0.0000	0.0000	0.0000	0.0000	0.0000
17.7	0.9621	0.9411	0.9115	0.8713	0.8191	0.7542	0.6773	0.5903	0.4969	0.4020	0.3108	0.2284	0.1585	0.1033	0.0627	0.0352	0.0181	0.0084	0.0035	0.0013	0.0004	0.0001	0.0000	0.0000	0.0000	0.0000	0.0000
17.8	0.9599	0.9381	0.9074	0.8660	0.8126	0.7465	0.6685	0.5810	0.4875	0.3929	0.3026	0.2215	0.1531	0.0993	0.0600	0.0335	0.0171	0.0079	0.0033	0.0012	0.0003	0.0001	0.0000	0.0000	0.0000	0.0000	0.0000
17.9	0.9577	0.9350	0.9032	0.8606	0.8059	0.7387	0.6598	0.5716	0.4780	0.3839	0.2946	0.2147	0.1478	0.0954	0.0574	0.0319	0.0162	0.0075	0.0031	0.0011	0.0003	0.0001	0.0000	0.0000	0.0000	0.0000	0.0000
18	0.9554	0.9317	0.8989	0.8551	0.7991	0.7307	0.6509	0.5622	0.4686	0.3751	0.2867	0.2081	0.1426	0.0917	0.0549	0.0304	0.0154	0.0071	0.0029	0.0010	0.0003	0.0001	0.0000	0.0000	0.0000	0.0000	0.0000
18.1	0.9530	0.9284	0.8944	0.8494	0.7922	0.7227	0.6420	0.5529	0.4593	0.3663	0.2789	0.2016	0.1376	0.0881	0.0525	0.0289	0.0146	0.0067	0.0027	0.0010	0.0003	0.0001	0.0000	0.0000	0.0000	0.0000	0.0000
18.2	0.9505	0.9249	0.8899	0.8436	0.7852	0.7146	0.6331	0.5435	0.4500	0.3576	0.2712	0.1953	0.1327	0.0846	0.0502	0.0275	0.0138	0.0063	0.0025	0.0009	0.0003	0.0001	0.0000	0.0000	0.0000	0.0000	0.0000
18.3	0.9479	0.9214	0.8852	0.8377	0.7781	0.7064	0.6241	0.5342	0.4408	0.3490	0.2637	0.1891	0.1279	0.0812	0.0479	0.0262	0.0131	0.0059	0.0024	0.0008	0.0002	0.0001	0.0000	0.0000	0.0000	0.0000	0.0000
18.4	0.9452	0.9177	0.8804	0.8317	0.7709	0.6981	0.6151	0.5249	0.4317	0.3405	0.2563	0.1830	0.1233	0.0779	0.0458	0.0249	0.0124	0.0056	0.0022	0.0008	0.0002	0.0001	0.0000	0.0000	0.0000	0.0000	0.0000
18.5	0.9424	0.9139	0.8755	0.8256	0.7636	0.6898	0.6061	0.5156	0.4226	0.3321	0.2490	0.1771	0.1189	0.0748	0.0438	0.0237	0.0117	0.0052	0.0021	0.0007	0.0002	0.0001	0.0000	0.0000	0.0000	0.0000	0.0000
18.6	0.9395	0.9100	0.8704	0.8193	0.7561	0.6814	0.5970	0.5063	0.4136	0.3239	0.2419	0.1714	0.1145	0.0717	0.0418	0.0225	0.0111	0.0049	0.0020	0.0007	0.0002	0.0001	0.0000	0.0000	0.0000	0.0000	0.0000
18.7	0.9365	0.9060	0.8652	0.8129	0.7486	0.6729	0.5879	0.4970	0.4047	0.3157	0.2349	0.1658	0.1103	0.0688	0.0399	0.0214	0.0105	0.0046	0.0018	0.0006	0.0002	0.0001	0.0000	0.0000	0.0000	0.0000	0.0000
18.8	0.9334	0.9019	0.8600	0.8065	0.7410	0.6644	0.5788	0.4878	0.3958	0.3077	0.2281	0.1603	0.1062	0.0659	0.0381	0.0203	0.0099	0.0044	0.0017	0.0006	0.0001	0.0000	0.0000	0.0000	0.0000	0.0000	0.0000
18.9	0.9302	0.8976	0.8545	0.7998	0.7333	0.6558	0.5697	0.4786	0.3870	0.2998	0.2214	0.1550	0.1022	0.0632	0.0363	0.0193	0.0094	0.0041	0.0016	0.0006	0.0001	0.0000	0.0000	0.0000	0.0000	0.0000	0.0000
19	0.9269	0.8933	0.8490	0.7931	0.7255	0.6472	0.5606	0.4695	0.3784	0.2920	0.2148	0.1497	0.0984	0.0606	0.0347	0.0183	0.0089	0.0039	0.0015	0.0005	0.0002	0.0000	0.0000	0.0000	0.0000	0.0000	0.0000
19.1	0.9235	0.8888	0.8434	0.7863	0.7176	0.6385	0.5515	0.4604	0.3698	0.2844	0.2084	0.1447	0.0947	0.0580	0.0331	0.0174	0.0084	0.0036	0.0014	0.0005	0.0001	0.0000	0.0000	0.0000	0.0000	0.0000	0.0000
19.2	0.9199	0.8842	0.8376	0.7794	0.7097	0.6298	0.5424	0.4514	0.3613	0.2768	0.2021	0.1397	0.0911	0.0556	0.0315	0.0165	0.0079	0.0034	0.0013	0.0005	0.0001	0.0000	0.0000	0.0000	0.0000	0.0000	0.0000
19.3	0.9163	0.8795	0.8317	0.7724	0.7016	0.6210	0.5333	0.4424	0.3529	0.2694	0.1959	0.1349	0.0876	0.0532	0.0301	0.0157	0.0075	0.0032	0.0012	0.0004	0.0001	0.0000	0.0000	0.0000	0.0000	0.0000	0.0000
19.4	0.9126	0.8746	0.8257	0.7653	0.6935	0.6122	0.5242	0.4335	0.3446	0.2621	0.1899	0.1303	0.0842	0.0509	0.0287	0.0149	0.0071	0.0030	0.0012	0.0004	0.0001	0.0000	0.0000	0.0000	0.0000	0.0000	0.0000
19.5	0.9087	0.8697	0.8196	0.7580	0.6854	0.6034	0.5151	0.4246	0.3364	0.2550	0.1840	0.1257	0.0809	0.0488	0.0273	0.0141	0.0067	0.0028	0.0011	0.0004	0.0001	0.0000	0.0000	0.0000	0.0000	0.0000	0.0000
19.6	0.9048	0.8646	0.8134	0.7507	0.6772	0.5946	0.5061	0.4158	0.3283	0.2479	0.1782	0.1213	0.0778	0.0467	0.0260	0.0134	0.0063	0.0027	0.0010	0.0003	0.0001	0.0000	0.0000	0.0000	0.0000	0.0000	0.0000
19.7	0.9007	0.8594	0.8071	0.7433	0.6689	0.5857	0.4971	0.4071	0.3203	0.2410	0.1726	0.1170	0.0747	0.0446	0.0248	0.0127	0.0059	0.0025	0.0010	0.0003	0.0001	0.0000	0.0000	0.0000	0.0000	0.0000	0.0000
19.8	0.8965	0.8541	0.8007	0.7358	0.6605	0.5769	0.4881	0.3985	0.3124	0.2342	0.1671	0.1128	0.0717	0.0427	0.0236	0.0120	0.0056	0.0024	0.0009	0.0003	0.0001	0.0000	0.0000	0.0000	0.0000	0.0000	0.0000
19.9	0.8922	0.8487	0.7941	0.7283	0.6521	0.5680	0.4792	0.3899	0.3047	0.2276	0.1617	0.1088	0.0689	0.0408	0.0225	0.0114	0.0053	0.0022	0.0008	0.0003	0.0001	0.0000	0.0000	0.0000	0.0000	0.0000	0.0000

Cumulative probabilities for the Poisson distribution (cont.)

Probability of success x =

λ	0	1	2	3	4	5	6	7	8	9	10	11	12	13	14	15	16	17	18	19	20	21	22	23	24	25
20	0.0000	0.0000	0.0000	0.0000	0.0000	0.0001	0.0003	0.0008	0.0021	0.0050	0.0108	0.0214	0.0390	0.0661	0.1049	0.1565	0.2211	0.2970	0.3814	0.4703	0.5591	0.6437	0.7206	0.7875	0.8432	0.8878
20.1	0.0000	0.0000	0.0000	0.0000	0.0000	0.0001	0.0002	0.0007	0.0020	0.0047	0.0102	0.0204	0.0373	0.0635	0.1010	0.1514	0.2147	0.2895	0.3730	0.4614	0.5502	0.6352	0.7129	0.7808	0.8376	0.8833
20.2	0.0000	0.0000	0.0000	0.0000	0.0000	0.0001	0.0002	0.0007	0.0018	0.0044	0.0097	0.0194	0.0356	0.0609	0.0973	0.1464	0.2084	0.2821	0.3647	0.4526	0.5413	0.6267	0.7051	0.7739	0.8319	0.8787
20.3	0.0000	0.0000	0.0000	0.0000	0.0000	0.0001	0.0002	0.0006	0.0017	0.0042	0.0092	0.0184	0.0340	0.0584	0.0938	0.1416	0.2023	0.2748	0.3565	0.4438	0.5325	0.6181	0.6972	0.7670	0.8260	0.8739
20.4	0.0000	0.0000	0.0000	0.0000	0.0000	0.0001	0.0002	0.0006	0.0016	0.0040	0.0087	0.0175	0.0325	0.0560	0.0903	0.1369	0.1963	0.2676	0.3484	0.4351	0.5236	0.6096	0.6893	0.7600	0.8201	0.8691
20.5	0.0000	0.0000	0.0000	0.0000	0.0000	0.0001	0.0002	0.0006	0.0015	0.0037	0.0082	0.0167	0.0310	0.0537	0.0869	0.1323	0.1904	0.2605	0.3403	0.4265	0.5148	0.6010	0.6813	0.7528	0.8140	0.8641
20.6	0.0000	0.0000	0.0000	0.0000	0.0000	0.0001	0.0002	0.0005	0.0014	0.0035	0.0078	0.0158	0.0296	0.0515	0.0836	0.1278	0.1847	0.2536	0.3324	0.4179	0.5059	0.5923	0.6732	0.7456	0.8078	0.8591
20.7	0.0000	0.0000	0.0000	0.0000	0.0000	0.0001	0.0001	0.0005	0.0013	0.0033	0.0074	0.0150	0.0283	0.0493	0.0805	0.1234	0.1790	0.2467	0.3246	0.4094	0.4972	0.5837	0.6651	0.7384	0.8016	0.8539
20.8	0.0000	0.0000	0.0000	0.0000	0.0000	0.0001	0.0001	0.0005	0.0013	0.0031	0.0070	0.0143	0.0270	0.0473	0.0774	0.1192	0.1735	0.2400	0.3168	0.4009	0.4884	0.5750	0.6569	0.7310	0.7952	0.8486
20.9	0.0000	0.0000	0.0000	0.0000	0.0000	0.0001	0.0001	0.0004	0.0012	0.0029	0.0066	0.0136	0.0257	0.0453	0.0744	0.1151	0.1682	0.2334	0.3092	0.3926	0.4797	0.5664	0.6487	0.7235	0.7887	0.8432
21	0.0000	0.0000	0.0000	0.0000	0.0000	0.0000	0.0001	0.0004	0.0011	0.0028	0.0063	0.0129	0.0245	0.0434	0.0716	0.1111	0.1629	0.2270	0.3017	0.3843	0.4710	0.5577	0.6405	0.7160	0.7822	0.8377
21.1	0.0000	0.0000	0.0000	0.0000	0.0000	0.0000	0.0001	0.0004	0.0010	0.0026	0.0059	0.0123	0.0234	0.0415	0.0688	0.1072	0.1578	0.2206	0.2943	0.3760	0.4623	0.5490	0.6322	0.7084	0.7755	0.8321
21.2	0.0000	0.0000	0.0000	0.0000	0.0000	0.0000	0.0001	0.0003	0.0010	0.0025	0.0056	0.0116	0.0223	0.0397	0.0661	0.1034	0.1528	0.2144	0.2870	0.3679	0.4537	0.5403	0.6238	0.7008	0.7687	0.8264
21.3	0.0000	0.0000	0.0000	0.0000	0.0000	0.0000	0.0001	0.0003	0.0009	0.0023	0.0053	0.0110	0.0213	0.0380	0.0635	0.0997	0.1479	0.2083	0.2798	0.3599	0.4452	0.5317	0.6155	0.6930	0.7619	0.8206
21.4	0.0000	0.0000	0.0000	0.0000	0.0000	0.0000	0.0001	0.0003	0.0009	0.0022	0.0050	0.0105	0.0203	0.0364	0.0610	0.0962	0.1432	0.2023	0.2727	0.3519	0.4367	0.5230	0.6071	0.6853	0.7550	0.8146
21.5	0.0000	0.0000	0.0000	0.0000	0.0000	0.0000	0.0001	0.0003	0.0008	0.0021	0.0047	0.0099	0.0193	0.0348	0.0586	0.0927	0.1385	0.1965	0.2657	0.3440	0.4282	0.5144	0.5987	0.6774	0.7480	0.8086
21.6	0.0000	0.0000	0.0000	0.0000	0.0000	0.0000	0.0001	0.0003	0.0007	0.0019	0.0045	0.0094	0.0184	0.0333	0.0563	0.0893	0.1340	0.1907	0.2588	0.3362	0.4198	0.5058	0.5902	0.6695	0.7409	0.8025
21.7	0.0000	0.0000	0.0000	0.0000	0.0000	0.0000	0.0001	0.0002	0.0007	0.0018	0.0042	0.0090	0.0175	0.0318	0.0540	0.0861	0.1296	0.1851	0.2521	0.3285	0.4115	0.4972	0.5818	0.6616	0.7337	0.7963
21.8	0.0000	0.0000	0.0000	0.0000	0.0000	0.0000	0.0001	0.0002	0.0007	0.0017	0.0040	0.0085	0.0167	0.0304	0.0518	0.0829	0.1253	0.1796	0.2454	0.3209	0.4032	0.4887	0.5733	0.6536	0.7264	0.7900
21.9	0.0000	0.0000	0.0000	0.0000	0.0000	0.0000	0.0001	0.0002	0.0006	0.0016	0.0038	0.0080	0.0159	0.0291	0.0497	0.0799	0.1211	0.1743	0.2389	0.3134	0.3950	0.4801	0.5648	0.6455	0.7191	0.7836
22	0.0000	0.0000	0.0000	0.0000	0.0000	0.0000	0.0001	0.0002	0.0006	0.0015	0.0035	0.0076	0.0151	0.0278	0.0477	0.0769	0.1170	0.1690	0.2325	0.3060	0.3869	0.4716	0.5564	0.6374	0.7117	0.7771
22.1	0.0000	0.0000	0.0000	0.0000	0.0000	0.0000	0.0001	0.0002	0.0005	0.0014	0.0033	0.0072	0.0144	0.0265	0.0457	0.0740	0.1131	0.1639	0.2262	0.2987	0.3789	0.4632	0.5479	0.6293	0.7043	0.7705
22.2	0.0000	0.0000	0.0000	0.0000	0.0000	0.0000	0.0001	0.0002	0.0005	0.0013	0.0032	0.0069	0.0137	0.0254	0.0439	0.0712	0.1092	0.1588	0.2200	0.2915	0.3709	0.4548	0.5394	0.6211	0.6967	0.7638
22.3	0.0000	0.0000	0.0000	0.0000	0.0000	0.0000	0.0000	0.0001	0.0005	0.0012	0.0030	0.0065	0.0130	0.0242	0.0420	0.0685	0.1055	0.1539	0.2140	0.2844	0.3630	0.4464	0.5310	0.6130	0.6891	0.7571
22.4	0.0000	0.0000	0.0000	0.0000	0.0000	0.0000	0.0000	0.0001	0.0004	0.0012	0.0028	0.0062	0.0124	0.0231	0.0403	0.0659	0.1018	0.1491	0.2080	0.2774	0.3552	0.4381	0.5225	0.6047	0.6815	0.7503
22.5	0.0000	0.0000	0.0000	0.0000	0.0000	0.0000	0.0000	0.0001	0.0004	0.0011	0.0027	0.0058	0.0118	0.0221	0.0386	0.0634	0.0983	0.1445	0.2022	0.2705	0.3474	0.4298	0.5141	0.5965	0.6738	0.7433
22.6	0.0000	0.0000	0.0000	0.0000	0.0000	0.0000	0.0000	0.0001	0.0004	0.0010	0.0025	0.0055	0.0112	0.0211	0.0370	0.0610	0.0949	0.1399	0.1965	0.2638	0.3398	0.4216	0.5057	0.5883	0.6660	0.7363
22.7	0.0000	0.0000	0.0000	0.0000	0.0000	0.0000	0.0000	0.0001	0.0004	0.0010	0.0024	0.0052	0.0106	0.0201	0.0354	0.0586	0.0915	0.1355	0.1909	0.2571	0.3322	0.4135	0.4973	0.5800	0.6582	0.7293
22.8	0.0000	0.0000	0.0000	0.0000	0.0000	0.0000	0.0000	0.0001	0.0003	0.0009	0.0022	0.0049	0.0101	0.0192	0.0339	0.0563	0.0883	0.1311	0.1854	0.2505	0.3248	0.4054	0.4889	0.5717	0.6504	0.7221
22.9	0.0000	0.0000	0.0000	0.0000	0.0000	0.0000	0.0000	0.0001	0.0003	0.0009	0.0021	0.0047	0.0096	0.0183	0.0325	0.0541	0.0851	0.1269	0.1800	0.2441	0.3174	0.3973	0.4806	0.5634	0.6425	0.7149
23	0.0000	0.0000	0.0000	0.0000	0.0000	0.0000	0.0000	0.0001	0.0003	0.0008	0.0020	0.0044	0.0091	0.0174	0.0311	0.0520	0.0821	0.1228	0.1748	0.2377	0.3101	0.3894	0.4723	0.5551	0.6346	0.7077
23.1	0.0000	0.0000	0.0000	0.0000	0.0000	0.0000	0.0000	0.0001	0.0003	0.0008	0.0019	0.0042	0.0087	0.0166	0.0297	0.0499	0.0791	0.1188	0.1696	0.2315	0.3029	0.3815	0.4640	0.5469	0.6266	0.7003
23.2	0.0000	0.0000	0.0000	0.0000	0.0000	0.0000	0.0000	0.0001	0.0003	0.0007	0.0018	0.0040	0.0082	0.0158	0.0284	0.0480	0.0762	0.1148	0.1646	0.2253	0.2958	0.3737	0.4558	0.5386	0.6186	0.6929
23.3	0.0000	0.0000	0.0000	0.0000	0.0000	0.0000	0.0000	0.0001	0.0002	0.0007	0.0017	0.0037	0.0078	0.0151	0.0272	0.0460	0.0735	0.1110	0.1597	0.2193	0.2888	0.3659	0.4476	0.5303	0.6106	0.6855
23.4	0.0000	0.0000	0.0000	0.0000	0.0000	0.0000	0.0000	0.0001	0.0002	0.0006	0.0016	0.0035	0.0074	0.0144	0.0260	0.0442	0.0708	0.1073	0.1549	0.2134	0.2819	0.3582	0.4394	0.5220	0.6026	0.6779
23.5	0.0000	0.0000	0.0000	0.0000	0.0000	0.0000	0.0000	0.0001	0.0002	0.0006	0.0015	0.0033	0.0070	0.0137	0.0249	0.0424	0.0681	0.1037	0.1502	0.2076	0.2751	0.3507	0.4313	0.5138	0.5945	0.6704
23.6	0.0000	0.0000	0.0000	0.0000	0.0000	0.0000	0.0000	0.0001	0.0002	0.0006	0.0014	0.0032	0.0067	0.0130	0.0238	0.0407	0.0656	0.1002	0.1456	0.2019	0.2684	0.3431	0.4233	0.5055	0.5864	0.6628
23.7	0.0000	0.0000	0.0000	0.0000	0.0000	0.0000	0.0000	0.0001	0.0002	0.0005	0.0013	0.0030	0.0063	0.0124	0.0227	0.0390	0.0632	0.0968	0.1411	0.1963	0.2618	0.3357	0.4153	0.4973	0.5783	0.6551
23.8	0.0000	0.0000	0.0000	0.0000	0.0000	0.0000	0.0000	0.0001	0.0002	0.0005	0.0012	0.0028	0.0060	0.0118	0.0217	0.0374	0.0608	0.0935	0.1367	0.1909	0.2553	0.3284	0.4074	0.4891	0.5702	0.6474
23.9	0.0000	0.0000	0.0000	0.0000	0.0000	0.0000	0.0000	0.0001	0.0002	0.0005	0.0012	0.0027	0.0057	0.0113	0.0208	0.0359	0.0585	0.0903	0.1324	0.1855	0.2489	0.3211	0.3995	0.4810	0.5621	0.6397
24	0.0000	0.0000	0.0000	0.0000	0.0000	0.0000	0.0000	0.0000	0.0002	0.0004	0.0011	0.0025	0.0054	0.0107	0.0198	0.0344	0.0563	0.0871	0.1283	0.1803	0.2426	0.3139	0.3917	0.4728	0.5540	0.6319
24.1	0.0000	0.0000	0.0000	0.0000	0.0000	0.0000	0.0000	0.0000	0.0001	0.0004	0.0011	0.0024	0.0051	0.0102	0.0189	0.0330	0.0541	0.0841	0.1242	0.1751	0.2365	0.3068	0.3840	0.4648	0.5459	0.6241
24.2	0.0000	0.0000	0.0000	0.0000	0.0000	0.0000	0.0000	0.0000	0.0001	0.0004	0.0010	0.0023	0.0049	0.0097	0.0181	0.0316	0.0520	0.0811	0.1203	0.1701	0.2304	0.2999	0.3763	0.4567	0.5378	0.6163
24.3	0.0000	0.0000	0.0000	0.0000	0.0000	0.0000	0.0000	0.0000	0.0001	0.0004	0.0010	0.0021	0.0046	0.0092	0.0173	0.0303	0.0500	0.0783	0.1164	0.1652	0.2244	0.2929	0.3687	0.4487	0.5297	0.6084
24.4	0.0000	0.0000	0.0000	0.0000	0.0000	0.0000	0.0000	0.0000	0.0001	0.0003	0.0009	0.0020	0.0044	0.0088	0.0165	0.0290	0.0481	0.0755	0.1126	0.1603	0.2185	0.2861	0.3611	0.4407	0.5216	0.6005
24.5	0.0000	0.0000	0.0000	0.0000	0.0000	0.0000	0.0000	0.0000	0.0001	0.0003	0.0008	0.0019	0.0041	0.0083	0.0157	0.0278	0.0462	0.0728	0.1090	0.1556	0.2128	0.2794	0.3537	0.4328	0.5135	0.5926
24.6	0.0000	0.0000	0.0000	0.0000	0.0000	0.0000	0.0000	0.0000	0.0001	0.0003	0.0008	0.0018	0.0039	0.0079	0.0150	0.0266	0.0444	0.0702	0.1054	0.1510	0.2071	0.2728	0.3463	0.4249	0.5054	0.5847
24.7	0.0000	0.0000	0.0000	0.0000	0.0000	0.0000	0.0000	0.0000	0.0001	0.0003	0.0007	0.0017	0.0037	0.0075	0.0143	0.0254	0.0426	0.0676	0.1019	0.1465	0.2015	0.2663	0.3390	0.4170	0.4974	0.5768
24.8	0.0000	0.0000	0.0000	0.0000	0.0000	0.0000	0.0000	0.0000	0.0001	0.0003	0.0007	0.0016	0.0035	0.0072	0.0136	0.0244	0.0410	0.0652	0.0985	0.1421	0.1961	0.2599	0.3317	0.4093	0.4894	0.5688
24.9	0.0000	0.0000	0.0000	0.0000	0.0000	0.0000	0.0000	0.0000	0.0001	0.0002	0.0006	0.0015	0.0033	0.0068	0.0130	0.0233	0.0393	0.0628	0.0952	0.1378	0.1907	0.2535	0.3246	0.4015	0.4814	0.5609
25	0.0000	0.0000	0.0000	0.0000	0.0000	0.0000	0.0000	0.0000	0.0001	0.0002	0.0006	0.0014	0.0031	0.0065	0.0124	0.0223	0.0377	0.0605	0.0920	0.1336	0.1855	0.2473	0.3175	0.3939	0.4734	0.5529

Table 4

Normal distribution

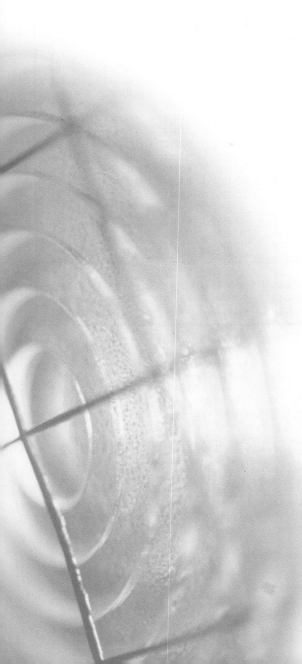

Cumulative probabilities for the standard Normal distribution

Z	0.00	0.01	0.02	0.03	0.04	0.05	0.06	0.07	0.08	0.09
−4.0	0.0000	0.0000	0.0000	0.0000	0.0000	0.0000	0.0000	0.0000	0.0000	0.0000
−3.9	0.0000	0.0000	0.0000	0.0000	0.0000	0.0000	0.0000	0.0000	0.0000	0.0000
−3.8	0.0001	0.0001	0.0001	0.0001	0.0001	0.0001	0.0001	0.0001	0.0001	0.0001
−3.7	0.0001	0.0001	0.0001	0.0001	0.0001	0.0001	0.0001	0.0001	0.0001	0.0001
−3.6	0.0002	0.0002	0.0001	0.0001	0.0001	0.0001	0.0001	0.0001	0.0001	0.0001
−3.5	0.0002	0.0002	0.0002	0.0002	0.0002	0.0002	0.0002	0.0002	0.0002	0.0002
−3.4	0.0003	0.0003	0.0003	0.0003	0.0003	0.0003	0.0003	0.0003	0.0003	0.0002
−3.3	0.0005	0.0005	0.0005	0.0004	0.0004	0.0004	0.0004	0.0004	0.0004	0.0003
−3.2	0.0007	0.0007	0.0006	0.0006	0.0006	0.0006	0.0006	0.0005	0.0005	0.0005
−3.1	0.0010	0.0009	0.0009	0.0009	0.0008	0.0008	0.0008	0.0008	0.0007	0.0007
−3.0	0.0013	0.0013	0.0013	0.0012	0.0012	0.0011	0.0011	0.0011	0.0010	0.0010
−2.9	0.0019	0.0018	0.0018	0.0017	0.0016	0.0016	0.0015	0.0015	0.0014	0.0014
−2.8	0.0026	0.0025	0.0024	0.0023	0.0023	0.0022	0.0021	0.0021	0.0020	0.0019
−2.7	0.0035	0.0034	0.0033	0.0032	0.0031	0.0030	0.0029	0.0028	0.0027	0.0026
−2.6	0.0047	0.0045	0.0044	0.0043	0.0041	0.0040	0.0039	0.0038	0.0037	0.0036
−2.5	0.0062	0.0060	0.0059	0.0057	0.0055	0.0054	0.0052	0.0051	0.0049	0.0048
−2.4	0.0082	0.0080	0.0078	0.0075	0.0073	0.0071	0.0069	0.0068	0.0066	0.0064
−2.3	0.0107	0.0104	0.0102	0.0099	0.0096	0.0094	0.0091	0.0089	0.0087	0.0084
−2.2	0.0139	0.0136	0.0132	0.0129	0.0125	0.0122	0.0119	0.0116	0.0113	0.0110
−2.1	0.0179	0.0174	0.0170	0.0166	0.0162	0.0158	0.0154	0.0150	0.0146	0.0143
−2.0	0.0228	0.0222	0.0217	0.0212	0.0207	0.0202	0.0197	0.0192	0.0188	0.0183
−1.9	0.0287	0.0281	0.0274	0.0268	0.0262	0.0256	0.0250	0.0244	0.0239	0.0233
−1.8	0.0359	0.0351	0.0344	0.0336	0.0329	0.0322	0.0314	0.0307	0.0301	0.0294
−1.7	0.0446	0.0436	0.0427	0.0418	0.0409	0.0401	0.0392	0.0384	0.0375	0.0367
−1.6	0.0548	0.0537	0.0526	0.0516	0.0505	0.0495	0.0485	0.0475	0.0465	0.0455
−1.5	0.0668	0.0655	0.0643	0.0630	0.0618	0.0606	0.0594	0.0582	0.0571	0.0559
−1.4	0.0808	0.0793	0.0778	0.0764	0.0749	0.0735	0.0721	0.0708	0.0694	0.0681
−1.3	0.0968	0.0951	0.0934	0.0918	0.0901	0.0885	0.0869	0.0853	0.0838	0.0823
−1.2	0.1151	0.1131	0.1112	0.1093	0.1075	0.1056	0.1038	0.1020	0.1003	0.0985
−1.1	0.1357	0.1335	0.1314	0.1292	0.1271	0.1251	0.1230	0.1210	0.1190	0.1170
−1.0	0.1587	0.1562	0.1539	0.1515	0.1492	0.1469	0.1446	0.1423	0.1401	0.1379
−0.9	0.1841	0.1814	0.1788	0.1762	0.1736	0.1711	0.1685	0.1660	0.1635	0.1611
−0.8	0.2119	0.2090	0.2061	0.2033	0.2005	0.1977	0.1949	0.1922	0.1894	0.1867
−0.7	0.2420	0.2389	0.2358	0.2327	0.2296	0.2266	0.2236	0.2206	0.2177	0.2148
−0.6	0.2743	0.2709	0.2676	0.2643	0.2611	0.2578	0.2546	0.2514	0.2483	0.2451
−0.5	0.3085	0.3050	0.3015	0.2981	0.2946	0.2912	0.2877	0.2843	0.2810	0.2776
−0.4	0.3446	0.3409	0.3372	0.3336	0.3300	0.3264	0.3228	0.3192	0.3156	0.3121
−0.3	0.3821	0.3783	0.3745	0.3707	0.3669	0.3632	0.3594	0.3557	0.3520	0.3483
−0.2	0.4207	0.4168	0.4129	0.4090	0.4052	0.4013	0.3974	0.3936	0.3897	0.3859
−0.1	0.4602	0.4562	0.4522	0.4483	0.4443	0.4404	0.4364	0.4325	0.4286	0.4247

Z	0.00	0.01	0.02	0.03	0.04	0.05	0.06	0.07	0.08	0.09
0.0	0.5000	0.5040	0.5080	0.5120	0.5160	0.5199	0.5239	0.5279	0.5319	0.5359
0.1	0.5398	0.5438	0.5478	0.5517	0.5557	0.5596	0.5636	0.5675	0.5714	0.5753
0.2	0.5793	0.5832	0.5871	0.5910	0.5948	0.5987	0.6026	0.6064	0.6103	0.6141
0.3	0.6179	0.6217	0.6255	0.6293	0.6331	0.6368	0.6406	0.6443	0.6480	0.6517
0.4	0.6554	0.6591	0.6628	0.6664	0.6700	0.6736	0.6772	0.6808	0.6844	0.6879
0.5	0.6915	0.6950	0.6985	0.7019	0.7054	0.7088	0.7123	0.7157	0.7190	0.7224
0.6	0.7257	0.7291	0.7324	0.7357	0.7389	0.7422	0.7454	0.7486	0.7517	0.7549
0.7	0.7580	0.7611	0.7642	0.7673	0.7704	0.7734	0.7764	0.7794	0.7823	0.7852
0.8	0.7881	0.7910	0.7939	0.7967	0.7995	0.8023	0.8051	0.8078	0.8106	0.8133
0.9	0.8159	0.8186	0.8212	0.8238	0.8264	0.8289	0.8315	0.8340	0.8365	0.8389
1.0	0.8413	0.8438	0.8461	0.8485	0.8508	0.8531	0.8554	0.8577	0.8599	0.8621
1.1	0.8643	0.8665	0.8686	0.8708	0.8729	0.8749	0.8770	0.8790	0.8810	0.8830
1.2	0.8849	0.8869	0.8888	0.8907	0.8925	0.8944	0.8962	0.8980	0.8997	0.9015
1.3	0.9032	0.9049	0.9066	0.9082	0.9099	0.9115	0.9131	0.9147	0.9162	0.9177
1.4	0.9192	0.9207	0.9222	0.9236	0.9251	0.9265	0.9279	0.9292	0.9306	0.9319
1.5	0.9332	0.9345	0.9357	0.9370	0.9382	0.9394	0.9406	0.9418	0.9429	0.9441
1.6	0.9452	0.9463	0.9474	0.9484	0.9495	0.9505	0.9515	0.9525	0.9535	0.9545
1.7	0.9554	0.9564	0.9573	0.9582	0.9591	0.9599	0.9608	0.9616	0.9625	0.9633
1.8	0.9641	0.9649	0.9656	0.9664	0.9671	0.9678	0.9686	0.9693	0.9699	0.9706
1.9	0.9713	0.9719	0.9726	0.9732	0.9738	0.9744	0.9750	0.9756	0.9761	0.9767
2.0	0.9772	0.9778	0.9783	0.9788	0.9793	0.9798	0.9803	0.9808	0.9812	0.9817
2.1	0.9821	0.9826	0.9830	0.9834	0.9838	0.9842	0.9846	0.9850	0.9854	0.9857
2.2	0.9861	0.9864	0.9868	0.9871	0.9875	0.9878	0.9881	0.9884	0.9887	0.9890
2.3	0.9893	0.9896	0.9898	0.9901	0.9904	0.9906	0.9909	0.9911	0.9913	0.9916
2.4	0.9918	0.9920	0.9922	0.9925	0.9927	0.9929	0.9931	0.9932	0.9934	0.9936
2.5	0.9938	0.9940	0.9941	0.9943	0.9945	0.9946	0.9948	0.9949	0.9951	0.9952
2.6	0.9953	0.9955	0.9956	0.9957	0.9959	0.9960	0.9961	0.9962	0.9963	0.9964
2.7	0.9965	0.9966	0.9967	0.9968	0.9969	0.9970	0.9971	0.9972	0.9973	0.9974
2.8	0.9974	0.9975	0.9976	0.9977	0.9977	0.9978	0.9979	0.9979	0.9980	0.9981
2.9	0.9981	0.9982	0.9982	0.9983	0.9984	0.9984	0.9985	0.9985	0.9986	0.9986
3.0	0.9987	0.9987	0.9987	0.9988	0.9988	0.9989	0.9989	0.9989	0.9990	0.9990
3.1	0.9990	0.9991	0.9991	0.9991	0.9992	0.9992	0.9992	0.9992	0.9993	0.9993
3.2	0.9993	0.9993	0.9994	0.9994	0.9994	0.9994	0.9994	0.9995	0.9995	0.9995
3.3	0.9995	0.9995	0.9995	0.9996	0.9996	0.9996	0.9996	0.9996	0.9996	0.9997
3.4	0.9997	0.9997	0.9997	0.9997	0.9997	0.9997	0.9997	0.9997	0.9997	0.9998
3.5	0.9998	0.9998	0.9998	0.9998	0.9998	0.9998	0.9998	0.9998	0.9998	0.9998
3.6	0.9998	0.9998	0.9999	0.9999	0.9999	0.9999	0.9999	0.9999	0.9999	0.9999
3.7	0.9999	0.9999	0.9999	0.9999	0.9999	0.9999	0.9999	0.9999	0.9999	0.9999
3.8	0.9999	0.9999	0.9999	0.9999	0.9999	0.9999	0.9999	0.9999	0.9999	0.9999
3.9	1.0000	1.0000	1.0000	1.0000	1.0000	1.0000	1.0000	1.0000	1.0000	1.0000
4.0	1.0000	1.0000	1.0000	1.0000	1.0000	1.0000	1.0000	1.0000	1.0000	1.0000

Cumulative probabilities under one tail of the standard Normal distribution

Z	0.00	0.01	0.02	0.03	0.04	0.05	0.06	0.07	0.08	0.09
0.0	0.5000	0.4960	0.4920	0.4880	0.4840	0.4801	0.4761	0.4721	0.4681	0.4641
0.1	0.4602	0.4562	0.4522	0.4483	0.4443	0.4404	0.4364	0.4325	0.4286	0.4247
0.2	0.4207	0.4168	0.4129	0.4090	0.4052	0.4013	0.3974	0.3936	0.3897	0.3859
0.3	0.3821	0.3783	0.3745	0.3707	0.3669	0.3632	0.3594	0.3557	0.3520	0.3483
0.4	0.3446	0.3409	0.3372	0.3336	0.3300	0.3264	0.3228	0.3192	0.3156	0.3121
0.5	0.3085	0.3050	0.3015	0.2981	0.2946	0.2912	0.2877	0.2843	0.2810	0.2776
0.6	0.2743	0.2709	0.2676	0.2643	0.2611	0.2578	0.2546	0.2514	0.2483	0.2451
0.7	0.2420	0.2389	0.2358	0.2327	0.2296	0.2266	0.2236	0.2206	0.2177	0.2148
0.8	0.2119	0.2090	0.2061	0.2033	0.2005	0.1977	0.1949	0.1922	0.1894	0.1867
0.9	0.1841	0.1814	0.1788	0.1762	0.1736	0.1711	0.1685	0.1660	0.1635	0.1611
1.0	0.1587	0.1562	0.1539	0.1515	0.1492	0.1469	0.1446	0.1423	0.1401	0.1379
1.1	0.1357	0.1335	0.1314	0.1292	0.1271	0.1251	0.1230	0.1210	0.1190	0.1170
1.2	0.1151	0.1131	0.1112	0.1093	0.1075	0.1056	0.1038	0.1020	0.1003	0.0985
1.3	0.0968	0.0951	0.0934	0.0918	0.0901	0.0885	0.0869	0.0853	0.0838	0.0823
1.4	0.0808	0.0793	0.0778	0.0764	0.0749	0.0735	0.0721	0.0708	0.0694	0.0681
1.5	0.0668	0.0655	0.0643	0.0630	0.0618	0.0606	0.0594	0.0582	0.0571	0.0559
1.6	0.0548	0.0537	0.0526	0.0516	0.0505	0.0495	0.0485	0.0475	0.0465	0.0455
1.7	0.0446	0.0436	0.0427	0.0418	0.0409	0.0401	0.0392	0.0384	0.0375	0.0367
1.8	0.0359	0.0351	0.0344	0.0336	0.0329	0.0322	0.0314	0.0307	0.0301	0.0294
1.9	0.0287	0.0281	0.0274	0.0268	0.0262	0.0256	0.0250	0.0244	0.0239	0.0233
2.0	0.0228	0.0222	0.0217	0.0212	0.0207	0.0202	0.0197	0.0192	0.0188	0.0183
2.1	0.0179	0.0174	0.0170	0.0166	0.0162	0.0158	0.0154	0.0150	0.0146	0.0143
2.2	0.0139	0.0136	0.0132	0.0129	0.0125	0.0122	0.0119	0.0116	0.0113	0.0110
2.3	0.0107	0.0104	0.0102	0.0099	0.0096	0.0094	0.0091	0.0089	0.0087	0.0084
2.4	0.0082	0.0080	0.0078	0.0075	0.0073	0.0071	0.0069	0.0068	0.0066	0.0064
2.5	0.0062	0.0060	0.0059	0.0057	0.0055	0.0054	0.0052	0.0051	0.0049	0.0048
2.6	0.0047	0.0045	0.0044	0.0043	0.0041	0.0040	0.0039	0.0038	0.0037	0.0036
2.7	0.0035	0.0034	0.0033	0.0032	0.0031	0.0030	0.0029	0.0028	0.0027	0.0026
2.8	0.0026	0.0025	0.0024	0.0023	0.0023	0.0022	0.0021	0.0021	0.0020	0.0019
2.9	0.0019	0.0018	0.0018	0.0017	0.0016	0.0016	0.0015	0.0015	0.0014	0.0014
3.0	0.0013	0.0013	0.0013	0.0012	0.0012	0.0011	0.0011	0.0011	0.0010	0.0010
3.1	0.0010	0.0009	0.0009	0.0009	0.0008	0.0008	0.0008	0.0008	0.0007	0.0007
3.2	0.0007	0.0007	0.0006	0.0006	0.0006	0.0006	0.0006	0.0005	0.0005	0.0005
3.3	0.0005	0.0005	0.0005	0.0004	0.0004	0.0004	0.0004	0.0004	0.0004	0.0003
3.4	0.0003	0.0003	0.0003	0.0003	0.0003	0.0003	0.0003	0.0003	0.0003	0.0002
3.5	0.0002	0.0002	0.0002	0.0002	0.0002	0.0002	0.0002	0.0002	0.0002	0.0002
3.6	0.0002	0.0002	0.0001	0.0001	0.0001	0.0001	0.0001	0.0001	0.0001	0.0001
3.7	0.0001	0.0001	0.0001	0.0001	0.0001	0.0001	0.0001	0.0001	0.0001	0.0001
3.8	0.0001	0.0001	0.0001	0.0001	0.0001	0.0001	0.0001	0.0001	0.0001	0.0001
3.9	0.0000	0.0000	0.0000	0.0000	0.0000	0.0000	0.0000	0.0000	0.0000	0.0000
4.0	0.0000	0.0000	0.0000	0.0000	0.0000	0.0000	0.0000	0.0000	0.0000	0.0000

Table 5

Student's *t*-distribution

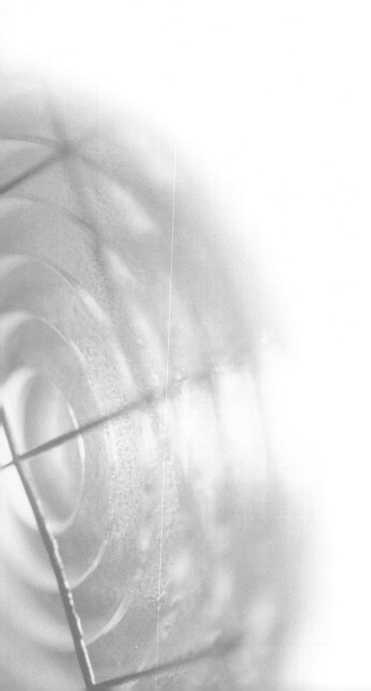

Probabilities for the two-tail Student's *t*-distribution

		Level													
Confidence		1%	5%	10%	20%	30%	40%	50%	60%	70%	80%	90%	95%	98%	99%
Significance		99%	95%	90%	80%	70%	60%	50%	40%	30%	20%	10%	5%	2%	1%
(parameter)		0.99	0.95	0.9	0.8	0.7	0.6	0.5	0.4	0.3	0.2	0.1	0.05	0.02	0.01
	1	0.0157	0.0787	0.1584	0.3249	0.5095	0.7265	1.0000	1.3764	1.9626	3.0777	6.3137	12.7062	31.8210	636.5776
	2	0.0141	0.0708	0.1421	0.2887	0.4447	0.6172	0.8165	1.0607	1.3862	1.8856	2.9200	4.3027	6.9645	31.5998
	3	0.0136	0.0681	0.1366	0.2767	0.4242	0.5844	0.7649	0.9785	1.2498	1.6377	2.3534	3.1824	4.5407	12.9244
	4	0.0133	0.0667	0.1338	0.2707	0.4142	0.5686	0.7407	0.9410	1.1896	1.5332	2.1318	2.7765	3.7469	8.6101
	5	0.0132	0.0659	0.1322	0.2672	0.4082	0.5594	0.7267	0.9195	1.1558	1.4759	2.0150	2.5706	3.3649	6.8685
	6	0.0131	0.0654	0.1311	0.2648	0.4043	0.5534	0.7176	0.9057	1.1342	1.4398	1.9432	2.4469	3.1427	5.9587
D	7	0.0130	0.0650	0.1303	0.2632	0.4015	0.5491	0.7111	0.8960	1.1192	1.4149	1.8946	2.3646	2.9979	5.4081
e	8	0.0129	0.0647	0.1297	0.2619	0.3995	0.5459	0.7064	0.8889	1.1081	1.3968	1.8595	2.3060	2.8965	5.0414
g	9	0.0129	0.0645	0.1293	0.2610	0.3979	0.5435	0.7027	0.8834	1.0997	1.3830	1.8331	2.2622	2.8214	4.7809
r	10	0.0129	0.0643	0.1289	0.2602	0.3966	0.5415	0.6998	0.8791	1.0931	1.3722	1.8125	2.2281	2.7638	4.5868
e	11	0.0128	0.0642	0.1286	0.2596	0.3956	0.5399	0.6974	0.8755	1.0877	1.3634	1.7959	2.2010	2.7181	4.4369
e	12	0.0128	0.0640	0.1283	0.2590	0.3947	0.5386	0.6955	0.8726	1.0832	1.3562	1.7823	2.1788	2.6810	4.3178
	13	0.0128	0.0639	0.1281	0.2586	0.3940	0.5375	0.6938	0.8702	1.0795	1.3502	1.7709	2.1604	2.6503	4.2209
	14	0.0128	0.0638	0.1280	0.2582	0.3933	0.5366	0.6924	0.8681	1.0763	1.3450	1.7613	2.1448	2.6245	4.1403
o	15	0.0127	0.0638	0.1278	0.2579	0.3928	0.5357	0.6912	0.8662	1.0735	1.3406	1.7531	2.1315	2.6025	4.0728
f	16	0.0127	0.0637	0.1277	0.2576	0.3923	0.5350	0.6901	0.8647	1.0711	1.3368	1.7459	2.1199	2.5835	4.0149
	17	0.0127	0.0636	0.1276	0.2573	0.3919	0.5344	0.6892	0.8633	1.0690	1.3334	1.7396	2.1098	2.5669	3.9651
f	18	0.0127	0.0636	0.1274	0.2571	0.3915	0.5338	0.6884	0.8620	1.0672	1.3304	1.7341	2.1009	2.5524	3.9217
r	19	0.0127	0.0635	0.1274	0.2569	0.3912	0.5333	0.6876	0.8610	1.0655	1.3277	1.7291	2.0930	2.5395	3.8833
e	20	0.0127	0.0635	0.1273	0.2567	0.3909	0.5329	0.6870	0.8600	1.0640	1.3253	1.7247	2.0860	2.5280	3.8496
e	21	0.0127	0.0635	0.1272	0.2566	0.3906	0.5325	0.6864	0.8591	1.0627	1.3232	1.7207	2.0796	2.5176	3.8193
d	22	0.0127	0.0634	0.1271	0.2564	0.3904	0.5321	0.6858	0.8583	1.0614	1.3212	1.7171	2.0739	2.5083	3.7922
o	23	0.0127	0.0634	0.1271	0.2563	0.3902	0.5317	0.6853	0.8575	1.0603	1.3195	1.7139	2.0687	2.4999	3.7676
m	24	0.0127	0.0634	0.1270	0.2562	0.3900	0.5314	0.6848	0.8569	1.0593	1.3178	1.7109	2.0639	2.4922	3.7454
	25	0.0127	0.0633	0.1269	0.2561	0.3898	0.5312	0.6844	0.8562	1.0584	1.3163	1.7081	2.0595	2.4851	3.7251
	26	0.0127	0.0633	0.1269	0.2560	0.3896	0.5309	0.6840	0.8557	1.0575	1.3150	1.7056	2.0555	2.4786	3.7067
	27	0.0126	0.0633	0.1268	0.2559	0.3894	0.5306	0.6837	0.8551	1.0567	1.3137	1.7033	2.0518	2.4727	3.6895
	28	0.0126	0.0633	0.1268	0.2558	0.3893	0.5304	0.6834	0.8546	1.0560	1.3125	1.7011	2.0484	2.4671	3.6739
	29	0.0126	0.0633	0.1268	0.2557	0.3892	0.5302	0.6830	0.8542	1.0553	1.3114	1.6991	2.0452	2.4620	3.6595
	30	0.0126	0.0632	0.1267	0.2556	0.3890	0.5300	0.6828	0.8538	1.0547	1.3104	1.6973	2.0423	2.4573	3.6460